John Goldingay is David Allan Hubbard Professor of Old Testament at Fuller Theological Seminary, Pasadena, California.

David Payne was formerly Director of Studies at London Bible College.

G. I. Davies is a Fellow of Fitzwilliam College and Professor of Old Testament Studies, University of Cambridge.

J. A. Emerton is a Fellow of St John's College and Emeritus Regius Professor of Hebrew, University of Cambridge, and Honorary Canon of St George's Cathedral, Jerusalem.

C. E. B. Cranfield is Emeritus Professor of Theology, University of Durham.

G. N. Stanton is a Fellow of Fitzwilliam College and Lady Margaret's Professor of Divinity, University of Cambridge.

The INTERNATIONAL CRITICAL COMMENTARY on the Holy Scriptures of the Old and New Testaments

GENERAL EDITORS

G. I. DAVIES, F.B.A.
Professor of Old Testament Studies in the University of Cambridge
Fellow of Fitzwilliam College

AND

G. N. STANTON, HON. D.D.
Lady Margaret's
Professor of Divinity in the University of Cambridge
Fellow of Fitzwilliam College

CONSULTING EDITORS

J. A. EMERTON, F.B.A.
Fellow of St John's College
Emeritus Regius Professor of Hebrew in the University of Cambridge
Honorary Canon of St George's Cathedral, Jerusalem

AND

C. E. B. CRANFIELD, F.B.A.
Emeritus Professor of Theology in the University of Durham

FORMERLY UNDER THE EDITORSHIP OF

S. R. DRIVER
A. PLUMMER
C. A. BRIGGS

ISAIAH 40–55

VOLUME II

A CRITICAL AND EXEGETICAL COMMENTARY

ON

ISAIAH 40–55

BY

JOHN GOLDINGAY
David Allan Hubbard Professor of Old Testament
Fuller Theological Seminary, Pasadena, California

AND

DAVID PAYNE
Formerly Director of Studies, London Bible College

IN TWO VOLUMES
VOLUME II
Commentary on Isaiah 44.24–55.13

t&t clark

T&T Clark International
A Continuum imprint

The Tower Building
11 York Road
London SE1 7NX

80 Maiden Lane
Suite 704
New York, NY 10038

www.tandtclark.com

ISBN: 0 567 04461 0 (Volume I)
ISBN: 0 567 03072 5 (Volume II)
ISBN: 0 567 04143 3 (Set)

Typeset by Data Standards Ltd, Frome, Somerset, UK
Printed and bound in Great Britain by Antony Rowe Ltd, Chippenham, Wiltshire

CONTENTS

III.

44.24–48.22: YHWH'S WORK WITH CYRUS

We have noted that Isaiah 44.24–45.8 forms a bridge between two major blocks comprising chapters 41–44 and 45–48 (†Mettinger, p. 25). It brings chapters 40–44 to a climax and leads into chapters 45–48. It thus faces both ways, and thereby half-justifies the strange medieval chapter division midway through 44.24–45.8. It makes specific links with 40.1–11 as a bracket round the block (cf †Beuken). Both passages bring encouragement for Jerusalem (vv. 26, 28; 40.2, 9) and the towns of Judah (v. 26; 40.9). Both speak of the leadership of a shepherd (v. 28; 40.11) whose road will be levelled (v. 2; 40.3–4), and of one whose word will be [made to] stand (v. 26; 40.8): but in each case in 40.1–11 the reference is to Yhwh, in 44.24–45.8 to Yhwh's human agents.

Retrospectively the words of v. 24 take up those of vv. 21–23, which summoned heaven and earth, declared that Yhwh has acted (*ʿāśāh*, here rendered 'make'), once again declared Yhwh to be the one who shaped Jacob–Israel, and twice more affirmed that Yhwh is restoring Jacob–Israel. In content there was little link between vv. 21–23 and what preceded. There is more with what now follows. Verse 24 introduces sections that will give more specific indication of how the one who shaped Jacob–Israel will bring about its restoration. This God relates to heaven and earth as actor/maker in a broader sense (cf 45.8). That underlies the summons to song in 44.23.

How far does the unit extend? While 44.24–28 could stand alone, in the present context it introduces 45.1–7. Verse 1 there comprises a resumptive opening that summarizes 44.24–28. Verse 8 then closes off 44.24–45.8. As a unit that could stand alone, but it is shorter than those in 40.12–44.23, and as we read on, we find vv. 9–13 taking up issues raised by 44.24–28 and grammatically requiring the 'Cyrus' of 44.28 and 45.1 as antecedent for the 'him' of v. 13. The topic under dispute in vv. 9–13 is obscure unless read in the light of 44.24–45.8. Yhwh is again one who stretches/stretched the heavens (vv. 24, 12) and is committed to building Jerusalem by means of Cyrus (vv. 28, 13). Typically, the overt confrontation in vv. 9–13 makes explicit the indirect confrontation in 44.24–28, in the light of the explicit oracle in 45.1–7.

In itself v. 13 is not a particularly strong ending, and once more vv. 14–17 continue to respond to the same agenda and grammatically require a noun from v. 13 as antecedent for the feminine suffix 'you', which recurs six times in v. 14. Its talk of wealth and treasure takes up from v. 13 as well as from v. 3, its confession in v. 14 is that anticipated in v. 6, its positive response to Yhwh provides an appropriate foil to vv. 9–13, and it shares links with chapter 29 that run through this material. Verse 17 would make a feasible strong ending to a chapter but once again vv. 18–25 link with what precedes, not only by means of the *kî* ('for') with which they open but in terms of the speakers/addressees and subject matter. They continue in the manner of these chapters to move on from allusiveness to greater explicitness, now with regard to the fate of the nations in relation to that of Israel. The section repeats motifs such as Yhwh's being sole God and restorer, and the contrast between the destinies of image-makers and Israel (compare vv. 24–25 with 16–17), and also takes further the new question of Yhwh's hiddenness from v. 15. With v. 25 we reach another strong ending and then something that looks more like a new start in 46.1.

We thus follow the medieval Christian chapter division at this point rather than any of the Hebrew divisions. A closes a section after 44.28. Most MT MSS, 1QIs^{a}, and 1QIs^{b} close one after 45.7. L and 1QIs^{a} close one after 45.13. The MT and 1QIs^{a} close one after 45.17. A and 1QIs^{a} begin the next new section at 46.3; L does not do so until 48.17. A new synagogue lection runs from 45.18 to 48.1.

III.a.

44.24–45.25: THE TRIUMPH OF CYRUS

It transpires that 44.24 thus introduces a unit that explicitly handles questions raised by Cyrus's advent, 44.24–45.25. We treat the unit as five sections, vv. 24–28, 1–8, 9–13, 14–17, 18–25 (on the delimitations, see the separate introductions below). In each the prophet passes on words from Yhwh. The messenger formula appears in vv. 24, 1, 11, 14, and 18. Yhwh addresses Jacob–Israel (44.24–45.1), Cyrus (45.2–7), heaven and earth (45.8), unnamed questioners (45.9–13), the exilic community (45.14–17), and the nations, who were themselves quoted in vv. 14–17 (45.18–25). Indeed, *Balentine (p. 113) sees 44.24–45.25 as 'an extended quasi-dialogue between God, the nations, and Israel'. Yhwh's self-announcement 'I Yhwh' recurs, in vv. 24–28, vv. 1–8 (five times) and vv. 18–25 (four times), the divine 'I' (*ʾānōkî/ʾănî*) in vv. 9–13 (three times), and a correlative 'you are God' in v. 14–17. The unique deity of Yhwh is asserted in all but the middle part. The claim 'there is no other' (*ʾên ʿôd*) recurs in vv. 6, 14, 18, 21, 22. Verbs for Yhwh's creativity appear in a number of combinations and patterns: *yāṣar/bārāʾ/ʿāśāh* ('form'/'create'/'make') in an ABCB pattern in 45.7, *yāṣar/ʿāśāh* in 44.24 and 45.9, *ʿāśāh/bārāʾ* in 45.12, *bārāʾ/yāṣar* in a BABA pattern in 45.18; other verbs for creation used in further combinations in these passages further illustrate the interplay of tradition and individuality.[1]

Within the whole, v. 8 forms a pivot. As well as closing off 44.24–45.7, it introduces the concerns that interweave in vv. 9–25, 'right'/'rightness'/'be right' (*ṣedeq/ṣᵉdāqāh/ṣaddîq/ṣādēq*) in vv. 8a, 8b, 13, 19, 21, 23, 24, 25, and 'deliver'/'deliverer'/'deliverance' (*yāšaʿ/môšîaʿ/tᵉšûʿāh/yešaʿ*) in vv. 8, 15, 17aα, 17aβ, 20, 21, 22 (†Hermisson). The prospect of deliverance, right, and rightness closes off 44.24–45.8, the prospect of right then closes off 45.9–13 and the prospect of deliverance 45.14–17, while subsequently right and deliverance together recur through 45.18–25.

The section incorporates elements from all five of †Kratz's layers (p. 217). From the period just before 539 BC come 44.24–26a; the bulk of 45.1–7; 45.20a, 21. From the Zion layer come the bulk of 44.26b–27 and 45.14. From 520–515 BC come 44.28; expansions in 45.1, 3, 5; the bulk of 45.11a, 12–13; 45.18, 22–23. Material from the images layer comes in 45.15–17, 20b. From the early fifth century BC come 45.8–10, 11b, 19, 24–25 and some expansions.

[1] Cf P. D. Miller, 'Studies in Hebrew Word Patterns', in *HTR* 73 (1980), pp. 79–89 (see pp. 88–89), building on an observation by S. Gevirtz, *Patterns in the Early Poetry of Israel* (Chicago, 1963), p. 44.

III.a.i. Yhwh designates Cyrus as shepherd (44.24–28)

In isolation 44.24–28 might be a self-contained oracle, but Yhwh's words lack a main verb, and at least in its written context vv. 24–28 forms the introduction to 45.1–8 (†Westermann; see also his *Sprache und Struktur*, pp. 144–51). The rhetorical impressiveness of its sequence of participial clauses heightens the significance of the statement they eventually introduce, while the lyrical exhortations of 45.8 have a parallel retroactive effect. Verse 8 links verbally with what precedes by the repetition of *pātaḥ* ('open'—an *inclusio* with v. 1), *bārāʾ* ('create'; cf v. 7), and *ʾănî yhwh* ('I [am] Yhwh'; cf v. 6). Formally the heart of 44.24–45.8 is thus the oracle in 45.2–6a, to which vv. 25–28, 6b–7 provide solemn introduction and conclusion, and vv. 24 (resumed in v. 1) and 8 an *inclusio* around the whole:

24 Yhwh speaks as lord of heaven and earth
  25–28 Yhwh as lord in events (participial self-descriptions)
    (1) 2–6a Yhwh's words to Cyrus
  6b–7 Yhwh as lord in events (participial self-descriptions)
8 Yhwh addresses heaven and earth as lord

In other respects v. 24 sets out the agenda for the whole and is the fountainhead from which it springs. Verses 25–28 offers a hymn-like (if also confrontational) response to it (†Merendino). In 45.1 its messenger formula is reprised. Verses 2–6a leads to Yhwh's self-description 'I am Yhwh and there is no-one else. Besides me there is no God', which takes up a theme of v. 24. Verses 6b–7 affirm 'I am Yhwh, maker of all these', taking up the words of v. 24. In v. 8 Yhwh calls on the heaven and earth that were the objects of Yhwh's creation in v. 24.

Verse 24 begins with a messenger formula, Yhwh's name being characteristically glossed with two familiar participial expressions, 'restorer' and 'shaper from the womb'. These already appeared in vv. 2 and 6 (see also 43.14 at a parallel point in the preceding spiral). In the divine self-designation 'I am Yhwh' that follows, the name is again glossed by a familiar participle, 'maker', one that also appeared both in 43.19 in that parallel spiral and in 44.2. This last participle is admittedly reused in a far-reachingly novel way, for Yhwh is now 'maker of all', not merely Israel's maker, but the participles in themselves nevertheless lull us into a false sense of familiarity. It is false because these three turn out to be only the first of a series that runs right though vv. 24–28 and constitute its distinguishing formal feature. Its series of participles that form Yhwh's self-description is the densest cluster of such participial ascriptions in Isaiah 40–55 (†Mauch). It is also false because of the scandalous novelty of the statement of intent that it introduces.

The symmetry of the section's structure is one consideration that leads †Merendino to the conclusion that it does not come from Second Isaiah but is a later imitation of the prophet's style. †Begrich and †Smart see vv. 27–28 as resuming and amplifying the content of what precedes it. †Begrich (p. 123 = 125) then sees v. 26b as an addition, †Smart vv. 27–28. For possible other earlier forms of vv. 24–28 see also †Kiesow; †Kratz; †van Oorschot, pp. 74–80. As we have them, the verses are structured with great neatness, such as may itself make such analyses and inferences difficult to believe:

24a	Introduction, beginning with the verb *ʾāmar* ('say') and glossing the name Yhwh with two participles
24b	Three parallel cola gloss the name further, each beginning with a qal participle
25–26a	Three parallel bicola, each chiastic, each beginning with a hiphil participle and each closing with a yiqtol verb
26b–28a	Three internally parallel lines, each beginning with the participle *hāʾōmēr* and relating Yhwh's actual words introduced by *l* and the identification of the subject/addressee, each closing with a yiqtol verb
28b	Conclusion: an infinitive form of the same verb *ʾāmar* introducing two parallel clauses.

This formal structure suggests an interpretation of the verses' content. The central three elements set Yhwh's present intentions in their widest context, gradually sharpening the focus:

24b	Yhwh's activity in relation to the world
25–26a	Yhwh's activity in relation to the realm of human wisdom in general
26b–28a	Yhwh's words regarding Jerusalem/Judah, the deep, and Cyrus in particular

The threefold presentation overlaps with schemes such as past, present and future; or creation, history and present; or creation, revelation and history; but its distinctiveness then needs observing. As usual in Isaiah 40–55 there is no suggestion that Yhwh's activity as creator (v. 24b) belongs distinctively to that past moment of initial activity that Genesis 1 portrays. The second stage (vv. 25–26a) concerns neither ongoing activity in general nor revelation in general but the ongoing activity whereby the pretensions of other alleged revelations are exposed and the revelations of Yhwh's own agents are vindicated. In the third (vv. 26b–28a) these capacities to speak and create are applied to the community's present needs. The introduction of the article on the final series of participles signals that the climax of the section lies here. A God who is creator and controller is the very one who now announces a message concerning the present (cf †Schoors and JM 1371, where 45.3 is noted as an example). The sequence as a whole elaborates major themes of earlier chapters—Yhwh as creator, as controller of events and therefore of access to their meaning, and as committed to the restoration of the community.

It is clear that the doctrine of creation is indeed not introduced for its own sake. While it would be an exaggeration to say that Second Isaiah does not distinguish between Yhwh's original creation, Yhwh's ongoing relationship with the world, and Yhwh's present activity in restoring Israel, it is true that the prophet is not directly interested in Yhwh's past or present relationship with the world as a whole but with the deliverance of Jacob–Israel as exemplifying the same divine dispensation.[2]

The three triads develop internally in three different ways. In the first, the opening summary colon is expanded into its two logical parts by the two succeeding cola. In the second triad, the initial two bicola parallel each other and the final bicolon offers a contrast and climax. The third triad moves in reverse order from the climax to which the story must move (v. 26b), via the central wonder (v. 27), both of which will be more prominent in later chapters, to the immediate event (v. 28a).

Once again, the participles formally parallel ones that sometimes appear in hymns. †Rendtorff (pp. 6–7) compared specifically Psalm 136. That psalm moves on from creation to Israel's originary experiences in history as a people, as is natural to descriptive praise (†Westermann). The prophet in turn does more than merely take over the creation tradition. As ever, the creation tradition is actualized in relation to questions raised by the present. By this very fact, however, at the same time the quasi-hymnic ascriptions necessarily make statements that are controversial and confrontational (†Gressmann, pp. 289–90). †Begrich (p. 42 = 49) thus classifies vv. 24–28 as an argument. But the structure of argument and conclusion (cf †Schoors) obscures the section's dynamic rather than illuminating it, and †Fohrer's view of it as a mixture of hymn and argument can only apply to its aim or ethos, not to its actual form. Noting that it begins with the messenger formula, †Melugin calls it a disputational promise. In the introduction to 43.22–44.23, in noting its parallel function to 43.14–15, we described it as a promise of deliverance in indirect form, for here, too, Yhwh makes promises and states their reasons. Promises of deliverance can take a variety of forms (cf †van Oorschot's comments on this passage, pp. 74–75).

Indeed, formally the participles are not hymnic in the sense of speaking to or of the deity, but self-predication. As such they are without parallel elsewhere in the Hebrew Bible. They do parallel the ascriptions of third-millennium Sumerian hymns such as Inanna's

[2] So G. von Rad, 'Das theologisches Problem des alttestamentlichen Schöpfungsglaubens', in *Werden und Wesen des Alten Testaments* (ed. J. Hempel; BZAW 66, 1936), pp. 138–47 (see pp. 140–42) = von Rad, *Gesammelte Studien zum Alten Testament* (TBü 8, 3rd ed., 1965), pp. 136–47 (see pp. 139–41); ET in von Rad, *The Problem of the Hexateuch and Other Essays* (Edinburgh/New York, 1966), pp. 131–43 (see pp. 134–36) = *Creation in the Old Testament* (ed. B. W. Anderson; London/Philadelphia, 1984), pp. 53–64 (see pp. 56–58).

hymn of self-praise.[3] Hearers familiar with such hymns would hear Yhwh once again disputing the claims of other gods to be creators and determiners and therefore announcers of events, and Yhwh's words might evoke a wry grin as they undermine the no-gods' pretensions by appropriating the genre designed to boost those pretensions. It would be a grin no doubt accompanied by an awareness of fear, anger, and frustration, as is often the case with the humour of the oppressed. The incongruity of the parallel is made explicit by the fact that a form of self-predication designed to enable a deity to claim superiority to other deities is used by a God who claims that there *are* no other deities, a God whose power in the world is absolutely and not merely relatively superior (cf †Westermann).

Yet we lack evidence that the prophets' hearers would be directly familiar with such hymns, whose extant examples come from 1500 years previously. We do have evidence that they might be familiar with their monarchic equivalent, the declarations regarding themselves by Sumerian, Assyrian, Babylonian, and Persian kings that appear in their inscriptions (*Dion, pp. 227–30; see, e.g., the Cyrus Cylinder, *ANET*, p. 316). To judge from passages in the Hebrew Bible such as Isa 10.8–14; 14.13–14; Ezek 28.2; 29.3, such monarchs' views of themselves were reckoned to amount to self-divinization. Countries and cities were reckoned to make quasi-divine claims for themselves, too: see Isa 47.8; Ezek 27.3; Zeph 2.15. Against this background, not least in Isaiah, Yhwh's self-declarations are set against the pretensions of Babylon and its king, of Persia and its king, and of Judah and its king. They mesh with the prophet's confining of the term 'king' to Yhwh. It is Yhwh who controls the nations' destinies. Nebuchadnezzar or Cyrus (or Jehoiachin or Zerubbabel) is the king's agent, not the king. If Yhwh seems self-centred, it is so as to be able to be Israel-centred, to be an effective restorer (*Dion, p. 234). The messenger formula in this particular context also emphasizes that the one who speaks is King, one who in his self-assertions speaks with divine–royal authority: so †Elliger, who sees the statement in its original form as addressed to the heavenly court.

It is the parallels between Babylonian and Israelite hymns with their common stress on the divine activity in creation and history that explain the simultaneously hymnic and confrontational nature of such sequences of participles. †Torrey compares the way 40.12–31 leads into 41.1–7. It also leads into the subsequent spiral that begins with 41.21–29, a section whose emphasis on Yhwh's distinctive capacity to speak about events on the basis of being controller of events is presupposed here in 44.24–28. Other deities cannot so speak

[3] *ANET*, pp. 578–79; for other examples see S. N. Kramer, *The Sumerians* (Chicago/London, 1963); S. Langdon, *Sumerian and Babylonian Psalms* (Paris, 1909), pp. 192–95; and esp. A. Falkenstein and W. von Soden, *Sumerische und Akkadische Hymnen und Gebete* (Zürich, 1953), e.g., pp. 77–79, 228–31.

of past or future events. Yhwh's distinctive lordship in these areas frustrates them (more accurately, their representatives) if they attempt to do so.

These parallels also hint at the intrinsic link between 44.24–28 and 45.1–7. The former can be read as a self-contained section, for although formally it contains no main verb and no message such as the messenger formula makes one expect, in substance its actual message appears in vv. 26b–28. But formally no message comes until 45.1–7. Formally the further significance of 44.24–28 lies in its preparing the way for 45.1–7. Verse 1 thus resumes the messenger formula, though it formally redirects the message to Cyrus, even if vv. 1–8 substantially continue to address Jacob–Israel. A converse implication is that the confrontational tone of vv. 24–28 that takes on the claim of Babylonian deities and their representatives has Jacob–Israel in mind. It cannot be assumed that Jacob–Israel automatically accepted the statements in vv. 24b–26a, except perhaps in some theoretical sense. Rather the opposite.

The introduction and conclusion with their shared use of *ʾāmar* also combine general and specific as they pair talk of Yhwh as Israel's restorer and shaper with talk of Yhwh building the city and establishing the temple. Some suspense is established by the introduction, with its reference to Yhwh's relationship with Jacob–Israel, or rather Yhwh's role in relation to Jacob–Israel. Jacob–Israel then disappears for the duration of the first two triads. Jerusalem–Judah features at the opening of the third triad, but arguably the conclusion then plays an important role in satisfying the expectations raised by the introduction.

44.24a. Yhwh has said this—your restorer, your shaper from the womb. The Syr adds *w'drk* ('and your help'), assimilating to v. 2.

Once again the messenger formula marks a new beginning, and once again it is immediately followed by participles. As usual these qualify the subject of the verb rather than constituting the beginning of Yhwh's own words. Although in picking up from vv. 21–23 the suffixes do establish that Jacob–Israel is addressed directly and not merely indirectly, the suffixes and messenger formula are unaccompanied by a naming of Jacob–Israel such as appeared in 'fear not' and other promissory oracles at 43.1, 14; 44.1, 6. This hints both at the fact that 44.24–45.8 as a whole focus on a formal addressing of Cyrus not Jacob–Israel and at the more confrontational nature of 44.24–45.13 as a further whole. With such usage the 'messenger formula' is indeed closer to being a 'citation formula' (Björndalen: 'Zeitstufen'). Another way to put it is to say that we are now two steps away from the social context of the literal delivery of a message. The messenger is a metaphorical one, and is delivering the message to someone other than the addressee.[4] †Elliger infers that the addressee

[4] See G. Fohrer's comments, 'Remarks on Modern Interpretation of the Prophets', in *JBL* 80 (1961), pp. 309–19 (see pp. 311–12).

is the heavenly court as in 42.1–4, but this presupposes too literal an understanding of the formula (the divine King must be addressing his court) and introduces an unnecessary complication.

The familiar participles both take us back to the beginning of Israel's life and by their nature hint that these are Yhwh's characteristic activities in relation to Jacob–Israel. In the context they also remind the people that their present restorer (cf vv. 22–23) is their original shaper (cf v. 21).

44.24b. I am Yhwh, maker of everything, stretcher of heavens alone, beater out of the earth of myself. The MT's accents imply 'I Yhwh am maker of everything. . .', but more likely the opening words constitute in themselves a complete self-declaration, 'I am Yhwh', which then introduces the first of the three triads of participial phrases in vv. 24b–28a (see the introduction to vv. 24–28). Such a self-declaration is not merely a phrase whereby someone unknown offers an introduction, and the fact that the audience knows Yhwh's name thus does not preclude such a self-declaration. It is unlikely that the divine name is '"only" an apposition' to be put in brackets (against *Fokkelman, pp. 305–6; his own inverted commas point to this).

The expression here is distinctive for the use of the long and thus perhaps more impressive form of the pronoun, *ʾānōkî* not *ʾănî*, as in 43.11 (but see the comment there); 51.15 (cf also 46.9); and in the Ten Words (Exod 20.2). It prepares the way for the extremely impressive sequence of participles that is to come. These continue the form of description in v. 24a and bridge the gap involved in the change of speaker (*Fokkelman, p. 303). †Thomas plausibly presents their beginning in v. 24b as two lines, 2–2 and 3–3, rather than a tricolon (†Kittel).

'Everything' is spelled out in the more familiar terms of the merism 'heaven' and 'earth'; anarthrous 'heavens' but '*the* earth' corresponds to common usage in Isaiah 40–44 (e.g. 40.22; contrast 42.5). Some LXX MSS thus narrow down *kōl* in rendering it πάντα ταῦτα, assimilating to 45.7 with its different reference. 'Stretcher' and 'beater out' similarly spell out 'maker', and do so in more vivid pictures. On the participles' lack of the article, see JM 138e. The Tg renders 'I suspended the heavens by my word', and thus suggests a more specific link between this statement about creation and what follows in vv. 25–28.

In turn, 'alone' and 'of myself' spell out 'I [am] Yhwh'.

רֹקַע: on the form, see GK 65d.
מֵאִתִּי 'of myself' (Q; cf Tg בגבורתי, 'by my power'; Syr *mny wly*, 'from me and for me') is preferable to מִי אִתִּי ('Who was with me?'; K, 1QIs[a], 4QIs[b], and some MSS; cf LXX τίς ἕτερος, Aq τίς σύν ἐμοί). A rhetorical question such as the latter is typical of Isaiah 40–55, but there are no other examples where the rhetorical question comes so late and so abruptly. Perhaps the less familiar Q text has been assimilated to such usage. From Vg *et nullus mecum* †Morgenstern infers ואין אתי, but Vg prefers negative statements when Heb.

has rhetorical questions. Vg thus supports K, though †Jerome uses both K and Q in his commentary (cf †Kedar-Kopfstein, p. 184).

44.25a. …frustrator of soothsayers' signs and enfeebler of diviners… 'Soothsayers' (*baddîm*) strictly refers to experts in hepatoscopy. By a nice coincidence, Hebrew has a homonym linked to the root *bādā*ʾ, which means 'devise' or 'invent' and thus suggests people whose words have no substance (cf 16.6; Job 11.3). At least by the time of Sym (which renders ψευδῶν) the distinction between the two words had apparently been forgotten (cf BDB), though there is no need to read this extra negative connotation into LXX ἐγγαστριμύθων ('ventriloquists'), Vg *divinorum* ('diviners'), Syr *zkwr'* ('mediums'), or Tg *bdyn* ('diviners'). In addition 'soothsayers' signs' alliterates with 'alone/of myself' in the previous line, suggesting 'the contrast between the validity and uniqueness of God's work, and the pretence of pluriform but powerless paganism' (*Fokkelman, p. 307). In turn, *qōsᵉmîm* ('diviners') strictly refers to belomancy, divination by means of arrows, but its root comes to provide Hebrew's most common terms for divination in general. If the reference to diviners were a new exodus motif (cf †Schoors), one might have expected some verbal overlap with Exod 8.14 and 9.11.

'Frustrate' (*pārar* hi) most commonly means to break or annul an obligation, but also to defeat a plan: in relation to the affirmations of vv. 25b–26, see classically 2 Sam 15.34 and 17.14. The parallel *hālal* (poel, also poal, hitpoel) is usually taken to mean 'madden' (cf Job 12.17; Qoh 7.7). It is likely a different root from *hālal* ('exult'; qal, piel, pual, hitpael—cf *HAL*); certainly the two are kept firmly separate in the way the stems are used. The folly the word denotes is not a mere intellectual shortcoming but a paralytic disablement (Jer 25.16; 46.9; 51.7). Indeed H. Cazelles suggests that it denotes weakness rather than stupidity.[5] In English 'feebleness' can denote either physical or mental weakness. But v. 25b parallels v. 25a and its second verb (for all its own problems) may disambiguate *hālal* here.

וְקֹסְמִים: LXX καὶ μαντείας ('and oracles') might represent וּקְסָמִים (*HUB*), Syr *wqṣmyhwn* ('and their divinations') וְקִסְמֵיהֶם (so †Morgenstern). LXX also adds ἀπο καρδίας ('from the heart'), perhaps displacing MT יְהוֹלֵל with an expansion from 59.13 (Goshen-Gottstein [see at 43.12], pp. 152–53).

44.25b. …turner back of wise and fooler of their knowledge… For *šûb* (hi), a stronger translation than 'turner back' might be justified—†Hessler suggests 'overturn'. 'Fooler' is the verb *sākal* (pi), which appears in parallel with *pārar* hi also in 2 Sam 15.31. L has *śākal*. That verb otherwise occurs once in the qal, commonly in the hiphil, but not in the piel (unless at Gen 48.14), and means 'be

[5] *ThWAT*, Vol. 2, cols. 441–44; ET Vol. 3, pp. 411–13.

circumspect/prudent/wise' and thus 'succeed' (cf 41.20; 44.18; 52.13). Here it might be understood as a piel privative (see GK 52h; *IBHS* 24.4f), 'to unwise', or as linked to *śākal* II ('to lay crosswise/entangle/confuse'; see *DTT*, p. 1574a), or as an ironic description of Yhwh's capacity to enlighten those who thought they were already enlightened. But later evidence (see *DTT*) suggests that both *śākal* and *sākal* could mean both 'be wise' and 'be foolish', and that *śākal* II became assimilated to *śākal* I with the latter meaning. L's reading reflects this later usage. The Tg has *mqlqyl* ('spoil/disgrace'—as at 2 Sam 15.31 for *sākal*), the Syr uses *skl*, LXX μωρεύων, Vg *stultam faciens* (both 'make foolish').

44.26a. ...confirmer of his servant's word and fulfiller of his aides' plan. As the prophet moves from the negative to the positive, the climactic significance of the third couplet in this triad is hinted by the change from 3–2 lines in v. 25 to a 3–3 line. The words 'confirm', 'word', 'plan', and 'aide' (*qûm* hi, *dābār*, *ʿēṣāh*, *malʾāk*) provide further links with 7.5–8 ('plan' [the verb], 'stand' [*qûm* qal]); 8.9–10 ('plan', 'word', 'stand'); 14.24–32 ('plan', 'stand', 'aide'); chapter 28 ('word', vv. 13, 14; 'stand', v. 18; 'plan', v. 29); chapter 29 ('plan', v. 15; 'words', vv. 11, 18); 40.8 ('word', 'stand'); 40.13 ('plan'); 41.28 ('consultant' [from the verb 'plan'], 'word'). The LXX has plural ῥήματα for singular *dābār*.

Each expression thus has a background earlier in Isaiah. This is even true of the verb *yašlîm* ('fulfil': cf v. 28), which was used with a different meaning in 38.12, 13. The meaning 'recompense' might make sense there, but surely not here (against Gerleman [see on 41.3], p. 11). The hiphil otherwise occurs only at Job 23.14, with another different meaning. The word thus still forms the novelty at the very end of the second colon. Its use here and in v. 28 is unique. It hints at something innovatory in content, though we may only notice the hint with hindsight (see on v. 26b).

The servant here has been identified as a self-reference to the prophet (†Ibn Ezra) or a reference to Moses (*Exodus Rabbah* 18.1, †Rashi), Isaiah ben Amoz (†Williamson, p. 52), Jeremiah (†Hitzig), the people (†Muilenburg), and Cyrus (*Spreafico). But the Tg (which also glosses with 'the righteous') and LXX^{A} render by the plural (cf NEB). While textually this looks like assimilation to the next colon, it rightly suggests that the term has no such specific referent, but applies to any servant—any prophet or leader, but anyone else, too—through whom Yhwh speaks and/or acts. This is supported by 'his aides' in the second colon, which as a plural both complements the singular 'his servant' (as happened in reverse order in 43.10) and disambiguates it. Such an interpretation fits the nature of this triad, which offers generalizations about Yhwh's sovereignty in events. The specific will come with the third triad in vv. 26b–28a. 'Servant' and 'aide' appeared in parallel in 42.19 (see the comment there).

44.26b. . . .the one who says of Jerusalem 'It will be inhabited', of the towns of Judah 'They will be built', 'I will raise its wastes'. Whereas 6.11 had warned that towns were to lie waste without inhabitant and the land was to be desolate, Second Isaiah declares that now Jerusalem is to be inhabited (the forms are *yôšēb* and *tûšāb*, participle and yiqtol from *yāšab*), Judah's towns are to be rebuilt, and Jerusalem's wastes are to be raised. †Korpel and de Moor take the niphal and hophal verbs as jussive, but it seems doubtful whether there are passive jussive forms in Hebrew. The hophal otherwise occurs only at 5.8, with a different meaning, but there is a general thematic link between 44.26 and 5.8–10 (†Williamson). The hiphil comes at 54.3. The usual meaning of *hāʾōmēr lîrûšālaim* would be 'the one who says *to* Jerusalem', but the following verb *tûšāb* is third person feminine (or second masculine, which does not fit). †Merendino takes the *l* as demonstrative (so also in vv. 27, 28), but it is uncertain whether this is a biblical usage. More likely *lîrûšālaim* would be understood to mean '*of* Jerusalem', as in vv. 28a, 28b; also 41.7 (†Elliger). In the second clause the form of the verb *tibbāneynāh* could be either second or third person feminine, but the hearer would more likely assume that the construction of the first phrase continues. This is confirmed by the third phrase where Jerusalem is again referred to in the third person. †Watts renders 'and [of] its wastes, I will raise [them]', but it is unlikely that the hearers could be expected to supply both the preposition and the suffix. Either way, the first person verb (assimilated to the others by the LXX's ἀνατελεῖ, '[its wastes] will arise') adds emphasis to the final phrase and introduces a feature running through the third triad as a whole. It will appear in the first person verb in v. 27b and in the first person pronouns in v. 28a and 28b. Here are Yhwh's actual words. This gives further emphasis to this climactic third triad as it resumes the first person of 'I am Yhwh' that introduced the three triads. It prepares the way, too, for the first person focus of 45.1–7 (†Muilenburg).

As the climactic significance of v. 26a in the first triad is marked by its being a 3–3 line after two 3–2 lines, so the significance of v. 26b as a statement of Yhwh's ultimate intention is anticipatorily underlined by its being a triplet. Verses 27 and 28a, which tell us how that intention will be realized, will be further 3–2 lines. The two emphasized lines, vv. 26a and 26b, also share the use of the verb *qûm* ('arise'; hi 'confirm', polel 'raise'), which begins v. 26a with a meaning appropriate to that line and closes v. 26b with a meaning appropriate to that line. Near the opening of Isaiah the verb *qûm* constituted a threat as Yhwh threatened to arise in response to the community's inclination to exalt itself (2.19, 21), for which Yhwh threatened to turn its towns to ruins (5.17) (†Miscall). But Yhwh's exaltation (cf 6.1) can also promise a capacity to raise ('confirm') a servant's word and raise a flattened city.

We have noted that †Begrich (p. 123 = 125) omits v. 26b as an anticipation of v. 28b. †Köhler omits the second colon, rendering v.

26b a line that fits neatly into the 3–2 sequence and giving the suffix on 'its ruins' a nearer antecedent.

תּוּשָׁב: Ehrlich repoints תִּוָּשֵׁב, 3 s. f. ni (pausal form). 1QIs[ab] have תשב, apparently the more familiar 3 s. f. qal, 'it will dwell'.
יהודה: LXX[B] 'Ιδουμαίας, a common slip for 'Ιουδαίας (†Ottley).

44.27. . . .who says to the deep 'Be wasted—I will dry up your streams'. In isolation, v. 27 could naturally be read as a return to talk of Yhwh's work in creation (an *inclusio* with v. 24b?) and/or in delivering the people from the Egyptians at the Red Sea (an *inclusio* with v. 24a?); cf subsequently 51.9–10. At the same time, such language has been used of Yhwh's imminent and present acts in the community's experience, not least in defeating Babylon and delivering the people from its bondage; cf 42.15, and subsequently 50.2, and 51.9–11 as a whole; also 43.2. With this significance the theme was already announced in 11.11–16 (†Williamson, p. 126). Further, we are used to such language being used to make statements that not merely refer to past or present in isolation from each other but that offer each as a mirror for understanding the other (cf 43.14–21). †Grimm and Dittert see v. 27 as a general statement of Yhwh's power over forces that overwhelm the community and that can effect what v. 26b promised. Yhwh always has power over the deep.

Verse 28a will thus disambiguate the line and suggest how at this point past and present, image and history are to be brought into relation, as it finally establishes the three-triad structure of vv. 24b–28a and invites us to read v. 27 in the context of vv. 26b–28a. In that context, placed between these other two lines, v. 27 can hardly be simply a reference back to creation or the Red Sea, nor is it poetically an *inclusio* with either v. 24a or v. 24b, nor is it merely a general statement. It heightens the effect of v. 26b by giving the concrete its mythic overtones.

Similar conclusions emerge from consideration of the particular nouns used in v. 27. The word 'deep', *ṣûlāh*, comes only here, but it is apparently a shortened form of the poetic term *m*[e]*ṣûlāh*/*m*[e]*ṣôlāh* used for the depths of the Red Sea (Exod 15.5; Neh 9.11), for the depths of ocean (Jonah 2.4 [3]; Micah 7.19; Pss 68.23 [22]; 107.24) or river (Zech 10.11; Job 41.23 [31]), and for the depths of distress (Pss 69.3, 16 [2, 15]; 88.7 [6]). It is one of a group of words used for 'deep' or 'flood' such as *t*[e]*hôm*, *ʿāmōq*/*maʿămaqqîm*, and *šeṭep*, along with more prosaic words for sea or waters or streams such as *yam*, *mayim*, *naḥal*, and *nāhār*. The poetic words and the prosaic words are commonly used in parallelism, as here, and this draws attention to the fact that they suggest some event that is at one level this-worldly and ordinary, but is so frightful and awesome to be experienced also as extraordinary and supernatural. But the nature of the this-worldly reality cannot be inferred from the use of the words themselves. It may not involve literal water, and if so, its literal reference has to be made explicit in some other way. Otherwise it remains unclear. Here in v. 27 there is no presupposition that the deep and its rivers have any literal connection with water, and it may be inappropriate to look for too specific a reference. The Tg, however, plausibly refers the flood to Babylon itself, rendering 'who says of Babylon, "It will be laid waste", and I will dry up its streams'; cf Jer 50.38; 50.36–37.

In the MT the second person suffix in v. 27b seems to require that the preposition *l* be rendered 'to' not 'of' in v. 27a, in contrast to v. 26. But the Tg's assumption that the 'deep' is Babylon encourages it to make the most of the recurrence of the root *ḥrb* from the end of v. 26. There may be three roots *ḥrb*, I 'be dry', II 'be waste', III 'smite' (so *BDB*; *DCH* conflates the first two), but their meanings give them scope to assimilate to each other (cf *DTT*). Here vv. 26b–27a utilize that possibility. We have used the word 'waste' both times to mark this, without implying a view on whether the prophet thought in terms of using the same root twice or of using homonyms. Some form of link with the exodus story is suggested by the fact that the root recurs from Exod 14.21 ('dry ground'), as *ṣûlāh* recalls *mᵉṣôlôt* ('deep/depths') in Exod 15.5. Yhwh is not merely recalling the exodus, but promising a repetition of its pattern (cf 43.16–21).

The second colon complements the first in a number of ways. The more common verb for 'be dry', *yābēš*, complements *ḥrb* and offers to disambiguate it in the opposite direction from the one to which v. 26b points. The verb is yiqtol instead of participle or imperative, and thus first person rather than second, and denotes deed rather than word. Again, †Watts's 'and [to] your rivers, "I will dry [you] up"' requires too much reading in.

חָרְבִי: on the form, see GK 46d, 63l.

44.28a. . . .who says of Cyrus, 'My shepherd: he will indeed fulfil all my desire'. At last Cyrus is mentioned, though he is merely Yhwh's underling and agent. The English version of the name is a Latinism, which itself had Latinized Greek Κύρος, which had Hellenized Hebrew *kôreš*, which had Semitized Persian *kurush*.

†Torrey views the reference to Cyrus here and in 45.1, and indeed v. 28 as a whole, as secondary additions to a Second Temple text that as such would hardly make reference to this exilic leader. †P. R. Davies agrees about the dating of the chapters but retains the text, understanding it to refer to the first Persian king as of key significance in the Persian period. R. K. Harrison sees the reference as secondary for the converse reason to Torrey, that the book as a whole comes from the First Temple period.[6] It is interesting and perhaps significant that Isaiah 40–66 never names Media/the Medes (contrast 13.17; 21.2; also, e.g., Jer 51.11, 28) or Persia/the Persians

[6] See his *Introduction to the Old Testament* (Grand Rapids, 1969/London, 1970), p. 794.

(contrast Second Temple writings, Chr, Ezra, Neh, Esther, Daniel, also Ezek 27.10; 38.5).

LXX φρονεῖν ('to think') implies that it reads the word *rōʿî* ('shepherd') either as *rēʿî* (cf Ps 139.2) from *rāʿāh* III or as a form from the root *yādaʿ* (cf †Jerome; and †Ziegler, p. 157, noting its appropriateness in the light of v. 18). That would suggest the translation 'my wish and all my desire he will fulfil', or would encourage the reader (rather than the hearer) to re-read the first colon along these lines in the light of the second. 1QIs[a] *rʿy* may imply that it read the noun as *rēʿî* ('my friend'), from *rāʿāh* II—otherwise one would expect the plene spelling. This would be an entirely plausible expression in the context.[7] The word is a different one from the word for 'friend' used of Abraham at 41.8 (where see), *ʾōhēb*, though the verb *ʾāhab* is applied to Yhwh's relationship with Cyrus at 48.14, and that in fulfilment of Yhwh's *ḥēpeṣ* ('desire'), as here. Here, too, Cyrus would then be designated as Yhwh's associate in a common task. While *rēaʿ* is commonly used in a weak sense to mean 'fellow-citizen/neighbour' (cf 41.6) or simply 'another person', it or related words can also denote lover, husband, or best man, and a high office at court in 1 Chr 27.33 (*rēʿeh* in 1 Kgs 4.5).

The MT, however, points the word *rōʿî*, from *rāʿāh* I ('my shepherd'; cf Sym, Th ποιμήν μου, Aq νομεύς μου, Vg *pastor meus*; Syr *r'yy*/*r'y* is ambiguous/ambivalent), a common middle-eastern description of a king. The Tg's paraphrase 'that he will give him kingship/a kingdom' presupposes the same understanding of the Hebrew, though the prophet, reticent enough about calling Yhwh 'king', does not call Cyrus king at all. As Jacob–Israel is designated Yhwh's servant and thus in some respects inherits the Davidic king's former position, so Cyrus is designated Yhwh's anointed shepherd and thus inherits the Davidic king's position in some other respects. It is a nice suggestion that etymologically 'Cyrus' means 'shepherd' and that the emphasis in the statement is that Cyrus is *my* shepherd (not Mithra's), but the philological evidence is circumstantial and the emphasis not obvious.[8] But the suffix does presuppose that Cyrus is 'merely' Yhwh's agent, a point the parallel colon goes on to develop. Yhwh is indeed the head shepherd, Cyrus the assistant shepherd.

We take the *w* at the beginning of the second colon as emphatic (see on 43.7); †Watts renders the clause as relative (see *IBHS* 39.2.4 on epexegetical *w*). 'He will fulfil' (*yašlim*) is then repeated from v. 26a, though spelled defectively (see GK 53n). Vg *complebis* 'you will fulfil' makes Cyrus instead of Jacob–Israel the addressee, anticipating 45.2–7. In taking up the themes of v. 26 and taking them further, v. 28 characteristically repeats some words and varies others. Thus *ʿēṣāh* ('plan') is succeeded by *ḥēpeṣ* ('desire'), a word that suggests the combination of attentiveness and a feeling of delight (see on 42.21).

[7] Cf A. Kuenen, *National Religions and Universal Religions* (Hibbert Lectures; London, 1882), p. 132.

[8] See †Elliger, against †Simcox, pp. 164–66.

Admittedly the parallelism and the contexts in Isaiah 40–55 suggest that the emotional aspect to *ḥēpeṣ* recedes. The element of will is more significant.[9] The English word 'desire' has parallel range. The suffix indicates that the desire is now Yhwh's and not merely the human agent's. The restoration is Yhwh's 'dream'.[10]

44.28b. . . .and that by saying of Jerusalem 'It will be built' and to the temple 'Be founded'. The allusion to the temple is a noteworthy addition to the concern with rebuilding in v. 26b. †Duhm views v. 28b as an addition, removing this novelty.

The three triads are neatly over. Yet †North comments that v. 28a would make an abrupt end. This is so because events have been announced in reverse order in vv. 26b–28a, for rhetorical reasons. In the MT, v. 28b has the effect of bringing us back to the event to which Yhwh's intent is ultimately directed, the restoration of city and temple, and which logically—because chronologically—belongs at the end of the story. The first explicit reference to Cyrus is closely followed by the first explicit reference to the rebuilding of Jerusalem and of the temple. †Grimm and Dittert see vv. 26b–28 as itself a chiasm, the outer limbs (vv. 26b, 28b) declaring the concrete acts Yhwh is committed to, the inner limbs (vv. 27, 28a) the power and the means by which they will come about.

LXX ὁ λέγων ('Who says. . .') assimilates v. 28b to vv. 26b–28a (cf Vg *qui dico*, which it also had in v. 28a; contrast Sym, Syr, Tg), and thus makes Yhwh the subject of the verb that governs v. 28b. †Ewald assumes this is so with the Hebrew. More likely the infinitive construct, even with *w*, depends on the previous finite verb and has the same subject (†Young, and cf *DG* 109). The *w* will again be explicative (†Elliger, comparing GK 114p; *TTH* 206). †Oort omits it with the Syr. So the words are Cyrus's, 'embedded speech of the third degree' (*Fokkelman, p. 310): Cyrus's words (v. 28b) come inside the self-quoted words of Yhwh (vv. 26b–28a) that come inside Yhwh's direct words (vv. 24b–26a) inside the prophet's words (v. 24a). But both rhetorically and chronologically this sequence of speeches comes to a climax with Cyrus and thus prepares for the act of commitment in 45.1–7.

As in v. 26b, it seems necessary to take the following *l* to mean 'of' rather than 'to', since the verb *tibbāneh* is third feminine not second feminine (contrast LXX οἰκοδομηθήσῃ, Vg *aedificaberis*). The parallel clause is then problematic. Its similar verb *tiwwāsēd* is difficult as third person, because *hêkāl* is masculine, and difficult as second person in the absence of a preposition. We have assumed that on this occasion the force of the *l* must carry over from the previous clause: cf Vg *templo*, hardly requiring that its text included an extra *l*

[9] So †Elliger (p. 286); cf G. J. Botterweck, in *ThWAT*, Vol. 3, col. 114; ET Vol. 5, p. 105.

[10] N. Lohfink's equivalent for חפץ (*Kirchenträume* [Freiburg, 1984], p. 36), as quoted by †Grimm and Dittert.

(against †Morgenstern). The two clauses then complement each other as third and second person.

תוסד: 1QIs[a] reads תיסד (first hand), יתיסד (second hand). †Dillmann emends to third person, יוסד. †Barthélemy notes that Akkadian *ekallu* is f.

III.a.ii. Yhwh designates Cyrus as anointed (45.1–8)

The messenger formula that opens v. 1 suggests a new beginning, and the overt addressee changes from (implicitly) Jacob–Israel to Cyrus, who was in the third person in the preceding verse. We come to a message formally addressed to Cyrus himself, Jacob–Israel being in the third person. But this is the first messenger formula in Isaiah 40–55 that lacks a participial qualification. That hints that this is not a straightforward new beginning. This in turn coheres with earlier indications that while 44.24–28 (where the messenger formula was qualified) also could be independent, it might not actually be so. Like other pairs of units such as 41.8–13, 14–16; 42.1–4, 5–9; 43.14–15, 16–21, each of these passages is just capable of standing alone, but they have the marks of belonging in pairs, at least in the form that we have them. We also noted in the introduction to 44.24–28 that there are certain *inclusio*s between the beginning of 44.24–28 and the latter part of 45.1–7. These continue in 45.8, which could be another self-existent unit, with new addressees and a different form but the same speaker, but is likely composed for this context.

The oracle declares that the events of which it speaks happen for Jacob–Israel's sake. It does not quite acknowledge that this is also true of the oracle itself, but it is so. The oracle brings Jacob–Israel good news (cf †Kratz, p. 81). Perhaps in a literal sense the oracle reports to it Yhwh's quasi-message for Cyrus (cf †Beuken).

The correspondence of a direct promise of deliverance in 43.16–21 and an indirect one by means of the designation of Cyrus in 45.1–8 parallels the correspondence in the first two spirals of direct deliverance oracles in 41.8–16 and indirect ones by means of the designation of the servant in 42.1–9. These parallels confirm the impression that one function of 44.24–45.8 is to bring the first four spirals to a close.

But 45.1–7 is formally addressed to an individual not a community, and specifically to a king. It is a quasi-royal oracle comparable with Israelite ones such as Psalms 2 and 110, addressed to Yhwh's Davidic anointed, with oracles addressed to individual Israelite kings in narratives such as 2 Samuel 7 and 1 Kings 3, with other middle-eastern royal oracles, and specifically with the one Cyrus recalls on the inscription on a clay 'barrel' known as the Cyrus Cylinder (see *ANET*, pp. 315–16). Here Cyrus (allegedly) speaks of the way Marduk commissioned him to attack Babylon in order to reverse recent religious innovations there.

It is impossible to know how far that text represents Cyrus's own convictions. Its terms follow those of Mesopotamian prototypes (see Barstad, *SJOT* 1987/2). It is also impossible to be sure about the relationship of Second Isaiah's oracle and the Cyrus inscription. If we take their dating at face value, the oracle cannot be dependent on the inscription, though †Morton Smith attributed the first part of the inscription, in which the closer parallels come, to the Marduk priesthood before the fall of Babylon. This would make dependence on that possible. It seems unlikely that Cyrus or his drafting committee depended on a Judean prophet's oracle (against Josephus, *Antiquities* XI, 1.2–3, and †Haller).

If the oracle postdates the inscription, this gives a plausible apologetic aim to the oracle. Their relationship comes to parallel that of Genesis 1 and the Babylonian creation story *Enuma Elish*. But it seems unlikely that the oracle then postdates the actual fall of the city and thus offers a retrospective interpretation of events. Isaiah 40–48 implies a very 'realistic' portrait of the prophet's purported involvement with the people's experience and concomitant claim to offer guidance on the significance of events, before and as they unfold. We would need to attribute to the prophet/poet an implausibly sophisticated (or devious) capacity to base arguments on Yhwh's ability to announce future events by means of material in which in reality Yhwh did not do so, and the subtlety or courage to attribute to Yhwh aims through Cyrus's achievements that the prophet/poet was in position to know were not fulfilled.

The links between inscription and oracle require no dependence of one on the other. They need only indicate that both are dependent on middle-eastern royal oracular style and ancient royal ceremony. In the present context, the significance of a comparison of oracle and inscription is to clarify aspects of the oracle's nature. It of course attributes Cyrus's achievements to Yhwh rather than Marduk and emphasizes Yhwh's capacity to frustrate the declarations of other gods and their agents. Taken at its face value, it backs Cyrus before events are over rather than with the wisdom of hindsight, though its hope that Cyrus will acknowledge Yhwh remains unfulfilled.

From 44.24–28 this section repeats, as well as the messenger formula, the asseveration 'I am Yhwh', the claim to unique and unrivalled deity, the concern with Jacob–Israel (now explicit), the reminder of Yhwh's special relationship with that people (now as 'chosen' rather than as 'shaped', though the verb 'shape' also appears in v. 7), Yhwh as 'maker' of everything, a concern with true knowledge, the motif of servant, and Cyrus as Yhwh's special royal agent (now 'anointed' rather than 'shepherd'). Distinctive to 45.1–7 is the direct address to Cyrus, the promise regarding his own destiny, victory, and profit, the aim that he and the world may acknowledge Yhwh, and his naming by Yhwh for Jacob–Israel's sake. The passage comprises a commission and promise to an actual king, and thus has many points of contact with the commission and promise to a metaphorical king in a passage such as 42.1–9. While anointing is characteristic of the designation of a king, this is not the case either with grasping by the hand or calling by name. The oracle does not mark the designation of someone. Cyrus is already the anointed. It is a declaration of what Yhwh intends to do through this anointed, specifically in connection with war. This is the context of the use of the rare verb *rādad* ('subdue') in Ps 144.1–2, of the stripping of loins in Isa 20.2–4, and of Yhwh's going before people in Deut 1.30 and 31.8.

†Begrich (p. 8 = 16) sees the oracle dividing into two parallel parts, vv. 1–3 and 4–7, which †Fohrer makes into two oracles. †Volz makes two oracles of vv. 1–3, 4bα, 5b, 6a, and vv. 5a, 7, 8, †Elliger of vv. 1a (beginning)7, and vv. 1 (rest), 3b, 5. †Merendino sees vv. 4a, 5aβ, 6b–8 as additions to the original Cyrus oracle. †Kratz sees vv. 1aβb, 3bα ('so that you may know'), 5 as additions to the original form of vv. 1–7 to adapt it to subsequent events. †Van Oorschot (pp. 89–91) sees the original oracle as vv. 1a, 2–4a, 5a, with v. 8 also being original (pp. 84–87).

†Kratz takes the threefold *l*^{e}*maʿan* as a key to the structure of vv. 1–7 as they stand, which suggests the outline

1 Introduction
    2–3 'I will go before you, *l*^{e}*maʿan*. . ., I Yhwh'
    4–5a '*l*^{e}*maʿan*. . ., I name you, I Yhwh'
    5b–7 'I gird you, *l*^{e}*maʿan*. . ., I Yhwh'
[8 conclusion]

Verses 1–8 may also be read chiastically:

1 Introduction (addressed to Jacob–Israel/heavenly beings?)
    2–3a Yhwh's promise
    3b–4 So that you may know
        5a Yhwh's self-predication
    5b Yhwh's promise
    6a So that they may know
6b–8 Conclusion (addressed to Jacob–Israel/heaven and earth?)

The chiasm and the repetition draw attention to the fact that the verses' ultimate concern is not Cyrus's victories but Yhwh's recognition. On the self-predication in vv. 5–7 see the introduction to 44.24–28.

45.1aα. Yhwh has said this to his anointed. As we noted in the introduction to vv. 1–7, the messenger formula is distinctive for its lack of participial qualification. At the point where we would expect such phrases, we encounter a description of Yhwh's addressee, Cyrus, which is at least as bold as that in 44.28. He is Yhwh's 'anointed', one designated by Yhwh like Saul or David.

In the MT, *lim*^{e}*šîḥô* ('to his anointed') is the immediate indirect object of 'said' and Yhwh's actual words begin after *lim*^{e}*šîḥô*. The chapter thus opens with a 4–4 line. The LXX, on the one hand (see below), begins Yhwh's speech one word earlier, while the Vg links 'to Cyrus' with 'to his anointed' (cf RSV). In the MT the same mildly disjunctive *zarqa* accent separates 'Yhwh' from 'to his anointed', then separates 'to his anointed' from 'to Cyrus'. By this accentuation, indeed, the MT probably intends the last expression to signify 'of Cyrus', to avoid identifying Cyrus as the anointed (†M. B. Cohen, pp. 3–6). Thus *b. Megillah* 12a has Yhwh speaking to the Messiah about Cyrus, while †Saadya, linking the opening clause with what has preceded, identifies the prophet as Yhwh's anointed. Conversely Aq, in keeping with policy elsewhere, replaces χριστῷ by ἠλειμμενῷ.

יהוה: LXX adds ὁ θεὸς, but it often has that (see on 41.17), so this is hardly grounds for adding האל m.c. (against †Duhm). The MT in any case reads this and the next colon (of Cyrus, the one whom I took by the right hand) as 3–3.
למשיחו: LXX τῷ χριστῷ μου, Vg *christo meo*, might imply למשיחי, which would then be the opening of Yhwh's actual words, 'To my anointed, to Cyrus…'. †Budde emends MT's אמר יהוה למשיחו ('Yhwh has said to his anointed') to למשיחי אמרתי ('I have said to my anointed'). Driver ([see on 43.14b] p. 164) simply repoints the verb אֹמַר ('I [Yhwh] will say [to my anointed]'). But †Ottley notes parallels in patristic writers that suggest that the first person suffix is influenced by Ps 110.1.

45.1aβ. …to Cyrus, the one whom I took by the right hand. The first person verbs mark this line as Yhwh's opening words, but Cyrus is still referred to in the third person rather than directly addressed. The words contain no main verb and comprise an honorific formal introduction to what follows. Writers such as †Torrey and Harrison (see on 44.28) again see the expression 'to Cyrus' as an interpretative gloss. We have just noted that the MT was scandalized by it, too. Early Christian writers such as Tertullian read the word as Κυρίῳ rather than Κύρῳ (so also some LXX MSS) and thus take this as an instance of God the Father speaking to God the Son (*Against Praxeas* 11; 28); so also Novatian (*The Trinity* 26). †Eusebius of Caesarea, who wrote the first extant Christian commentary on Isaiah, is the first writer to comment on the text more historically (see Hollerich, *Eusebius*, pp. 137–38).

As a pure relative *'ăšer* ('the one whom') would be surprising in poetry (†Köhler omits it). We have taken it as demonstrative (†Ehrlich)/deictic (†Merendino). Significantly, it follows the expression in 41.9 where the equivalent phrase describes Yhwh's servant.

45.1aγδ. …to put down nations before him and strip the loins of kings. In both form and meaning the rare verb *rādad* ('put down') recalls the slightly more common *rādāh* ('rule, have dominion over'). Speaker and hearer could then make links with the use of the latter at 41.2 (viewing it as a byform?) in connection with the conqueror who might be Abraham, Israel, or Cyrus. Indeed 45.1 disambiguates 41.1–

5. The latter verb also features in the significant promise of reversal at 14.2, 6, referring to Median termination of Babylonian domination over Israel, and in royal oracles at Pss 72.8 and 110.2 (cf also Num 24.19). Cyrus fulfils Yhwh's destiny for Media, Israel, and Israel's anointed king.

The more figurative 'strip the loins of kings' parallels the more literal 'subdue nations'. The verb comes at the end, making the line a chiasm that rhetorically suggests the reversal the words refer to. The metaphor reflects the loss of the ability to fight and rule. With some other verb such as 'shake' or 'break' (*māʿad* hi, *šābar*), 'loins' might be a figure for physical strength and morale (so †Calvin here), but the use of the verb *pātaḥ* (pi) suggests that the figure works in the more usual way, denoting the loosening of the (weapon belt/armoury around the) loins and thus the removal of the capacity to fight (†Luther): see 2 Sam 20.8, and contrast v. 5 below, and on the resultative piel, see *Piʿel*, pp. 201–2.

M. Dahood interprets the phrase in the light of Ugaritic and Akkadian equivalents, to mean 'I will open the legs of kings', that is, make them run (to open doors: see next line).[11] Either way, the phrase illustrates 'a kind of physical directness, to the detriment of the kings' about v. 1, alongside 'a certain physical proximity in favour of the victorious king' ('took by the right hand', acted 'before' his very eyes) (*Fokkelman, pp. 315–16).

לְרַד: from רָדַד one would expect רֹד, but see GK 67p; JM 82l. The pointing לְ for לָ results from the construct relationship with לפניו: see GK 102f. †Torrey sees LXX's ἐπακοῦσαι as an inner-Greek corruption. †Graetz reads לרדות from רדה (cf 41.2), †Klostermann לחרד ('so that [nations] tremble'), †Marti להחריד ('to terrify/rout'), Dahood לַרַד, a Phoenician-style yiphil (see at 41.2b).
אפתח: the yiqtol continues the inf. (cf GK 114r; *DG* 107). Given this regular idiom, it is unlikely that a hearer would interpret the (chiastic) clauses as meaning 'to subdue...I strip...' (†Watts), but the sequence of the clauses in v. 1b might justify '...and that I might strip...'.

45.1b. ...to open doors before him and that gateways might not close. Verbally 'to open doors before him' exactly corresponds to 'to subdue nations before him'. Each comprises infinitive with *l*, the phrase 'before him', and the plural noun (with rhyme at the end). Verse 1b itself forms another chiasm, while the repetition of the verb *pātaḥ* ('strip/open'), the last word in v. 1a and the first in v. 1b, with the stem changing from piel to qal, helps to make the link and the distinction between the two lines. The audience might guess that the double doors (*delātayim*) were those of cities that Cyrus would take, but this is made more explicit by the parallelism 'gateways' (*šeʿārîm*), a term that applies more distinctively to cities. Strictly the former are

[11] 'Hebrew and Ugaritic Equivalents of Accadian pitū purīdā', in *Bib* 39 (1958), pp. 67–69.

the elements that swing open and shut, the latter the whole structure around the doors, supporting them, and its environs (e.g. Gen 19.1, 6; Judg 16.3; Neh 3.1). A different parallelism appears in the verbs from that in the nouns, narrow and broad being replaced by positive and negative, the raising of a siege by the welcoming of an attacker.

דלתים: 1QIs[a] has pl. דלתות (cf v. 2) for MT dual, which does not appear in MH (†Kutscher, p. 295; ET p. 388).
שׁערים: LXX has πόλεις, but †Ottley doubts whether this suggests it read ערים; it is a common rendering in Deuteronomy (e.g. Deut 12.17, 18).
יסגרו: again the finite vb continues the inf. construction; see GK 114r. The negative is לא despite this being a purpose clause (JM 124q).

45.2a. I myself will go before you and level the city walls. The 'I' is expressed by the pronoun (the Tg characteristically has 'my word'), drawing attention to the fact that Cyrus's relentless advance reflects not merely his military expertise but Yhwh's preceding him.

הדורים: in form a passive participle; Vg *gloriosus terrae* implies a derivation from the verb הדר ('honour'). Syr *ʿrmʾ* ('uneven land'—as at 40.4 for העקב and at 42.16 for מעקשׁים) may infer that root here used in a more down-to-earth sense, 'what is upraised' (BDB). While the word is a *hapax legomenon* in BH, in MH it can mean a steep ascent requiring a circuitous path (*DTT*; also Reider [see on 44.88], p. 109, for an Arabic parallel). *DCH* has 'mountainous land'. 1QIs[a] has הררים ('the mountains'; cf LXX ὄρη), which looks like an easier reading, but Tov argues that it is original (*Textual Criticism* [see at 44.9b], p. 254). 1QIs[b] הדורים may be a composite of the MT and 1QIs[a] reading (†Elliger). †Houbigant emends to הדרכים ('the ways'). Tg; שׁוריא ('the fortified walls') suggests the word is an equivalent of Akkadian *dūru* ('city wall') (cf 29.3; *Hoffmann, *Southwood) and refers to the formidable walls of a city such as Babylon (see †Elliger). The pointing הַדּוּרִים is needed, and the art. is then suspicious in poetry.
אושׁר: K implies the hi form of an initial ו vb. It is implicitly supported by 1QIs[a] יאושׁר, which has emended the unfamiliar form (†Kutscher, pp. 168–69; ET p. 222). Q אֲיַשֵּׁר pi is the usual usage.

45.2b. I will break up bronze doors and cut up iron bars. If Babylon was reckoned to possess a hundred bronze gates (Herodotus 1.179), the first colon may provide clearer indication that vv. 1–2 refer to Babylon in particular. Both verbs are piel: see on 43.14 (and *Piʿel*, pp. 125–26, 181–83). The three piels at the end of each colon in v. 2aβb rhyme and reinforce each other. Walls, doors, and bars stand no chance against them (*Fokkelman, p. 317). If we were to repoint the word for 'fugitives' in 43.14 so that it read 'bars' (see note), this would support reference to Babylon here with what would then be the recurrence of the 'bars' that were specifically Babylon's there. The words occur as a qatal statement in Ps 107.16. The psalm also has a different (more prosaic?) form of the noun 'bronze' and a chiastic (more poetic?) word order. Here the verbs add to the prominence of first person yiqtol verbs in v. 2.

אֲשַׁבֵּר (pi): 1QIs[a] has the slightly more common qal אשבור ('I will break').

45.3a. I will give you dark treasuries and hidden hoards. While this follows logically from v. 2b, the verb is *w*-consecutive rather than simple *w* plus yiqtol to suggest purpose or result. The distinctive verb form marks the objective of vv. 2–3a and a different pair of plurals replace the sequence in vv. 1b–2, which have failed to block the way to these two rhetorically or substantially (*Fokkelman, pp. 316, 317). The word *ʾôṣār* denotes both treasure and treasury, as what is stored up and as a storage place. Here the construct, literally 'of darkness', suggests that the reference is to the place. The content of the place follows in the parallel colon.

'Hoards' (*maṭmôn*), the rarer word in the second colon, more inherently suggests hiddenness, often by being buried, sometimes with a hint of darkness (cf the passive participle in Job 20.26). 'Hoards' thus also links back to 'dark', and as 'dark' makes more explicit the inherent connotation of 'treasures', so the inherent connotation of 'hoards' is made more explicit by 'hidden'. It is a familiar enough root but again it appears in a rarer form, as the plural noun *mistārîm* (lit. 'hordes of hides'), and with an unusual reference (it usually applies to living things). In the context, the riches may suggest the financing of Cyrus's exploits rather than the reward of them.

מסתרים: LXX adds ἀνοίξω σοι ('I will open up to you'), which constitutes expansionist translation based on v. 1 (†Ziegler, p. 74; *HUB*) rather than suggesting an original אפתח לך (†Oort).

45.3b. . . .so that you may acknowledge that I am Yhwh. The one who calls you by name is the God of Israel. Cyrus is hardly expected to acknowledge Yhwh simply on the basis of receiving these treasures. †Duhm thus omits 'so that you may acknowledge', turning the 4–4 line into a 2–2–2 line. In the MT the logic might rather be that he will acknowledge Yhwh on the basis of Yhwh's having undertaken to act in a certain way and then done so. Further, the evidence is the activity indicated by vv. 1–3a as a whole, not merely that of v. 3a. Here lies a significance of the use of *w*-consecutive in v. 3a, linking this verb to those in v. 2 without implying that it forms any kind of climax. The aim of Yhwh's acts is not merely Jacob–Israel's deliverance but Cyrus's acknowledgment.

The MT's accents imply the understanding 'that I, Yhwh, the one who calls you by name...', but the sequence *ʾănî yhwh* more likely again suggests the self-designation 'I am Yhwh' (see on 41.4, 20). In isolation the second colon, notwithstanding the word order preserved in the version above, could be understood as a statement that 'the

God of Israel [is] the one who calls you by name' (cf the comment on the article on the participle in JM 137l). More likely the second colon parallels the first. 'I' is thus paralleled by 'the one who calls you' as subject, 'Yhwh' by 'the God of Israel' as predicate. 'Calling by name' again implies a sovereign summoning (cf 40.26; 43.1).

The Syr's 'who called you' anticipates v. 4.

45.4a. For the sake of my servant Jacob, Israel my chosen... The verse division implies that v. 4a begins a new sentence rather than constituting an enjambment. The word order is that of 44.2 (see comment) not that of 44.1, thus also taking the form of another chiasm (see GK 131g; but LXX changes to the more usual 'Jacob my servant'). Further, v. 4a comes at the centre of a chiasm comprising vv. 3b–4 as a whole:

3bα So that you may acknowledge Yhwh
3bβ The one who calls you by name
4aα my servant
Israel
4aβ Jacob
My chosen
4bα I call you by name
4bβ You do not acknowledge me

It thus transpires that while the aim of Jacob–Israel's deliverance is Cyrus's recognition of Yhwh, the beneficiary of Cyrus's recognition of Yhwh is—Jacob–Israel.

וישׂראל: *IBHS* 39.2.4 sees the ו (missing in 1QIs[a]) as epexegetical, Brongers ([see on 42.12] p. 275) specifically as compensating for the non-repetition of למען.

45.4b. I called you by name. I designate you though you do not acknowledge me. If we had read v. 4a as a continuation of v. 3, the *w*-consecutive with which v. 4b begins, which is rare in poetry, would have to be resumptive ('So I called you...'), which is possible but jerky. If v. 4a opens a new sentence, however, it turns out to form more idiomatically the protasis to a *w*-apodosis in v. 4b (†Saydon, p. 298; and see JM 176). It thus suits both bicola to read them as one sentence. It is implausible to stretch the construction further so that the whole of vv. 3b–4a leads into v. 4b, even if we see vv. 3b–4 as a strophe. GK 111b does not offer support or parallel for a purpose clause such as v. 3b so far preceding its main verb (against *Fokkelman, p. 318).

The LXX's καλέσω τῷ ὀνόματί μου omits the *w* and has Yhwh saying 'I will call you by my name'. In 1QIs[a] Yhwh says 'I called you and by [a] name (*wbšm*) I designate you'. In the MT Yhwh says 'I called you by your name', *bišmekā*. As well as called by name, Cyrus is 'designated', as Jacob–Israel's offspring 'designate themselves'

(44.5, where see). The verb *kānāh* appears only in these two verses and at Job 32.21–22. Here, at least, it must mean something like 'designate' rather than 'surname'.

As at 44.5 the verb is yiqtol. The fact that there, too, it stood in line-by-line parallelism with the yiqtol of *qārā*ʾ ('call') supports the suggestion that the yiqtol form is chosen to make a link with the (*w* plus) yiqtol form of *qārā*ʾ here (†Saydon, p. 295; cf also JM 113h). On the other hand the prophet declined further to assimilate these two verbs by making both either simple yiqtols or *w* plus yiqtols, and it is likely that a hearer would assume that there was some difference between them. We have preserved the difference by rendering the first past, the second present as a past act that lasts on into the present or continues to operate in it (cf GK 107h). †Young's suggestion that the second refers to nascent action fits the context less well.

In this context *wᵉlōʾ yᵉdaʿtānî* is then a circumstantial clause, 'though you did/do not acknowledge me', not a temporally consecutive clause 'but you did/do not…' like those in 42.20 and especially v. 25. Yet Cyrus and Jacob–Israel do have in common their not having acknowledged Yhwh. Verse 3bα contained the standard recognition formula which combines the objective that Yhwh should be acknowledged with Yhwh's self-presentation. By v. 4 these have come apart. Here appears the note that Yhwh has not been acknowledged. For the meaning 'acknowledge' here and in v. 5, cf Tg 'you do not know how to serve' ('revere' in some manuscripts).

אכנך: cf Syr *wknytk* ('and I gave you a second name'). In 1QIsa[a] הכנכה the initial ה might be simply an aural slip (†Kutscher, p. 186; ET p. 247), but a י above the line then makes it הכינכה, hi of כון ('he established you'). Tg has אתקינתך ('I prepared you'), which also recalls כון (*DTT*, *HUB*). LXX has καὶ προσδέξομαί σε ('and I will accept you'; following its rendering of רצה at 42.1—†Ziegler, p. 157), Vg *assimilavi te* ('I have represented you').

45.5. I am Yhwh and there is no other. Besides me there is no God. I gird you though you do not acknowledge me. The MT locates the mid-verse division after '…no God', but more likely the verse comprises two couplets, 2–2 ('I am Yhwh and there is no other') and 3–3. But v. 5a as a whole represents the centre-point of the chiasm comprising vv. 1–8 and comprises a succinct summary of much of the theology of chapters 40–45.

*Beuken (pp. 336–41, 350–54) takes as the contested point here 'Who is Yhwh', the answer being 'I am Yhwh and there is no other Yhwh', but this seems odd. The opposite view has been maintained by S. H. Blank (see *Prophetic Faith*, pp. 68–73). He sees 'I am Yhwh' as signifying in contexts such as this 'I am God', which leads quite logically into 'and there is no other'. But the fact that the prophet is quite capable of using the phrase 'I am God (*ʾēl*)' suggests that we should not lose the distinctiveness of the statement 'I am Yhwh'. Blank, like Beuken, may be trying to be too logical about the statement. The question behind the statement is, 'Who is God?', and the answer is 'Yhwh'. But it is true that in these chapters the point of Yhwh's self-presentation is the claim to exclusive deity. 'There is no other' (*ʾên ʿôd*) recurs in vv. 6, 14, 18, 21, 22; also 46.9; 47.8, 10. A more literal rendering would be 'otherwise there is not'. While *ʿôd* may be in origin a noun meaning 'continuance', this meaning does not fit here and the predominant usage is adverbial. The subject, 'God', has to be inferred from the parallel colon.

The yiqtol verb *ʾăʾazzerkā* presumably corresponds to the one in v. 4 (†Saydon, p. 295) and thus suggests 'I have been and am girding you'. Its meaning recalls and contrasts with v. 1a. The Tg renders less colourfully 'help' (perhaps implying *ʿzr* for *ʾzr*), Syr 'strengthen', while it is perhaps in order to avoid the anthropomorphism that the LXX simply omits the verb (cf v. 15).

זולתי אין: LXX omits אין, having added ὅτι ('for') at the beginning of v. 5 (cf v. 3b), and thus runs together the two middle cls. 1QIs[a] ואין implicitly links זולתי ('besides me') to the preceding cl. In contrast, 1QIs[b] reads וזולתי and cements the link to what follows.

45.6. ...so that people will acknowledge from the rise of the sun and from the setting that there is none apart from me. I am Yhwh and there is no other. The 2–2, 3–3 bicola of v. 5 are nicely followed by 3–3, 2–2 bicola in v. 6. The new 3–3 bicolon states the purpose of its predecessor, reusing its verb. The new 2–2 bicolon exactly repeats its twin. 'From the rise...and from the setting' is the first of four merisms in vv. 6–8. Here the two extremes cover everything in between. The two elements in the recognition formula again appear separately at either end of the verse, though now in the opposite order to that in v. 5. The verb is no longer negatived, but the bringing together of the two elements is still a matter of hope. Kennicott MS 150 omits 'of the sun' (see *HUB*); †Marti prefers the shorter text.

The spiralling subordination of aims continues. The aim of Jacob–Israel's restoration was Cyrus's acknowledgment of Yhwh. The aim of Cyrus's acknowledgment was Jacob–Israel's restoration. The aim of Jacob–Israel's restoration was the whole world's acknowledgment of Yhwh.

On 'I am Yhwh and otherwise there is not', see on v. 5; here, too, 'God' needs to be understood.

וממערבה: the ה looks like ה of direction (cf 2 Chr 32.30; 33.14), but if so the suffix must have lost its meaning—cf English 'from westwards' (see GK 90e). But ממערב usually occurs without the ה (e.g. 43.5. 59.19); so 1QIs[a], and †Köhler omits it. 1QIs[b] agrees with the MT. The addition of αὐτοῦ in some LXX MSS, Th, Sym may mean they read the pronominal suffix הּ ('from its setting') not the locative suffix ה; so also Syr and some Tg MSS. JM 94h takes the ה as a rare third f. suffix without *mappiq*.

45.7. Shaper of light and creator of dark, maker of well-being and creator of adversity, I am Yhwh maker of all these. As the assertion of Yhwh's unrivalled sovereignty is further extended by means of two further pairs of linked opposites to supplement sunrise–setting, the 2–2 pattern at first seems to continue. It then turns out to become a 4–4–4 pattern instead, as Yhwh's words come to a climax, though not yet to a conclusion. Like the prepositional phrase in v. 4a, the participial phrases in v. 7a more likely lead into v. 7b than hang onto what has preceded. Verse 6b has closed off a chiasm comprising vv. 5–6 and v. 7b is a rather brief self-contained interim ending. Once more there seems no reason to see the participles as especially hymnic (see on 40.22). If anything they more likely once again have the connotations of theological argument. Like others in these chapters, they resist being confined to referring to past events, without excluding such reference.

For Yhwh to be shaper of light and maker of well-being is unsurprising. By alliteration well-being (*šālôm*) takes up the verb *yašlīm* and the name Jerusalem from 44.28 (*Fokkelman, p. 322). If the meaning 'reparation' for *šālôm* is ever justified, the present context hardly points towards it.[12] As near the prophet's point is the comment in *Numbers Rabbah* 12.4 that the holy one created the world only on the understanding that there would be peace among created beings.

For Yhwh to be creator of dark is a new statement, though one in line with what has preceded. Darkness is a deprivation out of which people need to be delivered (42.6–7, 16). Yhwh is sovereign in relation to it, not only as one able to end its rule, but as one who imposes it in the first place (8.22 [9.1]). The idea that Yhwh is creator of adversity restates the point. 1QIs[a] replaces *šālôm* by *ṭwb* ('good'), drawing attention to the fact that there is no traditional link between the antonyms *šālôm* and *ra*ʿ ('adversity'; here *rā*ʿ, in pause). Each links with the antonyms light and dark, but links with the other only via these two. Thus *ra*ʿ appeared in the company of light and dark at 5.20, along with *ṭôb*, its natural antonym, with reference to people who will not face the dark/bad consequences of their policies and who pretend they will issue in light/good. In 41.23, other gods are challenged to do good or bad—to bring about blessing or disaster. In other contexts, *ra*ʿ can refer to moral evil, and the 1QIs[a] reading 'good and bad' may reflect Qumran belief in God's being the creator of both good and evil.[13] But reflection on whether God is the author of moral evil is alien to v. 7 in its original context (cf *Lindström).

Zoroastrian religion attributes sole deity to Ahura Mazda, and emphasizes an ongoing conflict between good and bad. That gives v. 7 new resonances in the Persian period, but for prophet and audience

[12] Against †Merendino, who follows Gerleman (see on 41.3).

[13] So Rubinstein, *JJS* 6 (1955), p. 194; cf H. Kosmala's comments on Qumran dualism in a review of H. W. Huppenbauer, *Der Mensch zwischen zwei Welten* (ATANT 34, 1959), in *VT* 11 (1961), pp. 356–59.

v. 7 rather resonates with such other connotations within Isaiah as a whole and within this prophet's thinking. In that context, describing Yhwh as shaper of light and creator of dark causes no surprises, though the use of the two familiar participles is extended and their collocation with the two nouns makes explicit or expresses incisively an assumption that is only implicit or is less succinct elsewhere. The parallel colon first adds the generalizing 'maker': cf this verb's appearance at the end of 43.7 after 'create' and 'shape', and indeed its reappearance here as the final participle, in v. 7b. Second, it adds *šālôm* as a novel parallel to 'light'. Third, it repeats 'creator', producing an ABCB pattern in the participles (cf 42.15),[14] and again lulling us into a false sense of familiarity. Fourth, it attaches to that participle the wide-ranging *raʿ* as an alternative and less metaphorical way of speaking of 'dark'.

The third colon repeats the declaration 'I am Yhwh', which opened and closed vv. 5–6, and appends to it a further participial qualifier, which at this further closure is appropriately longer than its predecessor and which sums up v. 7. 'All these', in other words, embraces the antithetical light/dark, well-being/adversity that have anticipated it, presupposing and making clear that the extremes stood for everything in between. The MT's 'I, Yhwh, do/make all these' is less plausible: cf v. 3. Syntactically v. 7 is not a *w*-apodosis sentence, but in substance it is. The fact that these words form an *inclusio* with the opening of Yhwh's words in 44.24 and thus round off the whole perhaps supports †Elliger's view that the 'all' is not only the double totalities of v. 7 but the total activity that the section has referred to.

יהוה: LXX again adds ὁ θεὸς without providing grounds for adding האל (against †Duhm): see on v. 1.
אלה: A. D. Corré suggests that אלה is an equivalent to *sic* ('thus'). It confirms that the text is as written and is not to be emended according to the *tiqqun* (the corrections proposed by the scribes).[15] If so, Yhwh simply claims to be 'creator of everything' and the parallel with 44.24 is exact.

45.8a. Rain, you heavens above. Clouds must pour down right. Verse 8 might be read as two tricola, in their distinctive form closing off 44.24–45.8, but in the MT it seems to comprise three bicola, 3–3, 2–2, 3–3, fitting the recurrence of 3–3 and 2–2 lines in vv. 5–7. In v. 8a each colon has a subject and a verb, but only the first has an adverb and only the second an object. The last word in each, 'above' and 'right', have force in both cola. Thus *ṣedeq* is the implicit object of the first verb as well as the second, but some suspense is suggested by the holding back of the noun so that it is the last word in the line. Only at

[14] See J. Kugel, *The Idea of Biblical Poetry* (New Haven/London, 1981), p. 20.
[15] '*ʾēlle, hēmma* = *sic*', in *Bib* 54 (1973), pp. 263–64.

the very end of the bicolon do we discover the object of the very first word and only then do we have any idea at all what the line is about. Further interest is sustained by the move from second person to third person verb, from hiphil to qal verb, from dual to plural subject, and from verb–subject to subject–verb order.

1QIs[a] begins *hryʿw* ('shout'), as in 44.23, to replace the less familiar *hrʿypw* (†Kutscher, p. 215; ET pp. 286–87); but cf LXX εὐφρανθήτω ('[heaven] must rejoice'), also the Tg *yšmšwn* ('[the heavens] must minister'). Such a reading would justify the description of this as an anticipatory hymn of praise (cf †Westermann). But in the MT the differences from 44.23 (and 42.10–13) are at least as significant as the similarities (†Beuken). Here heaven is not invited to worship, and the speaker is not the prophet. Yhwh speaks, and commissions heaven and earth to take a role in bringing about the fulfilment of Yhwh's right purpose. Perhaps we are to assume that the language constitutes a more poetic version of the commission to heavenly aides and earthly agents such as Cyrus, who have responsibility to see that Yhwh's right purpose is put into effect.

BDB suggests that *rāʿap* and *nāzal* both mean 'trickle' or 'drip', but more likely both suggest a much more abundant flow of water, as the present context requires: see the other occurrences of *rāʿap* (Ps 65.12, 13 [11, 12]; Job 36.28; Prov 3.20; all qal, not hi as here) and the use of *nāzal* in 44.3 and 48.21. Only here are the verbs used theologically in connection with right and deliverance. Heaven and earth and the verbs *ʿārap* and *nāzal* appear in a different metaphorical usage in Deut 32.1–2. In 55.9–11 heaven and earth are not the sources of right and deliverance. Rather their miraculous and abundant production of rain and crops provides a simile for the imminent miraculous and abundant accomplishment of Yhwh's purpose by the power of Yhwh's word (cf 54.9–10, where *šālôm* also recurs).

ממעל: although rain does come 'from above', the prep. should not be pressed, as the expression regularly means simply 'above' (see BDB, pp. 578b, 751b).

45.8b. Earth must open so that deliverance may fruit and rightness burst out, all at once; I Yhwh am creating it. In v. 8a the two cola had parallel subjects and implicitly the same object. Syntactically the novelty in the second colon was the jussive verb. It is then this that is immediately picked up in the next bicolon, while its subject changes from heavens/clouds to the correlative earth, and its number thus from plural to singular.

In the MT the point is made in three clauses that raise difficulties individually and in combination. The first verb *tiptaḥ* ('open') is elsewhere transitive, even where there is ellipse of the object; cf 28.24 (pi). We have assumed that it is here intransitive (so Driver [see on 40.12a], pp. 243–44). Syr *ttpth̤* and Vg *aperiatur* suggest repointing as niphal *tippātaḥ* (†Budde) or qal passive *tuptaḥ* (M. Dahood).[16] A further unique usage of this verb will come in 48.8.

The second verb *w^eyiprû* ('so that they may fruit') is plural. Its subject has to be inferred from what has preceded (so MT accents) or provided from what follows ('so that deliverance and justice may fruit'—†Qimchi), but this truncates the next colon. The Tg's 'so that the dead may live' likely witnesses to the MT's plural verb as well as constituting an interesting piece of theological interpretation, but 1QIs^a has singular *wyprḥ* from another verb for 'grow' that appears in 17.11; 27.6; 35.1–2; 66.14, while the Vg has singular *germinet* (with which it translates *prḥ* in 27.6; 35.2; 66.14). In the LXX singular ἀνατειλάτω ('grow') represents both verbs (though many MSS add καὶ βλαστησάτω). Goshen-Gottstein ([see on 43.12], p. 155) suggests it was wary of reference to earth opening because that usually suggests not blessing but disaster, as in the story of Korah. †Volz sees these two first verbs as variants and proposes *tipraḥ*/*taprîaḥ* to replace both, producing a neat 3-word line to lead into the next, 'earth must fruit in deliverance'; see further †Elliger (see on 41.15a) for an explanation of the text in terms of doublets. We have assumed that the versional evidence instead points to an original *w^eyēper* (cf †Houbigant). This also makes for a self-contained line, understood as 'so that deliverance may fruit' (cf 11.1). G. R. Driver further suggests that the problem is one of word division and redivides *w^eyēper w^eyešaʿ*, 'so that it may fruit, and deliverance [and rightness must spring up]'.[17]

This brings us to the third verb, *taṣmîaḥ*, for which one might have expected qal *tiṣmaḥ* (†Budde) (cf 42.9; 44.4; 58.8), or hiphil plural *yaṣmîḥû* ('make [rightness] bud'; cf 61.11). We have taken the MT as intensive hiphil; cf the parallel usage of *pāraḥ* (BDB; GK 53d). †Ehrlich deletes. The LXX repeats ἀνατειλάτω.

The collocation of *ṣedeq*, *yešaʿ*, and *š^edāqāh* is noteworthy. The latter two appear for the first time in chapters 40–55. While *ṣedeq* has a tendency to refer to God's activity (especially in these chapters) and *ṣ^edāqāh* to human activity, *ṣ^edāqāh* will refer to God's activity in (e.g.) 45.23, 24; 46.12, 13. It is a suggestive idea that Yhwh commissions both heavenly action in political events and an earthly response in the shaping of Jacob–Israel's life, but it is implausible to find such a distinction here in v. 8. This imposes an artificial disjunction upon the pair 'heaven' and 'earth' (†Reiterer, p. 104) and upon 'deliverance' and 'rightness' (which are linked by 'all at once').

Given that in these words Yhwh has been not merely speaking but acting (see on v. 8a), *b^erāʾtîw* ('I am creating it') might be taken as another performative qatal (see 42.1b). The Tg renders 'created them', the dead who were introduced earlier. The LXX renders 'created you'. The MT's *b^erāʾtîw* has a masculine suffix. The immediate masculine antecedent is the word for 'deliverance', but

[16] *Proverbs and Northwest Semitic Philology* (Rome, 1963), pp. 8–9.
[17] 'Hebrew Notes', in *JBL* 68 (1949), pp. 57–59 (see p. 59).

†Ibn Ezra takes it to refer to Cyrus (as indirect object)—as does †Bonnard. He then takes v. 8 as an introduction to vv. 9–13; cf the section break in 1QIs[ab]. More likely this is a 'dummy' impersonal pronoun with general reference to the events that have been described, but here masculine (see on 43.13).

תפתח ארץ: 1QIs[a] האמר לארץ—its original was perhaps unclear (cf †Muilenburg), as is its own equivalent to MT יזלו (Rowlands, *VT* 1 [1951], pp. 227–28). 1QIs[a] also lacks the closing words of v. 8, יחד אני יהוה בראתיו, but leaves a considerable space at this point. This again suggests that its text was difficult to read (†Martin, p. 14).

III.a.iii. Yhwh dismisses objections to this intention (45.9–13)

As v. 8 is intelligible as the close of a section, 'Oh' (*hôy*) regularly opens one, and thus marks v. 9 as a new beginning. *Leene (pp. 323–24) notes that v. 8 is rather a pronounced semi-closure part way through 44.24–45.25, which suggests that vv. 9–13 belongs more closely with what follows than with what proceeds.

The exclamation *hôy* can introduce an expression of dismay, reproof, warning, or even invitation.[18] Although most common in the prophets, its use in connection with grief (cf 1 Kgs 13.30; Jer 22.18) may suggest that it is of more popular background, and in terms of traditions that it has a background in wisdom—like other material in these chapters (e.g. within 40.12–26).[19] However that may be, its common association with death makes it strike a worrying note here,[20] though usage such as 55.1 may also suggest that by this period its connotations were less terminal. We might have expected the speaker to be identified, as at 30.1, but more often this is not so, as at 10.5; 29.1, 15; 55.1. In 55.1 the speaker is the same as in the preceding section. If that were so here, then Yhwh speaks. But in the other passages the speaker is unidentified even when it changes, and here the third person reference to Yhwh as 'shaper' of the addressees suggests that the prophet speaks, as in *hôy* oracles in 1.4; 5.8–23; 10.1–4; 17.12; 18.1; 29.15; 31.1; 33.1.

It is with v. 11 that once again the messenger formula marks a transition to Yhwh's own words. This leaves vv. 9–10 as the rhetorical equivalent to an extraposed clause, introducing the unit but not 'syntactically' related to it. The MT treats vv. 8, 9, and 10 as three separate units each closed by a setuma. After v. 13 is then the first petucha since 44.23. 1QIs[a] substantially indents v. 9 (perhaps partly to leave room for the last colon of v. 8: see comment), leaves a

[18] See W. Janzen, *Mourning Cry and Woe Oracle* (BZAW 125, 1972).

[19] See E. Gerstenberger, 'The Woe-Oracles of the Prophets', in *JBL* 81 (1962), pp. 249–63.

[20] On this association see H.-J. Krause, '*hôj* als prophetische Leicheklage über das eigene Volk im 8. Jahrhundert', in *ZAW* 85 (1973), pp. 15–46 (he disputes Gerstenberger's link with wisdom just noted); also H.-J. Zobel, in *ThWAT*, Vol. 2, cols 382–88 (ET Vol. 3, pp. 358–64).

space in the line before v. 11, and opens a new line after v. 13. In other *hôy* oracles at 5.9; 18.4; 31.4 the messenger formula appears part-way through the section rather than at the beginning, so that this feature is no pointer against vv. 9–13 being an intrinsic unity (against †Westermann). The resumptive, closing 'Almighty Yhwh has said' at the end of v. 13 and the new messenger formula at the beginning of v. 14, introducing material with a feminine singular addressee and a different tone and topic, suggest that the MT and 1QIs[a] are right to infer a section break after v. 13. The fact that the *hôy* statements refer to the complainant in the third person and vv. 11–13 then address hearers in the second also parallels other *hôy* oracles (cf 55.1, and significantly 29.15–16.[21] It is thus likewise no indication of a break between vv. 9–10 and 11–13.

The verbal links between the verses bind them closely together, counteracting any misleading impression that the rhetoric might give: 'work' (vv. 9, 11), children (compare the content of v. 10 with v. 11), questioning (compare the content of vv. 9–10 with v. 11), 'hands' (vv. 9, 11, 12), 'his/its shaper' (vv. 9a, 9b, 11), 'make' (vv. 9, 12). Within vv. 11–13 appear further links: 'Yhwh has said' (the *inclusio* around vv. 11, 13, where the formula is reprised), 'command' (vv. 11, 12), the first person pronouns 'I' (vv. 12, 13), 'armies' (vv. 12, 13). The closing references to 'creation' and 'right' (vv. 12–13) make the unit close in a fashion parallel to vv. 1–8. The content of Yhwh's declarations in vv. 12–13 concerning Cyrus and his role also corresponds to those in 44.24–45.8.

Some of the verses' repetitions provide formal patterning for the whole:

9a 'Oh'			
	9b 'Will…'		
		9b 'What…'	
10 'Oh'			
		10 'What…'	
			11a Yhwh has said this
	11b 'Will…'		
		12a 'I' (*ʾānōkî*)	
		12b 'I' (*ʾănî*)	
		13a 'I' (*ʾānōkî*)	
		13b 'He'	
			13bδ almighty Yhwh has said

In the section as a whole, the double 'Oh' and the double questions reinforce each other, and their content is confronted by the double declaration that Yhwh has spoken and by the double *ʾānōkî* and other pronouns. The force thus increases as the verses unfold. Within

[21] Cf †Williamson, pp. 58–63; also D. R. Hillers, '*Hôy* and *Hôy*-oracles', in *The Word of the Lord Shall Go Forth* (D. N. Freedman Festschrift, ed. C. L. Meyers and M. O'Connor; Winona Lake, IN, 1983), pp. 185–88.

the bracket around vv. 11–13, the sequence of clauses in which the verb never comes first is also noteworthy. Objects have the emphasis in vv. 11b and pronouns in vv. 12–13. Four chiasms also feature in vv. 12–13.

Although grammatical addressee changes along with speaker in v. 11, even vv. 9–10 with their third person reference can be vocative (cf 44.1, 23, as well as 55.1; 29.15–16) and we may infer from the content of v. 11 that the plural 'you' there is the same as the singular 'person' of vv. 9–10. 'You' are indirectly addressed individually by the third-person expression of dismay in vv. 9–10 (cf also 5.8–23). They are initially addressed by rhetorical questions that have a similar function to the participial phrases in 44.24–28. These presuppose that the affirmations that Yhwh makes will be disputed by their addressees. The threefold 'I' of vv. 12–13a and the closing statement of intent with regard to the building of Jerusalem in v. 13b also recall the threefold '[I am Yhwh] who says' in 44.26b–28a with its corresponding closing statement of intent in 44.28b.

As a counter-statement in the course of an argument, or a 'disputation' (†Begrich, p. 42 = 49), vv. 9–13 correspond to 40.12–31. *Naidoff sees them as combining two disputations in one speech. The wisdom connotations of the *hôy* statements (†Schoors) thus parallel the wisdom atmosphere of much of the material in 40.12–26. Like 40.12–31, it is a general statement, though of course one with an implicit application to a particular audience that the prophet sees as questioning the way Yhwh is running the world.

†Köhler sees vv. 9–10 and 11–13 as of separate origin. Elliger (*Verhältnis*, pp. 179–83) suggests that vv. 11–13 have been adapted from their original concern to reject the nations' objections to Yhwh's activity in relation to Israel. This coheres with the points of comparison between vv. 11–13 and Yhwh's challenges to the nations and their gods earlier. †Merendino sees vv. 11a, 12, 13abα as the original form of the oracle (so also †Kratz, †van Oorschot, pp. 80–82); vv. 16–17, then vv. 13bβγ, 14, then vv. 9–10, 11b, 15 represent later additions (†Kratz dates the whole in the Second Temple period). *Koole agrees that there is some unevenness about vv. 9–10 but suggests that they look odd as additions and are rather the convictions of the community, which believes that current affliction must be accepted. They are cited by the prophet in order to confront them in vv. 11–13.

45.9a. Oh the one who quarrels with his shaper, like a pot with earthen pots! The LXX's ποῖον βέλτιον κατεσκεύασα ὡς πηλὸν κεραμέως; ('how much better could I have shaped it like a potter's clay[?]') has a question rather than a *hôy* statement. This might suggest a differently pointed Hebrew text such as *hăyārîb* ('Does someone quarrel...') rather than *hôy rāb*. The question in v. 9b would then parallel that (†Oort). But the witness is not strong and Aq ὦ, Th οὐαὶ, Vg *vae*, Tg *yy*, Syr *wy* follow the MT. The LXX has likely assimilated the text to that of v. 9b. The 'oh' is the exclamation of a teacher reproving a resistant and stupid pupil. We might suspect that the entity with a shaper will be Jacob–Israel, but this will become explicit only in v. 11.

In the second colon there appear a second subject, the repeated preposition 'with' (*ʾet*), and a second noun governed by that preposition. In such a case one expects to infer that the verb in the first colon also applies to the second. Indeed, the subject of the second could in turn also apply to the first ('oh a pot quarrels with its shaper': cf 29.16).[22] We have thus taken the sentence as an implicit comparison, in which the 'like/as' is not expressed, as in 62.5 (cf GK 161; *DG* 130; JM 174). Human beings are quarrelling with their creator as if they were just quarrelling with fellow-creatures. It is not the case that translations that give *ʾet* the same meaning in both cola are 'devoid of sense' (†de Waard).

The KJV takes the phrase as a jussive exclamation, suggesting 'a pot [must quarrel] with earthen pots', while the Vg *testa de samiis terrae* assumes that the import of the preposition changes to 'with' in the sense of 'among' rather than 'against' (cf Syr *mn*), and takes the phrase as a whole as appositional to the subject of the first colon. These understandings require more reading into the text. Like English 'pot', *ḥereś* denotes fired clay as the material of which something has been made. On its own it normally denotes a fragment of pot, but in Prov 26.23 it may mean a whole vessel. While Jacob–Israel might compare itself with a bit of broken pot (†Morgenstern, following S. H. Blank), the parallel with the familiar imagery of 29.16 and Jer 18.1–11, taken further in v. 9b, suggests that the word here means a whole vessel.

The Tg takes the colon to refer to images that are merely earthly, while Th renders ἀροτριῶν τοὺς ἀροτριῶντας τὴν γῆν ('A plougher those who plough the earth'; cf LXX's question μὴ ὁ ἀροτριῶν ἀροτριάσει τὴν γῆν;, 'Does the plougher plough the earth?'). That draws our attention to the complexity of the Hebrew roots *ḥrś*/*ḥrš* and to the possibility that the passage is another that links with 28.24; cf the parallel of the motif of earth opening up in v. 8 with that of opening up the earth in 28.24 (Goshen-Gottstein [see on 43.12], pp. 153–55). The MT assumes the word is *ḥrś* (cf Syr *ḥṣpʾ*, Sym ὄστρακον), but the LXX and Th assume *ḥrš*. Aq κεραμίον σύν τέκτοσι χθονός implies one of each, while Tg *ṣlmy pḥrʾ dʿbydyn mʿpr ʾdmtʾ* ('the images of the potter made from the dust of the ground') seems ambiguous. At 28.24, *ḥrš* I has been used to mean 'plough', and it refers to image-making at 40.19, 20; 41.7; 44.11, 12, 13; 45.16, though it can denote skilled craftwork without that negative connotation; *ḥrš* II ('be deaf/silent') has also appeared at 29.18; 35.5; 36.21; 41.1; 42.14, 18, 19; 43.8. It seems likely that the MT's laconic and thus more difficult reading has stimulated the alternative readings, ancient and modern.

22 There is thus no need with Driver (*Festschrift für W. Eilers*, pp. 49–51) to add יֹצֵר at the close of v. 9aα to this end.

חרשׂ את־חרשׂי אדמה: †Volz links חרשׂ with the first colon then reads אֶת חֲרָשָׁו חֶרֶשׂ אֲדָמָה ('an earthen pot with its maker'); Driver (*JTS* 36, p. 399) חֶרֶשׂ אֶת חֹרְשֵׁי אֲדָמָה ('ploughland with ploughers of the earth'), perhaps anticipated by 1QIs[a] חרש את חורשי האדמה which *Johns follows but which †Kutscher (p. 180; ET p. 238) sees as misled by the אדמה that follows; Whitley (*VT* 11, p. 458) אֲדָמָה אֶת חֹרֵשׁ ('earth with a plougher'); †Thomas אֶת חֹרְשׁוֹ חֶרֶשׂ אֲדָמָה ('an earthen pot with its maker'). †Oort simply emends חֲרָשֵׁי to חָרַשׁ ('a pot with a maker of the earth'). E. Robertson ('Points of Interest', p. 38) repoints חֲרָשֵׁי to חֲרָשׁ ('a pot with workers in earthenware') — cf Driver's later suggestion חֶרֶשׂ אֶת חֹרֵשׁ/חֹרְשֵׁי ('sherd with scraper[s]', i.e. a person scraping away unevennesses from the work) (*Festschrift für W. Eilers*, pp. 49–51).

45.9b. Would clay say to its shaper 'What would you be making?' Or your work say 'he has no hands'? The link with 10.15 and 29.15–16 becomes more overt here. The everyday or wisdom background is also more evident in the rhetorical question used for reproof as an alternative to the *hôy* clause, a transition that parallels 29.15–16. As usual the rhetorical questions call attention to axioms that cannot be argued for but represent ground that is surely common to speaker and audience yet does not seem to be taken seriously in practice by the latter (†Gitay). At the same time the rhetorical question can be a form of prohibition ('Is clay to say...': *Leene), and this implication is appropriate after *hôy* with its connotations of disapproval (cf 10.15; 29.15–16). It is the potter who is the shaper addressed in v. 9b (rather than Yhwh—†Hitzig).

The internal reproving question *mah taʿăśeh* also appears in Job 9.12; Qoh 8.4; Dan 4.32 [35] (cf Exod 5.15; Jer 12.5) with the meaning 'What would you be doing' and it may be that the question would be understood in this familiar sense here. But Syr *'bd* more plausibly assumes that the context points to the meaning 'make' (cf Rom 9.20; also Tg *l' ʿbdtny*, 'you did not make me', assimilating to 29.16). The similarity of *ʿāśāh* to *ʿāsas* ('press') might underline the point. There might even be an etymological link between the two verbs, with the implication that *ʿāśāh* originally suggested the shaping of clay.[23] A yiqtol verb is often used in questions about activity in the present, apparently with deliberative or courteous or deprecatory implications (*TTH* 39γ; GK 107f; *IBHS* 31.4f; *DG* 63). †Bentzen compares the 'potential' yiqtol (GK 107r).

The Vg's *et opus tuum absque manibus est* takes the second colon as a continuation of the same reported question, 'and your work has no hands' (cf Syr, Aq, Th). †Korpel and de Moor do the same, taking it as parallel to 'clay' ('Or would your work that has no hands [say that]?').[24] There is no biblical parallel for *yādayim* meaning 'handles' rather than 'hands', probably not even passages such as 1 Kgs 7.35–

[23] So J. L. Palache, *Semantic Notes on the Hebrew Lexicon* (Leiden, 1959), p. 58.

[24] M. Dahood, 'Ezekiel 19, 10 and Relative *kî*', in *Bib* 56 (1975), pp. 96–99 (see p. 99), emends to achieve the same end.

36 where in any case the feminine plural *yādôt* is used; but see *DTT*. While *yādayim* can be used figuratively to mean 'power/freedom' (Josh 8.20) (so †Saadya), literal hands are key to a potter (cf Lam 4.2) and abstracting the word seems unnecessary.

*Leene notes that *pōʿal* elsewhere means 'work' in the sense of the activity not the result, and thus supports the idiomatic understanding in GK 152u, 'your work [is that of someone] who has no hands'. But *maʿăśeh*, the more prosaic equivalent to *pōʿal*, is capable of the concrete meaning, as is *pōʿal* in later Hebrew (see *DTT*). The MT's disjunctive accent on *ûpoʿolkā* ('and your work') implies that the verb 'would say' applies to the second colon, avoiding enjambment.

This last colon shows how these verses take up the form and motifs of 29.15–16 but take them in a new direction (†Williamson, p. 59). Chapter 29 concerned the self-deceit of people who thought they could hide their policies from Yhwh. It is the potter's stupidity that they presuppose. Chapter 45 concerns the arrogance of people who think they can tell Yhwh how to run the world. It is the potter's clumsiness that they presuppose. The prophet points out that it is paradoxical for the product of the potter's hands to question them.

היאמר: 1QIs[a] הוי האומר assimilates to vv. 9a, 10a. The art. ה might be seen as a witness to the original interrogative ה, an indication that this is a conflate reading. But though the art. does not otherwise appear in vv. 9–10 or generally with הוי (†Schoors), 1QIs[a] does already have it on the previous but one word (see above) and has the same phrase in v. 10.

ופעלך ('and your work'): †North repoints to ופעל כי ('and the work that'). †Houbigant emends to ולפעלו...לך (cf LXX, Th οὐδὲ ἔχεις χεῖρας; Syr *d'ydyk*). 1QIs[a] reads ...ופועלכה אין אדם ('and your maker is not a man [with hands]'); cf *Johns. †Oort emends ופעלך to ולפעלך ('and to your work'). Whitley (*VT* 11, pp. 458–59) emends to ולפעלו אין מידיך ('and to his work, it is not of your hands').

45.10. Oh the person who says to a father 'What would you be begetting?' or to a woman 'With what would you be in labour?' In the qal *yālad* more commonly refers to a woman's giving birth, in the hiphil (as here) more commonly to a man's begetting. The second verb *ḥîl* thus complements the latter, for it refers distinctively to a woman's labouring in childbirth, with its involuntary writhing and its associated fear and anxiety about the issue of the experience in a society where death in childbirth was common. The similarity to *ḥûl* ('dance') may mean the two roots are connected; both denote rhythmic movement and even if they are of independent origin, they might naturally coalesce (on both see *ThWAT*; BDB treats them as one). Prophets often spoke of God as the people's father (e.g. Jer 3.4, 19; 31.9); it is rare for the parallelism to be completed and for God to be compared both to father and mother (Gruber, *RB* 90 [1983], p. 354). The theme here is similar to that in 42.14, but the use of the verb *ḥîl* is distinctive, even if it is not quite the case that it is being predicated of God.[25]

The LXX has καὶ τῇ μητρί ('and to the mother'), improving the parallelism.

הוי אמר: 1QIs[a] הוי האומר; see note on v. 9. LXX ὁ λέγων omits הוי, as in v. 9; 55.1. †Oort again emends to a question, הֲיֹאמַר.

תחילין: the fuller ('paragogic') ן ending is emphatic and usually pausal. It is less common on the s. than on the pl. (GK 47o; *IBHS* 31.7; JM 44ef). 1QIs[a] תחולין is perhaps to make clear that the vb is qal not hi (†Kutscher, p. 177; ET p. 234).

45.11a. Yhwh has said this—the holy one of Israel, its shaper. The bite in the occurrences of the participle 'shaper' (v. 9) now becomes explicit. The 'shaper' that this pot is cross-examining is the holy one of Israel. Syr's addition 'the Lord of might is his name' (cf 47.4; 54.5) underlines the confrontational edge to the glossing of the messenger formula here.

45.11b. Ask me about the things to come. Over my children and over the work of my hands you may give me charge. The opening words have raised difficulties. 1QIs[b] corresponds to the MT but 1QIs[a] reads (from the end of v. 11a) *ywṣr hʾwtwt* ('shaper of the signs'), consonantally lacking a *w* at the end of the first word and a *y* in the second. One might dismiss this as pure miscopying (1QIs[a] also lacked *qᵉdôš yiśrāʾēl*, 'holy one of Israel', which was added above the line) or see *hʾwtwt* as a spelling variant with the same meaning as the MT (†Kutscher, pp. 164–65; ET p. 217). But LXX ὁ ποιήσας τὰ ἐπερχόμενα ('the maker of things to come') also presupposes that the first word of v. 11b belongs with v. 11a and probably that 'shaper' lacks a suffix—though the MT's text could be read to yield the LXX's meaning if the suffix is taken to be dative, 'shaper for it of things to come'.[26] The LXX's version pleased Augustine, who quoted it many times: three times in different connections in his direct discussions of predestination (*Rebuke and Grace* 23; 45; *The Predestination of the Saints* 19) and four times in his commentary on John (on 14.1–3; 15.15–16; 16.12–13; 17.1–5).

The MT's 'Ask me of the things to come' (*hāʾōtiyyôt šᵉʾālûnî*) takes up a familiar theme, Yhwh's claim to be able to speak of future events. The MT accents imply 'Ask me of the things to come concerning my children, and concerning the work of my hands give me charge', but as the line unfolds it becomes possible to link both *ʿal*

[25] Against J. A. Foster, 'The Motherhood of God', in *Uncovering Ancient Stones* (H. N. Richardson Memorial, ed. L. M. Hopfe; Winona Lake, IN, 1994), pp. 93–102 (see pp. 98–99).

[26] So M. Bogaert, 'Les suffixes verbaux non accusatifs', in *Bib* 45 (1964), pp. 220–47 (see p. 238). Alternatively the ending on יצרו might be an archaic emphatic construct (cf GK 90o).

('concerning/over') clauses to what follows and to leave 'the things to come' unqualified, as it usually is. If they will ask Yhwh about how the future is designed to work out, they may find it easier to let Yhwh's children and Yhwh's work be Yhwh's own responsibility. There is thus no need to take the imperative as permissive (so GK 110b) or ironical (cf GK 110a) though irony is built into the second, yiqtol verb. For the modal yiqtol used for permission, request, or command, see JM 123lm; *IBHS* 31.5.

The occurrence of *hāʾōtiyyôt* in 41.23 was followed by allusion to divine 'works' (*pōʿal*, v. 24), to Yhwh's 'arousing' the conqueror from the north (*haʿîrôtî*, v. 25a), and to the potter/shaper (*yōṣēr*, v. 25). Here 'shaper', 'the things to come', and 'work' come in v. 11, 'I aroused' in v. 13. The repeated *pōʿal* (41.24; 45.9, 11) deserves note because outside Isaiah 40–55 it is much rarer than the synonym *maʿăśeh*, which in Isaiah 40–55 appears only at 41.29 and 54.16. Verses 9–13, then, take up 41.21–29. The firmness of this evidence confirms the more circumstantial indications that they also take up the parallel 41.1–7 where Yhwh first asked the question who had 'aroused' the conqueror in connection with 'right' (*ṣedeq*) (cf v. 13). That might even further complicate the understanding of the forms of *ḥrś* in v. 9, for we noted that *ḥrš* II ('be silent') appeared in 41.1. Once again the community is challenged to recognize that Yhwh has the capacity to announce coming events and see that they happen, as is evidenced by the proven power to act and speak in the past, and that therefore it must let Yhwh be like a parent who exercises control of their children or a potter who exercises control of their work.

As v. 11a implicitly identifies the 'shaper' of v. 9, then, so v. 11b implicitly identifies the children in v. 10 and the 'work' in v. 9b. It also confirms that v. 9 questioned the skill of Yhwh's 'hands'. Yhwh is the parent who is being questioned as well as the potter who is being challenged. 'The work of my hands' suggests the value of the object to its creator. As an epithet, an equivalent term (*maʿăśeh yāday*, not *pōʿal yāday*) appears between 'my people' and 'my personal possession' (*naḥalāh*) in 19.25.

In this context, Yhwh's 'children' must be Cyrus and the Medes. The idea is unparalleled in the Hebrew Bible, and †Grimm and Dittert repoint plural *bānay* to singular *bᵉnî* ('my son'). But it represents only one further step beyond the unprecedented statements in 44.24–45.7 and completes a parallel with Psalm 2. If *pōʿal* is more easily understood to mean 'activity', then it is Yhwh's activity through Cyrus and the Medes that is referred to.

האתיות שאלוני: Syr has *šʾlwny ʾtwtʾ* ('ask me about the signs'), while Tg has אתון שאלין ('[future events] do *you* ask [of me]'). †Ehrlich infers Heb. האתם תשאלוני, but Tg does also have its equivalent to האתיות (†Williamson, p. 262). Driver ([see on 43.14b], p. 39) rather repoints the opening word הַאֹתִי, 'Do you question *me* concerning my children and command me concerning the work of my hands?'; †Skehan (pp. 54–55) notes the good link with the repeated 'I' that begins each of the next three lines.

Whitley (*VT* 11, p. 459) reworks as האתות תשאלוני ('do you ask me signs concerning my children'), †Morgenstern as אתיות תשאלוני ('do you ask me about the things to come [concerning my children]'). †Duhm accepts the noun but emends the verb to שלחוני ('send/commission') and takes 'over my children' as a gloss. †Volz emends to האתם תשכילוני בינה ('do you teach me insight?'). Gordis ([see on 42.14], p. 197), notes the possibility of understanding שאל in the light of its Aramaic meaning 'decide'. †Van der Kooij (pp. 88–89) sees 'signs' in 1QIs[a] as designed to make a link with the children who are signs in 8.18.

45.12a. I am the one who made earth and created humanity upon it. Particularly on some reworkings of v. 11, an audience might wonder whether v. 12 continues its rebuke for asking Yhwh questions. You cannot cross-question the creator (cf Job 38–39). But the content of v. 12 leads into that of v. 13, and vv. 12–13 together indicate that the rebuke issues from the substance of Yhwh's activity, not merely the fact of Yhwh's authority (cf Job 40–41). The argument is the clearer if we follow the MT's text in v. 11. It is possible to ask questions about the future and to trust Yhwh with it because of the power Yhwh has long shown in the world, not least as creator. The pronoun *ʾānōkî* does not emphasize Yhwh as opposed to some other deity, which is not the issue in vv. 9–13 (against *EWS*, p. 53; JM 146a). Rather it takes up the suffix in v. 11b: 'Ask *me*... give *me* charge [for] *I* am the one...'; the pronoun is thus extraposed (cf JM 146e, 156b).

Verse 11b had concerned humanity, as does v. 12aβ; v. 12b concerns the world, as does v. 12aα. Moving on from humanity to the cosmos as a whole adds force to the point. In working with the past tense rather than with participles, v. 12 more closely parallels Genesis 1 than Isa 42.5. 'Make' (*ʿāśāh*) is the more common of the two words for divine activity in Genesis 1, while 'create' (*bārāʾ*) is the more theologically freighted term used three times in connection with the creation of humanity in Gen 1.27. The Tg's typical gloss, '[I made earth] by my word', underlines the link, while the LXX and Syr omit 'created', perhaps to abbreviate the text. In context, however, v. 12a recalls 42.5, which leads into a statement on God's calling of the servant in the cause of right, so that the servant may be a covenant for people and a light for nations (cf v. 13 here).

45.12b. I—my hands stretched out heavens and I commanded their whole army. LXX's ἐγὼ τῇ χειρί μου ἐστερέωσα τὸν οὐρανόν implies 'I with my hands...', but the verb (reused in LXX from 42.5: †Ziegler, p. 157) is not first person; contrast Pss 3.5 [4]; 17.13–14; 44.3; 60.7 [5]. If the pronoun followed the suffixed noun it would emphasize the suffix and the meaning would be 'My own hands stretched out...' (cf Num 14.32; 2 Sam 19.1; 1 Kgs 21.19). Here the pronoun stands extraposed (see *DG* 149–51; JM 156b; *IBHS* 16.3.4). The function of this idiom can be to emphasize the pronoun (GK 135f, *EWS*, p. 95), which fits with the stress on 'I' in vv. 12a and 13a. The verb's agreement with 'my hands' also has the effect of stressing the transition from 'I' to 'my hands'. No such transition was needed or expected. Every other verb in vv. 12–13a is first person, and every other reference to 'stretching out' (*nāṭāh*) the heavens in Isaiah 40–55 has Yhwh as subject (40.22, where see; 42.5; 44.24; 51.13). The Tg (as well as having a first person verb) interprets 'my hands' to mean '[by] my might'. But the context points to the significance of the transition from 'I' to 'hands', which keeps its concrete reference, for it was the hands of the potter that were faulted in v. 9 and the hands of Yhwh that people were urged to trust in v. 11. The basis for such trust is the role of these hands in creation.

†Eitan takes the verb *ṣwh* to mean 'cause to shine', but it would more naturally be understood as the familiar *ṣiwwāh* ('command'). In what sense did Yhwh 'command' all the heavens' army? The LXX renders more prosaically τοῖς ἄστροις ('the stars'), while conversely Origen notes that if they can be commanded, they must be living beings (*Principles* I.7.3). While Yhwh continually commands the heavenly forces, in this context, especially with the past tenses, the verb more likely recalls the word that bade them into being (Ps 33.9; cf Gen 1). This fits with the allusion to the heavenly army in 40.26. Yet the difference may be an insignificant one. The point about asserting Yhwh's lordship over heavenly forces is to declare that Yhwh is lord of them now. If the verb indeed suggests 'call into being', it completes an impressive range of imagery for creation in vv. 9–12. Yhwh designs and shapes like a potter, begets like a father, travails like a mother, makes like a craftworker, creates like an artist, stretches like a sheikh, and commands like a king. In the present unit 44.24 adds that Yhwh beats out like a metalworker. Together these images emphasize the precision, purposefulness, pleasure, pain, care, effort, skill, sovereignty, and effectiveness of the restorer-creator's work.

45.13a. I am the one who aroused him with right and will level all his ways. *Leene (p. 322) comments that '*bᵉṣedeq* [with right] answers *ʾên yādayim lô* [he has no hands] in a single word'. Vg *ad iustitiam* perhaps has christological implications (†van der Kooij, p. 303).

The language parallels chapter 41; here, too, Yhwh does not actually name Cyrus, and the Tg renders the verb with a yiqtol *ʾytynyh*; presumably referring to the messiah. †Torrey hypothesizes that the suffix originally referred to the servant and was reapplied to Cyrus in the light of Ezra 1. The earlier explicit references to Cyrus then follow from that. Cyrus perhaps then merges with other figures called by Yhwh, and human kingship is further downsized in significance in relation to the kingship of Yhwh and the royal status of Israel itself (cf †Miscall). The point is then highlighted by the additional designation of 'him' as βασιλέα ('king') in some LXX MSS. But the difference over against chapter 41 is that Cyrus has now been named, and more likely we are to assume that the prophet refers to him here.

The verb *ʾăyaššēr* presumably has a similar meaning to that in 40.3 and 45.2—'I will level'—not 'I will show him the right way' or 'I will straighten' (remove obstacles on the horizontal rather than the vertical plane—a different metaphor, but with the same implications). We might have expected 'his ways', preceding the verb, to have its common moral connotation (as in 42.24), but those links suggest that it has a more literal meaning as it will in 49.9. The LXX has an adjective εὐθεῖαι for the verb 'level'.

העירתהו: two medieval MSS have ד for ר (see *HUB*), giving the sense 'bore witness'.

45.13bα. He is the one who will build my city and let go my exile community. Apparently the highways were ones that would lead to Jerusalem, again like that in 40.3. Once again a theme that has long been implicit—here the return of the exile community (*gālût*)—at last becomes explicit. The paraphrase τὴν αἰχμαλωσίαν τοῦ λαοῦ μου in the LXX and *glwt ʿmy* in the Tg may indicate a Hebrew text reading *glwt ʿmy* ('the exile of my people'), but if so, it is perhaps a text glossed in the light of the promise's fulfilment (†Ziegler, p. 127). It brings out the pathos inherent in the use of the noun itself with its suffix. One might compare, as well as 'my city' here, 'my sons/my daughters' in 43.6. Anticipating the spirit of gender-inclusive translation, the LXX also includes τῶν θυγατέρων μου ('my daughters') alongside τῶν υἱῶν μου ('my sons') in v. 11 here.

ישלח: LXX ἐπιστρέψει might imply ישיב (†Duhm) but more likely indicates its use of a standard phrase (†Seeligmann, p. 72).

45.13bβ. ...not for payment and not for inducement, almighty Yhwh has said. 'Payment' (*mᵉḥîr*) occurs more often with the preposition *b* meaning 'at a price' than without it (cf 55.1). 'Inducement' (*šōḥad*) is a more morally ambiguous term. It often denotes a bribe, a payment that causes someone to do something wrong (1.23; 5.23; 33.15). But in a political context such as the present its implication is slightly less dubious (e.g. 1 Kgs 15.19). Cyrus will act with apparent generosity.

A closing or intraposed formula of the form 'Yhwh has said', which is capable of varying expansions, appears here for the first time in Isaiah 40–66 (cf 39.6; 48.22; 54.1, 6, 8, 10; 57.19, 21; 59.21a, 21b; 65.7, 25; 66.9, 20, 21, 23). The title 'Almighty Yhwh' (see on 44.6) reinforces the claim to authority implicit in vv. 9–13.

שֹׁחד: 1QIsᵃ שוחוד is a dialectal form (†Kutscher, p. 41; ET p. 55).

III.a.iv. Yhwh explains the rationale of this intention (45.14–17)

Verse 13 closed with a resumptive messenger formula and v. 14 opens with the full version, which recurs in v. 18. The MT and 1QIsᵃ take the hint that vv. 14–17 comprise a section, though it is a confusing one. Like vv. 9–13 with their reference to an unnamed 'he', v. 14 refers to an unnamed 'you' (f. singular). The preceding verses suggest this is the exiled Jewish community of v. 13, which makes good sense—as the 'he' of v. 13 was the Cyrus of the preceding verses. At the end of v. 14 foreign peoples are speaking to the community, and again it makes sense to take v. 15 as the continuation of their words, though the addressee changes to God. Perhaps they continue speaking in vv. 16–17, though these might be understood as the prophet's words.

The other nations' words about the God who hides, the God of Israel, and the deliverer (cf also v. 17aα, 17aβ) echo Yhwh's words about hidden hoards (v. 3), the prophet's description of Yhwh as 'Israel's holy one' (v. 11), and Yhwh's commissioning of the process that will bring deliverance (v. 8). The motif of hiddenness also links with the *hôy* oracles in 29.15 and thus with vv. 9–10. It offers a response to Yhwh that contrasts with that described in vv. 9–10 and accepts Yhwh's sovereignty even when exercised in puzzling ways (cf †Merendino). 'You [are] God' also correlates with the repeated 'I [am] Yhwh' of vv. 24, 3, 5, 6, 8. The declaration regarding the shaming of image-makers forms an *inclusio* with the scorning of diviners (v. 25) but also looks behind that to the previous section, 44.9–20. Either way the point is heightened if the words are now on the lips of foreigners. In the broader context of the book it links with 41.11 and with 2.2–4. Verses 14–25 take up Lamentations 1–4 and Isaiah 14.[27]

The section does not fit form-critical categories (†Schoors, p. 112). †Melugin compares with other Zion-promises but establishes more a link of traditions than a formal category. †Westermann sees the verses as of separate origin. Verse 14 is a saying that belongs with chapter 60 where these themes are taken further (cf †Morgenstern). Verse 15 represents a positive response (perhaps an 'Amen gloss') to 44.24–45.7, which contrasts with that confronted in vv. 9–13 and accepts that from now on Yhwh's activity in history is no longer overt but works indirectly through the likes of Cyrus. Verses 16–17 are general comments on the fate of image-makers, parallel to 44.9–20. *Dijkstra sees vv. 14, 16 and 15, 17–19 as originally separate units. †Merendino notes the distinctiveness of the language and thought of vv. 14–17 as a whole, which relates intrinsically to vv. 9–13 but is, he believes, later comment on the words of Second Isaiah.

45.14aαβ. Yhwh has said this. The toil of Egypt and the profit of Sudan, and the Ethiopians, people of stature... The LXX has κύριος σαβαῶθ ('Lord almighty') as at the end of v. 13, and †Duhm therefore adds *ṣᵉbāʾôt*. The unaccustomed brisk unadornedness of the messenger formula in the MT compares with that in v. 1, where at least there is an addressee, and in itself suggests that v. 14 might resume from

[27] See K. Budde, 'Zum hebräischen Klagelied', in *ZAW* 11 (1891), pp. 234–47 (see p. 236).

what precedes rather than being a wholly new beginning. This is doubly confirmed by the content of what follows.

First, the financial theme of v. 13 reappears. †Duhm suggests emending 'toil' (*y*ᵉ*gîa*ʿ) to (collective) 'tiller' (*yōgēb*), †Oort repoints it to 'toilers' (*yōg*ᵉʿ*ē*), †Houbigant to collective 'toiler' (*yōgēa*ʿ), while D. N. Freedman (see †McKenzie) takes it as abstract for concrete and thus itself implying toilers. The LXX has ἐκοπίασεν ('he toiled') which might imply *yāga*ʿ. 'Toil' suggests the gain from work as well as the work itself, the more specific connotation of 'profit' (*saḥar*; cf 23.3, 18), which comes from a verb meaning to go about, for example, on business. Again †Duhm repoints to collective *sōḥēr* ('merchant'), †Oort to plural *sōḥ*ᵉ*rê* (cf Tg *tgry*; Syr *tgr*ʾ). These approaches to both nouns take their hint from the rest of v. 14 but obscure the link with v. 13. Produce, property, and profit might have been—indeed were—what Cyrus gained from his victories, but whatever Cyrus might have wanted or obtained, the world's wealth is on its way elsewhere. †Volz moves the bicolon back into v. 13. The possibility of making this suggestion stems from the substantial link between vv. 13 and 14 and the two sections to which they belong. †Merendino notes that this promise involves a reversal of the covenant warning of Deut 28.33 (*y*ᵉ*gîa*ʿ), which has been fulfilled with the exile, and a fulfilment of the kind of promise/warning that appeared in Isa 23.3, 18 (the only other occurrences of *sāḥār*/*saḥar* outside Proverbs).

In the MT it is in the second colon that the profit is replaced by the people who bear it. As the former links back with v. 13, this prepares the way for what will now follow. For the phrase 'people of stature' (ʾ*anšê middāh*—1QIsᵃ *mdwt*) cf Num 13.32, also 1 Chr 11.23; 20.6 in the singular. A homonym, *middāh* II, means 'tribute' (Neh 5.4; cf Ezra 4.20; 6.8 in Aramaic), and this understanding may be implied by Tg *sḥwr*ʾ ('trade'; cf the Hebrew noun in the previous colon). Egypt, Sudan, and Ethiopia might have been significant trading nations, but this is not a point the Hebrew Bible emphasizes. In 43.3 Egypt is the country of Israel's oppression and the country that paid a price for resisting its escape, and Sudan and Ethiopia appear alongside it as makeweights.

45.14aγ. —to you they will make their way and yours they will be, behind you they will follow. A nice assonance appears in the three clauses. 'To you' is ʿ*ālayik*, 'and yours' is *w*ᵉ*lāk*, 'will follow' is *yēlēkû* (lit. 'will walk'), while 'to you/yours/behind you' comes each time in emphatic position. †Jerome, †Ibn Ezra, and †Luther assume that the pronouns refer to Cyrus, and †Mowinckel repoints them to the masculine to that end. The MT's feminine singular might refer to Jerusalem (44.26, 28), the 'city' mentioned in v. 13, which fits with the motif of pilgrimage and offering that likely follows. But that Jerusalem was not the city of people but the city of stone and brick (to be rebuilt and repopulated), and the immediate feminine antecedent is the *gālût*, the 'exile community' (*Leene, p. 326). Usage hardly suggests that a *gālût* is too abstract to be addressed (so †Hermisson). But this community *was* the exiled Jerusalem community, the city of people, so that it will be natural for the meaning of Jerusalem and exile community to slide into each other, as seems to happen in what follows. Either way this forms a further indication that v. 14 carries on from vv. 9–13 rather than constituting a wholly new beginning.

The LXX adds δοῦλοι to the first colon, perhaps representing a dittograph of *yʿbrw* read as a form of *ʿbd* (†Ottley). Whether the subjects of these verbs come in any more than forced subjection to Yhwh and Israel is not yet apparent. The phrase *ʿābar ʿal* ('make their way to') can mean 'pass over', 'go against', 'come upon', or 'pass by'. This leaves unclarified the precise meaning of the expression here. But it is used for the journey to a place of worship or pilgrimage (Amos 5.5), and specifically for the journey to Zion in 35.8; cf 51.10; 62.10; Ps 42.5 [4]. This suggests a link with the oracle in Isaiah 18, with its talk of bringing offerings, as well as with the broader theme of the pilgrimage to Zion which forms a bracket round the book in 2.2–4 and 66.18–23.

The Tg's 'according to your word they will go' assumes that 'follow' has its straightforward literal reference, but it commonly denotes religious allegiance, especially in Deuteronomy (e.g. 13.5 [4]), but also, for example, in Jer 2.2, 23; Hos 11.10. If Deuteronomy required one place of worship for all Israel, Second Isaiah's monotheism implies one place of worship for all the world (†Wildberger, p. 513: he adds the rather frightening phrase 'a tightly centralized "churchly" organization').

45.14aδbα. In chains they will make their way and to you they will fall down. To you they will make their plea. In the MT the first clause belongs to v. 14a and completes a chiasm with the verb *yaʿăbōrû* ('make their way') in both outside clauses. The NRSV achieves a more plausible balance with its division into two 2–2–2 lines. Each begins with a *yaʿăbōrû* clause, the second being resumptive (LXX omits, perhaps to abbreviate). In this further set of three clauses, too, the verbs follow the prepositional expressions, while the second and third clauses with their *ʾēlayik* continue the assonance from the preceding line.

The foreigners' 'chains' (*ziqqîm*) could be turned into manacles (†North) but hardly into decorative anklets (†S. Smith); cf the addition of a word for 'bound' in the LXX and Vg. The root always refers to constraint: see Nah 3.10; Ps 149.8; Job 36.8; also *ʾăziqqîm* in Jer 40.1, 4. Nor can they be an isolated metaphor within the verse. On the other hand the idea that the chains are self-imposed as a sign of submission is a plausible one, and it might be the understanding presupposed in Isaiah 60 (see v. 11).

'Falling down' can be an act of obeisance to human beings (e.g. Ps 72.10–11); it need not imply worship. But 'pleading' (*pll* hit) has a human object only here. †Ehrlich emends to *wᵉʾel ʾĕlōheykā* ('and to your God [they will make their plea]')—an 'easier reading' if ever there has been one. The verb's legal background suggests that it would naturally have a non-religious usage parallel to that of 'falling down', even if this does not occur in the Bible.

ישׁתחוו: 1QIs[a] ישתחווה perhaps suggests the scribe is confused over this vb (see on 44.15; 46.6; and †Kutscher, p. 219; ET pp. 291–92).
אליך: 1QIs[a] adds ו, but the parallel (or at least comparable) third clause in the preceding line is similarly asyndetic. LXX and Syr 'in you' is perhaps assimilated to the subsequent בך.

45.14bβ. Yes, in you, God is in you and there is no other, no God. The words are presumably those of the plea just mentioned. They give the same prominence to the feminine singular object (lit. 'in you [is] *ʾēl* and there is no other, no *ʾĕlōhîm*'). In v. 24 *ʾak* ('Yes') has its restrictive meaning 'only', but here its adversative meaning fits better, 'contrary to what we have previously believed'.[28] It suggests a strong affirmation of something that was previously or is elsewhere denied; cf 19.11; 63.8 (*DCH*); Ps 58.12 [11] (†Delitzsch). It thus keeps its essential note of contrariness (cf 43.24) even when making an affirmation, and vice versa (cf *EWS*, pp. 129–30). The versions were unsure of the word's meaning.

Reading the line in the light of what has preceded, †Skinner renders not 'in you [is] God' but 'you [are] God', treating the preposition as pleonastic, *b* of equivalence/identity (see on 40.10a). More likely the text is now eventually fulfilling †Ehrlich's instinct to bring God in. In acknowledging the exilic community, the foreign peoples acknowledge Yhwh. 'And there is no other' (*wᵉʾên ʿôd*) exactly corresponds to v. 6. 'No God' is *ʾepes ʾĕlōhîm*, lit. 'nothing of God' (*ʾepes* being here a poetic synonym for *ʾên*). In v. 6 *ʾepes* came in the phrase 'nothing [apart from me]', its first occurrence since chapter 41.

For the second colon the LXX has 'and they will say "There is no God but you"', the Vg 'and there is no God but you', and the Tg, 'and there is no other God but he'.

אלהים: Tg adds בר מניה and J. Morgenstern suggests that בלעדיו ('besides him') was lost from the end of the line.[29]

45.15. But certainly you are God who hides, God of Israel who delivers. The LXX with its γὰρ plausibly invites us to assume that the speakers remain the same. Although the lament/confession in v. 15a would be appropriate on Judean lips, there is no indication of a change, and

[28] N. H. Snaith, 'The Meaning of the Hebrew אַךְ', in *VT* 14 (1964), pp. 221–25 (see p. 223).
[29] 'The Loss of Words at the Ends of Lines in Manuscripts of Biblical Poetry', in *HUCA* 25 (1954), pp. 41–83 (see p. 68).

that consideration also works against these being the prophet's own words, or Cyrus's words, or the sarcastic words of image-worshippers (†Morgenstern), or their being a question (NEB). Further, Israel is spoken of in the third person in v. 15b. †Klostermann emends 'you' (*ʾattāh*) to 'with you' (*ʾittāk*), so that the statement more clearly parallels that in the preceding line. In the MT the speakers now address God rather than speaking of God. 'But certainly' is *ʾākēn*, an asseverative like *ʾak*. It does not always imply a contrast—see, for example, 40.7 and LXX's γὰρ (cf *EWS*, p. 132)—and like 40.7b has been reckoned to introduce a gloss here. But it works well as implying a contrast and as integral to the section, as in 49.4 and 53.4. Its contrast is made not over against v. 12(!) (so *IBHS* 39.3.5d) but over against what immediately precedes (*Balentine, p. 109). The parallel with v. 14bβ points to that:

To Zion: 'Yes—in you—*ʾēl*—there is no other *ʾĕlōhîm*
To Yhwh: 'But—you—*ʾēl*—*ʾĕlōhîm* who delivers

It is this contrast with the preceding colon that explains why the pronominal subject in v. 15a precedes the predicate, the opposite to the usual order in a noun clause. It does also make a contrast with vv. 9–10 in offering the right kind of acceptance of the fact that Yhwh sometimes acts inscrutably.

The statement that God hides comes in this form (*sātar* hit) only here. †Ehrlich emends to a transitive verb (*mastîr* hi) parallel to that in v. 15b. God then hides in the sense of protects. The MT's expression has been subject to a number of interpretations, but in its OT context it is close to that of a plaint in one of Israel's laments about God hiding, in Ps 89.47 [46] (*sātar* ni). In other laments people similarly grieve over the hiding of God's face (*sātar* hi): for example, 13.2 [1]; 27.9; 44.25 [24]; 69.18 [17; 88.15 [14]; Job 13.24. Elsewhere it is assumed that human sin may be the reason for God's hiding (Isa 57.17) or for the hiding of God's face (8.17; 54.8; 59.2; 64.6 [7]; Jer 33.5, with respect to Jerusalem). The idea is the converse of that of God's appearing and the shining of God's face, and corresponds to a reality of human relationships. The literal occurrences of *sātar* (hit), in 1 Sam 23.19; 26.1 and the heading to Psalm 54, underline that the hitpael by its nature is reflexive ('to hide oneself') not passive ('to be hidden').

The subject and its implicit verb 'You [are]' likely carries over from the first colon to the second. The expressions in the second colon do not simply hang onto the noun expressions in the first. As a second predicate, 'God of Israel' balances *ʾēl* and the participle 'who delivers' balances the participle 'who hides'. This second predicate also marks another link with 45.3 ('God of Israel': otherwise the title has come only in 41.17) and 43.3 (*môšîaʿ*: otherwise the term has come only in 43.13). To 'restore' a six-beat line, †Duhm omits 'Israel', †Torrey 'who delivers' (as dittog.). The two verbs, 'hide' and 'deliver', are simply justaposed paratactically. Neither is subordinated to the other. The relationship between them is left unexplained

(*Balentine, pp. 110–11). But their background in the laments means that the hearers know how to relate them. The one who has been hider is now deliverer.

The LXX paraphrases the statement about God's hiding with the statement καὶ οὐκ ᾔδειμεν ('and we did not know'), perhaps in the light of vv. 4–5 (*HUB*). Aq, Th, and Sym replace by the more literal adjective κρυφαῖος, and Eusebius of Caesarea notes how they thus give clearer testimony to the mystery of Christ, the one in whom God was hidden, which he believed was explicit in the Hebrew.[30] †Simon links the expression to the characterization of the Egyptian god Amon—the name may itself mean 'hidden'—as mysterious and hidden, described thus partly because he is the deity who first came into being (see the hymns to Amon in *ANET*, pp. 367–72). In Egypt the doctrine of the mysterious, hidden God is all-pervasive.[31] Isaiah 45.15 then constitutes Egyptian acknowledgment of Yhwh as the real hidden God. *Heintz rather links it with the Babylonian practice of moving divine images about. When the image was absent, the god was absent. The foreigners describe Yhwh as a hidden God because Yhwh has no statue at all.

45.16. They are shamed, yes humiliated, all of them at once. Makers of figures go into humiliation. It again makes sense if we assume that the suppliants continue to speak, though they continue to voice the statements of faith that the prophet wishes to hear from the people's lips. The line is a solemn 4–4 (with the subject 'makers of figures' coming at the very end), if 'at once' (*yaḥdāw*) is as usual to be associated with what precedes, against the MT but with the LXX, Vg, Syr. Once again it holds the two verbs together (see on 40.5). The MT's verse division does, however, invite us to see it as modifying both cola (†Franke, p. 35). †Thomas suggests deleting 'all of them at once' (*kullām yaḥdāw*). The line is then 2–2–2. The LXX renders πάντες οἱ ἀντικείμενοι αὐτῷ ('all who defy/oppose him'), perhaps reading *yḥrw* for *yḥdw* (†Torrey) or for the two words *kol-neḥĕrāyw* (†Köhler) or *kol-qāmāyw* (†Duhm, who also keeps *yaḥdāw* to make a 3–3–3 line). But †Ziegler (pp. 151, 158) reckons the LXX assimilates to 41.11, as later its ἐγκαινίζεσθε assimilates 'makers of' (*ḥārāšê*) to 'be quiet' (*haḥărîšû*) in 41.1. 'All of them' (*kullām*) suggests 'the whole sorry lot of them' and is a characteristic feature of the image passages (see on 40.26).

Of the several homonyms *ṣîr*, the more common mean 'messenger' (18.2; 57.9) and 'pang' (13.8; 21.3), while a less common one means 'hinge' (Prov 26.14); *ṣîr* from the root *ṣûr*/*yāṣar* ('shape') occurs only

[30] See Εὐαγγελικῆς Ἀποδείξεως δέκα λόγοι 5.4 (§§ 225d–226a). Cf D. Barthélemy, 'Eusèbe, la Septante et "les autres"', in *La Bible et les Pères: Colloque de Strasbourg (1er-3 octobre 1969)* (Paris, 1971), pp. 51–65 (see p. 55) = Barthélemy, *Études d'histoire du texte de l'Ancien Testament* (Freiburg/Göttingen, 1978), pp. 179–93 (see p. 183).

[31] So R. J. Williams, 'Some Egyptianisms in the Old Testament', in *Studies in Honor of John A. Wilson* (Chicago/London, 1969), pp. 93–98 (see p. 95).

here and Ps 49.15 [14]. †Ehrlich emends to *y^eṣîrîm* (haplog.), 'creatures/creations' (*DTT*), which seems no improvement. †Qimchi infers that the images are pejoratively designated 'pains'; cf *ʿōṣeb* I ('pain' 14.3) and *ʿōṣeb* II ('image', 48.13) – *ʿāṣāb* is the more usual form (10.11; 46.1). †Cheyne emends to *ṣ^elāmîm*. In the context (cf vv. 9, 11; also e.g. 43.10) thc noun slurs images as lying on the human, created side of reality rather than the divine, creating side; cf Vg *errorum*. The point is underlined by making them the object of *ḥārāšê* ('makers of'): cf also v. 9.

הלכו בכלמה חרשי צירים: 1QIs[a] וילכו בכלמה חורשי צורים, probably without difference in meaning (†Kutscher, p. 180; ET pp. 238–39)—rather than implying that it intends צור ('rock').

45.17. But Israel is delivered through Yhwh, an everlasting deliverance. You will not be shamed or humiliated to everlasting ages. The Hebrew has no actual word for 'but', yet a contrast is made, by placing the subject first in the sentence; again the suppliants continue their confession. The Syr begins the verse 'Israel's deliverance is in its Lord, the deliverer for ever', a paraphrase perhaps owing something to Deut 33.29.

Verse 17a takes up the theme of deliverance from vv. 8 and 15 and gives it some emphasis. Deliverance is Israel's: the point is made not only by the positioning of the subject but by the use of the niphal verb. Given the likely original significance of the niphal as a reflexive, one is tempted to give it a middle sense, though niphals in general more often have a passive meaning. In the case of *yāšaʿ* only the niphal and hiphil occur, suggesting that the niphal operates as *the* passive. Nevertheless its use makes it possible to highlight the person (Israel) who is particularly in focus, whose centrality would be less evident if it were the object of an active verb. 'Finds deliverance' might convey some aspects of the idea. The verb is again qatal. In the context it hardly has past reference (e.g. to the exodus). The twinning of vv. 16 and 17 makes it more likely that this is another qatal verb that refers to the future that is becoming reality before people's eyes.

Israel is delivered 'through' Yhwh. Again the preposition is *b* (cf v. 14bβ). †Ruiz (pp. 89–90) sees this *b* as equivalent to *min* ('from/by'), but it is doubtful whether *b* can mean 'by', of a person (JM 132e).[32] It is significant that *b* is picked up again in v. 24. The notion seems to be a broader one than merely 'by' Yhwh. The Tg characteristically has 'by the word of Yhwh'. And Yhwh's act brings about 'an everlasting deliverance'; the phrase looks syntactically unrelated to v. 17aα. GK 117qr, JM 128a, *IBHS* 23.2.1b see such a phrase that uses a noun from the verbal stem as an internal object, though in a looser sense than is the case in 42.17. †Delitzsch also compares 14.6 and 22.17. It

[32] D. S. Tsumura takes it so here: see 'Niphal with an Internal Object in Hab. 3:9a', in *JSS* 31 (1986), pp. 11–16 (see p. 13).

strengthens the verbal idea, and is further strengthened by the intensifying attribute, and then by the fact that this attribute is plural *ʿôlāmîm* (lit. 'deliverance of ages'), presumably intensifying plural (†Beuken).

The closing colon expresses the contrast between image-worshippers and Israel in another way, by taking up the two verbs of v. 16a—negatived—as an *inclusio* for vv. 16–17. The 'you' (pl.) who are addressed are presumably the members of the Israel that is referred to in v. 17a and of the community that is addressed in v. 14. The change of person is not unusual in Isaiah 40–55; the LXX has third-person verbs.

The section closes with three words to suggest 'for ever' (*ʿad-ʿôlᵉmê ʿad*)—all beginning with *ʿayin* and underlining the lastingness of Israel's deliverance. Beyond and behind the fact that Yhwh's word stands *lᵉʿôlām* (40.8) is the fact that Yhwh is *ʾĕlōhê ʿôlām* (40.28). The first fact is the grounds for confidence that Israel's deliverance will become reality, the second for confidence that it will remain so. These are the first occurrences of *ʿôlām* with future reference since chapter 40. They affirm that the fact that Yhwh is *ʾĕlōhê ʿôlām* means that Yhwh's delivering also has ultimately lasting effects (cf 51.4–11; also 55.3, 13).

Midrash Tanḥuma (SB) quotes this verse in discussing both Exod. 20.2 and Lev. 17.3–4. In the world to come Israel will be delivered from slavery not by earthly agents and thus temporarily as one oppressor succeeded another (Egypt, Babylon, Media, Greece, Rome) but by the holy one in person and thus everlastingly.

III.a.v. Yhwh's challenge and invitation (45.18–25)

The sense of closure in v. 17 is matched by the sense of opening in v. 18 with its elaborately expanded messenger formula indicating that the speaker has changed. At the same time the self-introduction in vv. 18–19 resumes from 44.24, 26 (†Hessler) and the introductory *kî* ('for') also establishes a link with what precedes. The messenger formula reflects the fact that as usual the real though indirect addressee of these words is the Judean community, but the people is not the direct addressee. It is referred to in the third person in the *inclusio* 'offspring of Jacob/Israel'. The direct addressees are the 'fugitives of the nations'/'all earth's extremities' (vv. 20, 22). This also suggests a link with what precedes. Yhwh responds to the statements attributed to the nations in vv. 15–17.

Verses 18–19, 20–21, 22–23, and 24–25 are formally diverse and could all be seen as separate units. But in each Yhwh speaks, and in the text as we have it, they form a whole introduced by the messenger formula in v. 18 with its resumption/*inclusio* in v. 24; compare vv. 9–13. †Begrich (p. 42 = 49) sees the section as a disputation, but the messenger formula does not belong to this form, the challenge of vv. 20–21 is that of a court speech, and the exhortation in vv. 22–23 belongs to neither. Yhwh's unique deity is asserted in each subsection

(vv. 18, 21, 22, 24). 'Divine self-praise forms the dominant literary genre of the passage' (*Beuken, p. 350). In vv. 18–25 as a whole Israel's entire range of *ṣdq* ('right') words appears, *ṣedeq*, *ṣaddîq*, *ṣᵉdāqāh*, *ṣᵉdāqôt*, *ṣādēq*. 'Deliver' and 'deliverer' (*yāšaʿ*, *môšîaʿ*) also both come, in vv. 21, 22, and 23.

Within vv. 14–25 †Merendino attributes to Second Isaiah only earlier forms of vv. 18–19, 20–21, which he sees as relating back to vv. 9–13. †Hermisson adds vv. 22–23. In contrast †van Oorschot (pp. 38–41, 222–26) sees only vv. 20a, 21–23 as comprising the earliest form of vv. 18–25, vv. 20b being an expansion, vv. 24–25 a midrashic correction, vv. 18–19 part of the later 'near expectation' strand. †Kratz sees only vv. 20a and 21 as belonging to the earliest form of vv. 18–25 (leading into 46.9–11). Verses 18, 22–23, then 20b, then 19, 24–25 are subsequent expansions.

As v. 14 took up an issue raised in its preceding section, in v. 13, so vv. 18–19—in line with that opening *kî* ('for')—take up a number of issues raised in the preceding section. Is Yhwh really a God who hides? (v. 15): see v. 19, and vv. 18–19 in general. Does God really accept other peoples' acknowledgment? (vv. 14–15): see vv. 18, 23. Is Yhwh really a God who delivers, and if so, whom does Yhwh deliver? (v. 15): see vv. 20, 21, 22. Both sections affirm that 'there is no other' but Yhwh (vv. 14, 18, 21, 22, cf 24) and close with declarations on the shaming of those who do not acknowledge Yhwh and on Israel's safe destiny with Yhwh (vv. 16–17, 24–25).

Previous participial qualifications of the name Yhwh such as those in v. 18a have prepared the way for what would follow, in polemical fashion. Here the polemical point in vv. 18–19 as a whole (paralleling 44.24–28) introduces vv. 20–25 as a whole (†Westermann), particularly the stress on Yhwh's speaking (cf vv. 21, 23) and the reference to the offspring of Jacob (cf v. 25). †Rendtorff (pp. 9–10) suggests that the creation statement in v. 18 leads into and backs up the statement on Yhwh's power in history in vv. 19–25, without this point ever being quite explicit. †Stuhlmueller (p. 154) more precisely suggests that v. 18a leads into v. 19, while v. 18b leads into vv. 20–23. Verses 24–25 then have some features of *inclusio*. Further, v. 18a itself already intermingles statements about Yhwh's creativity and inferences about Yhwh's sole and powerful deity. The statement about Yhwh's creativity has just one verbal link with v. 19, the word *tōhû* ('emptiness'). But that also points to a link with Genesis 1–2, with its references to creating/shaping/making and to heaven and earth. Verse 19 also recalls Genesis 1–2 by its references to God's speaking and to darkness. Verse 18a thus indeed provides anticipatory support for v. 19. The manner of Yhwh's creation evidences the manner of Yhwh's likely relating to Jacob–Israel. In addition, v. 18a also links the creation of the world to Yhwh's unique deity. 'He is God' insofar as 'he established it'. This first anticipates and undergirds the claim in v. 18b. Then both underlie the challenge and claim in vv. 20–23 with its twofold 'there is no other'. In that last respect they are joined by v. 19 whose last colon also introduces the word *ṣedeq* whose variants will run through vv. 20–25. So Yhwh's activity involves power and right. These themes are announced in vv. 18–19 and interwoven in vv. 20–25. The section may be outlined as follows:

18a The prophet's introduction to the divine word
(what Yhwh says)
18b–19 Yhwh's claim about present and past
'I Yhwh, there is no other', 'offspring of Jacob'
    20–21 Yhwh's challenge about past and present
        'I Yhwh, there is no other'
    22–23 Yhwh's exhortation about present and future
        'I God, there is no other'
24aβ Yhwh's introduction to the human word
(what people say)
24–25 Yhwh's claim about present and future
'Only in Yhwh', 'offspring of Israel'

45.18aα. For Yhwh has said this, creator of the heavens—he who is God... On the assumption that even asseverative *kî* retains some causal link with what precedes (see on 40.2), this *kî* implies 'for', but what precise link does it indicate? Its absence from the LXX perhaps means that the LXX was uncertain on the matter. It hardly suggests doubts about *kî*'s place in the text, as †Hermisson implies (though *kî* is also missing from some late medieval Hebrew MSS; see *HUB*). It might relate to v. 17 in particular, understood as Yhwh's words put on the nations' lips. If so, it has in mind the comments in vv. 19 and 25 about Yhwh's relationship with Jacob–Israel, the 'audience in the house'. It might relate to vv. 14–17 more generally with its vision for the nations' recognition of Yhwh. If so, it leads into vv. 18–25 themselves in general. Perhaps the link between these means we do not have to choose. The section supports the overall perspective of vv. 14–17 in both its aspects. A *kî* at the beginning of a section is indeed unexpected and recalls the *weʿattāh* ('but now') of 43.1 and 44.1, which either indicates that originally separate units have been linked, or that the literary work from the beginning combined formally diverse sections.

For the typical participial qualification of Yhwh's name in the messenger formula, 'creator of the heavens', cf 42.5—†Duhm omits it. In the phrase 'he who is God' (*hûʾ hāʾĕlōhîm*) the first pleonastic pronoun anticipates the one that follows in the next line.[33] In isolation the article on *hāʾĕlōhîm* might be demonstrative ('that God'), but the only other instance in Isaiah, 37.16, points to the nuance 'the only/true God'; cf *hāʾēl* in 42.5 (†Hermisson).

[33] Cf NEB. See G. A. Geller, 'Cleft Sentences with Pleonastic Pronoun', in *JANES* 20 (1991), pp. 15–33 (see p. 32).

45.18aβ. ...shaper of the earth and its maker—he who is its establisher. The participles continue to compare with 42.5. On LXX's ὁ καταδείξας for *yōṣēr* ('shaper'), see on 40.26. The term 'make' with regard to earth recurs from v. 12 (where 'shape' also comes) and suggests that in v. 18 Yhwh is again claiming to work in a purposeful and effective way rather than a clumsy one (*Leene). But compared with v. 12 much more is said about earth than was said about heaven. This—and the particularity of what is said—leads into v. 18aγ. The polel of *kûn* ('establish') likely always means more than simply 'formed' (so even in Ps 119.73, in parallelism with *ʿāśāh*, 'make', as here) or 'founded' (Isa 62.7). It suggests 'not an act of creation as such but the shaping and establishing of an entity already present' (K. Koch, *ThWAT* on *kûn*, VI). It suggests that the object is secure (Ps 119.90, of the earth), and in addition made ready for its function, like the enemy 'set' on destruction (Isa 51.13). This in particular leads well into the next line. We take it that this and the subsequent finite verbs continue the participial construction (see GK 116x; JM 121j; *IBHS* 37.7.2; *DG* 113e).

עשׂה: 1QIs[a] עשׂיה retains the radical י, with the same meaning as the MT.

45.18aγ. ...(not creating it an emptiness, shaping it to be inhabited). The further references to creation further illustrate how important to the prophet is the past establishing of the earth (†Ludwig, p. 346). This occurrence of *tōhû* compares with that in Gen 1.2, as earlier occurrences do not, though †Stuhlmueller (pp. 156–57) describes the passage's relationship to Genesis 1 as indirect or tangential. Storyteller and prophet are independently beginning from Babylonian ideas. On the basis of a close examination of the use of the verbs in v. 18, †Holter (pp. 81–84) also argues against a particular link with Genesis 1. The Tg's 'he formed it for human beings to multiply on it' implies a commission to reproduce, and increases the link with Genesis 1. The line is often quoted in this connection in the Talmud (e.g. *b. Hagigah* 2b). But the LXX's ἀλλὰ κατοικεῖσθαι condenses and paraphrases the second colon; the Syr paraphrases differently, 'but that you might live in it I created it'.

1QIs[a] adds the preposition *l* to *tōhû* (cf LXX, Vg, Tg), bringing out the implicit 'to be an emptiness' and assimilating to the parallel colon as it does so (†Rubinstein, p. 316). In the MT the preposition appears in the second colon ('for inhabiting'), from which it may also operate backwards into the first colon.

לשׁבת: †Ehrlich emends to לא בשׁת and renders 'emptiness did not create it' (cf *Hirsch), 'shame did not shape it', the two nouns being terms for images.

45.18b. I am Yhwh. There is no other. The prophecy's characteristic 'I am Yhwh' opens God's actual words and will recur as an *inclusio* in

v. 19b. Indeed, vv. 18b–19 form a chiasm (†Beuken). 'I am Yhwh and there is no other' is restated as 'I am Yhwh, speaking right, announcing equity', and the two *lō*ʾ ('not') statements in v. 19a also balance each other. The corollary 'There is no other' corresponds to and confirms the words of recognition in v. 14. It will recur in vv. 21 and 22. Indeed vv. 20–23 as a whole take up this motif, though first in v. 19 there is another point to be made. †Rosenbaum (pp. 105–7) renders 'I, Yahweh (and there is no other)...': but the familiarity of the noun clause 'I [am] Yhwh' and the infrequency of such parenthetical clauses makes it unlikely that an audience could understand the line thus.

45.19aα. It was not in hiddenness that I spoke, in a place in a dark land. As the phrase from v. 14 recurs in v. 18b, now the root *str* from the next line (v. 15a) recurs in the next line of this section, in the form of the noun *sēter* (cf Vg *non in abscondito*). Yhwh had not hidden. The noun commonly means a hiding-place (16.4; 28.17; 32.8; cf the verb in, e.g., 49.2). With the preposition *b*, as here, it is commonly rendered 'in secrecy' (cf 48.16). Three related nouns also mean hiding-place, *mistôr* (4.6), *mastēr* (53.3), and *mistār* (45.3, where it was paralleled by *ḥōšek*, 'darkness', as here). Dahood ([see on 40.26b] p. 294) sees *sēter* as meaning concretely 'secret place' and as referring to Sheol. This would also fit the parallel phrase to come (see below), but there is insufficient indication in the context that the prophet was thinking in these terms.

If v. 15 made a general statement about God's relationship with the world, then v. 19 might well be another such general statement about a revelation in words that was accessible to people and was not made in vain. †Merendino renders the verbs as present. If v. 15 made a statement relating to concrete circumstances in the Babylonian world, then so might v. 19. †Watts sees an allusion to the Delphic oracle's secret prediction of Cyrus's conquest of Lydia. If v. 15 more likely makes a specific contextual statement that relates to Israel's traditions, the same may be true of v. 19. Yhwh claims to have spoken, not hidden.

What then is the dark land to which the second colon refers? Again, a general interpretation might infer that it simply denotes 'some spot in some dark land' (†Torrey), or Sheol the place of darkness (e.g. 1 Sam 2.6, 9; Job 17.13; Ps 88.4, 13 [3, 12]) as the source of oracles (cf 1 Sam 28) (†Delitzsch), or the divine realm to which mere mortals have no access—in Ps 18.12 [11] Yhwh makes 'darkness his hiddenness'. The context in v. 18 refers to creation, and this denial might alternatively disassociate Yhwh from the realm of darkness in the manner of Genesis 1—though this would be in tension with v. 7. In the context, the obvious more specific assumption is that darkness represents Babylon (cf 42.7; 45.3). †D. R. Jones construes the line to suggest that 'it was not in hiddenness that I spoke [as I did] in a dark land'—that is, Yhwh spoke openly there. But parallelism pushes us to assume that the force of the negatived verb carries over into the second colon. More likely the meaning of 'darkness' carries over from the first colon and denotes that Yhwh has spoken openly, in the light.

If the dark land is the realm of death, it would fit if the 'place' there (*māqôm*) is the tomb (so Dahood, [see on 44.2a], pp. 430–31). If not, *māqôm* might naturally have its common connotation of 'shrine', given the fact that the location of God's 'speaking' is commonly the shrine. This will be supported by the allusion to 'seeking' Yhwh in the next line: cf 18.7; 46.7; 60.13; 66.1; repeatedly in Deuteronomy 12; 16; 1 Kgs 8.29–35; Jeremiah 7.

45.19aβ. I have not said to the offspring of Jacob, 'Seek me in emptiness'. The LXX's μάταιον ζητήσατε ('seek emptiness') recognizes that the familiar *tōhû* lacks a preposition but ignores the suffix on the verb *baqqᵉšûnî* ('seek *me*'); *tōhû* surely must be taken adverbially. It occurs in association with 'darkness' in Gen 1.1–2, but both words must have different resonances from those of Genesis 1. Yet in the light of these links it is doubtful whether *tōhû* can be reduced to meaning merely 'in vain', '[for] nothing' (despite Tg *lryqnw*), here or anywhere else—even *lᵉtōhû* in 49.4; contrast *lᵉrîq* in 49.4; *lārîq* in 65.23. Indeed, these examples show that if *bᵉ* ('in') is to be provided (†Morgenstern) or—more likely—is to be understood from the previous line, this will not imply the meaning 'in vain', for which *lᵉ* is required, but 'in emptiness'; cf the distinction between the more common *bšqr* and *lšqr* (e.g. Jer 3.10; 1 Sam 25.21). 'I did not speak in hiddenness/darkness' is thus paralleled by 'I did not say..."seek me in emptiness"', or even—as the word order allows—'I did not say in emptiness "Seek me"' (†Calvin, *Tsumura). Koenig (*RHR* 173 [1968], pp. 25–27) links *tōhû* to the darkness of the desert where Israel first met Yhwh as the hidden God.

45.19b. I am Yhwh, speaking right, announcing true equity. For the simple *ʾănî* ('I [am]'), LXX repeats ἐγώ εἰμι ἐγώ εἰμι.

Yhwh speaks *ṣedeq*. This hardly refers to the manner of Yhwh's speaking with directness and clarity (against JB) nor in general to Yhwh's speaking truth as opposed to falsehood, any more than is the case in Ps 52.5 [3] (against †North). There *ṣedeq* belongs with *ṭôb* ('good') and both are set over against *raʿ*, *šeqer*, and in the context *rāʿāh*, *hayyût*, *rᵉmiyyāh* ('bad', 'deceit', 'bad', 'destruction', 'treachery') (see also Prov 12.17). As usual *ṣedeq* speaks of Yhwh's purpose to see that right is done by Israel (see on 41.2a). The parallel *mêšārîm* ('true equity') is a characteristic intensive or amplifying plural (GK 124e). The two words often appear together in Ugaritic (Watson, *VT* 22 [1972], p. 462) though they are not especially linked in Hebrew.[34]

[34] But see M. Weinfeld, *Social Justice in Israel and in the Ancient Near East* (Minneapolis, 1995), p. 25.

In the context *ṣedeq* and *mêšārîm* are set over against hiddenness, darkness, and emptiness. *Olley (pp. 449–50) sees *ṣedeq* as suggesting Yhwh's whole harmonious ordering of creation, bringing about what is right, including deliverance of Israel. One might compare H. H. Schmid's stress on the link between *ṣedeq* and world-ordering.[35] If these notions were interlinked in Israelite thinking, the connections lay in the background. The particular destiny of Israel within Yhwh's purpose stood firmly in the foreground when it used the word *ṣedeq*.

45.20a. Gather and come, come forward all at once, fugitives of the nations. The first and third verbs were used in the earlier summons to court in 43.9 and 44.11 ('gather', *qbṣ* ni, hit), and 41.1, 21, 22 ('come/bring forward', *ngš* qal, hi), while 'come/bring' (*bwʾ* qal, hi) is more broadly familiar. But the hitpael of the third verb is unique and adds variety to the parallelism. The LXX's βουλεύσασθε perhaps reflects the influence of 41.21 LXX (so †Ziegler, p. 158). The sequence conveys great vigour and the novelty at the end draws attention (†Gitay). The prophet's characteristic 'all at once' (*yaḥdāw*) then binds the three verbs (see on 40.5).

What kind of construct is *pᵉlîṭê haggôyim*? See GK 128; *DG* 32–35; JM 129; *IBHS* 9.5. In the expression *pᵉlîṭê ḥereb* the genitive is objective, 'those who have escaped the sword'. But there are no clear examples of this usage when the second noun is personal. 'Escaped from' involves *min*, in parallel to English. Here, then, 'people [i.e. Judeans] who have escaped the nations' is possible but would be unique. 'People who have escaped [and found refuge among] the nations'—again, that is, Judeans (†Hollenberg, p. 231)—requires too much to be read in, especially in an invitation to court proceedings such as is regularly addressed to foreign peoples. In Judg 12.4–5 the genitive is subjective or partitive (fugitives from Ephraim), and 'fugitives from among the nations' is the obvious meaning here.

Syntax, then, suggests that the fugitives are members of other nations who have escaped. In the context, this suggests people who have survived Cyrus's campaigns. The genitive is perhaps appositional or epexegetical, 'fugitive nations' (see on v. 20b). Or perhaps it refers by anticipation to people who will survive Cyrus's assault on Babylon.

יחדו: 1QIsᵃ has ואתיו ('come') from אתה, to which it is partial (†Kutscher, p. 169; ET p. 222), balancing באו in the first colon. Cf 41.5, 25, and for the imper. 21.12; 56.9, 12.

45.20b. They have not recognized, the people carrying their wooden images and making their plea to a god who will not deliver. If the construct in v. 20a is partitive, the sense continues cleanly as Yhwh continues to address them, and now points them to the non-survivors

[35] See his *Gerechtigkeit als Weltordnung* (Tübingen, 1968).

who went to their destruction carrying their images and calling on them in vain. Or perhaps v. 20b comments on the blindness of the people addressed in vv. 20a and 21. *MHP* (pp. 75, 156) sees the first of these two bicola as an aphorism that the prophet quotes, the second as one of the prophet's own 'concise and momentous phrases'.

†Westermann sees v. 20b as a gloss misplaced from chapter 46. In the MT it thus has the effect of announcing a theme that will be developed there, as well as continuing in vv. 19–20 allusions to vv. 14–15 and leading to the assertion that Yhwh is deliverer in v. 21. 'Their wooden images' is literally 'the wood of their images', an epexegetical genitive. 'Wooden' and 'images' take up references such as 44.17, 19, while 'making their plea' (*pll* hit: †Duhm adds the article to balance that on 'carrying') takes up v. 14 as well as 44.17, and the comment on these gods' inability to 'deliver' takes up the other participle from v. 15. Implicitly foreigners are invited to recognize that there is a destiny for pleas for deliverance where these pleas will receive a more effective hearing than they do from their gods—or from Israel if Israel is merely aggrandized by them, as vv. 13–14 might imply.

LXX has plural πρὸς θεοὺς for 'to a god', assuming a reference to polytheism.

45.21a. Announce and bring forward—yes, they must consult all at once. As in 41.1, once more there is a move from imperative to jussive between the two cola. The first colon stops short, both in comprising only two words and in lacking objects. †Duhm emends *ʾap* ('yes') to *ʾōt* ('a sign'), while †Morgenstern adds *ʾĕlōhêkem* and reverses the verbs (as in 41.22) so that 'announce' repointed (*wᵉhiggîdû*) links with the second colon. In the MT's order the implied object of 'bring forward' must be the same as that of 'announce', namely something such as arguments or strong points (cf 41.21). 'All at once' (*yaḥdāw*) again holds the preceding clauses together (see on 40.5).

יועצו: Syr *wʾtmlkw*, Tg אתמליכו, Vg *consiliamini*, all imper., suggest הועצו to assimilate the two cola to each other. The LXX conversely has εἰ ἀναγγελοῦσιν, ἐγγισάτωσαν, ἵνα γνῶσιν, all third person vbs. Geniza fragment Kb 13 has qatal נועצו.

45.21bα. Who informed of this beforehand, announced it in time past? Each word here has already occurred in the earlier court speeches, except *miqqedem* ('beforehand'). While temporal *qedem* often means 'of old' (cf 19.11; 23.7; 37.26; 51.9), etymologically it merely suggests 'before' and it need not carry the connotation of antiquity (cf Job 29.2; also Lam 1.7; 2.17; 5.21?). For the second colon the LXX has the paraphrase τότε ἀνηγγέλη ὑμῖν ('then it was announced to you'); cf 40.21. Syr 'and from the beginning I, even I, am the Lord' is drawn from other passages, for example, 43.13.

'In time past' (*mēʾāz*) if anything disambiguates *miqqedem*, for this term less often suggests any reference to distant time. Haller (Ευχαριστηριον, pp. 265–66) takes 'this' to be the creation of v. 18. The creation was indeed effected by Yhwh's word but it was not the subject of prediction. More likely 'this' is the right and equity of v. 19b, embodied in the rise of Cyrus.

45.21bβγ. Was it not I, Yhwh? There is no other God apart from me. Right God, who delivers, there is none besides me. The interrogative *hălōʾ* ('was it not') recurs from 44.8, 'I Yhwh' is a frequent collocation, '[and] there is no other' (*weʾên ʿôd*) came in vv. 14, 18 (where also it followed 'I [am] Yhwh'), and 'apart from me' (*mibbalʿāday*) in 44.6, 8. There are particularly close parallels with 45.5, 'I [am] Yhwh and there is no other. Besides me (*zûlātî*) there is no God', and with 43.11, 'apart from me there is no deliverer'. For Yhwh as *ʾēl* (the Hebrew behind the second occurrence of God above), cf 43.12; 45.14, 15. The irony lies in the way the context uses the same word *ʾēl* to refer to an image (cf v. 20b).

'Right' is the adjective *ṣaddîq*, as in 41.26 (the only two occurrences with regard to God in Isa 40–55); the noun *ṣedeq* came in v. 19. For Yhwh as the one who delivers, cf vv. 15, 17, 20. The collocation of the two words again underlines the connotations of doing 'right' as implying deliverance.

ואין עוד אלהים, an example of Hebrew's 'forgetting' that אין is by origin a construct (if it ever was) and therefore being able to insert a word between it and its n. (cf GK 152o)—treating it like an adv. (cf JM 154k).

אין: 1QIsª ואין (cf Syr), perhaps to make explicit that אין is prospective not retrospective.[36]

45.22a. Turn to me and be delivered, all earth's extremities. The summons in v. 20 implies the challenge to a contest, and there is a peremptory aspect to these imperatives. They are not a take-it-or-leave-it invitation. The imperative niphal of *yāšaʿ* occurs only here, and one is tempted to render 'deliver yourselves' to bring out the logic of an imperative as well as to reflect the likely original significance of the niphal. The reflexive translation would also work at v. 17 (where see) and at 30.16; 64.4 [5]. A tolerative niphal, 'let yourselves be delivered', would also be possible (†Duhm; cf GK 51c). After an imperative a yiqtol usually follows, but a second imperative commonly indicates the aim or result of the first and implies a promise—or a warning—as much as a command (GK 110cf; JM 116f; *DG* 86): cf 8.9; 36.16. So perhaps the idea is 'turn to me so that you may find deliverance'.

†Snaith (pp. 160, 185) sees this as an invitation to scattered

[36] See J. Carmignac, 'L'emploi de la négation אין dans la Bible et à Qumran', in *RevQ* 8 (1972–75), pp. 407–13 (see p. 408).

Israelites. He compares 43.6, which speaks of Israelites being gathered from earth's furthest bound (*miqṣēh hāʾāreṣ*). Here there is no indication of a change of addressee from vv. 20–21 and the expression 'earth's extremities' (*ʾapsê ʾāreṣ*) is arguably closer to the plural 'earth's furthest bounds' (*qᵉṣôt hāʾāreṣ*) in 41.5 where the term is also personalized as here and certainly refers to foreigners. The LXX omits 'all', abbreviating the text.

והושעו: 1QIsᵃ has the more usual if inappropriate hi והושיעו (†Kutscher, p. 32 [ET p. 43]); so also MS 150 (see *HUB*).

45.22b–23aα. For I am God. There is no other. By myself I swear. Linking the first clause of v. 23 with v. 22 (†Torrey) generates more equal lines through vv. 22–23 and a neater parallel structure in the rest of v. 23a. 'I am God (*ʾēl*)' is not directly a monotheistic statement but a claim to be the real God over against the manufactured *ʾēlīm* (*Holter, pp. 95–98). It is characteristically introduced by the explanatory and asseverative *kî* ('for'). †Rosenbaum (p. 107) again renders 'I, El (and there is no other)...': but see on v. 18b. The LXX omits 'for', abbreviating the text. On †Torrey's redivision of the lines, Yhwh is here close to making the point in Heb 6.13. It is as God and as the one who is alone God that Yhwh swears 'by myself'. The qatal verb is a classic performative (see *IBHS* 30.5.1d).

The motif of Yhwh's swearing an oath is most common with regard to the promises of blessing, and especially of land, to Israel's ancestors. The words here correspond most closely to the form in Gen 22.16–18, which specifically refers to other nations gaining blessing for themselves.

The Tg has 'by my word', one of a number of occurrences of the addition of *memrāʾ* in the context. Yhwh creates by this word, delivers by it, summons people to turn to it, swears by it, locates rightness and strength in it, draws people by it, and gives Israel acquittal and glory by means of it (vv. 12, 17, 22, 23, 24a, 24b, 25). Along with other periphrastic ways of speaking of God such as holy spirit, glory, and presence, talk in terms of God's word both safeguards against anthropomorphism and affirms the reality of divine revelation. In particular it represents God relating to human beings by addressing and responding to Israel, and by being addressed and responded to by Israel (see †Chilton, pp. 56–69).

45.23aβ. From my mouth rightness has gone out, a word and it will not return. 'Gone out' (*yāṣāʾ*) is masculine, and grammatical renderings would be 'from my mouth has gone out [in] rightness a word...' (cf Tg *bzkw ptgm*, suggesting *biṣᵉdāqāh* to †Graetz) or 'from [my] mouth of rightness has gone out a word...' (*pî* is both the construct of *peh* and the first person suffix form). But it is quite possible for a masculine verb to be followed by a feminine subject. An even more literal translation is 'there has gone out rightness' (cf GK 145o; JM

150j). The LXX precedes the words with the introductory oath formula Ἦ μήν. The Vg has future *egredietur*, making explicit that this is a promise relating to the future. However we construe the line, †Jerome correctly assumes that it implies that a promise about rightness (*iustitiae verbum*, Vg) has gone out from Yhwh's mouth and will be effective (cf Syr *mlt*ʾ *dzdyqwt*ʾ).

Reference to both 'word' and 'rightness' is connected with Yhwh's commitment to delivering Jacob–Israel (†Reiterer, pp. 46–51). Nearer to hand, *ṣᵉdāqāh dābār* takes up v. 19b, which describes Yhwh as *dōbēr ṣedeq*, 'speaking right' (see comment), and the word that creatively implements right in v. 8. †Morgenstern redivides *ṣedeq haddābār*, 'purposeful is the decree'.

What was this word and when did it go out (for the idea, cf 2.3; Dan 9.23, 25)? We are familiar with qatal verbs that announce what Yhwh is now doing or about to do (see on 41.10b), and this might be an instance. †Conrad (pp. 139–43) assumes that the qatal verb has literal past reference and alludes to the speaking that Yhwh has been undertaking earlier in Isaiah, with its concern for the destiny of the nations. The prophet's words about this destiny indeed need to be seen as a further outworking of words in Isaiah 1–39, but it is doubtful whether this bicolon can be expected to have such as specific reference. On the other hand, vv. 19 and 21 have already issued other reminders of Yhwh's past speaking, and in a broader sense this may be such. Isaiah 14.24–27 is a passage that especially expresses the notion that Yhwh had sworn an oath and formulated a plan regarding the destiny of the nations. The implementing of this oath will not be 'turned'. Once again earlier words from Yhwh are effective in this new present. Once again their significance changes. There was no hope for the nations in 14.24–27.

צְדָקָה דבר ולא: Vg and Syr transpose the nouns. The LXX has οἱ λόγοι μου οὐκ; cf †Duhm דברי לא ('my word [that] will not') and 55.11. For 'a word that will not return' we would expect simple לא (see GK 155n; †Oort supplies this). Job 29.12 is parallel and might be another example of relative usage with ו (†Feldmann); and see the discussion in JM 158ab. Dahood ([see on 40.12a] p. 5) sees this as an instance of emphatic ו. More likely in both occurrences the ו indicates a parallelism that interweaves the content of the two cola rather than the verse working by enjambment, as †Jerome assumes. But Vg may have christological implications (†van der Kooij, p. 303).

45.23b. To me every knee will bend, every tongue swear. The line begins *kî*. This might simply mean 'for'. It might mean 'that' (*DG* 156), but we are some distance from the word for swearing, and the content of the 'word' in the preceding bicolon is surely Yhwh's activity rather than human acknowledgment of Yhwh. It might mean 'certainly': see JM 165b in connection with oaths when the word is separated from the verb for swearing (cf Muilenburg 'Linguistic and Rhetorical Usages' [see on 40.2aβ, p. 156). The bending of the knee is a physical sign of homage and practical submission; cf Ps 72.9. 'Knee' (*berek*) occurs in the singular only here. 1QIs[a] has *bwrk* implying *bōrēk*, perhaps a participle, perhaps presupposing that spelling of the noun (†Nötscher, p. 301). 4QIs[b] has *brk*.

1QIs[a] prefixes *tšbʿ* ('swear') with a *w* (and; cf LXX, Vg). 4QIs[b] agrees with the MT. The LXX then renders the verb ἐξομολογήσεται ('confess'). This is probably not an indication that it read *tšbḥ* ('praise') but a loose translation reflecting the doxological character of the line so far (so Goshen-Gottstein, 'Theory and Practice' [see on 43.12], pp. 155–58). The LXX then adds τῷ θεῷ. In the MT the line thus ends with a surprise as the parallelism takes the thought on or clarifies it. The swearing of an oath—here *to* not *by*—is a sign of loyal commitment (cf 19.18; Ezek 16.8) parallel to bending the knee, and one that makes clear that the acknowledgment of Yhwh with which v. 23 is concerned is one of life and not merely of worship.

45.24a. Only in Yhwh—it is said of me—are true rightness and strength. On restrictive/asseverative 'only' (*ʾak*) see on v. 14. The reference to Yhwh in the third person might make us infer that the speaker has changed for vv. 24–25, but the parenthesis 'it is said of me' indicates that Yhwh continues to speak but is here quoting the words of others, of the peoples who come to bow before Yhwh.

Admittedly the words *lî ʾāmar*, literally 'to/of me one said', are jerky in the context. †Ibn Ezra takes them to mean 'who spoke to me'. But the parenthetic speech formula parallels that in 48.22, and for *l* meaning 'of', cf 41.7; 44.26, 28. Vg *in Domino dicet meae sunt iustitiae* links 'of/for me' (*lî*) with the main sentence ('Only in Yhwh—one says—are right deeds and strength for me'), while †North understands *lî* as an Arabism to make 'say' a command. 1QIs[a] reads imperfect *yʾmr*, by implication niphal *yeʾāmēr* (for the qal 1QIs[a] would have *ywʾmr*), 'it will be said'. †Schoors then sees the *l* as emphatic *lamed*. The LXX's τῷ θεῷ links 'only in Yhwh' to what precedes, as the direction of the oath, and then introduces v. 24 with λέγων (participle, 'saying') for *lî ʾāmar*. This might imply *lēʾmōr* (infinitive, 'saying'), but the expression is prosaic for these chapters (†Hermisson). †Koppe, retaining the MT's verse division, relocates this to the beginning of the line (cf Syr). †Cheyne emends it to *lᵉyaʿăqōb*, †Volz to *lᵉʾādām* (only in Yhwh are there right deeds and strength for Jacob/humanity). †Simon plausibly sees the MT as a composite of 1QIs[a] *yʾmr* and LXX's *lʾmr*. Cheyne and Volz apart, the meaning is hardly affected by any of these changes.

'True rightness' is plural *ṣᵉdāqôt* (LXX, Tg translate by singular). This probably denotes numerical plural ('right deeds') in 64.5 [6]; Judg 5.11; Mic 6.5, and here 'right deeds and strength' might form a hendiadys for acts of strength done in the cause of right (†Beuken). But the poet is fond of the intensive plural, and this usage fits well here as in v. 19b (cf GK 124e). Indeed, 33.15 has already likely used *ṣᵉdāqôt* in this way—and in the company of the word from v. 19b, *mêšārîm* ('true equity'). Here it refers once more to the one event on which these chapters focus.

For 'strength' (*ʿōz*) cf 12.2; 26.1; 49.5; 51.9; 52.1; 62.8. The singular complements the plural; cf singular 'right' and plural 'true equity' in v. 19b. The book's two preceding references to 'strength' already established its link with Yhwh's 'delivering', as here (cf 51.9; 62.8). The reference in 49.5 again makes a connection with the finding of honour, as here (cf 52.1 where it is a matter of beauty). But the link with *ṣᵉdāqôt* suggests that this strength is that exercised by the just God on behalf of the weak.

45.24b. To him will come to be shamed all who rage at him. Perhaps the MT offers another composite text, for it reads 'to him one will come and they will be shamed, all who rage at him': that is, the first finite verb is singular (following on from vv. 23–24a), the second is plural (leading into the second colon). The MT's *munah* accent on 'come' links it to the plural verb that follows. †de Boer infers that the verb refers to Yhwh's coming to Israel that brings the shame of those who rage at Israel, †Barthélemy that it should be understood impersonally. Only redivision of words is required to make both verbs plural with 1QIsᵃ, LXX, Vg, Syr, or both singular. In 41.11 'rage' belongs with 'quarrel' (v. 9), perhaps making these terms an *inclusio* round vv. 9–25 (*Leene).

If Yhwh continues to speak, 'him' is apparently someone else, presumably Jacob–Israel, though unmentioned since v. 19; cf Tg *bʿmmyh* ('at his people'). It was Jacob–Israel who was the object of rage (the same verb form) in 41.11 and who was the nations' destination (using different verbs) in v. 14. It was to Yhwh as well as to Jacob–Israel that the nations were implicitly to 'come' in v. 20. Coming and being shamed marks the end result of the challenge issued there; it is an alternative to turning and being delivered (*Beuken, p. 349).

†Beuken suggests that the prophet speaks in this sense as in the similar vv. 16–17. The prophet's speaking would then form an *inclusio* round vv. 18–25 as a whole. But we have reckoned that vv. 16–17 are the nations' words quoted by Yhwh, continuing from what precedes, and more likely the same is indeed the case in these similar and parallel lines. Yhwh's quotation of the words on every tongue continues through vv. 24–25.

יבוא ויבשו: coordinating simple ו (†Saydon, p. 300), or more likely purpose. 1QIsᵃ has יבואו יבשו. The LXX and Syr provide a copula, but for the asyndeton, cf 41.3 (†North). An alternative redivision is יבוא ויבש וכל..., 'let him come and thus be shamed, and all who are incensed at him'. The s. verb then continues from v. 24a, the assonance with בו at the end of the line is preserved more completely, and the less expected nature of the reading offers a clue regarding the textual variety. †Köhler omits יבוא ו (dittography), but also emends the preposition to עליו.

הנחרים בו: on the participle, see on 41.11. On LXX's οἱ ἀφορίζοντες ἑαυτούς ('those who separate themselves [from the Lord/Israel?]') see †Ziegler p. 152; †Seeligmann, p. 118. For בו, Syr has *lk* ('at you').

45.25. In Yhwh all the offspring of Israel will be right and thus will glory. The transition from v. 24 to v. 25 parallels that between vv. 14–16 and 17, while the reference to offspring also forms an *inclusio* with v. 18. †Elliot-Hogg plausibly sees vv. 24b–25 as an ABAB quatrain:

> To him will come and be shamed all who rage at him;
> In Yhwh will be right and will glory all the offspring of Israel.

The Syr has *by* ('in me'), perhaps reflecting abbreviation of the divine name.

†Olley (pp. 57–58) reads the LXX to imply that 'the offspring of Israel' can include people other than born Israelites, as born Israelites can surrender their membership of Israel. The fact that the subject 'all the offspring of Israel' comes at the end of the sentence makes it possible to take Yhwh's former enemies (v. 25) as the subject of the first verb and Israel as the subject only of the second. In contrast, †Volz describes vv. 24b–25 as a nationalistic gloss, and the passage as a whole as we have it does keep Israel's honour in mind even when envisaging the nations in some sense finding deliverance.

יצדקו ויתהללו: again, surely not merely coordinating ו (against †Saydon, p. 300), but here ו of result. The LXX and Vg make the verbs passive, and the LXX also adds ἐν τῷ θεῷ, improving the parallelism.

זרע: LXX adds τῶν υἱῶν, perhaps indicating that it read בני, or perhaps reflecting the influence of the familiar phrase בני ישׂראל ('children of Israel') (†Ziegler, p. 74).

Bibliography to 44.24–45.25

Balentine, S. E., 'Isaiah 45', in *Horizons in Biblical Theology* 16 (1994), pp. 103–20.

Beuken, W. A. M., 'The Confession of God's Exclusivity by All Mankind', in *Bijdragen* 35 (1974), pp. 335–56.

Broyles, C. C., 'The Citations of Yahweh in Isaiah 44:26–28', in †Broyles and Evans, pp. 399–421.

Clements, R. E., 'Isaiah 45:20–25', in *Interpretation* 40 (1986), pp. 392–97.

Deroche, M., 'Isaiah xlv 7 and the Creation of Chaos?', in *VT* 42 (1992), pp. 11–21.

Dijkstra, M., 'Zur Deutung von Jesaja 45 15ff', in *ZAW* 89 (1977), pp. 215–22.

Dion, H. M., 'Le genre littéraire sumérien de l' "Hymne à soi-même" et quelques passages du Deutéro-Isaïe', in *RB* 74 (1967), pp. 215–34.

Drinkard, J. F., 'Isaiah 44:24–45:7', in *RevExp* 88 (1991), pp. 201–4.

Fokkelmann, J. P., 'The Cyrus Oracle (Isaiah 44, 24–45, 7)', in †van Ruiten and Vervenne, pp. 303–23.

Haag, H., '"Ich mache Heil und erschaffe Unheil" (Jes 45, 7)', in *Wort, Lied und Gottespruch [Vol. 2]: Beiträge zu Psalmen und Propheten* (J. Ziegler Festschrift, ed. J. Schreiner), pp. 179–85. Stuttgart, 1972.

Heintz, J.-G., 'De l'absence de la statue divine au "Dieu qui se cache"', in *RHPR* 59 (1979), pp. 427–37.

Hirsch, S. A., 'Isaiah xlv. 18, 19', in *JQR* 14 (1901–1902), pp. 134–35.

Hoffmann, A., 'Jahwe schleift Ringmauern–Jes 45, 2aβ', in *Wort, Lied und Gottespruch [Vol. 2]: Beiträge zu Psalmen und Propheten* (J. Ziegler Festschrift, ed. J. Schreiner), pp. 187–95. Stuttgart, 1972.

Holter, K., 'The Wordplay on אֵל ("God") in Isaiah 45,20–21', in *SJOT* 7 (1993), pp. 88–98.

Hutter, M., '"Asche" und "Trug"', in *BN* 64 (1992), pp. 10–13.

Johns, A. F., 'A Note on Isaiah 45:9', in *AUSS* 1 (1963), pp. 62–64.

Kittel, R., 'Cyrus und Deuterojesaja', in *ZAW* 18 (1898), pp. 149–62.

Koole, J. L., 'Zu Jesaja 45, 9ff.', in *Travels in the World of the Old Testament* (M. A. Beek Festschrift, ed. M. S. H. G. Heerma van Voss and others), pp. 170–75. Assen, 1974.

Kosmala, H., 'Agnostos Theos', in *ASTI* 2 (1963), pp. 106–8.

Leene, H., 'Universalism or Nationalism? Isaiah xlv 9–13 and its Context', in *Bijdragen* 35 (1974), pp. 309–34.

Lindeström, F., *God and the Origin of Evil*, pp. 178–99. CBOTS 21, 1983.

Naidoff, B. D., 'The Two-Fold Structure of Isaiah xlv 9–13', in *VT* 31 (1981), pp. 180–85.

Ogden, G. S., 'Moses and Cyrus', in *VT* 28 (1978), pp. 195–203.

Olley, J. W., 'Notes on Isaiah xxxii 1, xlv 19, 23 and lxiii 1', in *VT* 33 (1983), pp. 446–53.

Pfeifer, G., 'Amos und Deuterojesaja denkformenanalytisch verglichen', in *ZAW* 93 (1981), pp. 439–43.

Pilkington, C. M., 'The Hidden God in Isaiah 45:15', in *SJT* 48 (1995), pp. 285–300.

Sawyer, J. F. A., 'Christian Interpretations of Isaiah 45:8', in Vermeylen (ed.), *Isaiah*, pp. 319–23.

Simon, U., 'König Cyrus und die Typologie', in *Judaica* 11 (1955), pp. 83–89.

Southwood, C. H., 'The Problematic *hadūrîm* of Isaiah xlv 2', in *VT* 25 (1975), pp. 801–2.

Spreafico, A., 'Jesaja xliv 26aα', in *VT* 45 (1995), pp. 561–65.

Texier, R., 'Le Dieu caché de Pascal et du Second Isaïe', in *NRT* 111 (1989), pp. 3–23.

Tsumura, D. T., '*Tōhû* in Isaiah xlv 19', in *VT* 38 (1988), pp. 361–64.

Virgulin, S., 'Un vertice dell'Antico Testamento', in *Parola e Spirito* (S. Cipriani Festschrift, ed. C. C. Marcheselli), Vol 1, pp. 119–28. Brescia, 1982.
Whitcomb, J. C., 'Cyrus in the Prophecies of Isaiah', in *The Law and the Prophets* (O. T. Allis Festschrift, ed. J. H. Skilton), pp. 388–401. Nutley, NJ, 1974.

III.b

46.1–47.15: THE FALL OF BABYLON'S GODS AND OF THEIR CITY

In the MT there is no break at 45.25. The next petucha comes after 48.16, though A also has one after 46.2; 47.3, 7; 48.11, while 1QIs[a] has one after 45.17; 46.2, 11, 13; 47.15, 1QIs[b] after 46.11 and 47.11, 4QIs[b] after 46.2. Even the LXX and Syr are more agreed on a break after 46.2 and 11 than after 45.25, 46.13, and 47.15. It is the medieval chapter divisions that rightly recognize that chapters 46 and 47 are self-contained sections. In complementary ways they together take forward the argument of chapters 40–55.

Chapter 46 begins with a vivid portrayal of the fall of the Babylonian gods, using a narrative descriptive form that has not appeared before. Chapter 47 less directly portrays the fall of Babylon herself (*sic*) with a vividness that comes from a sustained direct address to the woman who is collapsing. Chapter 46 opens with the Babylonian gods, supposedly sovereign authorities in the nation's destiny, incapable of saving the burden as they themselves (*napšām*) go into captivity. Chapter 47 closes with Babylonian science and religion, supposedly reflecting that sovereignty, equally unable to rescue themselves (*napšām*) at this moment. In 46.10 Yhwh can declare the outcome (*ʾaḥărît*) of events, in 47.7 Babylon for all her god-like pretensions cannot. Chapter 46 closes with deliverance in Zion, Chapter 47 with no-one able to deliver Babylon, though Jacob–Israel has as much difficulty as Babylon does over bearing Yhwh's purpose in mind (46.8, 9; 47.7). Chapter 46 includes a further declaration concerning Yhwh's plan and Cyrus as its means of execution, chapter 47 the last dismissal of the claims of other gods to make or reveal plans (v. 13). Both chapters forgo most of the subtlety, ambiguity, and indirectness of chapters 40–45 for concrete visionary portrayal and straight exhortation. The prophet has sought to draw the people to make their own journey away from their attraction to images and their acceptance of their place in Babylon, towards a new commitment to Yhwh and a recognition of what Yhwh is doing in events. Now the time has come for a direct challenge regarding these matters. The velvet glove is being cast aside.

†Franke includes a detailed study of the rhetoric of the chapters.

III.b.i. The fall of Babylon's gods (46.1–13)

We have noted that both the MT and 1QIs[a] associate vv. 1–2 with 45.18–25. A concrete instance of the bending required by 45.23 and the submission required more broadly by 45.14–25 is now portrayed by 46.1–2. This is presumably the instance the indirect audience especially wishes to hear of. †Luther, too, describes v. 3 as the true beginning to chapter 46, and †Mowinckel distinguishes 46.1–2 from vv. 3–13, while †R. H. O'Connell (pp. 187–88) sees 45.14–46.2 as a unit. This draws our attention to the fact that the characteristic feature of chapter 46 is the chiastic series of imperatives in vv. 3, 8, 9, and 12: listen, call to mind, call to mind, listen. These also make for a link with chapter 48—listen, listen, assemble, draw near, leave (vv. 1, 12, 14, 16, 20), as does the developing assertion of Jacob–Israel's rebellious nature.[1] Previously the dominant exhortation has been not to be afraid, though there have also been isolated commands to look up (40.26), to listen (42.18; 44.1), to forget (43.18), to remind (43.26), to call to mind (44.21), to turn (44.22). The imperative tone here, with its implication that Jacob–Israel will not listen, is thus new; these imperatives are different in addressees and function from those in 45.18–25, with which †Westermann links chapter 46.

Yet the medieval chapter division after 45.25 in turn draws our attention to the fact that there is something new about the description of an event in 46.1–2 over against what precedes, though partial parallels are provided by the 'audition' with which chapters 40–55 open and, significantly, by the narrative descriptions of the activities of image-makers (see esp. 41.5–7). So vv. 1–2 do not follow on seamlessly from chapters 40–45. †Simon describes the prophet as interrupting his theological flow. This procession is the reverse image of that in 45.14–25 (†Lack). But vv. 1–2 also stand out in relation to what follows, for their description of an event using mostly qatal verbs contrasts with vv. 3–13, which use mostly yiqtol verbs, imperatives, and participles (cf †Franke). Not that vv. 1–2 lack links with what follows. Indeed we might see vv. 1–2 as the 'text' for the subsequent exhortations:

1–2 The imminent event
3–13 The implications:
3 Listen (leading into 4)
8 Call to mind (leading from 5–7)
9 Call to mind (leading into 10–11)
12 Listen (leading into 13)

Another outline is suggested by the alternating of statements and imperatives that issue from them (cf †Grimm and Dittert):

[1] Cf Westermann's treatment of the two chapters, 'Sprache und Struktur', pp. 151–56 (rev. ed., pp. 68–73).

1–2 The gods are failing
    3–4 Listen to what Yhwh has done and will do (Yhwh carries)
5–7 Their images are useless
    8–9 Call to mind what Yhwh has said and is (Yhwh alone is God)
10–11 Yhwh alone speaks and acts
    12–13 Listen to what Yhwh has done and will do (Yhwh is bringing deliverance)

The chiasm in vv. 3–13 has some subtleties. In v. 3 the people bidden to listen are a remnant, which sounds gentle. In vv. 8–9 the people bidden to think are rebels. In v. 12 the people again bidden to listen are (merely) strong-minded, which likely contains a suggestion of perversity, but has withdrawn from the explicitness of v. 9. Furthermore, it is not only vv. 1–2 or even 1–4 that relate to what precedes. Verses 5–11 with their emphasis on Cyrus also do so, and vv. 12–13 take the chapter to a similar point to the one that chapter 45 reached. *Gaiser (p. 55) suggests a point by point parallel between vv. 3–13 and 45.18–25, while †A. Wilson (p. 161) pictures chapter 46 as having a square structure in which there are mutual relations between vv. 1–4 and 5–7, vv. 5–7 and 8–11, vv. 8–11 and 12–13, and vv. 12–13 and 1–4.

Form-critically, the three imperative sections belong to different *Gattungen*, but they are all more or less polemical. Yhwh is the speaker throughout. Verses 1–2 imitate a victory shout that provides the backing for a 'promise of salvation' in vv. 3–4. The anticipatory victory shout parallels that in Jer 50.2. It is but one of a number of parallels in Isaiah 40–55 with Jeremiah 50–51. Whereas †Cassuto infers from similar links with Jeremiah 10 and 30–31 that Second Isaiah is taking up the words of Jeremiah, here he makes the opposite assumption on the basis of Jeremiah 50–51 being later than Jeremiah (pp. 152–55), though the literary data seem similar. †Sommer (p. 36) excludes the chapters from his consideration of Second Isaiah's allusions to Jeremiah, suggesting that whatever the dating, the similarities reflect a common cultural background rather than the dependence of one on the other. The features of both works may nevertheless emerge from a comparison.

Whereas all the verbs in the five (breathless?) two-word clauses in Jer 50.2 are qatal, v. 1 includes two participles such as suggest an event taking place before the speaker's eyes (†Mowinckel describes vv. 1–2 as a seer's saying). This fits the fact that the 'you' who are directly addressed in the MT (denoted by the suffix in v. 1b) seem to be the Babylonians themselves, or the gods themselves, not people who will hear the shout as good news. The imperative in v. 3 then urges Jacob–Israel to listen to the promise. It is an unusual imperative for a 'salvation promise': see on 44.1, which at least goes on to a 'fear not'—as chapter 46 does not. The exhortation to listen hints that the audience is not doing so (cf e.g. 42.18; 46.12; 47.8;

48.1). This hint is underlined by v. 4, whose promises are confined to assertions of a general kind that are not cashed out in specific ways. Attention is rather given to the backing of Yhwh's fourfold *ʾănî* ('I'). This is indeed a 'polemical speech of salvation' (†Melugin, p. 24). While vv. 1–2 and 3–4 could stand on their own, as we have them they are mutually interdependent. Verbal links ('bear', 'carry', 'burden', 'free') support functional interweaving and contribute to the sense that this is one unit: so †Merendino, who sees the unit as a theological statement from a fairly late stage in the prophet's ministry. Verses 3–4 indicate who are the beneficiaries of the victory and bring home its implications, while vv. 1–2 provide something of the specificity that vv. 3–4's promise otherwise lacks.

Verses 5–11 are a disputation, characteristically combining rhetorical questions, sarcastic dismissal of alternatives, critical challenge, and personal claims on the part of the speaker. It recalls the content and order of 40.12–31 combined with the trial speeches that follow, though its distinctive stress on the images' incapacity to carry or deliver shows its link to this context. Indeed, the order of the constituents in this disputation overlaps notably with that of the salvation speech. Verses 5–7 parallel vv. 1–2 and vv. 8–11 parallel vv. 3–4. Its content also relates to what precedes. The sarcasm concerns carrying (both *sābal* and *nāśāʾ* occur in both vv. 4 and 7) and delivering, and the verb *ʿāśāh* recurs in each final line. But one must also note that the image of carrying which was more systematically explored in vv. 1–4 is less central in vv. 5–11, while the claim to speak and act which had been alluded to in vv. 3–4 is the theme that becomes more central as vv. 5–11 unfold. Further, the remnant of v. 3 have become the rebels of v. 8.

Verses 12–13 again urge people to listen to a promise of deliverance and in v. 12b perhaps allude to their lament (†Volz), but they address them as too strong-minded for their own good(?). They, too, affirm Yhwh's involvement with rightness/deliverance, in both qatal, yiqtol, and wᵉqatal verbs. They, too, express themselves in general terms. They, too, perhaps presuppose the specificity provided by what has preceded. Their imperative takes up that of v. 3. They have a 'compactness' (†Schoors) that recalls that of 43.14–15. That led into another promise of deliverance, this promise more obviously rounds off chapter 46 but perhaps also introduces chapter 47 (†Luther; also cf †Merendino, who thus sees it as secondary).

As well as holding 46.1–13 together, some of these verbal links, and some other verbal features make connections with what has preceded. 'Right' (*ṣᵉdāqāh*) recurs in 45.8, 23, 24, then 46.12–13, 'save/saviour/salvation' (*yāšaʿ/môšîaʿ/tᵉšûʿāh/yešaʿ*) in 45.8, 15, 17aα, 17aβ, 20, 21, 22; 46.7, 13a, 13b. From 45.18–25 there recur the motifs of the gods' incapacity to respond to prayer or to deliver, and their need to be carried (45.20; cf 46.1, 2, 3, 4, 7). The challenge to the 'fugitives of the nations' (45.20) is followed by one to 'what remains of Israel' (see on v. 3 below). The occurrences in 44.26, 28 of '[cause to] stand' (*qûm*), 'plan' (*ʿēṣāh*), and 'my longing' (*ḥepṣî*) are paralleled in 46.10–11. †Lack takes them as an *inclusio* round 44.24–46.13 and †Bentzen sees chapter 46 as closing off the Cyrus section begun at 44.24.

These also constitute a link with earlier material in Isaiah. We have noted that the motif of Yhwh's plan makes its final appearance here.[2] It featured first in 5.19 on the scornful lips of Judeans who sarcastically challenged this plan to come near (*qārab*: cf 46.13). In 8.9–10 Isaiah in turn scornfully challenged far countries (*merḥaqqē-ʾereṣ*) to formulate a plan or speak a word such as will stand (*qûm*) (cf 46.10, 11). In 14.24–27 Yhwh emphasizes the plan to break Assyria, part of a purpose affecting the whole world. In 28.29 the wonder of Yhwh's plan as implemented in the life of the nations is asserted, and in 30.1 the stupidity of people who plan in a way that ignores Yhwh's plan. In 36.5 the Assyrians ridicule Hezekiah's plan, while in 37.26 the tables are turned as they are reminded of what Yhwh had planned (cf 14.24–27). This is now being fulfilled. In 40.13 the prophet has hinted that there might be a man of Yhwh's plan, and 44.26, 28 have identified Cyrus as that man. See also 9.5 [6]; 11.2; 19.3, 12, 17; 23.8–9; 25.1.

†Melugin suggests that vv. 1–4 and 5–11 could originally have existed independently of each other. Within vv. 5–11, †Duhm reckons vv. 6–8 secondary, †Volz vv. 5–7, †Merendino vv. 6–7, 8b. †Kratz sees vv. 9–11 about Cyrus as the oldest material originally following 45.20–21. It was supplemented by vv. 1–4, then by vv. 5–7 with v. 8 to provide a link, and finally by vv. 12–13 with their orientation on Zion rather than Cyrus. Elliger (*Verhältnis*, pp. 183–85) attributes these to Third Isaiah. †Hermisson also sees vv. 9–11 as the verses most certainly deriving from Second Isaiah, though he is unwilling to specify their date. He sees them as originally following a shorter form of vv. 1–2 and offers a detailed discussion of the possible association of the development of vv. 1–7 with Xerxes's conquest of Babylon in 480. In contrast, Clifford (*CBQ* 42, pp. 456–57) regards vv. 5–7 as 'the centerpiece' that unifies the chapter.

46.1aα. Bel has bent down. Nebo is stooping. So far the prophecy has spoken of the gods in general terms, but now yet another of its generalizations becomes specific. For Bel as an equivalent to Marduk, see Jer 50.2; Nabu was Marduk's son. The LXX reads Dagon for Nebo, perhaps because the translator knew that Bel had been identified with Dagon in Babylon (†Seeligmann, p. 77), though this also draws our attention to parallels between this picture and the story in 1 Samuel 5. Another feature of the LXX is that it has two past verbs, ἔπεσε and συνετρίβη. So does 1QIs[a], to judge from the lack of a vowel letter in the second, *qrs*. The MT displays the variation effected by qatal *kāraʿ* followed by participle *qōrēs*, though they may be purely rhetorical variants. Meaning and sound thus

[2] See †Conrad, pp. 52–82; Jensen, in *CBQ* 48 (1986), pp. 443–55.

unite the two verbs even as form distinguishes them. †Torrey sees the line as a conflate text, but the phenomenon of such rhetorical variation is too common for this to be an advisable hypothesis. †Hermisson suggests 'Bel is bending as Nebo stoops' (cf GK 116o), but the verbs rather look coordinate.

The first verb is one that occurred four lines previously in 45.23, 'to me every knee will bend'. It commonly denotes religious prostration (e.g. 1 Kgs 8.54; 19.18; Ps 95.6), though also collapse in death (Isa 10.4; 65.12; Judg 5.27) as well as the crouching of an animal (Gen 49.9). The second verb occurs only in vv. 1–2 and thus provides the typical rarer variant in the second of two parallel cola. It also produces an alliteration. The LXX's συνετρίβη ('was shattered'—literally or metaphorically) is a guess (†Ottley) anticipating the way vv. 1–4 will develop but perhaps based on 21.9 where this verb also follows a form of πίπτω (see also 1 Sam 5.4); cf Tg *ʾtqṭyp* ('was broken off'; Vg, Syr also have passives). †Rashi takes it to mean dirtying oneself and to indicate the idea that the gods were not able to reach the toilet before defecating. This is the way in which the gods have become like animals (see v. 1aβ). *b. Megillah* 25b assumes such an interpretation in commenting that obscenity is forbidden except at the expense of images.

46.1aβb. Their images are coming onto animals or cattle. The things you bear are loaded as a burden onto weary ones. The MT divides v. 1 two-thirds of the way through, but this obscures the parallelism between the first two clauses (v. 1aα) and between these next two. †Westermann sees v. 1 as a sequence of 2–2 bicola. This assimilates v. 1aβb to v. 1aα with its brevity and rapidity and obscures the parallelism between vv. 1aβ and 1b as well as the long-drawn-out heaviness of the words and clauses in v. 1aβb, which mirrors the heavy loading of which the words speak (†Franke). †Thomas divides v. 1 into two six-word lines, obscuring the entire construction and dynamic of the lines. Syntax and parallelism suggest they are a 2–2 followed by a 4–4, though the 3–3–3 tricolon in v. 2 may invite us to read v. 1 as a 4–4–4 tricolon. This second line has a further parallel with the first in following a qatal verb with a participle, thus again expressing in two different ways the reality of something taking place before the speaker's eyes.

The word *ʿăṣabbēhem* is a new one for images in these chapters. The root *ʿāṣab* II ('shape') is rarer than *ʿāṣab* I ('hurt, pain, grieve, vex'), and the derived nouns are distinguished by their vowels (though 48.5 includes an exception). But it would not be surprising if the resonances of *ʿāṣab* I carried over to *ʿāṣab* II, of which this noun is by far the most common form. Words from the former occur at 14.3; 50.11; 54.6; 58.3[?]; 63.10. Idols imply pain, grief, and vexation (see 41.21). The antecedent of the suffix 'their' is the gods of the previous line whom the images represent, though the prophet does not elsewhere distinguish god and image thus and wherever else the word has a suffix it refers to the people to whom the images belong (cf esp. 1 Sam 31.9; 2 Sam 5.21; 1 Chr 10.9) or to their city (Isa 10.11; Jer 50.2, referring to Bel–Marduk; Mic 1.7). Thus 'their' might refer to the Babylonian people. †Torrey sees the word as an explanatory gloss.

Even in isolation *hāyû. . .laḥayyāh* (lit. 'became for/to the animal) would probably suggest 'have come to belong to an animal' rather than 'have come to be an animal': see BDB, p. 226, on *hāyāh* followed by *l*; *DCH*, Vol. 2, p. 99, adds the nuance 'be of benefit', which implies an irony by the time we get to the end of the line. The Tg renders *hww. . .dmwt ḥywn* ('have become the likeness of an animal') and the LXX's literal ἐγένετο. . .εἰς θηρία probably also implies 'became an animal'. But †Qimchi rightly reads the colon not in isolation but in association with its parallel and assumes that the word for 'burden' also applies in the first colon. His realization is the key to seeing how the line works as it stands as a 4–4, and it renders unnecessary attempts to identify glosses within it in order to make it work better (e.g. †Duhm, †Beuken).

The word *ḥayyāh* can denote any 'living creature', but particularly a land animal (cf Gen 1.28), and especially a wild animal as opposed to a domestic animal—the word is often qualified in this connection (cf 43.20) but not always (cf 40.16?). In Gen 1.24–25 'animals of the land' denotes wild animals, and in 2.20 'animals of the open country' is the equivalent. Both are set over against 'cattle' (*bᵉhēmāh*). But subsequently the same antithesis is simplified to simple *ḥayyāh* over against *bᵉhēmāh* (e.g. Gen 7.14, 21; 8.1; cf Lev 25.7; Ps 148.10). Here, then, while *laḥayyāh wᵉlabbᵉhēmāh* could suggest 'animals, namely cattle', it more likely denotes 'wild animals and/or domestic animals' (†Qimchi), though even the former are here used as beasts of burden (see further *ThWAT* on *bᵉhēmāh* and on *ḥāyāh*, iv.2).

The second colon begins with the passive participle *nᵉśuʾōtêkem* (lit. 'your borne things'). As 'bend' took up a verb from 45.23, this participle takes up the verb *nāśāʾ* ('bear/carry') from 45.20. The things borne may be the Babylonian people whom Bel and Nebo are supposed to bear, so that the 'you' is these gods (†de Boer), but the parallelism makes it more likely that the things borne are Bel and Nebo themselves. The 'you' then might be the 'earth's extremities' who were the last explicit addressees in 45.22, or the Jacob–Israel that is explicitly addressed in vv. 3–4 (†Franke). Yet to identify Jacob–Israel as image-carriers would be a scandalous novelty that might want more advertising (or is the hinting typical of this prophet?), and in vv. 1–2 it is the images' Babylonian bearers who are more in focus. They are likely the 'you', now in the second person to complement the third person of the parallel colon. Neither this participle nor the derived noun *maśśāʾ* ('burden') nor the verb itself suggest a burdensome carrying, though v. 20 has announced that it is a pointless carrying.

As a word for loading a beast of burden, the verb *ʿāmas* ('loaded') has more of that implication (cf Zech 12.3) (†Kissane; and cf Tg, just quoted). It is this imposition that makes the animals or cattle 'weary'. As the word 'burden' is needed to make sense of the first colon, the words *laḥayyāh w^e^labb^e^hēmāh* are needed to make sense of the second. The parallel between the *l* expressions at the end of the two cola works against the suggestion that the weary one is not the animal but the god that collapses and cannot save its load (†Torrey), nice picture though that is. It also works against the suggestion that here the feminine adjective is used for an abstract concept, with the meaning 'unto weariness'—cf Vg *ad lassitudinem* (†Morgenstern; cf *DG* 18; GK 122q; JM 134n; *IBHS* 6.4.2b).

Prosaically re-expressed, the line observes that the images that you/they Babylonians bear (in procession?) have been loaded as burdens (for a different kind of bearing) on weary animals or cattle (cf †Cheyne). The verb is likely again an instantaneous qatal and the description of the creatures as weary is likely proleptic. To be even more literal, the line observes that the images are being loaded as burdens on animals or cattle so as to make them weary. Like the fall of Babylon in chapter 43, of course, all this is so only in the prophet's vision. The picture will reflect the way images were brought into Babylon in time of war, the way images became trophies of war, and the way Nabu was carried from Borsippa to Babylon for the new year festivities.

נְשֻׂאֹתֵיכֶם עֲמוּסוֹת: an odd expression. Tg has יקירון על נטליהון מטולי טעותהון ('the burdens of their errors [images] are heavy on their bearers'), from which †Lowth and †Torrey infer נְשֻׂאֹתֵיהֶם, third person suffix. As usual we must suspect the instinct to tidy variation between lines and cola in this way. †Oort simply omits the suffix. †Volz repoints נְשֻׂאת כְּמוֹ, †North נְשֻׂאת כְּמַעֲמָסוֹת ('carried like burdens'), but the f. ptpl is then odd. The LXX has αἴρετε αὐτὰ καταδεδεμένα ('carry them bound'). The first two words suggest a misreading as נשׂאו אתם (†Hermisson). †Ottley suggests that the participle results from a misreading of עמס as אסר or עמר, while Goshen-Gottstein ([see at 43.12] pp. 144–45) sees LXX not as reflecting any variant reading but as translated in the light of Hos 10.5–6. †Ibn Ezra interprets the word as if it were pointed נֹשְׂאֹתֵיכֶם, 'your carriers', and †Ehrlich repoints it that way.
משׂא לעיפה: Whitley (*VT* 11, p. 459) sees this as the explanatory gl. It appears in 4QIs[b]. 1QIs[a] has משמיעיהמה ('their announcers'); cf the s. in 41.26. The word presumably refers to the worshippers of Bel and Nebo (see Rubinstein, *JJS* 6, pp. 194–96, who suggests that the word denotes musicians). לעיפה is doubly translated in the LXX, κοπιῶντι καὶ πεινῶντι.

46.2. They have stooped and bent all at once. They cannot save a burden. They themselves are going into captivity. Again the verbs are qatal and there is no indication that the subject has changed; *yaḥdāw* again holds together the verbs it follows (see on 40.5) rather than indicating that the beasts of burden (†Ibn Ezra) or the Babylonians (†Koole) are bowing together with the images. The opening two verbs come in the reverse of the order in v. 1. The Tg now has two words that mean 'be cut down' (*ʾtqṣyṣw ʾtqṭypw*), underlining the link with 1 Samuel 5.

One would expect the images also to be the subject of the following verb, literally 'they cannot free a burden'. If so, what is the burden that cannot be set free? In the previous line it was the images themselves, but it seems unlikely that Bel and Nebo are now so sharply distinguished from their images as to be envisaged as freeing them or not. There is no indication that the animals are now thought of as the burden rather than the burden-bearers. It is difficult to take 'a burden' as in apposition to the subject ('they, a burden, cannot free'; cf †Watts). If the images need to be the verb's object, its subject might possibly be impersonal ('No-one can free…'), for if the gods cannot rescue themselves, who is left to do so? The expression 'they themselves' (*napšām*) in the next clause might then be a resumptive reassertion of their position as subject. But in vv. 3–4 a deity's people will become the burden, the object of carrying (*nāśāʾ*) and freeing (*mlṭ*, resultative pi, as here: see *Piʿel*, p. 258). In retrospect it perhaps becomes clear that this statement in v. 2 forms part of the preparing of the way for vv. 3–4. The Tg thus renders '[they could not deliver] those who bore them' (cf Syr; Vg has the singular). The latter then become the subject of v. 2b. The images are in no position to rescue any burden. Poetry's omission of the definite article aids the ambiguity here. This applies not only to themselves, but to the people they are supposed to carry and set free and who have to carry *them*. †Hermisson takes *maśśāʾ* as secondary because of the change in reference.

The first word of v. 2b, *napšām*, can then be allowed to have more than mere resumptive significance, to be more than merely a substitute for a personal pronoun. It likely suggests 'their actual selves', their real beings (lit. 'their self goes in captivity'). Whatever the metaphysical difference between them, God and image are one in fate.

For the practice of taking images into exile, see on v. 1aβb. The phrase 'go in[to] captivity' (*baššᵉbî hālak*) recalls the one that comes in Lam 1.5, 18 (the former without the preposition) and thus marks this as a reversal motif. What was done to Jerusalem's children and to the pride of its youth will be done not only to Babylon's people (14.2, where the related verb comes) but to Babylon's very gods. The unexpected third colon makes the verse a neat 3–3–3 to complement the 2–2, 4–4 (or 4–4–4) of v. 1 and adds emphasis to the point.

קרסו כרעו: LXX's καὶ πεινῶντι καὶ ἐκλελυμένῳ οὐκ ἰσχύοντι has a vb too many. Either the first is part of a double translation of לעיפה at the end of v. 1, or the last is part of a double translation of לא יכלו which follows. Either way, the LXX then has the right number of words even if it is in difficulties over the meaning (as in much of vv. 1–2).

לא יכלו: the vb here governs the infinitive without ל as if an auxiliary verb (see BDB, p. 407b). 1QIsᵃ has ולוא יוכלו (yiqtol for qatal): see on 43.9.

משא: Syr *ṭʿwnyhwn* (†Oort thus infers נֹשְׂאֵיהֶם, 'their bearers'), Vg

portantem (†Kittel thus infers נֹשֵׂא, 'a bearer'). LXX's ἀπὸ πολέμου ('from battle') implies a misreading such as מצה (58.4; cf 41.12; †Ottley).
הלכה: 1QIs[a] has הלכו, making explicit that the subj. is the gods and not merely their images. 4QIs[b] agrees with the MT. The LXX renders by the more vivid ἤχθησαν ('were led'); cf Ezek 30.18.

46.3a. Listen to me, house of Jacob, all that remains of the house of Israel. The Tg 'listen to my word' is a logical enough gloss: cf v. 12, also 'my word stands' (v. 4aβ). 1QIs[a] has singular imperative as at 44.1—but contrast 48.1. In the second colon, the opening *w* is explicative. The LXX and Syr omit 'the house of', abbreviating the text. As 'listen to me' applies to the second colon as well as the first, 'all that remains of' applies to the first as well as the second.

†Qimchi suggests that 'the house of Jacob' denotes the northern tribes over against Judah, but such usage is very rare (Mic 1.5 is the most plausible example) and here 'Jacob = northern Israel, Israel = Judah' is not the obvious understanding. While Jacob can refer to the northern tribes, when it does so this is because Judah is irrelevant in the context rather than purposefully excluded. In Isaiah 'Jacob' and 'Israel' have similar reference. The people's being decimated so there are only its 'remains' to address at least hints that something still exists and has the possibility of some future. There are no pointers towards identifying this reduced community with (say) the people left behind in Judah rather than the people in Babylon, or vice versa. The point about the terms is what they say about the audience rather than about excluding anyone else.

46.3b. ...you who have been loaded from birth, borne from the womb. Two passive participles are repeated from v. 1b, except for a change of gender and another reversing of the order. 1QIs[a] reads the participles as active *ʿwmsym* and *nwśʾym* (see on v. 4a). The MT's version suggests that Jacob–Israel has long been carried in the way that the images now need carrying, even if they were a burden. They have been so carried from birth. Each time the preposition is the archaic poetic *minnî* for the usual *min*, misunderstood by 1QIs[a] as *mmny* ('from me'; Syr replaces it each time by 'in'). It contributes to a strong m-m-m-n-n/n-m-m-n-m pattern in the line (†Boadt, p. 458). In addition, it could perhaps have a stress of its own and thus render the line 3–3, though the MT does not construe it that way.

Birth is denoted by two anatomical terms, *beṭen* and *reḥem*. The first is a general word for the insides, applicable to males though also used for a woman's womb (cf 44.2, 24). The second has only the latter meaning and thus rhetorically gives precision in the second colon. The reference is presumably to the beginning of Israel's life at the exodus, though †Hermisson sees it as looking behind that to the time of Israel's first ancestors.

46.4a. Yes, until old age I am the one, until grey-headedness I am the one who will carry the load. The verse division invites us to read v. 3b as dependent on v. 3a and qualifying its nouns, but v. 4a suggests that v. 3b leads into v. 4a. This also perhaps makes the active participles in v. 3b in 1QIs[a] less unintelligible ('As for those who… I am the one').

First, 'from…yes, until' (*min…wᵉʿad*) is a common idiom for expressing comprehensiveness: see, for example, 1.6; 9.6 [7]; 10.18; 22.24; 27.12. The *wᵉ* can be omitted (cf 1QIs[a], LXX, Vg, Syr). The expression is mainly a prose idiom and significantly this single occurrence in chapters 40–66 reworks it. 'From' comes in an extraposed introduction to the main clause, which is opened by the *wᵉ* with which v. 4 begins. The effect is still to emphasize the totality of the period during which Jacob–Israel is carried. A further link between vv. 3b and 4a is that the former had left implicit who had done the carrying. Verse 4 makes the point explicit with great emphasis by means of its fivefold *ʾănî* ('I'). This feature begins with the strong 'I am the one' (*ʾănî hûʾ*). In v. 4a †Torrey takes the phrase to mean 'I am the same', but none of the occurrences of the phrase require this meaning (see on 41.4b). Here some difficulty has been felt with the phrase because it seems isolated in the context, but the difficulty arises from not seeing the interrelationship of the two cola. 'Until old age' and 'until grey-headedness' clearly parallel each other, the second providing a more concrete and vivid way of expressing the first. 'I am the one [who] will carry' is then divided between the two cola (D. N. Freedman, quoted in †McKenzie). The LXX hints at this understanding with its repeated ἐγώ εἰμι.

'Carry the load' (*sābal*) is a new verb. Like *ʿāmas* ('load') in vv. 1 and 3, it intrinsically suggests the carrying of a heavy burden, but it is more predominantly used in figurative ways. Related nouns denote the way Israel was burdened by Assyria (9.3 [4]; 10.27; 14.25) as it had once been in Egypt (Exod 1.11; 2.11; 5.4–7; 6.6). In a parallel way the Judeans of the exilic period saw themselves as carrying a load imposed by their ancestors' wrongdoing (Lam 5.7: note the context's references to Egypt and Assyria and the lack of deliverer). Other peoples carry the burden of their gods (v. 7); Yhwh bears the burden of Jacob–Israel (v. 4). Yhwh will do so until its old age—not until Yhwh's; the metaphor in vv. 3–4 envisages the people's lifetime, not Yhwh's.

שיבה: so L, without the diacritical point; other MSS have שֵׂיבָה. The LXX translates by a verb, καταγηράσητε ('you grow old').
אסבל: LXX's ἀνέχομαι (middle) suggests 'bear with' rather than 'bear' (†Ottley). The LXX adds an object, ὑμῶν—again at the end of the line.

46.4b. I myself made, I myself will bear. I myself will carry the load and free. The strong first person affirmation continues: a threefold *ʾănî* ('I') and four first person verbs, three beginning with *ʾaleph* like *ʾănî* itself, so that (ignoring the copulas) only the first verb fails to begin with *ʾaleph*.

This first verb raises questions independently of that. When used without an object in 41.4 and 44.23 we have rendered *ʿāśāh* with 'act'. In the latter case we took it as a performative qatal, and 'I am acting' would make good sense here. But *ʿāśāh* is much more commonly transitive, and here it is followed by three further transitive verbs for each of which an object must be inferred from the context. This is not difficult, as indeed is the case with the preceding verb at the end of v. 4a. †Melugin (p. 24) implies the rendering 'I have done it', which requires a different implied object from the one required by the verbs on either side and a less obvious meaning. More likely, then, *ʿāśāh* means 'make' and the qatal refers to the original act of Israel's making (cf 43.21; 44.21 with *yāṣar*, 'shape').

The train of thought in v. 4b parallels that in 44.2 where the participle was used. There the prophet moved from past making to future helping. Here the movement is from past making to future bearing/carrying/freeing (†Torrey; cf GK 106c). The first verb takes up from vv. 1 and 3. The LXX renders ἀνήσω, which †Ottley thinks a frequent LXX error for ἀνοίσω; the two were probably pronounced alike. The second verb comes from v. 4a. The third comes from v. 2; it lacks a *ʾănî* so that the *w* ('and') is directly linked to the verb in a coordinating role. The effect is to link the final verb closely with its predecessor, suggesting that setting free is not a matter of separate effort but is part of the service instinctively rendered by the burden-bearing God (†Motyer). Yhwh fulfils the role that the worshippers of images have to fulfil for their gods.

The Tg renders vv. 3b–4 '. . .you who are mercied more than all the peoples, dearer than all the kingdoms. Forever I am the one, to age after age my word stands. I created everyone, I scattered them among the nations. Yes, I will pardon their transgressions and forgive.' In general the thought here and when it partially recurs at 66.9 is rather generalized in the Tg and lacks the 'emotional thrill' (†Chilton, pp. 31, 133) that attaches to a situation where someone wishes to excite about the real possibility of the restoration of the community—though 'mercied' (*rḥymyn*) does pick up the word for 'womb' in the MT. To put it another way, the concrete, strongly human picture of Yhwh's relationship with Israel has disappeared for something more abstractly theological. In addition the notion of forgiveness has been introduced. It belongs in the broader context of Isaiah 40–55 noted above, perhaps facilitated by the use of the verb *nāśāʾ*, which can mean 'forgive' (cf †Grimm and Dittert). The one past and three future verbs in v. 4 have become two past and two future.

עָשִׂיתִי; †Klostermann emends to עמסתי (another word for 'carried'); cf vv. 1, 3. The spelling עמשׂתי (cf †Thomas) would be an easier change, but the form is doubtful (see BDB, p. 770b). †Duhm emends to נשׂאתי, repeating another vb from vv. 1, 3.

46.5. To whom would you liken me, make me equal, compare me so we might be alike? The words in v. 5a are variants on 40.18, 25 (where see). Typically the prophet achieves affect by accumulating words of related meaning and repeating them with variations. Those in v. 5b continue to express the same point in newer words. 'Compare' (*māšal* hi) comes only here, as the last of three coordinate verbs linked by simple *w*. It is the only one of the prophet's terms whose Akkadian cognate (*mašālu*) appears in Assyrian or Babylonian material on the incomparability of a god (so Labuschagne [see introduction to 40.12–31], pp. 33–57). The LXX has τεχνάσασθε, perhaps disliking the repetition of words of similar meaning, though the rationale for this particular verb is not clear. The Syr omits this and the last verb, the qal form of *dāmāh*. It was already used in the piel as the first verb and thus functions as an *inclusio*. It changes to first person and we have taken its further simple *w* as indicating purpose. Here the prophet has Yhwh speaking in a way that has elsewhere been avoided, for speaking thus in the first person plural risks compromising the point that the words make, the very claim to incomparability. For †Hermisson this is thus a sign that these are not Second Isaiah's words. 1QIs[a] also could not believe its eyes and substituted singular *wʾdmh* (cf 40.25).

תדמיוני ותשוו: the suffix on the first applies also to the second (1QIs[a] has ותשוני). On the form of תדמיוני, see GK 75dd. For ותשוו the LXX has ἴδετε, perhaps suggesting שׁורו/תשׁורו (†Ottley).
וְנִדְמֶה: †Oort suggests וְנִדְמָה (3rd s. ni). LXX's οἱ πλανώμενοι (cf Syr *ldṭʿyn*) might suggest הַנּוֹדדים (†Ottley); but see 41.10a on this verb, and note the LXX's general freedom in v. 5.

46.6. Those who lavish gold from a bag and weigh silver by the rod hire a smith to make it a god to which they may fall, and bow down. To back up the point made by the rhetorical question, the prophet again recalls the process whereby an image is made, here stressing the vastness of the investment in relation to the poverty of the return. The main verbs in vv. 6–7 are frequentative yiqtol with coordinate *w* (cf *TTH* 134; †Saydon, p. 300). But in both verses the main verb(s) lead into a purpose clause, 'so that he may make it into a god' and 'so that it may stand' (*wᵉyaʿăśēhû*, *wᵉyannîḥuhû*, each time simple *w* followed by yiqtol verb). Each of these is in turn qualified by an asyndetic relative clause, 'to which they will fall…' and 'which will not depart…'. The LXX makes the image-commissioners the subject of the making, so that the verb 'make' is plural, and takes the next clause as another main clause (καὶ κύψαντες προσκυνοῦσιν αὐτοῖς, and bending they do homage to them: cf EVV). But the lack of a *w* points to a relative clause without *ʾăšer* (cf GK 155; JM 158; *DG* 11–12). This is confirmed by the next verse, which relates how they take the image to its place. Verse 6 therefore hardly yet refers to their worshipping it (following Clifford, *CBQ* 42, p. 455).

†Alexander takes v. 6aα as the protasis of a *w*-apodosis clause, 'those who lavish...weigh silver...'. It would be more typical for the two clauses to be parallel, in keeping with their content, so that the finite verb in the second continues the participle (GK 116x). Vg *qui confertis*... takes the line as a whole as qualifying the subject of the previous line and translates by a second person verb (cf GK 126b; JM 138e). The MT verse division implies rather that the clauses qualify the subject of the verb at the beginning of v. 6b. †Hermisson takes v. 6a as a self-contained sentence parallel with the ones that follow, but it seems unlikely that an audience would hear the construction that way.

The word for 'lavish', *zûl*, comes only here, but it is a byform of *zālal*, meaning 'to make light of' and therefore 'to use freely'. In the OT it always refers to food and thus suggests gluttony, but *DTT* records more general usage with regard to liberality. There is thus no reason to emend *hazzālîm* to *hassōlîm* from *sālāh*, 'those who weigh' (†Perles). In Deut 25.13; Mic 6.11; Prov 16.11 a 'bag' (*kîs*) is the bag of weights used in business transactions. †Ehrlich thus here renders 'gold more than the bag', more than the weights can measure. This seem forced, and Prov 1.14 parallels the use of 'bag' to mean 'purse'. Thus 1QIs[a] has *bkys* ('by the bag'), assimilating the first colon to the second (†Rubinstein, p. 316). The Syr has 'from the bags'.

But the parallel expression in v. 6aβ does refer to means of measurement, which retrospectively invites us to render *mikkîs* with 'out of a bag' in the sense of 'by means of a bag [of weights]'; cf the parallelism of *b* and *min* in 28.7. The 'rod' is *qāneh*, the word for a cane in 42.3, used for anything stick-like and thus here for the beam at the top of the scales. The phrase 'rod of the scales' (*qnh m'znyym*) comes in the Mishnah at *Kelim* 17.16 (cf *DTT*). †Ehrlich suggests that the reference is to a means of weighing things out that handles much larger quantities than a bag of weights, and some such extravagance in the second colon would be appropriate enough, however we understand 'bag'.

The other terms in v. 6b have come earlier: 'the smith' (40.19; 41.7); 'the making' which contrasts with Yhwh's making of Israel (44.13, 15, 17, 19); the so-called *'ēl* that results, which cannot compare with the real *'ēl* (44.10, 15, 17; 45.20; pluralized by the LXX as at 44.15; 45.20); the strange subsequent 'falling' and 'bowing down' (44.15, 17) that now overtly contrasts with the talk of their falling down before the exile community and bending the knee before Yhwh and before their fate (45.14, 23; 46.1–2). The Tg makes 'the peoples' (*'mmy'*) the subject of v. 6, removing any possibility of thinking that there might be Israelite image-makers. But G. Mayer, at least (*ThWAT* on *kesep* III.2.c), assumes that v. 6 refers to an image of Yhwh in the private chapel of a wealthy Israelite.

ישקלו: LXX adds ἐν σταθμῷ to accompany ἐν ζυγῷ as at 40.12 (†Ziegler, p. 75).

יִשְׂכְּרוּ צוֹרֵף וְיַעֲשֵׂהוּ אֵל יִסְגְּדוּ אַף־יִשְׁתַּחֲווּ: 1QIs[a] ויעשה lacks the suffix (cf LXX, Vg). Its ישתחו substitutes what looks a more usual form of the vb שחה (†Kutscher, p. 219 [ET pp. 291–92]; and see on 44.15). This last vb is introduced by אַף, drawing attention to the 'in addition' of the extra vb—cf the comma in the translation (and see on 40.24). The LXX then adds αὐτοῖς (cf 44.15).

46.7a. They bear it carrying it on their shoulder and settle it in its position so it stands, without departing from its place. Literally, 'they bear it on the shoulder they carry it', though 1QIs[a] opens the line with a copula. The relationship between the two verbs is unspecified and the prepositional phrase could link with either verb as they are set alongside each other asyndetically; see *TTH* 163, *DG* 146–48. LXX's αἴρουσιν αὐτὸ ἐπὶ τῶν ὤμων καὶ πορεύονται probably assumes that the two verbs, *nāśā*ʾ and *sābal*, denote lifting and then carrying; cf Syr, which also provides a copula. We have rather followed Vg *portant illud in umeris gestantes* in seeing the second verb more idiomatically as subordinate to the first (other versions also replace the idiomatic singular 'shoulder' by the plural, and the Tg and Syr provide the implied 'their'). This assumption may also underlie the MT's linking of the prepositional phrase with the second verb, and it allows *nāśā*ʾ to mean 'bear' rather than 'lift', in line with the usage in vv. 1–4.

In the middle colon, *taḥtāyw* (lit. 'beneath it) is an idiomatic expression for 'in its position' (see BDB). The closing asyndetic clause (lit. 'it does not depart from its place') is a circumstantial one (see *TTH* 162; GK 156f). The Vg uses the verb *moveo* as it had at 40.20 and 41.7, missing the fact that the Hebrew verb has changed. It is no longer *môṭ*, which denotes accidental, unintended movement, but *mûš*, which can indicate deliberate, purposeful movement. The worshippers must take steps to make sure that the deity does not decide to leave.

וְיַעֲמֹד: †Ehrlich omits the ו as dittog. and links the vb with תַּחְתָּיו, 'they put it down; there it stands', comparing the LXX (which is, however, abbreviating). †Ehrlich argues that the suffix on תַּחְתָּיו needs to refer to the subject of its vb, as in 25.10: but see, for example, Exod 17.12 and Mic 1.4. Syr abbreviates the translation of the last four words of the line to 'and is unable to rise'.
יָמִישׁ: 1QIs[a] ימוש perhaps read this as hi (it would then mean 'from its place no-one moves it') and corrected to qal (†Kutscher, p. 192; ET p. 254).

46.7b. And someone can cry out to it, but it does not answer. It does not deliver him from his trouble. The line opens with another ʾ*ap* (see on 40.24) followed by a verb with a third person singular subject. Given that the image-maker of v. 6 is now some way away, this is more likely to be a vague personal subject (JM 155e). EVV take v. 7b as a conditional sentence (cf GK 159b), though the *w*[e] ('but') perhaps makes this less likely. Both lines in v. 7 are perhaps to be seen as tricola. It would even be possible to reckon both 3–2–3.

In the Psalms and Lamentations, with which Second Isaiah often links, the nature of a relationship with Yhwh is centrally that one cries out in trouble, finds a hearing, and experiences deliverance. So this line's accusation is another way of saying that these gods are no gods. Given that *ṣārāh* ('trouble') etymologically suggests being in straits, v. 7b provides a rare piece of evidence to support the tradition that *yešaʿ* ('deliverance') suggests spaciousness. The LXX has plural ἀπὸ κακῶν and omits the pronoun.

יצעק אליו: 1QIs[a] has the variant forms יזעק עליו. On the vb, see on 42.2.

46.8–9a. Think about this, be strong. Bring to mind, rebels, think about former events of old. The opening imperatival phrase (*zikrû-zōʾt*) corresponds to 44.21 (*zᵉkor-ʾēlleh*) except that the verb is now plural and the demonstrative singular, rather than vice versa. Its preceding verses, too, referred to the stupid activity of image-makers. There we concluded that the thinking that follows will take place in the light of the description that has preceded, but that the actual phrase 'these things' referred directly to matters about to be stated rather than to those just-stated facts about image-making. The same understanding makes sense here, though in part for different reasons, such as will emerge from v. 9a. †Thomas and †Merendino rightly suggest we take v. 9a with v. 8 (though they do so in the context of omitting v. 8a, with †Volz, or v. 8b). There in v. 9a the imperative 'think about' will be repeated, with a morc specific object. If the prophet had understood 'former events of old' as a different object from 'this' rather than as a specifying of what 'this' is, we would have needed that made clearer. Verse 9a surely restates rather than adds, as is presupposed by †Volz's inclination to omit v. 8a. Verse 8 is therefore not merely a conclusion to vv. 5–7 but rather a hinge between vv. 5–7 and vv. 9–11 (†Bonnard; a redactional one according to †Kratz). Habel ('Appeal to Ancient Tradition' [see on 40.21a], pp. 265–66) argues on a form-critical basis for the forward-looking reference of 'this'.

†Volz's proposal involved transferring to v. 7 the second verb. The verb *ʾšš* (hitpo) comes only here. *Leene (pp. 118–19) notes the relative frequency of rare and not-so-rare hitpael and related forms in Isaiah 40–55. Tg *ʾytqpw* and Vg *fundamini* plausibly presuppose the meaning 'found/be firm' also found in the noun *ʾăšîš* ('foundation'; 16.7); cf *DCH* on *ʾōš* at Qumran and *DTT* on *ʾăšaš*/*ʾûš*. While v. 8b cannot match the unfamiliarity of that verb, in other ways it does take v. 8a further. 'Bring to mind' (*šûb* [hi] *ʿal-lēb*) is a stronger expression than 'think about' (*zākar*, EVV 'remember'), while the address 'rebels' (*pôšᵉʿîm*) suggests that the command 'be strong' was ironical (cf the exhortation in 41.1aβ).

As 'rebels' disambiguates 'be strong', 'former events of old' (*ri'šōnôt mē'ôlām*) in v. 9a explains 'this'. Perhaps the prophet delayed this explanation as long as possible out of a sense of embarrassment, for the present exhortation is in more obvious verbal tension with 43.18 than was the case at 44.21. Evidently there is a kind of looking back that is forbidden and one that can be appropriate.

The parallelism of the tricolon as a whole thus works as follows:

8a	8b	9a
Think about this	Bring to mind	Think about former events of old
be strong	rebels	

'Bring to mind' strengthens 'think about'. 'Rebels' disambiguates 'be strong'. 'Former events of old' explains 'this'.

והתאששׁו: there are other suggestions for this vb. Syr *'tbynw* ('reflect') perhaps implies a vb linked with תושׁיה ('wisdom'). See 28.29 where תושׁיה is in parallelism with עצה ('purpose'); cf v. 10 here. †Dillmann emended to התבוננו with Syr. Some Vg MSS have *confundamini*, which has been taken to imply a link with אשׁ ('fire'), 'be red/blush/be shamed' (or 're-light your ardour'—†Bonnard, comparing Ps 39.4 [3]), but which might point to התבשׁשׁו ('be shamed'; †Graetz). R. Tournay then saw the MT as a deliberate alteration to safeguard Israel's honour.[3] LXX's στενάξατε ('groan') may suggest a link with Akkadian *ašāšu* ('be in distress'; cf *Cobb, and *DCH*'s suggestion that אשׁשׁ means 'grieve', also *DCH* אשׁ 6d). It also made G. R. Driver suggest התחשׁשׁו from חושׁ ('feel pain'), with the meaning 'be concerned'.[4] *Cobb himself suggested the meaning 'repent' (see further *HUB*); cf †Klostermann's emendation התאשׁמו ('acknowledge guilt'). †Qimchi took it as a denominative from אישׁ ('be men'; cf *HAL*; *Leene). This seems forced. Driver later suggested a link with Akkadian *aššīšu* ('be attentive'),[5] but *CAD* gives this vb the meaning 'be unruly', and still later (*JTS* 36, p. 400) Driver came to agree with †Volz.

השׁיבו...על־לב: LXX's μετανοήσατε...ἐπιστρέψατε τῇ καρδίᾳ is a double translation (†Ottley).

46.9b. For I am God. There is no other. I am God. There is none like me. As usual it is impossible or inappropriate to avoid rendering *kî* ('for'), but it is important to note that v. 9b is not merely an explanation of some other important statement. It is itself a main statement (†Kratz, pp. 55–56), one that reworks Yhwh's familiar claims, as usual in new combinations and with new variations. For the first 'I am God', cf 43.12; 45.22, though that was *'ănî 'ēl*, whereas this is *'ānōkî 'ēl*, which has even more emphasis. 1QIsᵃ and 4QIsᶜ

---

[3] 'Quelques relectures bibliques antisamaritaines', in *RB* 71 (1964), pp. 504–36 (see p. 529).

[4] 'Some Hebrew Roots and Their Meanings', in *JTS* 23 (1922), pp. 69–73 (see p. 70).

[5] 'Studies in the Vocabulary of the Old Testament. iii', in *JTS* 32 (1930–31), pp. 361–66 (see p. 365).

have *ʾănî*, the longer form having fallen out of usage (†Morrow, p. 173). In context this *ʾēl* contrasts with the pathetic *ʾēl* of v. 6; see on 45.21bβγ. This contrast is lost if vv. 6–8 are dismissed as a later addition.

'There is no other' was the repeated claim of 45.5, 6, 14, 18, 21, 22, each time following 'I [am] Yhwh/God' except at v. 14 where it appears on the lips of other peoples. The parallel colon then begins with the single word *ʾĕlōhîm*. We have assumed that the 'I [am]' of the first colon carries over into the second. This 'I [am] *ʾĕlōhîm*' is a new expression, one that implies a different contrast over against the images, for Yhwh had challenged the gods to do something that would prove that 'you [are] *ʾĕlōhîm*' (41.23) and had derided people who said to an image 'you are *ʾĕlōhênû*' ('you are our god[s]'; 42.17). Again, the assertion that there is 'none like me' (*ʾepes kāmônî*) restates the claim that there is 'nothing apart from me', 'no God' (45.6, 14, using *ʾepes* each time) and recalls the question 'Who is like me' (*mî kāmōnî*) of 44.7; also v. 5. The LXX has πλὴν ἐμοῦ ('except me') as at 45.6, 14. The Tg has 'besides me'.

46.10a. ...announcing outcome from beginning, deeds not yet done from beforehand. The participles in vv. 10–11 repeat the claims of those in 44.24–28, though here there is no explicit reference to creation, the prophet begins from the evidence of Yhwh's incomparable, exclusive deity that is provided by the capacity to declare ahead of time events that are to take place, deeds that are to be done, and Yhwh's agent is once again known only by epithets (while Zion is unmentioned until v. 13). *Midrash Tanḥuma* (SB) on Exod 7.8–9 includes a noteworthy long exposition of v. 10 that takes up its underlying assumption that Yhwh has a distinctive capacity to see and to determine where events are going, and to make this known, a capacity illustrated at the burning bush, at the exodus, and in telling Moses how Israel's history would turn out. It also observes that the 'desire' that Yhwh will see fulfilled (v. 10b) is that people find forgiveness rather than experiencing punishment (see also its comment on Lev 13.2).

Given the precedent in 44.24 that the first participles refer to creation, it is noteworthy that the announcement in v. 10a begins *mērēʾšît* as Genesis 1 begins *bᵉrēʾšît*. It is the only occurrence of this word for 'beginning' in Isaiah. The meaning is hardly very different from the use of *rōʾš* to mean 'the very first' in similar contexts in 40.21; 41.4, 26. But the uniqueness of the occurrence, the link with Genesis 1, and the precedent of 44.24 combine to suggest that v. 10a does refer to the beginning of creation. In turn this suggests that the term 'outcome' (*ʾaḥărît*: see *ThWAT*) should have a broader reference than it had at 41.22, without its being the technical term it eventually becomes in the context of the phrase *ʾaḥărît hayyāmîm* (lit. 'the end of the days'): see, for example, 2.2.

The parallel colon makes the first more concrete yet needs also to be understood in its light. 'From beforehand' (*miqqedem*) had narrow reference in 45.21 but in many passages *qedem* is reckoned to suggest 'of old' rather than merely 'beforehand' (see BDB). Further, *miqqedem*, like *rēʾšît*, appears in the creation story, though rendered 'eastward' (Gen 2.8; 3.24; also at significant points at 11.2; 12.8a, 12.8b). So the announcing of 'deeds not yet done from beforehand' again suggests a broad perspective on Yhwh's activity as sovereign of the world from the beginning.

מֵרֵאשִׁית אַחֲרִית וּמִקֶּדֶם אֲשֶׁר לֹא־נַעֲשׂוּ: on LXX's πρότερον τὰ ἔσχατα πρὶν αὐτὰ γενέσθαι, καὶ ἅμα συνετελέσθη, see †Troxel, pp. 20–23.

46.10b. . . .saying 'My purpose will stand. I will do all my desire'. Specifically, Yhwh has a purpose and desire for history. Here every word appeared in 44.24–28. The two nouns (*ʿēṣāh*, *ḥēpeṣ*) specifically and distinctively recall vv. 26 and 28, but the participle *ʾōmēr* also came there three times in vv. 26–28, the verb *qûm* ('stand') in v. 26 (hi, 'confirm'), and the verb *ʿāśāh* ('do') in v. 24 ('make'). The words are thus taken from all parts of 44.24–28, the segment concerned with creation, sovereignty in history, and Cyrus in particular. Here in their new combination they restate the middle of these two points, that Yhwh is lord in events in general—not merely reactive sovereign but initiator and planner. For *ʾeʿĕśeh*, 1QIs[a] has *yʿśh*. This might repeat the niphal from v. 10a, 'all my desire will be done' (†Grimm and Dittert); cf Vg *fiet*. Or it might be third person qal, '*he* will do all my desire', more likely a reference to Cyrus, assimilating to 44.28 as it will at 48.14 (†van der Kooij, p. 91), than an isolated indication that 1QIs[a] takes 'My purpose' as a messianic title (so †Chamberlain, p. 367). 1QIs[b] and 4QIs[c] agree with the MT. Some medieval MSS similarly have *ʿăṣātô* ('his purpose') for MT *ʿăṣātî* (see *HUB*), while LXX adds 'all' for vividness and parallelism.

It 'will stand' (*tāqûm*) also takes up a verb from 7.7,[6] and from 40.8. Whereas the purposes of the nations will be frustrated, Yhwh's purposes will be fulfilled. Syr has *mqdmʾnʾ* ('I predetermine'). For 'my desire', the LXX has a verbal expression ὅσα βεβούλευμαι ('what I have purposed'); †Ottley notes that the LXX seems careless in its use of βούλομαι and βουλεύω.

46.11a. . . .calling from the east a shriek, from a far country the man of his purpose. The participles now come to the specifics of the present. The one called is not named, as he is in 44.24–28. He has been identified in a number of ways, as is the case in 41.1–4. He has been taken to be Israel with the speed of a bird coming as the offspring of Abraham, whose own journey pointed to Israel's destiny (Tg; see †Chilton, pp. 46–48), or to be Abraham himself (†Rashi), or Sarah

[6] M. Fishbane, *Biblical Interpretation in Ancient Israel* (Oxford/New York, 1985, revised 1988), p. 498.

(see *Midrash Tanḥuma* [SB] on Gen 24.1), or a herald (†Hessler), or the Israel of the future as the agent of God's judgment (†Smart), or the messiah (Joseph Qimchi, as reported by †Qimchi). But we noted at 45.13a that omitting to name the one called before chapter 44 is one thing. Omitting to name him afterwards is another. In context one can hardly fail to infer that Cyrus is the primary referent of v. 11.

Etymology suggests that a 'shriek' (*ʿayiṭ*) is a bird that screeches, for that is what the (onomatopeic?) root suggests elsewhere (cf 1 Sam 25.14 for the verb). Usage indicates that it is a bird of prey, one that feeds on carcasses (e.g. 18.6; Gen 15.11). Xenophon says that Cyrus had the golden eagle as his ensign (*Cyropedia* VII.1.4), but it is a common military emblem, and one wonders why the prophet uses *ʿayiṭ* rather than the word for an eagle, *nešer*, which is also a bird of prey (cf Deut 28.49; 2 Sam 1.23; Jer 4.13; 48.40; 49.22; Ezek 17.3; Hos 8.1; Obad 4; Hab 1.8; Lam 4.19). Driver (*HW*, p. 60) links the word with an Arabic word for a massed army, *ġâṭu*, while †Simon thinks it suggests an obscure destroyer. †Rashi more significantly points to the fact that in Aramaic *ʿēṭāʾ* means 'counsel/purpose' (see Dan 2.14) and is equivalent to Hebrew *ʿēṣāh*. This comes in the previous line and in the next colon. †Ehrlich repoints to *ʿayyāṭ* in this connection. While familiar Hebrew usage rather indicates that an audience would assume that *ʿayiṭ* is a bird, familiarity with the Aramaic root might have encouraged the choice of this word in the light of the context. Emendation to *ʿabdî* ('my servant'; †Torrey), is unjustified.

'From the east' is if anything a reassuring rather than a threatening phrase (e.g. 43.5; 45.6). From 'a far country' (*ʾereṣ merḥāq*) can be a similarly encouraging phrase (Jer 31.10) but it more characteristically sounds a worrying note. Far off lands are the locations of powerful strange nations and supernatural hostile forces: see 8.9; 10.3; 13.5; 30.27 (and the adjective *rāḥôq* in 5.26). Jeremiah 4.16 and 5.15 also establish a link between 'far countries' and 'the north' as a traditional origin for such threats. Here 'a far country' may suggest 'the north', in keeping with the parallelism of 41.25. Before the threatening aspect to the shriek is qualified by the reminder that its name also hints that it has something to do with purposefulness, then, this threat is heightened by such a way of stating whence it comes. Conversely, the reassuring aspect to the reference to a man who is agent of Yhwh's purpose is subject to a double anticipatory qualification.

This apparently threatening figure from afar comes for restoration rather than for chastisement. Q has 'the man of *my* purpose' (*ʿṣty* not *ʿṣtw*; cf LXX, Vg, Syr) in v. 11aβ. This is what one might have expected and is therefore presumably a correction of the original. K characteristically, but also idiomatically in a participial construction like that in 44.26, moves from first person to third person (so also 1QIs[ab], 4QIs[d]).[7] The man of Yhwh's purpose or counsel is not one who

[7] M. Dahood suggests that Q is an instance of the third-person -i ending known in Ugaritic ('Hebrew–Ugaritic Lexicography ii', *Bib* 45 [1964], pp. 393–412 [see p. 398]). This seems an unnecessary complication.

formulates plans for Yhwh (see on 40.13) but one who is the means of executing plans that Yhwh formulates; cf v. 10b. The LXX's περὶ ὧν βεβούλευμαι further may presuppose *ʾăšer* ('that') for *ʾîš* ('man'), or may indicate an awareness that *ʾîš* can function as a relative,[8] or may indicate that the LXX takes *ʾîš* as collective (G. I. Davies).

46.11b. I both spoke and will also bring it about. I shaped and will also do it. The LXX's ἐλάλησα καὶ ἤγαγον, ἔκτισα καὶ ἐποίησα renders by all aorists, but the qatal verbs seem to refer to the past, the yiqtols to the future (cf Vg; and GK 106c). The threefold *ʾap* (see on 40.24) thus here suggests 'both…and'. The parallelism of 'spoke' and 'shaped' here contrasts with the occurrences of *yāṣar* in 22.11; 37.26; Jer 33.2, where the verb is parallel to *ʿāśāh* ('do') rather than succeeded by it. The occurrence in Jer 18.11 where it is parallel to *ḥāšab* ('think, devise') tests rather than disproves the rule. In the context of six references to the work of a 'shaper' whose activity is with the hands and not merely with the mind (Jer 18.2–6), *yāṣar* surely suggests the shaping of actual events (cf Vg *creavi*)—albeit as this takes place in Yhwh's intention. It is doubtful whether the verb *yāṣar* ever means 'plan', whatever may come to be true of the noun *yēṣer*.

1QIs[a] adds a suffix to produce a smoother reading *yṣrtyh* ('I shaped it'). At the end most LXX MSS add from 48.15 ἤγαγον αὐτὸν καὶ εὐόδωσα τὴν ὁδὸν αὐτοῦ ('I brought him and smoothed his way'). †Koenig (pp. 77–78) describes this as a midrashic underlining of the concrete temporal realization of Yhwh's word and of Yhwh's shaping.

46.12. Listen to me, strong-minded, far from rightness. It will not be surprising if human strength of mind (*ʾabbîrê lēb*, more literally 'heroes/bulls of heart') comes into conflict with Yhwh as the strong one, *ʾābîr* (e.g. 1.24; 49.26; 60.16). The vocalization may be artifically distinct (cf *HAL*). LXX's οἱ ἀπολωλεκότες τὴν καρδίαν suggests *ʾōbᵉdê lēb* ('lost-hearted'), involving only the minute consonantal change of *r* to *d*. The letters are distinguished only by a tittle, the corner of a letter. Unlike the MT's phrase, this phrase is unparalleled but is a fine alternative reading, though not necessarily therefore a more original one. It offers the audience a different form of ambiguity. They have to decide not whether they are being complemented or insulted, but whether they are being sympathized with or chided for their weakness. Contextually an argument for the MT is that sympathy/chiding for weakness was characteristic of earlier stages in the chapters (cf esp. 40.27–31). The address as rebels reflects the way the prophet has been moving towards a more and more confrontational stance, and an implicit insult is more in place than ambiguous sympathy.

[8] So R. Gelio, 'È possibile un *ʾîš* relativo/dimostrativo in ebraico biblico?', in *Rivista Biblica Italiana* 31 (1983), pp. 411–34 (see pp. 415–17). Koenig (*Oracles*, pp. 55–56) sees the Q reading as original and K as assimilation to 40.13.

'Far' is now the adjective *rāḥôq*, a nice alternative usage to that of the noun in v. 11, to be followed by the verb in v. 13. Neither adjective nor noun is used in the moral sense, but the verb is used to denote the need to keep far away from wickedness (Exod 23.7; Ezek 43.9; Job 11.14; 22.23; Prov 4.24; 5.8; 30.8). A contrasting description of the people as, instead, far away from right behaviour would thus be quite feasible and a nice usage; cf 29.13 (†North); also Ps 119.150. But nearer to hand is the plaint of the laments that Yhwh is far away (10.1; 22.2, 12 [1, 11]; 35.22; 38.22 [21]; 71.12; cf Lam 1.16). So, 'far from rightness' suggests 'far from the experience of having Yhwh do right by you'. Yhwh accepts the charge in their prayers, without accepting that their situation is undeserved.

46.13a. I am bringing near my rightness which will not be far away, my deliverance which will not hang back. It is not clear that there is movement in the meaning of 'rightness' in vv. 12–13 (so †Reiterer, pp. 84–85). Yhwh's affirmations about bringing rightness near also fit with the suggestion that v. 12 reflects the prayer that says it is far away or people feel far away from it. The LXX omits 'which will not be far away', to abbreviate the text. The Syr replaces by *lmʾtʾ* ('to come'), perhaps from 56.1.

For the first time here Yhwh explicitly promises that action is imminent. For *qērabtî* ('I am bringing near'), 1QIs[a] has the adjective *qrwbh* ('near [is my rightness]'). This may instance an inclination to avoid the instantaneous/performative qatal (†Rubinstein, p. 319) and/or the unusual piel verb. But the Tg has the equivalent *qrybʾ* and the Syr *qrbt*, while the adjective reappears in 51.5 and 56.1. There the LXX assimilates in the opposite direction by using the verb. 4QIs[c] has the hiphil *hqrbty*, with the same meaning as the piel; 1QIs[b] agrees with the MT.

'My deliverance' parallels 'my rightness', as *môšiaʿ* followed *ṣaddîq* at 45.21. The versions assume that the second colon is a self-contained clause: for example, Vg *et salus mea non morabitur* ('and my salvation will not delay'). We have rather inferred from the parallelism that the opening verb also governs 'my rightness' and that the two yiqtol verbs form parallel relative clauses (cf †Melugin) and parallel instances of litotes or understatement for rhetorical effect (†Franke). Like 'be far away', 'hang back' is a spatial metaphor. The verb *ʾāḥar* links with words for 'behind' or 'back' (cf 45.14, though also 43.14 for the temporal sense). The LXX replaces by first person οὐ βραδυνῶ to improve the parallelism.

46.13b. I will put deliverance in Zion, my attractiveness for Israel. This last line parallels v. 13a, and that might imply that the initial *w* should be taken as coordinating the opening words and that the verb should be rendered 'I am putting'. The use of the verb *nātan* recalls 41.19. In a sense 46.13b interprets its promise in pictures. As with v. 13a, the LXX τῷ Ἰσραὴλ εἰς δόξασμα assumes that the second colon continues the first with extra dependent phrases. The Tg does the same in the context of a messianic interpretation of 'deliverance' as 'deliverer' (*pryq*), which also implies that 'my attractiveness' is in apposition with 'Israel'. But 1QIs[a] and 4QIs[c] have *wlyśr*ʾ*l* ('and for Israel') at the beginning of the second colon; cf Vg *et*. . ., Syr *wl*ʾ*yśryl*, though 1QIs[b], 4QIs[d] agree with the MT. This points in the direction of seeing that the parallelism with v. 13a also means that the verb governs phrases in both cola. †Franke suggests that *nātan* means 'put' in the first colon and 'give [to]' in the second. The suffix on 'attractiveness' perhaps also implicitly applies to 'deliverance'.

In v. 13b there is an implicit parallelism between deliverance and attractiveness (*tip*ʾ*ārāh*) and between Israel and Zion. The prepositions are perhaps varied more for rhetorical reasons than to indicate significant differences in meaning. Admittedly †Hermisson suggests that 'deliverance' and 'attractiveness', 'in' and 'for', and 'Zion' and 'Israel' all imply more difference than the claim to parallelism recognizes (cf †Stone, p. 94). But alternating of prepositions is a common feature of Isaiah 40–55. It is one of the features that enables †Ruiz to speak of their 'ambivalence'. Lamentations 2.1 has daughter Zion under a cloud because Israel's attractiveness has been cast down, while 44.23 has the parallelism restore (*gā*ʾ*al*)/display attractiveness.

III.b.ii. The fall of Babylon herself (47.1–15)

In Isaiah 47 as a whole the speaker seems to be Yhwh, as in chapters 46 and 48, though this is explicit only in vv. 3 and 6. The addressee is Babylon, personified as a woman. This sets off chapter 47 from chapters 46 and 48, where Jacob–Israel is addressed. The exception that proves the rule is v. 4, as most MSS note with a setuma or petucha after v. 3 and 1QIs[a] with spaces either side of v. 4. There people or prophet speak about Yhwh in the third person and Jacob–Israel surfaces in the pronoun 'our', reminding us that people and prophet are the audience in the house and the human narrator throughout. 1QIs[a] treats chapter 47 as a single unit in that it begins 47.1 and then 48.1 with a new line and has none of its longer line spaces within chapter 47, but the MT does not see chapter 47 as a chapter in this way. In L it is part of 45.18–48.16, while A's divisions are 46.3–47.3, 47.4–7, and 47.8–48.11.

In the introduction to chapters 46–47 we noted features of chapter 47 that emerge when one looks at these two chapters alongside each other. The account of the fall of the Babylonian gods leads into an account of the fall of the Babylonian empire. The restoration of Zion in her finery presupposes the dethroning of Babylon in hers. Beauty for Israel (the root *pā*ʾ*ar*, 46.13) implies dust for Babylon (ʿ*āpār*, 47.1) (†Bonnard).

Like much of Lamentations, chapter 47 takes the form of a funeral dirge, broadly in 3–2 rhythm (Budde, 'Klagelied' [see introduction to 45.14–17], pp. 237–38). The word 'broadly' needs emphasizing. While two stresses in the second colon is a more consistent characteristic feature of the poem than three in the first, in neither case is the form strictly followed, and we do not have grounds for suspecting that this is because the text has been changed. Our assumption is rather that Hebrew poetry is consistent in following rhythmic forms only loosely.

This may be at least as much for further rhetorical reasons as for reasons of lack of interest in metre. Thus v. 1 opens with a standard 3–2, perhaps follows it with another that is obscured in the MT with a *maqqeph*, and perhaps closes with a third (v. 1b) where again the MT could be rescanned. But v. 2 comprises six two-beat cola, recalling the opening of chapter 46 with its jerky abruptness. It is not even the case that the poem is characterized by 'falling rhythm', lines where the second colon frustrates expectations by falling short of the length of the first. One of the poem's striking features is the number of 2–3 lines (e.g. both lines in v. 3, at least in the MT). One can at least say, however, that the average line-length, at just over five stresses per bicolon, is shorter than that in chapters 46 and 48, where it is just under six per two cola (†Franke, pp. 24, 104, 170). A further individual poetic feature of chapter 47 is groupings of three cola or three lines (†Grimm and Dittert refer to three-line parallelism): see v. 1 (3–3, 3–3, 3–3), v. 2 (2–2, 2–2, 2–2), v. 6 (in MT 2–2–2, 3–2–2; †Thomas 2–2, 2–3, 2–2), v. 8 (3–2, 2–3, 3–3), v. 11 (3–3, 3–3, 3–3), v. 13 (3–2, 2–2, 2–3 [?]), v. 14 (3–2, 2–2, 2–3). The MT also implies this understanding of vv. 10 and 11 but we have taken these as three double bicola.

As well as sitting loosely with the lament form, the poem links only very broadly to the themes of a funeral, contrasting 'then' and 'now', 'life', and 'death' like a dirge but not showing a dirge's specific characteristic features as David's lament over Saul and Jonathan illustrates them. Further, its 'grief' over Babylon's fall is of course not actually meant. It uses the lament form ironically. Its lament is actually a taunt.

Its account of Babylon's fall does not especially correspond to what actually happened in 539 BC. Indeed, †P. R. Davies (p. 215) suggests that the poem reflects Babylon's fall to Xerxes I in 482 when the Esagila was destroyed and Marduk's statue melted down. Cyrus is portrayed as responsible for what was achieved through his dynasty, as David is portrayed in Chronicles as determining all the arrangements for the temple worship. But Davies notes that we only have Xerxes's word for these events, as we only have Cyrus's for his being so welcome in Babylon. On the basis of its forty words that occur only here in chapters 40–53, its linguistic similarity to chapters 54–66, and its lack of phrases typical of chapters 40–53 such as 'I am Yhwh' and 'I and no other', Elliger attributed chapter 47 to Third Isaiah and thus to the Second Temple period (*Verhältnis*, pp. 105–16). †Merendino adds comments on its theological distinctiveness. In contrast to 46.1–4 it portrays the fall of the oppressor without accompanying this with promises of restoration for Israel (this seems to be another way of noting the fact that this is the only instance of an oracle against a foreign nation in Isa 40–66). The act of judgment works itself out immanently rather than being Yhwh's act, and it is unrelated to Yhwh's plan of salvation. It is also distinctive for the elaborate form it takes. It has a closer unity than sections such as 41.1–20 or 41.21–42.17.

In contrast †Morgenstern attributes it to the prophet's earliest period on the basis of its lack of key motifs such as image-making, sovereignty in events, and the significance of Cyrus, while †Hermisson and †Kratz (p. 217) date it to the eve of the fall of Babylon, the traditional critical view. †Muilenburg draws attention to features characteristic of chapters 40–55 such as the imperatives, assonance, and repetitions.

In the book called Isaiah as a whole, Babylon appears as follows:[9]

13.1–14.23 Announcement of Babylon's fall
14.24–27 Announcement of Assyria's fall, issuing from that (Yhwh's plan: 14.24, 26, 27)
21.9 Incidental reminder of the coming fall of Babylon and her gods
23.13 Incidental reminder of the responsibility of Babylon—not Assyria
36–39 Realization of Assyria's fall, issuing in a return to the theme of Babylon (Yhwh's plan: 36.5; 37.26)
40–48 Realization of Babylon's fall

Compared with Isaiah 21, the thinking of Isaiah 47 is more developed. Compared with Isaiah 13 it is less horrific but more concrete, less cosmic and more historical. Compared with Isaiah 14 it treats Babylon less as a symbol (*Martin-Achard, pp. 96–104). †Conrad (pp. 77–79) describes chapter 47 as the climax of the book's treatment of Babylon. Chapter 48 is concerned for the implications of her fall as it affects Jacob–Israel. *Franke sees it as having a pivotal role in the thinking and structure of Isaiah 40–55, set between the oppressed and demoralized Jacob–Israel of chapters 40–46 and the elevated and rejoicing Zion–Jerusalem in the chapters that follow. 'It is in ch. xlvii that the theme of downtrodden Israel is replaced by the prophecy of downtrodden Babylon' to make this transition possible (*VT* 41, p. 411). Chapter 47 constitutes a turning point. Nations such as Babylon have been Zion's assailants and the agents of her humiliation. They will now be the agents of her exaltation (†Darr).

There is wide variety in the analyses of chapter 47 (see †Franke, pp. 150–52). The outline below starts from the fact that, like chapter 46, it alternates imperatives with finite verbs that explicitly or implicitly ground the imperatives, though it alternates these in its own way. Here the imperatives (a) come first and are addressed to

[9] Cf †Conrad, pp. 77–79; C. T. Begg, 'Babylon in the Book of Isaiah', in †Vermeylen, pp. 121–25; *Franke, in *SBLSP* 1993 and in †Melugin and Sweeney.

Babylon rather than to Jacob–Israel or Zion–Jerusalem. The finite verbs speak about events to come, mostly in the yiqtol (b), and speak in the qatal or *w*-consecutive about the reasons for what is about to happen (c), in the manner of prophetic invective (cf †Beuken, p. 274). These reasons, in terms of Babylon's wrongdoing, actually appear only in connection with the middle two sets of imperatives, so that the two outer sections (without these) and the two inner sections (with them) form pairs. In content, however, the opening two and the closing two link, the first pair bidding Madam Babylon to sit as she will pay the price for wrong acts, the second pair focusing more on her unwise trust in her alleged wisdom.

(a) 1a, 2 — Sit in humiliation
(b) 1b, 3–4 — For you will be shamed

(a) 5a — Sit in silence
(b) 5b — For you will be dethroned
(c) 6–7 — You were heartless and thoughtless

(a) 8 — Listen, you who sit in security
(b) 9abα, 11 — Calamity will come upon you
(c) 9bβ–10 — You trusted in your wickedness and wisdom

(a) 12 — Stand in your chantings
(b) 13–15 — Your diviners will not be able to deliver you

Each of the four sections develops its point by means of a particular verbal, metaphorical, or theological framework (the main point emphasized in the following outline), but each framework then reappears in the next section so as to contribute to the binding of the whole:

1–4 *You are being taken from throne to servitude*
daughter–sit–you will no more be called
5–7 Daughter–sit–come–you will no more be called
you are being taken from power to imprisonment
you said, I will be queen for ever–in your mind
8–11 You sit–you say in your mind–I will not sit
'I am and there is none besides me' but disaster will come
you trust in spells and chants–you think you know
12–15 Stand–must stand–not for sitting–what will come
you have wasted so much energy on so-called knowledge, on chants and spells that cannot deliver you

Further binding, emphasis, and characterization is achieved by repetitions of words in close proximity: daughter (v. 1 twice), take (vv. 2, 3), expose (v. 2 twice, v. 3), mistress (vv. 5, 7), give/call (*śîm*, vv. 6, 7), say (vv. 4 emended, 7, 8, 10), heart (vv. 7, 8, 10), know (vv. 8, 10, 11a, 11b), bereavement (vv. 8, 9), widow[hood] (vv. 8, 9), enter/come (*bôʾ*, vv. 5, 9a, 9b, 11a, 11b, 13), be able (vv. 11, 12), upon you

(v. 11 three times), perhaps (v. 12 twice), stand (vv. 12, 13) (†Franke, p. 149).

Metaphors of movement run through the poem, with negative implications. These begin with a summons to go down (v. 1) in whose context the challenge to stand up (v. 12) gains further irony. Calamity falls down on Madam Babylon or simply comes upon her (*ʿal*, v. 11). The poem ends with distracted at-a-loss horizontal movement that is going nowhere (v. 15). Reversal is a key motif throughout (†Lack): from throne to dust (v. 1a), from finery to servitude (vv. 1b–3), from power to imprisonment (vv. 5–7), from security to loss (vv. 8–9), from confidence to disillusion (vv. 12–15). Verses 1–8 concern reality, vv. 9–15 illusion. The many references to knowing/knowledge in this section make the point that what Babylon thinks is reality is actually illusion. The judgments 'no throne' and 'no saviour' (*ʾên-kissēʾ*, *ʾên môšîʿēk*) form an *inclusio* round the whole. *Franke (*VT* 41, p. 413) notes also 'no one seeing me' and 'no coals' (*ʾên rōʾānî*, v. 10, *ʾên-gaḥelet*, v. 14), and the chapter's twelvefold *lōʾ* ('no/not') and Babylon's own double mistaken *ʾapsî* ('I alone', vv. 8, 10).

The various theories regarding earlier forms of the chapter and the process whereby it reached its final form may be illustrated from the work of †Merendino and †Hermisson, who posit rather different histories of development:

†Merendino

(a) Verses 1, 2bβ, 5–6abα, 7–8a, 10–12aα, 12b, 13bαβγ, 14a (less three words), 15bβγ.

(b) Verses 3b–4 (without 'Almighty Yhwh is his name')

(c) Verses 3a, 8b–9, 12aβ, 13a, 13bδ, 15abα.

(d) Verses 2abα, 6bβ and the other words in v. 4 may also belong to stage (c).

(e) The remainder of v. 14.

†Hermisson

(a) Verses 1–2, 5, 8–9abα, 10aβb, 11.

(b) Verses 9bβγ, 10aα, 12–14a, 15.

(c) Verses 3–4, 6–7.

(d) Verse 14b.

Such differences inspire scepticism regarding the feasibility of our tracing a process of development and of making this the basis for exegesis of the chapter.

47.1a. Get down, sit in the dirt, maiden daughter Babylon. Sit on the ground without a throne, daughter Chaldea. The command to 'get down' brings the fulfillment of the intention in 43.14. The addressee is to sit *ʿal-ʿāpār*, a nice alliteration to be immediately followed by another (†Boadt, pp. 359–61). The word *ʿāpār* most commonly denotes the loose dry earth that comprises the surface of the ground, but it can also refer to rubble or ash. Now *ʿāpār* is paralleled in the next line by *ʾereṣ* ('ground'). The two form a familiar word pair, though here their usual order is reversed. This has several results. One is to place *ʿāpār* in close juxtaposition with the verb *pāʾar*. We have already noted how chapter 46 thus ends with beauty for Israel and chapter 47 opens with dirt for Babylon (†Bonnard). Another is to mirror the reversal that the poem itself speaks of (*CHP*, p. 357). In addition, whereas the usual order places the less familiar word second, here the less familiar but more ambiguous word comes first. The effect is to tease with an ambiguity and then resolve it in the second line.

Why does Madam Babylon sit on the dirt/ground? Akkadian *erṣetu* and Ugaritic *ʾrṣ* can mean the underworld, and there are passages where this meaning would be appropriate to Hebrew *ʾereṣ*: see, for example, 26.19, in parallelism with *ʿāpār* (cf *ThWAT* on *ʾereṣ*, II.3; *HAL*). The fact that chapter 14 uses the verb 'get down' to denote a journey to Sheol circumstantially increases the possibility that the reference here is to a journey down to the underworld. But even in a passage such as 26.19, which certainly refers to death, the literal meaning of *ʾereṣ–ʿāpār* is appropriate. Further, *DCH* does not register this meaning of *ʾereṣ*, but does draw attention (Vol. 1, p. 396a) to the large number of phrases involving a verb for downward motion with *l* plus *ʾereṣ*, which provide circumstantial evidence in the opposite direction. They have literal, physical reference. It is indeed noteworthy that the preposition is *l* ('to') not *b* ('in'). 1QIs[a] has *ʿal* ('on'), assimilating to the parallel line. But it is also the case that people who die do literally go to live in the dirt/ground; see further on 44.23. Here in v. 1 there is no explicit allusion to death, but there may be a hint that the literal sitting in the dirt, on the ground, in humiliation and grief, points to something else.

For what does 'Babylon' stand? Babylon is a city, a country, a people, and an empire. In the parallel line 'Chaldea' (*kaśdîm*: see on 43.14) is the standard parallel to the more frequent and more general 'Babylon'. Although technically the name of the dynasty, it comes to be used as the name of the country and its people (e.g. 13.19; 23.13; Jer 25.12; 50.1, 8). The word is plural in form, so that in the parallelism it complements singular 'Babylon'. It thus usually refers to 'the Chaldeans', and †Skinner takes this construct as possessive rather than explicative. But *kaśdîm* can be treated as a singular noun for the country Chaldea (see BDB, *HAL*), and following *bat* ('daughter') this makes sense here. There is no indication that 'Chaldeans' has come to suggest diviners and astrologers rather than merely inhabitants or leaders of Babylon. At this point Babylon is the embodiment of oppression rather than of paganism (against Vermeylen, *Isaiah*, p. 41).

The title 'maiden daughter' applies elsewhere to Zion, Judah, and 'my people', but also to Sidon and Egypt (23.12; Jer 46.11). Its application to Babylon is thus not unprecedented. The OT also instances other expressions such as maiden Israel (e.g. Jer 18.13; Amos 5.2, in a dirge), daughter Zion (e.g. Isa 1.8; 10.32; 16.1; Lam

1.6; 2.1, 4, 8, 10, 18), and daughter Babylon (e.g. Jer 50.42; Ps 137.8). The frequency suggests that 'daughter x' is the primary form of the expression; the prefixing of 'maiden' is a rhetorical modification. In the form *b^e^tûlat bat-bābel* the alliteration is especially striking.

'Daughter' (*bat*) is both an absolute and a construct form. The LXX's παρθένος θυγάτηρ Βαβυλῶνος takes it as construct and perhaps implies the view that the people is personified as the daughter of the actual city, which is the people's mother (cf GK 122hi). More likely the construct is appositional and explicative, as in English 'city of Babylon' (cf *IBHS* 9.5.3h; *DG* 35; *HS* 42). Indeed, perhaps *bat* is absolute and in apposition, as must be the case when the word has the article in Lam 2.13.

Surprisingly, the LXX does seem to take *bᵉtûlat* as absolute and as in apposition (cf Vg *virgo*), perhaps rightly, for it is difficult to parallel the use of a construct in such a case of identical apposition, especially followed by another construct. Thus while both morphology and syntax allow *bat* to be either absolute or construct, syntax points to *bᵉtûlat* being absolute but morphology points to its being construct. The latter difficulty can be overcome if we assume that the form is an archaism,[10] perhaps chosen for the sake of the alliteration just noted (so Boadt: see above). But whether absolute or construct it initiates another appositional, explicative link with what follows. A *bᵉtûlāh*/*bᵉtûlat* is a young unmarried woman. The LXX παρθένος may seem to imply 'virgin', but it is doubtful whether this connotation does in principle attach to *bᵉtûlat*: see *DCH*. *ThWAT* on *bᵉtûlāh*, I–II, also notes that this connotation did not originally attach to παρθένος, and *bᵉtûlôt* are paired with *baḥûrîm* ('young men in the prime of youth') in Lam 1.18 and 2.21 (cf Jer 51.22; Zech 9.17; Ps 148.12).

'Without a throne' (*ʾên-kissēʾ*) is literally 'there is no throne', an asyndetic circumstantial clause (GK 152u; *TTH* 164; cf 9.6 [7]), missing in the LXX. 'From sitting upon the world throne Babylon comes down to sit in the dust' (†Young). The point is underlined by the Tg's 'without a *glorious* throne' (cf 13.19). On the basis of the place of the throne motif in chapter 14 and in an Ugaritic funerary liturgy, *Franke (*SBLSP* 1993, pp. 254–55; †Melugin and Sweeney, pp. 110–13) suggests that this also indicates a note of mourning and not merely humiliation.

שׁבי־לארץ: LXX's εἴσελθε εἰς τὸ σκότος ('go into the darkness') anticipates v. 5 but perhaps in part follows from rendering על עפר ('in the dirt') with ἐπὶ τὴν γῆν ('on the ground') and avoids repeating γῆν. It hardly warrants †Watts's repointing of שְׁבִי as שֻׁבִי ('return'). ישׁב ל is an

[10] Cf A. Fitzgerald, 'The Mythological Background for the Presentation of Jerusalem as a Queen and False Worship as Adultery in the OT', in *CBQ* 34 (1972), pp. 403–16 (see p. 409). Is the form a pure archaism/Ugariticism or would the word have been pronounced בְּתֹלֶת (JM 89i, 89o)?

archaism (Cross, *Canaanite Myth* [see on 40.3], p. 97) whose Ugaritic equivalent is well-attested.[11]

47.1b. For you will not continue to have people call you sensitive and delightful. The *kî* introduces not the grounds for the previous statement but some more explanation of its contents. Then the negative *ʾên* is succeeded by the negative *lōʾ*; the former will reappear in vv. 10, 14, and 15, the latter in vv. 3, 5, 6, 7, 8, 11 (three times), and 14. Between them they give the chapter the running negative tone noted already: Babylon will/did not, not, not....

The two adjectives (*rakkāh waʿănuggāh*) come together elsewhere in Deut 28.54, 56, in the telling context of a warning about exile and its consequences for civilized people. They suggest the discriminating fastidiousness of someone who has been brought up in a context of good taste and privilege. 'The terms conjure up the idea of luxury, the refinements of the court, the elegant life of carefree enjoyment' (†Westermann). They can have negative connotations, of softness (cf 7.4) and 'not knowing what real life is like' (cf 1 Chr 22.5) on the one hand, or lack of seriousness on the other (cf 57.4). But if the audience is tempted to assume these connotations here, what follows rather subverts that hearing. The impact of the prophet's words here and in v. 5, where a parallel phrase comes at the end of the verse, depends in part on the positive truth of the description of what Madam Babylon was, and indeed in reality still is. She is all a Judean might reasonably wish to be. She lives the life of a princess, the opposite of that of a slave, but her name for sensitivity and refinement is about to be taken away. There is no talk of any name to replace it, negative (contrast 34.12) or in due course positive (contrast, e.g., 1.26; 60.14; 61.3; 62.2, 4, 12). The verb *ʿānōg* and related words come with a positive sense in 13.22; 55.2; 58.13, 14; 66.11. 'The reader knows that Babylonia's army successfully laid siege to Jerusalem, creating the conditions that Deuteronomy envisioned (Lam 2:20; 4:10). But now, the tables are turned as tender, delicate Babylon goes down to the ground' (†Darr).

לא תוסיפי יקראו לך: lit. 'you will not add [that] they call you', formally a mixed construction in which the subject changes in the asyndetic subordinate cl.: cf 47.5; contrast 51.22; 52.1; also 42.21 (see GK 120c; JM 177c). 1QIs[a] has וקראו. The versions prefer to translate by a passive, to avoid the mixed construction.

47.2a. Take millstones and grind meal. Again removing the metaphor, the Tg paraphrases v. 2 in such a way as to emphasize the scattering and exile of Babylon's armies, and †Morgenstern understands vv. 1–3 to refer to Babylon going into exile as Zion had done. In isolation this would be an entirely natural approach to v. 2b but it is not

[11] M. Dahood, 'Ugaritic and Phoenician or Qumran and the Versions', in *Orient and Occident* (C. H. Gordon Festschrift, ed. H. A. Hoffner; AOAT 22, 1973), pp. 53–58 (see p. 57).

required by it and there seem insufficient grounds to take this as the key to the whole picture. Rather, Madam Babylon has to take on the life of hard work of an ordinary woman. Part of the problem for the Tg and other versions (as for us) was the rare vocabulary in the verse. The harsh assonance of the consonants (*qḥy rḥym wṭḥny qmḥ*) echoes the grinding the words refer to (†Muilenburg).

47.2b. Expose your hair. Uncover tresses. Expose legs. Cross streams. The rhythm of v. 1 looked irregular, though it could be read as 3–2. However this may be, it is clear enough that v. 2 forms six two-beat cola, recalling the opening of chapter 46 with its jerky abruptness. One might expect the six to form two 2–2–2 lines, but the MT divides them unevenly into two and four cola. This corresponds to the way in which the content of the first two (v. 2a) holds them together and the way in which the last four broadly belong together with their references to clothing, though they then naturally subdivide into two further pairs. The general point of v. 2b is thus also clear, with its further cola bidding Madam Babylon to behave like any other ordinary woman, but the details are less so.

The verb *gālāh* (qal and pi—here pi) can mean 'strip off [e.g. an item of clothing]'. The LXX thus renders *ṣammāh* by κατακάλυμμα ('veil'). A veil would normally be worn in public, especially by upper-class women and by married women generally, but not when one was doing hard domestic work, and not by slaves and prostitutes.[12] This understanding fits the picture of 3.18–23, and the other uses of the noun in Song 4.1, 3; 6.7 (and thus cf *Song of Songs Rabbah* III, 4.2). But *gālāh* more often means 'strip [e.g. a part of the body]', and this understanding is required for the second occurrence of the verb, and for v. 3. The Vg thus has *denuda turpitudinem* (guessing at the actual meaning of the noun?) while †Qimchi understands *ṣammāh* to mean 'hair', which Madam Babylon is bidden to uncover (by removing the veil). This understanding is possible if less obvious for Song 4.1, 3; 6.7. Sym σιωπηλόν ('silence') links the word with *ṣāmat* rather than *ṣāmam* (†Hermisson).

The verb in the next colon, *ḥāśap*, is also one that generally means 'strip' and can apply to a garment or a part of the body (the more familiar *ḥśb* in 4QIs[d] is presumably a slip). On its form, see GK 46d, 63l, JM 21e. Its noun, *šōbel* (see discussion in *HAL*), occurs only here. A similar Arabic root suggests something flowing (cf BDB), a similar Ugaritic root something twisting (round the body?).[13] This again could be an item of clothing (cf *Song of Songs Rabbah* III, 4.2; Driver [see at 44.9], p. 58), or could be a part of the body such as the

[12] Cf BDB, *HAL*, *DCH*; also S. M. Paul, 'Biblical Analogues to Middle Assyrian Law', in *Religion and Law* (ed. E. B. Firmage and others; Winona Lake, IN, 1990), pp. 333–50 (see pp. 339–42); K. van der Toorn, 'The Significance of the Veil in the Ancient Near East', in *Pomegranates and Golden Bells* (J. Milgrom Festschrift, ed. D. P. Wright and others; Winona Lake, IN, 1995), pp. 327–39.

[13] So M. Dahood, 'Philological Notes on Jer 18 14–15', in *ZAW* 74 (1962), pp. 207–9 (see p. 209).

hair. The LXX's τὰς πολιάς and Syr *ḥwrtky* ('grey hair') imply that part of the woman's shame is being exposed as grey-haired (*HUB*). Vg 'arm' (*umerum*) and Sym 'ears' (ὦτα) might indicate that all are guessing. The former might be inferred from the parallelism in 9.3 [4] (*HUB*). The latter may be inferred from its rendering of the previous phrase but might be a corruption of νῶτα ('back') (*HUB*). The MT's verse division suggests it linked this colon to the previous one, so 'flowing tresses' fits its understanding (cf †Ibn Ezra). To the guesses †Korpel and de Moor add the suggestion that that it links with the rare Akkadian word *šubulu* (a piece of jewelry?), *Beeston that it rather links with *šibbōlet* 'watercourse' (cf 27.12) and means a well, and that the verb here means 'draw water' (cf 30.14)—hence 'draw [from] the well'. 1QIs[a] solves the problem by reading *šwlyk* ('your skirts') as in Jer 13.26, but 4QIs[d] agrees with the MT. In the MT, the suffix on the first noun can no doubt be assumed to extend its application at least to the next one.

In the last pair of clauses, the individual words are clear, but there has been more uncertainty over the meaning of the total picture. Elsewhere, talk of baring legs could suggest rape, and *b. Berakot* 24a assumes that vv. 2–3 refers to exposure such as would encourage sexual excitement. Reference to rape thus fits with the language of v. 3, and it is a standard feature of invasion (†McKenzie). Implicitly Yhwh is the rapist (see *Franzmann, pp. 17–18). The removal of clothing has also been linked with the goddess's tearing of her garments in the ritual in which she bewails the fate of her city.[14] In the specific present context, baring the legs is more likely part of the picture of the inelegant behaviour that domestic activity requires of a woman. In the same way, here talk of crossing rivers does not suggest the long trudge of transportation, but contributes further to the picture of the drudgery of domestic duty—perhaps especially in Babylon with its many irrigation ditches. Yet 43.2 did refer to 'crossing' and to 'streams', and the words may be part of the suggestion that Babylon is changing places with Zion.

The philological considerations leave v. 2b puzzling at several points. The choices we have made have the advantage of coherently linking the first two cola and the second two.

47.3a. Your nakedness is to be exposed, yes your disgrace is to be seen. The sequence of paired verbs and nouns that ran through v. 2 continues with four more through v. 3, though in each line a particle in the second colon adds variety and makes for two 2–3 lines.

Exposure of someone's nakedness (*ʿerwāh*) is a euphemistic technical term for sexual intercourse in legal contexts (e.g. Lev 18.6–19) and in reference to Samaria and Jerusalem in Ezek 23.10, 29. As we noted in connection with v. 2b, in Isaiah 47 reference to rape in the context of military defeat would not be surprising, nor

[14] See F. W. Dobbs-Allsopp, *Weep, O Daughter of Zion* (BibOr 44, 1993), p. 112.

would reference to the sexual vulnerability of the female slave, but exposure of nakedness is not the obvious term to use to refer to either.[15] It means what it says in passages such as Lam 1.8, and suggests an experience of humiliation. For rape, Isa 13.16 uses the verb *šāgēl*, Jer 13.22 *ḥāmas*, Lam 5.11 *ʿānāh*.

E. Kutsch sees *ḥerpāh* ('disgrace'; plural in the LXX) as a synonym for *ʿerwāh* ('nakedness'; see *ThWAT* on *ḥrp* II, II.2), but there is no other example of such usage. Further, parallelism makes one expect some development rather than simple repetition in the second colon, and *gam* ('yes', conventionally 'also') points to some addition even if it also functions to underline (cf *EWS*, pp. 143–46; LXX omits). This is especially so here where *gam* makes the line an unexpected 2–3, unusual especially in a quasi-lament where one expects two stresses in the second colon. It adds to the emphasis on the second colon and brings vv. 2–3a to a climax (†Franke). Disgrace means disgrace (cf 51.7), the opposite of 'honour' (*kābôd*). The verb *ḥārap* played a key role in 37.4, 17, 23, 24; see also 65.7.

תראה: on the jussive with ה, see GK 109a, JM 114g. 1QIs[a] has תגלה for the first vb, assimilating the form to the second and implying that both are yiqtol and indicative (†Hermisson).

47.3b. I will exact punishment, and no-one will intervene. Who speaks? While words such as those in vv. 1–3a would be capable of being uttered by Jacob–Israel or Zion–Jerusalem, there has been no indication that the speaker has changed since chapter 46, and it is Yhwh who is the usual subject of the expressions 'punish/exact punishment' (*nāqam*/*lāqaḥ nāqām*; the more common noun *n*ᵉ*qāmāh* does not occur in Isaiah). One might especially compare Jer 50.15, 28; 51.6, 11, 36 for Yhwh's punishment of Babylon, and Deut 32.35, 41, 43 in a chapter with many links with Isaiah 40–55. In Isaiah, the scene has been set for this exacting of punishment by 34.8; 35.4 (for the simple verb, cf 1.24). The matter will be worked out further in 59.17; 61.2; 63.4, though not elsewhere in chapters 40–55.

The second colon raises difficulties. The MT reads *w*ᵉ*lōʾ ʾepgaʿ ʾādām*, which would mean 'I will not meet a human being' or perhaps '...meet as a human being' (cf Tg *mbny ʾnšʾ*, 'other than human beings'). What sort of meeting would be determined by the context. The verb *pāgaʿ* can take a direct object or govern a noun via the preposition *b*. It can mean to reach or meet accidentally (Exod 23.4) or deliberately (Gen 32.2 [1]), and to meet with friendly action and thus 'protect' (Isa 64.4 [5]), or with hostile action and thus 'attack' (Exod 5.3), or with a request and thus entreat (Jer 7.16). The hiphil can mean to cause to meet (Isa 53.6) or specifically to cause to 'entreat' (Jer 15.11), or actually to entreat (Isa 53.12; 59.16). In the

[15] Against F. R. Magdalene, 'Ancient Near Eastern Treaty Curses and the Ultimate Texts of Terror', in *A Feminist Companion to the Latter Prophets* (ed. A. Brenner; Sheffield, 1995), pp. 326–52 (see p. 331).

context here the verb could most plausibly thus signify 'I will not meet anyone', perhaps in the sense of getting into conversation with them and being deflected from the task, or more likely in the sense of meeting them with favour as in 64.4 [5]. But the usage is allusive. We have followed the Vg and Sym in reading a third person verb *yipgaʿ*, perhaps altered through dittography.

נקם אקח: interpretatively the LXX and Tg add 'from you': cf Jer 20.10 (*HUB*). Tg renders the vb 'I will avenge', perhaps implying **אקם**.
ולא אפגע אדם: Sym has καὶ οὐκ ἀντιστήσεταί μοι ἄνθρωπος, Vg *et non resistet mihi homo*. It seems unlikely that this is merely a paraphrase of the MT (so †Hermisson). The Vg in particular is not much inclined to such paraphrase. 4QIs^d reads hi **אפגיע** ('I will not intervene/entreat'), as in 53.6, 12; 59.16, and LXX παραδῶ may well presuppose this reading as that is the verb it uses in 53.6, 12 (though †Ottley notes its liking for this verb, which might simply be an equivalent for the qal in 47.3); cf also Syr *wlʾ ʾpgʿ bky ʾnš*. †Graetz emends to **אפרע** ('I will not let go of a man'). 1QIs^{ab} have *ʾpgʿ* (which could be read as qal, ni, or hi), and †Oort repoints the vb as ni **אִפָּגֵעַ** ('I will not be entreated'), †Torrey as hophal **אֻפְגַּע** with the same meaning (the understanding presupposed by †Ibn Ezra), while †Ehrlich emends to **אֵרָגַע** ('I will not rest')—all these need to understand **אדם** to mean 'as a man', or to emend it, on which see below. Dahood ([see on 40.12a], p. 31) sees the verb as an Ugaritic-style aphel.

47.4. . . .says our restorer, whose name is Yhwh almighty, holy one of Israel. In the MT v. 4 is an independent statement beginning with an extraposed phrase, 'Our restorer, his name is Yhwh almighty, holy one of Israel', or 'Our restorer, whose name is Yhwh Almighty, is the holy one of Israel', or 'The holy one of Israel is our restorer, whose name is Yhwh' (cf 1QIs^{ab}, Aq, Th, Sym, Vg, Syr, Tg). The statement is then apparently a comment by the prophet responding to the commitment in v. 3b. But the effect is choppy, as is reflected in †North's view that v. 4 is a gloss. The LXX, however, opens the verse εἶπεν (though †Barthélemy emphasizes the manuscripts that do not), suggesting Hebrew *ʾāmar*. †Duhm inferred that in the MT this had been corrupted into *ʾādām* ('human being') at the end of v. 3; we have followed the LXX in reading both words.

The hypothesis that the LXX points to the best Hebrew text fits with *Crenshaw's form-critical study of the refrain 'Almighty Yhwh is his name' (see p. 166), which notes that the refrain commonly appears within an oracular formula. As here, one context in which the refrain often appears is that of announcement of judgment. It expresses faith in Yhwh as creator and judge.

Either way the longer line (4–2 in MT, 2–3–2 as emended) brings the first section of the chapter to a powerful conclusion. Reference to Yhwh's being Israel's 'restorer' (*gōʾēl*: see on 41.14) fits well in the context. The plural suffix is unusual (see on 43.14). It perhaps invites the people to apply the prophet's words to themselves individually (see on the transition in 42.24). The LXX has the more usual second person singular, ὁ ῥυσάμενός σε (cf the varied renderings in 41.14; 43.14; 44.6, 24; 48.17; 49.7; 54.8).

47.5. Sit in silence, enter into darkness, daughter Chaldea. For you will not continue to have people call you mistress of kingdoms. '[In] silence' is *dûmām*. JM 126a takes the word as an adjective, 'sit silent', explaining the use of a masculine form as adverbial. GK 118o takes it as an actual adverb (see also GK 100g; *DCH*). BDB takes it as a noun in the adverbial accusative. Of the two other occurrences, any of these understandings fits Lam 3.26, though the construction there is odd and the text may not be in order; cf also the use of *dûmāh* in Ps 94.17; also 115.17. In Hab 2.19 *dûmām* seems to be a straightforward noun, functioning adjectivally after a construct. Here it could be adverbial but it could perhaps more straightforwardly be taken as this same noun implicitly governed by the preposition *b*, which appears in the second colon. The same understanding would apply to the noun *dmmh* in 1QIs[a]. The Vg has a verb, *tace*. Dumbfounded silence may be a natural reaction to defeat, but silence also links with death. The LXX sometimes renders *dumāh* by ᾅδης (e.g. Pss 93.17; 113.25).

The second clause speaks more specifically of 'entering into darkness', the verb being *bōʾ*. This verb has the effect of emphasizing the identity of the person's destination to a greater extent than do verbs that are regularly rendered 'go', such as *hālak* which draws attention to the journey and *yāṣāʾ* which draws attention to the setting out. Darkness, too, has the connotations of defeat and death.

The vocative 'daughter Chaldea' and the warning 'you will not continue to have people call you...' are repeated from v. 1 (see comment; the versions again translate by passive, while the LXX abbreviates by omitting 'continue to'). In the new appellative in v. 5b the word *g[e]beret* suggests the female head of a household. Elsewhere in the OT the word is always set over against *šipḥāh* ('servant'), in Gen 16.4, 8, 9; Isa 24.2; Ps 123.2; Prov 30.23, or *naʿărāh* ('[servant] girl') in 2 Kgs 5.3 (cf †Beuken). The use of *g[e]beret* rather than *g[e]bîrāh* ('queen') indicates that this is the metaphor the prophet uses—against BDB, which assumes that in Isaiah 47 alone *g[e]beret* means queen. *HAL* and *DCH* treat the two as forms of the same word. While *g[e]beret* might simply be the construct of *g[e]bîrāh*, the similar word *malkāh* ('queen') has a construct *malkat* as well as a byform *m[e]leket*. The latter admittedly occurs only as construct, but the word for 'wall' occurs in the absolute as both *g[e]dērāh* and *g[e]deret*. So there are parallels to support the possibility that *g[e]beret* might be a byform of *g[e]bîrāh*, which could occur both as absolute and as construct. The latter makes sense here, the former in v. 7.

It is suggestive that the states that are Babylon's underlings are referred to as 'kingdoms' (*mamlākôt*; LXX has singular). They had once been not merely *ʿammîm* ('peoples, ethnic groups') or *gôyim* ('foreign nations') but sovereign states that controlled their own destinies. They were ruled by a king or queen of their own. But they had ceased to be sovereign states and come to be ruled by Babylon like a servant ruled by a *g*[e]*beret*, with whom real power lay.

גברת: 1QIs[a] גבורת, perhaps construct of גְּבוּרָה ('might'), more likely construct of גְּבוֹרָה ('heroine'; *DCH*). Cf LXX's ἰσχύς.

47.6a. I was angry with my people. I profaned my heritage. So I gave them into your power. We have followed the MT in dividing v. 6 into two long lines, this first one 2–2–2. †Thomas redivides as three lines of shorter length more comparable with others in this poem, but this obscures the significant distinction between clauses with Yhwh as subject (closing with a *w*-consecutive) and ones with 'you' as subject, and produces not very balanced second and third lines. Budde ('Klagelied', p. 237) adds a verb at the beginning and one at the end to regularize the rhythm as three 5-stress lines, which draws our attention to the fact that the MT's rhythm is free rather than strict.

As at 43.28, the LXX resists making Yhwh the subject of the verb 'profane' and renders ἐμίανας ('you profaned'). As there, the Syr similarly has *ṭwšw* ('they profaned').

47.6b. You did not show them compassion. On an elder you weighted your yoke heavily. The argument here compares with that concerning Assyria in Isaiah 10, but it has its own distinctiveness. The indictment of Babylon concerns her failure to show compassion—*raḥămîm*, the quality whose linguistic association with the word for the womb (*reḥem*) suggests it is the quality that Babylon as a woman ought to have shown but did not.

The 'elders' (*zāqēn*) were among those who paid the price when Jerusalem was taken (Lam 2.21, singular; 2.10 plural; also 1.19; 4.16; 5.12, 14; Syr has plural here). Having declared the intention to pour out wrath on the elder as much as anyone else (Jer 6.11; cf Isa 3.2, 5; Ezek 9.6), Yhwh had commissioned Babylon to be the means of doing so (Jer 51.22), and that successfully. Now Babylon is under judgment for fulfilling the task. But the *zāqēn* may be not merely the aged person but the senior person. Elders are often mentioned alongside people such as priests, prophets, diviners, princes, judges, and warriors. Yet they are rarely mentioned on their own in any of these contexts (but see, e.g., Ezek 9.6), and in warning descriptions of invasion elders are not referred to (see, e.g., Jer 29; Ezek 26), while Isaiah 13–14 mentions women and children (13.16) but not old people.

After 46.4, the 'elder' on whom Madam Babylon has set a heavy yoke might be not a group within the community but might be Israel as a whole itself (†Ehrlich). This would also fit better with the fact that the critique of the king of Babylon in chapter 14 relates to his action in relation to the world as a whole and to his own people rather than to particular groups. Whatever the reference of 'elder', it is the word's meaning and connotation rather than its reference that makes the point. A woman ought to care about the fate of an old man.

Leviticus Rabbah 13.5 sees the closing words as fulfilled in the martyrdom of Rabbi Aqiba and his colleagues by the Romans.

47.7a. You said, 'I will be here forever, mistress in perpetuity'. The MT breaks the verse after 'mistress' and takes the word *ʿad* as a conjunction introducing v. 7b. As such it would usually mean 'until', or rather in this context 'so that' (cf Tg) or 'while' (†Korpel and de Moor). But these meanings are very rare (see BDB, pp. 725a) and more likely *ʿad* is a noun meaning 'perpetuity', parallel to *ʿôlām* in the first colon (†Hitzig; cf *HAL*, p. 742b). It might then link back to 'mistress' in the construct so that the phrase means 'mistress of perpetuity', 'perpetual mistress' (cf 9.5 [6]). More likely the word pair *ʿôlām* and *ʿad* (cf Hab 3.6) are in parallelism, with the less familiar word second as usual, and thus in reverse order to the Ugaritic example (*CHP*, p. 331); *ʿad* then presupposes the preposition on *leʿôlām* (cf *Freedman). The LXX, Vg, and Syr omit *ʿad*, more likely an indication of finding it difficult than of its being a gloss (against †Ziegler, p. 54); cf the substitution of *ʿwd* in 1QIsa, 'Still [you did not. . .]'. It is unlikely that an audience could be expected to recognize here a Hebrew word for 'throne' (Dahood, *Psalms II*, p. 81). †Lowth emends to *ʿal*.

'I will be [here]' is *ʾehyeh* (cf Exod 3.14) and implies a claim of some arrogance, reinforced by 'for ever/in perpetuity' (see, e.g., 9.6 [7], where the words are *ʿad-ʿôlām*; 40.8; 51.6, 8).

For *gebāret* ('mistress'), 1QIsa again has *gbwrt* (see on v. 5).

47.7b. You did not call these things to mind. You did not think about its outcome. Once again it makes sense to take 'these things' as primarily forward-looking even if taking into account what has preceded (see 44.21; 46.8). The two cola have parallel meaning, and 'these things' is thus initially explained by 'its outcome', *ʾaḥărîtāh* (†Torrey). For Zion's failure to 'think about its outcome', see 41.22 and 46.10; but also Lam 1.9. The pronoun has no obvious antecedent, because the wording follows that of Lam 1.9 but omits the antecedent. It seems forced to take it to refer to one of the preceding feminine nouns, for example, 'heritage' or 'mistress'. This may explain the versions' omission of it. The LXX has τὰ ἔσχατα, but this hardly refers to 'the last things' (see †Troxel, p. 23); Tg *swpʾ*, Syr *ḥrtʾ* ('the end') similarly, but singular. 1QIsa has *ʾḥrwnh*, 'its last' (cf 41.4), or 'at the last/afterwards' (but the use without a preposition would be unique), or 'at the last/latter thing' (Elliger: see †Hermisson). Many late medieval MSS have a second person suffix (see *HUB*): cf Vg *novissimi tui* ('*your* end'—some LXX MSS also have the second person pronoun). In the MT the pronoun apparently has the feminine's common neuter significance and refers to 'an abstraction:

the end result of Babylon's course of action' (†Willey, p. 169). The singular then complements the plural demonstrative in the first colon. The following verses will unfold what 'these things/its outcome' means.

47.8a. So now listen to this, delectable, you who sit in confidence, you who say to yourself 'I and I alone am still here'. 'So now' (*wᵉʿattāh*: see on 43.1a) suggests that again 'this' denotes what is about to be said. They are words that threaten an announcement of doom. †R. H. O'Connell (pp. 151–59) treats vv. 8–15 independently of vv. 1–7 as the 'structural axis' of chaps 40–54, without specific addressee and capable of applying to Zion or to Babylon. This seems to underestimate the significance of the way vv. 8–15 follow directly on vv. 1–7, addressed to Babylon. Though Zion was mentioned in 46.13, there is no indication that she might be addressed here, and the context suggests strongly that Babylon is still the addressee.

'Delectable' (*ʿădînāh*) comes only here (ignoring the difficult 2 Sam 23.8). An article on the vocative might have been expected (cf 46.12), though this is not invariable usage (see *IBHS* 13.5.2). Related words suggest that the central reference is to good food and its enjoyment (*ʿēden*, Jer 51.34; *maʿădān*, Gen 49.20; Lam 4.5; *ʿādan*, Neh 9.25), which can be a metaphor for sexual pleasure (*ʿednāh*, Gen 18.12), for inner delight (*maʿădān*, Prov 29.17), and then for rich spiritual provision (*ʿēden*, Ps 36.9 [8]). It suggests the enjoyment of the good life, without necessarily implying excess. Poet and hearers might also be aware of the similarity with the verb *ʿādāh* ('ornament oneself') and related words, including *ʿădî* (see 49.18) (†Hessler). There is another suggestion of reversal here.

Three times in 32.9–13 women at ease are warned about being *bōṭᵉḥôt* ('confident'). Here the point is made by combining the 'sit' of vv. 1 and 5 with adverbial *lābeṭaḥ* ('in confidence'). The words can suggest objective security (see the noun in 14.30; 32.17) or subjective trust and reliance, whether well-founded or false (see the participle in 36.6; 37.10; 42.17 as well as 32.9–13; also the finite verb in 36.4–9). Madam Babylon sits thus, unaware of the sitting that vv. 1 and 5 herald.

'You who say to yourself…' is literally 'the one who says in her heart…'. The Vg has 'in your heart', following the sense; anomalously, L has the accent on the penultimate syllable. The woman's words are individually ones with which we have become familiar in Isaiah 40–46. The LXX thus renders Ἐγώ εἰμι, καὶ οὐκ ἔστιν ἑτέρα ('I am and there is none other'); cf Tg *ʾnʾ wlyt br mny ʿwd*, Vg *ego sum et non est praeter me amplius*. For *ʾănî* ('I [am]'), see on v. 7a; for *ʾepes* ('[there is] none'), see, for example, 45.6, 14; 46.9. For *ʿôd* ('other'), see, for example, 45.5, 6, 14, 18, 21, 22; 46.9. But comparison with earlier passages reveals that each of the three words is used rather differently here in v. 8. Previously *ʾănî* always had a predicate, *ʾepes* was in that absolute form whereas here it has an ending (see the note), and *ʿôd* here follows that word rather than following *ʾên* ('there is not') as every other time in Isaiah 45–46. The three-word clause in fact needs to be interpreted in its own right rather than as a variant of earlier statements. Literally Madam Babylon says 'I and my exclusivity still [am/will be]'. The word *ʾepes* has a restrictive sense as in Num 22.35 and 23.13, while *ʿôd* has its frequent meaning 'yet' as in, for example, 1.5; 10.20; 14.1; 30.20; 32.5; 38.11; 51.22; 52.1; 54.4, 9; 60.18, 19, 20. Rather than constituting a separate statement of a claim to a God-like exclusivity of being, Madam Babylon's statement thus expresses the confidence to which the previous line refers and which the next line will re-express, and which her helplessness referred to in v. 15 will belie.

†Lack suggests that the words just discussed are Babylon's own slogan, but the whole of the words 'you who sit…still here' are identical with part of Zeph 2.15, where they are addressed to Nineveh. The distinctiveness of the usage of the words, just noted, would fit with the hypothesis that they are original there and have been adapted here as fitting well with the use of the individual words in this material. Indeed, †Sommer (p. 245) sees vv. 5–11 as a 'reprediction' of Zeph 2.13–15. On the other hand, †Hermisson notes that in Zephaniah 2 they can easily be read as a citation of this and other Isaianic texts that Zeph 2.15 declares to be fulfilled.

עדינה: †Hermisson takes עודנה in 1QIs^a as a participial form (also *hap. leg.*) with the same meaning, but †Nötscher (p. 300) understands עודנה to denote 'she still' (cf 1 Kgs 1.22), which used in the vocative would translate as 'you [who] still [sit…]', and prefers this reading.
אפסי: see JM 93q, 160n, which takes the ending as a first person suffix. P. Joüon queries the view expressed in GK 90kl that the ending is an old paragogic (fuller) case ending, which can be attached to the construct.[16] Either way, the use of **אפסי** makes for an alliteration with **אני** (†Boadt, p. 361).

47.8b. I shall not sit as a widow or experience the loss of children. Widowhood and loss of children are a fixed pair in Ugaritic (Watson, *VT* 22 [1972], p. 465). In a patriarchal society, her husband and her children are a woman's security, her protection, and her provision for the future. For Madam Babylon, her empire fulfilled that role, but it is about to disappear.

אדע: 1QIs^a אראה ('see'), to use a vb in its primary meaning (†Kutscher, p. 214; ET p. 284). 4QIs^d agrees with the MT.

[16] See P. Joüon, 'Notes de lexicographie hébraique', in *Mélanges de la faculté orientale* (Université Saint-Joseph, Beyrouth) 5 (1911), pp. 405–15 (see pp. 408–9).

47.9abα. But the two of these will come to you in a moment, in one day. Loss of children and widowhood in fullness are coming upon you. We follow †Thomas's division of v. 9 into three lines. While the LXX has χηρεία καὶ ἀτεκνία ('widowhood and childlessness'), in the MT the two abstract expressions come in reverse order to that of the concrete nouns in v. 8, reflecting the reversal that v. 9 speaks of (†Franke).

The sequence 'in a moment (*regaʿ*), in one day' suggests an anti-climactic movement, but this may be a prosaic response. †Morgenstern sees the second phrase as an explanatory gloss, but the double expression parallels one in 30.13 (instantly in suddenness). BDB suggests that *regaʿ* here denotes 'suddenly' rather than 'instantly': cf, for example, Ps 6.11 [10]; Job 34.20, passages that also suggest that it perhaps appears here not merely because of some intrinsic meaning but as a common rhetorical feature of declarations of judgment. Also significant is the fact that this word, too, reappears in Isa 54.7–8 and takes up from Lamentations (see 4.6). Syr *mḥwtʾ* ('blows') implies *negaʿ* rather than *regaʿ*.

The verb 'come' (*bōʾ*) opens the verse, in *w*-yiqtol form; †Saydon (p. 300) describes it as *waw* co-ordinate. The verb recurs in the second line, and three times more in vv. 11, 13, each time to refer to the way trouble is 'coming' to/on Babylon. The verb thus contributes to the unity of vv. 8–15. This second occurrence is qatal *bāʾû*. The LXX repeats the future ἥξει ('it/they will come'; LXX^B then omits the intervening words by homoioarkton); cf the Tg repeating *yytyn*, Syr *nʾtyn*. It is doubtful whether this is evidence for yiqtol *yābōʾû*, given the way in which cola or lines can complement each other, for example, in tenses. 'In fullness' is *k^etummām*, literally 'according to their completeness'. It is an unparalleled use of the noun. The LXX has ἐξαίφνης, the Syr *mn šlyʾ* ('suddenly'), which are their renderings of *pitʾōm* ('suddenly') in v. 11. They are surely interpreting rather than indicating that they read this word here; contrast Vg *universa*. †Köhler's *b^etummām* is hardly an improvement. More interestingly, A. Krochmal inferred the possible reading *k^etômim* ('like twins': see †Hermisson; and see BDB, p. 1060). Driver (BZAW 77, p. 47) links the usage with the word's connotation of 'innocence' or 'simplicity' and thus 'without definite aim' (BDB) or 'at random' and thus 'unexpectedly', but this seems forced.

ואלמן: 1QIs^a has ואלמנה, the more familiar word (†Kutscher, p. 29; ET p. 38). It usually means 'widow' but might be an alternative form of the noun meaning 'widowhood' (cf *DCH*).

47.9bβγ–10aα. In the midst of the multiplying of your chants and the great abounding of your charms you were confident in your wrong-doing, you said 'No-one is looking at me'. Until we reach the last word it is natural to render 'in the multitude of your chants and in the abundance of your charms...'. Then *m^eʾōd* ('very') closes the line and is difficult syntactically to relate to what has preceded (the Syr omits it). As an adverb it has no verb to qualify. Admittedly *mᵉʾōd*, like words such as *ʿôd* and *yaḥad*, is strictly not an 'adverb' but a noun used adverbially (see *IBHS* 14.5b). Here we might possibly render it 'a-plenty' (literally '[in] abundance'). But the usage is hard to parallel. BDB (p. 547a) this also allows for *ʿoṣmat* being not the construct of the noun *ʿoṣmāh* but infinitive construct from the verb *ʿāṣam*, which can then be qualified by *mᵉʾōd*. In turn this invites us retrospectively to recategorize *rōb* as also not a noun meaning 'muchness' but infinitive construct from *rābab* (cf *TTH* 118). The LXX omits the word, abbreviating the text.

This in turn eases another difficulty, the use of the preposition *b* ('in') at the beginning of each colon. The Vg renders *propter* ('on account of'; cf BDB, p. 90) and †Calvin 'despite': so BDB itself, p. 90b.[17] But the examples quoted hardly justify this rendering. Here these now become examples of the common use of *b* with the infinitive, probably purely temporal ('even while your chants are multiplying...').

In parallelism with *rōb* ('multiplying'), the less usual *ʿoṣmat* with other words from this root can suggest either strength or abundance. The former made sense at 40.29, but the latter is usual when words from this root are in parallelism with *rab* and associated words.

'Chants' (*kešep*) is an adaptation of Akkadian *kišpu*, a word denoting prayers designed to cause or protect from calamity. 'Charms' (*ḥeber*) are formulae that 'bind' people (*ḥābar* means 'join'). The Syr has 'chanters' (*ḥršyky*); a Geniza fragment similarly has *kaššāpayik* (see *HUB*). The Syr then follows that by 'charmers' (*mgwšyky*); cf 1QIsᵃ *ḥwbryk*, Vg *incantatorum tuorum*. Similar variations recur in v. 12.

Verse 10 then begins with a *waw* consecutive. The MT verse division implies that whereas v. 9bβγ depends on what has preceded, a new sentence begins with v. 10 (cf Vg). The LXX's τῇ ἐλπίδι τῆς πονηρίας, however, suggests the possibility that this clause continues the infinitival construction (so *TTH* 118; cf GK 114r, JM 124q, *IBHS* 36.3.2; πορνείας in some LXX MSS is an inner-Greek confusion). The sentence then crosses the division between vv. 9 and 10. The following clause might carry it on further. The structure of vv. 9bβγ–10aα is paralleled in 48.4–5a, even to the subsequent asyndetic clause with qatal verb. That is more unequivocally a *w*-apodosis construction (cf JM 176; GK 111h). This also makes for a good understanding of vv. 9bβγ–10aα. The construction points to a causal as well as a temporal relationship between the two lines. It was because of the multiplying/abounding that Babylon was so confident. The two lines then form less a footnote to v. 9abα than an introduction to v. 10aβb (†Hermisson).

The RSV has 'you felt secure in your wickedness' but it is doubtful whether *bāṭaḥ b*, which regularly means 'trust in', can be reduced to denoting the circumstances of trust rather than the grounds of trust.

[17] See also M. Z. Kaddari, 'Concessive Connectors in the Language of Isaiah', in †van Wyk, pp. 103–12 (see p. 106).

The verb presumably keeps the nuance of the noun *beṭaḥ* in v. 8; for such subconscious trust in wrongdoing, compare the comments on Judah in passages such as 30.12. For 'confident in your wrongdoing' (*brʿtk*), 1QIs[a] has 'confident in your knowledge' (*bdʿtk*)—the difference is only a tittle (see on 46.12). Verbally this fits well with the previous line, and with the next, to which 1QIs[a] has surely assimilated it (†Kutscher, p 173; ET pp. 228–29). The second colon fits with a preceding allusion to wrongdoing of the kind that v. 6b referred to (cf Ps 94.7).

אָמַרְתְּ: 1QIs[a] אמרתי (so also the Cairo fragment Kb 13—see *HUB*) is surely one of many examples of the plene spelling of the second f. in 1QIs[a], not a first person: cf Steck, *Die erste Jesajarolle*.
רֹאָנִי: perhaps a composite reading; see GK 61h, 75v on the form and the need to repoint רֹאָנִי, though †Delitzsch defends the MT. †Morgenstern emends to אין מיראני ('nothing frightens me'). The LXX assimilates to Madam Babylon's words in v. 8, repeated at the end of v. 10; its subsequent γνῶθι ὅτι suggests a reading such as רְאֵה ('see', imper.; †Hermisson).

47.10aβb. Your wisdom, your knowledge, it was this turned you. And you said to yourself 'I and I alone am still here'. The singular construction reflects the fact that wisdom and knowledge are a hendiadys (†Hermisson). They are near-synonyms (H.-P. Müller, *ThWAT* on *ḥākam*, III.1). The *w* on *daʿtēk* is explicative.

The verb 'turned you' is a polel form of *šûb*, a rare alternative to the hiphil (cf Jer 50.6). In principle the polel could have any of the meanings of the hiphil. The positive meanings such as 'bring back/restore' seem out of place. Tg *qlqyltyk* suggests 'lead astray': cf Vg *decepit*; also BDB, *HAL*, and the adjectives *šōbēb/šōbāb* ('back-turning', 'apostate'). On the basis of the collocation with reference to confidence as in 30.15, R. Gordis suggests 'made you confident',[18] but 'turn back' in the sense of 'defeat' seems more likely (cf 14.27; 44.25). This explains the LXX's ἔσται σοι αἰσχύνη, unless this implies a form of the verb *bôš*. The repetition in v. 10b from v. 8, except for the opening *w*-consecutive, underlines the fact that it was her intellectual, religious, and political resources that encouraged Madam Babylon's false confidence and thus her fall.

וְדַעְתֵּךְ: LXX's καὶ ἡ πονηρία/πορνεία σου implies ורעתך, the converse of the 1QIs[a] variant in the previous line.
היא reinforces the subject (*TTH* 123). It fulfils a resumptive and contrastive function (Geller, 'Cleft Sentences', pp. 32–33), suggesting 'it is that very wisdom/knowledge that…'.
שׁוֹבְבָתֶךְ: on the suffix, see GK 59g.

[18] See 'Some Hitherto Unrecognized Meanings of the Verb *shub*', *JBL* 52 (1933), pp. 153–62 (see p. 161) = Gordis, *The Word* [see on 42.14], p. 226.

47.11. Trouble will come upon you, of which you will not know the countercharm. Disaster will fall upon you, which you will not be able to counter. Desolation will come upon you suddenly, which you will not know about. The verse comprises three parallel lines. Each begins with a verb prefixed by *w* and followed by 'upon you' (*ʿālayik*). †Grimm and Dittert call the preposition hostile-aggressive. The first is a *w*-qatal that lacks a preceding yiqtol, but it is continued with simple *w* plus yiqtol verbs. Those must be co-ordinate (†Saydon, p. 300), and the first must surely then be taken as *w*-consecutive. Perhaps it is thought of as following on from and continuing v. 9a. In addition, the first and third of the verbs are from *bōʾ* ('come'), and a desire for variation may have contributed to the choice of *w* plus qatal at the beginning. The Vg and Syr omit the *w*.

The third verb is also qualified by 'suddenly' (*pitʾōm*), so that the three expressions increase in intensity ('come', 'fall', 'come suddenly'). The last does so in an unexpected way as we are given the impression that the verb stem is being merely repeated but are then surprised by a word that mirrors rhetorically the surprise it refers to. The equivalents of *bōʾ* and *nāpal* ('come', 'fall') are a fixed pair in Ugaritic (Watson, *VT* 22 [1972], p. 463).

The three nouns begin with the familiar *rāʿāh* ('trouble'). 'Disaster' is the stronger word *hōwāh*. The fact that it comes only here and in Ezek 7.26 may explain the change in 1QIs[a] to *hwyh*, though that raises problems of its own (†Kutscher, pp. 173–74; ET p. 229). There are several possible roots *hwh* with associated nouns *hawwāh* (*DCH* lists four). The most common itself means 'destruction'.[19] 'Desolation' is *šôʾāh* (cf 10.3), the most devastating of the words. Its effect is perhaps increased by its being the fourth word in the line, at the beginning of the second colon: 'there will come upon you suddenly—desolation that you will not know about'.

Three parallel asyndetic subordinate clauses beginning with *lōʾ* ('not') complete each line. In the first, Syr *bšprʾ*, Vg *ortum* take the object of Madam Babylon's knowledge as derived from *šāḥar* II, denoting 'dawn'. †Ibn Ezra then sees dawn as suggesting relief, †Qimchi as suggesting calamity. †Morgenstern takes it as from *šāḥar* I, which denotes 'blackness', comparing Lam 4.8. Neither is very appropriate here. The Tg has *lmbʿy ʿlh* 'how to pray against it', which perhaps supports the view that *šaḥar* is a homonym for *saḥar* (see on v. 15) and means 'charm': see BDB and cf Akkadian *sāḥiru* ('charmer'). This makes best sense in the context of vv. 10–11. The LXX's βόθυνος suggests *šaḥat* ('pit') (cf †Ottley). †Graetz suggests a form of *šāḥad* ('bribe'). Again, the difference is but a tittle (see on 46.12). †Hessler notes that *šōḥad* parallels *kōper* in Prov 6.35. Driver

[19] A. Guillaume in 'Magical Terms in the Old Testament' (*JRAS* 1942, pp. 111–31; *JRAS* 1943, pp. 251–54) argues that הוה in such contexts means 'evil of magical origin/curse'; contrast G. R. Driver, 'Witchcraft in the Old Testament', in *JRAS* 1943, pp. 6–16.

(*JTS* 36, p. 400) derived *šaḥar* from an Arabic root meaning 'laugh away' and thus 'overcome'.

In the second line's clause, 'which you cannot counter', *yākōl* ('can') again directly governs an infinitive (cf 46.2); 1QIs[a] has *lkprh*. The meaning of *kpr* (here as usual pi) is controversial. The LXX has intransitive καθαρὰ γενέσθαι, the Vg *expiare*, but neither 'wipe away' nor 'cover' nor 'expiate' makes very good sense in connection with something that has not yet happened. The equivalent meaning in this connection would be 'avert'.[20] The Akkadian equivalent *kupparu* refers to the work of a 'chanter', though in connection with purification rites (see B. Lang, *ThWAT* on *kipper*, I.1). But the previous occurrence of this root was at 43.3 where the noun *kōper* meant 'ransom', and †Marti sees the verb as here a denominative from that noun.

In the third line the equivalent clause reads simply *lōʾ tēdāʿî*. In isolation this might idiomatically signify 'without your knowing' (*TTH* 162; cf Ps 35.8; Prov 5.6), but in context the parallelism suggests '[which] you do not know'. The knowing will then refer not to previous experience but to the capacity to cope with the event. Perhaps the line-by-line parallelism invites us to understand 'its countercharm/its countering'. Rhetorically the sudden ending to the line mirrors its message in a complementary way to the unexpected addition of 'suddenly'. These relative clauses thus also heighten to a climax.

ובא: on the uninflected vb with subsequent f. subject, see JM 150j. 1QIs[a] ובאה conforms to later practice. It also removes the asyndeton in the first and last clauses by reading ולוא.

47.12. Do stand with your charms and with the multiplying of your chants, those with which you have laboured from your youth. Perhaps you may be able to succeed. Perhaps you may terrify. After the threefold bidding to 'sit', the irony of the challenge now to 'stand' is underlined by *nāʾ* (cf GK 110a, d). S. A. Kaufmann comments that *IBHS* 32.2.3d, which describes *nāʾ* as a particle of entreaty, is to be preferred to *IBHS* 40.2.5c, which suggests that the particle denotes that the command in question follows logically from what precedes.[21] But the latter observation illumines the usage here, given the irony: 'in the light of the uselessness of your wisdom, please do stand upright, firm, and confident in it'. Of the occurrences of *ʿāmad* ('stand') in the imperative, 2 Chr 20.17 sets up a nice ironical contrast with this one. Of the occurrences of *ʿāmad* followed by *b* ('in'), 2 Kgs 23.3 sets up a nice non-ironical contrast. On *rōb* ('multiplying'), see on v. 9.

1QIs[a] omits v. 12b and the first word of v. 13 and avoids giving the

[20] So B. Janowski, *Sühne als Heilsgeschehen* (WMANT 55, 1982), pp. 98–99; *DCH*.

[21] 'An Emphatic Plea for Please', in *Maarav* 7 (1991), pp. 195–98. *IBHS* refers to T. O. Lambdin, *Introduction to Biblical Hebrew* (New York, 1971), p. 170.

impression to the ordinary hearer who lacks an ear for irony that Madam Babylon really does derive any power from her charms and chants. In its place it adds *wʿd hywm* ('[from your youth] even to today'), conforming the text to Jer 3.25 (†Koenig, p. 268) and/or writing into the text the conviction that it relates to the copyist's own day when Babylon stands at the heart of the Seleucid Empire (†van der Kooij, pp. 92–93). The LXX omits 'Perhaps you may terrify', possibly finding the verb *ʿāraṣ* hard to understand in the context (cf †Ziegler, p. 50). The Vg has *fieri fortior* ('to become stronger'), the Tg similarly *lmtqp*, Syr *ttʿšnyn*. This is not far from the connotation of the adjective/noun *ʿārîṣ* in some contexts (see BDB). †Ewald infers from an Arabic root that the verb means 'resist'. †Hermisson more plausibly links it with the terrifying potential of demons and omens.

עמדו־נא; 1QIs[a] עמודינא, prefixed by ו above the line.
בחבריך וברב כשפיך: 1QIs[a] has בחובריך implying a participle; cf Vg *cum incantatoribus tuis*, Syr *bmgwšyky* and for the next noun *bḥršyky*. †Morgenstern repoints to two nouns חַבָּרַיִךְ and כַּשָּׁפַיִךְ ('your charmers/ chanters'). Cf v. 9 and comment. The MT resumes from v. 9 except for the reversal of the order.
בַּאֲשֶׁר: instead of this anomaly one would have expected אֲשֶׁר...בָּהֶם, except that the אֲשֶׁר would have been omitted in verse. GK 138f thus views it as demonstrative, though Cowley there seems to demur from this view. JM 158m sees it as another example of 'a kind of anticipation' involving אֲשֶׁר: see the note on 43.4a. 1QIs[a] has כאשר. The words in the clause reappear in v. 15, whence †Thomas sees them as interpolated.
יגעת: LXX's ἐμάνθανες may imply ידעת (†Ottley); but *HUB* notes the link of toil and study.
תערוצי: Vg, Tg, Syr are hardly grounds for suggesting תעצומי (†Morgenstern). †Ehrlich emends to the rather predictable תִּוָּעֲצִי ('take counsel').

47.13. You are collapsing in the midst of the multiplying of your plans. They must stand now and deliver you, the ones who observe the heavens, those who gaze at the stars, who make known for each month some things which would come upon you. The MT oddly divides the verse after the first colon. †Thomas also oddly attaches to it only the next verb (*yaʿamdû-nāʾ*, 'they must stand now'), which it thereby rather isolates from the verb dependent on it (*wᵉyôšîʿûkā*, 'and deliver you'). 'You...deliver you' surely comprises one 3–2 line. 'The ones who observe...stars' then forms a 2–2 line and 'who make known...–upon you' a third line, 2–3 or perhaps 2–2 (its second colon has three words but is shorter than its first).

The verb *nilʾêt* usually means 'you are weary [with]', but that statement does not fit well in the context, and with this meaning the verb is followed by *l* rather than *b*. The phrase 'in the midst of the multiplying of your plans' is parallel to the one in v. 9b, where it was introduced by a verb that we took as instantaneous qatal. The same understanding makes good sense here. This verb refers to a wearying and collapse that Babylon is about to experience. The nuance 'experience affliction/hardship' is suggested by the use of the noun *tᵉlāʾāh* (Exod 18.8; 20.14; Lam 3.5; Neh 9.32). The word for 'plans' looks like a composite of singular and plural (see note). The plural occurs elsewhere only at 25.1; Deut 32.28; Ps 13.3 [2], and in part of the tradition it thus became assimilated to the prevalent singular usage. The plural is another instance of the prophecy taking up Deut 32, with the nice reversal that it is now Babylon that is devoid of counsels—for all its multiplying of them.

Babylon's advisers are people who observe the skies and gaze at the stars. We follow the Tg in rendering *hābar* 'observe'. It uses the verb *skʾ/sky*. This gives good sense in the context and produces a good parallelism (indeed *Hommel takes 'those who gaze at the stars' as an explanatory gloss). BDB renders *hābar* 'divide'. The phrase then denotes the astrologers' skill at dividing up the sky into its various segments and spheres of influence. This gives fine sense in the context, but BDB notes that it is based on the existence of an Arabic word for 'divide' that refers to cutting meat into large chunks. †Rashi understands 'those who divine from the heavens', apparently presupposing a verb *bārar* with this meaning; cf †Caspari's suggestion that the word alludes to *baru* priests (so also †Morgenstern, despite commenting that they did not divine from the stars). †Ibn Ezra notes that the initial *h* on *hābar* is part of the verb, which would therefore need emending to give this meaning. †Saadya apparently connects it with the verb *bārar* with the meaning 'choose' (see on 49.2b), and M. Fishbane describes the form as a pseudo-hiphil from the root *br/brr*.[22] *Blau suggested 'those who worship the heavens' on the basis of Ugaritic *hbr*,[23] but (as he notes) *hbr* refers specifically to physical prostration rather than worship in an abstract sense, and anyway the idea of worship is not as apposite in the context. 1QIsª has *ḥwbry* from the verb noted in connection with charms in vv. 9, 12 (cf †Nötscher, p. 299). This looks a simplifying slip (*DCH*, Vol. 2, pp. 486–87, reads *hwbry* in 1QIsª, but the letter looks more like *ḥ* than *h*). G. F. Moore emended to *ḥōqᵉrê* ('those who search [the heavens]'; see BDB).

As etymology suggests, *ḥōdeš* can denote the 'new moon', the beginning of the (lunar) month (cf 1.13, 14; 66.23), and if Babylonian astrologers did offer their predictions at this moment, such a reference would make sense here. But the preposition is *l* not *b* (contrast, e.g., Ezek 46.3). The preposition is *l* in passages such as 1 Chr 23.31 in the rather different connection of offerings 'for/at' new moons and other occasions; contrast the use of *l* in Exod 12.2; Num 28.14; Ezek 47.12, which are among the vast majority of occurrences of *ḥōdeš* that mean the 'month' that the new moon introduces rather

[22] M. Fishbane, *Biblical Interpretation in Ancient Israel* (Oxford/New York, rev. ed., 1988), p. 457.

[23] Cf E. Ullendorff, 'Ugaritic Marginalia II', in *JSS* 7 (1962), pp. 339–51 (see pp. 339–40).

than the new moon itself. This meaning makes sense here. The advisers make things known 'for the months': that is, presumably for each month. H.-P. Müller (*ThWAT* on *ḥākam*, IV.3) takes 'the months' as the direct object, which seems a less likely use of *l*, though 'with regard to the months' would be possible. On the basis of their observations of the heavens, then, for/with regard to each month the advisers make known which days are auspicious and which inauspicious—thus make known 'some things that would come upon you'. 'Some things that' represents *mēʾăšer*, literally 'from [that] which'. The usage is uncommon but not odd (see, e.g., Gen 31.1; Jer 40.7; Ruth 2.9; cf BDB, p. 84a). *Genesis Rabbah* 85.2 quotes the passage and notes that the astrologers could reveal only some things. They could not reveal and deliver from all of them; cf †Saadya.

ברב: 1QIsa[a] ברוב makes poorer sense. LXX omits רב as in v. 9.
עֲצָתָ֫יִךְ: we take this as a conflate form, a cross between עֲצָתַיִךְ (pl. with suffix; cf LXX, Syr, Vg) and עֲצָתֵךְ (s. with suffix; cf Tg) (so †Torrey).[24] JM 94j identifies it as an example of the occasional confusion between s. and pl. suffixes. †Duhm repoints to refer to people, יוֹעֲצָיִךְ ('your counsellors').
יעמדו־נא: again enclitic נא; see on v. 12a.
הֹבְרֵי Q, הָבְרוּ K: the meaning will be the same, the latter implying a relative cl. without אשׁר (cf BDB).
מאשׁר: see comment. There is thus little ground to hypothesize the repointing מֵאֲשֶׁר as a 'compound relative' meaning simply 'that which' (so Dahood [see on 40.12], p. 414). LXX's simple τί ('what') might indicate that understanding or that the מ is dittog., or that it reflects haplog. or is rendering loosely. It also omits the preceding word לחדשׁים ('for each month'). Vg *ut ex eis* ('so that from them') takes חדשׁים as antecedent, but then has difficulty over verb and subject in the last cl. (cf Müller [see comment] who renders 'in which' and then lacks a subject). The prep. is surely too far away to be governed by ויושׁיעך ('deliver you [from what will. . .]') (†Ibn Ezra) or even to take its meaning from מודיעם in the sense 'inform concerning what' (†Gesenius; cf 2.3). More plausibly M. H. [Goshen-] Gottstein sees מאשׁר as equivalent to אשׁר. . .מהם ('what will come on you from them/from whom they come'): see on 43.4a.
יבאו: logically the LXX also follows the relative with a singular verb, now instanced in 1QIsa[a] (יבוא—metathesis one way or the other).
עליך: 1QIsa[a] עליהמה ('upon them').

47.14. There, they are like stubble. Fire is burning them. They cannot rescue their own selves from the power of the blaze. It is not coal for warming, flame to sit before. They are 'all' like stubble, the LXX adds (cf 50.9, 11). In the second colon the point is underlined by the juxtaposition of 'fire' (which comes first) and 'burns', which is language for calamity independently of reference to stubble (9.18–19). But it is down-to-earth language. The fire 'burns' (*śārap*: on the form, see GK 59g) rather than 'consumes' (*ʾākal*), as happened in a

[24] See also †Rubinstein, p. 320, referring to H. Yalon, 'מגילת ישעיהו', in *Kirjath Sepher* 27 (1951), pp. 163a–76a (see p. 167a).

down-to-earth way to the very cities of Judah when the country was invaded (1.7) and it was burnt with fire (Lam 1.13; 2.3, 4; 4.11). The experience of Zion will again become the experience of Babylon. †Koole takes the second colon as a relative clause, 'they are like stubble that fire burns'. The LXX renders by a passive to keep the same subject.

For v. 14b the Tg has 'there is no remnant or survivor for them, no, no place to survive there', which takes to an extreme language in Isaiah regarding Israel's own destiny. The LXX translates loosely and omits the negative, but may have intended a rhetorical question (see *HUB*). In the MT itself the description in terms of fire and the inability to find rescue corresponds to Judah's own experience at the hands of Babylon. Things are now reversed.

יצילו: 1QIs[a] has הצילו to parallel the previous line (†Rubinstein, p. 319). M. Dahood suggests that 1QIs[a] rightly understands the vb to have past reference,[25] but a modal understanding makes good sense.
לַחְמָם: on the form, see GK 28b, 67cc, but MT pointing might imply 'for their bread' and 1QIs[a] לחומם suggests a less unexpected לְחֻמָּם with suffix, 'for them to get warm' (†Brockington); cf Jer 51.39; also Syr *lnwrhwn*, Vg *quibus califiant*. *DCH* (Vol. 2, p. 342) also notes the emendations לַחֲמָם ('for warming') or לְחַמֵּם ('to heat') or לְחֹם ('for warmth'). Hummel ([see at 40.17] p. 103) unconvincingly sees this as an instance of enclitic ם; contrast Emerton ('Enclitic *mem*' [see on 40.17], p. 334). M. Dahood repoints לַחֲמִים ('diners').[26]

47.15. For you, such are those with whom you have laboured, your charmers from your youth. They are wandering each of them their own way. There is no-one to deliver you. The MT divides the verse after 'laboured', v. 15b then signifying 'Your charmers from your youth are wandering…', but †Thomas's division produces less unusual lines (4–2, 3–2); the Syr changes the word order so that the labouring is linked with the youth.

Hebrew *sāḥar* usually means 'go about on business', which would here imply 'merchants', but we have noted in connection with v. 11 that Akkadian *sāḥiru* refers to an expert in magical arts, a 'charmer', and this makes good sense here (cf Driver, *JTS* 36, pp. 400–1). *Ferron (pp. 437–38) defends the meaning 'trafficking' in the sense of facilitating 'traffic' between this world and the other world. By the time of Rev 18.15–17 the word seems to have been understood to mean merchants.

[25] 'New Readings in Lamentations', in *Biblica* 59 (1978), pp. 174–97 (see p. 177).
[26] 'Hebrew Lexicography', in *Orientalia* 45 (1976), pp. 327–65 (see p. 343).

אֲשֶׁר: 'those with whom'; see the comment on בַּאֲשֶׁר in v. 12, to which Tg, Syr, Vg assimilate v. 15. LXX's βοήθεια suggests to †Ottley עֵזֶר, but G. R. Driver posits that אֲשֶׁר itself here denotes strength or support (cf *DTT* on the vb אשׁר).[27]

יָגַעַתְּ: Dahood ('Hebrew Lexicography' [see note 26], p. 330) repoints as יֹגַעַתְּ, a Phoenician-style yiphil causative ('have worn out').

סֹחֲרַיִךְ: LXX's ἐν τῇ μεταβολῇ σου perhaps implies סְחֹרֵךְ (*HUB*), abstract for concrete.

Bibliography to 46.1–47.15

Avishur, Y., '"לֹא־שַׂמְתְּ לָהֶם רַחֲמִים"', in *Shnaton* 5–6 (1978–79), pp. 91–99, lxvi–lxvii.

Beeston, A. F. L., 'Hebrew *šibbolet* and *šobel*', in *JSS* 24 (1979), pp. 175–77.

Blau, J., '*Hōbᵉrē šāmājim* (Jes xlvii 13) = Himmelsanbeter?', in *VT* 7 (1957), pp. 183–84.

Brueggemann, W., 'At the Mercy of Babylon', in *JBL* 110 (1991), pp. 3–22. = Brueggemann, *A Social Reading of the Old Testament*, pp. 111–33. Minneapolis, 1994.

Cobb, W. H., 'On the Textual Crux in Isa. 48 8 [*sic*]', in *JBL* 39 (1920), pp. 168–70.

Cohen, C., 'The "Widowed" City', in *JANES* 5 (1973), pp. 75–81.

Crenshaw, J. L., '*YHWH ṣᵉbaʾôt šᵉmô*', in *ZAW* 81 (1969), pp. 156–75.

Ferron, J., 'La magicienne de Carthage', in *Le muséon* 79 (1966), pp. 435–41.

Franke, C., 'The Function of the Oracles against Babylon in Isaiah 14 and 47', in *Society of Biblical Literature 1993 Seminar Papers* (ed. E. H. Lovering), pp. 250–59. Atlanta: Scholars, 1993. Longer, revised ed., 'Reversals of Fortune in the Ancient Near East: A Study of the Babylon Oracles in the Book of Isaiah', in †Melugin and Sweeney, pp. 104–23.

—'The Function of the Satiric Lament over Babylon in Second Isaiah', in *VT* 41 (1991), pp. 408–18.

Franzmann, M., 'The City as Woman: The Case of Babylon in Isaiah 47', in *Australian Biblical Review* 43 (1995), pp. 1–19.

Freedman, D. N., '"Mistress for Ever"', in *Bib* 51 (1970), p. 538. = Freedman, *Divine Commitment and Human Obligation*, Vol. 1, pp. 249–50. Grand Rapids/Cambridge, 1997.

Gaiser, F. J., 'Remember the Former Things of Old', in *All Things New* (R. A. Harrisville Festschrift, ed. A. J. Hultgren and others), pp. 53–63. St Paul, 1992.

Hommel, F., 'The Word הברו in Isaiah xlvii. 13', in *ExpT* 12 (1900–1901), p. 239.

[27] 'Misreadings in the Old Testament', in *Die Welt des Orients* 1 (1947–52), pp. 234–38 (see p. 234).

Leene, H., 'Isaiah 46.8—Summons to be Human?', in *JSOT* 30 (1984), pp. 111–21.
Martin-Achard, R., 'Esaïe 47 et la tradition prophétique sur Babylon', in *Prophecy* (G. Fohrer Festschrift, ed. J. A. Emerton), pp. 83–105. BZAW 150, 1980. = Martin-Achard, *Permanence de l'Ancien Testament*, pp. 237–59. Geneva, 1984.
Rabinowitz, J., 'A Note on Isa 46 4', in *JBL* 73 (1954), p. 234.

III.c.

48.1–22: THE CHALLENGE TO JACOB–ISRAEL

Isaiah 48 closes off Isaiah 40–48. Babylon and Cyrus will no longer feature in the following chapters; neither will the clash with other gods. After the commission to leave Babylon/Chaldea, the focus moves from Jacob–Israel to Jerusalem–Zion.

Through the chapter a number of words recur and contribute to a sense of rhetorical unity: 'listen/inform' (*šāmaʿ*, vv. 1, 3, 5, 6a, 6b, 7, 8, 12, 14, 16, 20), 'call' (*qārāʾ*, vv. 1, 2, 8, 12, 13, 15), 'announce' (*nāgad* hi, vv. 3, 5, 6, 14, 20), 'command' (*ṣiwwāh/miṣwāh*, vv. 5, 18), 'do/fulfil/act' (*ʿāśāh*, vv. 3, 5, 11, 14), 'come out/get out/descendants' (forms of *yāṣāʾ*, vv. 1, 3, 19, 20a, 20b). The five occurrences of 'name' in the one chapter (vv. 1a, 1b, 2, 9, 19) is exceeded in the Prophets only by Malachi 1.

The Hebrew tradition does not treat Isaiah 48 as one chapter. In A the chapter divisions are 47.8–48.11, 48.12–16, and 48.17–22; in L they are 45.18–48.16 and 48.17–49.21. A synagogue lection runs from 48.2 to 49.25. In 1QIs[a] the chapter is divided neatly into two equal parts, vv. 1–11 and 12–22. Verse 12 begins in the same way as v. 1, but parallels between the two parts end there (against, e.g., †Muilenburg). Nor are the chiastic understandings of vv. 1–21 (†Franke) or vv. 1–16a (†Grimm and Dittert) convincing. The major marker in L after v. 16 does draw attention to the formal links between vv. 1–11 and 12–16 (though †Grimm and Dittert rightly assume that the latter unit closes before the enigmatic v. 16b). In form-critical terms, vv. 1–11 and vv. 12–16a begin by calling on people to listen, in the manner of prophetic invective. Both then ricochet into something more like a disputation or court scene (see, e.g., †Begrich, pp. 19–20, 42–43 = 26–27, 48–49), which recalls Yhwh's activity at the beginning and affirms Yhwh's activity in the present, and on this basis issues Yhwh's challenge about who has spoken about these events. The relationship between them parallels one that recurs in Ezekiel whereby a 'main oracle' is followed by a 'shorter echoing one' that resumes its themes with some heightening.[1] In this instance, in the second there is specific reference to Yhwh's friend and to Babylon/Chaldea.

It is a feature of vv. 1–11 that it combines forthright confrontation of Jacob–Israel itself with those recollections, affirmations, and challenges regarding Yhwh's activity. If the subsequent unit echoes vv. 1–11, we might expect to find confrontation also to be present and heightened there. In fact it does not feature in vv. 12–16a, but it

[1] See M. Greenberg, *Ezekiel 1–20* (AncB 22, 1983), p. 137.

does appear in vv. 16b–19 (v. 19 being the point after which 1QIs[a] indents the new line). In content, then, vv. 1–11 is paralleled by vv. 12–19 as a whole. The fact that vv. 12–19 as a whole manifest a complete set of parallels with Ps 81.6b–17 [5b–16] supports the contention that vv. 12–19 belong together. This is also suggested by the fact that vv. 16b–19 begin *wᵉʿattāh* ('but now'), a particle that indicates contrast but also invites us to link what follows with what precedes: see the comment on v. 16b.

The same phenomenon of promise and confrontation recurs again in vv. 20–22, on a yet briefer scale. In vv. 20–21 Yhwh's creative activity in the distant past is once more recollected and Yhwh's restoring activity in the imminent future is celebrated. Then v. 22 reaffirms the fruitlessness of that for wrongdoers.

A further element in the patterning is also particularly clear here. The affirmations to Jacob–Israel regarding God's activity in its history each time involve imperatives. The first and longest set of affirmations begins with just one imperative, 'listen' (v. 1). The middle, shorter section includes a tripled 'listen', 'gather...and listen', 'draw near...listen' (vv. 12, 14, 16). In turn the final, shortest section brings a multiplication of imperatives over a much shorter space, and also a movement from attention to action and from listening to speaking, 'get out...make haste...announce...inform... send out...say' (v. 20). Strikingly, in contrast none of the confrontations in the three sections include imperatives. They confine themselves to statements.

In terms of the combination of good news and confrontation, the chapter thus divides into three sections beginning with vv. 1, 12, and 20 (†Mowinckel, pp. 102–4, but see also pp. 257–60). Each has the same double theme and aim, the second being shorter than the first and the third than the second, yet the second heightening the first and the third the second. Both themes and aims have recurred through chapters 40–47. At the beginning, encouragement was more prominent, but confrontation has become more and more pressing: see 40.27; 42.18–25; 43.8, 22–28; 45.9–13; 46.8, 12. Jacob–Israel is now thoroughly and incurably rebellious throughout its history, as Ezekiel had emphasized. Verses 20–22 thus take chapters 40–48 to a resounding semi-closure. The obstacles to Jacob–Israel's restoration have been removed (the images, the power of Babylon). The only obstacle now is Jacob–Israel itself. To put it another way (†Smart), chapter 48 says little that is new but brings to a climax a stress on two contrasting certainties, God's purpose for Jacob–Israel and Jacob–Israel's obstinacy. The tension stands within chapter 48; its resolution will come only with chapter 49. In the confrontation of the community, there is no sign that it relates only to a part of the community—no sign of the existence of any 'faithful remnant' within it.

The comparison and development may be summed up as follows:

vv. 1–7	vv. 12–16a	vv. 20–21
Listen	Listen gather, listen draw near, listen	Get out, make haste announce, inform send out, say
They call themselves	Yhwh calls them	Yhwh's servant Jacob
Former events new events	Speaking of old Yhwh's friend Babylon/Chaldea	Rock once split Yhwh now restoring
vv. 8–11	**vv. 16b–19**	**v. 22**
No truth/right obstinacy perversity faithlessness rebelliousness	No attentiveness	Wrongdoers
Smelting	No well-being/right	No well-being

A further source of parallelism with variation within the three sections is the way in which the community is addressed or referred to. This is advertised by the opening half-verse, which combines a second plural verb ('listen') with a singular addressee ('house of Israel') that is then described by means of a plural participle and a third plural finite verb. While second singular dominates vv. 1–11, second plural and third plural also continue to feature. In vv. 12–19 the same combination appears. In vv. 20–22 there are again three forms of reference, but second singular is replaced by third singular. The phenomena are as follows:

	2nd s.	2nd pl.	3rd s.	3rd pl.
1	House of Israel	Listen		Called Came forth Swear, mention
2				Called, lean
4	You stubborn Your neck Your forehead			
5	Announced to you Informed you Lest you say			
6	You heard, see Informed you	You declare		

	You knew			
7	You heard			
	You say, knew			
8	You heard, knew			
	Your ear			
	You betray			
	You were called			
9	For you			
10	Refined you			
	Chose you			
12	Listen, Jacob			
	Israel, called			
14		Assemble		
		All of you		Listen
				Among them
16		Draw near		
		Listen		
17	Your restorer			
	Your God			
	teaches you			
18	You heeded			
	Your well-being			
	Your rightness			
19	Your seed			
	Your descendants			
20		Get out, flee		
		Declare		
		Announce		
		Send it, say	His ser-vant	
			Jacob	
21				They thirsted
				He led them
				For them

The chapter thus takes further the playing with number and person that—significantly—already appeared as a prominent feature of the earlier confrontational passage 42.18–25.

It is possible that (e.g.) vv. 12–16a existed as an independent unit before being combined with what are now the other sections of the chapter, though it is hazardous to argue (e.g.) that its opening imperative 'listen' must mark v. 12 as a beginning (so †Kratz): see, for example, 37.17 and 47.8. †Kratz (p. 217) sees only vv. 20–21 as belonging to the original Second Isaiah; vv. 12–15, 16b come from 520–515, the bulk of the chapter from the fifth century.

III.c.i. Listen, obstinate Jacob (48.1–11)

Verses 1–11 divide into four subsections, vv. 1–2, 3–6a, 6b–8, and 9–11. They may scan as follows.

1–2	3–3–3 (removing a *maqqeph* in the first colon) 3–3–3 3–3–3 (adding a *maqqeph* in the last colon)
3–6a	3–3–3 3–3–2 (adding a *maqqeph* in the first colon) 3–3, 3–3, 3–3
6b–8	3–3 3–3–3 (adding a *maqqeph* in the first colon) 4–4, 4–4 (adding a *maqqeph* in the first colon)
9–11	4–4 (moving an accent to the middle of the verse) 3–3 (adding a *maqqeph* in the first colon) 3–3–3

With increasing clarity the subsections manifest an ABA structure:

1a	Listen, ones who call themselves...
	1b Who worship not in truth or right
2	For they call themselves...
3	I announced/caused to be heard in time past
	4 Because you are obstinate
5–6a	I announced in time past, lest...; you heard, announce
6b	I cause you to hear...; you have not known
	7 Lest you should say
8	You have neither heard nor known, for...
9	For my name's sake
	10 I am refining you
11	For my sake, for my sake...for...

The first and third elements in each subsection match each other, though each time the third element takes the point further. Thus v. 2 in due course makes a link with Yhwh and not merely with Israel. Verse 5 adds the motivation that they should not attribute events to other gods, and adds the commission to the hearers to become announcers. Verse 8 adds the motivation of their deep unfaithfulness and rebelliousness. Verse 11 adds the concern that Yhwh's splendour should not be profaned.

There are close links between the two central subsections, vv. 3–6a and 6b–8 (†Hermisson):

The first events	New events
So that I could inform of them	I am informing you
In time past	Right now. . .not in time past
Suddenly I acted	They are being created now
Because of knowing	For I knew
Lest you should say	Lest you should say
You have listened; look at it all	You have neither listened nor known. . .

There are fewer close links between the first and last subsections. Formally, indeed, vv. 1–2 constitute the introduction to a message and vv. 3–11 the message itself, but substantially vv. 1–2 are part of the message and in some respects do form a pair with vv. 9–11. The third elements in these two outside subsections with their reference to Yhwh's name/splendour thus interlink, as do the third elements in the two central subsections.

In each of the subsections the first element (vv. 1a, 3, 6b, 9) is relatively friendly. The second element in each subsection then makes the confrontational point. This is clearly so in v. 1b. It is so in v. 4, though the point is taken further in the rhythmically unexpected longer third element (vv. 5b–6a). It is so in v. 7b, though again the point is taken further in the rhythmically unexpected longer third element (v. 8b), and it is given added emphasis by the fact that v. 8 is 4–4, 4–4 and not merely 3–3, 3–3. It is also so in v. 10, though probably more so in the third element with its own unexpected 3–3–3 form (which, however, forms an *inclusio* with vv. 1–2). As the subsections unfold, the confrontational element thus moves from being a passing motif to being the impression with which the subsection leaves the hearer.

Like 40.12–31 as a disputation and 42.18–25 and 43.22–28 as court speech, as a disputation vv. 1–11 may constitute a response to a challenge. If so, the implicit challenge was that Yhwh had not told the people about the events that were now unfolding in their experience. Once more, Yhwh grants the truth in the challenge, and offers the justification for it.

The interweaving of encouraging and confrontational material in vv. 1–11 is paralleled in Psalm 81, even though the more precise parallels with Psalm 81 come in vv. 12–19 (cf †Westermann). Verses 1–11 recollect a 'salvation oracle', which in itself presupposes a lament rather than a quasi-legal charge to which this responds. They challenge people to listen. They remind them of Yhwh's unique deity, demand, and promise. They also recollect the people's stubborn disobedience and judgment, and express the frustrated longing for them to listen and find Yhwh's provision (cf also Ps 95). Since †Duhm this interweaving has seemed implausible and the two main elements have been separated, in the conviction that they represent two independent oracles or the glossing of a hortatory oracle by confrontational material, perhaps to offer an interpretation of the failure of the promises (*Schmitt). †Schoors offers a list of seven different attempts to separate the two elements, to which he adds his own. *Schmitt and †Merendino provide two more. The scholars also provide varying accounts of the process whereby the text reached its eventual form. The diversity of these views reflects differences regarding criteria, and once again suggests that if the text did come into being by such a process, we lack the means to establish its actual nature. †Hessler argues strongly for the originality of the text as we have it, which she sees as essentially priestly rather than prophetic speech.

The patterned-ness of the text in its eventual form makes it seem profitable to focus on that, as well as itself raising the question whether the text can plausibly be reckoned to have come into being by that kind of process. The parallels with passages such as Psalm 81 more likely suggest that in both instances the interweaving is original than imply that in both it is secondary, while †Duhm's view has as one of its starting-points the conviction that Second Isaiah was exclusively a prophet of comfort. This seems to impose a view on the material.

The language of vv. 1–11 has points of contact with a range of other OT writings (see, e.g., †Hermisson), especially Deuteronomy, Jeremiah, and Ezekiel: for example, 'swear by/invoke' the name of Yhwh (v. 1), 'stiff neck/brass forehead' (v. 4), 'break faith/rebel' (v. 8b), concern for Yhwh's name (vv. 9, 11), and talk of refining (v. 10). The comments on these verses will indicate that superficially parallel usages turn out to be as marked by features that are distinctive to this prophecy as they are comparable to those other works. The case is similar to that with 42.18–25.

48.1a. Listen to this, house of Jacob, people who called yourselves by the name Israel, who came out of the waters of Judah. The plural exhortation to the house of Jacob is taken up from 46.3. If the community is thought of as a household or family, it is equally natural to speak of it as one entity or as a collection of individuals. Already the exhortation 'listen' presages confrontation, and the use of the name 'Jacob' hints at the people's self-will.

As in 46.3, 'house of Jacob' is paralleled by reference to Israel (see on 40.27). These people 'call[ed] themselves' or 'were/are called' by the name Israel. Given the use of the pual of *qārā*ʾ in vv. 8 and 12, and the reflexive niphal in the parallel clause in v. 2a, it is plausible to take the niphal here and in v. 2 as having its reflexive meaning. It might then be used as a straightforward self-designation. There is nothing pejorative about the use of the niphal in 35.8; 43.7; 61.6; 62.12. On the other hand, elsewhere when Jacob–Israel is qualified, this is by terms such as remnant/survivors (10.20; 46.3; 49.6; cf 41.14) or servant/chosen (44.1; 45.4). The new modifier 'who call[ed] yourselves' draws attention to itself and invites interpretation of some kind. This instance might, then, have pejorative implications: they call themselves Israel or call themselves after the holy city, whereas in reality they do not belong to either (contrast the qal of, e.g., 43.1; 45.4). The niphal will form a double contrast with the double pual 'called' of vv. 8 and 12 (also 58.12; 61.3; 62.2; 65.1; the only other occurrence of the pual is Ezek 10.13). Later developments in the chapter will perhaps confirm this connotation.

Something similar is true of the subsequent colon, which makes a triplet of v. 1a. The third colon is, of course, in itself unexpected, though the prophet likes tricola (†Volz), and long lines will emerge as a characteristic of chapter 48. It forms a chiasm with the preceding colon, the word order being 'and from the waters of Judah came/come out'. The *w* at the beginning of v. 1aγ is explicative, like the one at the beginning of v. 1bβ (which LXX and Tg omit).

The phrase *mimmê yᵉhûdāh* does not occur elsewhere. *Leene sees it as suggesting waters that overwhelm (cf 8.8; 47.2; 54.9; also the comment on v. 18 below), but this requires much inference. More likely the two cola comprising v. 1aβγ form a pair (cf †Thomas's layout) within the tricolon and this phrase parallels the one in the preceding colon. In connection with fatherhood, Isa 39.7 and 65.9 have simple *min* ('from') with this same verb *yāṣāʾ*, and *mimmê* might be a poetic variant for *min* (†Franke), though the LXX's ἐξ Ἰούδα hardly constitutes evidence that the LXX understood the word thus rather than that it was translating loosely. Forms of the root *yāṣāʾ* are more often used in combination with the plural of *mēʿeh* ('insides'): so v. 19 below, also 49.1; and 39.7 in 1QIsª. While *mimmᵉʿê* would thus be in place here (T. Secker, as quoted by †Lowth), *mimmê* with its more usual meaning 'from the waters of' looks the more difficult reading but one that is quite understandable. 'Waters' is a recurrent euphemism in connection with sex: see the reference to a 'fountain' in Deut 33.28 (*ʿayin*) and Ps 68.27 [26]; Prov 5.18 (*māqôr*). There is a more specific parallel with the 'waters' of Prov 5.15 and 9.17, though †Hermisson emphasizes that the reference there is to a woman not a man. Thus †Jerome takes the waters to denote semen, though the Tg's *zrʿyt* ('family') need not have this implication, unlike *zrʿ* (see *DTT*; against *Leene). It is telling that the Proverbs passages constitute warnings about irregular sex, of the kind that the ancestor Judah indulged in (Gen 38). This suggests that this sole allusion to Judah in Isaiah 40–55 refers not to the people but to the ancestor.

The qatal form of the verb *yāṣāʾû* need not in itself mean that it has past reference. Such a verb in a clause continuing a participial clause is regularly qatal and takes its time reference from the participle (cf *DG* 113e). The third person verb after a vocative is also quite regular (cf 47.8; GK 144p). The Vg idiomatically renders with a second person verb *existis* (so also in v. 1b, but not in v. 2). But the participial description of the people as taking their name from Israel could naturally have past reference, and this further description of the people as having their origin in Judah confirms this understanding. The string of participial clauses in v. 1 (two actual participles each continued by a finite verb) is the most substantial such sequence used to describe audience rather than speaker (compare and contrast

44.24–28; 46.3). If such appositional clauses are elsewhere always positive (†Schoors), that will add to the sharpness of the point as this one becomes negative.

It is a separable question whether the Jacob–Israel–Judah that Yhwh addresses represents the community over the years (so †D. R. Jones) or is simply the people of the prophet's day. There are no specific pointers to the former, while the chapter subsequently seems to address the contemporary generation, as was the case when 'house of Jacob' was paralleled by 'all that remains of the house of Israel' in 46.3. These considerations support the latter. On the other hand, it would be in keeping with the prohet's rhetoric elsewhere if the lack of specificity in vv. 1–11 makes it the generalization that is then applied to the current generation in vv. 12–21.

48.1b. ...who swear by the name Yhwh, who invoke the God of Israel—not in truth and not in rightness. The first two cola closely parallel the previous two. They comprise niphal participle, the phrase 'by the name', and the name itself, then 'and' plus preposition plus masculine plural construct, then further name, then third plural verb. This last is a hiphil yiqtol verb instead of a qal qatal, so that the parallelism is slightly less close for the second colon, and makes for the usual slight novelty in the second colon. That difference also reflects the fact that these two cola, unlike the previous two, do not refer to something in the past. They point to the people's present inclination and activity rather than their past origins.

The declaring of an oath is by its nature a religious act, but it can take place in a secular context or in the context of worship. Invocation of Yhwh can also belong in the context of worship (cf 12.4). †Marti suggests that this is the significance of the allusions here, and †Westermann adds that the phrases point to worship in word rather than sacrament. If so, they constitute one of the passage's links with 43.22–28, which recognizes that sacrificial worship was impossible in exile. In implying that the audience is involved in the worship of Yhwh, they might even suggest the actual delivery of this oracle in the context of worship. Yet the phrases do not particularly suggest that context. As plausibly the two cola refer to the invocation of Yhwh as God of Israel in oaths, so that their context is secular and legal rather than liturgical. The context in Lev 19.11–13 might be illustrative. The LXX renders the second colon by a passive construction.

In v. 1bγ the third colon is both expected and unexpected. By its nature the third line is unusual, though the tricolon in v. 1a might make us anticipate it or at least recognize its appropriateness retrospectively. In content its negativeness has been slightly hinted by preceding cola, especially v. 1aα with which it forms a bracket round the intervening pair of parallel closely related bicola, but those hints, too, would only be heard in retrospect. They did not presage critique as direct as this asyndetic 'not in truth and not in rightness'. The prophet declares that there is no match between words and reality, no doing of right by God that matches God's doing of right by them.

Verse 1 as a whole presents a subtly devised and ultimately disturbing ABCBCD pattern. Syntactically vv. 1–2 contain nothing that constitutes a message that the audience is supposed to 'listen to', nothing that explains 'this'. In that sense vv. 1–2 are not a self-contained unit but merely an introduction to vv. 3–6a (cf †Bentzen). But substantially the syntactically harmless participial clauses in vv. 1–2, and especially v. 1bγ, constitute that message, the 'this'.

†Duhm saw v. 1bγ as a question and then as introducing v. 2 rather than closing off v. 1: 'Surely it is not in truth and rightness that they call themselves…'. The phrase might indeed look forward as well as backward: †Franke notes that this line alone in vv. 1–2 includes no name (for God or the people or the city) and suggests that the one nameless line thus characterizes the whole. But its specific legal/verbal connotations suggest that the MT was right to assume that it had an intrinsic link with what precedes. It also seems a shame to destroy the MT's neat triple tricolon structure, by dissociating this final colon from v. 1. Further, there is no contextual reason for understanding the negative *lō*ʾ to have the meaning of the interrogative *hălō*ʾ. Significantly, when the Tg understands the colon as a rhetorical question about the reliability of Yhwh's word, it renders *lō*ʾ by *hl*ʾ. To understand the closing phrase as meaning 'not on the basis of truth and rightness' and as thus indicating that the people's election was not based on works (†Alexander) also both ignores the words' specific connotations and requires too much reading in.

48.2. For they call themselves after the holy city and lean on the God of Israel whose name is almighty Yhwh. A third 3–3–3 tricolon completes the first subsection. It relates back to v. 1a verbally by the recurrence of the niphal 'call themselves' and syntactically by the *kî* with which it opens. We have noted that 'not in truth and not in rightness' links intrinsically with the preceding cola. It is thus unlikely that we should see v. 2 as a noun clause dependent on it, with the *kî* meaning 'that' (†Klostermann). Nor is it likely that this opening *kî* could be heard to mean 'although' (†Muilenburg). *Leene takes it as asseverative, comparing 43.22. The comparison is apposite, but we have argued that in 43.22 as elsewhere (see on 40.2aβ) *kî* keeps some causal meaning. Here, too, it again has the regular meaning 'for', which holds in contexts such as these. The LXX has καὶ ('and').

†Duhm takes the link to be with 'not in truth and not in rightness', the calling/relying then being pejorative, but this seems too subtle. More likely the link is with the substance of v. 1 and perhaps specifically with v. 1a, the first tricolon. The pairing of divine names links v. 1bαβ with v. 2aβb. As the former was already linked in parallelism with v. 1aβγ, this tightens the interwoven relationships of vv. 1–2 as a whole. The divine names come in chiastic order in v.

2aβb and v. 1bαβ, with the development that in the last colon unqualified 'Yhwh' becomes 'almighty Yhwh'. These links make it unlikely that v. 2 refers to a different group from that in v. 1 (against D. N. Freedman, as quoted in †Franke).

'Call themselves after' (*qārā*ʾ ni followed by *min*) does not occur elsewhere, but clearly enough it suggests that the people identify with Jerusalem (cf Ps 87.5–6). The LXX's ἀντεχόμενοι ('cleave to') assimilates to the parallel colon (†Ziegler, p. 160). In the parallelism within vv. 1–2 as a whole and particularly that between vv. 1aβγ and 2a, the reference to 'the holy city' gives more precision to 'the waters of Judah' in v. 1aγ while repeating the verb from v. 1aβ. The phrase 'holy city' appears here for the first time—it is not yet a conventional characterization of Jerusalem. The Tg has 'for in the holy city is their portion'.

Verse 2aβ completes the parallelism between v. 2a and v. 1aβγ, at each point augmenting it. 'Lean' (*sāmak*) is a new verb to describe the people's attitude to God, and 'Israel' becomes 'the God of Israel'.

48.3. I announced the first events in time past. From my mouth they came out so that I could inform of them. Suddenly I acted and they came about. In returning to the claim to have announced events and made them happen, which now runs through vv. 3–8, Yhwh now addresses Jacob–Israel more overtly than was the case in earlier court scenes. The identity of the first events is again unstated, and we should likely not seek to give precision to the term's meaning. Verses 1–11 is a general statement.

The Tg reduces the anthropomorphism in v. 3aβ to 'from my word they came out'. 1QIs[a] has *yṣʾh*, which looks feminine singular, but the MT's *yāṣ*[e]*ʾû* repeats the form from v. 1a (except that the latter is in pause). The audience came out from Judah; words came out from Yhwh to meet them. The oddity in the next verb, *w*[e]*ʾašmîʿēm*, is the pointing of the copula. One would have expected *w*-consecutive with the meaning 'and I informed of them' (cf Vg, Syr, Tg, also LXX's καὶ ἀκουστὸν ἐγένετο). We have taken the MT as a purpose clause (so †Franke) rather than an example of the deliberate turning of *w*-consecutive into future (see *TTH* 174) or a frequentative (GK 107b). The masculine suffix presumably refers to 'the first events', even though *hāriʾšōnôt* is feminine.

The first colon has referred both to Yhwh's acts (the first events) and to Yhwh's anticipatory words about them ('I announced in time past'). The two succeeding cola amplify each in turn, chiastically and in parallelism with each other. The second has thus referred twice to Yhwh's speaking, while the third then refers twice to Yhwh's acting which issues from and fulfils those words. It is semantically and rhetorically less plausible to take 'I acted' to refer to Yhwh's speaking (with †Franke). Each time the colon comprises an adverbial expression, a qatal verb, and a wayyiqtol verb. In the second colon the verbs are third person then first, in the third the reverse. The difference between coordinating *w* and consecutive *w* makes for further variation within the parallelism, but it may also reflect a difference between words and acts. In v. 3aβ the two verbs refer to one act of communication, in v. 3b the two verbs refer to an act and its consequences. The pattern of word, word, act, and result recalls Genesis 1.

48.4. Because I knew that you are hard, your neck an iron sinew, your forehead brass... Yet another tricolon explains the background to v. 3, though syntactically v. 4 more likely leads into v. 5 than hangs onto v. 3 (cf Deut 7.7–8). As is the case in v. 3, the first colon makes the point in summary, and the second and third form parallel expansions of it, in chiastic word-order. The infinitival expression (literally 'because of my knowing') leaves open whether this is a past or a present knowing. If we have to choose, the past reference of the main verbs in v. 5a would disambiguate v. 4 and suggest a past reference here. The characteristic that Yhwh goes on to note is one that emerged clearly at a particular past moment, at Sinai, and this might imply that the noun clauses themselves refer to the past. But it is as significant that even Yhwh's past knowing related to an ongoing characteristic that importantly continues into the present of prophet and hearers, so we may appropriately render the noun clauses in v. 4 by a present tense.

'Hard' (*qāšeh*) commonly occurs in combination with a term for spirit, heart, face, or most often neck (e.g. Exod 32.9; 33.3, 5; 34.9). Now 'neck' (*ʿōrep*) appears in the next colon, and it seems likely that a standard phrase is here divided into two, with the word for 'neck' doing double duty and applying also implicitly to v. 4a. Jacob–Israel's hardness or stiffness lies in its unwillingness to turn its head to listen or to face in a new direction. The address reverts to the opening second singular of 'house of Jacob', making the most of the personification involved in speaking of someone with a neck and forehead.

'Sinew' (*gîd*) is used in a metaphor only here, while 'iron' (*barzel*) is used to apply to human beings elsewhere only in Jer 6.28. The two cola thus seem to represent the prophet's own reworking of the 'stiff-necked' cliché, by separating the elements and re-minting the metaphor in the second colon.

The third colon again changes the anatomical reference and speaks of the forehead, the location of the eyes. The people were of brazen look. Second Isaiah's use is again distinctive in its incorporation of 'brass' (*nᵉḥûšāh*), though this is a standard rhetorical accompaniment of iron (e.g. 45.2; 60.17; Jer 6.28). The adjective comes after the noun, the opposite to the norm in a noun clause, so that the two cola form a chiasm (*DG* 49c).

מדעתי: 1QIsᵃ's מאשר ידעתי prosaicizes and/or updates the syntax. LXX γινῶσκω ἐγὼ and Syr *ydʿ ʾnʾ* imply ידעתי. For מן meaning 'because of', see JM 170i.

48.5a. I announced to you in time past. Before it should come about I informed you. The resumption of vv. 3–4 comes in two 3–3 bicola, each closely parallel, with the second syntactically dependent on the first. The first two cola form asyndetic clauses arranged as a chiasm, whose beginning also links syntactically with v. 4, its *w*-consecutive following on that causal clause (*TTH* 127γ; *DG* 79). 'I announced' (*wāʾaggîd*) repeats the sound of 'sinew', the first word of v. 4b (*wᵉgîd*), but it and most other words in v. 5a also repeat the content of v. 3 with its first person verbs and suffixes. For variation, 'come about' (*tābōʾ*) is feminine singular (Vg has plural, as in v. 3): see the comment on v. 3a on incongruence, but also GK 145. The LXX adds the explicatory ἐπί σε. Further, the verb is yiqtol, as is required after 'before' (*bᵉṭerem*: see *DG* 62), while the informing is unambiguously past.

48.5b. . . .lest you should say, 'My statue did them, my image, my idol commanded them'. It is in such statements that the inflexibility lay. An inclination to images has characterized Jacob–Israel through its story, according to the Torah and the Prophets. In the parallelism the second verb tells us the way the action of the first verb was put into effect. In each colon the subject comes before the verb, for that is the emphasis.

'My statue' is *ʿoṣbî*. At 46.1 we considered the word *ʿăṣabbēhem* and noted the way in which the resonances of *ʿāṣab* I ('hurt, pain, grieve, vex') could have carried over into words from *ʿāṣab* II ('shape') so as to suggest that images are a pain, grief, and vexation. The word *ʿoṣbî* is indeed a homonym for a word for 'my pain' (cf 'your pain' in 14.3). The existence of the homonymy makes this the more likely explanation of this *hapax legomenon* than the suggestion that the original word has been bowdlerized by giving the vowels of *bōšet* ('shame') to a form of *ʿāṣāb* or *ʿeṣeb* (†Torrey; and cf 1QIs[a] *ʿṣby*, not *ʿwṣby*). In the second colon *ʿoṣbî* is paralleled by *pislî wᵉniskî*, usually reckoned to denote 'my graven image and/or my forged image' (see on 40.19). The verb that follows is singular, suggesting that only one image is in mind (†Morgenstern), perhaps one cast statue (see on 42.17). The LXX, Vg, Syr have plurals.

צִוָּם: LXX's ἐνετείλατό μοι may reflect צִוָּנִי; Syr also has a first s. pronoun. But Tg אתיכונון ('directed them') supports the MT.

48.6a. You have listened. Look at it all. You, will you not announce it? The NRSV follows the MT in taking this bicolon as the beginning of a new verse, and then divides the subsections as vv. 3–5 and 6–8. This has the advantage of reckoning all the subsections to be fairly equal in length. But Yhwh continues to refer to what has been said and done in the past. Thus v. 6a more likely closes the subsection. The theme of listening and announcing then forms an *inclusio* with v. 3, though the verbs come in chiastic order in a way that brings the subsection to a searching climax. In isolation and at the beginning of a subsection this occurrence of 'listen' would be somewhat enigmatic.

To what have they listened? †Simon suggests the reference is to the prophet's words (e.g. ch. 47), which Jacob–Israel has heard and whose implementation it can see before its eyes and is to announce. The more immediate context in vv. 3–5, specifically the 'caused to be heard' in v. 3, rather suggests a listening to Yhwh's word over the centuries announcing events in advance.

The LXX omits 'look at' (*ḥăzēh*), while the Syr renders by perfect *ḥzyt*. From this †Oort infers Hebrew *ḥāzîtā*, though †Torrey infers only the infinitive absolute pointing *ḥāzōh*. The usage would then compare with 42.20 (see comment). †Morgenstern redivides *šmʿ tḥzh* ('listen, you will see'). But the imperative is quite in place. †North sees the connotation as reassuring or promissory, in line with GK 110c, suggesting 'you *will* see it'. But the context is more confrontational, suggesting 'will you not look at what lies before your eyes?'. The verb *ḥāzāh* often refers to prophetic vision (1.1; 2.1; 13.1; 30.10a, 10b) but it can also suggest the correlative perception of people who see what prophets speak of (26.11; 33.17), and it can denote a quite everyday seeing (33.20; 57.8; Prov 22.29; 29.20). The prophetic use of *ḥāzāh* is developed by the Tg's 'has what is revealed to you been revealed to any other people?'.

The pronoun 'you' (*ʾattem*) which opens the second colon is plural, as is its verb. The bicolon thus corresponds to v. 1aα, though there the order was plural 'listen' then singular 'house of Jacob'. There is thus hardly need to emend the text for the sake of consistency. Here v. 6b will revert to the singular, as there v. 1aβ reverts to the plural. Thus on both occasions there appears an isolated phrase in the opposite number from the rest of the subsection (vv. 1–2 and 3–6a), in the one case in the opening colon, in the other in the closing colon. This again suggests we should hesitate about the double emendation (pronoun and verb) required to conform the colon to the context, but also about the suggestion that the audience changes to the nations for this second colon (†Franke). The plural might reflect the fact that Yhwh is now commissioning witnesses. The word 'witnesses' has been plural each time, in 43.9, 10, 12; 44.8. The alternation of singular and plural in 44.6–8 also compares with that here. So it is these witnesses who have (corporately) listened to Yhwh's words over the centuries and had them fulfilled in their lives who are to announce what they have had announced for them and seen with their own eyes. As in chapters 42–44, the mere fact that Jacob–Israel has failed Yhwh and failed to perceive what Yhwh is doing (42.18–25; 43.22–28) by no means implies that Yhwh abandons the intention that they should become witnesses.

כלה: *IBHS* 8.2d sees the ה as an instance of an old acc. ending, which would presumably suggest 'look at everything'. Whitley (*VT* 25, pp. 685–86) emends to כלם ('all of them').
ואתם הלוא תגידו: emendations include ואתה (s.; Whitley, *VT* 25, pp. 685–

86); ראתם ('you have seen'; †Duhm); ואת מה ('and why should you...'; †Oort); ראיתה ('you have seen it'; †Kissane); ועתה ('and now'; †Budde); אמת ('the truth'—metathesis; and cf 43.9; †Volz); וְאֹתָם ('and them'—simple repointing; †Ehrlich); ואתה ('and it'; †Torrey); then תָּעִיד ('repeat'; †Marti); תגיד (s.; †Oort); תעידו ('bear witness'; †Duhm). The LXX has ἔγνωτε here and εἶπας at the end of v. 6b, reversing the vbs. P. Wernberg-Møller redivides ואתמה לוא תגידו ('and you [the long form of the pronoun, which was then misunderstood] did not foretell it'; cf LXX).[2]

48.6b. I am informing you of new events right now, secrets which you did not know. The opening verb (*šāma*ʿ hi) appeared in the first bicolon of vv. 3–6a and it thus advertises a link between the two subsections, which refer to informing of past events and informing of new ones. It also occurred in the qal ('listen') in the last colon of vv. 3–6a, so it provides a more direct link between the two subsections vv. 3–6a and 6b–8.

These have a similar structure, each comprising a pattern whereby Yhwh speaks and gives reasons (vv. 3–4, 6b–7), then does the same again more briefly but in way that does more than merely summarize the first round (vv. 5–6a, 8). In subject matter they complement each other, vv. 3–6a focusing on the first events, vv. 6b–8 on new events. Here the link verb is accompanied by the verb 'know'. Both will reappear again in v. 7 and in v. 8. The form of the verb for 'inform' in v. 3 was unexpected (coordinating *w* plus yiqtol). Here the verb is straightforward qatal, and one would at first take it to refer to past revelation, in parallel to the other verbs in v. 3. But the rest of v. 6b shows that to be mistaken. The verb must be an instantaneous qatal (see on 41.10b).

Another puzzle at first sight is what further unannounced 'new events' and 'secrets' the prophet now refers to. *Condamin sees them as the work of the servant that is soon to be expounded. But the new events need not be ones that have not yet been announced in chapters 40–47. They are once again the new events that will set the Judeans free. The word *n*ᵉ*ṣurôt* is used only here, so that it characteristically adds some spice to the non-new word 'new' in the first colon. The verb means 'keep' or 'preserve' or 'hide', so these are events that were kept hidden until the prophet's ministry. 'You', the community before the exile and in the previous years of it, 'did not know of them'. In fact Jer 33.3 has already made this point in almost identical words (cf †Sommer, p. 226). The suffix following on two feminine nouns is masculine: see the comments on incongruence in v. 3a. On LXX's εἶπας, see on v. 6a.

חדשות: on the 'unmarked' obj. following on the suffixed hi, see *IBHS* 27.3b (and contrast Cant 2.14).
מעתה: LXX's ἀπὸ τοῦ νῦν ('from now') understandably takes the prep. to

[2] 'Pronouns and Suffixes in the Scrolls and the Masoretic Text', in *JBL* 76 (1957), pp. 44–49 (see pp. 44–45).

mean 'from'. This makes sense in 2 Chr 16.9, but in Jer 3.4; Dan 10.17 the *min* is more likely emphatic (on which see *HS* 325). Even its use in the phrase 'from/right now and for evermore' might work either way. Here, 'right now' makes better sense than 'from now on': see †Stuhlmueller (p. 140) and the comments on this prep. at 40.17a; 41.24a; 43.13a.

ונצרות: LXX's ἃ μέλλει γίνεσθαι may simply be interpretative, or may imply a form of יצר ('form'), and †Ehrlich repoints to וְנִצָּרוֹת, ni from יצר. 4QIs[b] has ונו[צר]ות.

ידעתם: 1QIs[a]'s ידעתן is grammatically more correct (see above). Syr does not render the pronominal suffix and may have read the verb as יְדַעְתֶּם (so the Cairo fragment Eb 10), though it translates it as if it were יָדַעְתָּ.

48.7. They are being created now, not in time past. Before today you had not heard of them, lest you should say 'There, I knew about them'. Although not in the first person, the opening verb that describes Yhwh's action may be seen as instantaneous qatal, while the subsequent qatal verbs refer to the past, to the period from creation to the exile. 'Heard of them' (*šᵉmaʿtām*) has another masculine suffix like that on 'you did not know [them]', but 'I knew about them' (*yᵉdaʿtîn*) has the feminine suffix we were expecting before, perhaps for the sake of alliteration (†Boadt, p. 361). Contrast 1QIs[a] *šmʿtym* (cf Tg), assimilating to what follows, and *ydʿtym*. The two verbs reappear from v. 6b.

The nearest parallel to the use of *bārāʾ* in the niphal to refer to events is Exod 34.10, a suggestive parallel as Jacob–Israel is encouraged to look for a return to its land parallel to its original entry. But for similar use of *bārāʾ* in the qal, see 41.20; 45.8, and for the thought using other words, cf 42.9; 43.19. These coming events are a further expression of the sovereign power Yhwh showed in creation (see on 40.26a).

Verse 7a makes generous use of the copula. It reads literally 'they are being created now and not in time past, and before today and you had not heard of them'. †Rashi thus suggests '...and before the day [I am informing you—carried over from v. 6b], and you had not heard of them [before now]'. †Franke suggests '...not in time past and [not] before today...', making v. 7a more parallel to v. 6b, which ends in a similar way. 1QIs[a] simply omits the final copula. But this final copula more likely follows 'and before today' as *w*-apodosis (*TTH* 128; and cf †Ibn Ezra).

יום: when the meaning is 'today', היום is usual. †Duhm redivides to יומו לא ('...its day you have not...'). †Klostermann emends ולפני־יום to ולפנים, while †Volz emends ולא מאז ולפני־יום to ולא [מ]לפנים (cf 41.26); but cf מיום in 43.13. LXX's προτέραις ἡμέραις ('in former days') translates loosely (†Ottley); cf Tg's וקדם יום מיתיהון ('and before the day of their coming'). †Althann gets the LXX's meaning by understanding יום to be capable of meaning 'time', thus (!) 'past time' (pp. 4–5). This seems implausible.

V.8a. You have neither listened nor known, nor in time past did your ear open at all. 'Neither…nor…nor' is a repeated *gam lōʾ*; compare and contrast the threefold *ʾap bal* of 40.24 and *ʾap ʾên* of 41.26. 1QIs[a] precedes the first *gam* with the copula. 4QIs[b] agrees with the MT. The first two clauses take up the familiar motif of listening and knowing (cf vv. 6b–7); The LXX's οὔτε ἔγνως οὔτε ἠπίστω translates freely. The Tg turns the three clauses into three separate accusations, of failing to respond to the prophets, the torah, or the Sinai covenant's blessings and curses.

The verb in the second colon is uncertain. Out of context the obvious meaning of MT *pittᵉḥāh ʾozneka* is 'she did not open your ear' (pi). In the context rather distantly, †Levy suggests that the subject of the piel verb is *ḥădāšôt* ('new events') in v. 6. The MT's pointing might imply niphal, 'your ear did not open', as if the form were *niptᵉḥāh* (†North), to which †Graetz emends the text; cf 35.5. The Cairo fragment Eb 10 has *puttᵉḥāh* (pu), '[your ear] was not opened' (*HUB*; cf Syr *ʾtpth*, Vg *aperta est*). M. Dahood, *Proverbs* (see on 45.8b), suggests this form, which he parses as qal passive. 1QIs[a] has *ptḥt*, apparently second person qal, 'you did not open' (cf Tg *ʾrkynt*ʾ, 'you did not bend'). This looks like assimilation to the first colon. The LXX's ἤνοιξα suggests *pātaḥtî*, 'I did not open' (†Duhm), but might be assimilation to v. 8b. †Budde suggests passive participle *pᵉtûḥāh*. According to GK 52k, 'intensive' piel can sometimes be intransitive, suggesting 'your ear did not open at all', it was tight shut. The expression is a litotes. GK then declares that this instance should be emended to niphal, though the recurrence in 60.11 (also Cant 7.13 [12]) would surely make it more likely that it should be understood in the light of GK 52k. But *Piʿel*, pp. 50–52, questions the existence of intransitive piel. Here, in the second colon and following the third *gam lōʾ*, one would expect some distinctive form to heighten the effect (†Franke), and it is noteworthy that 45.8 also contains a unique intransitive use of the qal of *pātaḥ*. The piel equivalent here might be resultative, drawing attention to the closedness of the ears rather than the act of closing them (many late medieval Hebrew MSS, LXX, and Syr do have plural 'ears'; see *HUB*).

שָׁמַעְתָּ: 1QIs[a] שמעתי, assimilating to the first person vb in v. 7b.

48.8b. For I knew you would keep breaking faith. Rebel from birth, you were called. Once again the *kî* likely keeps its causal significance (see on 40.2aβ) rather than being merely asseverative or concessive. The 'for' then relates to v. 7, both v. 8a and v. 8b being parallel explanations of v. 7.

'Keep breaking faith' is the verb *bāgad*, which is used for various forms of reneging on an obligation, going back on one's word, and being unfaithful in a relationship (see *ThWAT* on *bāgad*). The verb is repeated, infinitive absolute preceding qatal. This word order has been reckoned to emphasize the verbal idea, with the reverse word order suggesting repetition (cf GK 113). The doubling of the verb here would underline a sense of scandal at what is spoken of—'they actually break faith'; compare the varying repetitions of this verb and the noun *beged* in 24.16; 33.1; Jer 3.20; 5.11; 12.1; Mal 2.10–11, 14–16. But the distinction over word order is probably overstated, and in a number of passages the infinitive preceding the finite verb seems to denote repetition; JM 123k sees v. 8 as an instance (see further *EWS*, chapter 5; *IBHS* 35.3.1; *DG* 101).

While 'breaking faith' might suggest that the image here is that of marriage, 'rebel' disambiguates the verb and implies that the image is rather that of parent and children (cf 1.2–3). 'From birth' (*mibbeṭen*, lit. 'from the belly/womb': see on 44.2) in turn clarifies the form of emphasis provided by the repetition of the verb.

The verb *qōrāʾ* is qal passive (*IBHS* 22.6b); the expression is indefinite, literally '[it was] called to you'. 1QIs[a] has *yqrʾw* in accordance with its preference for active rather than passive impersonal forms (Rubinstein, *VT* 5, p. 187); cf Vg *vocavi te* ('I called you'), also Tg. †Jerome may have read it as *qārāʾ* (see †Kedar-Kopfstein, p. 182). 4QIs[d] agrees with the MT.

ידעתי: the כי to introduce the obj. cl. is omitted (cf GK 157a, *DG* 90b), as in the English. 1QIs[a] supplies כיא to make the construction easier (†Rubinstein, p. 319).

48.9. For the sake of my name I will delay my anger, for the sake of my praise I will muzzle it for you, so that I do not cut you off. The LXX has δείξω σοι ('I will show you [my anger]'), from which †Klostermann infers *ʾarʾekā* for the MT's *ʾaʾărîk*. The MT might be assimilating to 30.30 (†Ziegler, p. 160) †Feldmann understands the MT to indicate that Yhwh intends to 'hold onto' anger with a view to expressing it. The almost universal meaning of the verb *ʾārak* (hi) is 'prolong', which suggests a similar idea. Only in Prov 19.11 is the verb used in connection with anger to mean 'delay'. But the adjectival phrase *ʾerek ʾappayim* ('delaying of anger', 'slow to anger') is a familiar one, especially as a description of Yhwh beginning in Exod 34.6 in the context of the original assessment of Israel as stiff-necked (cf v. 4 here). Yhwh undertakes to continue to behave in line with Israel's experience in Exodus 32–34. Yhwh will not let the logic of vv. 1–8 work itself out. This will be 'for the sake of my name' (see on 43.25)—for reasons that emerge from Yhwh's own person, but they are good news for Jacob–Israel.

We take the line as a 4–4 one, against the MT, and assume that the force of the preposition *lᵉmaʿan* carries over into the second colon (†Ibn Ezra; GK 119hh; JM 132g), as does that of *ʾappî* as object. Conversely the 'so that' clause also applies to the first colon. The LXX, Tg, and Syr understandably assume that the unfamiliar verb *ʾeḥĕṭām*, which occurs nowhere else, governs *tᵉhillātî* ('my praise': 1QIs[a] has *tḥlty*, 'my beginning', *ḥ* for *h* being a common slip). They thus render 'I will bring in/establish/preserve my praise'. But in MH *ḥôṭām* can mean the nose or snout, and in Arabic a denominative verb means 'muzzle': see BDB. *DTT* links *ḥôṭām* with *ḥāṭam*, which can mean 'to seal (up)' and thus restrain. There are thus enough likely clues from usage that could also have been familiar in the audience's day, from sound association with *ḥāṭam*, and from the first colon, to make it possible for the audience to infer that the verb denotes 'muzzle' and thus 'restrain one's anger'; *ʾap* also means 'nose' as well as 'anger'. The Vg has *infrenabo* ('restrain'), though it takes *lāk* to indicate its object, as does †Ehrlich. To put it another way, 'I will delay my anger' is both explained by and explains 'I will muzzle it for you so that I do not cut you off'. For this last verb (*kārat* hi), contrast 9.15 [14]; 10.33–34.

אחטם: †Oort reads אחתם, †Graetz אחמל עלך ('I will spare you').

48.10. There, I smelted you, and not in the silver furnace. I chose you in the furnace of affliction. The verbs revert to qatal. The NRSV renders by the perfect, suggesting a reference to Yhwh's ongoing relationship with Jacob–Israel and to its experience in Babylon; cf the smelting motif in Ezek 22.17–22. The context rather suggests another reference back to the beginning of Israel's story, in Egypt. The meanings of the verbs match this, though they might actually have been heard with two different pairs of meanings. The first, *ṣārap*, is a familiar term for smelting and refining metal (cf 40.19; 41.7; 46.6) and thus for metaphorical testing and refining (cf 1.25). It often appears in parallelism with *bāḥan* ('test'): see, for example, Jer 9.7 [6], which Sommer ('Allusions', pp. 167–68) sees as 'confirmed' here. In v. 10b 1QIs[a] indeed has *bḥntykh*, but MT's *bᵉḥartîkā* is the unexpected and more difficult reading. To complicate matters, in Aramaic *bᵉḥar* can mean 'test' (cf BDB), though it seems an oversimplification simply to assimilate the meaning of the second verb to the first. The prophet could, after all, have used *bāḥan* and did not, unless the text has been assimilated to that of 41.8 and 44.1.[3]

There is a reverse complication. According to G. R. Driver, in Akkadian *ṣarāpu* can mean 'buy', and 'I bought you' would pair well with 'I chose you'.[4] But again there were familiar ways to make that point: cf *qānāh* in 1.3, which would have made a nice link with 43.24; *šābar* in 55.1; also 43.3–4. It seems likely, then, that the second verb makes for a surprise after the first, or vice versa, rather than the two being closely linked, though the alternative renderings of each may have pleased prophet and/or audience.

The LXX is open to joining in this dialogue in a quirky way. It has πέπρακα ('I have sold'); †Ottley suggests a corruption of πέπρηκα ('I

[3] So Robertson (see on 45.9a), p. 38. Palache (see on 45.9b), p. 14, sees both meanings of בחר as deriving from the idea 'distinguish'.

[4] See *JTS* 36, p. 401, and cf *AHw*, pp. 1514–15, on *zarāpu*; but this meaning for *ṣarāpu*/*zarāpu* is not mentioned in *CAD* (cf †Hermisson).

burned'), but †Ziegler (p. 161) sees assimilation to 50.1 and 52.3. †Jerome associates a christological understanding: it was what happened to Jesus, and to Paul (cf 1 Tim 6.8).

There is a parallel pair of possible interpretations for *b^ekāsep* (pointed thus in pause). That would usually mean 'with silver', indicating price (cf 43.24), and would thus follow well on a verb for 'buy'. The LXX has ἕνεκεν ἀργυρίου ('for silver'), the Vg *quasi argentum* ('like silver'). †Lowth inferred the preposition *k* for *b*, but the Vg may be assuming that *b*, when attached to a second object, could suggest 'consisting of' and thus 'as' (*b essentiae*; cf GK 119i). †Ehrlich compares Num 18.10 and Josh 13.6. But this requires *b* to have an unusual meaning and a different one from that in the equivalent, parallel phrase in the second colon. †Torrey emends *lōʾ* ('not') to *lî* ('for myself').

In the MT, after a verb for testing *b* rather suggests the place of testing. †Ibn Ezra thus understands 'in the silver refinery' (*bksp* = *bmṣrp ksp*). More likely the noun *kûr* in the second colon also applies to the first: 'I refined you, but not in the silver [furnace]'. The furnace did not produce anything of such value. The familiar construct phrase is *kûr habbarzel* ('the iron furnace'; Deut 4.20; 1 Kgs 8.51; Jer 11.4), a metaphor for Egypt. 'Iron' suggests 'affliction' (see Ps 107.10), so 'the furnace of iron' becomes 'the furnace of affliction' by the introduction of another word associated with Egypt, *ʿōnî*. Yhwh worked hard to produce something worthwhile at the beginning, but failed. It is this significance of v. 10 that gives it a similar function at the centre of the subsection to that of vv. 4 and 7 at the centre of theirs.

48.11. For my sake, for my sake, I will act, for how should my splendour be profaned? I would not give it to anyone else. As happens in each subsection, the last verse takes up its opening verse, here with the preposition *l^emaʿan*. The Syr omits the repetition of the preposition while the Tg has 'for my name's sake, for my word's sake', and the LXX 'for my sake I will act for you, for my name is profaned, and my splendour I will not give...'. At the same time the threefold *l^emaʿan* in vv. 9–11 recalls the threefold *l^emaʿan* in 45.3–6 (see also on 43.25).

Praise and name would form a pair as in 42.12, while all three words appear in 42.8. The word 'splendour' does not actually come until the third colon. The Hebrew reads literally 'for how should [it] be profaned? I would not give my splendour to anyone else'. We have assumed that 'my splendour' applies also in the second colon, like 'furnace' in the previous line. †Cheyne calls this a 'proleptic ellipse'. The LXX makes the construction easier by reading ὅτι τὸ ἐμὸν ὄνομα βεβηλοῦται ('because my name is profaned'), perhaps introducing the word 'name' from v. 9 and/or 52.5 and/or Ezekiel 20; 36.20–23 (so †Koenig, p. 373). †König takes this as the right way to construe the Hebrew, the name being the 'logical subject' of the verb from v. 9. †Volz moves 'my praise' (*t^ehillātî*) here from v. 9.

It is not particularly remarkable that the masculine verb *yeḥāl* precedes a feminine subject, especially one that does not appear until the next colon. Indeed *kābôd* ('splendour') precedes a masculine verb in 60.1. But 1QIs[a] and 4QIs[cd] have a first person verb *ʾyḥl*; cf the Reuchlin Tg MS *ʾtḥl* (†Koenig, p. 373, suggests that the other Tg MSS were assimilated to MT); Vg *blasphemer*; Syr *ʾttwš*. The Qumran reading could imply *yāḥal* ('wait'; cf 42.4; 51.5) rather than *ḥālal* ('profane', cf 43.28; 47.6; 56.2, 6). It would suggest a resolve on Yhwh's part not to continue the delaying of v. 9 (cf 42.13–17). It might then simply result from assimilation to the first person verbs of 43.28; 47.6, and/or from visual/aural error. The previous word is *ʾyk*, the third letter also sounding similar to the third letter of *ʾyḥl*. Syntactically a first-person verb would follow more easily on the previous colon and thus might be a correction (†van der Kooij, p. 309). But it might be that the MT results from theological hesitation about the idea of Yhwh's accepting profanation: cf the pointing at Ezek 22.16, though the word survives at Ezek 22.26. The LXX would then be an attempt to construe a theologically easier but syntactically more difficult text (cf †Budde; †Kutscher, pp. 182–83 [ET p. 242]; †Barthélemy). Dahood ('Hebrew Lexicography' [see on 47.14], pp. 185–86) takes the verb as a yiphil infinitive and translates 'how can there be a delay?'

III.c.ii. Gather, recalcitrant Jacob (48.12–19)

Verses 12–19 divide into vv. 12–16a and 16b–19, the two parts taking further the twofold aspect of vv. 1–11. The first part is also subdivisible into two with a new beginning at v. 14. †Kratz compares 44.24–45.7 with the first part leading into the second. Like 45.18–21, the passage opens in the manner of prophetic address (messenger formula or challenge to listen), but moves on to become something more like a disputation or court scene with the claims on Yhwh's part in noun clauses and qatal clauses, summons to assemble, challenges in the form of the question 'Who?', and further claims on Yhwh's part to be the answer to the question (cf †Melugin, p. 137). The fact that 45.18–21 also incorporates the claim not to have spoken in hiddenness (v. 19) supports the view that 48.16a, where the claim recurs, belongs with 48.11–15.

When vv. 12–16a are considered in isolation, their noticeable structural feature is the threefold interweaving of divine commands (vv. 12a, 14aα, 16aα) with divine claims in the form of noun clauses (vv. 12b, 16aγ), qatal clauses (vv. 13a, 14aβ, 15abα, 16aβ), and yiqtol/w[e]qatal clauses (vv. 13b, 14b, 15bβ). The first and third elements with their talk of Yhwh's action and speech going back to creation (vv. 12–13, 16a) form the frame and backing for the claim in the central element (vv. 14–15) that Yhwh will act now in Babylon–Chaldea through the one Yhwh espouses. The argument thus concerns not the propriety of Yhwh's using Cyrus, as in 45.9–13, but Yhwh's capacity to do so. At the same time 'Listen to me' belongs to the language of promises of deliverance, and this is where the heart of vv. 12–16a lies (†Merendino). While echoing vv. 1–11, this first subsection in vv. 12–19 heightens vv. 1–11 by making specific reference to the one Yhwh espouses and to Babylon–Chaldea, while the single 'listen' of v. 1 is taken up both in v. 12 (singular) and in vv. 14 and 16a (plural). The sevenfold pronoun 'I' (*ʾănî*) is an associated distinguishing feature of vv. 12–16a.

In vv. 16b–19 forthright confrontation of Jacob–Israel then follows up those recollections, affirmations, and challenges regarding Yhwh's activity. The form of (liturgical) prophetic critique recalls Psalms 50; 95; and especially 81 (*Westermann); also Deut 5.29–33 (†Grimm and Dittert).

The whole may scan as follows:

12–13	3–2
	3–3, 3–3
	3–2
14–16a	3–3 (adding a *maqqeph* in the second colon)
	3–2–2, 3–2–2
	4–4–4 (removing a *maqqeph* in the first colon)
16b–19	3–2, 3–3
	3–2, 3–3
	3–3, 3–3, 2–2

Once again the language of vv. 12–19, and especially vv. 17–19, may recall Deuteronomy (*van Arragon, pp. 14–16), Ezekiel (†Fohrer), Proverbs (†Hessler), or Third Isaiah (Elliger, *Verhältnis*, pp. 116–23), but links are generally superficial and neither close nor distinctive (see the comments). We have seen that vv. 16b–19 provide the confrontational element to vv. 12–19 that forms an integral feature to each section in the chapter and thus makes the verses 'indispensable' to its structure (†Beuken).

Most striking is the special relationship between vv. 12–19 as a whole and the bulk of Psalm 81. This psalm, too, alternates singular and plural and also second and third person; like Isaiah 40–55 it affirms that Yhwh spoke in hiddenness rather than remaining speechless (v. 8 [7]), and has Yhwh expressing regret in terms of 'If only' (v. 14 [13]). The prophecy and the psalm may be laid out in parallel:

vv. 12a, 14a, 16a	Ps 81.9 [8]:	Listen!
vv. 12b–13, 14b–15, 16a	Ps 81.7–8 [6–7]:	Yhwh's claims
vv. 16b–17a	Ps 81.6b [5b]:	The authority behind what follows
v. 17b	Ps 81.10–11 [9–10]:	The first command and its promise
vv. 18–19	Ps 81.14–17 [13–16]:	Regret and promise

The parallels with other parts of the OT are more superficial and general and seem likely to derive from the primary relationship with Psalm 81, as *Westermann hints. He suggests that the links with Psalm 81 are the key to the process whereby Isaiah 48 was turned from a salvation prophecy to an indictment and threat, but the points of contact are with vv. 12–19 as a whole. If the two passages are interdependent, that seems more likely to involve this whole. We have noted that the verb 'listen' is key for this chapter.

48.12. Listen to me, Jacob, Israel whom I called. I am the one. I am first, yes, I am last. The opening resumes v. 1 and thus puts us on the track of the possibility that v. 12 introduces a section parallel to vv. 1–11, though the repetition characteristically comes with variation. 'Listen [singular] to me' replaces simple plural 'listen'. The Tg characteristically interprets 'listen to my word', while 1QIs[a] has 'listen to these things' (*ʾlh* for *ʾēlay*). †Bonnard adds 'my servant', with some rabbinic texts and late medieval MSS (see *HUB*).

In the second colon a suffixed pual participle replaces a niphal participle, 'who were called by me' for 'who called yourselves'. The self-designation gives way to a designation by Yhwh which suggests Yhwh's sovereign authority in relation to the people and/or their special status. The present tense in the LXX and Vg, ὃν ἐγὼ καλῶ/*quem ego voco* ('whom I call') perhaps infers that this calling is a naming. But if that were the idea, we might have expected the phrase 'by name' (cf 43.1; 45.3, 4), and what would be the significance of such a naming here? Since chapter 40, most references to people being called have suggested summoning, often summoning to service (e.g. 41.9; 42.6; 43.7; 46.11), and this fits the significance of the verb when it recurs in v. 13. The participle thus more likely refers to Yhwh's original call of Jacob–Israel, and the aorist translation is appropriate.

In v. 12b the threefold *ʾănî* ('I') corresponds both to the threefold *gam* in v. 8 and to the repeated 'I/me/my' in the intervening vv. 9–11 (four preformatives, eight suffixes/sufformatives). The three noun clauses thus underline and undergird the claims of vv. 9–11. Having named Jacob–Israel, Yhwh moves to self-naming. The pronoun will recur in the company of *ʾap* ('yes') in vv. 13, 15 (where 'I' is repeated), and on its own in vv. 16, 17.

The line puts together the assertive 'I am the one' with which 41.4 closes and the succinct 'I am first/I am last' of 44.6, and adds a 'yes' (*ʾap*), to construct a particularly emphatic self-declaration. The Tg expands to 'I am the one who is from the first, yes the ages of ages are mine, and besides me there is no God'. In contrast, to simplify the text, the LXX and the Syr omit 'I am the one'. Indeed, †König insists that the first four words are not two clauses but one, meaning simply 'I am the first…', but the parallels with these other passages undermine such a construing of the line.

48.13. Yes, it was my hand that founded earth, my right hand that spanned heaven. When I call to them, they will stand all at once. In this characteristic assertion of Yhwh's sovereignty in relation to creation, the Tg once again modifies the prophet's anthropomorphism by replacing 'my hand/right hand' with 'my word/strength'. For the MT's *yāsᵉdāh*, 1QIsᵃ has plural *ysdw*, apparently assuming that the subject *ydy* is to be pointed as dual or plural, 'my hands', rather than singular, 'my hand'. As object Syr has *šṭʾsyh dʾrʿʾ* rather than mere *ʾrʿʾ*, assimilating to 40.21 (†van der Kooij, p. 286). Two rabbinic references also supply the definite article (see *HUB*); cf LXX.

In the parallel colon the subject is '[and] my right hand' (*wîmînî*). In some contexts the parallelism of 'hand/right hand' indicates that the first word refers to the left hand (e.g. Judg 5.26), and *Sifre on Deuteronomy* 35 (on Deut 6.8) turns this into a virtual rule that *yād* actually means 'left hand'[5] But in other contexts the parallelism rather suggests that 'right hand' gives specificity to 'hand' (e.g. Ps 138.7). The latter makes sense here. There need be no suggestion that Yhwh is undertaking the two actions in v. 13a with two different hands.

In the second colon, the LXX renders the rarer verb *ṭāpaḥ* (piel, 'spanned') in the second colon by the verb ἐστερέωσε ('made firm'), which gives it a similar meaning to the preceding verb. It is the verb the LXX used for *nāṭāh* ('stretch out', e.g., 45.12), but two nouns derived from *ṭāpaḥ* denote 'hand-breadth' and suggest that the verb more likely denotes 'span'; cf Vg *mensa est* ('measured'). †Franke's rendering 'produce' on the basis of Akkadian thus seems less likely. The picture is of a craftworker sizing up the task of creation. The fact that this second colon refers to the heavens is another unexpected element in this second colon, for 'heaven–earth' is the usual order: cf 40.12; 42.5; 44.23, 24; 45.8, 18. Here the reverse order corresponds to 45.12, where also heaven comes second as it leads into allusion to Yhwh's authority over the powers of heaven (cf also 40.25–26).

So v. 13b begins with a reference to God's summoning. The participial verb comes first, which in a circumstantial clause suggests emphasis (*TTH* 135.4). The recurrence of reference to God's calling resumes from v. 12a. The past verbs in v. 13a invite us to assume that this participle, like that earlier one, has past reference and denotes Yhwh's authoritative calling of creation into being: so the Tg. But the opposite implication is firmly given by the parallel colon which closes v. 13b, to which the circumstantial clause is linked by simple co-ordination. Thus following LXX καλέσω...στήσονται, Vg *vocabo...stabunt*, we have rendered *yaʿamdû* 'they will stand' to draw attention to the use of the yiqtol. But we assume that the colon as a whole suggests habitual activity, so that an English present would be quite appropriate. The qatal and yiqtol of v. 13b are then

[5] The view reappears in M. Dahood, *Psalms I* (AncB, 1965), p. 163; *Psalms III* (AncB, 1970), p. 281.

taken up in vv. 14a and 14b. 1QIs[a] *wyʿmwdw* is past in sense (cf Tg *qmw*).

48.14a. Gather all of you and listen. Who among them announced these events? Presumably Yhwh, the speaker in vv. 12–13, continues speaking in v. 14. It is Yhwh who issues summons such as this one in 41.1, 21. There the addressees are the nations or their gods, and here too it is they who are required to appear in 1QIs[a] (*yqbṣw kwlm*) and the LXX (συναχθήσονται πάντες). In the MT the court speech form is reworked. It is Jacob–Israel who is summoned to court. The plural 'listen' thus has the same subject as that in v. 1. The switch between singular and plural in vv. 12a, 14a, 16a, 17–19 compares with that within vv. 1–2 and 6; it is no pointer to a different audience (against †Melugin, p. 60).

In the second colon the Syr has *bkwn* ('among you'; cf some Tg MSS). Perhaps the MT conflates two traditions in v. 14a, one second-person and one third-person (†Armstrong, p. 147). But perhaps Syr is simply assimilating to the first colon through misunderstanding the rhetoric, an opposite assimilation to that in 1QIs[a] and the LXX. In this chapter, a change to third person is not surprising even if the entities referred to are unchanged (again, cf vv. 1–2). But in v. 14a, while the descendants of Jacob–Israel are the addressees, the question is not whether they themselves announced the events but whether the gods to whom they are tempted to transfer their allegiance did so.

וּשֲׁמָעוּ: for the vocalization of the (pausal) form, see GK 10g. 1QIs[a] has וישׁמעו, LXX καὶ ἀκούσονται, continuing their third person construction. Tg and Vg have straightforward imperatives, ושמעו/*et audite*.
הִגִּיד: 1QIs[a] has ויגיד.

48.14b. Yhwh espouses him, the one who will fulfil his desire for Babylon, and his arm will do so for Chaldea. Once again the prophet moves from claims about sovereignty in the original creation and in history in general to declarations about specific contemporary events. The Tg's rendering 'Yhwh because of his compassion for Israel will perform his pleasure. . .' points us to a number of questions regarding this difficult line.

First, in contexts such as this, *ʾāhēb* is a socio-political term (†Beuken). We have translated it 'espouse', a word that parallels *ʾāhēb* in being able to function both in the context of marriage and in that of politics.

Second, who is the speaker in v. 14b? It is Yhwh in vv. 12–14a and 15–16a, and there is no explicit indication of a change of speaker before and/or after v. 14b. The LXX omits 'Yhwh', which regularizes the metre (cf †Duhm). †Melugin (p. 138) takes v. 14b as a quotation of an older oracle about Cyrus, but there is no indication that this is so, and it would be preferable to understand v. 14b in a way that makes Yhwh the speaker there, too. It is difficult to take 'Yhwh' as the answer to the question in v. 14a (†Merendino), but quite possible to envisage that Yhwh is referring to 'the one Yhwh espouses'. Verse 15a shows how such an answer would feature on Yhwh's lips, in line with the first person statements in the similar passages 41.26–27; 43.9–11; 44.7–8; 45.21.

On the other hand, whose are the desire and the arm? So far in chapters 40–66, 'desire' (*ḥēpeṣ*) has belonged to Yhwh, not to a human being, even Yhwh's agent (44.28; 46.10; cf 53.10; and n.b. 58.3, 13a, 13b), while the only 'arm' that appears is also Yhwh's (40.10, 11; 51.5a, 5b, 9; 52.10; 53.1; 59.16; 62.8; 63.5, 12; 44.12 is a rather different usage). So the Tg is surely right to take the antecedent of each 'his' in v. 14b to be Yhwh rather than the friend.

Fourth, in isolation the opening phrase *yhwh ʾăhēbô* could be an independent clause meaning 'Yhwh espouses/espoused him' (cf Vg *Dominus dilexit eum*), but this is difficult to link to the context. In isolation the phrase might represent a name (†Volz compares 7.3; 8.1), but again there is no pointer to this in the context (contrast 62.2, 4, 12). More likely the phrase relates to the clause that follows. The noun could be extraposed, suggesting 'the one Yhwh espouses will...'. But that sounds odd on Yhwh's lips. This is less of a difficulty if we take the phrase as an asyndetic relative clause, '[One whom] Yhwh espouses...' (Sym); cf 41.2. †Rosenbaum (pp. 133–34) suggests rather that the construction involves the reverse of an extraposed clause (cf 41.12). 'Yhwh espouses' is then the main clause, and this leads well into the statement in v. 15. The extraposition of 'the one who will fulfil...' draws attention to this key statement.

Fifth, the Tg is surely again right to imply that *ḥepsô* leads into *bbbl* and that the force of the *b* carriers over to 'Chaldea' (GK 119hh). There is no need to add a second *b* (†Houbigant). For the preposition *b* the LXX has ἐπὶ ('against'), Vg *in* ('in'). While *b* can have a hostile meaning, this is hardly expected when it follows *ḥēpeṣ*, and in this sense the Vg is more plausible, especially if we may take it not locally (†Kratz) but in the sense of 'for', since this is such a common usage (e.g. 62.4; 1 Sam 15.22; 18.25; Jer 22.28; Mal 1.10; Ps 1.2). †Thomas apparently divides the line after *ḥepsô*, which would imply the less plausible understanding '...his desire, against Babylon and Chaldea is his arm' (†Thomas actually emends 'his arm' to 'seed'; see below).

Sixth, who is the one Yhwh espouses? The Tg assumes it is Jacob–Israel, the object of the verb on its only other occurrence in chapters 40–48 (see 43.4); cf LXX ἀγαπῶν σε ἐποίησα τὸ θέλημά σου... But the word also recalls the description of Abraham in 41.8 (*ʾōhăbî*: so †Duhm here); The Tg introduces Abraham into v. 15. 1QIs[a] also has *ʾwhby* and implies it is the prophet to whom Yhwh is committed and whose desire is fulfilled (see note); cf †Saadya and his version of 45.1aα. But †Theodoret inferred that (like that anointed) the one Yhwh espouses must be Cyrus. Although the description is different from that of Cyrus in 44.28–45.7, the role in this line looks like

Cyrus's. The description does recall that of the Cyrus Cylinder, where Cyrus says of himself, 'I am Cyrus...whose rule Bel and Nebo love, whom they want as king to please their hearts' (*ANET*, p. 316).

How the Tg construes the last two words in the line is unclear. Vg *et bracchium suum in Chaldaeis* seems to take *zᵉrōʿô* as a second object of the verb, parallel to *ḥepṣô*, but it is an odd noun to have as object of this verb, and *b* seems to need to change its meaning. GK 119hh takes the two words as a self-contained clause, 'and his arm [will be] on Chaldea'. This solves the first difficulty but not the second. †Delitzsch more plausibly assumes that 'his arm' is a second subject. 'Will fulfil his desire' also then carries over its force. 1QIs[a] omits the *w*, suggesting '...Babylon, whose arm is Chaldea'.

אהבו יעשׂה חפצו: in 1QIs[a] אוהבי וישה חפצי, the second word accidentally omits the quiescent ע while the first and third words look like an attempt to make the text more intelligible and/or a misreading of ו and י: see †Kutscher, p. 246 (ET p. 320); †Barthélemy; †van der Kooij, p. 91. †Klostermann emends אהבו to הֱבִיאוֹ, †Morgenstern repoints to אֲהֵבוֹ.
וזרעו כשׂדים: LXX's τοῦ ἆραι σπέρμα...might suggest the MT has lost a verb (†Klostermann) or suggest וזרע ('and [for] the seed [of Chaldea]'; †Feldmann). But LXX is likely to be trying to make sense of a puzzling line and may not have a different text. †Barthélemy suggests it is assimilating to 15.9, †Fritsch (p. 160) that it is avoiding the anthropomorphism. The repointing וְזַרְעוֹ would alternatively suggest 'and his [the friend's] seed [will fulfil his desire for] Chaldea'. G. R. Driver ('Notes on Isaiah', pp. 47–48) repoints וְזֹרְעוּ ('[the Chaldeans] are scattered').

48.15. I myself, I myself spoke. Yes, I called him, brought him. He is succeeding in his way. The further use of the verb *qārāʾ* makes more explicit the link between Yhwh's sovereignty over the heavens and Yhwh's sovereignty in current events. The sequence 'I myself, I myself...yes' (*ʾănî ʾănî...ʾap*) is also repeated from v. 12b (cf 46.4); again the LXX and Syr avoid the repetition and simplify the clause. We have inferred that v. 14b is a 3–2–2 line, and v. 15 is the same. Once again the prophet speaks of three stages in Yhwh's action. The first is Yhwh's declaration of intent. The next two verbs follow on without a *w* ('and'), conveying the swiftness of the sequence of actions (†North). But the second and third belong more integrally together—against MT, which locates the *athnach* between them—and refer to a second stage, the initiation of events that fulfil the declaration of intent. 1QIs[a] removes their asyndeton by dividing the words differently, *qrʾty whbyʾwtyhw*.

As for the fourth and final verb, in the context a reference to the consummation that lies ahead is appropriate and in prose we would take this as a regular *w*-consecutive. Vg *directa est* assumes rather that the final qatal verb is linked to what precedes by simple, coordinating *w* (cf †Saydon, p. 294). This perhaps makes for a more plausible view of the line as a whole, given the preceding sequence of verbs. But the verb could still then be taken as instantaneous qatal and as referring to a certain but strictly future event.

As well as typically adding the mediation of Yhwh's word, the Tg displays its tendency to add reference to Abraham: 'I myself, I myself by my word made a covenant with Abraham your father. Yes, I elevated him. I brought him up to the land of the house of my presence, and made his way prosperous' (cf †Chilton, pp. 46–48). The LXX's καὶ εὐόδωσα and Syr *wʾṣlḥt* also have a first person final verb, conforming to the previous three (†Watts) instead of letting the final phrase express itself differently as it makes its distinctive point. In the MT the one referred to is presumably still Cyrus. Vg *directa est via eius* understands the MT's expression *whṣlyḥ drkw* to mean 'his way has been successful' (cf Judg 18.5; also Isa 55.11 with Yhwh's word as subject) but it can equally be construed as 'he has made his way successful' (cf Deut 28.29; Josh 1.8; Ps 37.7). In the context the two preceding references to 'him' make the latter more natural.

והצליח: D. N. Freedman (see †McKenzie) points the verb as inf. abs. וְהַצְלֵחַ. †Torrey sees the MT's form as a composite from that inf. and a first person וְאַצְלִיחַ such as lies behind the LXX and Syr. 1QIs[a] has והצליחה; the f. form is puzzling.

48.16a. Draw near to me. Listen to this. Not from the very first was it in hiddenness that I spoke. From the time it came to be I was there. Verses 12–16a close off with a long 4–4–4 tricolon which re-expresses the content of v. 15 with its claims about Yhwh's activity. The speaker continues to be Yhwh, rather than the prophet (against †Qimchi) or Wisdom, whose speech in passages such as Proverbs 8 it does resemble (†Hessler). The addressee continues to be Jacob–Israel, as is the case through vv. 12–16a.

'Draw near' (*qirᵉbû*) is another way of challenging the people to 'gather' (*hiqqābᵉṣû*, v. 14a). 'To me' recurs from v. 12a, 'listen' recurs from vv. 12a, 14a, and 'this' recalls 'these events' from v. 14a. Yhwh's speaking and summoning 'from the very first' (*mērōʾš*) also recurs from 40.21; 41.4, 26, while in denying that Yhwh then spoke 'in hiddenness' (*bassēter*) the words also reaffirm 45.19. Some LXX MSS add 'nor in the dark places of the earth' from 45.19, to balance 'in hiddenness'.

Perhaps the history to which Yhwh refers is again the history that began with Abraham (cf Tg). Or the line might refer to the creation from which vv. 12–13 began. The antecedent of 'it' might then be the earth (v. 13; †Franke). Or it might refer to the fulfilling of Yhwh's assertions that has begun in the summons of Cyrus (†König). †Rubinstein (p. 321) suggests that 1QIs[a] *bʿt* ('at the time') for MT *mʿt* makes explicit that reference is to creation rather than the summoning of Cyrus. Yhwh's *šām ʾānî* ('I [was] there') recalls the *ʾattāh šām* ('you [are] there') addressed to Yhwh in Ps 139.8 (cf 10) as well as Wisdom's *šām ʾānî* addressed to Yhwh in Prov 8.27. This in itself undermines C. F. Whitley's suggestion that the unsuitability of the meaning 'there' supports the hypothesis that *šām* is here an asseverative.[6]

48.16b–17a. But now the Lord Yhwh has sent me with his breath. Yhwh has said this—your restorer, the holy one of Israel. The 3–2 bicolon in v. 16b has perplexed readers. If it is a later addition (†Oort), the question of its relationship with its adoptive context still arises. The MT verse division links it with what precedes, but we have seen that v. 16a has the marks of an ending, and the speaker now changes. Thus the Tg adds 'the prophet said' (*ʾmr nbyʾ*). That transition, unannounced in the MT, is easier if v. 16b belongs to a new subsection.

A look forward points in the same direction, for reference to being sent by Yhwh suggests a plausible if unique link with v. 17a as the introduction to a further address by Yhwh in vv. 17b–19. The parallel in 61.1 points in the same direction, as perhaps does Mic 3.8. Further, *weʿattāh* ('and/but now') characteristically opens a section or subsection in such a way as to establish a close link at the same time as a contrast with what precedes (†Grimm and Dittert): see 43.1a (and the comment); 44.1; 47.8; 49.5; 52.5; 64.7 [8]. While the first-person link between 48.16b and 49.1–6 is suggestive, the characteristic use of *weʿattāh* makes for a difficulty about seeing it as originally the introduction to 49.1–6 (so †Spykerboer). Admittedly *weʿattāh* can, on the other hand, function simply resumptively, and the occurrence in 1.21 might parallel this one as introducing a line that has been suspected of being an addition, but it would make an odd introduction to the *closing* line of a section or subsection. It is in the light of the content of vv. 17–19 that 'but now' seems the appropriate rendering, as is the case at 43.1 and 44.1. It is noteworthy that 43.1 and 44.1 both combine *weʿattāh* with the 'messenger formula'. Here the two elements appear in vv. 16b and 17a. This fact adds further support to the view that the new subsection begins with v. 16b.

The title 'the Lord Yhwh' (LXX omits 'Yhwh') will recur in the further prophetic testimonies in 50.4–9 and 61.1. Further, the suffixed qatal form *šelāḥanî* in 61.1 is exactly the same as that here; cf also 6.8. The form also recurs, for example, in Jer 26.12, 15; 42.21; Zech 2.12, 13, 15 [8, 9, 11]; 4.9; 6.15. On the other hand, the notion of sending is linked with the (deaf) servant in 42.19 and is probably implicitly linked with Cyrus in 43.14 (see comment).

The involvement of Yhwh's breath recalls its being put on Yhwh's servant in 42.1 (cf also 11.1–4). This, too, reappears in the testimony in 61.1. So, in the absence of other indications, the use of the first person here supports the Tg's assumption that the speaker is the prophet or a prophetic glossator. Eusebius of Caesarea takes the speaker as the Son of God and comments on how appropriately he

[6] See 'Has the Particle שם an Asseverative Force?', in *Bib* 55 (1974), pp. 394–98 (see p. 398).

uses the double title for the One who is greater than himself (Εὐαγγελικῆς Ἀποδείξεως δέκα λόγοι 5.6 [§ 231–232a]).

The MT is not clear on how the closing expression *w^e rûḥô* ('and his spirit') relates to the rest of the sentence. Vg *et spiritus eius* takes it as a second subject of the verb, which facilitates trinitarian observations on v. 16b: the Father and the Spirit send the Son (cf †Jerome; also, e.g., Origen, *Commentary on John* II 6) or the Father sent the Son and the Spirit (e.g. Origen, *Against Celsus* 1.46; Origen acknowledges the ambiguity in *Commentary on Matthew* XIII 18). In general terms, to make Yhwh's spirit the subject fits the way Ezekiel speaks of the activity of Yhwh's *rûaḥ*. In Ezek 2.2 and 8.3, Yhwh is the subject of the verb 'send' and the word *rûaḥ* appears as subject in the context (cf also 2 Chr 24.19–20; and the difficult Isa 27.8). But these links are not close. Only in Judg 9.23 and Ps 104.30 are the two words juxtaposed, and there *rûaḥ* is the object (in the latter the verb is piel); cf also Exod 15.7–8 (pi); Jer 51.1–2; Ps 147.18. There are other passages where *rûaḥ* is the object of broadly comparable verbs (e.g. 37.7; 42.1, 5; 44.3; Num 11.29; Ezek 36.26–27; Ps 51.12–14 [10–12]; Neh 9.20; see also 59.21), and a smaller number of passages where it is the subject of comparable verbs (e.g. 34.16; 63.14; 2 Kgs 2.16; Ezek 3.12, 14). Particularly interesting are Isa 61.1 where 'the breath of the Lord Yhwh is on me' is paralleled by 'he has sent me…', and Zech 7.12, 'the words that Almighty Yhwh sent by (*b*) his breath through the prophets'. Both passages might be dependent on 48.16b (though †Merendino sees 61.1 as the original). The use of the preposition in Zech 7.12 points to an understanding of *w^e rûḥô* as an adverbial accusative (cf †Saadya, and †Ibn Ezra's reference to Saadya), but the *w^e* may make it more likely that *rûḥô* is a second object. The Tg characteristically has 'and his word'.

After this novel pre-introduction to a word from Yhwh, v. 17a then gives a more conventional introduction to an encouraging message. The message's actual content will belie the introduction.

שׁלחני ורוחו: †Volz suggests אשׁלחנו לארחו ('I will send him on his way'), †Thomas שׁלח אני בחירי ('I am sending my chosen'), †Kissane שׁלחתי רוחה ('I have sent deliverance'), J. Bewer אהבי שׁלח אני ('I am sending my friend').[7] M. Dahood translates '…sends [to] me his spirit', taking the suffix as dative and the ו as emphatic.[8] It seems doubtful whether an audience could be expected to understand the line thus.
גאלך: on the form, see GK 93qq.

48.17b. I am Yhwh your God, one who teaches you to succeed, directs you in the way you should go. Yhwh's address begins precisely as the Ten Words (see Exod 20.2), and like them modifies the self-description by a reference to past acts and to Yhwh's commands. But

[7] 'Textkritische Bemerkungen zum Alten Testament', in *Festschrift Alfred Bertholet* (ed. W. Baumgartner; Tübingen, 1950), pp. 65–76 (see p. 66).
[8] 'Ugaritic and the Old Testament', in *ETL* 44 (1968), pp. 35–54 (see pp. 38–39).

the specific terms link more with Isaiah than with the Torah (e.g. 40.14; 42.16). †Qimchi renders 'teach you *for* [your] profit', which loses the parallel with the hiphil infinitive *hôʿîl* (admittedly without *l*) in 44.10 and 47.12. The LXX's 'I showed you [how] to find the way' is probably interpreting the same text as the MT. Syr apparently understands *yāʿal* as if it were *ʿālāh* ('go up').

1QH 6.20 alludes to this line: the Qumran community sees itself as directed in the holy way by God's commands (†Grimm and Dittert).

מלמדך: on the form, see GK 61h.
מדריכך בדרך תלך: one would have expected a retrospective pronominal expression (GK 155h). 1QIs[a] בה הדריכה בדרך אשר תלך provides that (cf LXX ἐν αὐτῇ) and אשר to help regularize the syntax (†Kutscher, p. 34; ET p. 44), as well as replacing the ptpl by a finite vb. 1QIs[b] מדרכיך is probably a slip for the word in the MT.

48.18a. If only you had attended to my commands. To judge from what follows in vv. 18b–19a, this three-word colon belongs more with what precedes than with what follows. It completes two 3–3 lines with v. 17bγ (cf †Thomas), as vv. 18b and 19a will complete two 3–3 lines. But at the centre of vv. 17b–18a, in form and content v. 17bβ and v. 17bγ form a parallel pair. Outside these paired cola, between v. 17bα and v. 18a there are then antithetical links in content: v. 18a indicates that the implication of v. 17bα had not been drawn. Verses 17b–18a thus form an ABBA quatrain.

The Tg reduces 'if only' (*lû/lûʾ*) to simple 'if'. Only Ps 81.14 [13] puts the word 'if only' on Yhwh's lips, but there Yhwh says 'If only you were listening to my voice', and leaves a door open for such listening to become reality. Here, the qatal verb excludes that. The people's not listening is a fact that cannot be altered (see *TTH* 140). The suggestion that *lûʾ* here is a slip for *lōʾ* (†Michaelis) thus seems implausible. Of course the facts may only be rhetorically unalterable. When people use this construction in prayer in 64.1 [63.19], it is designed to alter the facts.

The use of *lûʾ* and of *šālôm/ṣᵉdāqāh*, and the reference to attending to Yhwh's commands, hardly comprise a case for linking vv. 17–19 with Third Isaiah (against Elliger, *Verhältnis*, pp. 116–23). Indeed, the word 'command' has a context in Second Isaiah's thinking and vocabulary. Thus †Ehrlich, who repoints to singular *miṣwātî*, relates it to the command in v. 20. But this seems to depend on taking the clause to mean 'If only you would…'. L. Kopf takes it to mean 'counsel', but there is little ground for this in Hebrew.[9] Although the noun *miṣwāh* does not otherwise occur in Isaiah, the verb (*ṣāwāh* pi) comes in v. 5 and in 45.11, 12. These passages suggest that the commands that Jacob–Israel has ignored are Yhwh's commands about the events that will shape its destiny. Jacob–Israel's attending

[9] See 'Arabische Etymologien und Parallelen zum Bibelwörterbuch', in *VT* 8 (1958), pp. 161–215; 9 (1959), pp. 247–87 (see p. 197).

to them (*qāšab*) is then not a matter of obedience but of acceptance, trust, and proclamation (cf 42.23; 49.1; 51.4).

48.18b. Then your well-being would have been like a river and your rightness like the billows of the sea. The two cola form an ABCCB chiasm (*TTCHV*, p. 339). On the *w*-consecutive, see GK 111x; *TTH* 127γ. The reference continues to be to a past non-event, the past consequence of the unrealized wish (*TTH* 140). 1QIs[a] alters *wayyᵉhî* to *whyh* (see on 43.9).

Well-being and rightness (*šālôm*, *ṣᵉdāqāh*), which sum up the blessings Yhwh intended for Jacob–Israel, came close together in 45.7–8. These blessings are then characterized by means of the imagery of water that has recurred since chapter 41. On the generic use of the article on *kannāhār* (lit. 'like the river'), see GK 126o. There is no need to take 'the river' to be the Euphrates, with the Tg (as, e.g., 2 Sam 10.16; and, e.g., Isa 7.20 without the article), and earlier occurrences of this figure point away from this prosaic interpretation. In the Tg it may have been influenced by the references to Abraham in the context. In the same way, while 'river to sea' can suggest 'Euphrates to Mediterranean', that is hardly apposite to the figure here (here the LXX omits the article on 'sea'). River/sea is a common pairing, but usually in the reverse order (e.g. 19.5; 50.2; Pss 24.2; 66.6; 80.12 [11]; 89.26 [25]; Job 14.11).

48.19a. Then your offspring would have been like the sand, your own descendants like its grains. The construction continues that begun in v. 18a, and the word sequence is closely parallel to that in v. 18b. The two bicola thus form another quatrain. Both bicola run 'and your xxx would have been like the xxx, and your xxx like xxx': in other words the two bicola have in common the verb form, the preposition *k* followed by a definite noun, a noun with second singular suffix, the copula, a noun expression with second singular suffix, and a second *k* followed by a noun expression, and each line has an ABCCB word order.

Vg's use of *semen* here and in 1.9 prompts †Jerome to a happy contrast with that verse. As in 44.3; 61.9; 65.23; Job 5.25; 21.8, *zeraʿ* is followed by *ṣeʾĕṣāʾîm*. The passages comprise more than half the occurrences of the latter noun. As well as the effect brought by the introduction of this much less familiar if standard parallel noun, further variation is introduced by its being combined with *mēʿîm* (omitted by 1QIs[a] and some LXX MSS), to produce the phrase (literally) 'the issue of your insides'. The word first occurs in Gen 15.4 in a promise to Abraham, with the verb *yāṣāʾ* from which *ṣeʾĕṣāʾîm* derives. The context suggests the particular nuance of the word: it identifies offspring as the fruit of your own body (cf also 2 Sam 7.12; 16.11; 2 Chr 32.21). The use of this word, for variation, recalls the unique use of *mayim* ('waters') in v. 1, again with *yāṣāʾ*. The present phrase also forms a parallelism with variation in relation to that.

Then as a closing variation there follows the near-homonym *meʿōtāyw*, which occurs only here in the OT. In MH it means seeds, pips, or coins: cf *DTT*, which points to links in usage between the two similar words. Gray (*Legacy of Canaan* [see on 40.20a], p. 192 = 263) suggests Arabic and Ugaritic cognates. Presumably here 'its seeds' are the sand's grains; cf Tg *kprydwhy*, Aq, Sym, Th αἱ κέγχροι; contrast LXX's ὁ χοῦς τῆς γῆς, an inference from the parallel colon to make up for the word's unfamiliarity (†Ziegler, p. 94). Vg has *lapilli* ('pebbles'); *Brewer suggests 'shells'.

48.19b. Its name would not be cut off, would not be destroyed, from before me. The section closes with an isolated 2–2 line to give final expression to the grievousness of Jacob–Israel's position. The wayyiqtol verbs of the previous two lines give way to yiqtol. The LXX thus changes from aorist plus ἄν to aorist subjunctive, οὐδὲ νῦν οὐ μὴ ἐξολεθρευθῇς, οὐδὲ ἀπολεῖται.

Presumably there is some difference in meaning, and these verbs in the final colon leave the future more open. The LXX's τὸ ὄνομά σου ('your name') renders according to the sense rather than suggesting an original *šimkā* for MT *šemô*; the antecedent of the latter's suffix is presumably *zarʿekā* ('your offspring').

At the end the Tg adds 'for ever', which is doubtless implicit.

III.c.iii. Depart, rebellious Jacob (48.20–22)

A sequence of urgent commands characterizes this final brisk resumption of the chapter. Six positive imperatives dominate v. 20. These imperatives divide into two, a 2–2 bicolon urging action, and a sequence of further imperatives urging speech. The second part of the positive section comprises a sequence of qatal and wayyiqtol indicative statements about Yhwh's action that form the object of the verbs of speech, particularly the last ('say...'). These statements comprise four 4-word cola arranged 4–4 and 4–4. If we work back from these, we may ask whether v. 20a plus the first verb of v. 20b also comprise 4-stress lines. 'Get away from Babylon, flee from Chaldea' is clearly one. 'With ringing voice announce, inform of this' is another, if we hyphenate the second verb and the demonstrative. 'Send it out to the end of the earth, say' is a third.

The appropriateness for the sake of prosody of taking the imperative 'say' with the preceding verbs, against the MT, parallels that in 40.9, where 'raise it, do not be afraid, say, to the cities of Judah' forms a 3–2 line in sequence with two preceding ones. Each passage involves an urgent asyndetic sequence of verbs introducing the message.

By the end of vv. 20–21 it is clear in various ways that the speaker as well as the tone has changed. It is again the prophet, as in vv. 16b–17a.

But the section, and the chapter, and chapters 40–48 as a whole, close with a negative note in v. 22. That, too, could be read as a 4-beat line if we hyphenate ‘there is no well-being’.

48.20aα. Get out from Babylon, flee from Chaldea. With v. 20 comes a change from finite verb to imperative, once more from singular to plural (LXX keeps the singular), and from standard-length lines to a rather short and sharp one that is then doubled.

The familiar verb ‘get out’ (*yāṣā*ʾ) and the rarer verb ‘flee’ (*bāraḥ*) both appear in the exodus story (e.g. Exod 11.8; 12.31; 14.5). The latter occasionally means ‘hasten’ rather than ‘flee’ (see Cant 8.14), and assuming this meaning would reduce the tension between ‘get out’ with its connotation of joy (55.12; and cf 52.12) and ‘flee’ with its connotation of fear. But ‘flee’ is much the more common meaning of *bāraḥ*, and the prophet could have used a verb such as *māhar* (pi) to denote ‘hasten’ (cf 49.17; 51.14; 59.7). Further, *yāṣā*ʾ also occurs in the context of dangers (e.g. 52.11), confirming that both verbs suggest flight. To judge from what will follow, it is not the case that Babylon has actually fallen yet, but the community needs to be packed and ready to leave in mind and spirit.

48.20aβb. With ringing voice announce this, inform of it, send it out to the end of the earth, say... The four further imperatives make a transition from action to speech and run through two interwoven cola or lines, with a series of double- or multi-duty elements (†Franke). The two prepositional phrases apply to all the verbs, the demonstrative ‘this’ that actually comes after the verb ‘inform’ is also the object of the first verb, and the content of the message in vv. 20b–21 is the object of all the verbs, being in apposition to the demonstrative and to the suffix on ‘send it out’. The LXX omits the preposition ‘with’ and thus makes the ‘voice’ the verb’s object. The commands again call for people to be ready to leave in mind and spirit.

השמיעו: 1QIs[a], LXX, and Syr provide ‘and’. The LXX renders passive, ‘let this become heard’.
הוציאוה עד־קצה: 1QIs[a] omits the vb and has pl. (of קצו) קצוי as in 26.15; Pss 48.11; 65.6.

48.20b–21. Yhwh is restoring his servant Jacob. They are not thirsty as he leads them through the wastes. He is making water flow from a rock for them. He is splitting rock and water is gushing. The combination of a summons to praise and reasons/content in terms of Yhwh’s ‘recent’ action suggests to †Westermann the bringing together of a feature of hymns of praise such as Psalms 95 and 100 and a feature of narrative praise such as Psalm 40 (cf also Ps 126) to form an anticipatory hymn of praise or eschatological hymn of praise, though no longer in the first person (see the comments in †Begrich, p. 51 = pp. 57–58). As such its nature and its function in the context parallel 42.10–17 and

44.23 at earlier points of semi-closure in these chapters. Yet it does not take the actual form of praise in connection with an event that has indeed taken place. It takes the form of the instruction of a herald, like that in 40.9–11, though the person is rather the herald named in 42.19 (cf Crüsemann, *Studien*, pp. 50–55). The commissioning of a herald indicates clearly that the event is really happening.

The content of the message also involves verbs and images that have become familiar in the bulk of the material that has unfolded since 40.1–11. The opening verb is a 'prophetic' qatal. At the same time the reference to Jacob parallels vv. 1 and 12 (the beginning of of each section) and forms a fine contrast with the former. Although/because 'not in truth and not in rightness' is written over Jacob, Yhwh is restoring Jacob. Further, in case there were any doubt, Jacob retains the status of Yhwh's servant (the Tg has plural 'servants' for 'servant', while some LXX MSS have λαόν ['people'] for δοῦλον). It is the first time this has been noted since 45.4, and it will be significant in the light of what happens in 49.1–6.

The NRSV closes its quotation marks after this statement, at the end of v. 20. The content of the proclamation thus comprises that single 2–2 line 'Yhwh is restoring his servant Jacob'. It then renders v. 21 by an English aorist and implicitly invites us to refer the description to the events that followed the exodus from Egypt, which are implicit grounds for looking to Yhwh to care for the people after their leaving Babylon. It is clear enough that v. 21 recalls those events, not least in its use of very similar words to those in Pss 78.15–16 (†Simian-Yofre, p. 545) and/or 105.41–42 (†D. R. Jones).

But the continuity in syntax and content from v. 20 to v. 21 rather suggests that these verbs are also 'prophetic' qatal. The same significance then attaches to the closing instances of wayyiqtol (cf *TTH* 81; *DG* 82c). Whereas people thirsted after the first exodus, they will not do so after the second. The syntactical continuity, including the *w* that opens v. 21, makes it difficult to see the latter as the nations' response to v. 20 (so †Merendino, who sees the *w* as deictic). After its aorist ἐρρύσατο at the end of v. 20, the LXX changes to future with ἄξει ('he will lead') in v. 21. The subjects of the verbs in v. 21 are unspecified within them. It is natural to read them as continuing the message begun at the end of v. 20, thus providing the two subjects with antecedents, Jacob and Yhwh. Formally, v. 21 then continues the anticipatory praise to which most of v. 20 issued a challenge.

The LXX begins καὶ ἐὰν, suggesting it read *wᵉlûʾ* (*HUB*), and thus takes the first colon as the subordinate clause and the second as the main clause, which makes the entire message more of a unity as Yhwh is subject of every main verb. †Torrey suggests for the MT 'they are not thirsty in the wastes [where] he leads them'. The MT implies the ellipse of at least a conjunction but this requires the audience to supply both a relative particle and a retrospective pronoun. 1QIsᵃ has *hwlykw* for MT's *hôlîkām* (haplography).

'Wastes' (*ḥŏrābôt*) suggests the imminent wasting of Babylon and the longstanding wasting of Jerusalem with the danger and the challenge they represent, at least as much as the emptiness of any wilderness the people may have to travel through. But †Ehrlich suggests that the verb is a form from *ḥrb* I ('be dry') rather than *ḥrb* II ('be desolate'), perhaps to be vocalized *ḥărābôt* (cf †Simian-Yofre, p. 545). *HAL* does not see these as two roots (see discussion in *ThWAT* on *ḥārab*, § I). It is at least a plausible view that after a verb meaning 'be thirsty', these connotations might attach to *ḥŏrābôt*. The LXX has singular ἐρήμου.

The second pair of 2–2 lines (v. 21aβb) stand in parallelism. It is this that puts us on the track of the fact that the first two lines of the announcement in vv. 20b–21aα are also a pair of 2–2 lines—or in each case 4-stress lines. In v. 21b the word 'rock' (*ṣûr*) thus recurs, again in the first colon, 'gush' (*zûb*) corresponds to 'flow' (*nāzal*: see on 45.8a), being a rarer verb when used with this meaning, and the line closes with 'water' (*mayim*). This was also the opening word in v. 21aβ and thus forms an *inclusio* round the whole. The final *w*-consecutive conveys the logical consequence of the preceding verb: see GK 111l.

The LXX renders 'split' by a passive, σχισθήσεται, and adds καὶ πίεται ὁ λαός μου ('and my people will drink') from Exod 17.6: see references in †Koenig, pp. 3, 70–74. Fishbane (*Biblical Interpretation* [see on 47.13], pp. 220–21) sees this as instancing a 'tendency towards unifying the strands of Scripture'.

הזיל: 1QIsª הזיב, assimilating to the next line (†Kutscher, p. 176; ET p. 233). But Syr uses the same vb, *rdy*, to translate both words.

48.22. There is no well-being (Yhwh has said) for the wicked. If the line is more original at 57.21 (so †Williamson, pp. 210–11), it is also firmly embedded and indispensable here. It brings the chapters to an inevitable though grievous conclusion that takes into account the way Jacob–Israel's wickedness has come more and more into focus. The suggestion that it merely functions here and at 57.21 to divide chapters 40–66 into three equal parts (†Duhm) takes insufficient account of its integral role in chapter 48. Further, if it is derived from 57.21, it is odd that 'my God' was changed to 'Yhwh', for while 'Yhwh' fits v. 20, 'my God' would have made a fine *inclusio* with v. 16b. It constitutes a closing warning to the whole community at this dramatic moment.

The LXX renders *šālôm* by χαίρειν ('rejoice'), substituting the Hebrew word of greeting by the Greek equivalent (†Ottley).

Bibliography to 48.1–22

van Arragon, G. J., 'Reminiscenties aan Deuteronomium in Jesaja 40–55', in †Grosheide, pp. 11–16.

Brewer, A. J., 'וצדקתך כגלי הים', in *BetM* 11/4 (1965–66), pp. 94–95.

Condamin, A., 'Les prédictions nouvelles du chapitre xlviii d'Isaïe', in *RB* 19, n.s. 7 (1910), pp. 200–16.

Leene, H., 'Juda en de heilige stad in Jesaja 48:1–2', in *Verkenningen in een stroomgebied* (M. A. Beek Festschrift), pp. 80–92. Amsterdam, 1974.

Schmitt, H.-C., 'Prophetie und Schultheologie im Deuterojesajabuch', in *ZAW* 91 (1979), pp. 43–61.

Westermann, C., 'Jesaja 48', in *Studia biblica et semitica* (T. C. Vriezen Festschrift), pp. 356–66. Wageningen, 1966. = Westermann, *Forschung am Alten Testament*, pp. 138–48. TBü 55, 1974.

van Zijl, J., 'Is. xlviii 7 according to the Targum Br. Mus. Or. Ms. 2211', in *VT* 18 (1968), pp. 560–61.

Zolli, I., 'Eine Bemerkung zu Jes 48^{1}', in *Monatschrift für Geschichte und Wissenschaft des Judentums* 79 (1935), pp. 34–35.

IV

49.1–52.12: THE SERVANT AND JERUSALEM–ZION

The opening of chapter 49 has been widely regarded as marking a new division in the book, though it initially advertises no sharp transition. While A and 1QIs[a] open a new section, L, C, and R, and 1QIs[b] separate 49.1 from 48.22 with a mere setuma, while S and 4QIs[d] have no break at all. The summons of v. 1 corresponds to that in 41.1, the first person verbs recall 40.1–11 and 48.16b, and the calling of servant Israel parallels 41.8–10. Recollection in v. 1 of events that began with one's birth parallels 48.1, in the light of which the reversed references to Yhwh and calling gain new significance. In turn 48.12–19 had begun with another reference to Yhwh and calling, and had closed with a verse using the word 'insides' (*mēʿîm*) that now comes in 49.1. The bringing of Yhwh's deliverance 'to the end of the earth' in v. 6 corresponds to the declaring of Yhwh's restoring of Jacob–Israel 'to the end of the earth' in 48.20. Within vv. 7–13, the promise that people on the way to their land will not thirst but will have abundant water (v. 10) corresponds to what is implicitly such a promise in 48.21.

Following vv. 7–13, in v. 14 Zion is the speaker. While 49.14–50.3 thus introduces the theme of doubting Zion that now replaces disobedient Jacob–Israel, it in turn also links with 49.1–13. It takes up the motifs of Yhwh's being compassionate (*rḥm* ni, vv. 10, 13, 15: the verb has not come in chapters 40–48), of desolate [places] (*šōmēmôt*/*šōmᵉmōtayik*, vv. 8, 19), and of kings falling prostrate (*yištaḥăwû*, vv. 7, 23). The copula with which v. 14 begins (literally 'and/but Zion said') itself suggests a link with what precedes rather than a wholly new section (†Muilenburg). As vv. 1–6 move from the restoring of Israel to the bringing of light to the nations, so 49.14–50.3 moves from Zion's coming to acknowledge Yhwh (v. 23) to all the world's coming to acknowledge Yhwh (v. 26) (†Melugin). The theme of mother Zion and her sons runs through 49.14–50.3, as does Yhwh's use of rhetorical questions in response to Zion's doubts (49.15, 24; 50.1–2). These questions in each case then lead into positive affirmations by Yhwh.

Most MSS of the MT and 1QIs[a] begin a new section at 49.22. S and 1QIs[a] do so at 50.1, A and 1QIs[a] again at 50.4 (most MT MSS have only a setuma at these points). With 50.4–11 we come to another first-person passage, which as such parallels 49.1–6, and to further material addressing Zion in 51.1–52.12. After this, in 52.13–55.13 there are no more overt first-person statements by the servant and no more explicit references either to Jerusalem–Zion or to Jacob–Israel, though there is another servant passage, another address to Yhwh's spouse, and another exhortation to masculine plural hearers. We assume that the servant, the woman/city, and the male addressees in 52.13–55.13 have the same identity as before, but in the formal anonymity the rhetoric returns to that of chapters 40, and in a sense goes beyond it. Chapters 49–55 as a whole thus comprise three sequences in which servant passages alternate with material focusing largely on a mother/wife/daughter (though 51.1–8 and 55.1–13 exhort 'you' (masculine plural). Chapters 41–48 work with overlapping expectations and assessments of Cyrus, Jacob–Israel and the servant, with occasional explicit references to Jerusalem–Zion. Chapters 49–55 work with overlapping expectations and assessments of the servant and Jerusalem–Zion, with occasional explicit and implicit references to Jacob–Israel.

While the parallel with 57.21 carries a further suggestion that 48.22 marks the end of a section, the summons to praise in 49.13 also suggests an ending. †Lack sees the latter as closing off 40.1–49.12, using the verb *nḥm* ('comfort') as an *inclusio*. *Merendino (*Henoch* 4, pp. 297, 325), who believes that 49.1–13 concluded the original Deutero-Isaianic collection, sees 49.13 as closing off 44.24–49.13 as 44.23 closes off 42.14–44.23. This may suggest that 49.1–13 faces both ways, like 44.24–45.8. Both are 'gemstone passages' marked off by hymnic material on either side (†Mettinger, pp. 20–21). †Stassen gives precision to the way it does so: as 40.1–11 set the mainly Jacob–Israel material in 40.12–48.22 in the context of a concern with Zion–Jerusalem, so 49.1–13 sets the mainly Zion–Jerusalem material in 49.14–55.13 in the context of a concern with Jacob–Israel, for this is the concern that 49.1–13 shares with what has preceded. Thus †E. Nielsen (p. 199) sees it as forming a bridge between the two parts of the book. Alternatively we might see it as parallel to 44.24–45.8 in forming a bridge between the second and third parts of the book. Indeed, †Motyer sees 49.1–50.11 as a whole as parallel to 44.24–45.25. The fact that the voice in vv. 1–6 speaks of a development in the understanding of a vocation fits the development in thinking and motif between chapters 40–48 and 49–55 (†Williamson, p. 25). It will certainly transpire that 49.1–13 trailers themes that will be of increasing significance in 49.14–55.13.

IV.a.

49.1–13: THE SERVANT'S TESTIMONY AND ITS IMPLICATIONS

In due course it becomes clear enough that v. 1 introduces a new section with a different speaker from that in 48.22. A human 'I' speaks in vv. 1–6. A 'messenger formula' then introduces Yhwh as speaker in v. 7 and another short one introduces vv. 8–12, after which v. 13 summons heaven and earth to worship. 1QIs[a] begins new sections at 49.4, 7 (so also 1QIs[b]) and 14. The MT merely begins new paragraphs at vv. 7 and 14. Verses 7–13 follow closely on the servant passage in 49.1–6, somewhat in the manner of 42.5–9 or 5–17 after the servant passage 42.1–4. The phrase 'a light for nations' from 42.6 reappears in v. 6, and its companion phrase 'a covenant for people' reappears in v. 8. †A. Wilson (pp. 276–82) sees this as part of a chiastic patterning in vv. 1–13:

1 Peoples summoned far away
  5 Infinitival clauses
    6 'To raise', light for nations
      7 Centre highlights focus on nations
    8 'To raise', covenant of people
  9–10 Infinitival clauses
12 Captives come from far away

Verses 1–6 and 7–13 would be quite capable of standing on their own. They are formally quite different, the one a human testimony, the other a pair of divine speeches, and they have no syntactical connections. That would suggest that they are of separate origin. On the other hand, at the level of substance they have much in common and we have noted some verbal links and Wilson's chiastic understanding of them in the light of these. Both envisage Yhwh encouraging one who was discouraged. Both speak to the interrelationship of Yhwh's concern with Jacob–Israel and with the rest of the world. Both link with 40.1–11. It is again a question of whether material of separate origin was susceptible to being brought into mutual association or whether it is more likely that vv. 7–13 were designed (or adapted) to follow vv. 1–6. The close links between vv. 7–8 and chapter 42 might suggest that vv. 7–13 have been expressed or adapted to follow both servant passages. As we have the prophecies, at least, the prophet first makes explicit a commission in some way to minister to the world and not just to Israel, then implies that this calling is to be fulfilled by continuing to minister to Israel and declare to it Yhwh's deliverance.

IV.a.i. Yhwh called me to be a light for nations (49.1–6)

The passage alternates the statements of a human voice with that voice's reporting of Yhwh's words. It begins with an appeal to the world and closes with a promise for the world.

1–2 Testimony/confession (an address to be heard by the world)
  3 Yhwh's word to the speaker
4 Testimony/confession
  5–6 Yhwh's word to the speaker (events to be seen by the world)

Verses 1–6 might be described as a poem and/or an autobiographical narrative and/or a testimony. It is not a [servant] song. It utilizes resonances of several forms of speech.

First, the address to coastlands and peoples in v. 1a suggests a court speech with its original social setting at the city gate (cf 41.1; 48.14, 16). It hints from the beginning at the point where the passage will conclude, the fact that the announcement that is to follow has significance for the nations (cf 42.1–4).

Second, the testimony in vv. 1b–2 suggests the account of a prophet's call designed to buttress a prophet's prospects of being taken seriously by a community (cf 40.1–8; Jer 1.5) (†Westermann). Insofar as the passage links with 40.1–11 and forms an *inclusio* round chapters 40–48 it represents some heightening as the experience of overhearing and address by an anonymous heavenly voice is succeeded by the awareness of heavenly initiative explicitly exercised by Yhwh in person.

Third, the commission in v. 3 suggests the investiture of a king: cf 42.1–4 and Ps. 2.7–9 (†Kaiser, pp. 53–65; †Laato). The challenge to the nations (v. 1), the designation referring to birth (v. 1), the military imagery (v. 2, cf 11.4), and the role in relation to the nations (v. 6) also compare with Ps 2.7–10. Being called in the womb is a royal motif in Babylonian texts (Paul, *JAOS* 88, pp. 184–86) and several Egyptian texts speaking of the deity's involvement with the king even before his birth (see *NERT*, pp. 27–30). It could fit with the democratizing of the vision of kingship whereby Israel comes to have a kingly status and calling.

Fourth, the confession in vv. 4–6 suggests an individual thanksgiving in which before the community a person recalls a negative experience during which they spoke out concerning their travail, declared their continuing trust in Yhwh, and heard Yhwh responding to them (cf Pss 30; 116). †Begrich (pp. 49–50, 138–40 = 55–56, 140–41) sees vv. 1–6 as a whole in the light of this form. Although such laments and thanksgivings presuppose that Yhwh ultimately responds by acting, the suppliant's immediate experience is a response in word, as here (cf Ps 12).

†Duhm moves v. 5b to follow v. 3, and removes the resumptive opening to v. 6. This makes the length of the verses more even and

simplifies the complex syntactical structure of vv. 5–6. *Giblin sees the passage as combining two sayings comprising vv. 1–3, 5b and vv. 4, 5a, 6. *Merendino ('Jes 49 1–6') sees vv. 1–6 as a testimony put onto the lips of Cyrus, subsequently turned into a testimony put onto the lips of the prophet, and later still turned into a word of Israel personified.

49.1a. Listen to me, foreign shores. Attend, peoples far away. The Tg has '[listen to] my word' and '[attend] kingdoms', both common pieces of interpretation. The Syr has 'be silent' (cf 41.1). The LXX renders the end of the line διὰ χρόνου πολλοῦ στήσεται, λέγει κύριος ('for/after a long time it will come to be/he will stand, says the Lord') and thereby raises a number of issues. First, in the MT the line does sound like words of Yhwh (cf, e.g., 48.12, 14, 16, 18). Thus the LXX glosses v. 1a to indicate explicitly that Yhwh is speaking. †Ziegler (p. 76) compares 8.18 and 28.21. But the MT has no word for 'says' and assumes that the name Yhwh belongs with v. 1b, which will take hearers in a different direction.

Second, the LXX assumes that *mērāḥôq* refers not to distance in place but to distance in time, as in 22.11; 25.1; 37.26. Syr *mn rwḥqʾ* may make the same assumption (†van der Kooij, p. 277; cf *van der Kooij, p. 385). In the context of references to foreign shores, distance in space is more likely. On the other hand, the LXX is surely right to assume that *mērāḥôq* here denotes not 'from far away' (cf v. 12; 43.6; 60.4, 9; Tg *mrḥyq*; Vg *de longe*) but simply 'far away', as it more commonly does (cf 5.26; 22.3; 23.7; 59.14). The preposition *min/mē* thus here denotes 'off', 'on the side of' (see BDB, p. 578b). Verse 12 and the other occurrences offer clues as to what 'far away' might imply. Why distant peoples are being addressed will become clearer in due course (see vv. 6, 7, 12).

איים אלי: 4QIs[d] transposes, assimilating to the easier order in 41.1 (cf also 51.4–5) (†Skehan and Ulrich).
והקשיבו: 1QIs[a] lacks the copula.

49.1b. Yhwh called me from the womb. From the insides of my mother he pronounced my name. It transpires that Yhwh is not the speaker. The speaker is someone summoned into service by Yhwh, and that from before birth. In general v. 1b well illustrates the way in which the second colon in a line may repeat the content of the first in less familiar words. 'Insides' (*mēʿîm*; cf 16.11; 63.15) is less specific but rarer than 'womb' (*beṭen*; cf 13.25; 44.2, 24; 46.3; 48.8; 49.5, 15). While *beṭen* can apply to a man as the source of a baby's life or to his insides in other connections (see *ThWAT*), *mēʿîm* does so more often (cf 16.11; 63.15; Gen 15.4; 2 Sam 7.12). Here it is made explicit that it is the mother's 'insides' that are referred to. The LXX abbreviates the text.

'Pronounce [a name]' (*zākār* hi) commonly refers to the naming of

Yhwh (e.g. 12.4; 48.1), not least in connection with sacrifice (66.3). This is sometimes a naming of Yhwh by Yhwh (Exod 20.24), and †Duhm infers that here it refers to Yhwh's naming the speaker as Yhwh's servant. This seems unlikely as 'servant of Yhwh' is not a name. †Landy (p. 63) asks, 'Is he worshipping, celebrating my existence? or is the place of my coming-to-be that of YHWH's sacrifice?'. The paralleling of *qārāʾ* ('call') with *zākar* (hi) also recalls 48.1. This naming on Yhwh's part contrasts with the naming that 48.1–2 critiques.

Out of context, these could be the words of a prophet, a teacher, or a king. Here they appear in the midst of a prophet's words, and the natural way to take them is as the prophet's testimony.

אמי: 4QIs[d] seems to read יהואמי, the first three letters perhaps identifying God as the subject (G. I. Davies).

49.2a. He made my mouth like a sharp sword. In the shade of his hand he concealed me. The mouth could be a king's weapon (11.4) though the vision of a king's ministry in 42.1–4 put the emphasis elsewhere than on the destructive. The mouth is indeed also a prophet's means of acting. Perhaps we should assume that the first person suffix in the second colon applies also in the first, completing the chiasm: 'he makes my mouth like his sharp sword'. And perhaps the *k* denotes not mere comparison but identity: 'he makes my mouth into his sharp sword' (cf the use of *śîm k* in Nah 3.6). 1QIs[a] makes the point by omitting the preposition at first, though it is then added above the line. Psalm 57.5 [4], and perhaps Prov 5.3–4, suggest that the prophet is taking up an everyday expression that recognizes speech's capacity for piercing destructiveness, and applying this familiar image to the words of a prophet and indeed of Yhwh. The stinging closure to the previous chapter, and the stinging strand that runs through that chapter as a whole, have illustrated the way this applies to Second Isaiah.

What does the second colon add to the first? Shade (*ṣēl*) is regularly a positive metaphor, suggesting protection rather than the shadowy danger of darkness (4.6; 16.3; 25.4, 5; 30.2, 3; 32.2; 34.15). The shade of Yhwh's hand recurs in a similar context in 51.16. In the Psalms it is usually Yhwh's wings that provide shade (e.g. 17.8). The Tg renders *yādô* ('his hand') more abstractly 'his strength'; cf v. 22; 50.2. Since it is the prophet's mouth not the prophet as a person who is turned into a sword, the second colon probably does not suggest that the prophet is the sword hidden by Yhwh's hand, being tucked into a belt or concealed in a sleeve. It is the prophet as person not the prophet's mouth as sword that is hidden protectively by Yhwh. This fits with the fact that the notion of 'concealing' (*ḥābāʾ*/*ḥābāh*) implies more than mere location (cf 26.20; 42.22). The weapon is protected and/or kept secret.

49.2b. He made me into a burnished arrow. In his quiver he hid me. While the two cola within v. 2a and v. 2b do form pairs, in terms of actual parallelism the correspondence of vv. 2a and 2b as a whole is more obvious, so that v. 2 forms an ABAB quatrain. Both testify to Yhwh's preparation and also to Yhwh's protection. The opening verb is the same, except for the suffix. It is indeed now the prophet's whole person that is Yhwh's weapon. The preposition *l* replaces *k*, perhaps confirming the stronger understanding of *k* in v. 2a, and this time 1QIs[a] writes *k*, though it is then corrected to *l*. Perhaps the MT conflates two traditions, one with repeated *k*, one with repeated *l* (†Armstrong, pp. 148–49).

The arrow is much rarer than the sword, at least in the OT, and the arrow as a metaphor is correspondingly less familiar (but cf Pss 57.5 [4] just noted; 64.4 [3]; Jer 9.7 [8]). The burnishing referred to (cf Jer 51.11) is the smoothing of blemishes from the shaft to make the arrow fly true, and/or the shining brightness of arrows that makes possible an association between Yhwh's arrows and lightning (e.g. Hab 3.11; Zech 9.14) (H. A. Hoffner, *ThWAT* on *ḥēṣ*, § V.1). While Akkadian *barāru* means 'glitter' and the Hebrew finite verb *bārar* usually means 'cleanse', the qal passive participle more often denotes 'chosen', and this connotation may apply here (cf LXX ἐκλεκτὸν; Tg *bḥyr*; though †Ottley infers the reading *bāḥûr*). *HAL* and *DCH* distinguish a further root *bārar* meaning 'sharpen'; but see *ThWAT* on *bārar*, § III.1.

In the second colon the words once more come in chiastic order so as to continue the parallelism with v. 2a. The preposition is again *b*, it introduces another word with a suffix referring to Yhwh, and the verb is another hiphil in the same suffixed form with Yhwh as subject as occurred at the end of v. 2a. Only the actual root is different. 'Quiver' (*ʾašpāh*) is again a less common word than the expression it parallels. It occurs in connection with Yhwh only in Lam 3.12–13. 'Hide' (*sātar*), however, is more common than 'conceal' (*ḥābāʾ*), and the verb and related noun have been important words in these chapters (see 45.15, 19; 48.16).

49.3. Then he said to me, 'You are my servant, Israel in whom I will display my attractiveness'. The view that v. 3 brings the testimony to a first climax is supported by the way the line draws attention to itself by its form. It is longer than any line so far: although the MT punctuates it as 3–3, in words it is 4–4. It stands in isolation: whereas the two lines of v. 1 can be read together and the two lines of v. 2 must be so read, the single long line of v. 3 stands alone. It contrasts with the other lines in vv. 1–4 in being almost devoid of parallelism and therefore being unusually dense; it offers no breathing space. Whether read as 4–4 or as 3–3, it is a neater line than the three that proceed, which both in words and according to the MT's punctuation are 3–4, 4–3, and 3–2. At the same time the *w*-consecutive with which it begins is an unfamiliar form in chapters 40–48 (*Merendino,

'Jes 49 1–6', p. 240), though not a surprising one in a passage of testimony or narrative. It thus draws attention to the formal distinctiveness of vv. 1–6.

In other contexts 'You are my servant' could be the designation of a royal figure (cf Ps 2.7) (†Westermann), but 'my servant' is an equally natural description of a a prophet (cf 20.3, indeed) and we have seen that the natural way to read vv. 1–6 is as the prophet's testimony. This might be signalled by the standard word order with the pronoun in its unstressed position after the predicate; contrast 41.8a, which v. 3 closely parallels.

At what point did Yhwh thus designate Second Isaiah? †Whybray argues that v. 3 cannot be a re-statement of what happened at the prophet's commissioning, recounted in 40.1–8, because there it was a heavenly aide rather than Yhwh who spoke. This seems prosaic. One might expect a second account of the event that forms an *inclusio* round chapters 40–48 to heighten the presentation. On the other hand, after vv. 1–2 initially the natural way to read v. 3a is as recounting another aspect of an event that preceded the commissioning in 40.1–8, perhaps something like the commission recorded in chapter 6; v. 5a would mesh with that view. The second colon here, however, will point in a different direction. It begins with an astonishment, on most understandings of vv. 1–3a, though it is characteristic of vv. 1–6 that it keeps taking the audience in directions that we would not have expected, directions that do not fit what has preceded. The one designated is now addressed as 'Israel'.

One medieval MS omitted this word, and †Michaelis declared it a gloss (and see *Orlinsky, ' "Israel" '; †Orlinsky, pp. 79–89). This view has been urged on metrical grounds, but even if one were to grant such grounds in principle, we have noted that it is at least as easy to understand the word as contributing to a rhythmically neat line as to see it as spoiling one. A text lacking such a word might well have been glossed with it (e.g. from 44.21), as happened in LXX at 42.1, but this does not constitute evidence that this happened. Exegetically it makes for a more difficult reading and one likely to be simplified by omitting it.

The reference to Israel in isolation from parallel reference to (e.g.) Jacob is unusual (two LXX MSS have Jacob instead of Israel), though the usage in passages such as 44.21b; 45.17, 25 offers near-parallels. Yet the effect of this fact may be to make us look round for the completion of the usual parallelism. Jacob–Israel appeared in 46.3; 48.1, 12, and when Jacob comes alone in 48.20, that too is a rare usage that makes us look for a complementary 'Israel' such as this one (cf *Beuken, pp. 37–38). We do so the more expectantly, given the close correspondence between the clause in 44.23 ('Yhwh is restoring Jacob') and 48.20 ('Yhwh is restoring his servant Jacob'). The equivalent to the subsequent clause in 44.23 ('and will display his attractiveness in Israel') comes here in 49.3. If 'Israel' is not an addition to the text of Isaiah after the book came into existence but is a redactional addition to the original 'servant song' (*Lohfink), then the redactional addition effected this pairing.

The renaming of Jacob as Israel recalls Gen 32.29 [28] and 35.9–12. It is noteworthy that the second renaming leads into a reaffirmed promise of fruitfulness and land such as Isaiah 49 will once more reformulate. Yet the one designated Israel here is a different person from the one designated Jacob. Chapter 48 has made it clear that Jacob cannot function as Israel. The prophet is now to be the one who will do that. The implicit structure of the statement is, 'You are my servant, you are Israel, the one in whom...'[1] On the *ʾăšer* clause, see on 41.8aβ.

On the verb 'display my attractiveness' (*pāʾar* hit), see comment on 44.13b, 23b. In 44.23 it, too, it was linked with the vocation of Israel. †Westermann notes how odd is the notion of master glorifying servant rather than vice versa. Once again Yhwh's commitment to making human beings reflect the divine attractiveness replaces human commitment to making deity reflect their attractiveness. But the divine commitment expressed in 44.23 has moved further and further from realization through chapters 45–48. A fulfilment in the person of the prophet now replaces that—though only on a temporary basis, we will learn.

49.4a. I myself said, It was in vain that I toiled, for nothing and to no purpose that I used up my energy. The language now recalls that of a thanksgiving psalm with its recollection of a tough experience. The phrase 'I myself' renders *waʾănî*, the copula and pronoun with which the verse begins (1QIs[a] omits the copula). Elsewhere 'but/and I myself said' is indeed the language of a lament or of a thanksgiving that recollects one's travail: see Pss 31.23 [22]; 41.5 [4]; 116.11; Jonah 2.5 [4]. The content of the words recalls the prayers of Jeremiah, but also this prophet's own expectations as expressed in 40.6. It also contrasts with the promises in 40.28–31, and with the intention stated in v. 3b: 'instead of theophany...we have *tōhû*, "chaos"' (†Landy, p. 64). Indeed, both *tōhû* and *hebel* are words to describe images (e.g. 41.29; Jer 10.15). So instead of theophany we have an empty image. All three adverbial expressions come in emphatic position before their verbs. For *w[e]hebel* ('and [to] no purpose'), 1QIs[a] *wlhbl* makes the preposition explicit.

The unexpectedness of v. 4a is highlighted by the Syr. In an uncharacteristically frank and confrontational expansion it prefaces v. 4a with *wlʾ ʾmrt lzrʿh dyʿqwb* ('I did not say to the seed of Jacob'), then condenses what follows. The wording perhaps follows 45.19 (†van der Kooij, pp. 277–78; †Grimm and Dittert).

[1] Cf H. G. M. Williamson's discussion in 'The Concept of Israel in Transition', in *The World of Ancient Israel* (ed. R. E. Clements; Cambridge/New York, 1989), pp. 141–61 (see pp. 146–47).

49.4b. Yet my judgment was with Yhwh. My reward was with my God. The LXX and Vg render the opening *ʾākēn* ('therefore') with διὰ τοῦτο and *ergo*. One need hardly infer *lākēn* (cf †Ottley). 'Indeed' might be possible, as in 40.7 (another link with 40.6–8); 45.15, but the asseverative has adversative meaning in, for example, Zeph 3.7 and Job 32.8 (also Isa 53.4) and needs it here (*EWS*, p. 133; *IBHS* 39.3.5d; *HAL*; *DCH*). 1QIs[b] has *ʾk* (see on 45.14bβ). The adversative introduces a contrast between the attitude expressed by Jacob–Israel in 40.27 and that expressed by the present speaker.

EVV render the noun clause with present verbs, but the context suggests past (cf †Koole). The prophet's judgment (i.e. vindication) and reward (i.e. the glorification of which v. 3b spoke) were always secure with Yhwh, even when it did not look like it.

The LXX prefers more specific prepositions, παρὰ. . .ἐναντίον for the Hebrew's double *ʾet*. 4QIs[d] seems to prefix 'my God' with the name *Yhwh*.

49.5a. Now Yhwh has said, Yhwh who shaped me from the womb as a servant for him, to turn Jacob back to him, to stop Israel withdrawing. . . The *w[e]ʿattāh* ('now') advertises a new development (see on 43.1a), though it does not specify whether Yhwh's further words will constitute mere addition, consequence, or contrast ('and/so/but'). 1QIs[b] has *kh ʾmr yhwh*, LXX οὕτως λέγει κύριος, Syr *hknʾ ʾmr mryʾ* ('thus said/says Yhwh/the Lord'). In the MT the lack of *kōh* ('thus') means this is not quite the messenger formula, but the words make for a contrast with all that has preceded in vv. 1–4 (*Beuken, p. 27). Yhwh now speaks. The subsequent participial clause describing Yhwh's shaping of the prophet to be a servant recapitulates vv. 1–3. Shaping (see on 43.1a) summarizes v. 2, 'from the womb' takes up v.1b, while 'as a servant for him' takes up v. 3a. The whole verse will continue the long introduction that builds suspense on the way to the statement itself in v. 6.

†Westermann sees the bicolon as describing the work of the pre-exilic prophets, again because of the conviction that Second Isaiah preached comfort and not repentance. A more plausible possibility is that the clauses include in their perspective the work of Isaiah ben Amoz, which Second Isaiah carries on. But the line continues as essentially a description of Second Isaiah's own ministry. The prophet is called to embody the people's calling, but not because they have been finally cast off. How could that be? Yhwh is still concerned to bring them back, so that they can take up their calling. There are no grounds for limiting the references of Jacob–Israel here and in v. 6 to the Babylonian community (†Snaith, p. 198) or the relatively faithful within the community (†Hollenberg, p. 34).

Grammatically an infinitive such as *l[e]šôbēb* could be object of the opening verb ('Yhwh said. . .he would turn'; examples in BDB, p. 56), but the intervention of the words 'who shaped me from the womb as a servant for him' make this implausible. Bewer ('Textkritische

Bemerkungen' [see on 48.16b–17a], p. 67) ignores the subordinate clause in advocating this understanding. More likely the order of clauses suggests that *l^e^šôbēb*. . .links with the prophet's vocation. The infinitive might be understood as a gerund meaning 'in turning', as in 51.16 (cf GK 114o), but it is more naturally taken as indicating purpose. The Vg thus renders *ut reducam*. But whereas the Vg assumes that the subject of the verb is the speaker, the prophet, it seems more natural to see Yhwh as the subject, as in 51.16. †Hitzig takes this view as a way of avoiding the notion that Israel ministers to Israel, but it is doubtful whether this is any more effective than it is necessary. The bicolon still refers to the role that Yhwh seeks to fulfil to Jacob–Israel through the servant Israel.

'Turn' is the verb *šûb*, here polel, a stem of this verb that is much rarer than the hiphil and that presumably shares the piel's common focus on result rather than process (cf *IBHS* 27.2b). The verb occurs in the qal in passages with which vv. 1–6 resonate (6.10; 10.21; 44.22; cf also Jer 15.19). The LXX's τοῦ συναγαγεῖν ('to gather') suggests causing the people to return from dispersion in causing them to return to Yhwh.

The point is restated in the parallel colon, using as often a verb with a finite verb to continue and complement the infinitival expression (GK 114r). We have followed K and 4QIs[d] in reading *lōʾ* ('not'; cf also Vg, Sym, Th), rather than Q and 1QIs[a] *lô* ('to him'; cf also LXX, Tg, Syr). The latter reading implies the meaning 'and so that Israel might be gathered to him', which makes easier sense but thus seems to be a correction. †Jerome dislikes this reading, which he also attributes to Aq, because it obscures a testimony to the perfidy of Jewish people in Jesus's day. R. Tournay similarly sees K as an anti-Samaritan reading, one that affirms that (northern) Israel will indeed not be gathered.[2] K seems to imply a negative connotation for the verb, which is then reversed by the *lōʾ*.

†Sawyer suggests that the verb refers to being gathered to one's ancestors, that is, dying, as perhaps 57.1; Deut 32.50; Jer 48.33 (so Saadya, according to †Ibn Ezra, but this is not evident from †Saadya's own work). While Sir 8.7; 40.28; 44.14, and MH (see *DCH*; *DTT*) use the word absolutely with this meaning, the OT usually adds 'to their people' or some such phrase, or the context makes the point clear in another way. More plausibly the connotation is 'being withdrawn/taken away' (cf 16.10) or more likely reflexive 'withdrawing' (cf 60.20). The verb than repeats the statement in the parallel colon, with the usual variation by using a less familiar word. The speaker's task is to draw Jacob–Israel to turn to Yhwh rather than withdraw. Second Isaiah thus uses the terminology of 'Yahweh's gathering of the dispersed'[3] but gives

[2] See 'Quelques relectures bibliques antisamaritaines', in *RB* 71 (1964), pp. 504–36 (see pp. 529–30).

[3] The title of G. Widengren's article, in *In the Shelter of Elyon* (G. Ahlström Festschrift, ed. W. B. Barrick and J. R. Spencer; *JSOT* Sup 31, 1984), pp. 227–45 (a revised form of the article in *SEÅ* 41/42 [1976–77], pp. 224–34); see esp. p. 238.

both verbs a different meaning from that which attaches to them in the other context in the OT and (for instance) in Cyrus's inscription (for which see *ANET*, p. 316b).

יצרי; 1QIs[a] יוצרך 'who shaped you'. LXX MS 544 has ὁ καλέσας με ('who called me'): cf v. 1; Gal 1.15.

יאסף: LXX's συναχθήσομαι ('I will be gathered') might suggest אאסף ('I will gather'; †Torrey; he also omits לו/לא); Syr suggests לאסף (cf Robertson [see on 45.9a], p. 38). †Seeligmann (p. 116) rather sees the LXX as translating in the light of understanding Israel to be the servant (see on 42.1a), and *van der Kooij (p. 388) notes that the verb implies that specifically it is a dispersion community.

49.5b. ...as I am honourable in the eyes of Yhwh and my God has become my strength... The line begins *wᵉʾekkābēd*, simple *w* plus yiqtol, which one might see as continuing the construction and thus render 'so that I might be honourable in the eyes of Yhwh'. The gaining of honour in general might fit vv. 3b and 4b, and v. 5b does function resumptively in relation to both. But honour in Yhwh's eyes would be an odd object of Yhwh's aim stated in v. 5a. Further, the subsequent qatal clause is then difficult to interpret. Tg *wyqyrnʾ* and Syr *ʾštbḥt* suggest *waw* consecutive *wāʾekkābēd* ('so I was honourable'), which leads well into the qatal verb. But so does the MT's co-ordinating *w*. Again the prophet's description of what Yhwh intends recalls earlier description of Israel's destiny (see 43.4).

For *ʿuzzî* ('my strength') 1QIs[a] has *ʿzry* ('my support'); cf Tg *bsʿdy*. The verb *ʿāzar* will come in v. 8.

49.6a. He has said, It is slight, because of your being my servant, to raise the clans of Jacob, to turn the shoots of Israel... The long parenthesis separating the 'Yhwh said' of v. 5a from its object parallels the many long parentheses that simply qualify Yhwh's name before reporting Yhwh's actual words. In its complexity, formally abandoning the participial construction, the introduction especially parallels that in 43.16–21. Here, however, the construction is eased by a resumptive '[and] he said' (LXX adds 'to me'), which looks extra-metrical. Given the emphatic significance of the formula in v. 5a, the effect of this resumptive 'he said' is also further to underline the fact that we are about to hear Yhwh's words. The 'he said' thus heightens expectation. Verse 6a then comprises a 3–3–3 line; v. 6b seems to be 3–2–2. †Thomas links these as 3–3, 3–3, 2–2, but the second and third cola clearly form a pair, as do the fifth and sixth.

For the pairing of *qālal* ('be light/slight'; here ni ptpl: see GK 67t) with *kābēd* ('be heavy/honourable'; here also ni), which came in v. 5b, see 8.23 [9.1] (hi), an influential passage earlier in Isaiah (see on 41.4b); also, for example, 23.9; and the cognate nouns in Hab 2.16a, 16b (*Beuken, p. 29). Focus on some trivial task is excluded by the fact that the speaker was destined to be honourable in Yhwh's eyes.

The Vg renders Yhwh's opening words *parum est ut sis...* ('it is too little that you should be...'). It thus takes the verb *qālal* impersonally and implies that the succeeding *min* then suggests that this idiom is combined with the use of an attributive verb followed by *min* to express comparison (GK 133b; cf 49.19b; 50.2a). The infinitive is the effective subject of *nāqēl*: see the discussion of types of impersonal clauses in GK 144b. A similar expression occurs in Ezek 8.17. But both there and here a comparative understanding such as †de Boer's (p. 98) seems forced. JM 141i simply comments that the construction is not logically formed, but it seems appropriate to look for alternative understandings of the *min*. We have taken it to be causative (so J. Bachmann, according to *Beuken, p. 31); see *HS* 317, which notes the usage with an infinitive as here (e.g. Deut 7.7; 2 Sam 3.11).

Vg *servus ad suscitandas...*, LXX παῖδά μου τοῦ στῆσαι ..., and Tg *ʿbdy lʾqmʾ* all go on to express the same understanding of the two infinitival clauses that follow, taking these to spell out the nature of the servanthood that would be trivial. They thus seem to deny that the prophet's servanthood lay in what v. 3 specified. This is also implied by the causative understanding of *min* just suggested, because that makes these two clauses the effective, indeed actual subject of *nāqēl*. The prophet's servanthood is now being redefined in the light of the fact that for the time being it also represents the servanthood whose nature was announced in 42.1–9.

The clauses are arranged chiastically, verb–object, object–verb; the fact that the latter is an Aramaic word order (GK 142f; *TTH* 208) is surely coincidental. With a personal object the verb 'raise' (*qûm* hi) commonly means 'to bring on the scene' (e.g. Jer 23.5; 29.15; 30.9), but it can also suggest causing someone to stand firm (Ps 89.44 [43]) or elevating the fallen (e.g. 1 Sam 2.8; Jer 50.32). Especially suggestive is the use in this last connection in Hos 6.2 and Amos 5.2 with regard to the (doubtful) possibility of Israel's being raised from prostration or death. The word's precise connotation is unclear. It does not in itself clearly denote (e.g.) geographical or physical restoration (contrast the use with an impersonal object in v. 8) or restoration in relationship with Yhwh. 1QIs^b has a word ending *b*, perhaps *lhšyb* assimilating to what follows (†van der Kooij, p. 121).

The verb in the parallel infinitival clause is *šûb* as in v. 5a, though now hiphil rather than polel. LXX's τὴν διασπορὰν τοῦ Ἰσραὴλ ἐπιστρέψαι ('to return the dispersion of Israel'), as well as reflecting its concern for the dispersion to which its communities belonged, assumes that there is a substantive difference between the two forms and that this one denotes political as opposed to moral or religious restoration, as *qûm* might. But there are no grounds in usage elsewhere for making this distinction between the two forms; contrast Vg *feces Israhel convertendas* ('converting the dregs of Israel'). More likely the difference is one between a stress on result and one on process (see on v. 5a). There are thus insufficient markers for us to interpret these two clauses as having a different reference from the

Jacob–Israel clauses in v. 5a. They must have a resumptive relationship with them, in keeping with the resumptive character of vv. 1–6 as a whole. The variation in verbs is partly rhetorical. Within v. 5, the first two clauses took up vv. 1–3a while the last two took up vv. 3b–4. The middle two that define the servant's role were the new feature in between, in the middle of v. 5. It is they that are now in turn recapitulated in these two clauses in v. 6a in preparation and to raise suspense for the new statement in v. 6b.

'To raise' thus restates 'to stop withdrawing', and 'to turn' (hi) restates 'to turn back' (polel). Their resumptiveness is chiastic, as they are chiastic as clauses in relation to each other, all this mirroring in the rhetoric the reversal of the contents. As objects of the verbs, v. 6a sees the last occurrence of Israel in parallelism with Jacob. 1QIs[a] has these two in reverse order, perhaps because 'clans of Israel' is a more familiar expression (†Brownlee, p. 158). Reference to the Israelite clans (*šᵉbāṭîm*) in Isaiah comes only here and in 63.17. The actual phrase 'clans of Jacob' comes nowhere else in the OT (it is quoted in Sir 36.11).[4] It is not a stock phrase imported from elsewhere. Second Isaiah's liking for the name Jacob, not least on the way to being paralleled by Israel as here (and cf v. 5), makes the phrase quite natural on this prophet's lips. Von Rad (*Theologie*, vol. 2 [see on 40.8], p. 266; ET p. 253) infers an antithesis between the prospect of re-establishing the old clan alliance as opposed to the organization of the new Israel as a nation, but this seems alien to the context. The point of the reference to the clans lies in the anticipatory contrast with the shoots/preserved of Israel. 'Clans' by definition suggests the whole twelve-clan people. Syr has singular 'clan', though the difference from the plural is only a diacritical mark.

The people is currently a mere remnant. Here K presupposes *nᵉṣîrê* (cf 1QIs[a]), Q *nᵉṣûrê*. The former is an adjective that occurs only here, the latter a correction to the more familiar qal passive participle that would mean 'preserved/kept/protected' and seems more bland (against †Landy, p. 65). It occurs in 1.8; 48.6; 65.4, but with different meanings; for such a meaning of the finite verb, cf 42.6; 49.8; Ezek 6.12. This meaning is presupposed by LXX τὴν διασπορὰν ('the dispersion') and Tg *glwt* ('the exiles'). The prophet uses other words for a remnant/survivors in 45.20 and 46.3. †Michaelis plausibly suggested that K's *hapax legomenon* represents a word linked with the meaning 'branch' rather than 'preserve'; cf Syr, which has singular *nwrbh* to match singular *šbṭ*ʾ in the first colon. †Van der Kooij (p. 278) argues that this and other features of the Syr suggest that it has Christ in mind, but the evidence is thin. The noun *nēṣer* came in 11.1 (cf 60.21); †Ehrlich emends to its plural *niṣrê*. Historically these will represent a different root *nṣr* II, though prophet and audience might not make such a distinction. Talk of a

[4] See J. G. Snaith, 'Biblical Quotations in the Hebrew of Ecclesiasticus', in *JTS* n.s. 18 (1967), pp. 1–12 (see p. 9); P. C. Beentjes, 'Relations between Ben Sira and the Book of Isaiah', in †Vermeylen, pp. 155–59 (see pp. 158–59).

'branch' appears in 11.1 in the broad context of talk in 10.20–22 of a remnant/survivors (*šeʾār*/*pelîṭāh*: cf the words in 45.20; 46.3). This might support the possibility of seeing both meanings here. 'Clans' of Jacob would then contrast both with 'shoots' and with 'preserved' of Israel. Either way, the servant's ministry is one exercised to the remnant. Evidently this servant therefore cannot be identified with the remnant. For the syntax (object before infinitive), see GK 115a, 142f.

The LXX begins Yhwh's words μέγα σοί ἐστι... ('it is a great thing to you...'). Like the Syr at v. 4a, scandalized by the prophet's words it directly reverses the line's meaning. The Tg similarly turns the statement into a question, 'Is it a small thing to you...?' In contrast, the MT has Yhwh declaring that merely bringing Jacob–Israel back to God would be an insultingly trivial task(!) for one who is called to find honour as Yhwh's servant in the way that Israel was so destined. Honour lies elsewhere.

49.6b. I will make you into a light for nations, to be my deliverance to the end of the earth. In what, then, does the extra role consist? From the beginning Yhwh had in mind that the servant should have a role in relation to the nations. So Yhwh takes up the words of 42.6. Some LXX MSS further conform to 42.6 and to v. 8 by adding εἰς διαθήκην γένους, for a covenant of the people. The line begins with a weqatal verb that follows logically rather than chronologically on the preceding clause with its stative verb (*IBHS* 32.2.3d). Indeed, we have already implied that in a sense all vv. 5–6a and 6b do is restate vv. 3a and 3b.

The description of the servant's role in 42.5–9 did not include the term 'deliverance', but the expression could sum up that role. For the rendering 'to be my deliverance' rather than 'so that my deliverance might be ...', cf LXX τοῦ εἶναί σε εἰς σωτηρίαν; Vg *ut sis salus mea*; and cf 62.11. The servant is to 'be' deliverance as the servant in 42.6 was to 'be' covenant and light, and as Abraham was to 'be' a blessing (Gen 12.2). This may also clarify the implicit assumption regarding how Yhwh's deliverance reaches the world to its benefit. It is as it is embodied in prophet and people that the world comes to recognize it and to seek to share it. The prophet does not indicate any more concretely how light and deliverance reach the nations, though presumably it comes about in some way through the act of deliverance that Yhwh is about to bring about—the putting down of Cyrus and the restoration of the community to God and to its homeland.

קצה: 1QIsa has plural קצוי.

IV.a.ii. Yhwh makes you into a covenant for people (49.7–13)

We have noted that vv. 7–12 and 13 follow on vv. 1–6 in a fashion that is comparable to the way 42.5–9 and 42.10–17 follow on 42.1–4, reiterating the content of vv. 5–6. Verses 7–12 parallel 43.14–21 in comprising a short oracle introduced by a messenger formula, followed by a longer oracle similarly introduced which follows the theme of the first and takes it further. In each case the first, short oracle is quite complete in itself, and in each case has an envelope structure comprising a solemn introduction (virtually identical in the two cases) and conclusion which underline the significance of the oracle, belying its brevity:

7aα Solemn introductory substantiation
  7aβ The addressee
  7aγ The promise
7b Solemn concluding substantiation

As in 43.14–15 the balance of introduction and conclusion appears in their content, language, and rhythm as well as their function, as epithets reappear with subtle variation. Further, once more introduction and conclusion form 3–3 bicola (if we may move a *maqqeph* from the former to the latter), while the substance is more complex and thereby gains its own extra emphasis. Thus 43.14–15 can be read as an ABCBA chiasm, the promise being a tricolon. In 49.7 the inner two lines (2–2–2 and 3–2?) equal the length of introduction and conclusion. The first of these inner two lines (humiliation) is reversed by the second (exaltation), anticipating 52.13–53.12, so v. 7 might be seen as an ABBA quatrain.

In turn Yhwh's words in vv. 8–12 have a patterning expressed in the verbs and in the rhythm:

8–9a	I	9b–10	They
11	I	12	They

The resumptive I/they material in vv. 11–12 is noticeably shorter than the equivalents first time round; cf the comments on the structure of chapter 48 as a whole (and †Begrich, p. 12 = 20). This ABAB sequence in the verbs is enriched by an ABBA interweaving in content. The two outside units (vv. 8–9a and 12) concern the people's entering into their allocations—their being free to do so, and their journeying from the place of their estrangement to these allocations. The two inside units (vv. 9b–10 and 11) concern their provision for the journey.

Even aside from the markers of careful structure, in itself the shortness of v. 7 should hardly make us suspect the oracle's originality, though it is noteworthy that in both 43.14–21 and 49.7–12 the short oracle does not stand on its own. In each case, it would be possible to take the double oracle as a literary whole, the second messenger formula being resumptive. In the case of 49.7–12 this is supported by a possible outline of the whole:

7	Yhwh has said this:		about the nations
8–9a	Yhwh has said this:		about Israel
	9b–10	Concerning the way:	about Israel
	11–12	Concerning the way:	about far off peoples

The nations thus form an *inclusio* round vv. 7–12, as they do in a different sense round vv. 1–6, with v. 13 further broadening the horizon.

Verses 7–12 have links with the form of a priest's deliverance oracle (†Begrich, pp. 7–19 = 14–26), with that of a prophetic deliverance oracle addressed to the community (†von Waldow, pp. 86–90), and with a promise of deliverance (†Westermann):

Allusion to community lament (v. 7aαβ)
Yhwh's turning and acting—qatal verbs (v. 8a)
The future consequences of Yhwh's act (vv. 8b–12)
The aim (v. 7aγb)

The first two elements correspond to those of a deliverance oracle, but there is no 'fear not', a serious lack. Further, between these first two elements comes the aim of Yhwh's act, which belongs to the end of such an oracle. The yiqtol verbs of vv. 8–12 correspond to those of a promise of deliverance such as 41.17–20. The opening two, governing vv. 8b–9a, invite emending to *w*-consecutive. This would turn vv. 8b–9a into a statement of Yhwh's act such as belongs to the report of Yhwh's turning that comes in a deliverance oracle. †Westermann infers that the oracle has been expanded and rearranged in connection with its being linked to vv. 1–6. As it stands, by locating the statement of the aim of Yhwh's deed near the beginning, the double oracle puts the emphasis on that feature, while Yhwh's turning in v. 8a is also then given some emphasis by the resumptive messenger formula. It seems that the unit is the prophet's creation, like vv. 1–6. It utilizes the resonances of familiar forms, but precisely follows none of them (†Melugin).

After vv. 7–12, v. 13 uses the form of a small-scale imperatival community thanksgiving such as urges enthusiastic recognition of what Yhwh has done/is about to do. Yet these imperatives call for a wordless response from the cosmos rather than a musical and verbal recognition from humanity (Crüsemann, *Studien*, p. 48); see on 44.23.

There is a wide range of views concerning whether vv. 7–13 come from Second Isaiah, or from one of the subsequent redactors of the material, or from Third Isaiah (see, e.g., Hermisson, 'Einheit', p. 311; †van Oorschot, pp. 235–39; Steck, *ZTK* 90, pp. 123–25; Elliger, *Verhältnis*, pp. 38–56). *Merendino (*Henoch* 4 [1982]) sees the original oracle to have consisted in vv. 7aα, 8aβγ, 8bβγ, 9a, 11.

49.7aα. Yhwh has said this—restorer of Israel, its holy one. 1QIs[ab] have *ʾdny yhwh* ('Lord Yhwh') for the MT's *yhwh*, as in (e.g.) 48.16 and 49.22. Both subsequent titles have already appeared with the absolute noun and the suffix reversed, 'your restorer, the holy one of Israel', in the messenger formula at 43.14 and 48.17 (see comments). The Syr transposes them here. It was also 43.14–15 with its parallels to v. 7, noted above, that included the only other occurrence of 'holy one' with a suffix in Isaiah 40–55. Indeed, the only others in the OT are 10.17 and Hab 1.12. 1QIs[a] *gwʾlkh* and LXX ὁ ῥυσάμενός σε assimilate to the usual usage (e.g. 48.17; 49.26). The LXX's further ὁ θεὸς Ἰσραήλ assimilates to 48.1, 2 and thus makes for a nice link, for there Yhwh was critiquing the people for an acknowledgment of the God of Israel that lacked truth. Here Yhwh nevertheless affirms the relationship expressed by the phrase.

קְדוֹשׁוֹ: LXX's Ἁγιάσατε ('sanctify') implies the pointing קַדְּשׁוּ. MT's suffixed form (rather than 'Israel's holy one') is uncommon, though LXX preserved it at 43.15.

49.7aβ. —to one despised in spirit, loathed by nations, servant of rulers. The terms belong to a lament (e.g. Pss 19.13 [14]; 22.6 [7]; 88.8 [9]). They might describe the prophet, but more obviously resume descriptions of the community, and the reference to Yhwh's choice (v. 7b) adds to the indications that Yhwh is speaking to the people. It is quite usual for Jacob–Israel to be referred to in the third person in such descriptions of Yhwh that introduce speech to the people or appear within actual words to the people: again cf 43.14–15 as well as, for example, 41.14, 16; 43.3 (against *Merendino, *Henoch* 4, pp. 306–7). There is no need or grounds for the inference that they suggest a reinterpretation of the person of the servant as denoting Israel (*Merendino, *Henoch* 4, p. 303). This still falls foul of the fact that the servant speaks as 'I' there, whereas Israel is here 'you'. †Grimm and Dittert offer interesting accounts of the verse's reworking by Jesus for his disciples in Mark 10.42–45, by Aquila in relation to the circumstances of the Jewish people in the second century AD, and by Luther to the church in the sixteenth.

In detail the line raises difficulties. 'To one despised in spirit' is *libzōh-nepeš*. The verb form is infinitive construct (cf GK 75n), literally 'with regard to despising of the person/self/life' or '...a case of the despising of a person/self/life' (cf †Bonnard). The construction is thus abstract for concrete. Syntactically the construct might be objective (cf Gen 48.11), 'with regard to a person/self/life that people despise' (cf †Bonnard; and Vg *contemptibilem animam*). The singular word *nepeš* is used with reference to a corporate entity such as Israel in 3.9; 26.8; 43.4; 46.2; 51.23; 55.2, 3; 58.3; 66.3. But in the present context, such a reference by the use of *nepeš* would be very allusive. †Lindblom (p. 28) suggests 'one who loathed his life', comparing Job 9.21; but there the object is *ḥayyāy*, a different noun and one bearing a suffix. The LXX's τὴν ψυχὴν αὐτοῦ and Syr *npšh*, too, need to presuppose a suffix in order to understand the noun objectively. The LXX's φαυλίζοντα presupposes an active participle *bōzēh*, which looks like a grammatically easier reading as well as a contextually more difficult one. Driver (*JTS* 36, p. 401) reads *lᵉbōzēh napšô* ('to one who despises himself'). More likely the MT's construct is subjective (cf 47.9), 'with regard to a self's despising'. The *nepeš* is then not the person despised but the self that is doing the despising (cf 1.14; 38.15; 53.11; BDB, pp. 660b–61a). The self might be that of the victim, so that the phrase suggests a deep self-loathing; †Melugin renders 'to one despised of himself'. Or the self might be that of the oppressor, so that it suggests their deep loathing of Israel. Thus the Tg has *byny ʿmmyʾ* ('among the peoples'). For *nepeš* as suggesting depth of feeling, cf Ps 17.9 (†Volz).

R and Cairo fragment Eb 10 (see *HUB*) have *bᵉzēh*, apparently an Aramaic-type passive participle (cf Dan 2.22; 3.19) equivalent to the usual form *bᵉzûy* (e.g. Ps 22.7 [6]). 1QIs[a] *bzwy* then represents the same understanding. 4QIs[d] agrees, making it less likely that 1QIs[a] is 'modernizing' the form as is its inclination, still less replacing the infinitive with an easier form (see on 42.20); cf the passive ἐξουθενημένῳ in Aq, Sym, Th (so †Theodoret, though †Jerome says Th had active, LXX's reading), Syr *ldmstlyʾ*, and Tg's paraphrase (with plural *dbsyryn*). Perhaps the MT is then camouflaging the reference to the people's being despised (†Barthélemy). The participial phrase will imply 'despised as to person', that is, 'a person despised', or 'despised by a person'. †Ehrlich suggests that *nepeš* and *gôy* stand over against each other, referring to individual person and corporate nation, but the words are not used together elsewhere in this connection (42.1 is one of the few passages where they come in close collocation). They do come together suggestively in Deut 28.65, which envisages the people finding no rest among the nations and suffering from a languishing of its corporate *nepeš*. It is reduced to the status of servants or slaves (28.64, 68). The meaning here is likely similar.

'To one loathed by nations' is *limtāʿēb gôy*. Here the form looks like a piel participle, so that one would expect the phrase to mean 'to one loathing a nation'. It seems arbitrary to take the piel as uniquely intensive in relation to a hypothetical intransitive qal ('to a nation deeply loathsome'). It is less so to take it as causative, with BDB ('to a nation that causes loathsomeness'). After the preceding phrase, †Ewald plausibly takes it not as a verb form but as an abstract noun, 'with regard to a loathing of nation'. Following on his reading of the previous phrase, †Barthélemy plausibly sees the MT as another camouflaging of a 'misleading' (pu) passive that described Israel as loathed by nations. The original will then have been *limtōʿab* (†Oort). The LXX's τὸν βδελυσσόμενον ὑπὸ τῶν ἐθνῶν ('abhorred by the nations') then offers a plausible interpretation of this text. For its understanding of *gôy* as collective cf 55.5, and *ʿam* in 42.6. The Vg has *abominatam gentem*; Tg *dmṭlṭlyn byny mlkwwtʾ* ('to people cast out among the kingdoms'); Th, Aq τὸν βδελυσσόμενον [ὑπὸ τῶν—Sym] ἐθνῶν, Syr *ldmsly mn ʿmʾ*.

Most LXX MSS have plural τῶν δουλῶν (cf Syr, Tg).

למתעב: 1QIs[a] has pl. למתעבי (cf Tg, as throughout the line).

גוי: Ginsberg (*JBL* 69 [1950], p. 59) emends to גו ('back'), which provides good parallelism for נפשׁ taken to mean 'neck'. S. M. Paul suggests that the word functions Janus-like, suggesting 'neck' in the light of what precedes and 'nations' in the light of what follows.[5]

49.7aγ. Kings will look and stand up, leaders, and fall prostrate. Insofar as vv. 7–12 utilize the form of a deliverance oracle, v. 7aγ–b anticipates what follows. The LXX provides 'at him/to him' as object of the first and last verbs. In the MT it is vv. 8–12 that will tell us what the kings and leaders see to provoke their response, though the following bicolon will provide a clue in the meantime. The verb *rāʾāh* recalls 40.5 and anticipates 52.10, 15.

The reversal between vv. 7aβ and 7aγ is complete. Kings and leaders move from sitting in state to stand and then fall down in respect (as, e.g., Gen 19.1; 23.7). The second verb, *weyištaḥăwû* (see on 44.15), is even governed by co-ordinating *w* rather than *w*-consecutive, though the fact that one stands in order to bow might make it appropriate to see the clause as indicating purpose. There is no need to follow Syr's easier reading *wšlyṭnʾ nsgdwn*, which attaches the copula to the preceding noun (against Gelston, *VT* 21, pp. 522–23).

The LXX renders βασιλεῖς ὄψονται αὐτόν, καὶ ἀναστήσονται ἄρχοντες καὶ προσκυνήσουσιν αὐτῷ ('kings will see him, and rulers will stand up and fall prostrate to him'), a natural understanding in a prose context but one that makes for an odd 2–3 poetic line. 1QIs[b] rather (and uncharacteristically) juxtaposes the first two verbs asyndetically *yrʾw yqwmw* (Rubinstein, *VT* 5, p. 187). It points us to the rendering above, which assumes that the line is 3–2 and also that at least one verb in the first colon applies also in the second. The fact that 'stand up and fall prostrate' is a familiar linked pair of verbs facilitates this. Prosaically put, the line declares that kings and other leaders (*śārîm*) will look, stand, and fall down.

יראו וקמו שׂרים וישתחוו: 1QIs[a] has ראו וקמו ושרים יהשתחוו (see on 43.9).

49.7b. . . .for the sake of Yhwh, the one who is steadfast, the holy one of Israel: he chose you. With the final line of v. 7 we discover that the verse has an ABBA structure. Verse 7b reaffirms that there lies behind the intervening promise the person of Yhwh, Israel's God, the

[5] See 'Polysemous Pivotal Function', in *Texts, Temples* (see on 40.17), pp. 367–74 (see p. 370).

holy one. 'Steadfastness' and 'choosing' develop the title 'restorer', suggesting two facets of the background of this latter notion. In the MT the closing verb is third person *wayyibḥārekkā* (1QIs[a] omits the copula). The fact that the prophet is apparently the speaker—for the prophecy does not usually refer to God in the third person when God is actually speaking—also makes for a link with the first line. The LXX changes to the more usual first person ἐξελεξάμην (cf 41.8, 9; 43.10; 44.1, 2; 48.10), which brings the line to a fine rhetorical climax.

While *l[e]maʿan* occasionally means merely 'because of', once again the more common prospectively purposeful meaning fits here (see on 42.21a). Yhwh's act will testify to Yhwh's faithfulness. Such a use of *l[e]maʿan* fits with its use in connection with Yhwh and Yhwh's name in 37.35; 42.21; 43.25; 48.9, 11. In this sense, too, v. 7b goes beyond v. 7aα.

The line is in some ways syntactically similar to its predecessor. 'For the sake of' (*l[e]maʿan*) applies to the second colon as well as the first, and the line closes with a surprising *w*-prefixed verb, though this is a wayyiqtol. It thus ends more literally 'the holy one of Israel and he chose you'. Prosaically put, v. 7b thus suggests 'for the sake of Yhwh the holy one of Israel who is steadfast and chose you'. Elsewhere only in Deut 7.9 and Jer 42.5 is *neʾĕmān* ('steadfast'), or any other form of *ʾāman*, applied to Yhwh. On the *ʾăšer* clause, see on 41.8aβ.

The order of the two statements about Yhwh is surprising. In Deut 7.9 'steadfastness' naturally follows rather than precedes 'choice', and presumably the wayyiqtol verb here does not indicate a temporal relationship (so GK 111q?). *TTH* 76α sees it as 'a fresh idea loosely appended' by the help of *w*-, an epexegetical relationship whereby the wayyiqtol verb explains the preceding one (cf *IBHS* 33.2.2a). In other words, the *w* functions like a relative: so Vg *qui elegit te*. *Merendino (*Henoch* 4, p. 301) adds that the *w* is deictic. †Saydon sees this rather as a *w*-apodosis construction (see on 45.4b), implying 'As the holy one of Israel, he chose you'.

49.8a. Yhwh has said this. In a time of acceptance I am answering you, on a day of deliverance I am supporting you. The bare 'Yhwh has said this' is very unusual (cf only 45.14), which supports the view that—whether or not it is original—it is resumptive and not the beginning of an originally separate oracle. In the same way the nature of the following two cola suggests that they continue the oracle in v. 7 as Yhwh responds to the lament alluded to there, with a new attitude and a new act. For the verbs 1QIs[a] has *ʾʿnkh* and *ʾʿzrkh*, perceiving that the original qatal verbs *ʿănîtîkā* and *ʿăzartîka* are the instantaneous/'prophetic' qatals characteristic of the deliverance oracle and changing them to the easier yiqtols (†Rubinstein, p. 319); cf Tg.

Thus the words are ones that could have been addressed to the prophet and could re-state what was going on in vv. 4–6 (cf †Ibn Ezra). But the prophet does not report them as words addressed to 'me' but as words addressed to 'you', apparently Jacob–Israel, and this fits our reading of v. 7aβ. The addressee is singular, but at least some of the plurals in vv. 9–12 refer to the same people, and the closing hymn neatly combines the two in v. 13b. †Grimm and Dittert also compare prayers that concern the time and that interweave first-person and communal perspectives in Pss 102.3, 14 [2, 13]; 106.4.

The Tg's 'at the time that you do my pleasure' takes *rāṣôn* to refer to the people's pleasing Yhwh. The word can refer to people's freewill self-giving in worship of Yhwh (e.g. Lev. 1.3), but both noun and verb more commonly refer to Yhwh's acceptance and to what Yhwh approves, and it seems unlikely that here the phrase refers to the time of the speaker's prayer, of seeking Yhwh's 'Yes' (†Rashi), or to the time of the speaker's 'Yes' of commitment to Yhwh (†Qimchi). The notion of answering the people's prayer of lament comes explicitly in the verb in this colon, for which cf 30.19; 41.17; 58.9; Jer 23.35, 37; 33.3; Ps 118.5, 21; and contrast Isa 41.28; 46.7. The exile was a time of rejection, and specifically rejection of people's prayer; now that time is over.

49.8bα. I thus guard you and make you into a covenant for people, by raising the land. The Tg's 'and I will prepare you' takes the first verb *wᵉʾeṣṣorkā* as from *yāṣar* not *nāṣar*, as in v. 5; so also those LXX MSS that render this verb, καὶ ἔπλασά σε. This and the subsequent καὶ ἔδωκά σε ('I made you') suggest a wayyiqtol verb. The MT itself has simple *w* verbs, exactly repeating the forms in 42.6 (where see comment). *Merendino (*Henoch* 4, p. 308) once more sees the *w* as deictic.

The LXX's εἰς διαθήκην ἐθνῶν takes its genitive plural from the second of the two parallel phrases in 42.6, and some MSS expand it so as to include the whole phrase εἰς διαθήκην γένους εἰς φῶς ἐθνῶν ('into a covenant of people, into a light of nations'); cf Syr *wnwhrʾ lʿmmʾ*. This draws our attention to the way in which the MT splits this pair of phrases between vv. 6 and 8. The completing of the pair again points to the interweaving of the roles of prophet and people.

If the hearers expected *librît ʿām* ('into a covenant for people') to be followed within this line by *lᵉʾôr gôyim* ('into a light for nations'), once more the words unfold in such a way as to play with the audience's expectations and then frustrate them. There comes next not the phrase we expect, which the Syr and some LXX MSS duly provide, but another of similar shape in Hebrew, *lᵉhāqîm ʾereṣ* ('by raising the land'). Indeed, this phrase embodies a double tease, for the unexpected infinitive in turn sets up its own expectations. It, too, recurs from v. 6, where it had a personal object, the tribes of Jacob. Here the object is that people's land, with the implication that the verb's nuance is different.

Admittedly the MT probably implies a 2–2 line, 'I thus guard you and make you into a covenant for people', followed by a 2–3 line 'by raising the land, by allocating desolate properties'. This leads to the suggestion that a word such as *ṣiyyāh* ('dryness': cf 41.18; 53.2) is missing from the first half of the 2–3 line (†Kittel). We have rather linked 'by raising the land' with the preceding line, completing that as 2–2–2 (†Torrey). The verb is repeated from v. 6, now with impersonal object as in 44.26 (polel; cf also 58.12; 61.4). 'Raising the land' denotes the restoring of a land that has been devastated (*qûm* hi is a natural verb to refer to the (re-)erecting of buildings: see e.g. 23.13; 29.3). The usage thus neatly complements that in v. 6.

Now none of the 25 occurrences of *ʾereṣ* so far in 40.1–49.6 have referred to the land of Israel, and specifically *ʾereṣ* in 42.4 was not the land of Israel but the world. Second Isaiah does not speak of the land itself in the way that Ezekiel does (cf †D. Baltzer, chapter 7). If we read the raising of *ʾereṣ* in the light of this aspect of what has preceded, then, it would make good sense as denoting the restoring of the world, perhaps expressing a concern with other peoples whose lands have been the victims of the Babylonians' imperial policies as Judah's has been. The thought is not alien to the book of Isaiah as a whole (†Torrey). But it is difficult to maintain this focus on other peoples through the rest of the chapter. The language of vv. 8–11 is language usually used of Jacob–Israel, v. 12 is difficult except as a promise of a gathering of scattered Jacob–Israel, and v. 13 presumably refers back to vv. 7–12 and surely must mean Jacob–Israel by 'my people'. In turn 49.14–50.3 express doubts about Yhwh's commitment to Judah and its land, and v. 19 explicitly uses *ʾereṣ* of this land. In this context the raising of *ʾereṣ* is thus surely the raising of the land of Israel. It is the raising of the land of Israel that will give the world something to respond to. On the difficulty of determining when *ʾereṣ* means 'earth' and when 'land', see *ThWAT* on *ʾereṣ*, § II, introduction.

This issue relates to the question of the right understanding of *lᵉhāqîm*. The preposition *l* introducing an infinitive construct can have various connotations. LXX's τοῦ καταστῆσαι τὴν γῆν ('to raise the land') and Vg *ut suscitares terram* ('so that you may raise the land') take it as indicating the purpose or content of the covenantal commitment, which fits the usage in Exod 6.4; Josh 9.15; Jer 34.8 (†Begrich, p. 142 = 143), but the context in v. 8 ('*I make you* into a covenant *for people*') makes this understanding difficult here. The *l* plus infinitive thus has the common connotation 'by [raising]', exactly as in 42.7 where the LXX has a simple infinitive. It 'gives more details about or explains the preceding action' (JM 124o). Its subject is then the same as that of the preceding verb. Yhwh is the one who will do the raising as a means of making the people into a covenant (see †Schroten, p. 57).

The Tg has 'to raise the just who lie in the dust'.

49.8bβ–9a. ...by distributing desolate allocations, by saying to prisoners 'Come out', to people in darkness 'Appear'. The two further *l* clauses continue the construction, with v. 9a then syntactically recalling 44.28b. Yhwh will re-allocate the land in the way that Joshua allocated it when Israel first came to Canaan, but now to people who are 'prisoners' and in 'darkness'—the circumstances of those they were called to bring light to (cf 42.7). To provide some novelty at the end of the line, it closes with a familiar verb used in a new connection. The prophet began by envisaging Yhwh's splendour appearing (*gālāh* ni; 40.5). Now Yhwh bids the prisoners appear out of their darkness. The verb can also mean 'depart' and this fits as well in the context (*DCH*), suggesting a departing from exile to counter the departing into exile (*gôlāh*/*gālût*). The imperative conveys 'a distinct assurance...or promise' (GK 110c). 1QIs[a] provides a copula at the beginning of the colon ('and to people...').

לאשׁר בחשׁך: Syr *lḥbyš*ʾ ('to people shut in') may have been influenced by 42.7.

49.9b. Along the ways they will feed, on all bare places will be their pasture. We are perhaps to understand the prophet to be the speaker in vv. 9b–10, 12, describing the resourcing of the people as they make their way to the land. 'Bare places' (see on 41.18) suggests places without pasture and/or places of illegitimate worship (cf Jer 3.2): both connotations are denied here. The versions were apparently unfamiliar with the word and translated it by context. In 41.18 the LXX had ἐπὶ τῶν ὀρέων ('on the mountains'). Here it has ἐν... ταῖς τρίβοις ('on the paths').

In the first colon the LXX has ἐν πάσαις ταῖς ὁδοῖς αὐτῶν ('on all their ways'), which in itself would more likely be a pointer that *kol* applies in both cola than evidence for the addition of *kol* in the first. The line can be read as 3–3 rather than 2–2 by the removal of *maqqephs*. 1QIs[a] reads *ʿl kwl hrym* ('along all mountains'). This might reflect simple misreading, or might reflect the assumption that *šᵉpāyîm* ('bare places') in the subsequent colon meant 'high places' (†Kutscher, pp. 174–75; ET 230–31) or might add to the evidence that the MT has omitted a *kol* by homoioteleuton. There have been no bicola in chapters 40–48 where *kol* came in both cola.

דרכים: *Thomas emends to דככים ('sand-flats'), hypothesized on the basis of Arabic to balance the noun in the second colon. But the link with Jeremiah 3 (see above) works against this.

49.10a. They will not hunger, they will not thirst. Khamsin and sun will not strike them down. Not being hungry is implicit in having sufficient pasturage. Not being thirsty (*ṣāmēʾ*) resumes a more explicit earlier motif: see 48.21, also 44.3 for the adjective *ṣāmēʾ* and 41.17 for the noun *ṣāmāʾ*. 'Khamsin' (*šārāb*) occurs elsewhere only at 35.7 where the meaning 'mirage' or 'parched ground' would fit. Here the LXX more plausibly renders καύσων ('khamsin'), which corresponds with another Arabic usage. The Vg has *aestus* ('heat'). The motif corresponds with 40.7. For the sun 'smiting' (*nākāh* hi), cf Ps 121.6.

49.10b. For one who has compassion on them will drive them on. By springs of water he will guide them. 'Drive' (*nāhag*) is the ordinary word for driving animals, troops, and captives. The use of the piel rather than the qal suggests the result rather than the process of driving (*Piᶜel*, p. 201). The verb's possible negative implications are anticipated by the nature and the placing of the participle 'one who has compassion', which comes before the verb—as is the case with the prepositional phrase in the parallel colon. The LXX's παρακαλέσει might imply rather the verb *nḥm* (†Ottley), but this is another verb of which the LXX is fond (†Seeligmann, p. 68). Yannai (see Wallenstein, 'The piyyut' [see on 40.10a], pp. 474–75) implies the reading *mēreḥem* ('from the womb'), assimilating to the use of *mibbeṭen* in, for example, vv. 1, 5.

'Springs' (*mabbûaᶜ*) of water came in 35.7, along with 'khamsin'; see also 41.18, where the word was *maᶜyānôt*. There is some evidence of a homonym or development of *rḥm* meaning 'rain', and in the light of the reference to the burning sun in v. 10a and now the reference to waters, a reader who knew this root might perceive an instance of paronomasia in *mᵉraḥămām* which could also mean 'one who rains on them'.[6] 'Guide' (*nāhal*; cf 40.11) makes for a rhyme with the verb in the first colon (*yᵉnahăgēm*/*yᵉnahălēm*). The original reading in 1QIsᵃ was the more familiar *nāḥal* ('[cause to] inherit'), which occurred in v. 8.

49.11. I will make all my mountains into a way, and my highroads will rise up. On 'way' and 'highroad' (*derek*, *mᵉsillāh*), see on 40.3—but now the road is explicitly one for people to return by, and not just a road for Yhwh. The plural adds variety in the second colon rather than suggesting many highroads over against one way. The verbs are not the ones that were used in 40.3, but *rûm* ('rise up') nicely picks up the double use of this verb in the hiphil in 40.9 and thus further emphasizes the links between 49.1–13 and 40.1–11 as a whole. This highroad will soar over the mountains as the voice of Yhwh's herald does. Similarly *śîm* ('make') has played a frequent part in accounts of Yhwh's work of transformation in chapters 41–48. In 43.19 it referred to the making of a way in the wilderness; see also 41.15a, 15b, 18; 42.15, 16; 49.2a, 2b; and subsequently 50.2; 51.3, 10. The verb form *yᵉrumûn* with the fuller ending is an emphatic one at the end of the line (cf GK 47m). Despite the fact that the line is arranged chiastically, so that the subject precedes the verb, a feminine noun is followed by a masculine verb. This may reflect dislike of the third plural feminine yiqtol (GK 145u). Or should one render '[on] my

[6] Cf G. Rendsburg, 'Hebrew *rḥm* = "Rain"', in *VT* 33 (1983), pp. 357–62; he sees the final *m* as enclitic.

great highway they will walk high' (cf †Ibn Ezra), or '[into] my great highway [on which] they will walk high'? On the basis of an Arabic verb, D. Yellin hypothesizes a root *rāmam* ('repair') suggesting 'they will repair my great highway'.[7]

The LXX, Syr, and Tg lack the suffix on 'my mountains'. †Volz plausibly suggests that consonantal *hry* was an abbreviation for *hrym* and was misunderstood as the suffixed form. The suffix on *m*^{e}*sillôtay* could then be a consequential further slip (dittography; cf Syr *wšbylʾ*), but *m*^{e}*sillôtay* is more plausible than *hry* as an original reading. Yhwh is on this journey, after all (v. 10b; and cf Yhwh's way/a highroad for Yhwh in 40.3). Indeed, its influence might explain the misreading of *hry*. But the MT's two suffixes do suggest that as owner of the mountains Yhwh is in a position to do what the line speaks of. The second suffix, too, is missing from the LXX, but the LXX's reading of the colon as a whole is idiosyncratic, apparently assimilating it to vv. 9–10 and/or reading not *yrmwn* but *yrʿwn* (cf †Ziegler, p. 161) or *ymrwn* (*Goshen-Gottstein): καὶ πᾶσαν τρίβον εἰς βόσκημα αὐτοῖς ('and [I will make] every way into food for them').

49.12. There, these will come from far off, there, these from northward and seaward, these from the land of Syenites. As happened between vv. 8–9a and 9b–10, v. 11 makes another transition from first person to third person as Yhwh's speaking gives way to a description of the people's experience, perhaps from the lips of the prophet. The verse points in different ways to the worldwide nature of the return of peoples—Babylon by no means has all the focus. The Syr omits the 'There...there'; the LXX reworks to reduce the repetition. The Syr then accidentally repeats 'sea' in place of 'land'.

In the light of what follows, †Ibn Ezra and †Qimchi understand 'far off' to refer to the east, but this may be no more plausible than the understanding of 'hand' to denote 'left hand in 48.13 (see comment). †Ibn Ezra goes on to understand *ṣāpôn* ('north') to denote Babylon. 'Seaward' (*yām*) usually denotes westward, because the sea lies to the west in Palestine, but †Ibn Ezra refers it to the south (as in Ps 107.3) and takes it to denote Assyria, which he confuses with Ethiopia.

It is only with the last direction that the prophet specifically refers to a place. Ironically its reference is unclear. The MT has *sînîm*. In Gen 10.17 *sînî* refers to an obscure people on the Phoenician coast. The LXX's ἐκ γῆς Περσῶν takes it to denote Persia and thus as representing the east; the translators would have known of Jewish communities there (†Seeligmann, p. 79). More commonly the country to the east has been identified with China, which is historically possible but implausible (*Lambert; †Williamson, p. 263). In contrast the Vg has *terra australi*, Tg *ʾrʿ drwmʾ* ('southern

[7] 'Forgotten Meanings of Hebrew Roots in the Bible', in *Jewish Studies in Memory of Israel Abrahams* (ed. G. A. Kohut; New York, 1927), pp. 441–58 (see p. 456).

land'). There were two places south of Israel called *sîn*, the Egyptian border city otherwise known as Pelusium (cf Ezek 30.15) and the wilderness between Elim and Sinai (e.g. Exod 16.1). But 1QIsª has *swnyym*, which suggests the people of Syene/Aswan, *sᵉwēnēh* in Ezek 29.10 and 30.6 (cf †Michaelis), opposite the island of Elephantine with its Jewish colony.

49.13. Resound, heavens. Rejoice, earth. Mountains must break into sound. For Yhwh is comforting his people. He will have compassion on his weak. The command to a joyful response to Yhwh's promise recalls 44.23, and the first command exactly corresponds to its opening. The second corresponds to 44.23 in being addressed to earth; for the verb cf 41.16. The merism of heaven and earth might have seemed quite enough, but the third command again corresponds to 44.23 in its turning to the mountains and in its verb, though the latter is now jussive rather than imperative. For K *ypṣḥw*, Q *ûpiṣḥû*, 1QIsª *pṣḥw* (so also 4Q176 *Tanḥûmîm*, which also omits 'into sound'), and Vg *iubilate* assimilate to 44.23 (cf also Tg), though the K–Q distinction may reflect graphic confusion between *y* and *w* (cf Rubinstein, 'A Kethib-Qere Problem', p. 132).

By implication there is more reason for rejoicing than was the case at 44.23. The command to comfort Yhwh's people (40.1) is being fulfilled. The whole cosmos would have natural reason to rejoice in a restoring of Israel that had implications for the whole world. Verse 13b corresponds to 44.23b in being a double *kî*-clause arranged chiastically. The first verb is the instantaneous qatal *niḥam*, which 1QIsª characteristically changes to participle *mnḥm* (†Rubinstein, p. 319). Morgenstern (*HUCA* 36, p. 6) changes to yiqtol (haplog.). The second is indeed yiqtol. The sequence corresponds to 44.23b. It seems implausible to suggest that the second has past meaning, whether by hypothesizing the memory of an old past-tense yáqtul or by reckoning that this is a wayyiqtol verb with the *w* and the verb separated (against †Saydon, p. 296). The (partial) chiasm mirrors the reversal promised by the content (*TTCHV*, p. 371). The verbs seem to be reversed in LXX, ἠλέησεν...καὶ τοὺς ταπεινοὺς τοῦ λαοῦ αὐτοῦ παρεκάλεσεν.

L. Delekat suggests that here *ʿānî* means 'dependant' rather than 'poor' or 'afflicted'. 'His dependants' makes for good parallelism with 'his people'.[8] For the verb 'have compassion', see on v. 10a. All the expressions in v. 13b open the way to the message to Zion that follows as well as linking with what precedes and closing off vv. 7–13.

Exodus Rabbah 31.5 comments, 'When Israel asked God, "Who are your people?", the reply was, "The *ʿănāwîm*" '. But as we have noted, the LXX changes to 'the weak/humble ones of his people'.

[8] See L. Delekat, 'Zum hebräischen Wörterbuch', in *VT* 14 (1964), pp. 7–66 (see pp. 35–49).

Bibliography to 49.1–13

Beuken, W. A. M., 'De vergeefse moeite van de knecht', in †Grosheide, pp. 23–40.
Giblin, C. H., 'A Note on the Composition of Isaias 49, 1–6(9a)', in *CBQ* 21 (1959), pp. 207–12.
Goshen-Gottstein, M. H., 'Bible Exegesis and Textual Criticism. Isaiah 49,11: MT and LXX', in *Mélanges Dominique Barthélemy* (ed. P. Casetti and others), pp. 91–107. OBO 38, 1981.
Kissane, E. J., 'The Land of Sinim', in *Irish Theological Quarterly* 21 (1954), pp. 63–64.
Lambert, G., 'Le Livre d'Isaïe parle-t-il des Chinois?', in *NRT* 75 (1953), pp. 965–72.
Lohfink, N., '"Israel" in Jes 49, 3', in *Wort, Lied und Gottesspruch* Vol. 2: *Beiträge zu Psalmen und Propheten* (J. Ziegler Festschrift, ed. J. Schreiner), pp. 217–29. Stuttgart, 1972.
Merendino, R. P., 'Jes 49 1–6', in *ZAW* 92 (1980), pp. 236–48.
—'Jes 49, 7–13', in *Henoch* 4 (1982), pp. 295–329.
Orlinsky, H. M., '"Israel" in Isa. xlix, 3', in *Eretz-Israel* 8 (1967), pp. 42*–45*.
Rignell, L., 'Den s. k. andrea Ebed-Jahve sangen', in *StTKv* 28 (1952), pp. 26–32.
Thomas, D. W., 'A Note on דְּרָכִים in Isaiah xlix. 9b', in *JTS* n.s. 19 (1968), pp. 203–4.
van der Kooij, A., 'The Servant of the Lord', in van Ruiten and Vervenne, pp. 383–96.

IV.b.

49.14–50.3: YHWH'S RESPONSE TO ABANDONED ZION

In the last line of vv. 7–13 came reference to the comforting of Yhwh's people, which took up 40.1. There in 40.2 'Jerusalem' sat in parallelism with 'my people', and here in 49.14 Zion now becomes the speaker. In the second colon of v. 13 came the word *ʿānî* ('poor'). The noun *ʿŏnî* ('poverty, affliction') appears three times in Lamentations 1, a chapter that forms background to Isaiah 40 (see, e.g., vv. 3, 7, 9), to describe Jerusalem and Judah. So the Zion who now speaks has been in the wings in vv. 7–13. We are not surprised to hear her speak. Her words recall those of Jacob–Israel in chapter 40. Indeed, one can suggest a point-by-point reverse parallel with 40.12–31 (based on †Hessler):

49.14–17	40.27–31	Plaint and response
49.18–21	40.25–26	A challenge to lift eyes and look
49.22–23	40.21–24	Yhwh's sovereignty over kings
49.24–26	40.18–20	Yhwh's incomparable power
50.1–3	40.12–17	Yhwh's lordship over the created world

The reverse arrangement means that Zion–Jerusalem's question is in the forefront from the beginning and is addressed from the beginning, and the focus is as much on Yhwh's commitment to acting for her as on Yhwh's capacity to act.

The extended exchange between Madam Zion and Yhwh makes a number of references to her children, who comprise Jacob–Israel under another name (or non-name). Masculine plurals continue as subjects of third person verbs and as addressees in chapters 49–55 and this audience 'seems to correspond most closely to the prophet's actual audience' (†Willey, p. 180).

Formal markers suggest four subsection divisions. The first is 49.14–21; v. 22 begins with a messenger formula. The quoting of Madam Zion's contrasting words in vv. 14 and 21 forms an *inclusio* round the whole. Second, 49.22–23 opens with a messenger formula and closes with a recognition formula. A new messenger formula follows in v. 25. Third, 49.24–26 has a messenger formula in v. 25 near the beginning and a closing recognition formula. The content of v. 25 makes clear that it takes up v. 24 rather than being itself the beginning of the subsection. Fourth, 50.1–3 opens with a messenger formula and is followed by a change of speaker and form at 50.4.

These divisions are recognized in the MT, by petucha(!) before 49.22 and setuma before 49.24 and 50.1. A has an extra setuma before v. 25; 1QIs[a] has a number of extra division markers.

The speech of argument may be suggested by many of the rhetorical questions (49.14–15, 24; 50.1–2a; but not 49.21). Thus A. Graffy, for instance, sees vv. 14–25 (26) as a disputation,[1] and †Begrich (pp. 19, 45 = 26, 51) sees 50.1–3 as a disputation within which vv. 1–2a use the form of court speech, the speech of a defendant answering a charge and making a counter-accusation (and see †Melugin, pp. 50–53). *Merendino ('Jes 49, 14–26', p. 353) notes the characteristic wisdom connections of the questions in chapter 49. But the more pervasive and underlying tone of 49.14–50.3 is that of lament and of response in the form of a promise of deliverance, even where the language is confrontational (e.g. †Schoors). The section's explicit reference to Yhwh's entering into disputation in v. 25 concerns Zion's assailants not Zion herself (†R. H. O'Connell, pp. 21–22). †A. Wilson (pp. 282–83) finds a chiastic arrangement in vv. 14–26, but it is easier to see the characteristic elements of a promise of deliverance there:

	vv. 14–21	vv. 22–23	vv. 24–26
Messenger formula		22aα	25aα
Recollection of lament	14		24–25a
Yhwh's turning (mostly qatal)	15–16		
Yhwh's action (yiqtol)		22a	25b
The consequences	17–21	22b–23a	26a
The purpose of Yhwh's action		23b	26b

†Westermann is even able to identify the three classic directions of lament behind the overt words of vv. 14–26, 'You' (v. 14), 'I' (v. 21), and 'they' (v. 24). As a whole vv. 14–26 comprise three partial promises of deliverance that between them make one complete one (†Schoors). All three promise that Zion will regain her children. The same promise recurs in 50.1–3 but it has the more intrinsically disputational form and is addressed in the second plural masculine to a mother's children rather than to a mother herself. †R. H. O'Connell (p. 154) calls 49.14–50.3 a 'disputational consolation'. In its way *Pesiqta' deRab Kahana'* 17 anticipates this reading as it makes vv. 14–16 the answer to the plaint of Ps 77.7–13 [6–12].

Each of the four units would be capable of standing on its own, and at first sight they may seem to lack any specific or distinctive rhetorical links that would make them look designed to accompany each other. Their specific concerns vary. Verses 14–21 centre on the return of unexpected children. In vv. 22–23 the children are more incidental and the verses centre more on the way the children become the means of the nations expressing their submission to Zion. In vv. 24–26, in turn, the focus is on the overcoming of the children's oppressor. In 50.1–3 the children are addressed concerning their mother's status.

[1] *A Prophet Confronts his People* (AB 104, 1984), pp. 91–98.

Much of this provides circumstantial evidence for the view that each of the four subsections originally existed separately (†Melugin). If so, four units of similar theme now come together as an introduction to the Jerusalem–Zion chapters. Yet some subtle links between the subsections appear. At the opening of vv. 14–21 Zion bewails the way Yhwh/the Lord abandoned her, and at the opening of vv. 22–23 it is (unusually) 'the Lord Yhwh' who speaks in response. Apart from that double title, the messenger formulae in 49.22, 25, and 50.1 are only the brief and unadorned 'Yhwh says this', which is very unusual in Isaiah 40–55 and looks resumptive in each of these three passages as it is in 49.8. In 49.15–16, 24–25, and 50.2 there appears a striking patterning of particles in the sequences of questions, assertions, and affirmations:

49.15–16	*hă*		*gam*	*w*^{e}	*hēn*	(can		yes but	there)
49.24–25	*hă*	*w*^{e}*ʾim*	*gam*	*w*^{e}		(can	or	yes but)	
50.2	*hă*	*w*^{e}*ʾim*			*hēn*	(can	or		there).

Within vv. 14–21 appear a number of verbal links with 5.8–9 and 6.11–12 (†Williamson, pp. 53–54); see further below. These suggest that vv. 14–21 is in part a re-reading of those passages in which the prophet declares that earlier prophecies have come true and that their judgment is now being reversed. Behind vv. 22–23 and 24–26 similarly lies 5.25–29. Re-use of 13.2–3 also holds together vv. 22–23 and 24–26, and allusive contrast with chapter 47 runs through 49.14–26 (see on vv. 15, 18, 20, 21, 25). Chapter 60 will take the process of re-reading further. A further series of parallels with Jeremiah 2–3 appears in 49.14, 18, and 50.1 (see on v. 18), suggesting a link between these.

The relationship between the subsections of 49.14–50.3 parallels that between vv. 1–6 and 7–13 and it again seems more likely that the material was designed to go together than that it was of quite separate origin though susceptible to being brought into mutual association. Even adaptation of originally separate units seems inadequate as a model to explain the various links.

Verses 14–21 are divided by †Begrich (p. 18 = 25) into two parts, vv. 14–17 and 18–21, but by the NRSV into two paragraphs comprising vv. 14–18 and 19–21. More plausibly *Steck (pp. 36–38) sees the two accusations in v. 14 each answered, in reverse order, in vv. 15–18a and 18b–20. For him, v. 21 then begins the new subsection. We have seen reason to associate it rather with what precedes. Verses 14–21 then open and close with statements by Madam Zion, the second of which comprises questions in which she responds to her own plaint in the first. After that opening statement, Yhwh initially responds with a first-person account of commitment in vv. 15–16 with both yiqtol and qatal clauses and a noun clause, suggesting future, past, and present. Verses 17–21 with their account of the consequences of Yhwh's commitment characteristically divide into two parallel segments of which the first is longer than the second. Each comprises a promise in the third-person about Zion's children (vv. 17–18a, 20) and then a statement to Zion about the implications for Zion herself (vv. 18b–19, 21). The first (vv. 17–19) concerns the actions of the children and their mother, the second (vv. 20–21) their respective words. Diagrammatically put:

14	Zion	'He. . .me'		
15–16	Yhwh	'I will not. . .you/I have. . .you/you. . .before me'		
17–18a		'Your children. . .'	18b–19	'You will. . .'
20		'Your children will say. . .'	21	'You will say. . .'

The next two subsections (vv. 22–23 and 24–26) have structural similarities. Each incorporates a messenger formula. In each case this introduces a promise regarding Yhwh's coming action expressed in first-person singular yiqtol verbs. Its implications for those affected are stated in third-person plural yiqtol/w^{e}qatal verbs. In each case the subsection closes with the aim of recognition of Yhwh, by the community and by the whole world. The major difference between the two subsections is the introductory question with which vv. 24–26 opens. Yhwh apparently continues to speak and the question thus links the two subsections rhetorically. It also links them substantially, for it is a question that could be raised in the light of the undertaking in vv. 22–23. Only if that question is then satisfactorily answered can the promises in vv. 22–23 be delivered.

22aα	Messenger formula
22aβγ	Yhwh's promise
22b–23a	Zion's overlords' experience
23b	Recognition formula
24	A question that needs answering
25aα	Messenger formula
25aβ–26aα	Yhwh's promise
26aβ	Zion's overlords' experience
26b	Recognition formula

Then 50.1–3 has its own double structure. In v. 1 two lines of questions are followed by a *hēn* statement declaring the implications of the implicit answer to these, in qatal verbs. The same phenomenon appears in v. 2 closing with yiqtol verbs. Verse 3 then elaborates on this second question–answer sequence (cf *Merendino, 'Jes 50, 1–3 [9b.11]', p. 225).

1a	2a	Questions
1b	2b	Answers (*hēn*)
	3	Elaboration

Opinions vary as to whether the whole of 49.14–50.3 comes from Second Isaiah (e.g. †Westermann) or the whole is of later origin (e.g. †Morgenstern) or the material is of mixed origin. †Duhm, for instance, thought that 49.22–50.3 could not come from Second Isaiah both for stylistic reasons and because he found the talk of domination over the nations inconsistent with Second Isaiah's thought. But on this hypothesis redactors apparently found no irreconcilable tension between the nations' recognition of Yhwh in (e.g.) 45.22–23 and their submission in (e.g.) 49.22–26, and an individual prophet might equally find none. Arguably both perspectives appear within chapter 45. Elliger (*Verhältnis*, pp. 123–34) attributes 49.22–50.3 to Third Isaiah. Hermisson ('Einheit', pp. 304, 311) attributes 49.14–23 and perhaps 50.1–2 to the oldest layer of material and 49.24–26; 50.3 to the later 'Near expectation strand'; †van Oorschot links 49.14–23 with his 'first Jerusalem redaction', 50.1–3 with his 'Near expectation strand', 49.24–26 with his 'secondary Zion strand'. *Merendino ('Jes 49, 14–26', p. 345) sees the original text as vv. 14–17, 19b, 24–25.

IV.b.i. I will not forget you (49.14–21)

49.14. Then Zion said, Yhwh left me. The Lord forgot me. There is some ambiguity over who reports Zion's words. The continuity from v. 13 would imply the prophet, the continuity in v. 15 would imply Yhwh (*Merendino, 'Jes 49, 14–26', pp. 328–29). As 'he/Yhwh said' stood in contrast to the words of the speaker in vv. 3, 5, 6, in return '[and/but] Zion said' here stands in antithesis to 'Yhwh said' in vv. 7, 8. The rarity of *w*-consecutive in these chapters (see on v. 3) again draws attention to its significance here as for the first time Zion speaks. It is difficult to give precision to what 'Zion' refers to—the physical city personified, or the people as a whole, or the city's actual population, or its one-time population now deported, or a personification independent of all these that can exist over against its inhabitants. Like 'servant of Yhwh', 'Zion' is a plurivocal, tensive symbol.

As in v. 13b, the chiasm mirrors the reversal expressed in the contents (*TTCHV*, p. 371). An English perfect tense could also appropriately render the qatal verbs denoting an act that flows into a present state (*DG* 57d). A great 'leaving' (*ʿăzûbāh*) of the land of Judah was one of the Lord Yhwh's warnings in 6.11–13, a passage with a number of resonances in vv. 14–21. The power of Zion's plaint then comes from using Yhwh's own words, words that Yhwh can hardly refute. How can Yhwh talk in the terms of vv. 1–13 when the reality is as v. 14 describes it (cf Lam 5.20)? For 'left', the Tg has 'Yhwh removed his presence from me'. It avoids anthropomorphism by using the technical term for the presence of Yhwh in the temple, whose removal is the key problem after 587 BC or after AD 70 (†Chilton, pp. 69–75).

In parallelism with *yhwh* here is *ʾădōnāy*. Given the way the prophecy will develop, it would have been natural for the prophet to use the everyday expression *ʾădōnî* ('my husband'), and the fact that this is the only time *ʾădōnāy* on its own occurs in Isaiah 40–66 might make one wonder whether *ʾădōnî* has been misvocalized (†Klostermann). But in the MT the talk of leaving and forgetting does not yet specifically denote that of a husband abandoning a wife. The marriage relationship becomes explicit only at the close of this section, at 50.1, and only with 54.6–7 are 'leaving' and marriage brought together. The word *ʾădōnāy* is common alone in Lamentations (e.g. 1.14, 15), but the uniqueness of the usage may suggest that the compound expression *ʾădōnāy yhwh* (7.7; 25.8; 28.16; 40.10; 48.16; 49.22; 50.4, 5, 7, 9; 52.4; 56.8; 61.1, 11; 65.13, 15) is here divided between the two cola. The two terms come close together in 6.11–12, the passage just noted. 1QIs[a] has *wʾlwhy* ('and my God') above the *wʾdny*. This may imply that the Qumran community read out *yhwh* as *ʾădōnāy* and therefore provide an alternative in this second colon, as the MT does when the compound expression just noted occurs (e.g. v. 22). It also thereby further assimilates v. 14 to 40.27 (cf †Brockington). 4QIs[d] agrees with the MT.

49.15. Can a woman forget her baby, not having compassion on the child of her womb? Yes, these may forget. But as for me, I will not forget you. The LXX renders *ʾiššāh* by μήτηρ ('mother'); it uses γυνή later in the verse in the course of reworking the text (see note). The Vg translates more accurately if more generally *mulier* and the Syr *ʾnttʾ* ('woman/wife'). Dahood (*Questions disputées* [see on 40.27b], p. 27) understands *ʿûl* to refer to an unborn baby, as it can in Aramaic (see BDB), but this seems to fit ill in the context. In Hebrew it more naturally suggests a suckling, which heightens the force of the question. It is heightened further by the use of the verb *rāḥam* (pi; 'have compassion') which implicitly argues from a woman's nature; see 47.6.

The form *mēraḥēm* is another instance of *min* plus infinitive, here privative 'from having compassion', as at 44.18 (cf *HS* 321; *IBHS* 11.2e). The pregnant usage virtually implies 'so that she does not have compassion...' (cf LXX τοῦ μὴ ἐλεῆσαι..., Vg *ut non misereatur*...; and GK 119y). †Kittel suggests repointing *m*[e]*raḥēm* ('one who has compassion') to provide tighter parallelism. The form is masculine but such disagreements are possible and the form would thus take up that in v. 10; *IBHS* 6.5.2 views it as of common gender. R. Gordis ('Studies' [see on 44.8], p. 186 = p. 171) suggests that *mrḥm* is a word for woman or mother. D. N. Freedman (see †McKenzie) makes the same suggestion for the word *raḥam* ('womb'), here used to mean woman as in Judg 5.30 (on the root, see *HAL*). M. Dahood hypothesizes an occurrence of a verb *riḥḥam* ('to conceive, enwomb').[2] Such changes perhaps make the plural 'these' in the next line less surprising. However the word is understood, with its

[2] 'Denominative *riḥḥam*, "to Conceive, Enwomb"', in *Bib* 44 (1963), pp. 204–5.

links with the womb it is then juxtaposed with a more purely anatomical word for a woman's (or a man's) insides, *beṭen*, which is paired with *raḥam* in 46.3.

At the beginning of v. 15b, the MT's *maqqeph* implicitly links *gam* with the single word *ʾēlleh* that follows ('even these') as in 43.13, rather than with the whole sentence that follows as in 44.12; 47.3; 49.25. This would make good sense, yet *gam* followed by a pronoun often relates to the whole clause that the pronoun introduces rather than merely emphasizing the pronoun itself (see, e.g., 14.10; 30.33; 66.3, 4; and GK 153). Here rhythmic considerations might also incline the hearers to understand the word thus, as standing separately from the pronoun and making for a 3–3 rather than a 2–3 line. Either way this instance well illustrates how '*gam* is frequently employed when giving an exaggerated, aggravated or extreme case' (*EWS*, p. 143: the examples there include instances that link *gam* with one word and also ones that link it with a clause). Thus *DCH* renders 'even', C. van Leeuwen 'although'.[3] While the LXX and Vg render the construction as explicitly concessive (cf GK 160b), after the question in v. 15a it reads more naturally as a statement, and this understanding is encouraged by the subsequent *waw*-clause, 'but as for me…'.[4] Cf Tg *ʾp ʾm*.

For 'I will not…', the Tg has 'my word will not…'. The LXX adds εἶπε κύριος ('the Lord said') at the end.

תִּשְׁכַּחְנָה: Cairo fragment Eb 10 (see *HUB*) points the vb as ni, תִּשָּׁכַחְנָה ('these may be forgotten'), while the LXX has εἰ δὲ καὶ ἐπιλάθοιτο ταῦτα γυνή ('even if she should forget these'; cf Vg). To obtain this meaning Morgenstern (*HUCA* 36, p. 7) emends to תִּשְׁכַּח, while Driver (*JTS* 41, p. 164) repoints as תִּשְׁכָּחַנָּה, an energic form of the third s. But GK 47k warns against inferring this Arabic form in Hebrew. In addition, the word order with אלה preceding the vb hardly encourages this understanding. This order appears twice in v. 21b, but the context makes the meaning clear.

49.16. There, on my palms I engraved you. Your walls are before me continually. Whereas the LXX, Vg, Syr make explicit that these are 'my palms', in the MT the noun has no suffix. So v. 16a could be rendered 'on your palms I have engraved you [with my name]'. The verb *ḥāqaq* is used of the inscribing of decrees or decisions (10.1; 30.8); cf the nouns *ḥôq*/*ḥuqqāh* ('prescription, statute'), which 1QIs[a] *ḥwqwtyk* reads here (†Kutscher, p. 247; ET p. 322). It is nowhere else used of the inscribing of names. But Ezek 4.1 has used it for the engraving of a pictorial representation—of a city, indeed—and this fits with the second colon here. The inversion in the opening sentence

[3] 'Die Partikel אִם', in *Syntax and Meaning* (OTS 18, 1973), pp. 15–48 (see pp. 27–28); cf Kaddari, 'Concessive Connectors', p. 108.

[4] Cf C. J. Labuschagne, 'The Emphasizing Particle *gam* and its Connotations', in *Studia biblica et semitica* (T. C. Vriezen Festschrift; Wageningen, 1966), pp. 193–203 (see p. 201).

draws attention to the inversion in its contents, from negative in Ezekiel to positive and from hands that punish (40.2) to palms that remind. The Tg avoids the anthropomorphism by rendering 'as upon hands you are depicted before me'.

The back of the hand might be a more natural place for a tattoo or an aide-mémoire, but it seems unlikely that *kap* can denote an enclosed hand or fist (see P. R. Ackroyd, *ThWAT* on *kap*, § II.4a). †Korpel and de Moor suggest that the outline of the city is marked on Yhwh's palm because it has been resting on the city for so long. Perhaps the distinctiveness of *kap* lies more in its lacking the connotation of power and violence that attaches to *yad* (†Grimm and Dittert). †Eitan repoints to *kēpîm* ('rocks'). Dahood (*Ugaritic-Hebrew Philology* [see on 40.2aβ], p. 34) sees the ending as enclitic *m*.

A city with its walls can be thought of as a deity's crown, but it is not clear that this motif lies in the front of awareness here. There is no reference to the crown image. If it is present, it has been reworked. Instead of the walled city being the deity's mural crown, her children are her mural crown.[5]

1QIs[a] and 4Q176 *Tanḥûmîm* add *w* to begin the second colon. The LXX brings 'your walls' into the first colon and then has to supply εἶ ('you are') to complete the second.

49.17. Your children are hurrying your devastators. Your destroyers will get out from you. The MT takes the verb *māhar* (pi) in its common intransitive sense. Its accents then imply 'your children are hastening. Your devastators and your destroyers will get out from you.' The LXX's rendering καὶ ταχὺ οἰκοδομηθήσῃ ὑφ' ὧν καθῃρέθης, καὶ... ('and soon you will be built by your devastators, and...') more plausibly construes the line as 3–3 than as 2–4, with devastators/destroyers in parallelism. Keeping the MT's pointing but ignoring its accents we can thus take *mihărû* transitively, as in 1 Kgs 22.9 (and see BDB). The verb is a 'prophetic' qatal, a natural tense for a description of promised future deliverance, while a yiqtol in the second colon once again makes the meaning more explicit.

For the piel participle *m[e]hār[e]sayik*, 1QIs[a] *mhwrsyk* might be a dialectical variant (†Kutscher, p. 41; ET p. 56) but could imply preposition *min* plus the more common qal *horsāyik* ('than your devastators'; *Flusser). Aq ἀπὸ καθελόντων σε also implies the *min*, as may the LXX (†Torrey). As usual, the qal would suggest the process of devastation, the piel the result. The repointing to introduce the preposition produces the nice idea that Zion's rebuilders outdo her devastators so that the city is rebuilt more quickly than it was devastated. But this is allusively put, the use of the verb followed by *min* in this way is unparalleled, and there is no link with the second colon.

[5] See M. E. Biddle, 'The Figure of Lady Jerusalem', in *The Biblical Canon in Comparative Perspective* (ed. W. W. Hallo and others; Lewiston, NY, 1991), pp. 173–94 (see pp. 182–84); also K. Baltzer, 'Stadt-Tyche'.

The LXX also reads the first noun *bōnayik* rather than *bānāyik* (the difference in the middle vowel comes from the noun's no longer being in pause), with 1QIs[a] *bwnyk* (cf Th/Aq οἰκοδομοῦντες, Tg *ybnwn*, Vg *structores*). There is also some plausibility about this understanding, given that building and devastation are natural antitheses. In general the context focuses less on building and more on the return of inhabitants, though a reader (as opposed to a listener) might have continued to infer a paronomasia (see on v. 16). 'Your children' in the MT (cf Sym οἱ υἱοί σου, also a minority Tg tradition: see Sperber's apparatus) are these returners. They are the subject and object of verbs in v. 18, which otherwise lack subjects and objects. The term makes more explicit the metaphor of Zion as mother. The antithesis settlers–devourers in v. 19 parallels the antithesis children–devastators here; and children and settlers are equated in vv. 20–22.

49.18a. Lift your eyes about and look. All of them are gathering, they are coming to you. The Tg makes explicit that the imperatives, which are second singular feminine, continue to address Jerusalem, as in Jer 3.2 (see the end of the comment on v. 18b). The LXX construes the middle words to mean 'look at all of them' and the line as a tricolon, but the MT accents more plausibly make it a long bicolon in which the second colon answers the question raised by the first, 'look at what?'. It is the children of v. 17 who are the antecedents of the 'all of them' in the second colon.

שְׂאִי: 1QIs[a] סאי is MH spelling (†de Boer).

49.18b. As I am alive (Yhwh's oracle), certainly you will don all of them like jewellery and bind them on like a bride. The line has a triply solemn extra-metrical beginning, underlining the certainty of that to which it refers. 'As I live' (*ḥay-ʾānî*: on the pausal form in this expression, see GK 32c) is Yhwh's equivalent to the human oath 'as Yhwh is alive' (e.g. Jer 4.2). If the latter might be a construct nominal expression '[by] the life of Yhwh' (H. Ringgren, *ThWAT* on *ḥāyāh*, § III. 9), evidently this must be a verbal one (cf *DCH* on *ḥay*). As in 41.14; 43.10, 12, the asyndetic 'Yhwh's oracle' comes not at the beginning of a unit but resumptively nearer its end. The LXX's ὅτι and the Vg's *quia* take the particle *kî* that follows to mean '[I swear] that', but this requires some inference and 'certainly' is more likely: see on 45.23b.

Either way, the remainder of the line is the first of a series of five shorter lines that run through vv. 18b–20. The length of the opening cola varies, but each line has a two-stress second colon. After the opening *kullām* ('all of them') this first reads as a chiasm, once more mirroring the reversal suggested by the content (cf vv. 13b, 14). Literally it reads 'all of them like jewellery you will don and you will bind them on like a bride', or prosaically 'you will don and bind all of them on like a bride her jewellery'. The LXX's ...πάντας αὐτοὺς ἐνδύσῃ καὶ περιθήσῃ αὐτοὺς ὡς κόσμον νύμφης partly implies this understanding and hardly indicates the need to move *ʿădî* ('jewellery'); cf Tg . . .*kqšwṭ klt*ʾ. Co-ordinating simple *w* opens the second colon (†Saydon, p. 301).

The referent of *kullām* ('all of them') is again the children of v. 17, the proud finery of their mother who is (paradoxically) arrayed like a bride. For the apparently definite *kakkallāh* ('like *the* bride'), if we may trust the MT vocalization, see GK 126o; JM 137i; *IBHS* 13.5.1f.

ותקשׁרים ככלה: †Williamson (pp. 264–65) suggests omitting, as a marginal cross-reference to 61.10; v. 18b can then work as a 3–3 line. †Ehrlich suspects simply the last word on the basis of the comparison not fitting this woman with many children, and sees it as a misplaced misreading of כָּלּוּ from the end of the next line. Cairo fragment Eb 10 has qal וַתִּקְשְׁרִין for MT's piel (*HUB*). Qal 'bind' suggests process while piel 'bind on' suggests result (see *Piʿel*, p. 189).

49.19a. For your wastes, your desolations, your devastated land. . . The opening *kî* might resume 'that/certainly' from v. 18b, but the common 'for' makes good sense in the spelling out of a promise. Verse 19 as a whole will make clear how it explains both v. 17 and v. 18 from which it takes up words. 'Your devastated land' (*wᵉʾereṣ hărisutēk*—literally 'and the land of your devastation') is a unique phrase and a more out-of-the-way one than 'wastes' and 'desolations', though the verb came in v. 17. In one way or another the line thus resumes familiar expressions and sums up painfully familiar realities, yet closes in such a way as not to make the words mere makeweight. Preceding v. 19b, the line forms an anacoluthon. The words will be resumed in the second singular verb there (cf *TTH* 197). The effect of the anacoluthon is to reflect in the disjointedness of the syntax the disjointedness of the experience of wasting, desolation, and devastation, and the pathos of the community's awareness of the state of the land. As was the case in v. 8, the rarity of reference to the restoration of the land is counterbalanced by the unusual form of the allusion. The prophet is not merely reproducing a standard motif.

חרבתיך ושׁממתיך וארץ הרסתיך: to remove the anacoluthon, the MT's nouns can be repointed as verbs, הֲרַסְתִּיךְ חֵרַבְתִּיךְ וְשִׁמַּמְתִּיךְ. . ., ('I wasted you, I desolated you, I devastated you [to] the ground'; cf †Torrey, with †Williamson's comments, pp. 264–65: instead, at the beginning he adds יְכַלּוּ, 'they will be completed'; haplog.). The LXX does not render ארץ but it is surely paraphrasing, as when it resolves the anacoluthon by making the three nouns in v. 19a the subject of στενοχωρήσει ('will be straightened'); cf Vg *angusta erunt*. The Tg follows the MT.

49.19b. For now you will be too constricted for inhabitants. Your devourers will go far away. The *kî* ('for') is omitted by the LXX, Vg, and Syr (see on v. 19a). It resumes the one at the beginning of v. 19a, while the 'now' (*ʿattāh*) as usual sets up a contrast with what has preceded, though doubtless the two give force to what follows (cf Muilenburg, 'Linguistic and Rhetorical Usages' [see on 40.2aβ], p. 138). The context in vv. 18–21 speaks of Zion by means of a series of synecdoches ('your eyes', 'your wastes', 'your ears', 'your heart'), each accompanied by direct reference to 'you'. This suggests another significance in the anacoluthon in v. 19 (†Lack), though its resolution in the LXX and Vg means that they remove that direct address here. On the form *teṣᵉrî* ('be slight, constricted'), see GK 67dd. The verb might mean 'crowded *by* inhabitants', but more likely the *min* is again comparative (see GK 133c); compare v. 6a, and with this root 2 Kgs 6.1; Josh 19.47 (in the text presupposed by LXX). For the singular collective *yôšēb* ('inhabitants'), cf Gen 4.20; Amos 1.5, 8, also the feminine *yôšebet* in Isa 12.6. But the more direct background may again be 5.9 and 6.11 with its warning that cities will be without inhabitants (*mēʾên yôšēb*).

The inhabitants of v. 19b are the children of v. 17a. There is no reason to introduce the gentiles, who will appear in vv. 22–26. The destroyers of v. 17b are now the devourers of v. 19b. The verb is *bālaʿ*, again piel to suggest result rather than process, swallow up and thus annihilate rather than simply swallow (*Piʿel*, p. 192). If it has a background for prophet and hearers, this may lie in Lam 2.2, 5, 8, 16, though in three of these occurrences Yhwh is the subject. The finite verb neatly reuses *rāḥaq* from 6.12 with a nice reversal of use. There the inhabitants of Judah were being sent far away. Here the compliment is returned to Judah's devourers. Nearer to home are the occurrences of the adjective *rāḥôq* in vv. 1, 12, the location of the prophet's rhetorical audience and of Judeans due to return, changing places with their devourers. The LXX adds ἀπὸ σοῦ ('from you').

49.20. Further, the children of your bereavement will say in your hearing, 'The place is constricted for me. Move over for me so that I can live here.' The initial *ʿôd* parallels the use in promises of restoration such as Jer 31.3a, 3b, 4, 22, 38 [4a, 4b, 5, 23, 39]; 32.15; 33.10, 12,13; Zech 1.17; 8.4 (e.g. †Marti). There, however, it means 'again', which does not fit here. Once more the poet sets up expectations that the words that follow belie, for what the children will say does not merely repeat what was said before the destruction. In typological fashion, it goes beyond that. Vg *adhuc* takes *ʿôd* to denote continuance, while the LXX has γὰρ ('for'). †Feldmann renders 'the time will yet come when' (cf †Muilenburg), but this is difficult to justify. Of the usual meanings of *ʿôd*, addition is thus the one that makes best sense here (*DG* 53). It is the regular sense in chapters 40–55, where the word comes most often in statements of Yhwh's unique deity (e.g. 45.5, 6, 14, 18, 21, 22). Linked to the verb, the words it introduces add to the bare facts of v. 19. †Oort emends to *ʿad* ('until').

The children of v. 17 now explicitly reappear. Grammatically these could be 'your bereaved children', or the children of whom the mother understandably but mistakenly thought she had been bereaved but who now astonishingly return (†Rashi: cf LXX . . .οὓς ἀπολώλεκας). More likely the children of her bereavement (*šikkulîm*: see on *šᵉkôl* in 47.8) are ones born after the mother had lost her first children. JM 136h suggests that the plural is one of extension in time, suggesting a state that is prolonged, GK 124d that it is an abstract plural suggesting the various concrete manifestations of a state (cf *IBHS* 7.4.2). In truth, for the most part the people who 'return' to Zion will be people who had never lived there before.

Whereas the promise in v. 19b used the expression *ṣārar min* ('to be too constricted for'), here for variety the people's own words use the adjectival phrase *ṣar lî* ('constricted for me'), which with the different preposition does not explicitly indicate comparison. It is evidently an individual 'child' who speaks (the Syr has plurals), apparently to another of the children, as the verb *gᵉšāh* is second person singular masculine. So, as v. 20a suggests, Madam Zion is overhearing her children speaking to each other. The verb *nāgaš* usually means 'draw near' but like some other verbs for motion it can suggest movement from the perspective of the speaker or of the destination. So here it means 'draw near [to somewhere else]', that is, 'draw away [from me]'; cf the use of *ʾāsap* in v. 5a. The LXX's ποίησόν μοι τόπον ('make space for me'; cf Vg) translates according to the sense. 'Live here' is the verb *yāšab* (cf *yôšēb*, 'inhabitant[s]', in v. 19b).

49.21. You will say to yourself, 'Who fathered these for me, seeing I was bereaved and barren, gone into exile and passing away. Who reared these? When I was left on my own—where were these?' Madam Zion's first statement was a plangent, succinct 2–2 lament. The closing statement is a poignant three-line set of rhetorical questions, questions of wonder that contrast with the aggressive rhetorical questions in which the prophet specializes. †Thomas lays out the whole verse as three lines, the introduction then being part of the first bicolon. This gives it a place in the rhetoric equivalent to that of the opening colon of v. 20, but otherwise there is little poetic shape to the resultant arrangement. The MT divides the verse after 'barren', and this points us towards treating 'you will say to yourself' as another extra-metrical introduction like that to v. 18b. Following that, the bulk of v. 21 then becomes a 6-colon ABBABA sequence. The MT's division comes after the first two cola.

Each 'A' colon comprises a question, announced by the interrogatives *mî*, *mî*, *ʾēpōh* ('who', 'who', 'where'). The RSV renders *ʾēpōh* ('whence'), but this is difficult to parallel. In Judg 8.18 *ʾēpōh* may mean 'how/of what kind' (BDB) and †Volz extends that meaning to here, but the LXX and Vg assume the more usual meaning 'where', which fits. It raises the question of the children's location when the mother seemed alone. Each question also incorporates the demonstrative *ʾēlleh* ('these'). It is natural to refer this to the children who have been prominent in vv. 17–20.

Each 'B' colon comprises a statement about the state of Zion. They form a double and a single circumstantial clause, marked as such by their opening with the pronominal subject (cf *TTH* 160). The single clause is introduced by *hēn*. The particle's regular deictic meaning does not work well here (NRSV and NIV simply omit it), and we have followed Labuschagne (*Syntax and Meaning* [see on 40.15], p. 11) in taking it as the introduction to a circumstantial clause. The pronouns also function to make clear the subject of the clause when it changes. In addition, in the first the order means that the pronoun precedes the predicate, the reverse of the regular order. This has the effect of emphasizing the contrast with what what has preceded (see *IBHS* 8.4.2). In the second, the pronoun is expressed even though the clause has a finite verb and thus does not need the pronoun to establish the meaning.

'Gone into exile and passing away' follows asyndetically from what precedes and is succeeded by a *w*-clause. 1QIs[a] adds a *w* to remove the asyndeton and omits the subsequent *w*. The final question also begins asyndetically, though here the LXX and Vg provide a copula. Both the *w*-clause and the asyndetic clause are cleft sentences, opening with the deictic/demonstrative, the latter being a clause with pleonastic pronoun (Geller, 'Cleft Sentences' [see on 45.18a], p. 22).

The LXX lacks the second 'B' colon, *gōlāh wesûrāh*, which has been seen as a corrupt dittograph of the preceding word *galmûdāh*,[6] or simply as a prosaic gloss that makes Zion an exile when it is not (†Duhm). LXX's ἐγὼ δὲ ἄτεκνος καὶ χήρα... ('but I [was] childless and a widow...') in fact assimilates the second line to 47.8–9 (Jeppesen, 'Mother Zion', p. 114).

In terms of their connotations, the words *gōlāh wesûrāh* are not prosaic. In content they are more so. For a moment they abandon the metaphor of motherhood and bereavement for literal description of the community's experience, though other verses also do that (e.g. in vv. 16–18). But the words are taken up from Amos 6.7 (*yiglû berōʾš gōlîm wesār mirzaḥ serûḥîm* 'they will go into exile at the head of those who go into exile, and the revelry of the carefree will pass away'), so that they fit the prophet's practice of taking up earlier prophecy and declaring that it has been fulfilled but can now be reversed. †Thomas's layout shows how the phrase occupies the exact midpoint of the verse around which everything else clusters, and is thus potentially the interpretative centre for understanding the whole.

The first question uses the verb *yālad*, which more often means 'bear' than 'beget', but it is here masculine. The masculine might be used with a feminine subject and meaning: perhaps cf Gen 20.17,

[6] According to †Barthélemy this was first proposed by P. Ruben in his *Critical Remarks Upon Some Passages of the Old Testament* (London, 1896).

though Abimelech may be included in the subject there, and there is not the same ambiguity as here. The feminine *yālᵉdāh*, which the prophet has avoided, is the more common form, so it seems more likely that the masculine is significant and that the question relates to who begot these children. The LXX's ἐγέννησε and the Vg's *genuit* are ambiguous.

The verb *giddēl* in the second question is again masculine (on the form, see GK 52l). Both masculine verbs contrast with 51.18 where Zion is the subject and both are feminine. 'When *gdl* in the piel denotes the rearing of children, not only does it have reference to keeping them alive in spite of the great infant mortality rate, but also to "making something out of" the children', as is reflected in the usage in parallelism with *rûm* in the piel (R. Mosis, *ThWAT* on *gādal*, II.4b). In the parallelism in the present context, bringing up thus goes beyond giving birth.

The 'I'-clauses, and that central phrase 'gone into exile and passing away' which is grammatically dependent on the first, are the kind of statements that might appear in a lament. Yet the words have few actual parallels in laments and are more obviously creations carefully crafted for this context. Indeed, each subsection of vv. 14–26 is provided with an allusion to a lament (see †Westermann, †Schoors).

'Bereaved' comes from the verb *šākal* which occurs in Lam 1.20 in the piel, but the qal is rare and its passive participle comes only here. It is accompanied by the even less familiar *galmûd* ('barren') which comes otherwise only in Job, and not in lament contexts. 'Gone into exile' comes from the verb *gālāh* which appears in Lam 1.3, but its participial form corresponds rather to Amos 6.7, just noted. There the accompanying verb *sār* ('pass away') also occurs. †Ibn Ezra takes *sûrāh* as a verbal adjective rather than a participle (cf GK 72p, Vg *captiva*, Sym, Syh αἰχμάλωτος—which however imply *ʾăsûrāh* 'imprisoned'). *IBHS* 37.4e takes it as passive 'rejected', but notes that it is rare for such a participle to indicate a state rather than a process. Further, *sûr* is an intransitive verb, and Aq ἀφισταμένη invites us to take the passive participle as intransitive rather than passive in meaning, as in Jer 17.13 (BDB; cf GK 50f). This also corresponds to the meaning of the wᵉqatal form in Amos 6.7, to which 1QIsᵃ *wsrh* assimilates the reading. The precise connotation of *sûrāh* is as open as is that of 'pass away' in English. It might be very gloomy.

While the verb *šāʾar* ('be left') and related nouns are used in explicit connection with the exilic communities in passages such as 11.11 and 46.3, they are often used of Jerusalem and Judah (e.g. 4.3; 28.5; 37.4, 31–32). The usage here, however, is distinctive, as it works within the image of Zion as mother. Given other indications that vv. 14–21 presuppose a re-reading of 5.8–10 and 6.11–13, it is striking that in 6.11 the LXX apparently presupposed *tiššāʾēr* ('[the land] is left [desolate]') for MT *tiššāʾeh*, while 'on your own' (*lᵉbaddᵉkem*) came in 5.8 (†Williamson, p. 54).

IV.b.ii. I will summon bearers for your children (49.22–23)

49.22a. The Lord Yhwh has said this. There, I will raise my hand to nations, lift my signal to peoples. The composite title *ʾădōnāy yhwh* means that this new segment opens in a parallel way to v. 14 (see comment). There Zion spoke about *ʾădōnāy yhwh*; here *ʾădōnāy yhwh* speaks about Zion. In effect the promise begins 'these are the words to Zion of the one who was being questioned earlier'. In this way v. 14 continues to set the agenda for vv. 14–26. 1QIs[a] and the LXX lack *ʾădōnāy* and thus conform the messenger formula to its usual form elsewhere—though not in these chapters where the short form without any qualification is very unusual (see comment on 45.14). 1QIs[a] also prefaces the verse with *kyʾ* ('for'); cf v. 25.

The first two cola within Yhwh's words are neatly parallel, with the word order verb–indirect object–object, indirect object–verb–object. Yhwh is now acting as general, summoning nations/peoples to play their part in bringing about the events that Yhwh has determined. Nearly half the occurrences of the word 'signal' (*nēs*) come in Isaiah, most in mutual dependence in 5.26; 11.10, 12; 13.2; 49.22; 62.10 (the others are 18.3; 30.17; 31.9; 33.23) (cf †Clements, pp. 108–9; and on the relationship of the passages, see †Williamson, pp. 63–67, and his references).

עמים: LXX τὰς νήσους ('the islands') hardly implies איים. It is translating loosely (†Ottley). 1QIs[a] העמים perhaps generalizes the statement—virtually 'all peoples' (cf †Koenig, p. 22).

49.22b. They will bring your sons in their embrace, your daughters will be carried on their shoulder. The nations are summoned to fulfill the promise in 14.2, where Yhwh declared *wehĕbîʾûm ʾel meqômām* ('and they [peoples] will bring them to their place'). Now is the moment when they will indeed bring them (*wehēbîʾû*), to a place that (we have already seen) will turn out to be too small (v. 20). Verses 14–21 have spoken only of *bānîm*, which we have assumed to suggest 'children' rather than merely 'sons'. Here in the parallelism *benōtayik* (your daughters) explicitly accompany *bānayik* ('your sons'); cf 43.6. The merism emphasizes that *all* the offspring are covered (†Bonnard).

In the only other occurrence of *ḥōṣen* ('embrace'), in Neh 5.13, the word suggests the fold in the front of a person's outer clothes (cf *ḥēṣen*[?] in Ps 129.7). The Syr guesses 'hands'. The second colon pictures the young ones either clasped to the chest or hoisted on the shoulder (*kātēp*): H.-J. Zobel (*ThWAT* on *kātēp*, § II.1) suggests that *kātēp* denotes the front of the shoulder area or 'chest', which makes good sense of this occurrence, but poorer sense of others. The double masculine in the first colon is paralleled by the double feminine in the second (*TTCHV*, p. 222). The Tg gives the children a splendid rather than a homely ride, in carriages and litters.

49.23. Kings will be your foster-fathers, their queens your nursing mothers. Faces to the ground they will fall down before you. They will lick up the dust of your feet. Then you will acknowledge that I am Yhwh. Those who wait for me will not be shamed. As if she was a queen, Madam Zion will have substantial help in bringing up her children—kings and queens will do it for her (the LXX has 'queens' without 'their', giving more exact parallelism). Their falling to the ground before Madam Zion will be another sign of their recognition of her. It is an extravagant middle-eastern sign of homage, like Abraham falling to the ground before the Hittites (Gen 23.7, 12). The piel *yᵉlaḥēkû* again points to result rather than process (*Piʿel*, pp. 146, 192–93).

Like the messenger 'formula', in these chapters the recognition 'formula' (v. 23b) is never a mere formula. It is always qualified in the light of the context. So it is here, though this is difficult to bring out in translation. The line reads '...that I am Yhwh, the one whose waiters will not be shamed'. On the *ʾăšer* clause, see on 41.8aβ. One aspect of the reversal which v. 23 promises is that the shaming which has been Zion's experience is now due to be that of her enemies and not that of Zion and her children (see 41.11; 42.17; 44.9, 11; 45.16, 17, 24). Once again waiting is a lament motif and a matter of waiting for Yhwh rather than merely for help (Westermann, *Forschung*, pp. 219–65). The qal participle 'those who wait for me' (here *qōwāy*, with suffix; Vg *eum* implies *qōwāw*) is missing from the LXX, which also continues the second person construction from the previous clause.

אפים ארץ: **אפים ארצה** is more usual (see GK 156c).

IV.b.iii. I will overcome their oppressor (49.24–26)

The subsection begins by speaking of a warrior and a just one, and of plunder and captives. It is not immediately clear to whom these terms refer. By the end of the subsection it will be clearer that the warrior is Babylon, who is 'just' because it is Yhwh's agent in bringing its deserved calamity on Zion. The captives and plunder are thus Zion's people. But the passage works by not making this clear immediately.

49.24. Can plunder be taken from a warrior? Or can captives escape from a just one? The continuity with v. 23 suggests that Yhwh continues to be the speaker. To make Zion the speaker, *Merendino ('Jes 49, 14–26', pp. 341–42) has to add 'Zion said'.

While a recognition statement like the one in v. 23 might well signal the end of a subsection (cf 41.20) it need not do so (cf 45.6), and a rhetorical question like this one could well signal the beginning of a new subsection but it need not necessarily do so (cf on v. 15a). It will be the resumptive messenger formula in v. 25 that will confirm that a new subsection begins in v. 24, covering another aspect of the prophet's implausible promise. How is it possible for those children to come home to their mother?

The alternatives offered by the two questions are introduced by the particles *hă-* and *wᵉʾim*, the standard way to introduce alternative questions. They are more common when the apparent alternatives are merely rhetorical, as here. They are then usually questions that expect the answer 'No', also as here, so that the second particle makes the nature of the question quite clear insofar as the first has not already done so (see BDB, pp. 50, 210). The verse then opens and closes with the two verbs, both yiqtol, one pual or qal passive *yuqqaḥ*, the other niphal *yimmālēṭ*.

For the first, 1QIsᵃ has impersonal active plural *yqḥw* for the MT's *yuqqaḥ*, in keeping with its dislike for the impersonal passive (†Rubinstein, p. 319). The LXX's μὴ λήμψεταί τις might imply *yiqqaḥ*. It then renders the second by passive σωθήσεται ('be saved'), but the niphal is regularly intransitive (see BDB), perhaps invariably so (so *HAL*?; cf 20.6; 37.38). Further, a verb meaning 'save' begs questions regarding what kind of person holds the plunder and what is the significance of its being held by them.

'Plunder' is a noun from the verb 'take' (*malqôaḥ* from *lāqaḥ*) and thus constitutes a paronomasia here. The noun designates people or things 'taken' in war and comes otherwise only in Numbers 31. Isaiah 5.29 referred to the nations who responded to Yhwh's raising a signal as seizing plunder, but used different words (Davies, 'Destiny', p. 115). The singular collective 'captives' (*šᵉbî*) accompanies *malqôaḥ* in Numbers 31 but appears elsewhere alone, and more commonly as an abstract noun for captivity. Here the second noun gives precision to the first by making it clear that we are talking about human (or at least live) booty. These two nouns come next to each other, except for the intervening introductory *wᵉʾim* (1QIsᵃ omits the *w*).

We are left with the two middle elements in this chiastic bicolon, literally 'can be taken–from a warrior–plunder?': or 'can captives–just–escape?'. Evidently the people are captives, but is their captor Yhwh (cf 42.13) (so that as prey they are secure), or is it Babylon (cf Jer 50.36; 51.30, 56, 57) (so that as plunder their situation is hopeless)?

Any hope that the second colon might clarify this question is frustrated, but at least the setting of the verse as a whole does clarify the more ambiguous equivalent word there, *ṣaddîq*. In isolation this might naturally be taken as an adjective qualifying *šᵉbî*, 'or can a just captive…' (so †Ibn Ezra), but the required meaning 'just' in the sense of 'rightful/lawful' cannot be paralleled. Sym has αἰχμαλωσία δικαίου ('the captivity of a just one'). This might be an objective genitive identifying the exilic community as *ṣaddîq*, but it seems unlikely that the prophet would identify the community thus. Or it might be a subjective genitive, denoting people captive *to* a just one, which works with the parallelism in seeing *ṣaddîq* and *gibbôr* as having comparable roles in the two cola. So †Qimchi thinks of the captives of a strong and just conqueror; cf the Tg, though it has plural *zk*ʾ*yn*. Rather than implying a genitive relationship, however, it would be more characteristic for the line to presuppose that the preposition in the first colon applies also in the second.

Either way, the 'just one' is the same person as the 'warrior'. It was again Yhwh who was the just one in 45.21, though in 13.3 the similar *m*ᵉ*quddāšāy* ('my consecrated ones') referred to human warriors, actually Babylon's conquerors, and stood in parallelism with *gibbôr*. Neither parallel points to the just warrior being Israel's captors. For *ṣaddîq* 1QIsᵃ has ʿ*ryṣ* ('terrifier'); cf Vg *robusto*, Syr *nšyn*ʾ. This is surely assimilation to v. 25 rather than suggesting that *ṣaddîq* was originally a marginal gloss (so Allen, 'Cuckoos' [see on 42.10b], pp. 147–48). The LXX solves the problem of the scandal of the word *ṣaddîq* for its translators' own communities by a paraphrase that incorporates the word ἀδίκως ('unjustly'): see †Seeligmann, p. 112.

שְׁבִי: *HUB* suggests that the LXX, Aq, and Th read a qal ptpl שֹׁבֵי; but the expected form would be שֹׁבֵה.

49.25a. For Yhwh has said this. Yes, a warrior's captives can be taken, a terrifier's plunder can escape. By its nature the further unusual unadorned brief messenger formula suggests more of a link with what precedes than the prophet's characteristic amplified formulae do. We have taken the *kî* ('for') to make that link explicit even if it is also asseverative (see on 40.2aβ). If so, the causal link is with a presupposed positive answer to the question in v. 24, which comes explicitly in what then follows. The sequence of vv. 24–25 otherwise parallels that within v. 15. After the *hă*- question in v. 24 there comes the unexpected answer in the *gam* ('yes/even') assertion in v. 25a and the contrasting *w*ᵉ-... ʾ*ānōkî* ('but I myself') reassurance in v. 25b. The unexpected reversal of 'captives' and 'plunder' compared with v. 24 mirrors the unexpected reversal the line speaks of. 1QIsᵃ assimilates v. 25a to v. 24, and this time replaces the pual or passive qal *yuqqaḥ* by the then more familiar niphal *ylqḥ* (†Kutscher, p. 33; ET p. 43). The Tg prefers the explicit 'I will restore... rescue'.

Apart from these unexpectednesses, the novelty in v. 25a is the occurrence of the noun ʿ*ārîṣ* ('terrifier') instead of *ṣaddîq* in the second clause. The great terrifier in Isaiah is Yhwh (see the verb in 2.19, 21; 8.12–13; 29.23; 47.12; also the noun *ma*ʿ*ărāṣāh* in 10.33). This may make it unlikely that the MT felt the need to replace ʿ*ārîṣ* by *ṣaddîq* in v. 24 because the former seemed an inappropriate epithet for Yhwh (so de Waard, *Bible Translator* 41, p. 312). On the other hand, Ezekiel uses the noun to refer to Babylon (see, e.g., 32.12), and this could suggest that the terrifier here is Babylon, or Persia. The next line will suggest it is Babylon, as in Ezekiel.

49.25b. But your assailant I myself will assail and your children I myself will deliver. RSV's 'for' is neither justified nor necessary. The *w*ᵉ link suggests a contrast with what has preceded, as in the parallel

v. 15. But a difference from v. 15b is that there the verb was repeated, so that the 'but' related solely to its subject ('yes a woman may, but I will not'). Here v. 25b contrasts more systematically with v. 25a. The 'I' is again expressed, indeed twice, but first the objects come in emphatic position before the two verbs. The word order is reflected in the translation above. The logic is thus that v. 25a first makes an assertion that runs contrary to the expectation set up by the question in v. 24, then v. 25b makes an affirmation that in turn runs contrary to the expectations set up by this assertion. In a sense it could have followed more directly from v. 24 with a 'thus' rather than a 'but', as the second colon in v. 15b could have followed in this way directly from v. 15a. Even if a terrifying warrior might lose his plunder, this situation is different: it is Yhwh in person who will make that happen. The Tg anticipates this point by introducing first person active verbs into v. 25a.

'Assail/assailant' (*rîb*/*yārîb*) can refer to ordinary quarrelling or fighting, but that meaning hardly applies to the relationship between a 'warrior' and his 'plunder', and more often the verb has legal connotations (see on 41.11b). This fits the description of the warrior as *ṣaddîq* in v. 24b (†Motyer). Thus the LXX renders ἐγὼ δὲ τὴν κρίσιν σου κρινῶ (cf Vg). The LXX's noun actually means 'judgment' and might reflect a reading such as *rîbēk* ('your judgment') rather than *yᵉrîbēk*, but its rendering through vv. 24–26 is very paraphrastic. 1QIsᵃ lacks the initial *y* but it is not clear whether it reads *rybk* or *rwbk*, presumably the former. In addition it seems to have an extra *y* above the line, which suggests plural *rybyk*. But these readings may only reflect the much greater familiarity of the phrase *rîb rîb* ('plead a cause'), for example, in laments Pss 43.1 and 74.22. The LXX re-words the text in the same way at Jer 18.19. The MT's phrase opens the way to a neat point-by-point parallelism in v. 25b as a whole (see the translation), which the LXX loses. In addition the alliteration in the line is noteworthy. Every word either begins ᵓ or contains *k* or both (†Boadt, p. 362). The MT also compares with Ps 35.1, another lament, though there the word is plural *yᵉrîbayik*. The Vg's noun phrase suggests this plural here. A Cairo Geniza MS reads *yᵉrîbayik* (see *HUB*), the Syr *wdynyky*, and 1QIsᵃ has its supralinear *y*. Either way, paradoxically it is the just warrior against whom Yhwh is now bringing a case.

In the parallel colon the metaphorical point is made more straightforwardly, though still metaphorically. 'Deliver' (*yāšaᶜ* hi) is another verb with legal connotations (see on 43.3a), so the act of freeing is again designated as one that brings the just liberation of someone who cries out for justice—in this case, for her children. It is only with the suffixes on 'assailant' and 'children' that Madam Zion surfaces in vv. 24–26.

So far in vv. 24–25a the just warrior/terrifier might be Yhwh, or Babylon, or Babylon's coming conqueror. What happens when we come to v. 25b? If the warrior is Yhwh, or Yhwh's agents in defeating Babylon, then the sequence of thought is that contrary to what people might expect, Israel as booty/captives might in one sense not be as secure as it thought, but is nevertheless finally secure because Yhwh will after all rise to assail and deliver. The thought then links with that of the earlier passage where Yhwh was characterized as a warrior, 42.13–17. Like that passage, too, it intertwines the apparently contrasting images of Yhwh as mother and Yhwh as warrior. The strengths and the incompletenesses of each image makes them balance each other. There, too, Yhwh seemed to be capable of defeat by default and to require raising from inactivity in order to act in deliverance; for Yhwh's capacity to be defeated by determined human resistance, cf also Ezek 29.17–21. If the warrior stands for Babylon's conqueror, the transition to v. 25b is subtle in another respect. A witness to this is the RSV's introducing of that causative link between the two lines, 'for I will contend…'.

Whether the warrior is Yhwh or the conqueror, however, the assailant has to be a different person. This seems difficult. Rather, the (formerly) just warrior/terrifier/assailant must be Babylon from whom Zion's children have to be freed. †Miller (pp. 81–82) draws attention to the transition in the oracles from conflict with the prophet's own community to conflict with Babylon, while †Hessler raises the question whether the warrior/terrifier is Death itself (of which Babylon might be an embodiment), than whom Yhwh is indeed more powerful (cf v. 26b).

49.26a. I will feed their flesh to your oppressors. They will be drunk on their blood like new wine. In this poetic context, this is hardly a mere prosaic account of cannibalism like that envisaged in Deut 28.53–57 and Jer 19.9, and portrayed in 2 Kgs 6.24–31. Dahood (*CBQ* 22, pp. 404–6) points to a parallel with a Phoenician inscription where the language suggests being reduced to the last extremity. There may be a stress on the suffixes, 'their *own* flesh/blood' (so GK 135l). Such language can be a vivid way of describing people coming to a self-inflicted death (see Qoh 4.5), though if so the Tg avoids it along with something of the line's inherent gruesomeness by having the oppressors' flesh fed to the birds and their blood to wild animals. 'Oppressors' (*yānāh* hi) normally refers to the illegal ill-treatment of the poor and weak within Israel (e.g. Lev 19.33). Again it thus has legal connotations. Yhwh is promising the relief that the law required for the oppressed.

Here *ʿāsîs* ('new wine') strictly suggests the newly pressed juice of the grape (*ʿāsas* means 'crush'), without implying that it has not yet fermented since it is evidently intoxicating (cf Joel 1.5). As well as hinting at large-scale drinking such as might naturally accompany the first winemaking of the season, the image recalls that of treading grapes with the process's blood-like results; again cf 63.1–3. But these people are treading themselves.

והאכלתי: If 1QIs[a] ואוכלתי is qal ('and I will eat') it is a slip. It might be poel with the same meaning as hi, or an Aramaizing aphel. The LXX simplifies and improves the parallelism with φάγονται ('[your oppressors] will eat').

49.26b. All flesh will acknowledge that I am Yhwh your deliverer, the strong one of Jacob, your restorer. The closing line of vv. 24–26 parallels that of vv. 22–23, but in the manner of parallelism takes it further. It is a tricolon (3–3–3?) whose extra length matches the extra extent of its reach.

The word 'deliverer' (*môšîaʿ*) is familiar enough in such contexts (see 43.3a), though here it picks up the verb 'deliver' in v. 25b. The action there promised is the specific event that brings about the recognition of Yhwh as deliverer. The equally familiar 'restorer' similarly came in v. 7 (see on 41.14b). The second and third cola are arranged chiastically so that the two participles come together at the centre, and as a novelty at the end comes the new title in parallel with the name Yhwh, 'the strong one of Jacob' (cf only 1.24; 60.16; also Gen 49.24; Ps 132.2, 5; and Sir 51.12). The usage suggests this may be a Jerusalem title for Yhwh. The pronunciation *ʾăbîr* (construct of *ʾābîr*) is likely an artificial way of distinguishing the word from *ʾabbîr* (see on 46.12). Each time the phrase appears in Isaiah, the LXX tones down the anthropomorphism. Here it renders 'the one who upholds the strength of Jacob'. It might reflect redivision of the words as *wgʾl kʾbyr* (*HUB*).

IV.b.iv. I have been reaching out to you (50.1–3)

50.1a. Yhwh has said this. Where, then, is the divorce-paper belonging to your mother, whom I sent off? Or, which of my creditors was it to whom I sold you? In the English Bible a new chapter begins, hardly because vv. 1–3 and 11 form an *inclusio* (†Torrey), for the links are slight, nor solely because of the new messenger formula (†Alexander), which again takes brief and perhaps resumptive form, nor solely because 49.26 looks like an ending (†Cheyne), for it looks no more final than 41.20, but perhaps because of these in combination with the change of addressee, for now the children are questioned about their mother. The real exilic audience is thus now two moves away from the rhetorical audience. In the MT 50.1 is more appropriately marked merely by a setuma (a petucha comes at 49.22 and 51.1).

Divorce is a new image for the problematic situation Madam Zion finds herself in. For the giving of a divorce-paper, see Deuteromy 24, where the verb 'send off' (see 43.14) appears three times. The LXX renders the relative clause ᾧ ἐξαπέστειλα αὐτήν ('with which I sent her off'; cf Vg), but *ʾimmekem* ('your mother') is the nearer antecedent and the above understanding corresponds to the unambiguous construction in the next line.

After the messenger formula, the two questions that occupy the rest of v. 1a may be seen as long lines in parallelism with each other. 'Where, then' represents *ʾê zeh*, the interrogative followed by the enclitic (see BDB, p. 261). 'Or' (*ʾô*) is rare in poetry (but see 41.22), alternatives normally being expressed by means of the copula *wᵉ* (e.g. 44.8, 10, 14, 20). Perhaps it, too, carries some emphasis here, or perhaps it is part of a prosaic tone to v. 1a as a whole (compare the double *ʾăšer*, and the nouns). It introduces a different metaphor, independent of that in the first question. Now Yhwh is like a man who has sold his children into slavery because of debt (see, e.g., Neh 5.1–5). Obviously money has not changed hands in this 'sale'; *mākar* refers to the handing over of something in payment of the existent debt.[7] The reality is that as well as the city being desolated, its inhabitants have been taken away. LXX's ὑπόχρεῳ means a debtor rather than a creditor. The LXX knew that in reality Yhwh has only debtors, not creditors.

50.1b. There, for your wrongdoings you were sold. For your rebellions your mother was sent off. The verbs from v. la recur in the latter part of each colon in v. 1b, but they are preceded by a prepositional expression that changes their force. Yhwh responds to the charges in reverse order, so that v. 1b has a chiastic relationship with what precedes. Yes, they were sold, but the reason lay in them, not in Yhwh's lack of resources. Yes, their mother was sent off, but a look at the divorce paper will clarify the reason. In a sense, the logic breaks down, or rather the metaphor does so. Yhwh's reason for sending off the mother was the rebelliousness of the children—who in reality are the addressees, seen as one with their literal parents.

שִׁלְּחָה: Vg repeats the active verb 'I sent away', while Tg interprets the metaphor, 'your congregation was sent away'.

50.2a. Why did I come and there was no-one, call and there was no-one answering? Has my hand really become too short for redeeming? Do I have no strength to rescue? The word for 'why' is not *lāmāh* but the rarer *maddûaʿ*, which suggests an incredulous question. It commonly follows on earlier questions that imply a negative answer. We have seen that v. 1b seems to exclude this understanding of v. 1a, and A. Jepsen thus sees v. 1b as a mistaken gloss.[8]

Characteristically, v. 2a reopens the question from v. 1a and asks

[7] See Z. W. Falk, 'Hebrew Legal Terms: ii', in *JSS* 12 (1967), pp. 241–44 (see pp. 242–43); and in general, R. de Vaux, *Les institutions de l'Ancien Testament* (2 vols; Paris, 1958 and 1960), Vol. 1, pp. 130, 263; ET *Ancient Israel* (London, 1961), pp. 83, 172.

[8] 'Warum', in *Das Ferne und nahe Wort* (L. Rost Festschrift, ed. F Maass, BZAW 105, Berlin, 1967), pp. 106–13 (pp. 110–12).

the hearers to look at issues in more than one way. It is also characteristic that the poet should go on from responding to an accusation by making a counter-charge, which takes up the broader question which underlies 49.14–50.3 and responds to it robustly as Yhwh suggests that the boot is on the other foot.

In the first pair of questions, idiomatically the 'why' comes at the beginning, and just once, applying to both cola. Strictly it relates to the second phrase each time, 'there is no-one/no-one answered'; cf 5.4b (GK 150m; JM 161k). There is another implication of the interdependence of the cola. The NRSV glosses *ʾên ʾîš* in the first colon, '[there was no-one] there', presupposing that the phrase is a complete statement. More likely *ʾên ʾîš* is completed by *ʾên ʿôneh* ('there was no answerer'), so that prosaically the line asks 'When I came and called, why was there no-one answering?'. For this latter construction in parallelism see also Isa 59.16; also in prose and thus not undivided 1 Kgs 8.46. The latter uses *ʾādām*, the other word for 'man'. This marital context includes the word *ʾîš*, which also does not recur in 66.4 (†Korpel and de Moor).

*Merendino ('Jes 50, 1–3 [9b.11]', p. 229) suggests that the addressees in v. 2 are no longer Zion but her foes. In a court scene where Yhwh issues a challenge to the nations, the questions would draw attention to the incapacity of the nations or their gods to respond to Yhwh's question about who acts and speaks in the world (cf 41.21–29), and would implicitly reassert Yhwh's unique power to act. The verb *bôʾ* ('come') is indeed used of Yhwh's coming to give judgment in 3.14; 5.19; 35.4, though Yhwh comes to Jerusalem more comfortingly in 40.10. The verb *qārāʾ* ('call'), too, occurs in connection with a summons to trial in 59.4, and *ʿānāh* ('answer') in connection with a response to such a challenge in 41.28, while these two verbs come together in this connection in Job 9.16 13.22.

Another pair of questions follows. Like 49.24 (see comment), they open *hă-* and *weʾim* (1QIsa omits the *w*), which are signals for questions that expect a negative answer, and the questions they introduce once again relate to the question whether Yhwh has the ability to restore the people. The LXX's 'is not my hand strong' avoids even raising the question whether Yhwh's hand might be short and incapable of reaching out to act (†Fritsch, p. 167). The Syr's 'has my hand indeed cut short and delivered' may also be a theological change (*HUB*). The qatal verb is preceded by the infinitive absolute. Whereas at 48.8b (see comment) this usage suggests repetition, here it strengthens the verbal idea, a recurrent usage in rhetorical questions (*EWS*, p. 87; *DG* 101a; *IBHS* 35.3.1g). It is followed by another comparative *min* (see on v. 19). The point is put more prosaically in the parallel colon by the question *weʾim-ʾên-bî kōaḥ* (lit. 'and is there not in me strength'): cf 40.26, 29, 31, as well as the language of the exodus/Red Sea event (e.g. Exod 9.16; 15.6; 32.11).

For 'redeeming' (*pedût*), LXX τοῦ ῥύσασθαι, Tg *mlmprq*, Vg *redimere* might imply rather a form of the verb *pādāh*, presumably infinitive *pedôt*. Dahood ('Phoenician-Punic Philology' [see on 41.2b],

p. 464) sees *pᵉdût* itself as a Phoenician-style infinitive. The monetary metaphor presumably links with the talk of selling in the context.

50.2b. There, by my blast I can dry up sea. I can make rivers desert. Their fish will smell for lack of water. They will die of thirst. Once again a particle, this time *hēn* ('there'), witnesses to some neat patterning in the questions and strong affirmations in 49.14–50.3. First, within 50.1–2 it completes a double sequence of repeated questions in vv. 1a and 2a and contrasting *hēn*-affirmations in vv. 1b and 2b. In addition, it completes another sequence in 49.14–50.3 as a whole: see the introduction to 49.14–50.3. The occurrence of *ḥārab* ('be dry') here means that if there are three roots *ḥrb* (so BDB: but contrast *HAL*; *DCH*; O. Kaiser, *ThWAT* on *ḥārab*, § I), all three have appeared in 49.1–50.3 (see 49.2, 17).

The language in the previous line could have suggested reference to the exodus. Thus †Múgica (pp. 202–3) understands the verbs in vv. 2b–3 as instances of past yiqtol. Yet the way the language develops in v. 2b moves away from suggesting any specific link with the exodus. It refers more generally to Yhwh's power over forces of disorder. The people had seen these forces at work in their own experience; Yhwh still has power over them. For 'by my blast' (*bᵉgaʿărātî*), LXX τῇ ἀπειλῇ, Vg *increpatione*, Tg *mzwpyty* begin a process of moralizing and diluting the word's force that is continued in EVV 'rebuke'.

Implicitly this final colon states the purpose of the previous line, the first verb being unusually without *w* (*TTH* 64). If there is a recollection of another motif in the exodus story (see Exod 7.18, 21; Ps 105.29; also Ezek 29.4–5), it is an imprecise one. On the understanding presupposed above, presumably the first colon states the end result of Yhwh's action and the second colon explains how this comes about. †Torrey suggests that *tibʾaš* comes not from *bāʾaš* ('smell' assumed by Vg *conputrescent*) but from *bāʾaš* ('be bad/be badly off'; cf Sir 3.26 [24 in Lévi's ed.]; *DTT*), which is also known in Ugaritic (Driver, *JTS* 31, pp. 276–77) and in OT Aramaic (cf Dan 6.15).

תבאש: 1QIsª has תיבש ('dry up') as in 42.15; 44.27; Nah 1.4. The fact that א has become a quiescent letter may have facilitated the change (†Kutscher, p. 182; ET p. 241). Cf LXX's ξηρανθήσονται, which presupposes the lack of א (†Seeligmann, p. 65).
תמת: on the quasi-jussive form, see on 42.6a. Morgenstern (*HUCA* 25, pp. 62–63) adds בהמתם ('their animals') at the end of the line as a more natural subject for the verb. Syr omits בצמא which follows.

50.3. I can clothe heavens in black. I can make sack their covering. The language again has parallels with exodus motifs (see Exod 10.21–22), but more closely links with the language of death and mourning. It suggests a contrast with the bridal finery of 49.18. Verse 3 thus constitutes a solemn ending to 49.1–50.3, driving us to look on forward.

The LXX and Syr have 'like sack'.

Bibliography to 49.14–50.3

Blythin, I., 'A Note on Is xlix 16–17', in *VT* 16 (1966), pp. 229–30.

Flusser, D., 'The Text of Isa. xlix, 17 in the DSS', in *Textus* 2 (1962), pp. 140–42.

Grether, H. G., 'Translating the Questions in Isaiah 50', in *Bible Translator* 24 (1973), pp. 240–43.

Merendino, R. P., 'Jes 49, 14–26', in *RB* 89 (1982), pp. 321–69.

—'Jes 50,1–3 (9b.11)', in *BZ* 29 (1985), pp. 221–44.

Philonenko, M., 'Sur l'expression "vendu au péché"', in *RHR* 203 (1986), pp. 41–52.

Rosenrauch, H., 'Note on Is. 49.16', in *JQR* 36 (1945–46), p. 81.

Steck, O. H., 'Beobachtungen zu Jesaja 49, 14–26', in *BN* 55 (1990), pp. 36–46. = †Steck, pp. 47–59.

IV.c.

50.4–11: THE AWAKENING OF YHWH'S SERVANT

The MT puts a setuma or petucha either side of vv. 4–11 and 1QIs[a] begins new lines at these points. Both thus assume that vv. 4–11 are to be distinguished from their context and belong together. The reason for this is clear enough at the beginning. Through 49.15–50.3 the prophet has been reporting Yhwh's words. Verse 4 begins a paragraph in which the prophet again speaks as 'I'. Matters become more complicated in vv. 10–11. In v. 10 Yhwh's servant is referred to in the third person, as is Yhwh. Then in v. 11 there appears a first person suffix that implies that Yhwh is now the speaker—as we will suggest is the case in v. 10. Thus A provides a setuma after v. 9.

The 'I' form of the prophet's testimony in 50.4–9 corresponds to that of 49.1–6, and vv. 10–11 in due course treat vv. 4–9 as words of Yhwh's servant like 49.1–6. In a parallel way 51.1–52.12 with its focus on Madam Zion then suggests comparisons with 49.14–50.3. Looking on, we discover a further passage about Yhwh's servant in 52.13–53.12, again followed by address to Yhwh's wife in 54.1–17.

The framework of 49.14–50.3 is Zion's accusation that Yhwh has forgotten her and the counter-accusation that her children have been unresponsive to Yhwh's call. The one who speaks in 50.4–9 declares a contrasting confidence and responsiveness, claiming in this connection to have been 'aroused' by Yhwh (50.4). That introduces a motif for 50.4–52.12, as this verb (*ʿûr*) will recur three times, summoning to action that will address the three issues of bondage, punishment, and shame (†Grimm and Dittert). Each time it is repeated and then reinforced. Each time in due course further words of Yhwh follow.

First, in 50.4 the prophet is aroused by Yhwh (yiqtol hi verb repeated, followed by qatal 'opened'). These words introduce 50.4–11. Yhwh's words follow in 51.1–8.

Second, in 51.9 Yhwh's arm is urged to arise (imperative qal verb repeated, followed by a further repetition). These words introduce 51.9–11. Yhwh's words follow in 51.12–16.

Third, in 51.17 Jerusalem is urged to arouse herself (imperative hitpolel verb repeated, followed by 'stand'). These words introduce 51.17–20. Yhwh's words follow in 51.21–23.

Fourth, in 52.1 Jerusalem is urged to arise (imperative qal verb repeated, followed by 'put on your strength'). The words introduce 52.1–2. Yhwh's words follow in 52.3–6.

As the section closes with the prophet's own words in 52.7–12, in 50.4–52.12 as a whole the prophet's own speaking has unusual prominence, occupying about as much space as Yhwh's speaking. At the same time, Yhwh's own 'I/me' and Yhwh's commands have significant prominence (51.1–8, 9[?], 12, 15–16, 22–23; 52.4–6; *Kuntz, pp. 146–47).

The structure of the section as it leads into 52.13–53.12 may also be expressed as a chiasm:

50.4–11	Yhwh's servant
51.1–8	Exhortation (plural): listen
51.9–16	Yhwh's arm urged to act in deliverance
51.17–23	Exhortation to Jerusalem: arise
52.1–6	Exhortation to Jerusalem: arouse yourself
52.7–10	Yhwh's arm bared to act in deliverance
52.11–12	Exhortation (plural): leave
52.13–53.12	Yhwh's servant

The repetition of forms of the verb *ʿûr* is accompanied by other repetitions: 'the Lord Yhwh. . .for me' (50.4, 5, 7, 9); 'disciples', 'in the morning', 'my ear' (50.4–5); 'the Lord Yhwh helps me' (50.7, 9); 'like clothing', 'consume' (50.9; 51.8); 'listen to me' (51.1, 7); 'look to' (51.1–2); 'is comforting' (51.3); 'peoples' (51.4); 'my arm/arms' (51.5); 'my right/deliverance' (51.5) 'then my deliverance' (though a different form of this word)/'rightness' (51.6); 'my deliverance'/ 'rightness will be for ever' (51.6, 8); 'joy' (51.11); 'I' (51.12); 'the fury of the oppressor' (51.13); 'founding earth' (51.13, 16); 'drank' (51.17); 'his chalice/fury cup. . .the chalice/shaking cup' (51.17, 22); 'there is no-one to. . .among all the children she. . .' (51.18); 'put on' (52.1); 'Zion/Jerusalem' (52.1, 2); 'depart' (52.11). Although such repetitions are a feature of Isaiah 40–55, there are more than usual here. They convey urgency and excitement as they tighten the screw of the rhetoric. They facilitate a process whereby themes of chapters 40–49 are resumed and their demand on God and people underlined.

The RSV plausibly divides vv. 4–11 into three subsections of very similar length. Each of the first two (vv. 4–6 and 7–9) contains two of the section's distinctive occurrences of 'the Lord Yhwh' (1QIs[a] has 'the Lord God' the second time). Two link with Yhwh's speaking, two with Yhwh's helping. In each case the second fulfils a resumptive function, closing off a chiasm in v. 5 and introducing a summary in v. 9. Each of these two subsections refers to the speaker's face. Each works with courtroom imagery. Of the latter two subsections (vv. 7–9 and 10–11), each moves from 'Who' to 'There' (*mî*, *hēn*), doubled in vv. 8 and 9, then repeated in vv. 10 and 11. While the section does not have a consistent rhythm and some lines are difficult to construe, most of its lines have only two stresses in the second half (vv. 4aα, 5aα, 5aβb[?], 6a, 6b, 8b, 9a, 9b, 10bβ, 11a, 11bα, 11bβ). In other words, it is written in lament metre. *Van der Lugt offers a systematic poetic reading of vv. 4–11 as three balanced stanzas, while †Melugin (p. 153) suggests that the point of vv. 4–9 is to lead into v. 10–11—though historically, vv. 10–11 have been widely reckoned to be additions to the original servant passage.

The speaker's testimony makes a link with what precedes by taking up that naming of God as 'the Lord Yhwh' (vv. 4, 5, 7, 9: cf 49.14,

22). The equipping, speaking, and responsiveness of vv. 4–5 compares with 49.1–3 and contrasts with the resistance and unresponsiveness of 49.14–50.3. Yhwh's opening of the speaker's ear contrasts with the non-opening of the people's ear in 48.8. Yhwh saw no point in sending them to school, but does so send the speaker (†Bonnard). The ministry of encouraging the weary with a word (v. 4) corresponds to that exercised by the prophet in 49.14–50.3. It is designed to effect that restoring of Jacob–Israel to which the prophet was commissioned in 49.5, 6. The persistence despite opposition of v. 6 corresponds to that of 49.4a, though it goes beyond it. The experience of humiliation and spitting on the part of one who will be identified as Yhwh's servant (vv. 6, 10) corresponds to the community experience of being despised and loathed as a servant in 49.7. The confidence of vindication in vv. 7–9 corresponds to that in 49.4, though it goes beyond it, and also to the promises of 49.22–26. It contrasts with the loss of confidence in 49.14 to which those promises respond.

This passage thus has points of correspondence and contrast with 49.1–6 as that had points of correspondence and contrast with 42.1–4. The servant's relationship to the nations in 42.1–4 reappeared in 49.1–6, but the latter contrasted with 42.1–4 in seeing the prophet as embodiment of the servant calling and in seeing that calling as also one exercised to Israel itself. In 50.4–11 there is a correspondence to 49.1–6 in that the prophet is again Yhwh's servant, but a developing of the focus on that calling as one exercised in relationship to Israel. This has the consequence of suspending any concern for the nations here—though this will reappear in 51.4–5 in terms linking directly with 42.1–4. The 'Who/There' sequence in 50.8–9, 10–11 has already appeared in 50.1–2 and thus binds the two units.

Verses 4–9 do not identify addressees, nor make explicit what is the point of this testimony. A prophetic testimony is characteristically designed to make the audience attend to the prophetic words that follow. A psalm of trust of the kind to which vv. 4–9 formally correspond is designed to encourage the faithful and confound the wicked (see, e.g., Ps 31.24–25 [23–24]). Such purposes become overt in vv. 10–11 where the testimony's implicit audience(s) are directly addressed.

Since †Duhm, the servant passage 50.4–9 has been widely regarded as later than the surrounding material, and 50.10–11 as a yet-later addition. E. Haag (*Gewalt*, pp. 164–66) sees vv. 5b–6, 7b, 9b as original; vv. 4b, 7a, 8–9a, 10–11 are later, and vv. 4a, 5a are subsequent expansions. *Merendino (*ZAW* 97; *BZ* 29) offers an alternative account.

50.4aα. The Lord Yhwh gave me a disciple's tongue. It is customary to question the text of vv. 4–5aα (see *Schwarz). In the MT it works substantially as a chiasm. More literally:

The Lord Yhwh gave me a tongue
of disciples
for knowing how to aid the faint
[with] a word
he wakens
in the morning
in the morning
he wakens
an ear for me
for hearing
like disciples
the Lord Yhwh opened my ear

The testimony works in reverse order (hysteron–proteron; †Grimm and Dittert): chronologically, opening the ear and hearing precedes using the tongue for speaking. By its nature, such a testimony offers an individualized portrait of the one who speaks, but this individual could still be a figure for a community (cf 1.5–6; also Lamentations). Yet as was the case in 49.1–6, in the absence of indications to the contrary the natural assumption here is that 'I' means 'I'. It is again 'the Lord Yhwh' who speaks to 'me' (cf 49.22; cf the reference to the Lord Yhwh's sending in 48.16; also 40.10; 49.14; and cf 51.22; 52.4).

'A disciple' represents the distributive plural *limmûdîm* ('like one of the disciples').[1] It thus links with the occurrences in 8.16 and 54.13, the only other occurrences of the word with this meaning. In 8.16 it is Isaiah who is the master, in 54.13 it is Yhwh; here in 50.4 both might apply. The prophet reckons to be among the disciples to whom Isaiah entrusted his teaching (8.16) but looks to the whole people following Yhwh's teaching (54.13). The Tg renders 'teachers', which in the context makes good sense in connection with the tongue and speaking rather than the ear and hearing (contrast v. 4b). But it misses the hysteron–proteron and the influence of 8.16, to which this testimony perhaps suggestively adds the awareness that only a disciple can be a teacher.

Outside the context of the link with 8.16 and 54.13 we might follow the LXX's παιδείας (cf Syr *ywlpn*ʾ; LXX[A] has σοφίας) in taking the plural noun as intensive rather than numerical plural, an abstract noun, as in Sir 51.28 (see GK 124df). It then resembles those in 43.28; 49.20; 51.7; 63.4. †Olley (pp. 46–47) sees παιδείας as an allusion to the disciplinary function of diaspora experience. The Vg similarly has *linguam eruditam*. The form *limmûd* itself more naturally suggests an abstract noun (Payne, *JSS* 12, p. 221).

50.4aβbα. . . .for knowing how to aid the faint: with a word he wakens each morning. The MT, 1QIs[a], LXX, and Tg link '[with] a word' with what precedes: in the MT it closes v. 4a; 1QIs[a] makes this explicit by

[1] So R. Gordis, 'Job xl 29', in *VT* 14 (1964), pp. 491–94 (see pp. 492–93). Cf the pl. to denote an indefinite s. in GK 124o.

reading the next verb as 'and he wakens'; the Tg understands 'faint for the word'; the LXX has 'speak a word'. But †Kittel more plausibly takes 'for knowing how to aid the faint' as a complete three-word colon. We know 'the faint' from 40.29; it is another way of speaking of Jacob–Israel as needing the ministry 49.5–6 described.

†Kittel then takes 'with a word he wakens' as the next complete colon, but at this point we may follow the MT's accents and link the verb with the next word to produce the colon 'with a word he wakens in the morning', which makes for a neat 3–3 line at the centre of v. 4, one that comes to an end at the centre of the chiasm outlined above.

Syntactically it would be possible to take 'a word' as subject of 'wakens', preceding it like the subject of the previous line. But there is no other passage where 'a word' is subject of such a verb (15.5 with 'a cry' comes nearest) or where this verb has such a subject. Again, syntactically we could take the noun as the object ('a word he wakens…'), but such objects are usually part of the person (spirit, wrath, love, jealousy, power, heart)—as happens in the next line here. The 'word' is the message Yhwh gives the prophet to encourage the fainting people.

The idiomatic repetition *babbōqer babbōqer* means 'every morning' (e.g. 28.19), the beginning of the day which is the time to seek a word from Yhwh (e.g. Ps 5.4 [3])—or the time for Yhwh to take an initiative in giving one. Here (against the accents) we take the words as belonging to separate lines in the chiasm. The phrase naturally accompanies frequentative yiqtol verbs, but here the yiqtol also indicates that the prophet moves from an account of an original call ('the Lord Yhwh gave') to an account of an ongoing experience (†Grimm and Dittert). The LXX's apparent lack of one *babbōqer* more likely suggests haplography there than dittography elsewhere. †Barthélemy suggests that the prepositional prefix on προσέθηκέν is a corruption of a repeated πρωί, so that the LXX's text corresponds to the MT.

עות: the vb comes only here in BH, but means 'help' in Aramaic; and cf עוש which also comes once in BH, in Joel 4.11 [3.11]. See BDB and *DTT* under עות and עוש. Thus Vg renders *sustentare*, Aq ὑποστηρίσαι. The more familiar עות (pi) means 'bend', 'twist', and then 'subvert', but such a meaning (e.g. †Rignell) seems to require a *tour de force* of interpretation, as does 'adapt' (†S. Smith). LXX[A] ἐν καιρῷ…εἰπεῖν ('to speak in time'; cf KJV) takes עות as denominative from עת ('time'). †König links it with Arabic *ġâtha* 'refresh/quicken'. Ibn Bal'am links it with another Arabic root that means to talk fluently or excessively—thus 'to teach' (see Greenspahn [see on 44.8], p. 89). †Korpel and de Moor see it as a variant of עוד ('to make witnesses'). Simple εἰπεῖν ('to speak') in other LXX MSS, Tg לאלפא ('to teach') are paraphrasing. †Ehrlich emends לענות ('to answer'), †Klostermann לרעות ('to shepherd'); he sees לדעת and לעות as a double reading. *Merendino (*ZAW* 97, p. 350) omits לעות את־יעף because ידע is not elsewhere followed by ל (only Exod 36.1).
את־יעף: the prose obj. marker before the indeterminate noun makes

explicit that this is the obj. (JM 125h; this explanation may apply even if the word is determinate). Cairo fragment Eb 10 (see *HUB*) has inf. יעוף.
דבר: Tg takes as obj. of יעף and envisages people fainting for the word of Yhwh's torah, but as a vb this would be intr. LXX's εἰπεῖν λόγον links it with the preceding vb (see above). †Lindblom takes as obj. of לדעת ('for knowing the word to aid the faint') but the distance from the vb makes this difficult. Vg *verbo* more plausibly takes it as adv. acc. (cf GK 118m).
יעיר: in 1QIs[a] ויעיר (also when the word recurs), making the backward link of דבר more explicit. On the basis of an Arabic homonym Driver hypothesizes a Heb. vb עיר and renders 'bores [my ear]' (see *JTS* 41, p. 164; *CP*, pp. 126, 333). †Ehrlich obtains a similar result by hypothesizing a vb ערר whose hi would mean 'hollow', related to the word מערה ('cave'), comparing כרה in Ps 40.7 [6]. LXX has ἔθηκέ...προσέθηκέ for the two occurrences, suggesting to †Ottley יעל ('he offers', עלה hi) for יעיר. †Budde emends נעים ('delightful'), †Kissane יעיל ('avails').

50.4bβ. Each morning he wakens an ear for me for hearing like a disciple. The Tg assumes that the reference is to the opening of the ear of the prophets' hearers. It has 'he sends his prophets early in case the ears of transgressors may be opened...' (see note). The MT's point is rather that Yhwh's servant's distinctive attribute is the capacity to hear what Yhwh is shouting. The final word is the repeated *limmûdim*, again distributive plural. The Vg has *magistrum* ('[so that I might listen as] to the master') this time instead of *eruditam*.

יעיר: in Chilton's understanding, Tg takes this as inwardly transitive/intensive/internal hi (GK 53def; *IBHS* 27.2fg; cf BDB, p. 735b), 'he rises early to send', but Tg's use of קדם for עור seems designed, characteristically, to avoid such anthropomorphism. Stenning's 'he sendeth forth...early' is more likely.
אזן: Tg takes as directly adv. acc., 'with the ear'. This is possible when the word is taken in isolation but hardly in this context, where it looks like the obj. of the vb. Tg links it with what follows.

50.5. The Lord Yhwh opened my ear. And I did not resist. I did not turn away. Given the much greater familiarity of the expression 'opening the mouth', reference to the opening of the ear is unexpected, though it is a Babylonian metaphor in connection with a god's revelatory speech (so †Grimm and Dittert; and cf BDB's reference to Assyrian *uznâ puttû* with which cf *AHw*, pp. 859b, 1448a). The Tg paraphrases 'Yhwh God sent me to prophesy'.

Once again the prophet speaks as one called to model the response to Yhwh that Jacob–Israel failed to give: contrast 42.20.

50.6a. I gave my back to floggers, my cheeks to beard-pullers. Willingness to obey Yhwh (v. 5) has to issue in willingness to be humiliated, but the two are not yet identified. Nor is there reason to see a link with ritual humiliation of the king in the Babylonian new-year festival (for which see *ANET*, p. 334), or with the discipline of a school. This is obedience not drama, and the floggers are enemies not teachers (†Kaiser). Flogging and beard-pulling suggest formal symbolic shaming (see, e.g., Neh 13.25), and vv. 6–9 as a whole suggest a legal or quasi–legal process. It might be that the Judean community was in a position to charge and punish the prophet in this way, and it might be that the prophet could nevertheless describe the community as 'faint', but it seems more likely that such formal and concerted attack comes at the hands of the Babylonians. It is easy to imagine their affront at a Judean prophet's declaration that Babylon's attacker is destined to win the victory and be the Judean community's saviour, and their desire to silence and/or discredit the prophet.

למרטים: 1QIs[a] has למטלים, perhaps by dissimilation and metathesis (Guillaume, *JBL* 76, p. 43). In BH מטל would mean 'to hammer', while on the basis of Arabic, Driver (*JTS* 2, p. 27) posits a homonym that would suggest metal-beaters. Or the word might come from טלל ('to roof'). But none of these make good sense. Ugaritic *ṭll* would suggest 'knock over' (*Hempel), while in MH מטל might mean stone-throwers (see *DTT*). Syr has *lšwqp*ʾ ('to strikers') and LXX εἰς ῥαπίσματα ('to blows'), the impersonal expression matching the impersonal εἰς μάστιγας ('to scourges') in the first colon. The LXX may be paraphrasing an unfamiliar expression (†Ziegler, p. 127), but *Gundry suggests that the LXX and Syr have the 1QIs[a] reading which they understood to mean 'beat' along the lines of Driver's Arabic cognate and which then underlies Mark 14.65. Carmignac ('Six Passages', pp. 44–46) emphasizes that the cognate is dubious and suggests that לסטרים from סטר ('slap': see *DTT*) underlies 1QIs[a], Syr, and LXX. This would generate a nice paronomasia with הסתרתי in the next line.

50.6b. I did not hide my face from deep humiliation and spit. 'Hide the face' usually indicates rejection or anger (e.g. 8.17; 53.3; 54.8; 59.2; 64.6 [7]). But it is used in other connections (Exod 3.6; Pss 10.11; 51.11 [9]) and here suggests that the prophet did not shrink from facing up to the cost of prophesying. 'Turn my face' (1QIs[a], LXX, Syr, Vg: see note) reflects the removal of an unusual usage rather than indicating that the MT has introduced one.

הסתרתי: 1QIs[a] has הסירותי, LXX ἀπέστρεψα, Vg *averti*, Syr ʾ*pnyt*; and cf 2 Chr 30.9. But the LXX and Syr use their vbs for סתר in passages such as 8.17; 53.3; 54.8. Vg does not, and its reading might correspond to 1QIs[a]. Dahood (*Ugaritic-Hebrew Philology* [see on 40.4], p. 64) sees הסתרתי as a form of סור with infixed ת.
כלמות: we have taken this as intensifying rather than numerical pl.

50.7a. But the Lord Yhwh supports me. Therefore I have not been humiliated. The first clause with its yiqtol verb recurs (less the copula) in v. 9. The past verbs in the Tg and LXX fit the context where the verb in the second colon is qatal, though if the yiqtol refers to the past it more likely has imperfect meaning ('was supporting/used to support'). But when the phrase recurs, the LXX renders as present, while the Vg has *auxiliator meus* ('my helper'), without a verb, both times. It seems likely that the Vg is right that the verb has the same meaning both times and that each time the yiqtol is habitual present. †Kaiser's future (both times) is harder to relate to the succeeding qatal verb.

†Eitan suggests that this is not the common verb *ʿāzar* but a homonym meaning 'justify'. This is probably an unnecessary complication (see *CP* 332), though if the homonym was known, it could be more easily understood to appear in v. 9 given the parallelism, and it would be a paronomasia that would have pleased Second Isaiah. But the verb and the related noun often denote support in a legal setting which ensures that people get their rights (e.g. Ps 71.12–13). The support thus often involves deliverance from humiliation (e.g. Ps 70.2–6 [1–5]).

In the second colon the LXX's further aorist implies that the pressure of v. 6 is over. What will follow indicates that this is not so, and an English perfect is more likely appropriate. The link with the present implication of the yiqtol verb, with which poetry often pairs a qatal verb, is then the closer. But so far, the willingness to accept humiliation (v. 6) has not become actuality, and the prophet is living by the convictions earlier urged on Jacob–Israel (see 41.10–13), once more 'being' Israel (cf 49.3).

50.7b. Therefore I set my face like flint. I knew I would not be shamed. This setting of the face presumably refers back to the refusal to hide the face of v. 6, and the tense reference is thus the same. It is less likely that the verb has perfect meaning (against *IBHS* 33.3.1b). This second 'therefore' thus parallels its predecessor or even goes behind it rather than following from it. It was Yhwh's help that both guaranteed safety from humiliation and had thus provided the basis for the face-setting. Thus not only is the repetition typical of Second Isaiah, or (in the case of a repeated 'therefore') of the Isaiah redaction.[2] So is the subtle difference in meaning, and the further hysteron–proteron. The LXX simplifies matters by rendering ἀλλὰ ('but'), hardly grounds for positing a different original such as *kî* (†Duhm).

The second colon begins with a wayyiqtol. This hardly implies that the 'knowing' follows on the 'setting'. The relationship with the preceding verb might be seen as epexegetical (*IBHS* 33.2.2; *TTH* 75–76), though 'for I know' (*IBHS* 33.3.1b) is hard to justify. More likely we should see this last clause in v. 7 as another consequence of the first. It parallels the one it succeeds rather than following on it. The statement could have been expressed by means of another

[2] See B. W. Anderson, '"God with Us"—In Judgment and in Mercy', in *Canon, Theology, and Old Testament Interpretation* (B. S. Childs Festschrift, ed. G. M. Tucker and others; Philadelphia, 1988), pp. 230–45 (see p. 235).

'therefore', but the wayyiqtol construction makes for variation. Yhwh's support of the prophet has the three results affirmed in v. 7aβb. The clause thus constitutes another instance of the hysteron–proteron aspect of the passage. A wayyiqtol can have any of the meanings of a straightforward qatal, which in the case of the stative verb *yādaʿ* can indicate present, 'I know' (cf *IBHS* 33.3.1b). But placed in a sequence of past tenses, 'I came to know' and thus 'I know' (*TTH* 80), or better strictly past 'I knew', makes good sense. Through v. 7aβb the prophet describes the past result of the truth stated in v. 7aα. The chronological order of events is knowing, setting, and not being humiliated. While the prophet takes responsibility for making a firm stand, this is possible not because of some personal strength but because of Yhwh's own commitment.

כחלמיש: the word completes a paronomasia running through vv. 6b–7, following on מכלמות and נכלמתי.

50.8. My vindicator is near. Who will arraign me? Let us stand together. Who is my accuser? He must come forward to me. The RSV attaches the first colon to v. 7, which turns vv. 8aβ–9 into a sequence of bicola. The first two begin 'Who?' (*mî*), the second two begin 'There' (*hēn*). The LXX opens v. 8 with ὅτι ('because'). This could retrospectively link with v. 7 or introduce v. 8. On the MT's arrangement, it is vv. 6–7 that form a sequence of bicola, which is disturbed by the RSV's assessment. Either way v. 8aα stands out. Elliger (*Verhältnis*, p. 34) sees it as a short line on its own. It stands in exposed and emphatic position at the centre of the prophet's account of the experience of trial in vv. 6–9, and indeed, makes explicit the legal framework of thinking in the passage. Earlier court disputes about who is in control of history have assumed that a court which listens to the witnesses will agree that Yhwh is in the right over against other gods and their representatives. Here the prophet is similarly confident of having someone to testify to the truth of the declarations we have been reading, about current events and their significance for the Babylonians and for the Judeans. We might compare the way Job speaks about vindication, with varying degrees of confidence, in, for example, Job 13.18–19; 19.25–27a; 31.35. Here Yhwh is not a protagonist in the court scene (as in chapter 41) but the key witness who is near in a spatial sense, metaphorically standing nearby in court, and/or in a chronological sense, about to intervene.

The ABCBC formation of v. 8 with this opening short line is paralleled in passages such as 43.25–26 and 44.8, as well as others where the short line is the messenger formula, such as 42.5; 43.14–15; 49.22, 25 (*van der Lugt, pp. 113–14).

The 'accuser', *baʿal mišpāṭî*, is literally 'master of my decision/judgment'. Given that the servant's decision/judgment is Yhwh's business (cf 49.4), the phrase might refer to Yhwh and be equivalent to 'my vindicator'. In the context of the question 'Who…' parallel to that in the previous line, this meaning is difficult here, and the expression also recalls the 'people who arraign me' (*ʾanšê rîbekā*) of 41.11 as well as the use of *mišpāṭ* in 41.1; cf also the 'person with business' (*baʿal dᵉbārîm*) of Exod 24.14. The less familiar phrase parallels the more familiar one in v. 8a and may be an Akkadianism (cf *Avishur).

If *mî* can sometimes mean 'whoever' in a non-interrogative sense, this is hardly an instance (against BDB). The context points to a question, albeit rhetorical (*DG* 8). In turn, 'come forward' (*nāgaš* hi) recalls 41.1. Here the third singular complements the first person cohortative of v. 8a (LXX conforms the first colon to the second).

50.9a. There, the Lord Yhwh supports me. Who is the one who will condemn me? The first colon repeats v. 7aα with the copula replaced by deictic *hēn* ('there'), a common feature of court and other argumentative speech in these chapters in connection with the clinching of a point (see 40.15a, 15b; 41.11, 24, 29; 44.11; 50.1, 2). †Begrich (p. 10 = 18) compares the declaration 'There, God is my helper' in Ps 54.6 [4], taken to be a response to a priestly salvation oracle. This draws attention to the difference from the prophet's word here, which involves *hēn* not *hinnēh* (1QIsᵃ has *hnh* both times). It fulfils a different function in this argumentative context, and introduces a finite verb not a participle. The verb, moreover, is yiqtol, not qatal. Followed by the further yiqtol verb, in isolation one might have rendered this one 'will support me'. But that following verb is as much modal as future, and there are no pointers away from giving this word the same significance as in v. 7. After v. 8 it does more than merely repeat v. 7aα. The prophet has not explicitly identified the vindicator of v. 8 (cf the anonymous restorer of Job 19.25). It might have been that Cyrus would be the vindicator when he takes the city. In this key short line the identification becomes explicit. Labuschagne (*Syntax and Meaning* [see on 40.15], p. 9) takes the *hēn* to mean 'if', but this usage is less familiar and there is no specific pointer towards it.

The second colon then repeats the form and content of the two questions in v. 8, though it strengthens it. The demonstrative *hûʾ* underlines the 'Who?' (see JM 144a), and the verb 'condemn' (*rāšaʿ* hi) is a stronger one than 'arraign' or 'accuse'. Strictly it is the act of the court itself, not of the plaintiff, though it is also used in this looser sense in Job 9.20; 15.6; 34.17, as in English. There is therefore no need to assume a meaning such as 'have me condemned'.

50.9b. There, all of them will wear out like clothing. Moth will consume them. A further *hēn* clause parallels v. 9a and offers a contrast to it. Verse 9b pairs with v. 9a as the preceding pair of bicola are similar and contrasting. Both instance parallelism between lines as well as parallelism within lines: the judgment on the attempt at false condemnation, which would naturally lead to execution, is that the agents of condemnation meet their own death. 'All of them' perhaps suggests 'the whole sorry lot of them' (see on 40.26). The LXX has πάντες ὑμεῖς ('all of you'). Its verb is then παλαιωθήσεσθε ('grow old'), arguably always an undertranslation of *bālāh*. The Tg follows the word order and renders 'are like clothing that wears out, that a moth eats', but this involves ignoring the plurals.

כַּבֶּגֶד: generic use of the article, esp. common in comparisons (*IBHS* 13.5.1f).

50.10a. Who among you reveres Yhwh, listens to his servant's voice? The 'Who/There' interweaving of vv. 8–9 continues in vv. 10–11, though this third pair of occurrences of the words works in a different way. The 'Who' directly addresses those to whom it refers, who are friends rather than foes. The 'There' likewise directly addresses those to whom it draws attention and thus discomforts rather than comforts its dramatic audience. The LXX closes the question after the first colon and renders the second verb ἀκουσάτω ('he must listen'), which might imply a jussive verb, but both phenomena may simply reflect the difficulty of construing v. 10 as a whole. In association with the LXX's supposed reading, GK 137c takes the 'who' as indefinite, while †Duhm takes it as relative. But these are rare uses of *mî*, if they exist (on the former, see †Alexander; cf on v. 8). In the absence of other pointers from the context, the presupposition must be that *mî* is grammatically interrogative, though rhetorically the reference is doubtless indefinite. The question invites people to identify with this category (*Beuken, pp. 170–74). The question 'Who among you' recurs from 42.23, where it had the same significance.

In accordance with later usage the Tg takes 'those who revere Yhwh' to denote the community as a whole and asks who among them listens. Like the LXX this works against the parallelism, but it does draw our attention to the implication of the address for the community as a whole. Verse 10a need not imply an acceptance of the idea that the community is divided into a group that looks at things the prophet's way and another that does not. More likely it is an appeal to the whole community to identify itself as revering and obedient, even though walking in darkness. Only here in Isaiah 40–55 does *yārē*ʾ have positive meaning ('revere' rather than 'fear'), and Elliger takes that as an indication that this line is an addition from Third Isaiah (*Verhältnis*, pp. 31, 37; he notes many other verbal links with Third Isaiah in v. 10).

For 'his servant' the Tg characteristically has 'his servants the prophets'. 1QIs[a] offers a striking interpretation. Its participle is plural, requiring the rendering 'Who among you revere Yhwh, who listens to his servant's voice?' 'God heeds the voice of his Messianic Servant' (†Chamberlain, p. 372). In this asyndetic line, syntactically the MT itself might be understood thus, but we do not otherwise hear it suggested that listening is Yhwh's business between 1.15; 30.19; 37.4, 17; 38.5 and 59.1–2; 65.24.

Who speaks in vv. 10–11? In chapters 40–55 as a whole, the main speakers are Yhwh and the prophet, though their words are set in the context of the voices of an author or narrator or editor or glossators. In v. 10a both Yhwh and the prophet are referred to in the third person, which might imply that the speaker is one of that latter company. Thus Elliger (*Verhältnis*, pp. 33–38) sees v. 10 as from Third Isaiah and v. 11 as a later gloss on v. 9b, while *Merendino (*ZAW* 97; *BZ* 29) sees v. 10 as belonging with vv. 4–9a but v. 11 as part of a later oracle continuing vv. 1aα, 2–3, 9b. But if something like this is so, whom do such speakers address—who are the 'you' of v. 10 and the 'you' of v. 11? Editors and glossators do not usually address the audience on the stage but the audience in the house, the book's audience rather than the prophet's audience. Thus Elliger assumes that in v. 10 Third Isaiah addresses the Second Temple community (*Verhältnis*, p. 37). But there is no indication that the referent of 'you' has changed from a sixth-century audience to a later one. Further, in v. 11 it is Yhwh who speaks, even if via an editor or glossator.

So do vv. 9–11 involve three speakers, prophet, editor, and God? It is simpler to assume that Yhwh speaks throughout vv. 10–11. References to Yhwh in the third person on Yhwh's own lips are common enough, and a transition to direct address and to Yhwh's speech, particularly as it is unannounced, adds to the intrinsic power of vv. 10–11. The prophet would also be capable of third-person self-reference, but this would make for a less plausibly complex jerkiness about vv. 9–11. Either way, the audience is the implicit audience of the prophet's testimony, Second Isaiah's own community in Babylon. This 'you' is different from the 'them' of v. 9b (against †Ibn Ezra).

שֹׁמֵעַ: LXX might imply juss. יִשְׁמַע; cf Syr *nšmʿ*.
כֻּלְּכֶם: 1QIsª has כולם ('all of them').

50.10bα. One who has walked in deep darkness and had no brightness... The Vg and Tg take the whole of v. 10 as one sentence. In the Vg v. 10bα then refers to the servant ('...who has walked..., he must hope...'), while the Tg's pluralizing the servant (see above) makes this singular relative clause refer back to the reverer. Either way, this long question is then a rhetorical one, though it is not clear whether as such it comprises an open challenge to people who might say 'I am', or an indirect declaration that there are no people in this category. In the latter case, v. 11 would then take up this declaration. But we will note that v. 11 would be an unparalleled negative statement to the prophet's own community. The verses also seem to exclude the idea that the answer to the question is 'No-one'. The question would be an open challenge.

The Vg's might be a more plausible understanding if the words were prose, but long complex sentences of this kind are unusual in Hebrew poetry, and *ʾăšer* ('[one] who') understood as a pure relative is also a prose usage, especially relating to the immediately preceding word. Deuteromy 20.5–7; Judg 10.18, and Hag 2.3 offer close prose parallels to the present sentences; contrast the usage in, for example, 41.8, 9; 43.10. We thus follow the LXX, which takes this middle line as an independent relative clause (cf GK 138; *IBHS* 19.1d, 3c; *DCH*, Vol. 1, pp. 428b–29b). It does not continue to describe the servant but introduces the subject of the main verb in v. 10bβ, who is by implication the reverer of Yhwh in v. 10a. If the relative directly refers back to this person, it makes little difference. The LXX signals this change by a move from third person singular and jussive in v. 10a to second person plural imperative in v. 10b, οἱ πορευόμενοι...πεποίθατε...('[You] who walk..., trust...').

1QIsa[a] also implicitly takes this line as a new start. It has another plural verb (*hlkw* for *hālak*), perhaps suggesting 'Who [among you] walk in darkness...' (†Chamberlain, p. 372). The MT similarly divides the verse so as to link this bicolon with the one that follows. The question at the beginning of the verse thus ends after the first bicolon not after the first colon (LXX) nor after v. 10bα (†S. Smith, p. 71) nor at the end of v. 10 (Vg). The asyndetic move from qatal to yiqtol without change of subject is paralleled in 52.8 (†Saydon, p. 293).

הָלַךְ: there is hardly need or warrant for Elliger's repointing of the qatal to ptpl הֹלֵךְ, though this conforms the text more closely to 9.1 [2] (*Verhältnis*, p. 29). In the MT the n. cl. complements the qatal cl. as s. נֹגַהּ complements pl. חֲשֵׁכִים.

50.10bβ. ...must trust in Yhwh's name and lean on his God. The LXX's πεποίθατε...ἀντιστηρίσασθε and the Vg's *speret...innitatur* rightly assume that the verbs are jussive rather than yiqtol. The latter seems to require a 'Yet' to open the line (cf RSV), and there is no such adversative in the text. The Vg's *speret* turns trust into hope, which fits Second Isaiah's general emphasis (the verb *bāṭaḥ* comes only here in Second Isaiah). But it is hardly justified by the usual usage of *bāṭaḥ*, or supported by the parallelism with *šāʿan* (ni, 'lean'), which is linked to *bāṭaḥ* by co-ordinating *w*. 'Yhwh's name' is equivalent to 'Yhwh in person', a usage that reappears in Third Isaiah (see 56.6; Elliger, *Verhältnis*, p. 31).

Genesis Rabbah 60.1 applies the verse to Abraham as one who indeed revered Yhwh, listened to the voice addressing him as servant, and walked from Mesopotamia to Canaan without any light except Yhwh's guidance, trusting and leaning on Yhwh.

50.11a. There, all of you who kindle fire, who gird firebrands... The MT's verse division perhaps implicitly understands v. 11a as a self-contained sentence, as the LXX does, but the Vg more plausibly takes this line, like the first of v. 10, as a sequence of noun expressions in apposition, forming the subject of the verbs in v. 11b. The 'all of you' who are formally addressed are presumably now the Babylonian community which threatens the prophet, though the 'real' addressees are no doubt Judeans for whom such a warning to those trouble-makers would be an encouragement.

מאזרי: the pi vb governs זיקות as its direct obj. (cf Ps 18.33 [32], 40 [39] = 2 Sam 22.40; Ps 30.12; cf *Beuken, p. 175), rather than being reflexive ('gird themselves with'). This is the meaning of the hit (8.9; Ps 93.1) to which †Volz assimilates it, emending to מתאזרי. Syr *mgwzly* might imply מאירי (T. Secker, as quoted in †Lowth), a simpler and surely less original reading (*Holter). Syr may merely be assimilating to v. 11bα where it uses *gzl* for בער ('light'). From LXX's κατισχύετε ('overpower') †Oort infers מעזרי ('helping'), but girding and strength are closely connected (Pss 18.33, 40 [32, 39]; 93.1) and more likely the LXX is paraphrasing (†Ottley); cf Guillaume's comments on the link between אזר and אדר (see on 42.21). *Joüon ('Notes philologiques', p. 196) rather emends to מורי ('shooters'), as Prov 26.18.

50.11bα. Walk into your fiery flame, walk among the firebrands you lit. The attackers' tactic is an inherently dangerous one, and they will pay the price for it. The LXX's τῷ φωτὶ, Vg's *in lumine*, and Syr's *bzhr*ʾ assimilate to the more familiar *ʾôr* and to 2.5. The LXX and Vg also assume that the preposition *b* means 'in' rather than 'into', but the latter is the more common meaning after 'walk' (*hālak*; cf 45.16; 46.2) and here the phrase contrasts with v. 10bα, where the phrase 'walk in darkness' has no preposition. We have repeated the verb as a way of representing explicative *waw*.

50.11bβ. This is coming from my hand for you. You will lie down in pain. For 'from my hand', the LXX has 'through me', avoiding the anthropomorphism (†Fritsch, p. 159). The Tg renders 'from my word', often Yhwh's agent of punishment in the Tg: cf 8.14; 33.11; 40.24; 41.16 (†Chilton, pp. 58–60). In the MT Yhwh is more directly involved.

'Lie down' can refer to the sleep-like position of the dead (e.g. 14.18; Ps 88.6 [5]); *maʿăṣēbāh* is then a place of pain after death, like the later Gehenna. Thus *Midrash Ecclesiastes* on Qoh 3.9 pictures God declaring v. 11 to people complaining to find themselves there. But it can also suggest the process of dying (cf 43.17), and in the context of Isaiah, more likely the imagery of the previous lines continues. The word *maʿăṣēbāh* comes only here. While the *m* preformative on the root *ʿṣb* could suggest location (cf BDB), it could equally denote abstraction (thus simply 'pain') or instrument (thus perhaps 'torment') (see *IBHS* 5.6b; JM 881). Either of the latter fits here. The hearers will lie writhing as they are tormented by the fire they have kindled; cf 66.24, where again the reference is hardly to Gehenna, though it might be to the geographical Ge-hinnom, or at least to some place outside Jerusalem where dead bodies lay rotting and burning. †Rignell rather links the word with *ʿāṣab* II and takes it to mean '[a place of] idolatry', but this is hardly suggested by the context. The preposition is actually *l*, thus literally 'lie down into torment'; cf 47.1a. The usage is the familiar pregnant one rather than an indication that *l* has the same meaning as *b* (contrast †Ruiz, p. 95). The Tg paraphrases 'to your stumbling you will return'.

תִּשְׁכָּבוּן with paragogic ן, omitted by 1QIs[a], closes the line and the chapter.

Bibliography to 50.4–11

Avishur, Y., '"מי־בעל משפטי יגש אלי"', in *Leshonenu* 52 (1987–88), pp. 18–25.
Beuken, W., 'Jes 50 10–11', in *ZAW* 85 (1973), pp. 168–82.
Corney, R. W., 'Isaiah 1 10', in *VT* 26 (1976), pp. 497–98.
Grether, H. G., 'Translating the Questions in Isaiah 50', in *BTranslator* 24 (1973), pp. 240–43.
Hempel, J., 'Zu Jes 50 6', in *ZAW* 76 (1964), p. 327.
Holter, K., 'Die Parallelismen in Jes 50, 11abα', in *BN* 63 (1992), pp. 35–36.
Joüon, P., 'Notes philologiques sur le texte hébreu d'Isaïe 11,13; 42,14; 50,11', in *Bib* 10 (1929), pp. 195–99.
van der Lugt, P., 'De strofische struktuur van het derde knechtslied', in †Grosheide, pp. 102–17.
Merendino, R. P., 'Allein und einzig Gottes prophetisches Wort', in *ZAW* 97 (1985), pp. 344–66.
—'Jes 50,1–3 (9b.11)', in *BZ* 29 (1985), pp. 221–44.
Morgenstern, J., 'Isaiah 50:4–9a', in *HUCA* 31 (1960), pp. 20–22.
Schwarz, G., 'Jesaja 50 4–5a', in *ZAW* 85 (1973), pp. 356–57.

IV.d.

51.1–52.12: THE AWAKENING OF YHWH AND OF JERUSALEM–ZION

On the setting of 51.1–52.12 in chapters 49–55, see the introductions to 49.1–52.12 and to 50.4–11. Its material has commonalities of theme and language that give it some internal unity and some distinctiveness over against its context—notably its focus on Zion–Jerusalem. At the same time it is varied in form; it is not a unified composition in the manner of a passage such as Amos 1.3–2.16 (even allowing for some expansion of the latter). So either the prophet was content with a slightly jerky composition, or materials of varying form and origins have been brought together on the basis of commonalities. The MT MSS agree on providing either a petucha or a setuma after 50.11; 51.3, 6, 8, 11, 16, 21, 23; 52.2, 10, 12. Some of these MSS have a petucha after 50.3, 11; 51.21; 52.6, 12, but there is no broader agreement on the divisions (see *PuS*, pp. T 23–25). In L there is no further petucha after 50.11 until 65.12; in A petuchas follow 50.3; 51.6, 21, 23; 53.12. 1QIs^{ab} offer further permutations. A synagogue lection runs from 49.26 to 52.6.

As commonly happens, the community's lament is often reflected in the prophecy: see especially 51.9–11, though our understanding of this passage suggests that this once again takes place in an innovative way. Here the prophet's own response to the lament is not merely promise that it will be answered (51.12–16, 21–23; 52.3–10) but challenge to the city and to the deportees to behave as if it is being answered (51.17–20; 52.1–2, 11–12). In their own way 50.4–11, and 51.1–8 at the beginning of the section, initiate this process (see 50.10–11 and the imperatives in 51.1–8). Like the prophet's experience, the community's experience is now portrayed in tougher terms, though it is a matter of disagreement whether this means that life is actually tougher for it or whether this is a feature of the rhetoric of the chapters. Similarly, the focus on Zion–Jerusalem might indicate that these prophecies were uttered there, but might rather indicate that the prophet is communicating with the Babylonian community in a new way (or even has been communicating with the Jerusalem community throughout). Again, the fall of Babylon is now pictured as imminent, or even as having actually happened. That might indicate that real time has moved on, but might rather be another feature of the rhetoric (on these issues, see, e.g., †Haran, pp. 148–53; †Williamson, p. 229). L. R. Fisher notes how the themes of conflict and kingship appear together here, as they appear together in the Ugaritic understanding of creation, which goes on to picture the ordering of chaos and the building of a temple. Chapters 51–55 may be an OT equivalent to this sequence.[1]

Elliger (*Verhältnis*, pp. 198–213) sees 51.4–5, 10b, 12–14 as from Third Isaiah and 51.11, 15, 16 as later additions. †Mowinckel sees vv. 4–5 and 7–8 as later additions. For †Kiesow, within 51.9–52.12 the original material is 51.9–10, 17, 19; 52.1–2, 7–10. Hermisson ('Einheit', p. 311) distinguishes between an earliest strand of material (51.9–10, 17–23; 52.1–2, 7–12), a strand emphasizing the nearness of Yhwh's action (51.1–2, 4–8, 12–14 [15–16]), and later additions (52.3–6). For *Steck (*BN* 44, pp. 74–86; 46, pp. 58–90), 52.7–12 are the first strand; subsequently there were added 51.9–10a, 17, 19–23; 52.1–2; then 51.18; then 51.12–15; 52.3; then 51.4–5; then 51.1–3, 6–8, 10b–11; 52.4–6; then 51.16. For †van Oorschot, 51.9–10, 17, 19; 52.1–2, 7–10 belongs to his 'first Jerusalem redaction', 51.4–5 to his 'imminent expectation' strand, 51.1–2, 7–8, 12–15, 18, 20–23, to his secondary Zion strand; other verses are miscellaneous additions.

IV.d.i. Listen, pursuers of right (51.1–8)

In principle and out of context, v. 1 might be a prophet's words, but the antecedent to the 'me' of v. 1 is Yhwh, and it is Yhwh who speaks in v. 2 and in vv. 1–8 in general. *Stevenson has the servant speaking in vv. 4–6. This seems implausible, but see the comment on v. 5b in 1QIs[a]. More likely, then, Yhwh also speaks in v. 1, again self-referring in the third person in v. 1b. The LXX tidies the sequence by having Yhwh address Zion in v. 3, but the combination of first- and third-person reference follows that in 50.10–11. Three times, then, in vv. 1–8 Yhwh summons people to hear: 'Listen to me', 'attend to me/pay heed to me', 'listen to me' (vv. 1a, 4a, 7a). Each time this imperative is followed by another: 'Look', 'lift up your eyes/look', 'do not be afraid' (vv. 1b–2a, 6aα, 7b). Each time these commands are grounded in clauses beginning 'for' (vv. 2b–3a, 4b–5, 6aβ, 8a). Each of these sequences of clauses closes with yiqtol verbs promising joy or deliverance (vv. 3b, 6b, 8b). The three exhortations to attentiveness might suggest that vv. 1–8 comprise three oracles (†Gressmann), but their links invite us to look at them together (†Mowinckel).

†Bonnard divides vv. 1–8 into four subsections (vv. 1–3, 4–5, 6, 7–8), each comprising exhortation to attentiveness and reasons, but v. 6 in isolation stands out from the other exhortations as it points to heaven and earth rather than to Yhwh, and it looks more like a continuation of the second subsection. Verses 1–8 thus divide into vv. 1–3, 4–6, and 7–8. Each refers to Yhwh's 'right' (*ṣedeq*), the object of people's seeking and knowing in vv. 1 and 7, and of Yhwh's bringing near in v. 5. Verses 1–3 and 4–6 have in common the exhortation to listen and look. Verses 1–3 and 7–8 have in common the exhortation

[1] 'Creation at Ugarit and in the Old Testament', in *VT* 15 (1965), pp. 313–24 (see pp. 323–24).

'listen to me' and the concern with the community's destiny. Verses 4–6 and 7–8 have in common their reference to Yhwh's *tôrāh*, their closing grounds for their exhortations, both negative and positive, and their (contrasting) concern with the destiny of other peoples. The parallelism throughout the subsections is particularly systematic. All but vv. 5a and 6aβ comprise classic 'synonymously parallel' bicola. Further verbal links with vv. 1–3 will appear in vv. 9–11, and *Holmgren sees vv. 1–11 as a chiasm, but vv. 7b–8 do not fit the chiasm and the substance of vv. 9–11 takes a new direction. The internal binding of vv. 1–8 is more substantial. Similarly the way this new direction is taken further through 51.17–52.6 works against the suggestion that vv. 1–16 are 'a poem' (*Kuntz). The section brings together the prophet's typical rhetorical devices in concentration. It gives prominence to Yhwh's speaking in the first person and specifically uttering commands. It incorporates a sequence of metaphors and similes. It makes use of repetition and contrast.

Verses 1–8 manifest a number of verbal links with what precedes in 49.1–50.11: 'listen' (v. 1, cf 50.10); 'right' (*ṣedeq*, vv. 1, 5, 7, cf 'my vindicator', *maṣdîq*, 50.8); 'wastes' (v. 3, cf 49.19); 'light of peoples' (v. 4, cf 49.6); 'decision' (v. 4, cf 50.8); 'clothing/moth' (v. 8, cf 50.9). Verses 4–6 take up 42.1–4, while the combined concern with the community's destiny and with the world's recalls 45.18–25. While †Lack exaggerates in seeing 42.18–25 as the inspiration of vv. 4–8, links with that section are also noteworthy. Verses 1–8 extend to the people as a whole the assurance regarding the prophet's destiny in 50.4–9 (†Bonnard).

51.1a. Listen to me, pursuers of right, seekers of Yhwh. The need to press for attentiveness is paradoxical in the light of the description of them that follows. This need is a first indication that it is unlikely that the prophet here addresses a group who are already specially identified with the message of previous chapters and see themselves as 'the bearers of the true faith' over against the bulk of the community (†R. R. Wilson, p. 63). They are not people whose responsiveness the prophet can assume. The Tg characteristically has 'Listen to my word' in vv. 1, 4, and 7 (cf also v. 5).

Elsewhere 'pursuing right' might suggest an ethical commitment, but in Second Isaiah—especially when 'right' is *ṣedeq*—it will rather describe people who are pressing for Yhwh to act to deliver them. In a sense the Tg 'pursuers of truth. . .seekers of teaching' is thus nearer to the prophet's meaning, as in a different way is Paul's talk of pursuit in Phil 3.12–14. The parallel description 'seekers of Yhwh' confirms this understanding (see 45.19a), since that expression also suggests seeking Yhwh's intervention (cf, e.g., Ps 69.7 [6]). A related noun *baqqāšāh* ('request') generates the modern Hebrew word for 'please'. The trouble is that these pursuers/seekers are still the kind described in (e.g.) 40.27 or 49.14. D. N. Freedman (see †McKenzie) takes 'right' as abstract for concrete and as referring to Yhwh as the just one, but this seems too much to read back from the second colon into the first. The versions all take the word impersonally, though exegetes such as †Cyril understand vv. 1–8 as a whole christologically (see Krašovec, *Merismus*, pp. 105–6).

51.1b. Look to the rock from which you were hewn out, to the cavity, the hole, from which you were dug out. At first we might assume that the challenge to look to the rock would suggest looking to Yhwh (e.g. 44.8); for the confrontational use of the verb *nābaṭ* (hi), cf 42.18. But the second colon undermines that understanding; there is no precedent for describing Yhwh as a cavity or hole. The Tg's paraphrase 'you were cut like rock from stone, dug like rubble from an empty pit' does begin to make clear the point of the challenge. 'Hole' is missing from the Syr and may be an explanatory gloss on the less familiar word (Driver [see on 40.1], p. 137). The Jerusalem Talmud, *y. Sôṭah* ii, exploits the similarities between the words for 'hole/cistern' (בור), 'well' (באר), and 'create' (ברא) (†Koenig, pp. 188–91).

חֻצַּבְתֶּם, נֻקַּרְתֶּם: LXX has active ἐλατομήσατε and ὠρύξατε, perhaps implying the active pointing חֲצַבְתֶּם and נְקַרְתֶּם, variant ways of speaking of people's taking initiative in relation to Yhwh in continuity with v. 1a (†de Boer, pp. 58–67). This makes for easier Hebrew, as the MT lacks the twofold 'from', though the asyndetic usage is entirely possible (GK 155k; JM 158c; *IBHS* 19.6a). חצב pi/pu comes only here, and *IBHS* 22.6b sees the form as qal passive. נקר pi/pu is common enough. In both cases here the pu will be resultative (*IBHS* 25.3b).

מקבת בור is a construct phrase ('the cavity of the hole' or 'hole-cavity'). מקבת with the meaning 'cavity' (cf LXX τὸν βόθυνον) comes only here in the OT, though several times in the Siloam Tunnel inscription (and see *DTT*, p. 930). Elsewhere מקבת and מקבה mean 'hammer', perhaps originally as a tool that facilitates piercing or boring. The vb נקב means 'pierce/bore'. מקבת does not elsewhere mean 'quarry' (KJV). נקבה means 'female', which will turn out to be an appropriate connotation here (see v. 2a). Syr omits בור, perhaps taking it as a synonym of מקבת and abbreviating the text; †Thomas follows.

51.2a. Look to Abraham your father and to Sarah who would bear you. It turns out that (unprecedentedly) the rock is Abraham, who had set an example of looking in hope for God's promises to be fulfilled for him, and had thus pursued right and sought Yhwh.

And the cavity is Sarah. The verb *ḥîl* means 'to be in pain' and the resultative polel thus suggests one born as a result of labour. The Tg, Syr, and Vg render the yiqtol by an ordinary past tense. †Saydon takes it as a reminiscence of a preterite yáqtul form (p. 295). *TTH* 27 takes it as a vivid poetic usage (cf *DG* 62). The LXX renders by a participle (τὴν ὠδίνουσαν ὑμᾶς), suggesting an equivalence between this verb and the noun 'father' which it parallels (*CHP*, p. 346). The two expressions are then rhetorical equivalents, varying as is the nature of parallelism. †Duhm thus assumes that it simply means 'mother'. But what is the significance or effect of using the verb rather than the noun, or of using the yiqtol rather than the qatal (contrast Jer 2.27)? R. Jonah (see †Ibn Ezra) understands the yiqtol to have its conventional future meaning. It suggests Sarah's capacity to mother yet further children, good news for the exilic community. It takes the promises in 49.14–26 yet further, implicitly answering the question in 49.21. GK 107b suggests that the yiqtol is a past imperfect, denoting an action that has continued over the centuries. Thus †Dillmann took it to denote Sarah as the ever-bearing mother of an ever-renewed people.

תחוללכם: on the form see GK 60f. †Graetz emends to חוללתכם to obtain a past meaning.

51.2b. For as one I called him, so that I might bless him and make him many. A similar ambiguity recurs to that in v. 1b. As in our English translation, the 'one' could be Yhwh or Abraham. To describe Yhwh as 'one' would parallel Deut 6.4 and constitute an appropriate appeal to the integrity of Yhwh who has been pursuing one purpose over the centuries through bringing about the earlier and later events to which Second Isaiah has referred (*Janzen, 'An Echo'). But this seems over-subtle, and it is undermined by the succeeding invitation to the audience to link the 'one' and the verb 'make many'. The word *ʾeḥād* ('one') does sometimes carry the connotation of 'only one' (cf *DCH*), though the Tg's gloss 'alone in the world' perhaps makes this too explicit; rather cf 2 Sam 7.23 (†Grimm and Dittert). But the Tg rightly assumes that 'called him' means 'brought him into my service' (as at 48.16; and cf 41.2, 9). The audience is urged to consider Abraham's example as someone who committed himself to Yhwh (†Chilton, p. 46), but also Yhwh's commitment to taking Abraham from being one to being many. Yhwh can do it again.

The verbs that comprise the second colon begin with simple *w*. The LXX, Vg, Tg, and Syr render them as if they were wayyiqtol, suggesting 'I blessed him and made him many'. The third verb might be taken as an instance of co-ordinating *w*, but this does not apply to the middle one. *TTH* 27, 84, *DG* 62, 85 take the two as further instances of yiqtol with straightforward past meaning, GK 107b as dogmatic emendations to turn the text into an explicit promise. †Ehrlich takes them as frequentative yiqtol. The MT corresponds to Gen 12.2, particularly closely in the case of the first of the two. It more explicitly encourages the hearers to see themselves in the same position as Abraham on his way from Mesopotamia. We have thus taken them as suggesting purpose.

ואברכהו: 1QIs[a] ואפרהו ('so that I might make him fruitful'), perhaps assimilating to the usage of פרה and רבה as a standard pair (†de Boer, p.

76). It appears not least in promises to people such as Abraham: for example, in Gen 17.6 (†Grimm and Dittert).

וארבהו: LXX's καὶ ἠγάπησα αὐτὸν καὶ ἐπλήθυνα αὐτόν ('and loved him and made him many') might suggest ואהבהו instead of or alongside וארבהו (†Seeligmann, pp. 19–20) but may reflect the influence of 41.8 and/or indicate that the LXX's is a composite text (see †Zillessen, p. 245; †Ziegler, pp. 76, 162).

51.3aα. For Yhwh is comforting Zion. He is comforting all its wastes. In form and content the *kî* clauses declaring Yhwh's action of comfort parallel the one in the hymn at 49.13; cf the similar clauses with the verb 'deliver' in 44.23. Subsequently 52.9 will combine these two. But in overt function v. 3 is quite different. The clauses are not the grounds for an exhortation to praise, though they will lead to praise (v. 3b). The *kî* introduces a clause that brings a section to its climax, in this case like a statement that concludes a parable and brings home its meaning (Muilenburg, 'Linguistic and Rhetorical Usages' [see on 40.2aβ], p. 146). In covert function the clauses may be little different, for an exhortation to anticipatory praise is an invitation to faith and hope just as vv. 1–3 are.

Once again the verbs are 'prophetic' qatal. The Tg paraphrases with verbal expressions that explicitly refer to the future, 'Yhwh is about to comfort'; cf Vg *consolabitur*. The LXX has a future verb in the first clause alone, καὶ σὲ νῦν παρακαλέσω... Syr keeps the tense but (as Brock reads it) renders by the more concrete verb *bn*ʾ ('build'), as at 49.13. That draws attention to the fact that here 'comfort' refers to action rather than mere words: contrast the LXX's use of παρακαλέω, and the meaning of the Hebrew verb in 40.1, where the Syr has *by*ʾ*why*—though the doubling of comfort also makes a link with 40.1.

51.3aβ. He is making its wilderness like Eden, its desert like Yhwh's park. The MT's wayyiqtol continues the construction of the previous line. This time the LXX, Vg, and Tg have future verbs, but these are hardly strong evidence for continuing simple *w* ('so that he might make'). The suffixed forms 'its wilderness/desert' come only here. The LXX abbreviates, but some MSS complete the translation, incorporating a phrase such as τὰ πρὸς δυσμὰς αὐτῆς ('to its west') and thus taking the word 'desert' as a homonym meaning 'setting, west' (cf *ma*ʿ*ărāb*, 45.6). Syr renders this word *pq*ʿ*th* ('its valley') as at 40.3 and 41.19: hardly an old reading, then, as †van der Kooij (p. 266) speculates.

'Eden' and 'Yhwh's park' suggest two complementary ideas, that of abundance and fertility and that of a place where God spends time. The usage here links more closely with Ezekiel (see 28.13; 31.8–9, 16, 18; 36.35) than with Genesis 2. The specific connotations in Ezekiel and elsewhere of 'God's park' make it unlikely that the recurrent expression 'Yhwh's/God's park' is merely a superlative phrase for 'a splendid park'.[2]

51.3b. Joy and gladness—it will be present in it, thanksgiving and the sound of music. *CHP* (pp. 181–83, 205) takes this as a chiastic tricolon (2–2–3), a distinctive form such as might close a section. But v. 3 is not such a close, and the singular verb may suggest that the preceding subject 'joy-and-gladness', which very often occur as a word-pair, is thought of as a hendiadys. 1QIs[a] pluralizes *yimmāṣēʾ* to *ymṣʾw*; on such disagreement in BH see GK 146de. The LXX also has plural but translates as if qal, 'they shall find'. The Syr has a stronger verb, 'shall be heard'.

'Joy and gladness' accompanying transformation came in 35.10 towards the close of that vision, and so it is in vv. 1–3. H. Graetz thought chapter 35 originally came here.[3] 'Present' also recurs from 35.9, but reversed. That promised there would be no wild beasts there, 51.3 promises there will be joy there. When 35.10 recurs as 51.11, the further words 'sorrow and sighing are fleeing' also come, and 1QIs[a] adds those words (though with singular verb) here at the end of v. 3. On the other hand, 'thanksgiving' (*tôdāh*—the words) and 'music' (*zimrāh*—the sound) come only here in Isaiah.

51.4a. Attend to me, my people. My nation, pay heed to me. The line forms a perfect ABCCBA chiasm ('. . .to me pay heed'), repeating the content of the opening words of v. 1 in different words. Elsewhere 'attend' forms a word-pair with 'listen': for example, 28.23; 42.23; 49.1; Jer 18.19; Hos 5.1; Pss 17.1; 61.2 [1]. Following on v. 1a, the present occurrence thus functions somewhat like that in a second colon, repeating the first by means of a less familiar word. The LXX then repeats the verb here, ἀκούσατέ μου, ἀκούσατε. 'Pay heed' functions in a similar way as a word-pair with 'attend' (Ps 86.6; Prov 17.4) and with 'listen' (e.g. 1.2, 10; 32.9) and as a word-triplet with both (e.g. 28.23; 42.23; Hos 5.1; Ps 17.1).

We might expect that the objects of the two verbs also repeat v. 1a. If v. 1a had referred to a faithful element within the community as a whole, then v. 4 might designate this 'remnant' as the real 'people of Yhwh', but there has been no indication of this novel idea. We would expect 'my people/nation' to designate the whole people of Yhwh, even if it has particularly in mind those among whom the prophet lives, and this fits with the conclusion that the 'pursuers of right/seekers of Yhwh' are the people as a whole—even if described thus with irony.

The Syr has plural nouns 'peoples/nations', the LXX a plural for the second noun only, οἱ βασιλεῖς ('kings'): see on 41.1. These fit with the plurals that follow in vv. 4b–5 (†Gressmann). The singular

[2] Against P. A. H. de Boer, 'יהוה as Epithet Expressing the Superlative', in *VT* 24 (1974), pp. 233–35 (see p. 235); also *IBHS* 14.5b.

[3] See 'Isaiah xxxiv. and xxxv.', in *JQR* 4 (1891), pp. 1–8.

might then reflect misunderstanding of an abbreviated plural (†Lowth) or be a nationalizing dogmatic emendation (†North). On the other hand, the Syr and LXX's plurals might be assimilating to 49.1 and vv. 4b–5, and the former might be universalizing dogmatic emendation in a passage that as a whole is nationalist (†Snaith). The LXX's plural fits with its universalizing tendency elsewhere (†van der Kappelle, pp. 129–32). †Hollenberg (p. 34) suggests that the plurals in vv. 4b–5 refer to the singular 'my people/nation'. 'My nation' (*lᵉʾûmî*) comes only here; *Midrash Rabbah* (e.g. Exod 52.5) understands the word as 'my mother' (*lĕʾimmî*). In Isaiah the plural comes in 17.12, 13; 34.1; 41.1; 43.4, 9; 49.1; 55.4a, 4b; 60.2. The unsuffixed singular comes only in Gen 25.23 (twice); Prov 11.26; 14.28. But the alternative parallelism for *ʿammî* is *gôyî*, and this also comes only once in the OT (Zeph 2.9). Further, *gôy* is used of Jacob–Israel in Isaiah only at 1.4; 10.6; 65.1, all pejoratively; 9.2 [3]; 26.2, 15a (twice); 58.2; 60.22; and thus never in chapters 40–55. The MT's usage is intelligible and coherent.

51.4b. For teaching will issue from me, my decision for the light of peoples. The grounds for the exhortation recall 42.1–4 and remind the people that Yhwh is still concerned for the whole world. In 42.1–4 the teaching/decision issue from the servant, but here the speaker can hardly be the servant. Even if this unannounced transition were hypothesized for v. 4, like that in 48.16b, it could hardly be sustained for v. 5. The declaration that the teaching issues directly from Yhwh thus also contrasts with chapter 42. Indeed the suffix on 'my decision' perhaps applies retroactively to '[my] teaching'. The decision is explicitly Yhwh's. In the context this may reflect the fact that for a while the servant's attention is being given to matters concerning Jacob–Israel itself (see 50.4–11). But the identification of servant and Lord will be taken further in 52.13–53.12.

The expectation here parallels the Babylonian claim in a hymn to the sun god that the whole of humanity bows to him, the universe longing for his light (cf *BWL*, pp. 128–29). †Koenig argues that therefore here as in 42.6 and 49.6 it is *the* teaching, the *tôrāh* of Moses, which is to be the world's enlightenment;[4] cf LXX νόμος, Vg *lex*. But the context does not point to this connotation of *tôrāh*, here any more than at 42.6.

The MT reads v. 4b as a 4–4 line whose length reflects its significance and constitutes a parable of the fact that Yhwh's concerns extend beyond what might have been expected. In each colon the verb then comes at the end. The closing verb, which should probably be rendered 'I will settle', constitutes the rhetorical surprise in the second colon. But the LXX links this word with the next line,

[4] †Koenig, pp. 356–57; also Koenig, *RHR* 173 (1968), pp. 33, 133–34; and see the discussion between M. A. Sweeney ('The Book of Isaiah as Prophetic Torah') and G. T. Sheppard ('The "Scope" of Isaiah') in †Melugin and Sweeney, pp. 50–67, 274–81.

and we have followed its understanding (see the following note, and the comment on v. 5a).

ארגיע: On the basis of the MT's verse division, Vg *requiescet* is right to take the vb as רגע II ('rest'; cf 34.14). The usage is odd, but the idea parallels the use of שׂים in 42.4. The vb's meaning should hardly be reduced to 'render' (Kopf [see on 48.18], p. 202). Tg יזדמנון ('join themselves') takes 'peoples' as the subj. †Volz emends ארגיע to אגיה ('shine'; נגה hi); cf 13.10.

51.5a. In a flash my right is near. My deliverance is issuing. My power will decide for peoples. As we have just noted, the LXX's opening ἐγγίζει ταχὺ ('draws near quickly') suggests that it read *ʾargîaʿ*, the last word of the MT's v. 4, as the first word of v. 5. Taken as a verb, in this context the word will be from *rāgaʿ* I; cf Sym ἐξαίφνης ταχύνω and the noun *regaʿ* ('a moment/twinkle/flash'). The verb would then literally signify 'I will make momentary [the bringing near of my right]'. But more likely the word is a noun used adverbially, as in Jer 49.19; 50.44; Prov 12.19.[5] The LXX's verb reappears (in the perfect tense) in the NT declaration that God's reign has come near (e.g. Mark 1.15). On the other hand, a statement involving the adjective ἐγγύς (e.g. Luke 21.31; Rev 1.3) more closely resembles the MT both in form and in content, for it more unequivocally refers to an event that is believed to be imminent.

Expressions from 42.1–9 (and subsequent chapters) continue to recur, suggesting that the passage functions to affirm once more that the intent declared in chapters 40–50 is about to be implemented. 'Right' and 'deliverance' came in parallelism as here in 45.8, and the Vg repeats the christological personification *justus/salvator* (see 41.2a; also v. 7a). The third colon (which †Ziegler, pp. 140–41, sees as an addition) repeats the point again in terms that are subtly more novel. It adds a third form of clause. The first colon is a noun clause, the second a qatal clause, the third a yiqtol clause. My 'power' is the plural of *zᵉrōaʿ* ('arm'), here unusually treated as masculine, and here alone is it plural (or dual: see JM 91c) when used of Yhwh's activity (Deut 33.27 may refer to Yhwh, but if so in a different connection). The plural complements the singular in v. 5b; the LXX and Syr have singular as in the next line (see *HUB* for variants in Hebrew MSS). Applied to a human being the word would concretely suggest the use of two arms to wield a bow (Gen 49.24; 2 Sam 22.35/Ps 18.35 [34]). But in Hos 7.15; Ps 37.17; and Job 22.9 the NIV apparently takes it as an abstract plural for strength, in accordance with a hint in BDB. This would also fit Deut 33.27. Here the specific concrete sense does not especially fit, and Second Isaiah is fond of abstract/intensive plurals (cf 40.26b). This might also link with the use of the masculine (cf Dan 11.31).

[5] So Delekat ('Wörterbuch' [see on 49.13], p. 56); cf J. Barth, *Die Nominalbildung in den semitischen Sprachen* (2 vols, Leipzig, 1889–91; 2nd ed., 1894), p. 138, for ארגיעה in Prov 12.19.

The LXX's paraphrase is in the spirit of the MT when it assimilates this line to the next, εἰς τὸν βραχίονά μου ἔθνη ἐλπιοῦσιν ('for my arm nations will hope'), while again instancing its inclination to add explicit references to hope for foreigners (†Ziegler, pp. 140–41). The Tg and Syr render as if the Hebrew read 'by my power peoples will be judged'.

קרוב: G. R. Driver, repointing קָרֵב (pi inf), commends the LXX's verse division on rhythmic grounds, but this argument holds only if we also omit the middle phrase from v. 5a to produce two 3–3 lines, and he later abandoned the proposal.[6] Some LXX MSS add ὡς φῶς ('like light') to the middle colon. If this represented an original כאור or כנגה, the line would become 3–3–3. More likely the words are an addition from 62.1 (כנגה; †Ziegler, p. 76) or Hos 6.5 (אור; †Torrey) or Ps 37.6 ([LXX 36.6]; כאור; †Zillessen, p. 246). †Cheyne also emends קרוב to אקריב to match the asyndetic construction in Jer 49.19 (cf GK 120gh), 'I will twinkle [and] bring near'. †Duhm emends the phrase to הרגיע קרב, †Oort to ברגע קרב; cf the compound ברגע [קטן] ('during a [little] moment') in 54.7. †Ehrlich emends to simple רגע, the adv. acc. ('in/for a moment') which comes in 47.9 and 54.8, to which on Delekat's view (see above) ארגיע is an alternative.

51.5b. Foreign shores will wait for me. They will hope for my arm. We have noted that 'foreign shores...will hope' takes up the words of 42.4, except that the verb has a paragogic nun (see on 41.5). Reference to their 'waiting' applies to them the verb applied to Jacob–Israel in 40.31 and 49.23, but using resultative piel with the stress not merely on the act of waiting but on waiting *for* something (*Pi'el*, pp. 171–73)—namely, Yhwh's arm. Singular complements plural. †Torrey further suggests that a metaphorical significance ('strength, help') complements the earlier literal. Perhaps rather this occurrence confirms the view that the first was itself metaphorical.

For the MT's 'my power/for me/my arm', 1QIs[a] has 'his power/for him/his arm'. Barthélemy (*RB* 57, p. 548) thought this might be original, the MT reflecting a rejection of the notion of an earthly Messiah. More likely it is a reinterpretation of the verse, perhaps applying it to the Messiah in the light of the community's interests (so, e.g., †Chamberlain, pp. 366–67; see on 42.1b), perhaps to Cyrus in the light of earlier passages such as 46.11–13 (so, e.g., †Bonnard), perhaps to the servant (†Brownlee, pp. 193–99). The effect of the MT is thus to focus attention on Yhwh's own person rather than on an earthly figure. That is its contrast with the servant passages that it recalls.

As foreign peoples are not elsewhere the subject of 'waiting', so they nowhere else look to 'Yhwh's arm' as their hope rather than a threat. But it is in keeping with vv. 4–5 as a whole and with the prospect encouraged by 42.1–9; 45.20–25; and 49.1–6, so that there is

[6] See 'Studies in the Vocabulary of the Old Testament. viii', in *JTS* 36 (1935), pp. 293–301 (see pp. 298–99); and see p. 401.

no more reason here than there for seeing this waiting/looking as implying dread rather than hope (see Van Winkle, *VT* 35, pp. 447–48; against †Snaith). Jacob–Israel's deliverance is also their deliverance. But their coming to Yhwh is also their glorifying Jacob–Israel.

זרעי/אלי/זרעי: 1QIs[a] text (see above) is זרועו/אליו/זרועו.

51.6aα. Lift your eyes to the heavens, look at the earth below. The sequence 'attend' and 'lift your eyes/look' follows that in v. 1, but the direction of the 'look' changes. Heaven and earth are again a standard pair, a merism suggesting the whole cosmos. The 'earth below' might be this inhabited world or the world below (see on 44.23a). The next line indicates that the former is meant. 1QIs[a] *mtḥth* adds a pronoun or locative.

51.6aβ. For heavens are shredding like smoke, the earth will wear out like clothing, its inhabitants will die in like manner. There is no problem about the opening *kî* having its usual causal meaning (Aejmalaeus, 'Function and Interpretation' [see on 40.2aβ], p. 199). It introduces three exactly parallel cola that make up a 3–3–3 line, comprising noun, *k*-clause, and verb. Once more, 'are shredding' is a 'prophetic' qatal referring to an event that cannot yet be seen, and once more further yiqtol verbs make this more explicit. 'Heaven/earth' hold together the first two cola, the yiqtol verbs hold together the second two cola, and the plural nouns and verbs hold together the first and third. Rhetorically the middle colon thus looks both ways.

While earth/its inhabitants might be a natural pair in its own right (cf 40.22), heaven/earth is a more familiar one. It is here taken up from v. 6aα. Thus the first two cola could form a quite coherent line in their own right, and the third is unexpected and has particular rhetorical impact. The fact that its content links it most directly with the hearers, who are among the inhabitants to which it refers, also gives its substance corresponding impact. The three subjects already appeared together in 42.5, though in two bicola, with a whole line given to earth's inhabitants. Further, there Yhwh's creative involvement with heaven, earth, and its inhabitants functioned as an encouragement, a support for the claim that Yhwh was concerned for all the peoples. In this line the point is turned on its head, though the context still expresses that concern.

The verbs link in a similar way. An ambiguity about the first, which could mean 'be salty' or 'be ragged', is resolved—or at least played on—by the second (on the LXX, see on 50.9). The third then adds prosaic literalness; the Syr softens the verb to 'will be'. The downside to the fact that the heavens are like a tent (e.g. 40.22) is that they can wear out (contrast the LXX's use of στερέωμα elsewhere: see the note). They can dissolve like smoke. The Tg takes this instance of *beged* to mean covering rather than specifically clothing (cf Num 4.6–13; 1 Sam 19.13), but the context gives no pointer to this less familiar reference

מלח (ni, 'are shredding') comes only here. A similar Arabic vb denotes 'tear to shreds' and a Heb. n. מלחים means 'rags'. Thus †Rashi has 'decay, rot'. The more familiar מלח denotes 'salt' and Aq and Sym render ἁλιοῦσι 'be salty', perhaps in the sense of 'be grey', the colour of salt: see Driver, *JTS* 36, p. 402. Driver later noted a similar Arabic vb meaning 'be grey'.[7] LXX's ἐστερεώθη ('are made firm/solid') gives poor sense. It would make a nice irony, but the LXX is not given to irony (cf *HUB*). It may reflect puzzlement, assimilation to 45.12 (נטה); 48.13 (טפח), and the use of στερέωμα ('firmament') in Genesis 1 (†Ziegler, pp. 157–58). The idea of making firm the creation is a 'stereotype of prophetic thought' in the LXX, utilized when the translator is in difficulty (*CP*, p. 252). But *Jacobson suggests that Jerome and the LXX both had a text that read נמוגו, which could naturally mean 'dissolve', but could apparently also mean 'solidify'. 1QIs[a] replaces the first two cola by וראו מי ברא את אלה ('and see who created these'), assimilating to 40.26. The words are followed by a space and may constitute an attempt to make up for a defect in the original (†Martin, p. 14), but may also reflect the importance of astrological thinking at Qumran (†Koenig, pp. 249–69).

כמו־כן: ('like thus') is another unique expression, but comparable to אחרן] כן] ('after thus, afterwards') and the common על־כן ('upon thus, therefore'). The versions understand the MT to mean 'in like manner'. 1QIs[b] כמוכן implies 'like locusts', מוכן apparently being yet another Heb. n. for 'locusts', like most of them a collective n.[8] †Dillmann understands כן as such a collective for gnats, but notes that the regular s. of כנים is כנה. J. Weir thus emends כן to כנים (dittog.): see †Cheyne, who suggests that כן might be an abbreviation for the pl. But elsewhere in the OT, creatures such as moth, gnat, grasshopper, and locust are images not for frailty but for destructiveness (e.g. v. 8) or smallness (e.g. 40.22). Robertson ('Points of Interest' [see on 45.9a], p. 39) emends to כמוהן ('like them'), †Ehrlich to יתמון from תמם ('they will come to an end, be destroyed').

51.6b. But my deliverance will be forever. My rightness will not fall. The point about the comments on the cosmos is to make a contrast with Yhwh's lasting-ness. The nouns resemble those in v. 5a, but they are not identical and they come in reverse order: *ṣedeq*/*yešaʿ* are succeeded by *yᵉšûʿāh*/*ṣᵉdāqāh*.

תחת: the vb could derive either from חתת ('shatter') or נחת ('descend'). The former is not elsewhere used with such a figurative meaning and gives a poor sense here. The latter denotes descent to Sheol in Job 21.13 while the Aramaic ho is used for deposement in Dan 5.20 (cf also *DTT*; and Driver, *JTS* 36, p. 402). LXX ἐκλίπῃ, Vg *deficiet* ('fail'), Syr *tʿbr* ('pass away'), and

[7] 'L'interprétation du texte masorétique à la lumière de la lexicographie hebraïque', in *ETL* 26 (1950), pp. 337–53 (see pp. 349–50).

[8] See J. Reider, 'Contributions to the Hebrew Lexicon', *ZAW* 53 (1935), pp. 270–77 (see pp. 270–71).

Tg תתעכב ('be detained, delay') more likely imply נחת. They are hardly grounds for hypothesizing תחדל ('fail'; †Oort), תחר ('delay'; †Ehrlich), or תאחר ('delay'), as 46.13; †Perles)—where a word for 'delay' fits as it does not here.

51.7a. Listen to me, you who acknowledge right, a people with my teaching in its mind. Once more the prophet urges attentiveness, but once more the audience is differently characterized—though we conclude that once more the prophet has the whole people in mind. That is confirmed by the very use of the word 'people' (cf 'my people' in v. 4a, which the LXX also has here). Those who pursue right are now those who acknowledge right, who recognize Yhwh's purpose. It is in this sense that they have Yhwh's teaching in their mind. Whereas the LXX renders *tôrāh* by νόμος, and by Vg *lex*, here Yhwh's 'teaching' does not refer to behavioural or religious expectations (as in, e.g., Jer 31.31–34). It refers to the same 'teaching' on Yhwh's intention for coming events as is suggested by 'right' or 'decision', the intention Yhwh is pursuing through Cyrus. As in v. 1, some irony attaches to the designation of the audience as wanting to see Yhwh's intention fulfilled. The prophet urges them to live up to their claim to be thus open to Yhwh's will. †Spykerboer suggests that throughout vv. 1–8 the prophet makes a conscious attempt to distinguish Israel as a whole and Yhwh's faithful followers. The opposite is the case.

On the incongruence in the relative clause, contrasting with the congruence in v. 17, see on 44.1. On the asyndetic noun clause, see JM 158b.

51.7b. Do not be afraid of human reproach. Do not be shattered by their taunting. The exhortation not to be afraid again confirms that the prophet addresses the people as a whole (cf, e.g., 41.10–14). The fact that the verb is here plural may simply reflect the dominance of the plural in v. 7 as a whole (for the plural elsewhere, cf, e.g., Deut 20.3; 31.6; Isa 35.4; Jer 42.11). The grounds for the encouragement are also new, reflecting the fact that the crisis is now (portrayed as) sharper and the moment of deliverance is now (portrayed as) imminent. The form of speech requires no assumption that these verses speak 'eschatologically' or 'pessimistically' or 'dualistically', and therefore cannot come from Second Isaiah (against †Grimm and Dittert), any more than was the case with vv. 4–6.

The second colon makes the point again in more unusual words. The prepositional phrase comes first, making for an ABBA pattern in the line. 'Be shattered' often pairs with 'be afraid' (e.g. Jer 30.10), though not elsewhere in Isaiah. Here it repeats the last verb form in v. 6, except that it is now plural. Whichever is the right meaning there, it has a different one here. If it meant 'shatter' in v. 6, one might compare the literal and metaphorical meanings of the verb 'shatter' in English (and LXX's ἡττᾶσθε). 'Their taunting' takes up

43.28. Here, too, the plural complements the singular in the first colon.

51.8a. For moth will consume them like clothing, grub will consume them like wool. The imagery might seem surprising because this might seem a mild comparison compared with others (e.g. 41.15–16), but perhaps it carries the connotations of the speedy and devastating destruction of a locust plague (cf Joel 1). The second word for moth, translated 'grub', comes only here in the OT. Each of the words is pointed as having the article: syntactically it is regular for the article to be used to denote a whole class, especially in comparisons (*DG* 31e).

עשׁ: LXX's ὑπὸ χρόνου might imply the LXX read עשׁ as עת (†Ottley), but J. de Waard ('Homophony', p. 554) suggests that the idea of time as waster underlies the translation (cf *HUB*).
יאכלם: for the repeated vb two different forms appear in Vg (*comedet*, *devorabit*) and Tg (איכ׳ד, אה׳יל), and in Jer 10.25 אכל is paralleled by כלל, but the MT's repetition is so unusual that it is more likely to be retained as the more difficult reading than replaced by יכלם (Driver, 'Hebrew Notes', p. 165). Syr restructures the line as a whole.
סס: on cognates, see Cohen, *Hapax Legomena* [see on 40.5], p. 114. LXX is happily able virtually to transliterate using σής.

51.8b. But my rightness will be forever, my deliverance to all generations. The Vg has the nouns in the same order as v. 6, but the MT reverses them; the phrase 'will be forever' also recurs. In contrast to v. 6b, here the *w* with which the second colon begins is an explicative that draws attention to the need to take the verb in the first colon as applying also to the second (Brongers, 'Alternative Interpretationen' [see on 42.12], p. 275). The closing phrase in vv. 1–8 (lit. 'to generation and generations') is the new element in this line. The precise phrase comes only here, though without the preposition it appears in Ps 72.5 and with a different preposition in Ps 102.25 [24]. But the terms also recall Gen 17.7, and another recollection of Abraham would make for an *inclusio* round vv. 1–8.

As well as repeating v. 6b, v. 8b completes an ABBA structure within vv. 7–8. The first and last lines draw attention to the commitment to the lasting achievement of a right purpose that has been the subject of Yhwh's teaching. The middle two lines draw a practical implication (v. 7b) with its own basis in a negative corollary (v. 8a).

IV.d.ii. The awakening of Yhwh's arm (51.9–16)

We noted that vv. 1–3 find parallels in vv. 9–11 but concluded that these denote parallel beginnings rather than pointing to a chiastic structure in vv. 1–11. 'Split' is the same root as 'cut'; 'dry up' is a homonym of 'waste'; drying up Sea reverses making the desert flourish; 'joy and gladness' recur; creation/exodus/new creation pairs with creation/Abraham/new creation. Verses 1–3 urge a remembering of Abraham and Sarah; vv. 9–11 urge a remembering of Egypt and the Red Sea (†Bonnard). More broadly, vv. 9–11 assume four lines of tradition, victory over chaos at creation, Yhwh acting in history as warrior, the deliverance at the Red Sea in particular, and the crossing of the Jordan at Gilgal (†Simian-Yofre, p. 551). Like vv. 1–8 the section conveys an immediacy and forcefulness which derives from the presentation of Yhwh speaking, and specifically commanding, from the use of imagery, from repetitions and contrasts, and also from the use of rhetorical questions and quotation (*Kuntz, pp. 146–50).

The first two lines have the 3–2 rhythm of a lament, while the succeeding four lines (vv. 9b–10) also have two-beat second cola, and †Begrich (p. 167 = 166) reworks v. 11 to comprise three 3–2 cola. In other respects, the passage does not look like the quotation of a lament. 'Wake up', for instance, belongs at the end of a lament, not at the beginning (†Vincent, p. 111), and the future statements in v. 11 do not naturally fit the lament form (see †Melugin, p. 160). The prophet makes the matter explicit when quoting a lament elsewhere, in 40.27 and 49.14 (cf also 40.6). There is no instance in preceding chapters of a lament's being quoted without this being made clear. Further, in the context on both sides Yhwh is the speaker, and there is no specific indication of a change here. This suggests that vv. 9–11 take up the form of a lament, perhaps combined with forms of speech from other expressions of pre-exilic worship celebrating the reign of Yhwh (see †Vincent, pp. 111–23), but that typically the prophet transforms its significance. It becomes words uttered by rather than to Yhwh (see further on v. 9aα). Thus vv. 9–16 begin and end with our overhearing Yhwh's words, of self-encouragement and of encouragement to Zion.

Understanding the structure of vv. 12–16 itself is complicated by the internal changes in number and gender (see on v. 12). We have concluded that before accidental changes the whole addressed a (rhetorically) singular listener, to be identified with the community. Out of context, such a reworked text might be reckoned a servant passage (so Sellin, *NKZ* 41, pp. 157–58), but in the context it is difficult to match with other accounts of the relationship between Yhwh and the servant. Since chapter 42 we have not heard of features such as the servant's abject fear or forgetting of Yhwh, whereas we have heard of these attitudes on the part of Jacob–Israel and Zion–Jerusalem. In the MT v. 16 alone might be less implausibly read as addressed to the prophet. In this case v. 16 would likely be an introduction to vv. 17–23, analogous to 48.16b as an introduction to 48.17–19. But this spoils the patterning of the introduction of sequential sections by the verb *ʿûr* ('wake up/wake yourself').

On the assumption that vv. 12–16 belong together, they divide into two parts, each introduced by a double self-declaration by Yhwh (vv.

12a, 15). The first self-declaration introduces the 'Fear not' oracle, which occupies most space in vv. 12–16. It has a more rebuking cast than these usually have, and thus also recalls the form of a disputation. †Melugin (p. 160) comments that 'the use of disputation style is a typical Deutero-Isaianic way of adapting the form of cultic speech to meet the kind of doubt prevalent in the exile'. The second introduces a positive statement to balance the negative of vv. 12–14.

Such a reworked version of a 'fear not' oracle, its grounds mixing noun clauses and qatal and yiqtol verbs, could naturally follow on a lament. The link with a 'fear not' oracle made †Begrich designate vv. 9–11 as an individual lament, specifically a prophet's lament, which receives its reply in vv. 12–16 (see pp. 167–68 = 166–67): cf the appeal to 'Awake' in Pss 7.7 [6]; 35.23; 59.5 [4]. †Von Waldow (pp. 23–25) then suggested that rather the extent of the reworking of the 'Fear not' oracle parallels the reuse of the individual lament form to express the challenge of a community, the appeal to 'awake' in Ps 44.24 [23]. Either way, out of context the promise would form a response to the lament in vv. 9–11, reasserting the proved transitoriness of humanity and specifically the proved vulnerability of oppressors, and the power of the creator, which were the subject of vv. 9–10 themselves. For the combination of lament and promise, cf 26.16–21; 33.7–12; 40.27–31; 49.14–50.3.

As we have understood vv. 9–11 to involve an even more radical reworking of the lament form, however, in the context the promise instead builds on the self-commissioning of vv. 9–11. Second Isaiah's characteristic rhetorical questions appear in both parts (vv. 9, 10, 12, 13: 'Was it not', 'Why', 'Where'), as do participles, especially relating to Yhwh's work as creator (vv. 9b, 12, 13, 15); cf also the infinitival phrases (v. 16b). The section once again links with what precedes. With v. 10, cf 50.2; with v. 13, cf 49.14; with v. 16a, cf 49.2; with v. 16b, cf 49.13–14.

†Duhm sees vv. 10b, 15–16 as later additions to Second Isaiah's work. Elliger (*Deuterojesaja*, pp. 204–13) sees vv. 9–10a as from Second Isaiah, vv. 10b, 12–14 from Third Isaiah, and vv. 11, 15–16 as later. †Fohrer sees vv. 11–16 as scribal expansion of Second Isaiah's work. Hermisson ('Einheit', p. 311) sees vv. 12–14 (15–16) as belonging to the 'Near' stratum which declares that the salvation promised by Second Isaiah but delayed is now imminent.

51.9aα. Wake up, wake up, put on strength, arm of Yhwh. The LXX adds Ἰερουσαλήμ to the 'wake up' call here, assimilating to 51.17 and 52.1 (cf †Zillessen, p. 245; †Ziegler, p. 76). We have noted that in the context, the 'wake up' call is self-addressed, like Deborah's 'wake up' call (Judg 5.12). Yhwh does not need to be aroused to battle by someone else (cf 42.13). The verb 'put on' usually refers to clothes, including armour (1 Sam 17.5, 38; Jer 46.4; Ezek 38.4). But there is no need to take 'strength' here to denote armour, as if were abstract for concrete. 'Put on' often refers to qualities such as justice, majesty, and beauty (e.g. Ps 93.1; 104.1). Abstract pairs with concrete in 52.1 and 59.17. In a significant parallel Ps 89.11 [10] reminds Yhwh, 'you pierced Rahab; with the arm of your strength...'. The compound expression is divided here, though the words come together and the LXX understands them as a composite, 'the strength of your arm' (τὴν ἰσχὺν τοῦ βραχίονός σου). Each word in Ps 89.11 [10] ('you', 'pierced', 'Rahab', 'arm', 'strength') reappears in v. 9 (Ginsberg, *JBL* 77, p. 153).

The Tg's 'reveal yourself, reveal yourself...put on might from before Yhwh' represents a threefold toning down of the prophet's words

עוּרִי: the stress on the second syllable each time (*milra*) is unusual (GK 72s); cf 52.1. The following line has the accent on the first syllable, which makes it look as if the stress is in the more usual place (*milel*), perhaps just for variety (cf †Ibn Ezra; GK 72s). But †König suggests that rather this accent is not another conjunctive *mahpak* but the disjunctive *jethib*, which is similar in appearance but is located at the beginning of the word wherever the stress lies (prepositive). Thus the stress can still be *milra*.

51.9aβ. Wake up as in days of old, generations of long ago. The previous colon's challenge might have been implicitly for a raising of Yhwh's arm like that at the Red Sea. This next colon almost makes that explicit. Plural-singular 'days of old' is complemented by plural-plural 'generations of long ago', an unusual usage (see GK 124q). While 'days of old' could denote creation, it commonly refer to the great days of Israel's own history (e.g. 45.21; 46.9–10). N. Wyatt personalizes the generations as referring to heavenly beings who witnessed the ancient struggle,[9] but it is not clear why they should be urged to wake up.

51.9b. Are you not the very splitter of Rahab, slayer of the dragon? †Kiesow (p. 169) sees 51.9–10 with 43.16–21 as one of the two prophecies of Second Isaiah that unequivocally refer to the exodus—or rather to the deliverance from the Red Sea (cf Tg). While this fits the identification of Rahab with Egypt in 30.7, talk of 'splitting' her rather suggests a link with stories of world origins that involve splitting a mythic female figure—Tiamat in *Enuma Elish* (see *ANET*, pp. 61–68, 501–4). Within the OT it thus suggests a link with the Rahab of Job 9.13 and 26.12. The dragon (*tannîn*) in turn recalls a parallel Ugaritic story which uses the word *tnn*. If the beginning of v. 9 referred to the Red Sea event, then, that is now described in terms of those stories about the origins of the world itself.

The participles revert to the prophet's earlier common practice in referring to creation, to the beginnings of Israel, and to subsequent events (e.g. 40.22–23, 26, 28–29; 42.5; 43.1; 44.2, 24–28; 45.7, 18).

9 *Myths of Power* (Münster, 1996), pp. 186–87.

They hardly imply that these are timeless events but they do point to the linkage between them and to their present implications. The participles thus recall Second Isaiah's previous appeals to creation and the beginnings of Israel, though in content they constitute a very different way of referring back to those events (contrast v. 13 which follows).

The LXX omits the line by homoioarkton.

אַתְּ־הִיא is f., agreeing with זרוע ('arm'). The pleonastic היא perhaps extraposes the את, and gives it emphasis (*DG* 1b, *IBHS* 16.3.3, *EWS*, pp. 72–74, JM 154ij): hence 'the very…'. The construction recurs in the next line. It recalls the Israelite conviction that Yhwh not Marduk is the real victor over powers of disorder.
מחצבת is the sole occurrence of חצב in such a theological connection (contrast v. 1 above) and the sole occurrence of the hi—a pseudo-hi, since the meaning is the same as that of the qal (see JM 54f). I. L. Seeligmann sees the word not as derived from a genuine four-letter stem but rather as combining חצב and מחץ, both meaning 'pierce'.[10] If it is, the assonance with המחרבת in exactly the same position in the next line makes it unlikely that the form results from conflation in the course of textual history. One might also imagine readers recalling a link with the use of מחץ in this connection in Job 26.12. The parallel vb here, חלל (but see below), is the vb in Job 26.13. 1QIs[a] and 4QIs[c], with המוחצת, assimilate the text to Job 26.12 (cf †Kutscher, p. 215; ET p. 287).
רהב: 1QIs[a] רחוב, a misreading; cf Th πλάτος.
מחוללת: Vg *vulnerasti* links this with חלל (so *BDB*; *DCH*) but the form could as easily come from חיל (see BDB, p. 297a; *DCH*, Vol. 3, p. 212). Thus Cross (*Canaanite Myth* [see on 40.3], p. 137) renders 'the writhing dragon'. As the dragon was characterized in this way in myths (cf 27.1), this gives an excellent sense and provides a more consistent parallelism with the next line, but the ptpl should then be m. The f. ptpl continues to agree with 'arm'. Perhaps the polel of חיל could then have a causative meaning, 'twister of the dragon'. The equivalent passive, the polal, is capable of both resultative and causative significance (see BDB, p. 297b; *DCH*, Vol. 3, p. 212). Further, when the OT characterizes the dragon in this way in 27.1 it uses עקלתון and בריח (cf Job 26.13).
תנין: 1QIs[a] has תנים, a mistaken 'correction' (†Kutscher, p. 222; ET p. 296); so also Geniza fragment Eb 10.

51.10a. Are you not the very dryer of Sea, of the waters of the great Deep? The Red Sea event continues to be described in terms of the events that brought the world into being. The line corresponds very closely to its predecessor. After the pairing of the two lines of v. 9a, the two lines of vv. 9b–10a also pair. Each addresses Yhwh's arm. Each begins 'Are you not the very…'. Each follows this with a participle, the two rhyming and differing only in their central letter.

[10] 'Voraussetzungen der Midraschexegese', in *Congress Volume: Copenhagen 1953* (*VT* Sup 1, 1953), pp. 150–81 (see p. 169); cf *HAL*; Tov, *Textual Criticism* (see on 44.9b), p. 243.

Their object, Rahab or Sea, comes next, completing the first long colon in each. Both the second, short cola then open with an expression beginning *m*, but in other respects the second cola are not parallel, so that the rhetoric works by accompanying similarity with distinctiveness.

After v. 9 one might initially be inclined to understand the verb as *ḥārab* III ('destroy'—put to the sword). Putting Sea to the sword might seem an implausible idea, though in the Ugaritic texts the primeval victory over the powers of disorder can be symbolized simultaneously as the slaying of the Dragon or as the smiting of Sea. Anat asks, 'Did I not smite El's beloved, Sea? Did I not destroy El's River, Rabbim? Did I not muzzle the dragon (*tnn*)? I smote the crooked serpent...'[11] Here in v. 10 Sea similarly features, as does the great (*rabbāh*) Deep (cf Gen 1.2; 7.11; 8.11). As v. 10 unfolds, it suggests that 'dry' is the dominant meaning, but the resonances of *ḥārab* III are also present (see also v. 19).

Fitzgerald (*CBQ* 34, pp. 407–8; see introduction to chapter 47) sees *tᵉhôm* as the name of a deity (cf Tiamat) and *rabbāh* as a title, rendering 'Great Tehom'.

51.10b. ...turner of the depths of Sea into a way for the restored to cross? Once more the prophet's use of a participle encourages the hearers to understand this activity of Yhwh's as not confined to creation or the origins of the people. Yhwh continues to be such a turner. The further reference to Yhwh's creating a 'way' makes that more explicit (cf, e.g., 49.11).

'The restored' is the last word in the verse and opens a repetition from 35.9–10 which runs into v. 11. †König sees this as a floating oracle like 2.2–4.

הַשָּׂמָה: The MT accents on the penultimate syllable, presupposing that it comprises the article functioning as a relative followed by qatal. The LXX's ἡ θεῖσα more plausibly takes it as another ptpl, whose accent should be on the last syllable (cf GK 138k; *DG* 31, †Marti).
מַעֲמַקֵּי: 1QIs[a] has במעמקי to produce '[who puts] in the depths...', avoiding the MT's double accusative construction (cf †Rubinstein, p. 319).
מַעֲמַקֵּי־יָם: †Begrich (p. 167 = 166) emends to simple מעמקים ('depths').

51.11a. So Yhwh's redeemed will return, will come to Zion with ringing voice and eternity's joy on their head. Initially it might be an open question whether the verbs in v. 11 are jussives, and 1QIs[a] might be read thus throughout, but in the MT the final verb is unequivocally qatal.

Behind v. 11 is 35.10 and behind 35.10 is Jer 31.11–13. In such contexts v. 11 functions to add to the challenge of vv. 9–10 rather

[11] Quoted from A. Herdner, *Corpus des tablettes en cunéiformes alphabétiques* (Paris, 1963), 3.3.35–39, in Cross, *Canaanite Myth* [see on 40.3], p. 119.

than to respond to it. It has this function even if it is an addition from 35.10 here: for example, †Spykerboer notes that vv. 9–10 wholly focus on Jerusalem and its restoration and sees v. 11 as an addition incorporating reference to the return of the deportees. In context the reference to this return thus becomes part of the promise of Zion's restoration. It is the first explicit reference to the people's return in these chapters.

The description of the people as Yhwh's 'redeemed' picks up from 50.2, with its allusion to Yhwh's 'hand' as still having the power to act. The construct might suggest both agency and possession, both the main aspects of the subjective 'genitive' (*DG* 33). Ignoring its rendering at 35.10, the LXX links this opening word with v. 10. Its treatment of what follows then comes to stress Yhwh's agency in what will happen (*HUB*): 'by the Lord they will return...'.

A ringing voice or sound (44.23; 48.20; 49.13) concludes the two cola. Three further cola follow to make v. 11 as a whole a pentacolon (*CHP*, p. 188). At its centre v. 11aγ links to the bicola on either side. In content it introduces v. 11b, with which the LXX links it syntactically. The MT accents link it with v. 11a, and two considerations support this. Rhetorically it qualifies the last word of v. 11aβ. As the second colon explains where it is that the redeemed return to, so the third colon explains the nature of the 'ringing voice'. Then syntactically v. 11aγ is more plausibly understood as dependent on v. 11aαβ. It is a circumstantial noun clause introduced by *w* (see GK 141e; JM 159d), followed by a new asyndetic beginning to v. 11b. In linking v. 11aγ with what follows, the LXX provides a καὶ. The asyndetic clauses may nevertheless be seen as explicative (cf JM 177a; and *DG* 146–47 on apposition).

'Eternity's' is *ʿôlām*, the word rendered 'of long ago' in v. 9b, and Jarchi (see †Alexander) renders 'olden joy' here. It is a suggestive idea, but if we are to see a time allusion, the forward reference of the word is much more common: cf the notion of rejoicing forever in Ps 5.12 [11]. But the time reference seems irrelevant here, and we have taken this as an example of the word's use as one of Hebrew's way of expressing the superlative.[12] To judge from 61.3, the joy on their heads takes the concrete form of garlands, or more likely oil. To 'eternity's joy' the Tg adds 'a cloud of glory shall cover their heads', recalling 4.5 and also the promise of the cloud covering the place of Yhwh's presence (e.g. Exod 24.15–16; 40.34). The Tg thus emphasizes the link with v. 11aαβ and the coming of the redeemed to Zion, the place where Yhwh's glory dwells. The joy of v. 11aγ is the joy of worship and the heads are those of Zion's worshippers.

פדויי: 1QIs[a] has פזורי ('scattered'), perhaps under the influence of Jer 50.17 (†Kutscher, p. 207; ET pp. 274–75).
עולם: 4QIs[c] adds [ת]היה; cf 61:7 (†Skehan and Ulrich).

[12] So G. Brin, 'The Superlative in the Hebrew Bible', in *VT* 42 (1992), pp. 115–18 (see p. 117).

51.11b. Joy and gladness will overtake. Grief and sighing are fleeing. We have noted that the link in content with the preceding colon would make it possible to see v. 11aγb as a tricolon closing off vv. 9–11, but the syntactical binding of v. 11aγ to what precedes means that v. 11b is syntactically self-contained. As a bicolon in its own right it then forms a chiasm with antithetic parallelism to close the subsection (*TTCHV*, pp. 370, 390). The Vg renders the first colon *gaudium et laetitiam tenebunt* ('they will gain joy and gladness'). In isolation this makes good sense. The verb can mean 'reach' and the Vg's understanding gives the verb an object. But the LXX's καὶ εὐφροσύνη καταλήμψεται αὐτούς ('and gladness will overtake them') utilizes the verb's other meaning. This usually involves an object, but that can be understood: see Exod 15.9 (the further link with this chapter is striking); 1 Sam 30.8; Ps 7.6 [5] (we have already noted the link with the next verse of this psalm); 1 Chr 21.12. The verb is masculine despite the fact that 'gladness' is a feminine noun, but 'joy' was masculine and either feminine or masculine would thus be possible.

So the clause can be read either way, but the second colon clarifies the question. The asyndetic 'prophetic' qatal verb first complements the yiqtol verb (see *TTH* 14γ). The meaning also does so. 'Overtake' (*nāśag*) is commonly a military word, paired with 'pursue'. 'Flee' (*nûs*) appears most commonly in battle contexts (see J. Reindl in *ThWAT*): it is as if grief and sighing are running away in a panic, in shame. †Cocceius renders 'they will flee grief and sighing', but the verb is not elsewhere used transitively.

ישׂיגון: with paragogic nun (see on 41.5), missing from 35.10.
נסו: preceded by ו consecutive in 35.10. Syr has the *w*. 1QIs[a] and 4QIs[c] have ונס, ו consec. with s. vb complementing the earlier pl.; cf Vg *fugiet*, Tg ויסוף. These variants doubtless reflect dittog./haplog. of ו and/or confusion of ו and ן. We cannot know what text is original.
יגון: LXX's ὀδύνη καὶ λύπη repeats its double translation from 35.10 (†Ziegler, pp. 70–71, 76).

51.12. I myself, I am the one who comforts you. Who are you to be afraid—of a mortal who will die, a human being who will be made grass? After v. 12a the Syr adds 'the Lord has said', reflecting the fact that if vv. 9–11 were words addressed to Yhwh, a transition to Yhwh's words without announcement or summons to listen would be difficult. If vv. 9–11 are Yhwh's self-challenge, the lack of any indication who speaks here ceases to be a problem. Yhwh continues to speak.

The text does make clear that the addressee changes, though it does so in a confusing way. The first 'you' is masculine plural, the second feminine singular, whereas v. 13 is masculine singular. The masculine plural follows on the plurals of v. 11, while the feminine singular follows on the reference to Zion in v. 11. The transition to masculine singular after the feminine corresponds to that in 41.14–15, though there Jacob/Israel is the addressee. Masculine might reappear as the default gender, especially in material that recalls a lament (†Schoors). The combination of all three with the same reference would be a *tour de force*, distracting rather than rhetorically effective. Variation also appears in 1QIs[a] and the versions, but in different combinations. The Vg may correspond to the MT but it looks less odd (because *timeres* in v. 12b can be either masculine or feminine). The Tg has masculine plural through v. 12. 1QIs[a] has feminine singular for the first verb in v. 13. The Syr has feminine singular through v. 13. The Greek translations have no plurals at all. Thus the LXX's παρακαλῶν σε suggests that the plural suffix on 'who comforts you' (*m*[e]*naḥemkem*) is assimilated to the preceding plurals by dittography from the succeeding 'Who' (*mî*). It is then naturally followed by 1QIs[a], Syr and Vg, as well as by the Tg, which assimilates the second colon. If the singular suffix on 'who comforts you' is thus original, it should perhaps be pointed feminine. Verse 12 as a whole then addresses Zion, as will the beginning of 51.17–23 and 52.1–10.

The LXX's σε could suggest that Yhwh was comforting the prophet (cf †Ibn Ezra). Rather the self-description of v. 12 is not a response to a (non-existent) prophetic or communal lament in vv. 9–11 but to an actual lament in Lamentations 1, where the same participle occurred five times, each time negatived (vv. 2, 9, 16, 17, 21). 'The shape of the oracle is its message' (†Motyer). The people of God opposed and oppressed are surrounded by Yhwh's reality as comforter and creator. The force of this response is increased by the way 'I myself, I am the one who comforts you' stands alone, on the MT's division of the verse, with v. 12b forming a bicolon of its own.

'Who are you to be afraid' is a slightly odd expression, and elsewhere *mî* sometimes seems to need translating as 'how'. Ruth 3.16 is the best example. But 'who' is as satisfactory here (cf Amos 7.2, 5); see further v. 19 and comment. The LXX goes on expansively, γνῶθι τίνα εὐλαβηθεῖσα ἐφοβήθης ('know whom dreading you feared'), the double verb assimilating to 57.11 (†Ottley). Its rendering of the verb for 'fear' by an aorist is followed by the rendering of the further *w*-consecutive in v. 13aβ by past imperfect ἐφόβου. The verbs then refer back to the fear of v. 7, and the noun clause will derive its tense from the succeeding verb: hence 'Who were you that you were afraid' (†König). But more likely such a *w*-consecutive denotes a logical rather than chronological sequence and the wayyiqtol cannot be assumed to have past significance. In the context the present significance of the noun clause in v. 12a carries over into the succeeding noun clause, 'Who [are] you', and on into the wayyiqtol verb (†Saydon, p. 298; GK 111m, v; *DG* 79; *IBHS* 33.3.4; JM 118h). *TTH* 79 hints that one might rather see it as an illogical consequence: 'who art thou, *and* (yet) thou *fearest*'.

On the asyndeton 'a mortal [who] will die', see JM 158a. The closing phrase *ḥāṣîr yinnātēn* might be understood in two ways, with little difference in meaning. Either it means 'is given up [to destruction like] grass': for this use of *nātan*, cf 2 Sam 20.21; 1 Kgs 14.16; Hos 11.8. But the usage is rare, especially without a phrase such as 'to death', and the preposition 'like' has to be presupposed (contrast Pss 37.2; 90.5; 103.15). The LXX, Syr, Vg provide it. 'Made grass' presupposes a more common meaning of the verb (BDB, p. 681a) and no need for a preposition; 40.6–7 (see comment) has already declared that 'all flesh is grass. . .the people is grass' and made specific the implications of the metaphor. The link with 40.6–8 suggests either that this passage also comes from Babylon (†S. Smith, p. 170) or that it indicates the same way of thinking in Jerusalem as held in Babylon.

מנחמכם: on the form, see GK 61h.
מי את ותיראי: †Oort emends to m. אתה ותירא, to assimilate to v. 13. Tg renders 'of whom are you afraid?' and †Ehrlich and Freedman (see †McKenzie) redivide the centre of v. 12 מנחמך ממי ('. . .comforts you [s.]. Of whom. . .'). This involves emending to ירא or taking the ו on ותיראי as emphatic, which seems a forced way of preserving the MT. The LXX may have read את מי (*HUB*). 1QIs[a] has אתי.
ינתן: 1QIs[a] has נתן. The LXX paraphrases ἐξηράνθησαν ('are dried up'), assimilating to 40.7 and 42.15 (†Ziegler, p. 162); cf Syr, Vg. Gelston (*VT* 21, pp. 523–24) less plausibly sees all these as arising from misreading of Tg's interpretative חשיב ('are reckoned').

51.13aα. . . .and to forget Yhwh your maker, extender of heavens, founder of earth? As we have noted, in the MT v. 13 brings a transition to masculine singular verbs and suffixes. Masculine is the default gender, but parallels in vv. 11–16 with 41.8–16 may suggest that the suffix's tacit reference is Jacob–Israel. The further *w*-consecutive hardly indicates chronological sequence from the preceding verb, but rather a further (il)logical sequence. They are afraid because they have put Yhwh out of mind. Specifically, they have declined to reflect on the fact that the one who brought them into being as a community is the very creator of the heavens and the earth.

ותשׁכח: so also 4QIs[c]. 1QIs[a] ותשכחי את assimilates to the f. of v. 12a, as well as adding the object marker. Syr does so to the whole verse. †Duhm sees the MT as resulting from the misunderstanding of such a sufformative, taken as an abbreviation for יהוה.
נוטה: †Ehrlich suggests נוטע ('planter'), assimilating to v. 16. LXX repeats τὸν ποιήσαντα ('maker').

51.13aβ. . . .and to be fearful continuously, all day, because of the fury of the distresser when he is setting himself to destroy? Yet another *w*-consecutive still further develops the scandal of Zion's failure to take account of who it is (v. 12b). The reference is thus hardly to the past, whether Egypt (van Hoonacker, according to †Schoors), or

Jerusalem at the time of its fall, but rather to the present. It suggests the real or assumed situation of the deportees in Babylon in the 540s.

Rhetorically the line takes v. 12b further by using the rarer synonym *pāḥad* ('fear') for *yārēʾ* ('be afraid'; see on 44.8a), and then by using it in the piel: GK 52k sees it as intensive, *Piʿel* (p. 224) as resultative and suggesting the activity of living fearfully. The only other occurrence (Prov 28.14) also qualifies the verb with 'continuously'. With that word and the subsequent synonymous adverbial expression 'all day', the line also takes v. 12b further in substance: cf 52.5 for the combination of expressions. The word *tāmîd* can denote merely 'regularly/continually' (e.g. Jer 52.33, 34), but it has meant 'continuously' at 49.16 (cf 60.11; 62.6) and this makes for a telling contrast; 58.11 and 65.3 are more ambiguous. Similarly *kol-hayyôm* can mean merely 'every day', but more often means 'all day' (e.g. 28.14; 65.2, 5). Zion's own self-description in Lam 3.62 is that it is under attack 'all day' (cf 1.13; 3.3, 14). Since the people have been encouraged by the reminder of who Yhwh is, the 'distresser' here can hardly be Yhwh. It might be Nebuchadnezzar (†Bonnard) or Xerxes (*Morgenstern, 'The "Oppressor"') or Cyrus, or more likely Babylon in general or Nabonidus in particular. Whoever it is, the prophet's point is that the threat is now over.

The verb 'setting' might involve the ellipse of an object, perhaps 'arrow' (cf Pss 7.13 [12]; 11.2; and for the ellipse 21.13 [12]), perhaps 'mind' (for the ellipse, cf Job 8.8). But Aramaic *kûn* can mean 'intend' and a derived MH noun means 'intention' (*DTT*, p. 622). Verse 13 here may instance that meaning (†Ehrlich).

וַתְּפַחֵד: †Duhm emends to qal f. וַתִּפְחֲדִי.
מִפְּנֵי: LXX's τὸ πρόσωπον is surprisingly literal. Perhaps it reflects פני without the מ (i.e. haplog.).
כַּאֲשֶׁר: the word can be of comparative, causal, or temporal force. The last makes best sense here. Many late medieval MSS, Vg, Syr omit the כ (see *HUB*).
לְהַשְׁחִית ואיה: LXX has τοῦ ἆραί σε, και νῦν ποῦ ('to destroy you, and now where'). †Oort infers Heb. לְהַשְׁחִיתֵךְ. But the LXX adds σε earlier in the verse, too.

51.13b–14a. But where is the fury of the distresser? One stooping is hastening to be released. The MT links the first clause with what precedes, but a more usual division of the cola takes vv. 13b–14a and v. 14b as two bicola. The first opens by affirming that the era of destruction is indeed over (cf 49.14–26), whether the fury is the human distresser's or directly Yhwh's. In the latter case, Yhwh asks this rhetorical question about Yhwh's own fury.

Verse 14a might then provide an alternative description of the distresser's downfall, and might do so in several ways. In MH 'release' can denote the opening of the bowels, and *b. Berakot* 57a, 57b see this meaning here. Verse 14a might then mean 'one stooping is hastening to relieve himself', referring to the common motif of the involuntary loss of bodily control in a situation of danger and fear (cf Dan 5.6). The only other occurrence of intransitive qal of the verb for 'stoop' relates to bending down, in connection with sexual intercourse (Jer 2.20). †Rashi alternatively suggests 'one who girds [cf the use in 63.1] is hastening to be stripped [cf the use in 45.1]'; cf the antithesis in 1 Kgs 20.11. The Tg also assumes that an 'avenger' is the subject of v. 14a. But it then has to provide 'the righteous' as a new subject for v. 14b.

In the MT the subject of v. 14a seems to continue to be the subject in v. 14b, so this person must be the one distressed (as 1QIs[a] makes explicit) rather than the distresser or a third party. †Ibn Ezra assumes it is the prophet. †Bonnard pictures someone bent for running, rushing for the gate. †Hessler interprets in the light of Jer 48.11–12, 'the cooper is hastening to empty [the vessel of its wine]'. This requires that Jeremiah 48 uses an image that would be familiar and involves reading much into the allusion. Further, the niphal verb is odd. Linking with the same passage †Korpel and de Moor suggest 'soon the cellarman will be released'.

צֹעֶה: 1QIs[a] has צרה ('distress?', 'one distressed?'). Vg *gradiens* implies צעד. The LXX does not render the first two words; see on v. 14b.

51.14b. He will not die for the Pit, nor will he lack his bread. 'Die for the Pit' is a pregnant expression implying 'die [and go] to the Pit', an alternative term for Sheol as the abode of the dead; cf 47.1a; 50.11b; Pss 74.7; 89.40 [39]; Cant 7.13. There is thus no need to hypothesize that *l* has the meaning of *b* ('in'; †Ruiz, p. 95).

For v. 14 as a whole the LXX has only ἐν γὰρ τῷ σῴζεσθαί σε ('for in your deliverance', corresponding to *l*[e]*hippātēah*) οὐ στησέται ('he will not halt', corresponding to v. 14bα) οὐδὲ χρονιεῖ ('or tarry', corresponding to v. 14bβ). It is presumably an interpretative paraphrastic guess at a tricky text rather than implying a different original. *HUB* suggests the influence of 63.1. For the last verb, cf 13.22 and Hab 2.3, whose messianic significance reappears here (†Ziegler, pp. 112–13). Going further, Sym (as quoted by †Jerome) *cito infernus aperietur et non morietur in corruptionem* ('quickly one below will be revealed...') introduces reference to the doctrine of resurrection, reflecting conflict between Jews and Samaritans;[13] cf Vg *cito veniet gradiens ad aperiendum et non interficiet usque ad internicionem nec deficiet panis eius.*

The Vg thus takes 'his bread' as subject of the second colon and takes the verb as intransitive (cf BDB, *DCH*). One might have expected the subject to precede the verb if it was to change thus, and the Tg rather suggests 'he will not lack his bread'. 'Bread' often

[13] †Van der Kooij, pp. 243–44, following D. Barthélemy, 'Qui est Symmaque' (see p. 461).

stands for food in general, so that the colon can imply an understated promise that all life's basic needs will be met.

לַחְמוֹ: †Volz emends to לחו ('his vigour'). Driver (*JTS* 36, pp. 402–3) obtains the same meaning by repointing לֶחָמוֹ, the noun לח with the long third person suffix (cf 53.8). †Simon repoints לְחָמוֹ ('his fighting'), but this does not fit as well, and לחם is usually niphal. For v. 14b †Duhm hypothesizes לא יעמוד ולא יאחר on the basis of LXX.

51.15. Yes, I am Yhwh your God, stiller of the sea when its billows roar: Almighty Yhwh is his name. One might at first hear Yhwh's further self-declaration as an *inclusio* for vv. 11–15, but it will turn out to introduce the subsequent statement in v. 16. It begins emphatically, with a *w* and the pronoun 'I'. Better sense is gained by taking the *w* as affirmative (JM 177n; cf LXX ὅτι) than as suggesting contrast (Vg *autem*) or as a dittograph (1QIs[a] lacks it). 'Your' is masculine singular, implying the same addressee as in v. 13: for masculine singular 'your God', cf 41.10, 13; 43.3; 48.17, each time referring to Jacob–Israel. That last passage and this one fit W. Zimmerli's dictum that this expression suggests Yhwh's might rather than Yhwh's consolation, yet it is Yhwh's might applied to the security of Yhwh's relationship with the people.[14] But the singular also makes this the same expression as that which opens the Ten Words (Exod 20.2; Deut 5.6), and the words that follow suggest further comparison and contrast as they refer back to the Red Sea deliverance.

LXX ὁ ταράσσων, Vg *conturbo* assume that *rāga*ʿ means 'stir' not 'still'. Followed by a wayyiqtol verb, this is immediately the obvious translation. The billows' churning results from Yhwh's stirring. But the Tg renders 'rebuker of the sea'; Yhwh is more commonly the quietener of churning than its cause (cf Ps 93), and another verb *rāga*ʿ means 'be still' (see on v. 4b). With a causative meaning 'still' makes good sense (†Snaith; cf Job 26.13; also 34.14; and the noun in 28.12) if we take the following wayyiqtol as epexegetical (cf *TTH* 75–76; *IBHS* 33.2.2; JM 118j). Either way the wayyiqtol after a participle with present reference itself has present rather than past reference (see on v. 12, also JM 118r; again contrast †König). 'It is characteristic of *hāmāh*/*hāmôn* to be employed to designate both the raging of the sea and the raging of hostile nations; it even serves in many instances to link both manifestations of the forces of chaos' (A. Baumann in *ThWAT* on *hāmāh*, III.1). The Syr follows the Tg's understanding of the participle but renders *hāmāh* ('be still') in line

[14] 'Ich bin Jahwe', in *Geschichte und Altes Testament* (A. Alt Festschrift; Tübingen, 1953), pp. 179–209 (see p. 201); ET in Zimmerli, *I Am Yahweh* (Atlanta, 1982), pp. 1–28, 138–43 (see p. 21).

with its rendering of *rāga*ʿ as 'rebuke'; cf also Mark 4.39. It might be assimilating to Ps 107.29.[15]

רֹגַע: on the form see GK 65d. To gain the meaning 'rebuked', there is no need to emend to גֹּעֵר (cf †Thomas): see comment.
שְׁמוֹ: cf, e.g., 47.4; 48.2; 54.5. LXX ὄνομά μοι implies assimilation to the context (see v. 14aα) rather than an original שְׁמִי. The word-order emphasizes the title (see on 48.2).

51.16a. I put my words in your mouth. With the shade of my hand I covered you. The Tg has 'And I have put the words of my prophecy in your mouth'. We have noted that the words beginning from v. 12 could—with a little emendation—be understood as addressed to the prophet. These words in v. 16a are such as are spoken to the prophet in 49.2 (cf also 50.4; Jer 1.9), and 48.16 illustrates the way in which these chapters can incorporate a sudden transition to material addressed to the prophet. But the situation there is rather different. At 48.16b a transition is explicitly involved as there is a change of speaker and hearer. Yhwh moves from being 'I' to being 'he' and the 'me' in 48.16b has to have a corresponding new referent. Further, the substance of the content absolutely required such a change even if the syntax did not. Here there is no change of speaker and no indication in the rhetoric that the addressee changes. The apparent need to presuppose a change of addressee arises from the words' content. The words do resemble ones earlier spoken to the prophet. The prophet embodies the people's vocation, and Yhwh's commitment to the prophet thus also applies to them. The Syr has second feminine pronouns.

Formally, the line forms a chiasm of two parallel cola. It opens and closes with first-person verbs (wayyiqtol then qatal), the second word in each colon has a first-person singular suffix (with a plural then a singular noun), and the two central words open with the preposition *b*. Yet in substance, the two sets of words are hardly parallel at all. 1QIs[a] omits the *w* (haplography?, but see on 43.9) on the opening verb and thus turns it into a yiqtol. The LXX similarly renders θήσω (having not represented the *w* at the end of v. 15: see comment) and then σκεπάσω. 4QIs[b] has the *w*. In keeping with earlier expressions of commitments to the community, we might take the verbs as further instantaneous/performative wayyiqtol and qatal; they would thus express Yhwh's present commitment to the people. But what follows in v. 16b will make it more likely that they have past reference. 'Covered you' is a different verb from 'concealed you' in 49.2, though the meaning seems similar and the difference to be for the sake of variation. The piel is resultative (*Pi'el*, pp. 204–5).

[15] So A. Gelston, 'Was the Peshitta of Isaiah of Christian Origin?', in †Broyles and Evans, pp. 563–82 (see pp. 573–76).

51.16b. ...in planting heavens and founding earth, and in saying to Zion 'You are my people'. For epexegetical infinitive with *l* to state motives or circumstances, see GK 114o; *DG* 108; *IBHS* 36.2.3e. 'Plant' is a surprising verb for the establishing of the heavens. It is used commonly of people (e.g. Exod 15.17), once of nails (Qoh 12.11) and of tents (Dan 11.45). LXX's ἐν ᾗ ἔστησα looks like a loose translation along these lines.

For the last colon LXX has καὶ ἐρεῖς Σίων ('and you will say to Zion'), implying a change of subject for the final infinitive and making clear that divine creation and prophetic speech are two different matters (cf †Seeligmann, p. 109). This reflects a surprising sequence in v. 16b, from creation straight to Zion, but the MT offers no hint of a change of subject and this way of approaching the line will not do. *Midrash Tanḥuma* (SB) on Gen 1.1 refers the first colon to the original creation (effected through the Torah: see v. 16a). If it refers to coming events, it must denote the creation of a new heaven and earth, a motif that will become more explicit in 65.17; 66.22 (so, e.g., †Delitzsch). The Tg's 'to establish the people of whom it was said that they would increase like the stars of the heavens and to establish the congregation of whom it was said that they would increase like the dust of the earth' takes it as a figure for the renewing of Israel. But too much is required to read this meaning into the words, and the mere fact of an unaccustomed verb (contrast 40.22; 42.5; 44.24; 45.12; 51.13) is insufficient to signal a different temporal reference.

More likely they are a restatement of the words in v. 13, with the customary variation: the construction is different (infinitive rather than participle), the first verb different. Once again the prophet links reference to the creation of the world and the creation of Israel, here by picturing Yhwh having in mind the designation of Israel when involved in the act of creation. In keeping with the talk in terms of Zion–Jerusalem rather than Jacob–Israel in chapters 49–55, however, Yhwh actually refers to designating Zion 'my people'. Zion can be both the city that people left and the people who left it.

לנטע: Syr assimilates the verb to v. 13 and earlier passages, suggesting לנטת ('in stretching'; †Houbigant). †Ehrlich repoints לְנֹטֵעַ ... וּלְיֹסֵד ('as one who plants/founds').
שָׁמים: †Rendtorff (p. 10) emends to שׁממה ('desolation').
לציון: T. Penar sees the ל as vocative.[16]

IV.d.iii. The awakening of Jerusalem (i) (51.17–23)

The difference between vv. 17–23 and vv. 9–11 is that Jerusalem rather than Yhwh's arm is addressed. Both have a part to play in the fulfilling of Yhwh's purpose of restoration. †Begrich (p. 56 = 62) calls

[16] '"Lamedh vocativi" exempla Biblico-Hebraica', in *VD* 45 (1967), pp. 32–46 (see p. 45).

this renewed address to Jerusalem a *Trostwort* or word of encouragement for mourners, while †von Waldow (pp. 21–22) sees it as a form of salvation oracle. Both forms of language indeed appear, again with Second Isaiah's typical creativity (†Melugin, p. 161). The bicola are all 2–2, 3–2, 4–2, or 5–2, except for vv. 19a, 21 (which could be read that way with the aid of extra *maqqephs*) and v. 22b.

Verses 17aβ–20 work chiastically:

17aβb Madam Zion the object of Yhwh's fury
  18 The absence of her children
    19 Her multiple devastation
  20a The death of her children
20b Her children the object of Yhwh's fury

Verse 17aα stands outside the chiasm, to have its theme taken up in vv. 21–23. Verse 19 in its own complexity of structure stands at the centre of the chiasm. Each of the opening two elements are taken further when their motifs recur in v. 20. The children are revealed to be absent because dead (not merely deported), and they as well as the city itself are the object of Yhwh's fury. Thus the exhortation again takes up the characterization of Jerusalem in Lamentations 1, but also the prospective characterization of Babylon in chapter 47—Madam Zion is to stand as Madam Babylon falls to sit in the dust.

51.17aα. Wake yourself, wake yourself, stand up Jerusalem. The repeated verb picks up that in 51.9 but appears in the hitpolel rather than qal form and thus as both reflexive and resultative, though the reversion to qal in 52.1 suggests that the variation may be mainly stylistic. The bidding is the opposite of that issued to Babylon in 47.1. In vv. 17–23 as a whole the prophet seems to be the speaker until explicitly quoting Yhwh in vv. 22–23, though there is no hint of this change, which is also mainly rhetorical.

51.17aβ. ...you who drank from Yhwh's hand his fury cup. Part of the reason for Jerusalem's present prostration is indicated. As at 40.2 (and v. 16 here), the Tg softens the anthropomorphism to 'you who accepted before Yhwh...'. For the metaphor, metonymy, and synecdoche involved in the talk of drinking a cup of wine that stands for God's anger, see †Lack (pp. 180–83). Perhaps the prophet implies that the people have been the victims of Yhwh's angry feelings, but it may be that the fury represented by the cup denotes its toxic effects rather than or as well as the emotions of the one who gave it. It is the opposite of the blessing cup that a company shared on happier occasions.

אשׁר: we take the opening conjunction as a demonstrative (cf GK 138a).

51.17b. ...who drank, who drained, the chalice, the shaking cup. The line completes a chiasm with v. 17aβ: literally, 'you who drank from

Yhwh's hand his cup of fury—the chalice, the cup of shaking you drank, drained'. The repetitions are noteworthy. A noun from the previous line reappears in the first colon, the verb from the previous line in the second colon. These are in any case familiar words. They are now glossed by less familiar ones. The chiastic word order of v. 17b itself is thus new noun–old noun–extra noun–old verb–new verb.

'Chalice' (*qubbaʿat*) occurs only here and in v. 22. It might be an Akkadianism (cf BDB), though it is known from Ugaritic, where 'cup' and 'chalice' are a fixed pair (Dahood, 'Hebrew-Ugaritic Lexicography ix' [see on 43.9], pp. 341–42). Cohen (*Hapax Legomena* [see on 40.5], pp. 86–87), argues against any link with *gābîaʿ* ('cup, bowl'). †Thomas deletes *kôs* ('cup') here and in v. 22 as a gloss on the unfamiliar word, but the textual evidence for its being a later addition is poor; it is represented in the LXX.[17] If it is an explanatory gloss, it is a failed one, for the Vg does not understand *qubbaʿat* and renders from the context *fundum* ('bottom'). The Tg has the compound expression, which itself recurs in v. 22, though Syr does not.

The construct 'cup of shaking' is a genitive of effect (*IBHS* 9.5.2c) or purpose (GK 128q). Cohen (*Hapax Legomena*, pp. 85–86) suggests that *tarʿēlāh* actually means 'poison'; the Tg has 'cursing'. Again, it points to the drink affecting people in the manner of alcohol or poison. 'Drained' (*māṣāh*) is another rare word for the verse's closure. The two verbs come together in Ps 75.9 [8] in the opposite order. There this word is accompanied by specific reference to the 'dregs', and here the Vg renders the asyndetic construction by the adverbial phrase *usque ad faeces*. It is doubtful whether we should see the Hebrew as quasi-adverbial (cf *IBHS* 39.3.1b; contrast JM 177g). For the thought, cf also Ezek 23.32–34.

51.18. There was no-one to guide her, of all the children she had borne. There was no-one to take her by the hand, of all the children she had brought up. The Vg renders *ʾên* by a present, *non est* ('there is no-one'), but the past verbs in v. 17aβb suggest rather that we follow LXX οὐκ ἦν in taking the noun clause as having past reference. Like v. 17aβb, the two lines in v. 18 parallel and repeat each other. P. Haupt suggests that the verb *nāhal* means more than merely 'guide' and proposes 'settle/take to rest',[18] but here as on earlier occasions (e.g. 40.11; 49.10) parallelism does not seem to support this.

In the second colon in each line, 'borne' is complemented by 'brought up', which thus takes further rather than merely clarifying. It also makes explicit that the children are grown-ups rather than young people: contrast Lam 2.11–12 and 4.3–4. It is customary to note that in the story of Aqhat it was specifically the children's job to guide mother home when she was the worse for drink (see Aqht A, 1.31–32; *ANET*, p. 150).

[17] Against †Thomas; see Tov, *Textual Criticism* (see on 44.9b), p. 280.
[18] 'The Hebrew Stem *nahal*, To Rest', in *AJSL* 22 (1905–6), pp. 195–206 (see p. 196).

מנהל: 1QIs[a] מנחל ('allocate') is presumably a misreading. LXX's παρακαλῶν (cf Syr, Tg) might similarly imply misreading for מנחם, but compare 40.11; 49.10 LXX (*HUB*).
לה: 1QIs[a] 'corrects' to לך and the LXX expresses the whole of v. 18 as second-person address, leading neatly into v. 19. They thus make explicit that the third-person forms in v. 18 (which †Fohrer takes as an addition) are those of a quasi-relative, like 54.1 (†Schoors; cf JM 158n), implying '...you for whom there was no-one to guide her...'.

51.19. There were two things that were happening to you (Who was to mourn for you?): destruction, devastation, famine, sword (Who was I to comfort you?). The cola could have come in the sequence v. 19aα, 19bα, 19aβ, 19bβ and thus formed two standard bicola with internal parallelism. Instead the cola are interwoven to produce another ABAB pair of parallel whole lines that belong closely together. Like the noun clauses in v. 18, the participial clause should again derive its time reference from the context, which suggests past. This makes entire sense: the experiences in v. 19aα are associated especially with the Babylonian reduction of Jerusalem. The subsequent yiqtols then make good sense as past imperfects or as modal uses. The Tg's 'two afflictions came upon you, Jerusalem—you cannot stand; when four come upon you, despoiling, breaking, famine, and sword, there is no-one who will comfort you but me' apparently refers the first bicolon to the first fall of 587 BC, the second to that of AD 70.

The Tg goes on to understand the MT to mean 'there is none who would comfort you but me'. The 'Who' question indeed implies 'No-one' (cf BDB, p. 566b), but the Tg's understanding of the sentence as a whole cannot be paralleled. The same is true of †Ibn Ezra's 'By whom shall I comfort you?' This matches the sense of Lam 2.13 but also corresponds in wording to Nah 3.7, of which the clause here seems to be a compressed version (†Cassuto, p. 169). But that does not mean we can assimilate the meaning to Nahum's.

The four forms of calamity suggest totality. We are apparently to make two calamities out of v. 19bα, but there is no obvious way to do so. †Calvin even suggests that the four specific instances of calamity constitute one whole while the absence of mourner/comforter constitutes the other. The sentence links the four nouns with threefold *w* and thus points in no particular direction. The LXX omits the middle *w* and thus plausibly pairs devastation and destruction, then famine and sword. The first two alliterate, as do the second two (*haššōd, haššeber*; *hārāʿāb, haḥereb*). While the latter two clearly relate to persons, it is not the case that the former two relate rather to land or buildings. While some passages could be read either way, in many passages destruction and devastation (for the combination see 59.7; 60.18; Jer 48.3) must apply to human beings, whether the words come alone or together. Usage does not suggest that the two pairs of words denote respectively moral decay and outward distress (†Torrey). If there is a distinction between destruction and devastation, the former more suggests outer death, the latter inner shattering, as in English. Further, while the first two could be read as a hendiadys for devastating destruction, it seems forced to see the second two as another hendiadys.[19] Famine and sword sum up the concrete form that death took when Jerusalem was besieged and reduced. They form a pair in, for example, Jer 5.12; 11.22; 14.13, 15, 16, 18; 16.4; 42.16; 44.12, 18, 27 (elsewhere they are accompanied by pestilence). Another way of making two out of four is thus to take the twofold disaster to denote devastating destruction that takes a twofold concrete form, though the fact that destruction/devastation is a pair of its own suggests that there is no need to go on to link destruction specifically with famine and devastation with sword (†Ibn Ezra). This fits the warning in 47.9, where the prospective double calamity for Madam Babylon is focused on her people. Closing off the list, 'sword' (*ḥereb*) recalls the address to Yhwh as drier/destroyer (*maḥărebet*) of Sea in v. 10. The sword that should be exercised on Israel's enemies has been exercised against the people itself.

However we reconfigure the four disasters as two, the fact that four are listed, as the Tg makes explicit, makes one ask why they are numbered two. The number recalls the 'double' of 40.2. The further doubling to four in v. 19b makes the point in 40.2 once again. More recently and more directly it recalls the two disasters threatened for Babylon in 47.9. The further doubling then hints that two disasters is the very minimum that Babylon deserves. Further, they may well be two because the first pair fulfil one warning of Jeremiah's, the second pair another warning (cf Jer 4.20; 15.2) (cf Paul, 'Echoes', pp. 116–17).

שתים הנה: LXX renders δύο ταῦτα, but we would then expect the words to have the article or to be in the opposite order; or cf the expression שתי־אלה in 47.9. שתים might be extraposed, suggesting 'two things, these were happening to you' (cf the comment on the use of the f. in GK 122q?). But the parallel passages Prov 6.16 and 30.15 exclude that and suggest that הנה is rather a copula. They also establish that this is an expression designed to introduce a list. 1QIs[a] has m. המה.

אנחמך: 1QIs[a] has the more predictable ינחמך; cf LXX's παρακαλέσει, Vg *consolabitur*, Syr *nby'ky*. Tg seems to have read as the MT, and †Jerome seems aware of its reading (see †Kedar-Kopfstein, p. 193). GK 47b suggests that the MT's form reflects the Babylonian pronunciation of ינחמך, but it is not clear why one isolated instance should be misspelled. M. Dahood first parsed as a third-person aphel[20] then reworked as אנח מך ('has groaned over you'); cf Lam 1.4, 8, 21. This requires an unparalleled use of the qal, an unparalleled assimilation of the נ in מנך, and an unparalleled meaning for מן where we would expect על. *Dahood compares Exod 2.23, a suggestive parallel for the vb, but there מן has a different meaning. A more plausible possibility is that the reading is a composite of נחם and אנח.

[19] So *CHP*, p. 326; cf M. Z. Kaddari, 'A Semantic Approach to Biblical Parallelism', in *JJS* 24 (1973), pp. 167–75 (see p. 169).

[20] 'Some Aphel Causatives in Ugaritic', in *Biblica* 38 (1957), pp. 62–73 (see p. 70).

51.20. Your children were overcome, they lay at the entrance to all the streets like a snared oryx, the people who were full of Yhwh's fury, of your God's blast. The length of the line that indicates why the children cannot help their mother has suggested that the phrase 'at the entrance of all the streets' is an addition. But it forms another link with Lamentations (see 4.1) of a kind that is characteristic of this subsection, and in the MT v. 20 thus ends with a pentacolon, like v. 11 at the equivalent half-way point in vv. 9–16. For *rōʾš* the LXX has ἄκρου ('top'), and the Vg *capite* ('head'), common meanings (cf 42.11; 51.11), but the point of this reference is not obvious unless this is simply an equivalent to 'at every street corner'. *DCH* (Vol. 3, p. 175) rather suggests 'entrance': cf the use for the beginning or head of a river (Gen 2.10) or of a period of time (Isa 40.21; 41.4, 26; 48.16). *Terian suggests the term denotes 'dead-ends' of the kind an oryx would be cornered into in a pen, but 'head' is an odd word for that.

The word *tôʾ* ('oryx') comes only here and at Deut 14.5 (as *t*ᵉ*ʾô*). The versions paraphrase or misunderstand as a word for 'beet'. *IDB*, Vol. 2, p. 251b, calls it 'absolutely unidentifiable'. At Deut 14.5 the Tg takes it to mean 'wild ox' (cf *DTT*; *Bilik), the LXX and Vg, to mean 'oryx' (cf also Syr *dyṣʾ*), an animal related to deer, gazelle, and antelope, which was hunted with nets (*IBD*, p. 57) and fits better here (cf *HAL*). On hunting and nets, see Keel (*Welt* [see on 42.10], section II.2c.) The Tg paraphrases 'those who are thrown [into nets]'.

Verse 20b in turn corresponds to v. 17aβb. The image of being 'full' is thus given precision by the link with a cup and drinking. Yet the last colon typically introduces a new word, 'blast'. That was supposed to be exercised on the sea (50.2). Its exercise on these children is thus grievous.

עלפו: *DTT* plausibly distinguishes עלף I ('cover') and עלף II ('overcome'). In the MT the pual comes only here, but see BDB; for the hitpael, Amos 8.13; Jonah 4.8. LXX's ἀπορούμενοι might be a paraphrase (†Ottley) or might be a corruption of ἀπερριμένοι (†Ziegler, p. 128). Sym's ἐπορεύθησαν may then be a further corruption.
שכבו: 1QIsᵃ שוכבו is assimilated to its עולפו (†Kutscher, p. 274; ET pp. 358–59).
כתוא מכמר: literally 'like the oryx of the snare'. LXX has ὡς σευτλίον ἡμίεφθον ('like a half-cooked turnip'), Syr *ʾyk slqʾ dkmyr* ('like cooked beet'). †Jerome suggests that LXX's noun presupposes another 'Syriac' word *thoreth*: cf *DTT* on תרדא/תרד ('beet'). The adj. presupposes that מכמר is not 'snare/net' from כמר III, but a form of כמר I ('heat', †Ziegler, p. 99; see BDB).
גערת (see on 50.2): LXX ἐκλελυμένοι ('weakened') may suggest it read the root גרע (G. I. Davies).

51.21. Therefore do listen to this, you who are weak, drunk but not with wine. Second Isaiah does not deal much in 'therefores', in the manner of First Isaiah. This exception only proves the rule, because there is no inevitable logic about vv. 21–23. In 47.8 *w*ᵉ*ʿattāh* ('so now') introduces the same verb form as here—though without the enclitic *nā*ʾ—and the same object, ‘listen to this’ (the LXX omits ‘this’). Babylon is then characterized as *ʿădînāh* (‘delectable’), Zion as *ʿăniyyāh* (‘weak’). The summons thus draws attention to the contrast between the two passages addressing Babylon and Zion. On the other hand, the ‘do listen’ (with the enclitic) repeats the exhortations in vv. 1, 4, 7. It can be a pleasant experience to be under the influence of alcohol, but not to be under the influence of the cup that these people have had to drink.

שִׁכֻרַת וְלֹא מִיָּיִן: the phrase is a cross between a constr. phrase in which the second n. denotes the cause (cf 1.7, ‘burnt by fire’; GK 1161) and a pass. ptpl. expression with the cause/agent denoted by מִן (cf 28.7; GK 121f). The pure forms would be שִׁכֻרַת לֹא יַיִן or וְלֹא מִיַּיִן שְׁכֻרָה. †Torrey takes it as a composite reading. But see JM 129m for other instances of the constr. ptpl. followed by a prep. GK 130b suggests that שִׁכֻרַת is an old abs. form used to avoid the hiatus שְׁכֻרָה וְ, and GK 50f suggests that it is not really a pass. ptpl. (because the vb is intr.) but an adj., but JM 50e more plausibly sees such pass. ptpls with an act. sense as Aramaisms.

51.22aα. Your Lord Yhwh has said this, your God who defends his people. The lines continue to work in pairs. This one pairs with v. 21 in forming an extended solemn introduction to the words that follow in vv. 22aβ–23. The previous line introduces these words by characterizing the addressee, like 45.1. This line does so by characterizing the one who speaks, as usually happens (e.g. 42.5). For the combination of the two, see 44.1–2.

‘Your Lord’ is an expression to describe someone’s husband (cf Ps 45.11 [12]; also Isa 49.14). Madam Zion’s husband is also her God: the *w* prefixed to ‘your God’ draws attention to the fact that the second colon’s predicate is the verbal expression in the first. 1QIs[a] omits it, as do 4Q176 *Tanḥûmîm* and the LXX, but the LXX’s κύριος ὁ θεὸς is probably abbreviating (†Elliger). Sym’s ὑπερμαχήσει for *rîb* suggests a reference to the last great battle, corresponding to the exodus at the End (†van der Kooij, pp. 240–41). †Volz sees the passage itself as eschatological.

It is a husband’s or a God’s business to defend his wife. The breakdown in the relationship has meant that matters have not been working out that way, but Yhwh affirms that the proper arrangement will be re-established.

51.22aβb. There, I am taking from your hand the shaking cup. My chalice, the fury cup—you will not continue to drink it. The pair of lines takes up the expressions from v. 17, though it reverses the motifs and generates another chiasm. On the extraposed clause, see on 42.3a. Unusually in verse the object marker is used, to signpost the construction at the beginning of the extraposed clause (cf *TTH* 197). The verbs are another instantaneous/performative qatal and a yiqtol, and the second promises another converse of the experience destined for Babylon: see 47.1, 5.

לשתותה: 1QIs[a] לשתותו changes the gender to match the fact that the immediately preceding noun כום is more often m. in MH (see *DTT*; †Kutscher, p. 33; ET pp. 43–44).
כום: the second occurrence is again absent from the LXX and Syr.

51.23. I will put it in the hand of your tormentors, the ones who said to your neck 'Bow and we will pass over', and you made your backs like the ground, like the street for people passing over. Once more a pentacolon closes the section and once more the promise takes up the plaints of Lamentations, this time about torment (e.g. 1.12)—though here the torment comes from other people rather than from Yhwh. †Simon sees these tormentors as other Judeans.

†Alexander takes *nepeš* ('neck') to refer to the spirit, to a paining of the inner person (cf BDB, p. 660b), but the context refers to physical pain. In isolation the word would most likely constitute a simple intensification (†Volz), a paraphrase for the personal pronoun (so BDB, p. 660a). But L. Dürr refers it to neck or throat, which fits the parallelism.[21] An ambiguity about the first colon (what does *nepeš* mean?) is then characteristically resolved by the second. †Stone (p. 85) sees the last three cola as referring to the rape of Madam Zion by her attackers. But 'pass over' is not the obvious verb for the making of that point, and the words also recall the language of Amos 1.3; Zech 10.5; Ps 129.3, and the symbolic action of Deut 33.29; Josh 10.24; Ps 110.1. 'Making your back…' indeed recalls 'giving my back…' in 50.6, adding another dimension to the parallel between the calling and experience of servant/prophet and people. The reference to the street then takes up that in v. 20.

ושמתיה: 1QIs[a] ושמתיהו again prefers m. pronominal suffix.
מוגיך: 1QIs[a] adds ומעניך ('and of your humiliators'), LXX's καὶ τῶν ταπεινωσάντων σε. †Zillessen (p. 242) and †Ziegler (p. 76) derive the extra word in the LXX from 60.14 where the message of 51.23 is reworked, though 60.14 might be a witness to an original מעניך at 51.23. Tg has simply דהוו מונן and T. Secker (see †Lowth) sees מוניך from ינה ('your oppressors') as the original reading (cf 49.26). Perhaps 1QIs[a] and the LXX witness to a double reading. But the less familiar MT term is more likely original (Talmon, 'Aspects of the Textual Transmission' [see on 40.18a], p. 108).
אשר: again demonstrative (cf GK 138a), hence 'the ones who'.
שחי: the only qal occurrence of this vb (see on 44.15).
גוך: Tg has יקריך ('your dignity'). Zion's humiliation was the putting down of human worth. Syr *lʿmky* implies גֵּיךְ (*HUB*).

[21] See 'Hebr. נֶפֶשׁ = akk. *napištu* = Gurgel, Kehle', in *ZAW* 43 (1925), pp. 262–69 (see p. 267). But contrast H. Seebass in *ThWAT* on *nepeš*, IV.1.

IV.d.iv. The awakening of Jerusalem (ii) (52.1–6)

As the repeated verb 'wake up/wake yourself' introduced a section at 51.9 and 51.17, the recurrence of the repetition suggests another new section. The appearance of *kî* ('for') clauses through vv. 1–6 matches the dynamic of 51.9–16 and 51.17–23, though their content is not what one would expect—but then Isaiah 40–55 delights to frustrate expectations. While the MT provides a setuma after v. 2 and modern editors see a transition from verse to prose there, it is possible to see v. 3 as completing the structure of vv. 1–3 and as a tricolon closing off the subsection:

1abα Summons to Zion/Jerusalem to wake up
  1bβ Reasons: *kî* plus yiqtol verbs
2 Summons to Jerusalem/Zion to stand
  3 Reasons: *kî* plus yiqtol verb

The middle three lines comprising vv. 1bβ–2 once again have the rhythm of lament, with two-beat second cola. Oddly, the opening line is 2–3, as are the actual words of Yhwh in v. 3aβb.

Verses 1–3 might again reflect the language of encouragement to mourners (see on 51.17–23) but they also suggest an investiture like Athena's: for instance, with the invitation to put on strength/attractive clothes, K. Baltzer compares Athena's ornamented armour or shield ('Stadt-Tyche', p. 116; ET p. 55). The prophet promises the restoring of Madam Zion's beauty (v. 1) and her freedom (vv. 2–3). The opening and closing lines reflect the prophet's distinctive forms of expression: 'wake up/put on strength', 'sell' (50.1), 'restore'. Inside this bracket the language again reflects that of Lamentations 1–2. 'Attractiveness' was what Yhwh took from Jerusalem in throwing her from heaven to earth (2.1). Foreigners who were forbidden to enter the congregation have invaded the holy place and stained it (1.9–10; cf 2.7). Zion sits in the dust (2.10). Wrongdoing and its consequences weigh on her neck (1.14). Daughter Zion (the word *bat* in such connections comes 14 times in Lam 1–2) is a captive (1.5, 18). All this is now reversed. Once more, what is to happen to Zion is also the opposite to what happens to Babylon, another 'daughter', who is to move from sitting on a throne to sitting in the dust, her fine clothes stripped off.

Verses 4–6 develop v. 3 in more certainly prose form, taking up the 'for nothing' of v. 3 (see vv. 4, 5).

Verses 3–6 form a pattern of their own:

3–4 Past: You were sold/oppressed
  'Yhwh said this' recurs
  'For nothing' 'My people'
5 Present: Rulers boast, Yhwh's name stands despised
  'Yhwh's oracle' recurs
  'My people' 'For nothing' 'My name'

6 Future: You will acknowledge
'Therefore' recurs
'My people' 'My name'

The reiterated phrases confirming that these are Yhwh's words recall the speech of Haggai and Zechariah, though they have also appeared in Isaiah 40–55. As 51.9–16 promised an end to bondage and 51.17–23 an end to punishment, 52.1–6 promise an end to shame (†Grimm and Dittert). Verses 3–6 have commonly been seen as a series of glosses on vv. 1–2 (see, e.g., †Whybray).

52.1abα. Wake up, wake up, put on your strength, Zion. Put on your attractive clothes, Jerusalem, holy city. In 51.17–23 the prophet was the speaker, quoting the words of Yhwh in vv. 22–23. The same pattern likely continues in 52.1–10. So the prophet urges Zion to wake up and put on strength, as Yhwh had urged Yhwh's arm to wake up and put on strength (51.9). The LXX adds an extra Σιών in the first colon, whereas 1QIsᵃ omits the word altogether. The qal form 'wake up' is shorter and sharper and thus more urgent than the hitpoel in 51.17 ('wake yourself').

For 'your attractive clothes', the LXX has simply 'your glory' (τὴν δόξαν σου). The Syr omits the pronominal suffix.

עזך: 1QIsᵃ lacks the suffix. †Budde emends to עדיך ('your jewellery') to make a better pairing with the next colon; cf 49.18. But עז and תפארת/תפארה are a pair in Pss 78.61 and 89.18 [17]. Syr omits 'put on strength', by accident or to abbreviate the text.

52.1bβ. For uncircumcised and stained will not continue to enter you. The reference to the uncircumcised is almost unique in the prophets. Ezekiel 44.6, 9 condemns the profaning of the sanctuary by the presence of the uncircumcised, but here critique has become promise and the sanctuary has become the city as a whole. Once more it reverses a plaint in Lamentations (see 1.10). Similarly the reference to stain (*ṭāmē*ʾ) is new in these chapters (but cf vv. 11–12). Furthermore, there are no other passages that link uncircumcision and stain. Uncircumcision belongs to the antithesis 'holiness/profaneness', the divide between Israel and other peoples. 'Purity/stain' is an antithesis that works within Israel itself. So the prophet promises that the city will be preserved from both uncircumcised gentiles and stained Israelites, but perhaps thereby implies that the latter are no different from the former.

If the language of v. 23 could suggest rape, then the same is true of the promise in this line (†Stone, p. 85; cf †Darr, p. 177).

יוסיף יבא בך עוד: 1QIsᵃ resolves the asyndeton by prefixing the second vb with a ו (†Rubinstein, p. 319). The *Tanḥuma* Lech Lecha includes the reading לעבר for יבא, which is supported by the LXX, Vg, Tg, but may derive from the influence of the parallel wording in Joel 4.17 [3.17]; Nah 2.1 (see *HUB*). 1QIs[a] and some Kennicott MSS omit עוד (see *HUB*).

52.2a. Shake yourself off, arise from the dust, sit, Jerusalem. 'Sit on the throne of splendour', the Tg characteristically but appropriately paraphrases; Zion and Babylon are indeed changing places. For the sequence 'stand' in order to 'sit', see 1 Sam 2.8; 28.23; 2 Sam 19.9 [8]; Ps 113.7–8, and the Ugaritic texts quoted by Dahood (*CBQ* 20, pp. 43–45). 'From the dust' comes between the opening two verbs and may apply to both; cf the 'intervening' expressions between related verbs in 40.30; 41.15; 42.21; 43.17; 44.11, 17; 46.7; 53.4. But the above passages show that it more naturally links with 'arise' (see †Rosenbaum, pp. 154–56). †Westermann assumes that the addressee is now the deportee community rather than the city (see on v. 3), but there is no suggestion of such a change.

שְׁבִי: in 46.2; 49.24, 25, this was the n. 'captivity/imprisonment', but that makes poor sense here. In the next line comes the f. adj. שְׁבִיָּה, which †Oort reads here (and cf †Qimchi's 'prisoner'). This makes good sense but regrettably removes the paronomasia that binds the two words with contrasting meaning.[22] The same is true of A. Berlin's suggestion that the two forms as they stand both mean 'captive', this being an instance of 'morphological parallelism'.[23] 4Q176 *Tanḥûmîm* has שובי. L has שְׁבִּי, with euphonic strengthening *daghes* (see GK 20).

52.2b. They are loosing the bonds from your neck, prisoner, Daughter Zion. As Daughter Babylon (47.1) is taken from power to constraint, Daughter Zion is taken from constraint to power. City goddesses were portrayed in chains, perhaps a sign of their certain link with their cities. Zion is the opposite of a chained goddess (K. Baltzer, 'Stadt-Tyche', p. 116; ET p. 55–56).

התפתחי: hitpael, which with a direct obj. suggests performing an action on one's own behalf (GK 54f). There is thus no need to add מ ('from') before מוסרי (†Kissane). In the MT, Q has s. f. imper. התפתחי ('loose for yourself'); cf 4Q176 *Tanḥûmîm*, LXX, Aq, Sym, Th, Syr, Vg. This looks like assimilation to v. 2a (†Barthélemy). K has התפתחו: cf 1QIs[a], Tg. In form this might be m. pl. imper., which does not fit the context, or more likely third pl. 'prophetic' qatal, a statement that grounds the exhortation in v. 2a. Tg 'are broken' assumes that this form has passive meaning. Perhaps the hitpael form is chosen to parallel the one in the previous line, though it hints at an irony—the liberators are freeing Zion 'for themselves'.
שְׁבִיָּה: Dahood ('Hebrew Lexicography' [see on 47.14], p. 190) understands

[22] Cf *Holter; S. M. Paul, 'Polysensuous Polyvalency in Poetic Parallelism', in *"Shaʿarei Talmon"* (S. Talmon Festschrift, ed. M. Fishbane and others; Winona Lake, IN, 1992), pp. 147–63 (see pp. 154–55).
[23] *The Dynamics of Biblical Parallelism* (Bloomington, 1985), pp. 42–43.

the extra syllable as an Ugaritic-style vocative particle. †Bevan redivides שְׁבִי הבת, assimilating to v. 2a.

52.3. For Yhwh has said this. For nothing you were sold and without money you will be restored. As happened within v. 1, the grounds for the challenge in v. 2 come in the form of a statement about the future, but that statement about the future is anticipated and undergirded by the assertion that it is Yhwh's statement. The 'messenger formula' comes twice in vv. 3–4, an oracle formula twice in v. 5. The word *ḥinnām* ('for nothing', lit. 'gratuitously') can mean 'to no purpose' or 'without cause' or 'for no money', and the various possibilities are utilized in vv. 3–6. Verse 3b makes clear that the last meaning applies here.

The addressees are plural and what follows will make it inescapable that they are the members of the deportee community. Does this mean that 'Zion' must denote that deportee community? That seems to impose an artificial understanding on vv. 1–2. Rather the movement between the one and the other reflects the fact that both Zion and the deportee community feature as audience, either on the stage or in the house.

52.4. For the Lord Yhwh has said this. My people went down to Egypt at the beginning to stay there, and lately Assyria oppressed them. 1QIs[a] omits 'the Lord'. The combination of Egypt and Assyria, the first two great oppressors in Israel's story, corresponds to 11.11–16; 19.23–25; Hos 9.3; 11.5, 11, and the two peoples may form a merism, standing for south and north (so Krašovec, *Merismus* [see on 41.19], p. 121). Surprising reference to Assyria reappears in Ezra 6.22 where the name apparently denotes Persia as the power that was 'the Assyria of the day' (cf Neh 9.32). Seleucid Syria is perhaps 'the Assyria of the day' in 11.11–16 and 19.23–25.[24] So either 'Assyria' means Babylon as the community's present oppressor, or v. 4 refers to Israel's two great historical oppressors and briskly summarizes their significance in the past.

מצרים opens the second cl.; an accusative of motion often comes first in a cl. (JM 155s).

באפס (lit. 'by/in extremity/nothing') is open to the same range of meanings as חנם in v. 3. Tg and Vg render 'for no reason'. But Isaiah 10 would hardly support the notion that Assyria had no reason for acting against Jerusalem. Isaiah 37.36–38 might imply 'to no purpose/profit' (cf חנם in v. 5). †Ruiz (p. 92) sees here as an instance of ב used like ל for purpose; but see BDB, p. 90. LXX βίᾳ ('with force') might imply בחמס but more likely indicates paraphrase; for the succeeding עשקו ('oppressed them') LXX has ἤχθησαν, taking the verb as passive. †Ehrlich emends to באפי ('in my anger'). †Saadya

[24] See O. Kaiser, *Der Prophet Jesaja: Kap. 1–12* (Göttingen, 1960; 2nd ed. 1963; 5th ed. 1981; ET *Isaiah 1–12* [OTL, 1974; 2nd ed. 1983]) and *Der Prophet Jesaja: Kap. 13–39* (Göttingen, 1973; ET *Isaiah 13–39* [OTL, 1974]), on the passages.

suggests the meaning 'at the end', that is, 'at the last'. This is unique to this passage, and V. Hamp (*ThWAT* on אפס) therefore rejects it. But it pairs well with 'at the beginning' in the parallel clause (cf *DCH*).

52.5a. Now, what was I doing here (Yhwh's oracle), that my people were taken for nothing? Either way, the prophet returns to the people's present oppression under Babylon. The first clause is literally '...what [*mah*] for me here' (Q; also 1QIs[a]) or '...who [*mî*] for me here' (K). 'Who' is even more difficult to account for than the one in 51.19b (cf that in Ruth 3.16) but it is similar to the one in Gen 33.8. This suggests it is an idiomatic usage that may well be original; *mah* is then the easier reading. The expression in 22.16 with both 'what' and 'who' denotes 'What place do you have here? Who belongs to you here?' The latter usage is common enough (see, e.g., Ps 73.25) and hardly fits the present context.

The LXX's τί ὧδέ ἐστε and the Vg's more literal *quid mihi est hic* ('what do I have here') supply a present verb, while †Ibn Ezra suggests 'What reason is there for me to be silent?' and †Delitzsch 'What do I need to do here?', 'What do I find here?' The Tg supplies a yiqtol verb, rendering 'Now I am about to deliver'. But a noun clause commonly takes its time reference from an associated verb clause, and this fits with the fact that when a question is followed by a *kî* clause, the latter usually indicates the unexpected result and evidence of the former (e.g. 7.13; 22.1; 36.5; Gen 20.9; 31.15; Judg 14.3; 1 Sam 20.1; Mic 4.9). So Yhwh asks, 'How did I come to let my people be taken for nothing?' (cf Tg's interpretation of 'taken' as 'sold') or '...to no purpose'.

On '[But/and] now', see on 43.1a; on 'Yhwh's oracle', see on 41.14b.

52.5b. Its rulers boast (Yhwh's oracle) and continually, all day, my name stands despised. The double expression for this ongoing contempt ('continually, all the day': the LXX abbreviates by omitting the second phrase) corresponds to that in 51.13. The dishonour is equal to the fear. A third instance of the first person suffix is thus added to the two in v. 5a: 'to me', 'my people', 'my name'.

The Tg renders 'the peoples who rule over them', while †Ibn Ezra renders 'its poets' rather than 'its rulers' (*māšal* II rather than *māšal* III), but more likely these are the Babylonian rulers we have met before (49.7; cf 14.5). In the MT the verb is the hiphil of the onomatopeic *yālal* ('howl'—on the form, see GK 53q, 70d). Elsewhere the verb invariably denotes a howl of anguish (e.g. 13.6; 14.31; 15.2, 3; 23.1, 6, 14; 65.14; Jer 25.34; 51.8), but 'its rulers will howl [when Yhwh judges]' does not fit the context and 'its rulers howl [in cruel exultation]' (BDB) requires the verb to have a meaning peculiar to this passage. Aq δακρύουσιν, Sym, Th ὀλολύζουσιν suggest a present howl, which would have to be that of the deportee community's leadership, as in 28.14. But whence the sudden reference to people of whom we have not heard before, and what leadership? †Qimchi takes the meaning as causative ('makes them howl'; cf Vg *inique agunt* 'act unfairly'?), which gives good sense but is otherwise uninstanced. More plausibly the Tg's 'boast' suggests the repointing *yᵉhallᵉlû*, piel from *hālal*, which can mean 'boast' as well as 'praise' (see Ps 10.3, also more commonly the qal and hitpael). The fact that the verb usually means praise might have led to its repointing (†Torrey).

The second colon may clarify the meaning of the first and confirm our understanding of the verb, for the despising (see *THAT* on *n'ṣ*) of Yhwh's name (cf Ps 74.10, 18) is an implication of the Babylonian rulers' boasting.

The Syr and Tg prefer an active construction to run on from the first colon. Concerning the LXX's θαυμάζετε καὶ ὀλολύζετε, †Seeligmann (p. 54) calls the use of θαυμάζειν 'inscrutable', though †Ziegler (p. 162) notes other passages where it uses θαυμάζειν when the Hebrew is difficult, but this might be a double translation reflecting the meaning of both *yālal* and *hālal*. The LXX goes on to add δι' ὑμᾶς and at the end ἐν τοῖς ἔθνεσι ('because of you...among the nations'). The thought, and in the latter case the wording, appears in Ezek 36.20–23 (†Seeligmann, p. 74); cf 20.9, 14, 22; and Paul's application of the text in Rom 2.22–24.

יהילילו: 1QIs[a] has והוללו, apparently poel of הלל ('make fools of them'; cf 44.25), perhaps supporting Driver's repointing יְהֹלָלוּ (pausal, 'are gone mad'; *JTS* n.s. 2, p. 26) or †Ehrlich's יְחֻלָּלוּ ('are profaned').
נאם יהוה: *Blank sees as a mistaken resolution of a first person suffix on thc vb, יחללוני ('they defame me').
מִנֹּאָץ: if a real word, this is a variant on a hitpael, with the preformative's ת assimilated (GK 54c). In isolation the final qamets suggests the preformative plus the rare poal (the passive equivalent of the poel and thus a variant on pual), producing a hitpoal, but there are no other instances, and more likely it is a hitpoel (a variant on the hitpael itself) in pause; cf BDB and the pausal hitpael forms יִתְפָּאָר and אֶתְפָּאָר in 44.23 and 49.3. For background, see JM 53; 59; *IBHS* 21; 26. Even this is a combination of rarities, and more plausibly the word is a composite of the pual מְנֹאָץ (cf 1QIs[a] מנואץ) and the hitpael מִתְנָאֵץ (†Qimchi) or hitpoel מִתְנֹאֵץ (GK 55b). The reflexive conjugation is then odd. †Luzzatto sees it as a Masoretic repointing of the pual to avoid speaking of Yhwh's name as reviled; cf Tg's 'over the service of my name they blaspheme'. But why should the Masoretes take exception to this particular instance of the regular usage of this vb? Dahood ('Hebrew Lexicography' [see on 47.14], pp. 359–60) sees the מ as a misunderstood enclitic belonging to שְׁמִי ('my name') and repoints the vb נֹאָץ (qal passive).

52.6. Therefore my people will acknowledge my name—therefore that day they will acknowledge that I am the one who speaks. Here I am. The link claimed by the repeated 'therefore' is elliptical, and 'therefore'—along with 'my people' and the expression 'that day'—does not otherwise appear in the setting of the 'recognition formula', 'and you/we/they will acknowledge that I am Yhwh/acknowledge that I have spoken'. The Tg substitutes the more usual 'the peoples', in the context of a passive construction. Indeed, the phrase '...will acknowledge my name' and the participial form ('the one who speaks') do not occur. Thus with the last exception we have a collocation of familiar phrases, brought into a new and elliptical combination.

At the end, the Tg typically paraphrases 'Here I am' as 'My word abides'. †Hessler renders '...who says "Here I am"': but the actual expression is as unusual as English '...who speaks "Here I am"'. *DCH* (Vol. 2, p. 388a) includes a list of passages where 'speak' introduces direct speech. Some might be queried, but the list does not include this passage.

לכן (second occurrence): 1QIs[a], LXX, Syr, Vg omit. †Ehrlich emends to ויבן or ייבין, †Kissane to יבין ('[and] will understand'), the verb that pairs with ידע in a connection such as this in 43.10.
הוא (second occurrence): on the demonstrative, see on 51.9. H. Kosmala suggests that in contexts such as this הוא is equivalent to the divine name יהוה, which Yhwh is envisaging the people acknowledging: אני הוא is equivalent to אני יהוה elsewhere.[25]

IV.d.v. Listen to the lookouts (52.7–10)

Suddenly, from down-to-earth prose we are in verse as lyrical as any lines in these chapters. Surprisingly, vv. 7–10 work in lament metre. With the possible exception of v. 8b, each line has a two-beat second colon. It has this feature in common with the 'vision speech' of Num 24.3–9, with which †von Waldow (pp. 49–50) compares vv. 7–10. There also the visionary proclaims 'How lovely...', even if using *ṭôb* not *nāʾāh*, though that is hardly enough to proclaim the phrase a marker of vision speech (against †Grimm and Dittert). If it is that, the links with other biblical passages will suggest that it is vision speech consciously shaped as scriptural lyrical poetry rather than instinctive unpremeditated exclamation.

Whereas Yhwh spoke the prose, the prophet speaks the verse, which closes with Yhwh's arm bared to act in deliverance. This recalls the exhortation in 51.9–16 and presupposes that it has been heeded. But the statement about Yhwh's arm is part of the grounds for the reactions of vv. 7–8 and the exhortation to break into enthusiastic sound that occupies the second half of the section (vv. 9–10) and marks this as a climax or turning point in the prophecy as a whole: cf 42.10–17; 44.23; 48.20–21; 49.13. Verbally the exhortation links specifically with 44.23 ('resound/break into sound'); 48.20–21 ('resound, is restoring'); 49.13 ('resound/break into sound, for Yhwh is comforting his people'); and also 51.3 ('wastes, for Yhwh is comforting').

[25] 'The Name of God (Yhwh and huʾ)', in *ASTI* 2 (1963), pp. 103–6 (see pp. 105–6).

As well as thus linking with 51.9–16 within this larger unit, vv. 7–10 comprises a reworking of a number of existent passages in prophecy and psalmody (cf Willey, 'Servant', pp. 286–88).

First, it links with 40.1–11 and with 40.9–11 in particular, which also began *in medias res* with the messenger, before later revealing what had happened and required announcement. It, too, comprised four sub-sections (though one less line) dominated by five-stress cola. There already the wielding of Yhwh's arm had been promised (40.10). Once again the messenger to Zion on the mountains (40.9) reappears, though here the word is masculine. In both passages the word 'messenger' comes twice. Once again mighty rule (40.10) is declared. Once again voices raise themselves (cf 40.3, 6). Once again people are to see Yhwh appearing to the world and coming to Zion (cf 40.5, 10). The comfort of 'my people' commissioned in 40.1 is declared to be here for 'his people'. †Van Oorschot (pp. 105–27) sees it as playing the epilogue to the prologue that comprises 40.1–5, 9–11 within his 'first Jerusalem redaction' of Second Isaiah.

Second, it links with Nah 2.1–3 [1.15–2.2], from which comes the picture of the feet of a messenger on the mountains proclaiming that all was well. Second Isaiah declares, 'That prophecy in Nahum: its time has now come'. The fact that the downfall Nahum had in mind was that of Assyria (cf v. 4) might heighten the significance of the allusion, by facing the disappointment of the rise of another oppressor and/or by assuming that the prophecy that had been fulfilled before could be fulfilled again because of 'the vitality of the word of God'.[26]

Third, it links with the joyful praise of Psalms 98–99, whence come the declaration that Yhwh reigns as king in Zion and the phrases in v. 10. It links with Ezek 20.33–44 where Yhwh declares the intention of raising his outstretched arm in order to act as king over Israel and bring Israel to Yhwh's holy mountain so that Yhwh's holiness is manifested in the sight of the nations (*van der Woude, pp. 188–89).

Fourth, it links with Lam 4.17, declaring that people who once kept watch but saw nothing will now see (v. 8).

Fifth, it links with Psalms 9 and 50 and others that declare that Yhwh sits enthroned in Zion and governs the world from there and asks that Yhwh may activate that lordship, and it declares that Yhwh's reigning is not merely something Israel believes in as theological principle or hopes to see, but something that is about to become visible reality. It also conspicuously omits from its vision the Davidic king whose election by Yhwh is commonly inseparable in the Psalms from Yhwh's commitment to Zion: see, for example, Ps 132.

Sixth, it recalls the declaration in Exodus 15 that Yhwh has acted as Israel's king, itself an Israelite application to historical events of a pattern in the faith of Israel's contemporaries that they located in the

[26] See P. R. Ackroyd, 'The Vitality of the Word of God in the Old Testament', in *ASTI* 1 (1962), pp. 7–23 = Ackroyd, *Studies in the Religious Tradition of the Old Testament* (London, 1987), pp. 61–75, 263–66.

relationships between the gods and the warring that protected the stability of the cosmos (*Hanson, pp. 389–90).

Seventh, it recalls the plaint that ruined Zion has no prophets (Ps 74) and that Babylonian victors ask for a Zion song to be sung when such songs only underline grief (Ps 137), and shows that a prophet is here and that Zion songs can be sung again.

The section thus provides a striking illustration of the way in which Second Isaiah reworks earlier material—Psalms, Lamentations, sayings from earlier in Isaiah, earlier sayings of Second Isaiah's own, and the words of other prophets. It also illustrates the significance of what distinguishes Second Isaiah's prophecy. Compared with Ezekiel, the exodus language (e.g. the mighty hand and outstretched arm) is less prominent and the declaration about Yhwh reigning is qatal rather than yiqtol. Whereas in 40.9–11 Yhwh bade the (feminine) messenger to address Zion, here the prophet bids Zion to heed the (masculine) messenger. Whereas there the messenger was commissioned, here the messenger is already at work. Thus here the first verb describing the messenger's work is qatal, and the verbs describing Yhwh's ruling, coming, and caring for the people, and specifically the acts of Yhwh's arm, are now qatal not yiqtol. There 'comfort' was an imperative, here it is qatal. Here ruined Jerusalem is thus explicitly called to respond in exultation. Here the prophet puts 'his people' in clearest parallelism with 'Jerusalem'. Here the people who come with Yhwh are unmentioned; vv. 11–12 will relate to them. In 40.9–10 the interjection *hinnēh* ('there') was implicitly visual (cf EVV 'behold'), here in 52.8 *qôl* ('listen', but lit. 'a voice') is aural. At the same time other verbs ('resound', 'see' [twice]) remain yiqtol or w^{e}qatal and thus locate the prophecy dramatically between initiation and consummation.

At Qumran, 11Q Melchizedek 2.15–16 applies v. 7 to Melchizedek as the one in whom God's reign is embodied, though this need not imply that Melchizedek was (a) god.[27] The account of the preaching of John the Baptist and of Jesus (e.g. Mark 1) similarly reflects the language of vv. 7–10 and apparently the conviction that Jesus brought the presence or the appearance of God. Christians might have thought it was self-evident that Second Isaiah's vision was being fulfilled in Jesus's preaching of the gospel of God: with the word εὐαγγέλιον compare the LXX's εὐαγγελιζόμενος in v. 7, and with the phrase βασιλεία τοῦ Θεοῦ, the LXX's βασιλεύσει σου ὁ θέος. Jesus declares the good news that God's reign has come, in language in the Greek that †Grimm and Dittert see as instancing a NT tendency to turn theologically significant verbs into nouns. Noting that nevertheless the passage is not actually quoted in the Gospels (but see Rom 10.15), they further suggest that this reflects the fact that Jesus proclaims the nearness of God's reign, like 51.5, rather

[27] See, for example, M. de Jonge and A. S. van der Woude, '11Q Melchizedek and the New Testament', in *NTS* 12 (1965–66), pp. 301–26 (see p. 305); P. J. Kobelski, *Melchizedek and Melchireša'* (*CBQ* Monograph 10; Washington, DC, 1981), esp. p. 54.

than its initiation. Whatever may be true of the interpretation of Jesus, in Second Isaiah the difference between the two forms of speech is surely rhetorical rather than substantial.

52.7a. How lovely on the mountains are the feet of the herald, announcer that 'All is well', herald of good, announcer of deliverance. We have noted that one of Balaam's oracles begins 'How lovely...' (though using the more prosaic verb *ṭôb*). The expression is the first parallel with the love language of the Song of Songs: nearly half the occurrences of the verb *nāʾāh* ('be lovely') and the related adjective come there. The subsequent words, 'on the mountains... "All is well"' follow Nah 2.1 [1.15], though behind that is the experience of a messenger's arrival described in a passage such as 2 Sam 18.19–28. The Tg's addition '[on the mountains] of the land of Israel' draws our attention to the poetic lack of overt specificity in the prophet's words.

The LXX's εὐαγγελιζόμενος ('bringer of good news') obscures the fact that a herald's news would not always be good, as is underlined by its subsequent adding of the apparently redundant object ἀγαθά ('good'); contrast Vg *adnuntiantis*, and see 40.9. What makes these feet lovely is the fact that they do bring good news—*šālôm*, *ṭôb*, *yešûʿāh*. The threefold *m*-participles in the second line ('one who announces...brings a message...announces') would have seemed typically Second Isaiah if we had not known that they are adapted from elsewhere.

1QIs[a] has the order 'herald', 'herald', 'announcer', 'announcer'.

נאוו: BDB takes this as pilel of נאה. GK 75x takes it as ni of אוה, suggesting 'be desirable' and here 'How welcome' (†North). This makes good sense here, but it does not fit the adjective נאוה, which must mean 'lovely/fitting'. The verb is one like ידע used in the qatal to denote something achieved in the past but continuing effective in the present (GK 106g). The LXX apparently attaches the last word of v. 6 to v. 7 to give the sense 'Here I am as beauty on the mountains' (see †Ottley).

52.7b. ...who says to Zion, 'Your God is reigning'. After the two six-word lines in v. 7a the verse comes to an abrupt end with a 2–2 line whose shortness draws attention to it (the MT treats v. 7aα as 2–2 but it is still longer than this last one). It begins with another of the prophet's participles (e.g. 40.6; 41.13; 44.26, 27, 28; 46.10), characteristic especially of the earlier chapters. Proclamation to Zion again recalls 40.9, and the content of the subsequent message restates that in 40.9–11. The Tg repeats its rendering from 40.9 (see comment), 'the reign of your God is revealed'. It has the message announced to 'the congregation of Zion', which presupposes one answer to the question of the referent of 'Zion'.

There is some disagreement over whether the verb *mālak* is a fientive verb, one that describes a change of state ('become king'), or a stative verb, one that describes an ongoing state ('reign'). In the first case, in the context of Second Isaiah it is natural to take the verb as another of the prophet's 'prophetic' qatals, referring to an event that is spoken of as having happened, like the actual accession of a human king (see, e.g., 1 Kgs 15.1, 9, 25). Here the qatal presupposes the conviction that the event is about to happen. In the second case, the qatal can refer to the present, and the same translation allows alternatively for this view.[28] But if there is disagreement in our day about whether the verb is fientive or stative and what rules therefore apply to it, it may well be that there was uncertainty in OT Israel, or that it was used in both ways. The application to kings of Judah and Israel just noted more suggests the fientive than the stative use. Similarly the very fact that the verb is here part of the content of a messenger's announcement of an event supports the view that it is a fientive verb referring to a punctiliar event (†Grimm and Dittert).

Psalms 93.1; 96.10; 97.1; 99.1 declare *yhwh mālak* ('Yhwh is reigning'), the noun preceding the verb. If the verb is a stative the phrase in the Psalms may effectively be a noun clause in the usual word order.[29] If the verb is a fientive, the word order rather affirms that Yhwh and not some other god reigns.[30] Second Isaiah's phrase *mālak ʾĕlōhāyik* ('your God is reigning'), with the verb first, has closer OT parallels in 24.23 and Ps 47.9 [8]. In 24.23 the qatal verb is the basis for yiqtol statements that more overtly refer to the future, to consequences of the statement in the qatal, as is less explicitly so here. In Ps 47.9 [8] the statement *mālak ʾĕlōhîm* ('God reigns') is set in the context of a series of qatal statements in 47.6–10 [5–9]. It is difficult to tell whether such statements made in worship simply express religious conviction about the present or about the future, or reflect historical events. Second Isaiah is declaring that such statements are at this moment becoming historical reality. There are varying views regarding whether these psalms are earlier or later than Second Isaiah, and whether the same answer must apply to all of them or whether rather some may be earlier, some later.[31] This makes

[28] See D. Michel, 'Studien zu den sogenannten Thronbesteigungspsalmen', in *VT* 6 (1956), pp. 40–68 (see pp. 49–52); also the discussion in A. Gelston, 'A Note on יהוה מלך', in *VT* 16 (1966), pp. 507–12.

[29] So J. Ridderbos, 'Jahwäh malak', in *VT* 4 (1954), pp. 87–89, referring to GK 142a.

[30] So L. Köhler, 'Syntactica iii', in *VT* 3 (1953), pp. 188–89.

[31] For example, S. Mowinckel argues that they come as a group from the First Temple: see *Psalmenstudien II* (Oslo, 1921; reprinted Amsterdam, 1961). H.-J. Kraus believes that Pss 93 and 99, and perhaps 95, come from the First Temple; Pss 96–98 are dependent on Second Isaiah: see *Psalmen 60–150* (Neukirchen, 1961; 5th ed. 1978); ET *Psalms 60–150* (Minneapolis, 1989), on the Psalms. E. Lipiński believes that Pss 93; 97; and 99 come from the First Temple: see *La royauté de Yahwé dans la poésie et le culte de l'ancien Israel* (Brussels, 1965; 2nd ed., 1968), pp. 91–335; cf '*Yāhweh mâlāk*', in *Bib* 44 (1963), pp. 405–60. Broadly like Kraus, J. Jeremias believes that Pss 93; 95; and 99 are earlier but Pss 96 and 98 are dependent on Isa 40–55 and Ps 97 is Hellenistic: see *Das Königtum Gottes in den Psalmen* (Göttingen, 1987), pp. 121–36. H. Leene ('History and Eschatology in Deutero-Isaiah', in †Van Ruiten and Vervenne, pp. 223–49 [pp. 238–49]) argues that Second Isaiah utilizes Pss 96 and 98 rather than vice versa, but can allow for the possibility that nevertheless they were composed after 539 because he dates Second Isaiah from later in the century.

nodifference to the meaning of v. 7 in itself though it generates a different understanding of how the conversation on these matters progressed within Israel.

The word order here does not make a point of affirming that Yhwh (as opposed to Bel) reigns, which would have been an understandable point to make. If the verb is a stative, and in effect this is a noun clause with the usual word order reversed, then on the contrary it makes a point of affirming that Yhwh reigns rather than being dethroned (cf 63.19, though there the verb is *māšal*). If the verb is a fientive and the clause has the regular word order, then the verb has the emphasis inherent in this being a verbal clause, and the end result is not very different. Either way the prophet is declaring that Yhwh is now asserting sovereignty in the community's life against the background of this not having been so.

Other texts affirm that Yhwh *will* reign (yiqtol or w^{e}qatal). In Ezek 20.33 Yhwh declares the intention to reign, to act sovereignly in the future (cf Mic 4.7). The context is similar to that in Isaiah 52 though some crucial decades earlier. In Exod 15.18 the affirmation begins from the fact that Yhwh has acted sovereignly, which in the context it can take for granted (cf Balaam's reference to Yhwh's being acclaimed as king among them, Num 23.21). The affirmation builds on it a statement regarding a continuing exercise of that sovereignty (cf Ps 146.10). In 1 Sam 8.7 Yhwh regrets the fact that the people 'have rejected me from reigning over them'. The sense that kingship is a theologically questionable institution lies under the surface in Ezekiel (where the human ruler is called 'prince' rather than 'king') and in a different way in Second Isaiah (where Yhwh is king and no Israelite ruler features) (†D. Baltzer, pp. 141–42). Micah 2.13 promises a restoration when Yhwh as Israel's king and shepherd will pastor and lead the people, and Mic 4.6–7 a moment when Yhwh will reign over the people on Mount Zion; cf also Zeph 3.14–19 (*van der Woude, pp. 192–93). In relation to all these, Second Isaiah's qatal stands out in its affirmation made at the moment when Babylon is about to fall.

לציון: Penar again finds vocative ל here ('Lamedh vocativi').

52.8a. Listen. Your lookouts are lifting voice. Together they will resound. The imagery changes, from messengers who come to a city to tell it what they have seen, to lookouts on the city walls relating what they can now see. 'Resound', previously qal, is piel in vv. 8–9 (resultative: *Pi'el*, p. 155): here alone in chapters 40–66, but as in 35.2; Ps 96.12; 98.4, 8.

קול צפיך: LXX's φωνὴ τῶν φυλασσόντων σε takes as a construct, which suggests that the colon as a whole is an exclamation; so also Tg, which renders 'your leaders'. GK 146b rather takes קול as an interjection, as it did

40.3.[32] 1QIs[a] has קולם for the second קול. Cross ([see on 40.3], p. 109) sees the two occurrences of קול as reflecting a conflate text.
נשאו: LXX ὑψώθη καὶ implies נשׂא ו; it takes the vb as ni, the 'voice' (previous note) being the subject.

52.8b. For with both eyes they will look at Yhwh's return to Zion. The opening expression (lit. 'eye with eye') comes elsewhere only in Num 14.14 (also Deut 19.21 with different meaning). The LXX's ὀφθαλμοὶ πρὸς ὀφθαλμοὺς ('eyes to eyes') suggests 'face to face'; cf Jer 32.4. But there the expression is (lit.) 'his eyes [will see] his eyes'. Further, the meaning 'eye to eye' is surely inappropriate. The lookouts' task does not involve looking in the eye but seeing with the eye and hastening to witness, on the basis of 'a real personal revelation of God' (F. J. Stendebach, *ThWAT* on *ʿayin*, col. 36). The Tg thus better paraphrases 'with their eyes' and Sym with ὀφθαλμοφανῶς (cf Morgenstern, *HUCA* 29, p. 13), and †Ruiz (p. 92) is unwise to suggest that *b* here equals *l*. *Lamentations Rabbah* 1.23, 57 make a link with Lam 1.16: both eyes ran with tears, now both eyes see their comfort. *Pesiqta' deRab Kahana'* 16 adds that they sinned with the eye (3.16), were smitten in the eye (Lam 1.16), but were also comforted through the eye (cf the comments on 40.2).

'Eye to eye' would be a strong anthropomorphism. Strong anthropomorphism indeed follows, probably twofold. The Vg renders *videbunt cum converterit Dominus* ('they will see when the Lord turns...'). The preposition *b* following the verb 'see' can indeed mean 'when', but it can also designate the object of (careful) seeing, suggesting 'look at'. The only other occasion when the verb is followed by *b* plus an infinitive, Ps 37.34, is an example. The vivid anthropomorphism involved in the notion of looking at Yhwh certainly appears in the talk of Yhwh's returning to Zion. The anthropomorphism is again the clearer when the MT is compared with other versions of the text, which all tend to tone down the anthropomorphism (†Koenig, pp. 269–74). 1QIs[a] adds *brḥmym* from Zech 1.16 (†Kutscher, p. 433; ET p. 543). 'Returns in compassion' sounds more figurative, implying as it does 'restores the compassion that has been missing' (cf BDB, p. 89b). It is this form of the text to which the Eighteen Benedictions refer, which might suggest that it is more than a 1QIs[a] invention but might also suggest liturgical influence in both texts (cf †Barthélemy). The LXX similarly renders ἡνίκα ἂν ἐλεήσῃ ('whenever he has compassion on'). The Vg's *cum converterit Dominus Sion* and Aq, Sym, Th ἐν τῷ ἐπιστρέψαι κύριον τὴν Σίων ('when the Lord restores Zion') take the verb as transitive (see BDB, p. 998b) rather than as an instance of a verb of motion governing a noun that indicates the destination of the motion (GK 117a). The same double possibility arises in connection with Nah 2.3 [2], where *ʾet* follows the verb: tantalisingly this can be read as the

[32] See C. Peters, 'Hebräisches קול als Interjektion', in *Bib* 20 (1939), pp. 288–93 (see pp. 292–93).

object-marker or as the preposition 'with' (see *van der Woude, p. 191). The Tg doubly safeguards against the anthropomorphism, providing an object for the verb 'see', 'the mighty acts that Yhwh will do' and a paraphrase for what follows, 'when he restores his presence to Zion'. In the MT the picture of Yhwh's own return forms a heightened *inclusio* with 40.3–11.

52.9a. Break out, resound all together, wastes of Jerusalem. The agent of resounding is now the city itself (cf 54.1). Specifically, they are the devastated parts of the city—it would be artificial to take 'wastes of Jerusalem' as an epexegetical genitive ('wasted Jerusalem') rather than an attributive genitive ('Jerusalem wastes') (see *IBHS* 9.5.3bc). Nor is there any need to take the term as a metonymy for the city's population (so †Grimm and Dittert). It is even less likely that the phrase refers either to the Babylonian community (†Westermann) or to a community in need primarily of spiritual renewal (†Motyer).

רננו: instead of the vb, 1QIs[a] has the n. רינה, which is the more familiar expression after the vb פצח (†Kutscher, ET p. 323 [not in the Hebrew ed.]). Cf LXX's εὐφροσύνην.

52.9b. For Yhwh is comforting his people, restoring Jerusalem. The Tg replaces the 'prophetic' qatals with the more literal 'is about to comfort', while the LXX represents the first with ἠλέησε ('had compassion'), as at 12.1 (*HUB*). The LXX also omits 'his people'. This solves the problem of the relationship between 'his people' and Jerusalem, which also reappears from 40.1–2. †Ziegler (p. 156) sees the word as an addition from 49.13, but the absolute usage of the verb would be unparalleled. †Thomas notes that two late medieval MSS have 'Israel' rather than 'Jerusalem', which solves the problem in an alternative way.

52.10a. Yhwh is baring his holy arm before the eyes of all the nations. In speaking of Yhwh's actual action in v. 10, the prophet's language systematically corresponds to that of Ps 98.1–3. As there, the further strong anthropomorphism is qualified by the description of Yhwh's arm as 'holy'. It is like no human arm.

52.10b. All earth's extremities are looking at our God's deliverance. In isolation one would see the opening verb as a *w*-consecutive following a 'prophetic' qatal and render it in the future tense (*TTH* 113 [1]). But the line exactly corresponds to Ps 98.3b and more likely the qatal retains the same sense as its predecessors. Whether or not the qatals here in Isaiah and in the Psalm have the same sense, within each they surely have the same sense. The *w* is thus co-ordinating.

IV.d.vi. Get out from there!(52.11–12)

Once more the prophet turns to address people in Babylon directly. Structurally these verses thus pair with the exhortation in 51.1–8, but their repetitions now convey an urgent exhortation to leave Babylon (couched in terms that come from earlier scriptures), not merely to listen to the prophet speaking of what Yhwh will do.

52.11a. Depart, depart, get out from there. Stained, do not touch. The bidding 'depart, depart' takes up Lam 4.15, and †Theodoret takes vv. 11–12 as God's prophetic warning to the Christian community to leave Jerusalem on the eve of its fall in AD 70 (and Tertullian to leave the Jewish community: see *Against Marcion* 3.22). †Simon also assumes that people are here urged to leave Jerusalem, thus breaking with the faithless there, while †Torrey suggests that the addressees are urged to break with their Egyptian-style bondage. They might thus be leaving Jerusalem to go to meet the approaching king, like the inhabitants of a city welcoming its liberators.

But 48.20–21 surely sets the interpretation of this exhortation (cf also 49.9; and Jer 50.8; 51.45). 'Get out from there' resumes the 'get out from Babylon' of 48.20: 'Babylon' is the antecedent of 'there'; cf the Tg's amplifications in v. 12. There were later urgings to leave Babylon, promises that people would do so, and actual leavings (e.g. Zech 6). Here, too, the call is addressed as from a Jerusalem perspective, but there is no other indication that this urging relates to a different prospective leaving from that in 48.20–21—as †Spykerboer suggests, seeing this as a later addition like 51.11. †Wilkie (p. 38) similarly associates this with the relief of the period after Cyrus's victories, which discouraged deportees from returning to Judah.

'Stain' also featured in Lam 4.15, but here the hearers are warned not about bringing to others the stain they are affected by, but about contracting stain as they leave—perhaps the stain of involvement with Babylonian gods. The people need not bring stain from exile back to Judah, but they must take care not to do so.

טמא: 1QIs[a] בטמה spells the word differently and prefixes with the preposition ב, as is usual with the vb נגע (including Lam 4.14, which leads into the verse that has close links with this line).

52.11b. Get out from its midst, purify yourselves, Yhwh's vessel-bearers. The prophet speaks like the Egyptian king bidding the Israelites get out from the midst of his people (Exod 12.31) but also takes up Ezekiel's words about Yhwh's threat to come to purify the community (20.7, 10)—it would be better off taking action to purify itself (cf also 49.2). The word for 'vessels' means 'weapons' in, for example, 13.5; 54.16, 17 (cf †Alexander), but the regular reference to vessels and instruments used in worship fits here: cf the Tg's 'you who bear the vessels of Yhwh's sanctuary' (also Ezra 1.7–11). Cross ([see on 40.3], p. 109) sees these vessels as substitutes for the covenant chest.

P. C. Beentjes notes that 2 Cor 6.17 quotes v. 11 in 'upsidedown form'.[33]

צאו מתוכה: missing in 1QIs[b].
הברו: on the vb form see GK 67t. †Ehrlich repoints הָבֵרוּ (hi imper.) so that the exhortation urges the community as a whole to purify the vessel-bearers, but this presupposes that the vessel-bearers are a defined group.

52.12a. For you will not get out in haste. You will not go in flight. There is no problem about *kî* retaining its causal sense here and in v. 12b: the people will not be under pressure when they leave (contrast the fear of Exodus 14), and therefore be compromising over purity. 'Not. . .in haste' reverses Exod 12.11 and Deut 16.3: this exodus will be better than the exodus from Egypt.

The Tg makes specific 'from among the peoples' and 'to your land'.

52.12b. For Yhwh is going before you, the God of Israel is bringing up your rear. †Ehrlich suggests that the line implies a merism: Yhwh will always and everywhere be there as Lord for the people. This may obscure the furthering of the military–royal metaphor that reappears from vv. 7–10. It is the king who leads the people in battle.

The term 'bringing up the rear' is here turned for the first time into a metaphor, marking this major section close, though it is striking that the reference to the rearguard in Num 10.25 relates to a journey with worship vessels (the procession in Joshua 6 involves only ark and trumpets). Indeed, outside the special circumstance of Exodus 14 there is no reference to *Yhwh*'s being behind the people. It is perhaps the parallelism that generates the point here. The Tg removes it by reinterpreting the form of the root *ʾāsap*, with its 'the God of Israel is about to gather your exiles'; cf LXX ὁ ἐπισυνάγων, Vg *congregabit*. But at least these versions preserve the awareness that the word is a participle that still functions verbally and thus balances the participle in the first colon; contrast EVV's use of the noun 'rearguard'.

Once again the passage forms an *inclusio* with 40.10–11: the rare explicit allusion to the people's return to Zion is common to 40.10–11 and 52.12 (also 48.21; †D. Baltzer, pp. 60–71).

מאספכם: on the form, see GK 60f, 61h; the pi is used for a profession (*Pi'el*, pp. 58–60).
ישראל: at the end 1QIs[a] adds אלוהי כול הארץ יקרא from 54.5, adding further to the heightening of the picture of the new exodus over against the first (Rubinstein, *JJS* 6, pp. 196–97).

[33] 'Discovering a New Path of Intertextuality', in *Literary Structure and Rhetorical Strategies* (ed. L. J. de Regt and others; Assen, 1996), pp. 31–50 (see p. 43).

Bibliography to 51.1–52.12

Bilik, E., ‘התוה איננו עוף’, in *BetM* 21/3 = 66 (1976), pp. 458–61.

Blank, S. H., ‘Isaiah 52.5’, in *HUCA* 25 (1954), pp. 1–8.

Cerfaux, L., ‘L’évangile éternel’, in *Mélanges Gonzague Ryckmans*, pp. 672–81. BETL 20, 1963.

Dahood, M., ‘Is 51, 19 and Sefîre, III 22’, in *Bib* 56 (1975), pp. 94–95.

Fichtner, J., ‘Jesaja 52, 7–10 in der christlichen Verkündigung’, in *Verbannung und Heimkehr* (W. Rudolph Festschrift, ed. A. Kuschke), pp. 51–66. Tübingen, 1961.

Freund, J., ‘“סורו, סורו, צאו משם”’, in *BetM* 34/1 = 116 (1988), pp. 50–58.

Gundry, R. H., ‘למטלים’, in *RevQ* 2 (1959–60), pp. 559–67.

Hanford, W. R., ‘Deutero-Isaiah and Luke–Acts’, in *CQR* (1967), pp. 141–52.

Hanson, P. D., ‘Isaiah 52:7–10’, in *Interpretation* 33 (1979), pp. 389–94.

Helberg, J. L., ‘Nahum–Jonah–Lamentations–Isaiah 51–53’, in *Biblical Essays: Proceedings of the Twelfth Meeting of “Die Ou-Testamentiese Werkgemeenskap in Suid-Afrika”... 1969* (ed. A. H. van Zyl), pp. 46–55.

Holmgren, F., ‘Chiastic Structure in Isaiah li 1–11’, in *VT* 19 (1969), pp. 196–210.

Holter, K., ‘A Note on שׁביה/שׁבי in Isa 52,2’, in *ZAW* 104 (1992), pp. 106–7.

Jacobson, H., ‘A Note on Isaiah 51:6’, in *JBL* 114 (1995), p. 291.

Janzen, J. G., ‘An Echo of the Shema in Isaiah 51.1–3’, in *JSOT* 43 (1989), pp. 69–82.

—‘Rivers in the Desert of Abraham and Sarah and Zion’, in *HAR* 10 (1986), pp. 139–55.

Koch, K., ‘Damnation and Salvation’, in *Ex auditu* 6 (1990), pp. 5–13.

Kuntz, J. K., ‘The Contribution of Rhetorical Criticism to Understanding Isaiah 51:1–16’, in *Art and Meaning* (ed. D. J. A. Clines and others), pp. 140–71. *JSOT* Sup 19, 1982.

Martin, W. C., ‘An Exegesis of Isaiah 51:9–11’, in *Restoration Quarterly* 9 (1966), pp. 151–59.

Melugin, R. F., ‘Isaiah 52:7–10’, in *Interpretation* 36 (1982), pp. 176–81.

Morgenstern, J., ‘The “Oppressor” of Isa 51 13’, in *JBL* 81 (1962), pp. 25–34.

Ringgren, H., ‘Die Funktion des Schöpfungsmythos in Jes. 51’, in *Schalom* (A. Jepsen Festschrift, ed. K.-H. Bernhardt), pp. 38–40. Stuttgart, 1971.

Seidl, T., ‘Jahwe der Krieger—Jahwe der Tröster’, in *BZ* 21 (1983), pp. 116–34.

Steck, O. H., ‘Beobachtungen zu den Zion-Texten in Jesaja 51–54’, in BN 46 (1989), pp. 58–90. = †Steck, pp. 96–125.

—‘Zions Tröstung’, in *Die Hebräische Bibel und ihre zweifache*

Nachgeschichte (R. Rendtorff Festschrift, ed. E. Blum and others), pp. 257–76. Neukirchen, 1990. = †Steck, pp. 73–91.

—'Zur literarischen Schichtung in Jesaja 51', in *BN* 44 (1987), pp. 74–86. = †Steck, pp. 60–72.

Stevenson, W. B., 'The Interpretation of Isaiah xli. 8–20 and li. 1–8', in *Exp* VIII/6 (1913), pp. 209–21.

Terian, A., 'The Hunting Imagery in Isaiah li 20a', in *VT* 41 (1991), pp. 462–71.

van Uchelen, N. A., 'Abraham als Felsen', in *ZAW* 80 (1968), pp. 183–91.

Williamson, H. G. M., 'Gnats, Glosses and Eternity', in *New Heaven and New Earth* (A. Gelston Festschrift, ed. P. J. Harland and C. T. R. Hayward), pp. 101–11. *VT* Sup 77, 1999.

van der Woude, A. S., 'Hoe de Here naar Sion wederkeert...', in †Grosheide, pp. 188–96.

V.

52.13–55.13: YHWH'S ACT OF RESTORATION AND TRANSFORMATION

Once more, 52.13 has been widely regarded as marking a significant transition in the chapters, yet the wording of the verse also suggests continuity, and a synagogue lection runs from 52.7 to 55.12(!). The particle *hinnēh* ('there') which opens 52.13–53.12, like *hēn*, never marks a wholly new beginning; both particles suggest a new section, but one which links with what precedes (cf, e.g., 42.1; 54.11; †Spykerboer). If the transition at 52.13 at first seems a sudden one, then, like that at 49.1 and 50.4, it is not surprising that there emerge links with what has preceded. Yhwh's arm is being revealed (52.10): upon whom (53.1)? It is being revealed before the eyes of all the nations (52.10): they have seen (52.15).

Through 42.18–52.12 the prophecies have been explicit in their reference to Jacob–Israel, Babylon, Cyrus, and Zion–Jerusalem, and they have identified both Jacob–Israel and the prophet as Yhwh's servant. 52.13–55.13 comprises three closing sections which as a whole return to the anonymity which was more characteristic of the opening sections, 40.1–42.17. Indeed, there is no naming at all in 52.13–55.13, and Yhwh's servant is once again described but not explicitly identified, as in 42.1–4. Of course the preceding chapters have been explicit about the identity of the servant (cf 52.13–53.12), the woman-city (cf 54.1–17a), and the covenant community (cf 54.17b–55.13), yet this return to anonymity opens up the possibility that each of these figures may be more (or less) than was the case before. It seems unlikely that the servant in 52.13–53.12 is some person who has not been mentioned before and who is not actually identified here (e.g. Jehoiachin or Zerubbabel or the Messiah)—or if this is so, the book does not give us enough information to come to a conclusion on the matter. More likely the starting point for identifying the servant is the interplay between people and prophet that has characterized preceding chapters. The chapter describes the vocation of the servant which is thus the vocation of both prophet and people. In the same way, the woman/city of 54.1–17a is Zion, but the effect of not naming her is to focus attention on the metaphor rather than the referent. And the addressees of 54.17b–55.13 are the community that has been addressed before, whose departure is commissioned one last time.

The anonymity of 52.13–55.13 is one of the features of it that links it with chapters 56–66, and Elliger attributes it to Third Isaiah (*Verhältnis*, pp. 6–2, 135–67). If this is correct, the book presents the chapters to us as an extension to the message addressed to the exilic community. Without these chapters, 40.1–52.12 would now seem truncated, because they offer a more far-reaching take on the problem of the people's rebellion (left unresolved at 48.22), a more far-reaching commitment to the woman/city, and a more far-reaching statement of the 'democratization' of Yhwh's covenant commitment to David (which also incorporates an *inclusio* with 40.1–11). Conversely, if the chapters were first addressed to the exilic community, they are expressed in such a way as to be immediately accessible to the later community.

V.a.

52.13–53.12: THE FRUITFULNESS OF THE SERVANT'S MINISTRY

The passage's structure

Modern translations make a chapter division after vv. 13–15, and 52.13–53.12 has been analysed as two units, a proclamation by Yhwh about the servant (Israel) and a song of testimony or thanksgiving about the prophet as Yhwh's servant (so, e.g., †Orlinsky, pp. 17–23). The Hebrew manuscript tradition shows some variation, but it broadly reflects the same two possibilities, of treating 52.13–53.12 as one unit or as two. Thus some MT MSS provide a setuma before 52.13, again before 53.1, and then before 54.1. 1QIs[a] similarly begins new lines at 52.13 and at 53.1, though it also begins and indents a new line at v. 9, slightly indents the line for v. 10aβ (v. 10aα had extended to the end of the preceding line), has slight spaces before vv. 6b and 12, then begins a new line at 54.1. Other MT MSS treat 52.13–53.12 as one whole, lacking the setuma at 53.1, while 1QIs[b] likewise has a space division before 52.13 and none before 53.1. On the other hand, no MT MSS have a petucha at both 52.13 and 53.12, and none has a petucha at 53.1.

The break at 52.13 is suggested by differences in speaker and addressee. In 52.7–10 and 52.11–12 the prophet was addressing Jerusalem and its exiled residents, urging the one to rejoice and the other to set off, as if Yhwh's act of restoration has actually happened. In 52.13–15 Yhwh speaks, about 'my servant' and his success; the identity of the addressee never becomes clear in 52.13–53.12. The modern chapter change comes with a further change in speaker, though now the identity of the speakers as well as that of the audience is unclear. But on their own, vv. 13–15 seem truncated. Conversely, the third-person verbs beginning in 53.2 are deprived of an antecedent identifying their subject if chapter 53 is separated from what precedes. The further reference to the servant's 'look' and 'appearance' (53.2, cf 52.14) specifically links 52.13–15 and 53.1–12. Then, whereas 'we' speak throughout vv. 1–6, and 'I' speaks in v. 8b and perhaps thus throughout vv. 7–9, by v. 11b Yhwh is the speaker again in such as way as to make the closing lines an *inclusio* with 52.13–15. Further, the subject is again the exaltation of 'my servant' (52.13; 53.11). There are further references to the 'many/great' (*rabbîm*) who featured in 52.13–15, and a recurrence of the verb *nāśā'* in the very last line which balances that in the first. The verbs throughout vv. 1–9 are qatal; they are more mixed in the LXX, Vg, and also in vv. 12–15 and 10–12 MT. Exhortation to Jerusalem then resumes in 54.1.

All this suggests that the inference that a new unit begins at 53.1 was understandable but that as chapter 53 unfolds, it makes clear that the inference was false. 52.13–53.12 is one section. As †Calvin says of the opening of a new chapter at 53.1, 'this division, or rather dismemberment, of the chapter, ought to be disregarded'. Certainly Justin Martyr disregards it in quoting 52.13–53.12 as a foretelling of Jesus (*First Apology* 50–51; see also *Dialogue with Trypho* 118), though he does elsewhere also quote 52.10–54.6 as one seamless whole (*Dialogue with Trypho* 13), while Augustine later does the same with 52.13–54.5 (*Harmony of the Gospels* i.31). Such attitudes by Christian exegetes may reflect their Christian convictions about the reference of the passage; Augustine's reason for reading on into chapter 54 and stopping where he does is his desire to affirm the significance of Jesus for the whole world (see 54.5). The context implies that the 52.13–53.12 refers directly to the prophet and indirectly to Israel.

Within chapter 53, the subdivisions in 1QIs^a seem implausible. To begin at the end, it is odd to divide Yhwh's first-person statements in vv. 11aβb–12. In v. 10, the reference to Yhwh's determining holds the two lines together. On the other hand, linking v. 9 with v. 10aα does draw attention to the fact that the KJV's 'Yet' overtranslates the *w* at the beginning of v. 10. The RV divides the fifteen verses into five subsections of three verses; at the centre of vv. 1–9 this does nicely highlight v. 5b, which is also marked out by its language in relation to what lies either side of it. But it also obscures the apparent transition within vv. 10–12 from speech about Yhwh to the speech by Yhwh which corresponds to that in 52.13–15. It seems forced to turn the whole of vv. 10–12 into Yhwh's speech by inferring that Yhwh is self-referring in v. 10, and it seems rather subtle to infer an unmarked transition from the prophet's speaking to Yhwh's speaking within v. 10, corresponding to a transition from Yhwh's speaking to the prophet's speaking within 52.13–15 (†Motyer). *Fohrer reworks the section as six five-line subsections, but this implausibly separates v. 6b from v. 6a with which it is bound by an *inclusio*.

A good starting-point for understanding the section's structure is surely the material where Yhwh speaks in the first person, which forms an *inclusio* of four lines each (52.13–15 and 53.11aβ–12). *Steck sees this as following a threefold pattern that appears in 1 Kgs 22.19–22 and then in 42.1–4; 49.1–6; 50.4–9. Far from its being impossible to determine the end of the report begun in v. 1 (†Spykerboer), the transition from third-person to first-person reference to Yhwh and the resumptive 'my servant' in v. 11aβ signals that this report has ended, though one must grant that the Masoretes' verse-division shows that this was not evident to them. Indeed, strictly it is vv. 2–9 which comprise the actual report of something which (in the perspective of the vision, at least) has already happened. Verse 1 then introduces this report and vv. 10–

11aα close it. Another firm point is the coherence and distinctiveness of of vv. 4–6 at the poem's centre. This begins with a 'Yet' which signals the new insight they will record and itself centres on the distinctive formulation in v. 5b; it closes with a further statement of this insight in v. 6, incorporating an *inclusio* which also contains the only reference to Yhwh in vv. 2–9. All this suggests the following outline:

52.13–15 My servant will triumph despite his suffering

  53.1 Who could have recognized Yhwh's arm?
    53.2–3 He was treated with contempt
      53.4–6 The reason was his suffering for us
    53.7–9 He did not deserve his treatment
  53.10–11aα By his hand Yhwh's purpose will succeed

53.11aβ–12 My servant will triumph because of his suffering

While a chiasm can follow a linear course, one would not especially expect it to do so—form and content would then be in tension. The poem moves from the prospect of triumph to the reality of suffering and the reasons for that suffering, and then back again. Verses 2–3, 4–6, and 7–9 thus do not constitute a quasi-narrative account of the servant's life, from youth to adulthood and death, but a series of parallel accounts of the servant's experience and its significance.

The passage's poetic form

The metre of the section is particularly irregular. In the MT the lines might be reckoned to scan as follows:

52.13–15:	3–4, 4–3–3, 4–4, 5–3
53.1:	3–4
53.2–3:	3–3, 4–3, 3–4, 3–3
53.4–6:	4–2, 3–3, 3–2, 3–2, 3–3, 3–3
53.7–9:	3–2, 3–4–3, 3–3, 4–4, 3–2, 3–3
53.10–11aα:	4–3, 4–4–4
53.11aβb–12:	5–3, 3–3, 5–3, 3–2

While some tidying could be done by manipulating *maqqephs*, it seems that in general a regular stress pattern is not intrinsic to this poem as we have it, any more than a regularity in the lengths of subsections. Alongside this fact may be set another. The poem contains an above-average number of exegetical difficulties. Sometimes individual words are obscure. Sometimes their meaning is clear enough but it is not clear how they fit with other words in the context. Sometimes the syntax is obscure.

All this might suggest that the text has suffered malformation to an unusual degree. But it is doubtful whether text-critical evidence suggests this. One crude measure is the space which *HUB* gives to textual material concerning different passages. While that given to 52.13–53.12 is more extensive than that occupied by sections of equivalent length on either side, it is not uniquely so, and page-for-page more space is required for (e.g.) 46.1–47.3. The fact that there is no great evidence of textual diversity over the passage in antiquity is especially striking given the controversial status of the passage in the early Christian/Masoretic period. It suggests that either the text became corrupt at a period before that for which we have any evidence, for reasons which are inexplicable, or that the section was in origin free in its metre, innovative in its philology, and oblique in its syntax. On the former hypothesis, the text has generated a huge number of proposals for emendation on metrical, philological, or syntactical bases (as well as some on purely text-critical grounds), but none of these have generated any consensus as authentic readings. We will therefore proceed by seeking to come to an interpretation of the oldest Hebrew texts that we have, represented by the MT and other ancient textual traditions, while then noting the implications of some modern proposals for making the text easier. The section is form-critically unique, and this may cohere with the other unusual features which we have noted, and all these may cohere with the apparent uniqueness of the theological point which the section makes.

The absence of regular metre does not raise any questions regarding whether the section is poetry. It has poetry's denseness and allusiveness, and a key role is played by simile and metaphor, particularly the similes in vv. 2, 6, and 7, and the sacramental and political/military metaphors in 52.13 15 and 53.10 12. Its word order is often not that of prose (e.g. 52.15aβ; 53.1b). It has many examples of parallelism (e.g. each of the thirteen pairs of lines from 52.14aβ to 53.6a), which is a characteristic formal feature of Hebrew poetry. Verses 4–6 in particular are especially characterized by 'synthetic' parallelism, while in many other lines the second colon differs quite markedly from the first (see, e.g., vv. 13, 15a, 1a, 7a, 8a, 10a, 11aβb, 12aγδ). Both these aspects of the poem's rhetoric in its use of parallelism relate to its content: the repetitions underline points, the unexpected differences underline the unexpected nature of its content.

The poem makes considerable use of repetition: 'my servant' (vv. 13, 11); 'exalt/bear' (*nśʾ*, vv. 13, 12); 'many' (vv. 14, 15, 11, 12a, 12b); 'appearance/look' (v. 14 and then in reverse order in v. 2); 'mouth' (vv. 15, 7a, 7b, 9; 'he would not open his mouth' recurs in vv. 7a, 7b); 'see' (vv. 15, 2, 10, 11); 'Who' (vv. 1a, 1b, 8); 'before [lit. 'to the face of]/face' (vv. 2, 3, 7); 'ground/land' (vv. 2, 8); '[he was] despised' (vv. 3a, 3b); 'we esteemed him' (vv. 3, 4); 'great suffering/weakness (v. 3; then in reverse order in v. 4—also 'weakened', v. 10); 'he' (vv. 4, 5, 7, 11, 12); 'wrongdoing' (vv. 5, 6, 11); 'rebellion' (vv. 5, 8), and 'rebels' (vv. 12a, 12b); 'he bore' (vv. 4, 12); 'all of us' (opening and closing v. 6); 'share out' (v. 12aα, 12aβ); different forms of the verbs 'afflict'

(vv. 4, 7), 'carry' (vv. 4, 11), and 'crush' (vv. 5, 10); also 'hear/what we heard' (vv. 15, 1); 'know/knowledge' (vv. 3, 11); 'Yhwh determined/Yhwh's determination' (vv. 10a, 10b). One or two very common words also recur, such as 'not', 'for', 'self', 'to him', 'thus/so', 'man', the preposition *ʿal*, and the name Yhwh. The section makes particular use of repetition with variation between the 'theological' subsections, vv. 4–6, 10–11aα, and 11aβ–12 ('bear/carry', 'hurt', 'crush', and the double use of *pāgaʿ* hi).

The effect of repetition is to bind the poem as a whole together, to draw attention to links between particular sections, to emphasize particular motifs, and to suggest connections between motifs and entities which might not look related. These include humiliation and exaltation, and the speakers' mistaken earlier assumptions about the servant and their eventual realizations (*Raabe). Repetitions of words from earlier in the chapters also suggest such connections between this unnamed servant and both the prophet as Yhwh's servant and Israel as Yhwh's servant.

The poem includes a number of unusual idioms (e.g. 53.3bα, 8bβ, 10aα) and a number of instances of asyndeton (e.g. 53.5a, 6a, 10b, 11aα). Both of these mirror a central feature of its content, a note of contrast—between affliction and triumph, between misunderstanding and realization, between the servant and other people, between the one and the 'many'. The contrast between misunderstanding and realization, between past experience and new insight, is also mirrored in the recurrent pronouns and pronominal suffixes (he–we, his–ours, him–us). It is also reflected in another aspect of the section's language. C. R. North counts 'some forty-six words or expressions... not otherwise found in Deutero-Isaiah' (*Suffering Servant*, p. 168); he does go on to note that this is not so much greater a proportion than is the case with chapters 40, 47, or 54, and in detail contests Elliger's argument (*Verhältnis*, pp. 6–27) that the passage's language is closer to that of Third Isaiah.

Links with preceding passages in Isaiah

The nature of the section and its problems are clarified if we compare it with some other passages with similarities or other links.

First, it has links with the first part of the book called Isaiah. The section contains a number of verbal points of contact with 6.1–13. While most involve common words, the number of these makes them significant, as does the related beginning of the two passages.

(1) The description of the servant's exaltation (52.13) corresponds to the description of Yhwh's exaltation (6.1).
(2) The common words 'wrongdoing' and 'failure', but also the double occurrence of the less common word 'touch' (6.7), recur in 53.4, 5, 6, 8, 11, 12.
(3) Three of the verbs in 6.9b ('hear', 'see', 'consider') recur in 52.15b, the fourth ('know/experience') in 53.3a, 11aβ.

(4) The words 'heal', 'desolate/appal', and 'seed' in 6.10, 11, 13 recur in 52.14; 53.5, 10.

Thus *Gosse describes 52.13–53.12 as modifying the gloom of chapter 6. Sin, obduracy, and desolation are to be replaced by healing, insight, fruitfulness, and exaltation. The connection with chapter 6 recalls both the community's position as Yhwh's servant (because chapter 6 concerns the community) and the prophet's position as Yhwh's servant (because the prophet there identifies with the community in its sin, and suffers for it).

The section also has a more subtle relationship with chapter 11. A notable verbal link is the word 'root' (11.1; 53.2), but such links are also pointers to a more ambivalent relationship of substance. This is epitomized by this use of that word 'root', because its significance is positive in 11.1 but negative in 53.2. That corresponds to the way in which 52.13–53.12 takes up the motif of the Davidic king as Yhwh's servant but inverts many of its implications.

The section is more systematically clarified by a comparison with passages within chapters 40–55, particularly 40.1–11; 42.1–4; 49.1–6; and 50.4–11.

It resembles the very opening passage in chapters 40–55, 40.1–11, in being very visual in its expression; there are two senses in which we might describe it as visionary. Yet technically it is an audition rather than a vision. We are being given a report of something which the prophet heard rather than saw. The prophet resembles a blind person who hears voices and knows exactly what they say, can repeat their description of what they see and can recreate the scene in the mind's eye, but has personally only heard the voices and does not always know who they belong to. The result is to put the emphasis on the content of their words rather than the speakers' identity. As in 40.1–11, however, the prophet is clear that Yhwh is the person who initiates the speaking; and as in 40.1–11, the focus on the content of the words rather than the speakers has the effect of emphasizing their promissory nature. In 40.1–11 that was achieved by verbs in the imperative, here by yiqtol verbs.

A second passage for comparison is 42.1–4 with its 'There is my servant'. Once again a servant is being pointed to, and comment is being made not on who he has been but on who he will be. Once again the poem is very visual. Once again the form is that of the designation or presentation of a king as the one to whom God's promise attaches; 52.13–53.12 offers even less hints than 42.1–4 regarding who the 'king' is being presented to. This would be quite natural if the oracle is designed to be an encouragement to servant–prophet or servant–people: see the comment on the intercalated 'you' of 52.14 (and compare the movement to 'you' in 42.5–9). The point does not lie in the context of the presentation but in what it signifies for the person being presented and for the audience in the house. In other words, the royal form is again more background than foreground to the section, which is the prophet's poetic creation.

Once again there is a lyrical tone to the passage, but it is no more a 'song' than any other passage, and less so than many. Once again the language and idiom are not characteristic of Isaiah 40–55, though the language links with the rest of this material.

Once again, in response to Yhwh's 'There...' we want to say 'Where?', and we receive no answer. The passage's nature as a vision means that its internal meaning may be clear enough without its external reference being at all clear. One might compare visions in Zechariah 1–6, or later visions in Daniel or Revelation. Some of those are interpreted to the visionary in such a way that the reference becomes clear, but in this case the prophet passes on no interpretation. In both 42.1–4 and 52.13–53.12 the content of the vision is implicitly more significant than its reference: the vision describes the way Yhwh's servant (whoever that is) undertakes his task and how it finds fulfilment.

Nevertheless we have suggested that in 42.1–4 the context points to an answer concerning the servant's identity, and the same is so with respect to 52.13–53.12. On the one hand, chapters 43–48 continued to affirm Jacob–Israel's position as Yhwh's servant, yet also made it increasingly clear that Jacob–Israel was in no position to fulfil the servant's calling. Chapters 49–50 thus testified to the prophet's realization of receiving the commission to fulfil the role of servant as a means of bringing about the community's restoration. Speaking of the servant in the third person takes up the speech of 50.10–11 and is thus no barrier to this being a description of the prophet's vocation, even one composed by the prophet. We do not have to infer that the vision comes from someone other than the prophet; there is no reason why a prophet should not envisage his or her own suffering and death and incorporate it in a third-person vision. But the third-person form does slightly distance the prophet from the servant role. That role in 52.13–53.12 continues to be one that Jacob–Israel can hardly fulfil, though the third-person form of speech points to the fact that it is still Jacob–Israel's vocation.

The passage's form and background

Formally the passage does not correspond to a known genre. Elliger (*Verhältnis*, p. 19) calls it a prophetic liturgy, in which words of God frame words of mourning, thanksgiving, and penitence; in a sense such descriptions constitute simply a restatement of the problem. It is also the passage's failure to fulfil standard expectations which encourages theories such as *Ruppert's ('"Mein Knecht"') that 53.1–10aαβb represent its original form; it was later supplemented by 53.10aγ, 11aα, then by 52.13–15; 53.11aβb-12. *Sekine (e.g. *Transcendency*, pp. 367–71) identifies seven stages in the redactional development of the passage.

Understandings such as Elliger's correspond in part to that suggested by †Begrich (pp. 55–59 = 62–66) and developed by *Whybray. Behind 52.13–53.12 is the form of a thanksgiving psalm such as Psalm 30 which recalls the experience of affliction and deliverance. The comparison also suggests a number of instructive contrasts.

First, the deliverance and vindication have not yet happened, so that these words belong more in the context of the situation presupposed by a lament than that presupposed by a thanksgiving, and the passage has similarities to a lament (†Begrich, p. 56 = 63). Other form critics had indeed identified the passage as a penitential psalm (Gressmann, *Der Messias*, pp. 305–6) or a dirge (Mowinckel, *He That Cometh*, p. 200, following H. Jahnow). If the passage's context is one of lament rather than thanksgiving, it belongs with Psalm 6 or 22 rather than Psalm 30.

Much of the detailed language of the passage is that of the laments, and we therefore need to be wary of inferring from it a picture of the concrete nature of the servant's suffering. Description in terms of illness, violence, and legal conviction all belong to the tradition of such portrayal: in itself the description does not give us grounds for taking any one, or the whole as a composite picture, as literal description (†Westermann).

*Whybray argues that the passage uses two groups of expressions. One comprises the 'stock vocabulary' of lament, used here to refer to the servant's being unimpressive, isolated, and despised. The other comprises more distinctive terms to describe the servant's affliction and humiliation; 'there is no reason to doubt that they refer to actual events in which the Servant was involved' (p. 96). Examination of Whybray's lists of terms leads to a different conclusion. While one may see the language of lament behind the first group, in each case (as we would expect) the prophet uses this language in a distinctive way. One cannot precisely parallel the phrases in the laments. Conversely, six of the seven expressions in the second group also belong to lament language (the exception is *nāgaś* in v. 7a). There are indeed two groups of terms, one perhaps more figurative, one more concretely referring to physical ill-treatment, but they form part of one novel whole. Further, given that this is a poem (and given the kind of poem it is), there is no more reason to assume that it does refer to actual events than there is to doubt that it does; there is no presumption about the matter.

A second distinguishing feature of this 'thanksgiving' is that its promise is expressed in the third person rather than the first. This is in principle no strange feature for a lament or thanksgiving. Prophetic laments such as those in Jeremiah 15 and Hosea 6 make explicit what we may suspect was a common feature of laments in ordinary usage, that people prayed them on behalf of others. Occasionally this is explicit in the Psalms in prayers for Yhwh's anointed which may reveal that the whole psalm was the people's prayer for their king. It is then a feature of the thanksgiving in Psalm 118. In isolation, then, the passage might well be one in which disciples lament the prophet's death (or near-death) as they hope for a return to life. It is the context and the continuity with what precedes, including the third-person reference in 50.10–11, which makes it more likely that we are to take this as the prophet's own third-person lament and thanksgiving. That might support the possibility just noted that the passage's talk of death and restored life need not refer to the coming of death in our sense but to deliverance from a deathly experience in life, such as Psalm 30 describes (cf *Soggin).

Third, the section is framed as a word from God not as human words of thanksgiving or lament. Admittedly the anticipatory account in vv. 13–15 deserves comparing with the introductory summary to a thanksgiving psalm (†Westermann). It would have been quite possible for the statements about the future to be expressed as the convictions of the human speakers, as happens in a lament, but instead they are expressed as divine promise. They thus differ from such statements in being more a promise of deliverance such as might occupy the space between the cry to God in a lament and the anticipatory praise with which a lament such as Psalm 6 or Psalm 22 closes, or inviting comparison with the word from Yhwh at Ps 12.6 [5] (cf †Kaiser, p. 88). At the same time they differ from a 'salvation oracle' in being mostly declaimed in the third person rather than addressed to the beneficiary (except in v. 14aα).

The passage constitutes the prophet's final attempt to picture how the problem of Jacob–Israel's rebellion may be resolved. How does forgiveness and renewal come about? The prophet brings together four existent images or fields of metaphors. One is the image of Israel as an afflicted people (see, e.g., 1.5–6), or Jerusalem as an afflicted woman (see, e.g., the preceding passage 51.17–52.12). Another is the experiences of a prophet, who is one who goes through affliction in the course of ministering to people. A third is the field of metaphors associated with the king of Israel, which is prominent at the opening and close of the passage.

In the historical context, this servant forms a positive counterpart to Jehoiachin and Zedekiah. The passage has a number of links with Jer 22.24–30, suggesting that it constitutes a promise that the servant's destiny will not simply follow Jehoiachin's (cf †E. Burrows, p. 73; cf also Cazelles, 'Le roi Yoyakin'). Jehoiachin was despised (v. 28, the same word as in 53.3); no determination/desire attached to him (v. 28, the same word as in 53.10); there is no future for his offspring (v. 28, the same word as in 53.10); neither he nor they will succeed (v. 30, the same word as in 53.10). In each case the word form is exactly identical in the two passages. In the light of these links, other less precise ones are probably significant: 'he will not return to the land' (vv. 27–29; compare 'cut off from the land of the living', 53.8); 'his days' (v. 30; compare 'he will have a long life', literally 'prolong days', 53.10). Comparison with Jer 23.5–6 also suggests links with the promise of one who will be a just branch who will act with insight, unlike Zedekiah. The image of the kingly plant has already also been developed in Ezek 17.5–10 (*Begg). Second Isaiah envisages a quite different form of fulfilment from the one implied by these prophecies.

A fourth field of metaphors is first signaled by the reference to 'spattering' in v. 15, most of whose occurrences come in Leviticus 1–16. The passage has other links with these chapters, such as the references to being 'touched' in the sense of stricken (vv. 4, 8), the reference to the reparation-offering (v. 10), and the talk of 'bearing wrongdoing' (v. 11).

Beyond the fourfold OT background to 52.13–53.12, some background for the portrait has been identified in Babylonian texts about the the god Tammuz's dying and rising (see, e.g., Engnell, *The 'Ebed Yahweh Songs*) and/or in Babylonian kingship texts (see *ANET*, pp. 267, 331–34). While the vision might have gained resonances from this background, there is nothing distinctively comparable with this material and nothing that requires such a hypothesis (see critiques in *Scharbert; †Kaiser, pp. 96–99). And it would then be odd for the passage to make a point of describing the servant's affliction and exaltation as something of which nations and kings had never heard (†Westermann). Israelite ideas about the nation and its suffering, prophecy and its cost, kingship and its promises, and priesthood, cleansing, and recompense are all that is required as background to the vision. What these do is make possible a complex innovative description of the means whereby forgiveness and renewal come. We have seen that the pattern of the chapters as a whole as well as that of 52.13–53.12 in particular is to move in spiral rather than linear fashion. Here 52.13–53.12 once more takes up issues that have preoccupied us since chapter 40 and offers one more treatment of them, or makes one more attempt to bring the people to forgiveness and renewal.

The afterlife of the passage

Isaiah 52.13–53.12 has had a more colourful afterlife than most of the OT. Within the OT itself, the enigmatic vision in Zech 12.10–13.1 of people mourning over one(s) who has (have) been slain, and of the opening of a fountain for people's cleansing, parallels its motifs, though there are no verbal links.[1] More explicitly Daniel 10–12 simply identifies the wise teachers of its day as the contemporary embodiment of Yhwh's servant (*Ginsberg, *VT* 3). The passage's influence later in the second century can be seen in *1 Enoch* in the *Book of Heavenly Luminaries* 72–73 and in the *Similitudes* 46.[2] Wisdom 2–5 incorporates another appropriation of the passage in the next century: encouragement for the persecuted comes from the passage's implicit call to a righteous life which is its own reward, and its promise that death is not the end.[3]

In the LXX and in Syr, the servant is an individual person who

[1] See D. R. Jones, *Haggai, Zechariah and Malachi* (London, 1962), p. 162.

[2] See G. W. E. Nickelsburg, *Resurrection, Immortality, and Eternal Life in Intertestamental Judaism* (Cambridge, MA/London, 1972), pp. 70–78.

[3] See *Wolff, pp. 45–47; *Suggs; *Ruppert, 'Der leidende Gerechte'.

belongs to the future, in effect a messianic figure, but not one with specifically Christian features. Indeed, D. A. Sapp notes that the LXX's rendering is relatively unamenable to the understanding of the significance of Christ's death in a writer such as Paul.[4] The Tg similarly glosses 'my servant' in 52.13 with the expression 'the anointed'; if v. 14aβ originally referred to 'ruin' rather than 'anointing' (see comment), the 1QIs[a] reading at v. 14aβ may have the same implication (so Chamberlain, *VT* 5, p. 309). The Tg then separates the description of the servant's exaltation (e.g. 52.13, 15; 53.12) from the description of suffering and humiliation. The latter is assumed at the moment to apply to Israel (e.g. 52.14) but to be the destiny of the nations (e.g. 52.15; 53.3). The servant is 'an exalted, proud, and aggressive personality, a champion who takes up the cudgels for the despised and downtrodden and suffering Israel, who wields destructive power over their enemies and subjugates mighty kings in their behalf. He also restores Israel to national dignity, rebuilds its sanctuary, is a champion of Torah, metes out judgment to the wicked, and consigns them to Gehenna' (*Levey [see on 53.2aγb], pp. 66–67). But the anointed servant's task is to pray for his people in their sin and affliction, to work and to risk his life for them (e.g. 53.11–12). The stress on the last note does not give the impression that the Tg's interpretation is affected by the need to stand over against Christian interpretation.[5]

The significance of the passage for Jesus and the early church is a much-controverted question. While later Christian interpretation came to treat the whole passage as a prediction of Jesus, the nearest to a concerted exposition within the NT appears in 1 Pet 2.22–25. It is a matter of dispute whether this is the first concerted exposition (so *Hooker) or whether the passage had been of crucial importance for Paul or whether Jesus had already seen himself as the suffering servant (see, e.g., *Wolff); the debate is reprised in *Bellinger and Farmer. Certainly other NT references are more atomistic. Jesus's healing ministry made people recall the servant's taking people's illnesses (v. 4; Matt 8.17). In Luke 22.37 he himself speaks of the need that scriptures which were written 'about' him, such as talk of the servant's being 'counted with rebels', should find fulfilment (cf v. 12). A Christian evangelist can be portrayed as making this passage a basis for talking about Jesus (Acts 8.32–33).

It is in Justin's *First Apology* 50 and his *Dialogue with Trypho* 13 that the passage as a whole is first systematically treated as referring to Jesus. In his argument *Against Celsus* (e.g. 1.54–55; 6.75) Origen similarly takes 52.13–53.12 as a prophecy which must apply to Jesus

[4] 'The LXX, 1QIsa, and MT Versions of Isaiah 53 and the Christian Doctrine of Atonement', in *Bellinger and Farmer, pp. 170–92. Cf *Levey, p. 67; more generally *Hegermann, pp. 128–30; *Litwak.

[5] See Chilton, *Isaiah Targum*; cf *Betz; *Syrén; contrast, e.g., *Wolff; *Levey, p. 67. On the tradition of a suffering Messiah in Judaism, see *Hruby; M. Fishbane, 'Midrash and Messianism', in *Toward the Millennium* (ed. P. Schäfer and M. Cohen; Leiden/Boston, 1998), pp. 57–71.

and cannot (for instance) refer to the Jewish people. †Eusebius 3.2 [97c–100a] later sees a detailed correspondence between the vision and the virgin birth, sinless suffering, atoning death, and resurrection of Jesus, a vision which is (as it were) given from the perspective of Holy Saturday when Jesus has died but has not yet risen.

When the African politician in Acts 8 asked his question, Philip the evangelist did not simply say 'the passage is about Jesus' but 'starting with this scripture, proclaimed to him the good news about Jesus'. The statement lends itself to the modern reader's finding some hermeneutical sophistication in this formulation, as if Philip knew he was providing a readerly response to the text rather than a piece of historical-critical exegesis. The developed Christian conviction that Jesus 'fulfilled' the prophecy in 52.13–53.12 risks robbing the passage of much of its power; the passage is simply a prediction of Jesus which has been fulfilled and has therefore fulfilled its function. This is not the nature of the exposition in 1 Peter 2. It indeed parallels with Isa 52.13–53.12 the fact that Jesus did no wrong in deed or word, so that his death constituted a taking of people's sins; whereas they were like wandering sheep, they have been healed through his being wounded (vv. 5–6, 9). Yet the point about this exposition is to urge the Christian community to be like Jesus in its handling of attack (cf the argument of Phil 2.4–11 with its connections with Isa 52.13–53.12). The fact that the vision had come true in Jesus meant that it now needed to come true in the church. 1 Clement 16 (and Origen himself, e.g., *Against Celsus* 8.55) reads the passage in this way as well as seeing it as a prophecy. Similarly, while Jesus met a response which made people recall v. 1 (John 12.38), so did Paul and other Christian Jews (Rom 10.16) as they operate like the servant in a mission to people who have not yet heard (Rom 15.21; cf v. 15).[6] The servant illumines the experience of the community as well as that of Jesus.

The NT's stance is thus comparable to the perspective inherent in the passage itself, that if it constitutes God's promise to the prophet, it is not only that. From a Christian viewpoint some irony attaches to the fact that the one entity which is outside the purview of 52.13–53.12 is an individual future redeemer, a 'Messiah'; but the openness of the text enables a Christian like Philip to look at Jesus through the prism provided by this passage to see if it is illuminating, and to look at the passage through the prism provided by the story of Jesus to see if that is illuminating, see if he might have made it come true.

The patristic/rabbinic period saw flourishing interest in Isaiah 53 on the part of Christian theologians for similar reasons to those which drew first-century writers: it helped them handle a question they needed to handle, the significance of Jesus. Conversely, Jewish sources show no particular interest in the passage, partly because they have no such strong reason to be drawn to it, partly because the

[6] For more subtle links between the NT and Isa 53, see, e.g., *Hoad; *Betz; and on John 12.38, *Beauchamp, pp. 347–55.

focus of their own interest lay more in halakah and haggadah, partly in reaction to Christian preoccupation. As is the case in the NT, rabbinic sources could use the figure of the servant to illumine the vocation of the people of God, though they more characteristically assume that the chapter refers to the Messiah.

This configuration changed in the medieval period, when Christian polemic which asserted that Jewish suffering issued from God's casting off the people for their sins, and the increased intensity of Jewish suffering at Christian hands, drew Jewish writers to the passage for an equivalent reason to that which had drawn Christians to it a millennium earlier. It helped them handle the question they needed to handle, the need to understand Jewish suffering. Beginning from the identification of the servant and Israel made elsewhere in these chapters, †Rashi and subsequent interpreters could see their people's exile as enabling the spreading of their witness to Torah in the world and (in the aftermath of the First Crusade) see their people's suffering as imposed for the sake of making atonement for the nations' sin as well as for its own (see *Rembaum). On the representation of chapter 53 in art in the medieval and later periods, see Sawyer, *Fifth Gospel*, pp. 83–99.

Much later Eliezer Berkovits describes Isaiah 53 as 'the description of Israel's martyrology through the centuries. The Christian attempt to rob Israel of the dignity of Isaiah's suffering servant of God has been one of the saddest spiritual embezzlements in human history. At the same time, the way Christianity treated Israel through the ages only made Isaiah's description fit Israel all the more tragically and truly. Generation after generation of Christians poured out their iniquities and inhumanity over the head of Israel, yet they "esteemed him, stricken, smitten of God, and afflicted" '.[7]

The tenth-century Jewish exegete *Saadia referred the whole passage to Jeremiah and showed how this works exegetically in some detail, in a manner parallel to Christian application to Jesus's story. In contrast, one contemporary Karaite scholar, *Salmon ben Yeruham, referred the humiliation to Israel in the past and the glory to the Messiah. Another, *Yephet ben 'Ali, opposed both of these. Saying that he follows the interpretation of the earlier Karaite master Benjamin Al-Nahawandi, he refers the whole to the Messiah, who is humiliated on Israel's behalf and later exalted. †Ibn Ezra then argued from the context (52.12 and 54.1) that neither Saadia nor Yephet can be right. He personally thinks that the servant is always the prophet, but he shows how the whole can apply to Israel. Implicitly he is doubtless responding to Christian application of the prophecy to Jesus, but it is Abrabanel who offers the most systematic such critique, emphasizing (for instance) that he was not buried with the wicked, had no seed, did not lengthen days, and did not divide spoil (see *Neubauer). If it be argued that this language is figurative, then in his notes to †Ibn Ezra's commentary M. Friedländer

[7] *Faith After the Holocaust* (New York, 1973), pp. 125–26.

comments that 'the whole argument is destroyed which is based on the supposition of a minute coincidence of the facts here predicted with the incidents in the life of Jesus'. Abrabanel applies the passage to Israel but also to Josiah. †Rashi refers it to the righteous remnant within Israel.

52.13. There, my servant will act with insight. He will arise and exalt himself and be very high. The servant poem in 42.1–4 began 'There', but the word was *hēn*; here it is *hinnēh* (elsewhere in the OT the latter is much more common, but Isa 40–55 includes seventeen instances of the former and fourteen of the latter). In 42.1 *hēn* introduced a noun clause, which also made for a link with the noun clauses about the servant in 41.8–9 (cf 50.11); in 52.13 *hinnēh* introduces a verbal clause, the verb coming between the particle and the subject. It makes a statement about the servant rather than pointing to him. The passage does not itself indicate who is speaking or who is spoken of. But 'my servant' picks up from 42.1; 49.3, 6 ('my servant'), and 49.5; 50.10 ('his servant') and signals that it is Yhwh who speaks. Further, the fact that the latter four passages refer to the prophet signal that Yhwh also speaks about the prophet here, even if the link with 42.1 also reminds us that this is not all that needs to be said about the servant's identity; 'my servant' was Jacob–Israel in (e.g.) 41.8–9.

†Torrey takes *yaśkîl* as the servant's name ('There is He-acts-with-insight, my servant') but the word is a straightforward verb form applied to David and Hezekiah in 1 Sam 18.5 and 2 Kgs 18.7. The verb suggests that the servant has a David-like role or experience (see also 1 Sam 18.14, 15, also v. 30 for the qal). If he comes under pressure like David, he will act with insight and come out on top like David. Torrey's suggestion is thus an unnecessary extravagance, as is †Engnell's suggestion (p. 77) that the word might be a denominative 'will execute a maskil' (the title for a kind of psalm which comes in some Psalm headings).

Although the verb usually denotes the giving of attention or the exercise of insight (cf 41.20; 44.18), the Tg renders *yṣlḥ* ('succeed') here; when the verb is applied to David, modern translators also conventionally give the word this meaning. Implicitly it thus denotes success which results from behaving in a way which shows insight. But the LXX renders συνήσει, Vg *intelleget*, Syr *mstkl*. Aq has ἐπιστημονισθήσεται, strictly 'will be caused to understand', but Aq is inclined to use passives for verbs which look transitive but are intransitive (*Hegermann, pp. 28–29). In taking up this verse, Dan 11.33, 35; 12.3, 10 also implies the meaning 'have insight', though it gives it a causative meaning (also 9.22). This would follow well from the previous servant passage (see 50.4, 10) and would lead well into what eventually follows here (*Beauchamp, p. 334). But there is no other instance of the verb used absolutely with this meaning and it is unlikely that an audience could have inferred that the verb was causative, especially in the context of the line's continuation in v. 13b.

In this present context either 'show insight' or 'succeed' would fit. But when the David story uses the verb it implicitly contrasts David's insight with Saul's stupid folly as well as David's success with Saul's failure. Indeed, most occurrences of this verb which may be translated 'succeed' appear in contexts which suggest having insight, so that this is also a plausible rendering there (Deut 29.8 [9]; Josh 1.7, 8; 1 Kgs 2.3; 2 Kgs 18.7; Jer 10.21; 23.5; perhaps not Jer 20.11; Prov 17.8). The verb refers to knowing what you are doing (cf Kosmala [see on 44.18]). The servant, then, will demonstrate such wisdom, and this will lead to his exaltation (v. 13b). The closing description of the servant's exaltation in 53.11–12 will speak of his knowledge and his success, again using terms which recall a king like David.

Meanwhile, the three following verbs give ascending and cumulative definition to the results of the servant's acting with insight: he will arise (ingressive, suggesting the beginning of a process), exalt himself (niphal, suggesting his personal involvement), and thus finally be high (stative)—indeed, very high. While the LXX renders the three verbs by two passives (Aq, Th, Sym by three passives), the Hebrew verbs may as easily suggest the servant's achievement. He is acting, not being acted on.

*Baltzer suggests that v. 13 may actually have Moses in mind and be taking up Deuteronomy 34; it will then itself in due course be taken up by *Testament of Moses* 10–11.

ישׂכיל: *Driver repoints to ni יִשָּׂכֵל from שׂכל II ('he will be bound'). †Budde neatly emends to ישׂראל (but †Torrey notes that the converse corruption would be more likely); Morgenstern (*VT* 11, p. 313) emends to ישׂקל ('he is suspended'). †Duhm omits.
עבדי: †Duhm sees as a misunderstood abbreviation for עבד יהוה. *Dahood ('Phoenician Elements') parses the suffix as a Phoenician-style third-person.
ירום ונשׂא וגבה מאד: 1QIs[a] וירום (cf Syr). NEB repoints to יֵרוֹם ('will be raised up'). M. Dahood takes ירום as qal passive participle from the by-form ירם and then takes the colon as a description of Yhwh who 'will prosper his servant'[8] 1QIs[b] reverses the last two verbs. The LXX has καὶ ὑψωθήσεται καὶ δοξασθήσεται σφόδρα. †Ottley infers that the last Heb. vb is missing, and the Hexaplaric group of MSS does add καὶ μετεωρισθήσεται at the end, but the position of σφόδρα would rather imply that the second Gk vb represents the last Heb. vb. †Marti thus suggests that the first vb is omitted, and *Hempel sees it as a gloss on נשׂא (which he takes as a denominative from נשׂיא). Aq, Th, and Sym replace the second vb by ἐπαρθήσεται καὶ μετεωρισθήσεται. Most likely the LXX is paraphrasing and it is inappropriate to attempt to specify which two verbs are represented. Elsewhere ὑψόω can render both the first two vbs (e.g. 30.18; 33.10).

[8] 'Hebrew–Ugaritic Lexicography iii', in *Bib* 46 (1965), pp. 311–32 (see p. 323); also *Dahood, 'Phoenician Elements'.

52.14aα. Just as many were appalled at you... After the talk of insight and exaltation, the statement about humiliation is a surprise. At first sight Yhwh seems now to be addressing someone other than the servant who has been put down and has thus been the subject of horror, and comparing the addressee's experience with the servant's. The identity of this addressee is not specified, and inference about it would depend on prior inference regarding the servant's own identity. If the servant is someone other than the prophet, then this 'you' might be the prophet; if the servant is the prophet (or a promised future king), it might be Jacob–Israel. The Tg's understanding of the whole vision as divided in its reference to the servant and to Israel could have found a starting-point here, and the Tg does refer vv. 14aβb to Israel rather than the servant, though for this first colon it has an interpretative rendering, 'as the house of Israel hoped for him for many days'. *Driver makes this the basis for reconstructing a supposedly missing colon; *Hegermann suggests the influence of Hos 3.4.

The Syr and Th also render '...at him'. This might imply that their text (and Tg's) had this reading, but the textual change in the MT is then difficult to comprehend, and more likely they, too, are interpreting the text in a way which accurately reflects its meaning (it is the same person who is referred to throughout v. 14), though not its rhetoric. A sudden switch from third to second person and back again also appears in 1.29–31 and 42.20 (another servant passage); cf GK 144p. Here the prophet-servant appears both as 'he' and as 'you', both as addressee of Yhwh's words and as subject of them. But the change also hints that we should not identify servant and prophet too unequivocally.

The 'many' will reappear in v. 15 and in 53.11b–12 (cf also 54.1). Little that has preceded 52.13–53.12 has prepared us to infer who the term refers to. Their 'appalment' is a standard feature in portraits of disaster (e.g. Lev 26.32), but the term is also applied to Job in a passage which J. C. Bastiaens sees as a reminiscence of v. 14.[9] The LXX has a future verb, ἐκστήσονται (cf Syr *ntmhwn*); contrast Aq, Th, Sym.

עליך: *Dahood ('Phoenician Elements') redivides as עלי (understood as third person) followed by כי (understood as emphatic).

52.14aβb. ...so his appearance is anointed beyond that of anyone, his look beyond that of any other human being. Two different understandings of the line are suggested by the MT and by (for instance) Aq, Th, Sym, Syr. Both involve some syntactical oddity; the latter

[9] 'The Language of Suffering in Job 16–19 and in the Suffering Servant Passages in Deutero-Isaiah', in †van Ruiten and Vervenne, pp. 421–32 (see p. 426). Bastiaens finds a concentration of references to Deutero-Isaiah in Job 16–19, esp. to 50.4–9 and 52.13–53.12 (see p. 432).

perhaps has better textual support, but the MT's understanding makes better sense contextually.

The MT's verse subdivision holds together the first two cola in v. 14 and suggests that they constitute a comparison, 'Just as...so...' (*kaʾăšer...kēn*). This sequence comes about 55 times in the Hebrew Bible. It can suggest various forms of straightforward comparison (e.g. 55.11), but especially a comparison between word and event, or a comparison/contrast between blessing and trouble or vice versa (e.g. Jer 32.42; Zech 8.13). The MT implies that a variant on the latter comparison appears here: as people were appalled at the servant, so he is now or soon will be anointed like a king or priest (and therefore the object of reverence rather than horror). The reference to anointing parallels the account of David's anointing as a person good in appearance (though the noun there is *rōʾî* [in pause], not *marʾeh*) and a man of (good) looks (*tōʾar*, as here) (1 Sam 16.12–13, 18; cf †Grimm and Dittert); cf also Ps 89.20–21, 51–52 [19–20, 50–51] and the designation of Cyrus as Yhwh's anointed in 45.1. While prophets were not usually anointed, priests were, and this reference to anointing fits the priestly aspect to 52.13–53.12, not least the next verse.

More literally the verse reads 'just as many were appalled...so his appearance [is/will be] an anointing beyond that of a human being'. '[Is] anointed beyond' thus represents the construct noun *mišḥat* followed by the preposition *min* (cf GK 130a). The noun usually refers to the 'anointing' oil. 1QIsª reads *mšḥty*. That might be a first person form of the related verb, suggesting more straightforwardly '...so I anointed his appearance...'[10] Or it might be the same construct as the MT's with a conjunctive *-i* sufformative, instanced elsewhere in 1QIsª (e.g. 49.7). It then functions to underline the construct relationship (see GK 90klmn; so *Rubinstein, pp. 478–79).

In contrast, the versions implicitly construe *mišḥat* as a form of the verb *šāḥat* ('ruin') not a noun from *māšaḥ* ('anoint'), while BDB takes *mišḥat* as the sole occurrence of a noun meaning 'ruining'. On this assumption, EVV translate the preposition *min* by an English comparative (compare the usage in Ps 45.8 [7]), and thus give the impression that he was disfigured 'beyond human beings' and ceased to look human. This is probably misleading. If a comparative is to be used, in English the word 'other' needs adding, as in comparable passages such as Gen 3.1; Exod 14.7; 33.16; Lev 11.23; Deut 7.7; Prov 30.2; Est 3.8 (cf BDB, p. 582b): his appearance was disfigured more than that of any other person. To put it another way, the *min* is more equivalent to a European superlative (cf *IBHS* 11.2.11e), as the LXX recognizes at Gen 3.1 (contrast NIV); Prov 30.2 (contrast NRSV). If this interpretation is right, the point of the line is then not necessarily that the servant suffered more than any other human being, nor that he ceased to look like a human being, but that he suffered in a way

[10] So, e.g., †Barthélemy; Barthélemy, in *RB* 57 (1950), pp. 546–47 = Barthélemy, *Études*, pp. 17–18; †Brownlee, pp. 204–15.

which marked him more than any other human being. Implications of this appear in vv. 2, 3, and 8: because he has suffered as if he were the worst of human beings, people can treat him as such.

If the word indeed means 'ruining', this will reflect the link between the servant and Israel/Zion. The related verb often applies to the destroying of Israel/Zion by Yhwh or by enemies (e.g. 51.13; 54.16; Jer 13.9, 14; 15.3, 6; Lam 2.5–8). At the same time, describing the servant's appearance and form as ruined would make for a telling contrast with what should be true of a king, who was ideally a person of attractive appearance and form (1 Sam 16.18; 17.42). He would be no David, this servant. Indeed, the word 'appearance' comes ten times in Leviticus 13, and the passage would then already be advertising that his appearance is more that of someone with a skin disease than that of a handsome king.

Was a reference to anointing original, or was a reference to ruining original? There are no other references either to anointing or to ruining someone's 'look' or 'appearance'. There are no other occurrences of a noun *mišḥat* meaning 'ruin' and the prophet could have used one of the three other nouns from that root which have this meaning (*mašḥît*, *mašḥēt*, and *mošḥāt*), but there are no other occurrences of *mišḥāh* except in connection with the anointing oil. Daniel 8.24–25 and 9.24–27 refer both to ruining and to anointing, which may imply that the author was aware of both ways of understanding the present passage (Brownlee, *BASOR* 132, pp. 13–14), and †Koenig (pp. 370–71) sees the passage as inherently ambiguous. On the other hand, the connotations of the notion of 'ruining' just noted might explain how this idea came to replace 'anointing'. Or, 'anointing' could have replaced 'ruining', to avoid the idea that the servant was disfigured (†Luzzatto); this removes the chief obstacle to an interpretation of 52.13–53.12 which dissociates the servant about whom Yhwh speaks in 52.13–15 and 53.11aβ–12 from the figure whose affliction unnamed speakers describe in 53.1–11aα.

Yet the 'so' clause becomes very difficult to construe if it explains the appalment rather than contrasting with it. It is no longer possible to hold together the first two cola in v. 14 as a comparison. 'Just as many were appalled at Yhwh's servant, so Yhwh's servant was ruined' does not work as a comparison: ruining and appalment might work, but the reverse order does not. If one begins from the literal difference in pronouns, 'just as many were appalled at *you*, so *his* appearance was ruined' works better, but we have seen that it is unlikely that the change in pronouns suggests a change in the person referred to. The Tg rather takes the *kēn* of v. 14aβ as independent of the comparison; it introduces a somewhat cumbersome periphrasis explaining the appalment of the 'many'.[11] Applying the line to the people rather than to the servant, it thus begins (literally) 'who their appearance was dark among the peoples and their face beyond

[11] See M. J. Mulder, 'Die Partikel כֵּן im Alten Testament', in *Remembering All the Way...* (OTS 21, 1981), pp. 201–27 (see pp. 222–23).

human beings'. This is hardly evidence for reading *kî* ('for') for *kēn* (†Kittel), but it represents the way the line must be construed if the MT's *mišḥat* means 'ruining' rather than 'anointing'.

We have seen that the Tg, Syr, and Th keep a third person suffix in v. 14aα. In contrast, the LXX renders in the second person throughout v. 14, and in isolation this might correctly interpret v. 14 in the light of the idiom which also features in English whereby a relative clause will use third person suffixes to refer back to a second-person antecedent (cf 5.8; 51.7; 54.1). OT poetry is capable of making that transition from second to third person in other situations (cf 45.8, 21; 61.7), like that from third to second (GK 144p). The existence of this idiom then makes it easy to effect a transition back to the third person in v. 15. Jewish exegetes such as †Ibn Ezra take the line as the content of what the 'many' say rather than simply as the reason why they were appalled.

But a further complication will then be introduced by v. 15, which opens with another *kēn*. If v. 14aβb is a periphrasis, v. 15a is the apodosis of the comparison, but 'Just as many were appalled at you...so he will spatter many nations' does not constitute much better a comparison with v. 14aα; we will note possible emendations of the second verb, but the need to emend raises questions about the proposed understanding of the text as a whole. This point becomes sharper when †Marti moves v. 14aβb to an easier position at the end of 53.2. †North hypothesizes that it was moved here to v. 14 to make up for the loss of a colon which has made v. 14aα seem isolated. †Volz instead removes v. 14b which he sees as originally a gloss to 53.2–3; we have noted that *Driver devises a new colon to complement v. 14aα.

BDB assumes that the periphrasis reads more literally 'such [was] the ruining of his appearance, beyond a man...'. EVV 'so disfigured was his appearance' give a misleading impression of the straightforwardness of the construction presupposed by the 'periphrasis' hypothesis. The use of *kēn* which is required is somewhat unusual: see *DCH*, Vol. 4, pp. 430b–431b on the use in noun clauses, and p. 432a on the possible use as an adverb of quantity as well as of manner. On either interpretation of *mišḥat* the use of the noun is also unusual, though a similar instance comes in v. 3bα. The basis for arguing that the noun construction is not original is textual rather than syntactical (see note).

So the colon which at first looks isolated eventually finds its pair in v. 15aα (see comment); the delay in resolving the question it raises mirrors the nature of the experience it describes. The fact that there are other passages where *kaʾăšer* introduces a double comparison (see Exod 1.12; Josh 11.15; †Barthélemy) further supports the MT's understanding of the passage. The present instance is not as neat a sequence as those earlier ones, but it is less problematic than the alternative understanding just considered, and it is quite intelligible: as they were appalled, so he is anointed and so he can therefore spatter. Syntactically the protasis of the comparison in v. 14aα thus finds a double apodosis in vv. 14aβb and v. 15a. Metrically, however, v. 14aα finds its pair in v. 15aα, while a complete bicolon comprising v. 14aβb intervenes.

In Ps 49.3 [2] *b^e^nê ʾādām* and *b^e^nê ʾîš* seem to be contrasted as upper-class and lower-class or vice versa, but most other occurrences of such pairings occur in parallelism which does not obviously imply such a contrast (e.g. Num 23.19; Jer 2.6; 49.18, 33; 50.40; 51.43; Pss 8.5 [4]; 62.10 [9]); 90.3; Job 35.8; 1QH 4.30; 10.3) and there are no pointers to this contrast here (against †Young).

מִשְׁחַת: Aq, Th, Sym *corrupta est*, Syr *mḥbl* imply the ho ptpl abs. מָשְׁחָת (*Hegermann) or constr. מָשְׁחַת (cf †Luzzatto). The LXX's paraphrase ἀδοξήσει ('[your form] will be inglorious') which contrasts with its δοξασθήσεται in v. 13 (*HUB*), Vg *inglori[os]us erit*, and Tg חשוך ('darkened') can all be loose renderings of מָשְׁחָת. Geniza fragment Kb 13 has מָשְׁחָת (in connection with †Barthélemy's questioning, see *Rubinstein). This is also a ho ptpl form (see GK 53s), and it thus indicates awareness of this reading in the Masoretic tradition. †Torrey sees מִשְׁחַת as a composite reading, perhaps of the ho ptpl and נִשְׁחַת (ni, 'he was disfigured'), to which Morgenstern (*VT* 11, p. 314) emends the MT. *Komlosh renders 'his stature' (reading 1QIs^a^ as משחתו) on the basis of Aramaic משחא ('measure', *DTT*, p. 851; cf BDB, p. 602b). Guillaume (*JBL* 76, pp. 41–42) links 1QIs^a^'s vb with an Arabic vb meaning 'mar'. *Dahood ('Phoenician Elements') understands the prep. as denoting the agent, 'disfigured by human beings'.
תארו: on the form, see GK 93q; JM 96Aj. 1QIs^b^ has תרו. LXX ἡ δόξα σου again reflects its liking for this root (cf Tov [see on 44.9b], p. 127) rather than suggesting an underlying תפארתך (†Zillesen).
אדם: 1QIs^a^ has האדם, LXX pl.

52.15aα. …so he will spatter many nations. This further 'so' statement, then, pairs with v. 14aα and completes a bicolon structured ABBA (another follows in 53.10), while also taking further the 'so' statement in v. 14aβb; in a rendering such as the Tg's it pairs more exclusively with the 'as' clause in v. 14aα, after the periphrasis comprising v. 14aβb. Either way, 'many nations' corresponds to (simple) 'many', 'will spatter' contrasts with 'were appalled', and 'at' recurs in the next clause. The addition of 'nations' offers some clarification of the 'many' in v. 14aα and points to the 'many' of 2.2–4 or Ps 89.51 [50].

'Spatter' (*nāzāh*) denotes the splashing of blood, oil, or water over people or objects in connection with their dedication or cleansing (e.g. Lev 8.10–11, 30, where the object is 'oil of anointing'—the word in v. 14). Readers might at first not only wonder what spattering nations means, but also wonder over what the servant is spattering them. †Ibn Ezra takes the verb to denote the shedding of their blood (cf the qal in 63.3) and the Tg renders 'scatter' (*ybdr*);[12] but this requires a bigger jump than the assumption that the verb refers to

[12] See also T. C. Vriezen, 'The Term *hizza*', in *OTS* 7 (1950), pp. 201–35 (see p. 204).

spattering something *on* the nations. Aq and Th have ῥαντίσει ('sprinkle'), Vg *asperget* ('sprinkle'), Syr *mdkʾ* ('purify'). These renderings suggest that the versions were able to work out that this is a distinctive usage of the verb without the usual preposition, and presumably other readers could also do so. There is no need to infer that the Vg and Syr reflect the influence of Christian convictions (†van der Kooij, pp. 277, 303)—the Vg also uses *aspergo* in Leviticus 8. The verb in any case seems to govern the thing spattered in Lev 4.6, 17, though the text there is difficult. The significance of the spattering will be clearer when we get to the end of the poem, though it never makes explicit what the servant is spattering the nations with.

*Nyberg (p. 47) posits that the Masoretes misunderstood the line in linking 'at him' with the second colon (contrast LXX). He renders 'many nations will spatter on account of him'—that is, perform a purification rite to avoid contamination from him. This involves assuming that the singular verb has a plural subject (cf GK 145o), with the LXX, that the transitive verb is used intransitively, and that the preposition has a different meaning from usual: elsewhere when *ʿal* links with this verb, it designates the object over which a liquid was sprinkled. This collocation seems unlikely. An Arabic homonym of *nāzāh* means 'leap' (see BDB; *TTH*, pp. 227–28), but there is no evidence for its existence in Hebrew or for its being capable of generating the meaning 'startle'. There seems no need to hypothesize these possibilities, and no advantage because it provides a poor contrast to 'be appalled'. It might be supported by LXX θαυμάσονται ('will be astonished'), but the latter is as likely a loose translation: see comment on 52.5b, also †Ziegler, pp. 162–63. †Grimm and Dittert suggest that the LXX presupposes a form of the Aramaic verb *twh* ('disgust'). More likely it derives from the parallelism; *HUB* compares Job 21.5.

*Dahood ('Phoenician Elements') sees the yiqtols through v. 15 as having past reference.

יזה: 1QIs[a] divided יז הגואים, though it was corrected to the MT's division. Sym ἀποβαλ[λ]εῖ ('cast off') suggests יזנח ('he will spurn'). †Rashi explains as a by-form of ידה ('cast down') as used in Zech 2.4 [1.21]. †Lindblom hypothesizes a root יזה of which this is then the qatal (qal or hi). †Cheyne emends to יַתֵּר ('startle'), †Klostermann to יזה[י]ר ('instruct'), †Duhm (in his first edition) to יזהיר מ ('shine more than'), †Marti to ישתחוו ('bow down'), †Ehrlich to יתמהו ('be startled'), *Moore to יִרְגְּזוּ ('shake'—cf Exod 15.14), †Zillessen to יתמו ('be astonished'), †Köhler to ישעו ('gaze'), †Kissane to ידמו ('be amazed'—cf Exod 15.16), *Treves (p. 106) to יזהר or יזהרו ('be enlightened/instructed/admonished'), *Kutsch (p. 17) to יזוחו which he takes to denote astonishment (though this is to replace one uncertainty by another: see *DCH*), K. Fischer (see †Grimm and Dittert) to ינוו ('glorify'–cf Exod 15.2).
גוים רבים: †Torrey omits גוים and renders רבים 'mighty', which is hardly how an audience would hear it, especially after the occurrence in v. 14.

52.15aβb. Kings will shut their mouths at him, for what had not been told them they will have seen, what they had not heard they will have considered. The MT implies that v. 15a is a bicolon in which 'many nations' and 'kings' form a pair, though in other respects these two cola do not balance very closely. We have suggested that v. 15aα additionally pairs with v. 14aα in forming a bracket round v. 14aβb. Verse 15aβ then also links with what follows. Read in this way, vv. 13–15 closes with a long tricolon (4–5–4 in MT!) about the kings, which balances the four lines about the many. *Dahood ('Phoenician Elements') also links this phrase with v. 14aα and then again refers the yiqtol verb to the past, but it is more difficult to relate that to what follows. Shutting the mouth could be a further expression of appalment, but if we do take the yiqtol as having future reference, here more likely it suggests restraint, respect, and submission (e.g. Job 5:16; and cf 49.7).

The LXX again renders the qatal verbs as futures, and here they surely do refer to future events (cf *DG* 59); the seeing and considering have not yet taken place, but their being qatal reflects the fact that they will precede and lead to the shutting of the mouth which v. 14aβ describes. The prophet's promise contains an ellipse, a jump in the rhetoric: not 'they will hear what they have not heard' but 'they will see what they have not [even] heard'. The experience of seeing and hearing (see, e.g., 6.9–10; 40.21, 28; 42.20; 52.7–10) is extended from Israel to the nations.

יקפצו: 1QIs[a] וקפצו (see on 43.9).
אשר (both times): 1QIs[a] את אשר. Contrast the LXX and Vg, which take the אשר to refer to the kings ('those who have not been told of him [supplied from the context: *HUB*] will see and those who have not heard will understand'). On independent relative clauses introduced by אשר, see on 41.8a.

53.1. Who believed what we heard? Upon whom did the arm of Yhwh reveal itself? The LXX begins κύριε ('Lord'), providing its answer to the question who is now addressed (cf John 12.38; Rom 10.16). But who now speaks? Is it the nations and kings, who speak of what they have indeed now heard (v. 15)? Verse 15 admittedly attributed silence rather than speech to them, and said that they saw rather than heard, but this contradiction would be only of a superficial kind. And the nations have admittedly not spoken before, but it would be typical of the prophet to introduce a novel note at this novel moment. On the other hand, the speaker(s) eventually refer(s) to 'my people' (v. 8). Further, in vv. 13–15 the nations' acknowledgment lies in the future and will be based on the servant's exaltation; while v. 1 might indicate that that future has come, the exaltation has not come, so that it is too soon for the nations to speak (†Stalker), or at least the whole of their speech has to be projected into the future.

Most significantly, (dis)belief in Yhwh's word is a motif which relates to the people of God, not to the nations, and they are the usual referents of 'we/us/our' (e.g. 40.8; 42.24; 47.4). The only obstacle to a simple identification of the speaker as Jacob–Israel is the occurrence of that expression 'my people', but it is entirely plausible to see that as marking the prophet's identifying with Jacob–Israel as happens in the passages just noted (cf especially 40.6–8). Verses 12–15 and 1–11aα thus express two responses to the servant, one on the part of nations and kings, the other on the part of Jacob–Israel. Of course neither response is yet actual; they take place in a vision.

Once more the prophet begins a subsection with a rhetorical 'Who?', which is followed by a qatal verb. The qatal can be used modally in rhetorical questions indicating astonishment and implying a negative answer, here 'Who would have ever believed' (see Gen 21.7; †Giesebrecht, p. 159; cf GK 106p). Admittedly †König questions the parallels and doubts whether the modal translation is ever compelling. But in any case the LXX's aorist ἐπίστευσε ('Who believed'; cf Vg) is the more obvious rendering. Presumably it constitutes an indirect acknowledgment by the speakers that they themselves had not at first believed what they were told about the servant, which on the prophet's account is of course true of their response to everything they had been told. Either way, the implied answer to the rhetorical question is 'No-one'. At the exodus, the people had believed (14.31), at least sometimes. Not so here.

The word *šᵉmûʿāh* ('what we heard') always denotes a report received rather than one given (even 28.9, 19); cf LXX τῇ ἀκοῇ ἡμῶν, Vg *auditui nostro*. What was the content of this report? In isolation the first colon might refer to the message which had come to the prophet (cf 28.9, 19) and the words might be the prophet's lament, though here, at least, the plural works against that. Or it might refer to many things outside the passage—earlier material in this book as a whole or material uttered in worship as happened in the Tammuz liturgy; this would presuppose that nations and kings speak here, though †Bentzen notes that they could hardly speak in such terms of something not previously heard.[13] In the context *šᵉmûʿāh* takes up the 'hearing' of v. 15, and behind that the people who cause others to hear about the baring of Yhwh's arm (52.7–10)—to which v. 1b then refers. This in itself hints that the report is the one we are about to have amplified in vv. 1–11aα.

For one might have thought that a revelation of Yhwh's arm was inescapable, but v. 1b presupposes that this need not be so. It asks its question in subtle fashion. The preposition is *ʿal*; elsewhere it is *l* or *ʾel* (cf 52.10, and 1QIsᵇ here), to which Morgenstern (*VT* 11, p. 315) emends the MT. Thus here Aq, Th, and Sym have ἐπὶ τίνα for LXX's τίνι. 'To' is a possible meaning of *ʿal*, but *ʿal* is not the obvious preposition to use to convey this meaning. In 52.14–15 *ʿal* meant 'at' or 'because of', while *Dahood ('Phoenician Elements')

[13] See further Bentzen, *Messias*, pp. 54–56 (ET pp. 56–58, with additions).

renders 'before', but other meanings fit better here. In 42.13 *ʿal* denoted 'against', so that the preposition might raise the question whether Yhwh's arm *has* been raised against Babylon (52.10)—or whether it has been raised against the servant (cf 53.4–6, esp. 5b). But the much more common meaning of *ʿal* is 'on': see especially 52.7. Alongside the question who received the message is the question where did the revelation come. Given where the revelation came (in this humiliated servant), it is not surprising that the people failed to see it. *Nyberg (pp. 48–49) nicely runs the two cola together, 'Who could have believed what we heard [about] the one on whom Yhwh's arm revealed itself', but this seems to require *mî* to function as a relative pronoun.

Yhwh's arm is here virtually hypostatized and is the subject of a verb as in 40.10 (cf also 48.14, and the address to Yhwh's arm in 51.9); contrast 52.10 and 42.11. The revelation is indeed a revelation of Yhwh, but it is a revelation of a part of Yhwh in some sense representing Yhwh and distinguishable from Yhwh.

Verse 1 is used to interpret the rejection of Jesus in John 12.37–38 and Rom 10.16. *Evans indeed sees John 12.1–43 as a midrash on 52.7–53.12.

53.2aαβ. He grew before him like a sucker or a root out of dry ground. After the *w*-clause in v. 1b explaining the implicit answer to the question in v. 1a, a *w*-consecutive then opens v. 2 and introduces the sequence of verbs which follows. The LXX and Syr omit the *w*, and it might simply be the idiomatic introduction to a narrative, with no particular connection with what proceeds (cf GK 111f; JM 118k). †Marti suggests that it conveys a sense of astonishment, as initial 'And' can in English. The KJV's 'for' gives the *w* a similar significance to the *w* in v. 1b: it is implicitly an epexegetical *w*-consecutive answering the question in v. 1b and/or continuing the explanation of that in v. 1a (cf *IBHS* 33.2.2; *TTH* 76; GK 111d; JM 118j; *DG* 78: Gen 31.26 is a parallel in following on a question). Indeed †Budde emends to 'for he grew' (*kî ʿālāh*).

The suggestion that the *w* makes no particular connection with what precedes is difficult in the light of the fact that neither v. 2a nor what follows identifies the subject of its verb. If it were not for the *w*, we might assume that the subject is some unnamed person; but the *w*-consecutive points to a continuing reference to what precedes. The subject of the verb, then, is the servant who was the subject of 52.13–15. In turn that confirms the reference of the 'upon whom' in v. 1b. That, too, must refer to the servant, the subject of 52.13–15, rather than (e.g.) to Babylon. The antecedent of 'he' is the 'whom' of v. 1b, which itself refers back to the 'him' of vv. 14–15, the 'my servant' of v. 13. Verses 2–3 will begin to explain why 'we' could not believe the prophet's message or recognize Yhwh's arm at work.

Initially this is expressed by means of a figure. The verb *ʿālāh* already implies the image of a plant growing; it is not used of human beings 'growing', as it is of plant growth. Its literal meaning 'ascend' is reflected in Aq, Th ἀναβήσεται, also Sym ἀνέβη—which *Hegermann sees as intended to refer to Christ (on the LXX, see the note). There is no reason to take v. 2a to describe the servant's youth. More likely it describes his ministry.

This plant grew 'before him'. Again there is the question of an antecedent, which we take to be 'Yhwh' in v. 1b. Both third person pronouns thus continue from the preceding line and from vv. 13–15. †Klostermann suggested that *lᵉpānāyw* rather means 'before himself', that is, 'straight up', and compares Jer 49.5; but there it means something more like 'straight down'. †Ehrlich rather compares with *negdô* ('straight ahead'; Josh 6.5, 20) and *Gordon provides Syriac parallels, but that again seems inapposite; the term needs to suggest an essentially upward direction. Such explanations seem both inappropriate and unnecessary. The common expression would surely be understood to have its usual meaning (cf *Driver, who was once attracted to Klostermann's understanding but apparently later abandoned it).

There are some striking parallels to the use of the phrase here. We have noted that the expression 'before Yhwh' comes 49 times in Leviticus 1–16. In Hos 6.2 'before him' denotes Israel's beginning a new life before Yhwh (†Bonnard). In Gen 10.9 Nimrod is a mighty warrior 'before Yhwh' (†Grimm and Dittert). But it seems more significant that the expression commonly suggests 'under his eye'. In the context of the plant simile, it hardly implies 'under his surveillance' and therefore with his own eye fixed on God and aware of his holy calling (e.g. Gen 6.11, 13; 7.1; 17.1; †Duhm). Rather it implies that he was watched over by God (e.g. Ps 61.8 [7]).

The servant grows before Yhwh 'like a sucker' (*yônēq*). The word elsewhere denotes a baby boy; the feminine equivalent is more common with this meaning, being applied to ordinary people in Job 8.16; 14.7; 15.30, to a people in Hos 14.7 [6]; Ps 80.12 [11], and to a king in Ezek 17.22. The prophet presumably chose to use the masculine form in order to apply it to the male figure of the servant. The LXX, Aq, Th, and Syr pardonably infer that it refers to a child as a suckling (the LXX renders παιδίον, Aq τι[τ]θιζόμενον, Th θηλάζον, Syr *ylwdʾ*) and †Eusebius 3.2 [97c–98a] perceives a mysterious allusion to the miraculous nature of Jesus's birth; contrast Sym κλάδος, Vg *virgultum* ('shoot'), Tg *lblbyn dprn* ('shoots which sprout'), though such terms could also be seen as messianic. 'Root' (*šōreš*) can similarly apply to an ordinary individual, to a people, or to a king (e.g. Job 8.17; Ps 80.10 [9]; Isa 11.1, 10).

The first, rarer word thus usually appears in the company of the second. Etymologically the first suggests a sucker, a shoot from a plant's root rather than from its stem. Presumably the same is true of the second word, though *Dahood ('Phoenician Elements') assumes that the two words rather complement each other, referring to a shoot above (cf Ezek 17.22) and a root below. In contrast, H. L. Ginsberg suggests that *šōreš* can refer to the bottom part of a tree trunk which is above the ground and not just to the part below the ground,[14] so that both words might refer to growth above ground, but only 11.1 suggests this meaning for *šōreš* and that occurrence may be an instance of metonymy.[15]

Until we come to the end of the line, we would naturally take it to indicate that the servant developed a ministry which manifested God's care and blessing. But at the end it transpires that the growth takes place 'out of ground that is dry' and therefore not very healthily. This begins to explain why people would not find it easy to believe that he was the locus of Yhwh's revelation. The Tg infers that the line describes a flourishing growth which belies the nature of the ground in which it takes place, but it is significant that its paraphrase has to reverse the imagery. Its '. . .like a tree which sends its roots by streams of water' reminds us of the contrast with Ps 1.3. The Tg then adds interpretatively 'so holy generations will increase in the land that needed him [the servant]'.

ויעל: extant LXX MSS have ἀνηγγείλαμεν ('we announced') (cf †Rahlfs), which is difficult to explain as a rendering of the Hebrew. Ziegler (*Isaias*) sees it as an inner-Greek corruption of an original ἀνετείλε μέν.
לפניו: †Ewald suggested לפנינו ('before us'), †Marti לפנים ('previously'), †Lindblom לפני ('before me': dittog.), †Volz יפה לא ('unlovely'), Mowinckel (*He That Cometh*, p. 197) בחרבה ('in dry ground'), *Schwarz (*ZAW* 83) מפנה ('from a battlement').
מארץ: LXX and Th ἐν γῇ, Tg בארעא ('in the earth') imply ב for מ.

53.2aγb. He had no look, no majesty so that we should look at him, no appearance so that we should want him. The next line confirms the meaning of the previous one. It makes three parallel statements about him. These could be read as a 2–2–2 or 3–3–3 line (see the note on the middle colon), but it is also noteworthy that (visually, at least) each of these cola is slightly longer than the preceding one. The negative *lōʾ* in each colon instead of *ʾên* (usual in a noun clause) conveys some emphasis (GK 152d), suggesting that the servant 'was the very reverse of attractive' (†North). The three statements take up two terms from v. 14 and also specify that he had no 'majesty', no royal dignity.

While the Tg might have continued to relate v. 2 to the people, as it did the similar phrases in 52.14, instead it reverses their meaning, as it did in v. 2aαβ. The unusual appearance of the servant makes him superhuman rather than subhuman: 'his appearance is not a common appearance and reverence for him is not an ordinary reverence, and his face will be a holy face, so that everyone who sees him will consider him'.

[14] '"Roots Below and Fruit Above"', in *Hebrew and Semitic Studies* (G. R. Driver Festschrift, ed. D. W. Thomas and W. D. McHardy; Oxford/New York, 1963), pp. 72–76 (see pp. 74–75). Cf *Millard.

[15] Cf J. Becker, 'Wurzel und Wurzelspross', in *BZ* 20 (1976), pp. 22–44 (see pp. 26–27).

ולא הדר: 1QIsa ולא הדר לו, conforming to previous cl. †Marti omits.

ונראהו: 1QIsa has ונראנו. †Duhm omits. MT's *athnach* on the preceding word implies something like '…nor majesty. We looked at him, and he had no appearance, but we wanted him'. †M. B. Cohen (pp. 9–11) suggests that the MT is seeking to reduce any implication that the servant was deeply degraded, a desire taken further in the Tg which sees the vb as ירא rather than ראה. But Sym ἵνα ἰδῶμεν αὐτὸν works with the parallelism between this vb and the one which closes v. 2 and rhymes with it (cf Vg). The *athnach* thus needs moving, though not onto this word (*Thomas), but rather to the end of v. 2aαβ which marks the mid-point of v. 2. If we were also to hyphenate ולא־הדר to parallel the approach in the first and third cola (or to remove each maqqeph from those cola) we would have a neat 2–2–2 (or a 3–3–3) line. For the consecutive cl. construction (ו plus jussive/cohortative), see GK 166a. *DG* 87 rather sees it as purpose. LXX's καὶ εἴδομεν αὐτόν, καὶ οὐκ εἶχεν εἶδος οὐδὲ κάλλος divides the line as the MT but presupposes a ו consec and paraphrases the second colon (rather than implying a different text?—see †Ziegler, p. 128); cf Vg and Syr. *Dahood ('Phoenician Elements') renders 'that we should envy him'.

ונחמדהו: 1QIsa again has a נו suffix. Syr *wdglnyhy* ('and we disowned him') paraphrases out of uncertainty (*Hegermann; and see *HUB*). Following the MT's construing of the preceding clauses, †Rashi interprets this verb as a question, 'Now shall we desire him?' †Qimchi takes the negative in v. 2a to apply here too—'and we did not want him'.

53.3a. …despised and most frail of human beings, a man of great suffering, experienced in weakness. The LXX takes v. 3 as an independent sentence ('He was…'), but in that case in a participial clause we would expect 'he' to be expressed. In GK 116s, most of the examples where the pronoun is omitted are clauses introduced by a particle such as *hinnēh* or *kî*, though one spectacular exception is Job 12.17–25 (see also Isa 40.22–23?). The Vg and Aq rather take it as a series of phrases dependent on v. 2b and thus an illustration of the prophet's fondness for enjambment.

Once more the description of the servant as 'despised' takes up that of the people (cf esp. 49.7). The subsequent *w* is perhaps then explicative, suggesting 'despised as…'.[16] But 'most frail of human beings' is a difficult expression. The verb *ḥādal* means to refrain or cease from an act or from a person (cf Exod 14.12; Job 7.16; 19.14); cf LXX ἐκλεῖπον, Tg *ypsyq*. The adjective might thus here mean 'ceasing from human beings'.[17] G. R. Driver compares 2.22.[18] The idea could link with the coming picture of the servant as like a person with skin disease, though the term is not used of such a person's confinement and the expression is allusive. Further, there is little other indication that the servant turned away from people. Rather people turned away from him (cf v. 3b). 'Rejected by human beings' would thus make

[16] M. Dahood, *Proverbs and Northwest Semitic Philology* (Rome, 1963), p. 59.

[17] See D. W. Thomas, 'Some Observations on the Hebrew Root חדל', in *Volume de Congrès: Strasbourg 1956* (*VT* Sup 4, 1957), pp. 8–16.

[18] 'Linguistic and Textual Problems', in *JTS* 38 (1937), pp. 36–50 (see pp. 48–49).

better sense, but it is hard to get this meaning out of the expression. †Rignell suggests 'lacking human beings', which would make good sense if the servant were afflicted Israel (†Mettinger, p. 40). P. Calderone's suggestion that the adjective means 'fat' and thus 'stupid' seems to build speculation on speculation.[19]

We have rather followed the use of the adjective in Ps 39.5 [4] to mean 'ceasing' in the sense of transient or frail (cf †Luzzatto). And we have followed translations such as Sym's ἐλάχιστος ἀνδρῶν ('least of men'), Syr *mkykʾ dʾnšʾ* ('[most] lowly of men'); also LXX's παρὰ πάντας ἀνθρώπους (†Qimchi) which assume that the adjective is turned into a superlative by the subsequent plural (see *IBHS* 14.5, and on the omission of the article in verse, n. 30); cf also the Vg's *novissimum virorum*, which †van der Kooij (p. 303) sees as reflecting Christian convictions. The genitive is then not objective or subjective but defining.

The first phrase in the second colon supports this understanding. 'A man of much suffering' is literally 'a man of sufferings/pains' and the expression thus complements 'a frail one of men': the word for 'human beings/men' reappears in the singular, another construct introducing a defining genitive in the plural. In parallelism with *makʾōbôt* is *ḥōlî*, which commonly means 'illness': cf Sym νόσῳ. But the context speaks more explicitly of harm from other people than of disease. The noun and the verb *ḥālāh* do occasionally mean 'wound' (significantly 1.5) and this would thus fit well. But more often the noun denotes 'weakness' (cf LXX μαλακίαν, Vg *infirmitatem*).

Whereas *ḥădal* has been interpreted as passive though it looks active, *y*^{e}*dûaʿ* has been interpreted as active ('knowing weakness') though it looks passive ('known by/to/for weakness'): cf the other occurrences in Deut 1.13, 15 and Tg *mzmn* ('destined'). So the LXX has εἰδὼς φέρειν μαλακίαν, Syr *ydʿ ḥšʾ*, Vg *scientem infirmitatem*; contrast Aq γνωστὸν ἀρρωστίᾳ, Th γνωστὸς μαλακίᾳ, Sym γνωστὸς νόσῳ. 'Acquainted with weakness' presupposes that the verb is one of a small number of instances where the passive participle expresses 'a state which is the result of the subject's own action'; cf 26.3; Ps 103.14; Cant 3.8 (*DG* 113, remark 6). GK 50f, 84^{a}m goes further in drawing attention to other examples of *qātûl* forms which cannot be taken as passive participles; it sees them as instances of a distinct *qātûl* ('ground-form'). 1QIs^{a} offers the active *wywdʿ* (cf 1QIs^{b} *wydʿ* [?]), but that looks like a correction. G. R. Driver (see above) saw this as an instance of *yādaʿ* II and took it to mean 'humbled',[20] but the Arabic basis of this theory has now been demolished.[21]

[19] See 'Supplementary Note on *ḥdl* ii', in *CBQ* 24 (1962), pp. 412–19 (see pp. 416–19).

[20] Cf, e.g., J. A. Emerton, 'A Consideration of Some Alleged Meanings of ידע in Hebrew', in *JSS* 15 (1970), pp. 145–80 (see pp. 175–76); *DCH* under ידע II.

[21] See W. Johnstone, '*ydʿ* ii, "be humbled, humiliated"?', in *VT* 41 (1991), pp. 49–62; cf J. A. Emerton, 'A Further Consideration of D. W. Thomas's Theories about *yādaʿ*', in *VT* 41 (1991), pp. 145–63. See already J. Reider, 'Etymological Studies: ידע or ירע and רעע', in *JBL* 66 (1947), pp. 315–7; D. F. Payne, 'Old Testament Exegesis and the Problem of Ambiguity', in *ASTI* 5 (1966–67), pp. 48–68 (see pp. 60–62).

The Tg apparently begins by taking the 'human beings' as the subject of the sentence; it assumes they are people in general and that the verse speaks of the way 'the splendour of all their kingdoms' will be for contempt and will cease. 'They will be sick and afflicted' like a person of suffering, one destined for sickness, despised and not esteemed, like Israel when God's face was hidden from it. That might be seen as the converse of the promise in Deut 7.15 that the 'dread diseases of Egypt' will be turned away from Israel. *Ceresko (pp. 49–50) notes that the description of the servant as 'experienced in weakness' takes up the language there applied to Israel's suffering in Egypt, where the people 'experienced' such 'weakness'.

נבזה: LXX reads ἀλλὰ τὸ εἶδος αὐτοῦ ἄτιμον: an expanded translation taking up the n. from v. 2 (†Ziegler, p. 77).
אישים: the rare form of the pl., Phoenician according to *Dahood ('Phoenician Elements'), generates an alliteration with s. איש (1QIs[a] ואיש) which follows (†Torrey). Hummel ([see on 40.17], p. 101) identifies an enclitic ם on the s. noun.
מכאבות: 1QIs[b] מכאבים, assimilating to v. 4a. LXX's ἐν πληγῇ assimilates to v. 4b.
וידוע: J. Reider (see footnote) emends to וירוע ('and weakened [by suffering]'); see BDB, p. 438b.

53.3b. As when people hide their face from someone, he was despised and we did not esteem him. Syntactically the line continues to depend on what precedes: literally, 'and like the hiding of the face by/from him/us, despised, whom we did not esteem'.

In the first colon, preposition and suffix are both ambiguous. The LXX refers the phrase to the servant's hiding his face from us (cf Vg). †Cheyne suggests this would be because he had a skin disease, but there are no parallels for such a meaning; a person with a skin disease had to warn people of the danger of pollution through contact (Lev 13.45), but not to hide the face—which would risk the opposite effect. In 50.6 it referred to refusing to face attack and shaming, and †Whybray links v. 3 as a whole to the consequences of the prophet's arrest and ill-treatment by the Babylonians because of his work as a prophet. †Qimchi sees this hiding as a reflection of Israel's shame in exile, and this at least draws our attention to the fact that while the speakers themselves will in due course identify this suffering as undertaken because of them or for their sake, it was not undertaken instead of them.

Hiding the face is more commonly an act of rejection, and in this context *min* regularly refers to that from which someone hides (e.g. 8.17; 54.8). The Tg's 'as when the face of the Presence was taken up from us' implies that God was the subject of the 'hiding'; God's face was hidden 'from him' (cf Aq, Th, Sym; *Heller). This is indeed the usual connotation of the phrase (see, e.g., 59.2, with absolute 'face'; also 8.17; 54.8; 64.6 [7]; Ps 13.2 [1]), but the context here refers to human reactions to the servant. This understanding is confirmed by the repetition from the opening of the verse in the second colon.

כְּמַסְתֵּר: perhaps a composite hi form combining the ptpl מַסְתִּיר (cf 1QIs[a]) and inf הַסְתֵּר. With Tg's 'taken' might be compared LXX and Syr's 'turned'; in Isaiah they regularly translate הסתיר reverentially, as if it were הסיר (contrast Vg) (Rowlands, *VT* 9, pp. 188–89). Aq ὡς ἀποκεκρυμμένον might suggest ho ptpl כְּמֻסְתָּר (†Marti). †Ehrlich emends to נסתיר [פנינו]. †Zillessen suggests כִּי מִסְתַּר.
נבזה: 1QIs[b] ונבזה; 1QIs[a] ונבוזהו, perhaps a form of בזז ('and we despoiled him'—though NEB renders 'we despised him', presumably parsing as from בוז rather than בזה); cf Syr *wšṭnyhy* ('and we attacked/despised him'?) Perhaps each time (49.7; 53.3a, 3b) the prophet hoped the audience would hear overtones of בזז (cf †Miscall). †Ehrlich emends to ונבזהו.
לא: M. Dahood sees as a noun meaning '[we considered him] nothing', comparing BDB, p. 520a.[22]

53.4a. Yet it was our weaknesses that he bore. Our great suffering—he carried it. 'Weakness' and 'suffering' reappear from v. 3, though the 'yet' (*ʾākēn*) with which the line begins advertises that vv. 4–6 testify to a new understanding of these which the speakers have now come to.

'Bore our weaknesses' is an allusive expression. 'Our weaknesses' comes first, before the verb. The pronoun *hûʾ* (strictly 'he') then follows; it also functions to draw attention to the contrast between what people originally thought and what they now realize, perhaps by adding emphasis to the preceding suffix 'our' (so †Rosenbaum, pp. 82–83), perhaps by contrasting with it (so Geller, 'Cleft Sentences', p. 31); compare the further 'unnecessary' pronouns in vv. 4b, 5a. The patterning of the word endings in v. 4 is also noteworthy: *-ênû* twice in v. 4a, then *-nû*, *-nuhû*, and *-unneh* in v. 4b.

In what sense did the servant 'bear' (*nāśāʾ*) the speakers' weaknesses and 'carry' (*sābal*) their great suffering? Matthew 8.17 applies this verse to Jesus's taking away people's pains, but *nāśāʾ* is not otherwise used metaphorically with this meaning. The context rather suggests that he shared in the experience of them when he did not need to do so, in the manner of Jeremiah.

For 'bore our weaknesses', the LXX has 'he bears our sins', which might have suggested the influence of Christian stress on sin subsequent to Matt 8.17 (*Euler); but the Tg similarly has 'he will pray concerning our transgressions'. More likely the translations assimilate to the stress on sin elsewhere in the section (†Ziegler, pp. 24–25; *Hegermann), including vv. 11–12 where the tense also changes from qatal to yiqtol. But they may also point towards another possible implication of the line. Does it imply that the suffering that comes to him is caused by the people's sin in the sense that they inflict it on him?

[22] 'Hebrew–Ugaritic Lexicography iv', in *Bib* 47 (1966), pp. 403–19 (see p. 408).

ומכאבינו: †Thomas adds הוא with 20 MSS, Syr, Vg (*ipse*). But Vg and Syr also repeat הוא in a similar way in v. 11b. †Thomas's suggestion apparently arises from metrical considerations. The extraposition of the subject and the resumptive suffix have the effect of signalling pause (Khan, *Studies*, p. 92). The word is now in its more usual m. form.

53.4b. ...when we ourselves had esteemed him smitten, struck by God, afflicted. The link and the contrast with what has preceded continues. 'We ourselves' stands in counterpoint to 'he himself' (the Tg makes 'we' the subject of the descriptions here—we were esteemed smitten, struck, afflicted). Each time the pronoun is expressed; we follow *TTH* 160 in seeing this line as a circumstantial clause. 'Esteemed' takes up the last verb in v. 3: 'we did not esteem him, or rather we esteemed him in the following way...'. The link and contrast continues further in the three subsequent participial expressions, though they also suddenly make explicit the explanation of what the speakers had previously thought was happening.

The verb 'smite', lit. 'touch' (*nāgaʿ*), recurs in Job to denote God's 'touching' someone with devastating results: for example, 19.21, which Bastiaens ('Language of Suffering' [see on 52.14a], p. 429) thinks is a reminiscence of this verse. For the pregnant use of the participle without the agency being identified, cf Ps 73.14 (also the pual in v. 5), though here the agency is made explicit in the parallel colon. In 2 Kgs 15.5 the verb refers to being afflicted with skin disease, and the related noun *negaʿ* (cf v. 8) can refer to skin disease (see Lev 13–14), though this is hardly enough to indicate that the servant has skin disease (cf Vg *leprosum*). Further, this would have been visible and not a matter of what people 'esteemed' (*Driver).

The second verb (*nākāh* ho; 1QIs^a, LXX, Syr prefix with a copula) explicitly suggests hitting or beating someone, but it can also suggest being hit by disease (e.g. Deut 28.22, 27, 35). Here it is explicit that God is the agent. In such phrases the word for God sometimes suggests a superlative, so that the phrase might mean 'dreadfully beaten'.[23] But it would be pointless for the speakers to say that they esteemed him dreadfully beaten when there was no question of that; what is new in their confession is their recognition of the cause of this, not the fact of it (*Clines, p. 17). The references to God's agency in vv. 1, 6, and 10 also support the assumption that 'struck of God' is a genitive indicating agency (cf GK 116l; *IBHS* 9.5.1; *HS* 45; JM 121p; *DG* 33). Admittedly such use of the absolute word for 'God' is unusual; there are no other occurrences in Isaiah 47–55 and †Kaiser asks whether it might mean 'gods', as in 41.23. A consideration here may be that *ʾĕlōhîm* ends with *m*; each word in the colon thus begins or ends with *m*, as each of the four main words in the next line will begin with *m*. The incorporation of the construct at this point has the effect of defamiliarizing the hendiadys (†Rosenbaum, pp. 153–56).

[23] D. W. Thomas, 'A Consideration of Some Unusual Ways of Expressing the Superlative in Hebrew', in *VT* 3 (1953), pp. 209–24.

The LXX omits ‘[by] God’, perhaps for theological reasons that reflect the dualism of the Hellenistic period (cf v. 10) (Lust, *Bijdragen* 40 [1979], p. 13; S. E. Porter and B. W. R. Pearson, ‘Isaiah Through Greek Eyes’, in †Broyles and Evans, pp. 531–546 [see p. 538]); contrast Aq, Th, Sym.

נגוע: on Aq ἀφημένον, see *Hegermann, and on Sym ἐν ἀφῇ ὄντα, see †van der Kooij, p. 237.

53.5a. . . .when he was someone wounded because of our rebellions, crushed because of our wrongdoings. After the opening *w* (omitted by Syr) and pronoun, the line comprises two participles and two nouns prefixed by the preposition *min*. Thus all four main words begin with m, and each of the cola closes with the suffix *-ēnû/-ênû*.

The *w* introducing a participial clause suggests that v. 5a is another circumstantial clause (cf GK 141e), which restates v. 4a. For ‘wounded’ (*mᵉḥōlāl*) Syr has *mtqṭl* (‘killed’). J. P. Brown suggests that the verb refers to impalement, a frequent form of execution for political crimes in the ancient world.[24] But it is not the usual word, and *Ceresko’s suggestion (pp. 45–46) that it was used to avoid attracting the authorities’ attention seems fanciful. For ‘crushed’ (*mᵉdukkāʾ*; 1QIs[a b]; Syr again prefix with *w*—cf LXX), The LXX has μεμαλάκισται (‘made sick’). †North takes the line to refer to the servant’s inner identification with people, but the recurrence of several of the words in the line in Psalm 88 and in Lam 3.30–34 argues against that.

In what sense does he suffer ‘because of’ (*min*) them? This might simply mean that as Israel had been struck by God and had experienced weakness or wounding for its rebelling and for its wrongdoing (1.2–6), so the servant is also wounded and crushed ‘because of’ these. He shares in that experience. The preposition then denotes the ‘remoter cause’ of something (cf BDB, p. 580a). But the passage implies that there is more to his suffering than merely sharing theirs. The further possibility is that *min* denotes ‘the immediate or efficient cause’. Their rebellion and wrongdoing found one expression in attacks on him (cf the discussion in †Orlinsky, pp. 57–58).

This time the Tg takes the subject of v. 5a to be the temple, defiled and abandoned in AD 70 because of Israel’s sin; the Tg then prefaces the verse with a promise of its restoration based on one concerning the Branch in Zech 6.13 (*Hegermann): ‘He will build the sanctuary that was defiled. . .’. This promise might presuppose a double reading of the first participle in v. 5, understood to suggest both wounded and defiled (*HUB*; and see the following note).

[24] ‘Techniques of Imperial Control’, in *The Bible and Liberation* (ed. N. K. Gottwald and A. C. Wire; Berkeley, 1976), pp. 73–83 = *The Bible and Liberation* (ed. N. K. Gottwald; Maryknoll, NY, 1983), pp. 357–77 (see p. 374).

מְחֹלָל: Aq βεβηλωμένος, Tg אִיתְחַל link with חלל III ('defile') rather than חלל I. This would give good sense and a good link with 43.28 and 47.6: the servant shares in the deserved defilement of leadership and people as a whole. But one would then expect
מְחֻלָּל (cf †Marti) and the parallelism supports LXX's rendering ἐτραυματίσθη. †Qimchi rather links with חיל (cf v. 10).
מִפְּשָׁעֵינוּ: so C and other Masoretic MSS (see *HUB*), also 1QIs[a b]. A and L have מִפְּשָׁעֵנוּ ('because of our rebellion'); cf v. 8.

53.5b. Chastisement to bring us well-being was on him; by means of his beating, there was healing for us. The line stands at the centre of vv. 2–9 and sums up the realization they express. 1QIs[a] and Tg begin with *w* ('and') but this probably assimilates to verses on either side. In the MT the line begins with yet another word beginning *m* and another word whose stem ends *m* and which then ends with the suffix *-ēnû*, while the third word ('on him') refers back to the opening word in v. 5 ('when he'). While the second colon could have continued the pattern, instead continuity with variety is achieved by a colon that has parallel meaning to the first but has a different structure. This involves another prepositional expression, but with *b* rather than *min*, and an impersonal verbal idiom that makes the line close with the further prepositional expression 'for us' which compares and contrasts with the opening 'when he' and also takes up the *-nû* ending of each of the cola in v. 5a and of (lit.) 'our well-being' in the first colon here. In sound, 'for us' (*lānû*) also generates a repetition in *kullānû* ('all of us'), the first word of v. 6, and also its last word.

The question of 'well-being' was left unresolved at the end of chapter 48. Here well-being for the people is brought about by the servant's 'chastisement' (*mûsār*: 1QIs[a] again prefixes with *w*). The RSV renders 'punishment', but the word does not especially suggest the action of a court undertaken for the sake of justice. It is more a word for the disciplining of a pupil by a teacher or a child by a parent with a view to the recipient's growth or reform. The LXX renders παιδεία ('education'); the Tg's 'by his teaching his well-being will multiply upon us' assumes that the discipline is the teaching itself. †Kaiser compares Gen 50.20 with v. 5a; one might also see Joseph as someone who experiences chastisement and wounding to bring other people well-being and healing.

For 'by means of', *Zimmerli (p. 238) suggests 'at the cost of' (*b* of price; cf BDB, p. 90a). For such use of the commercial metaphor, see Josh 6.26 and 1 Chr 12.19. But there is insufficient hint that the commercial metaphor is operating here, and more natural and frequent parallels are the use of *b* to denote that by means of which people may be delivered (e.g. 1 Sam 14.7) or by means of which they may die (e.g. the sword: Jer 21.9). Paradoxically, the means of death has become the means of deliverance.

EVV have a plural for 'his beating', taking the singular as collective (cf BDB). The plural of *ḥabburāh* would comprise a natural complement to the masculine singular 'chastisement', and 1QIs[a] *ḥbwrtyw* with its suffix for a plural noun may imply plural (*Dahood, 'Phoenician Elements', p. 68). Perhaps this consideration was overriden by the desire to make a link with 1.6; at least this is the effect of the use of the singular here. The healing of which v. 5b speaks is the restoration of a wounded people.

The Tg's 'By our attachment to his words our transgressions will be forgiven us' starts from the more common meaning of *ḥbr* ('unite, join'). The Syr also closes with a future verb, implying the idea that forgiveness is a gift that belongs to the End (*Hegermann; cf Rom 11.27).

שלומנו: J. Weir (see †Cheyne) suggests שִׁלּוּמֵנוּ ('our retribution'); Gerleman ('Die Wurzel', p. 10) sees this as the meaning of MT. On the genitive of purpose or effect, see GK 128q; *IBHS* 9.5.2c; *HS* 44.
נרפא לנו: on the passive construction, see GK 121a; *IBHS* 11.2.10g, 23.2.2e; JM 128ba, 132f. †Graetz reads מַרְפֵּא ('healing').

53.6a. All of us had wandered like sheep. We had turned, each person, to their own way. As 'all of us' forms an *inclusio* round the verse as a whole, so perhaps does this reference to wandering in the first colon and the reference to 'wrongdoing' in the last colon, for the two roots overlap in form and meaning (*tāʿāh* and *ʿāwōn* from *ʿāwāh*: if there are two roots *ʿāwāh*, they themselves overlap in meaning). In contrast, the LXX repeats the verb πλανάομαι ('wander') in the second colon from the first. The Tg sees this wandering to refer to the people's scattering in exile; it is influenced by Zech 13.7 (the two passages appear together in the NT: see *Hegermann).

כצאן: for the article in comparisons, see GK 126o; *DG* 31.

53.6b. And Yhwh let the wrongdoing of all of us fall upon him. The MT construes this as a 3–3 line by giving the object marker a stress of its own. This is an unlikely reading, but even so the line is visibly shorter than the the closing line of any other subsection. The object marker is very unusual in poetry; it adds to the distinctive emphasis of the colon's sparseness.

The verb is *pāgaʿ* (hi). It is a unique usage, though one explicable as a metaphorical extension of the qal. Sym thus renders literally, κύριος δὲ καταντῆσαι ἐποίησεν εἰς αὐτὸν τὴν ἀνομίαν πάντων ἡμῶν ('but the Lord made to arrive at him the lawlessness of us all'). The qal means 'meet', in friendly or hostile fashion; it is often used with the preposition *b*, as here, particularly when the verb denotes a hostile encounter. The people's point is then that Yhwh causes or allows their wrongdoing/responsibility/penalty to meet or hit the servant. The Tg renders 'But before Yhwh it was a delight to forgive the transgressions of us all for his sake' (the LXX and Syr also have a plural noun).

The LXX's rendering paraphrases but expresses the point well, παρέδωκεν αὐτὸν ταῖς ἁμαρτίαις ἡμῶν ('he gave him over to our sins'). The Vg expresses it more literally, *posuit in eo iniquitatem omnium nostrum* ('he placed on him all our iniquity').

את: Mowinckel (*He That Cometh*, p. 197) emends to האתהו ('brought on him'); Elliger also assumes that the text is corrupt ('Textkritisches', pp. 115–19).

53.7aα. He was put in subjection, though he was one who would let himself be afflicted and who would not open his mouth. Verses 7–9 make it quite explicit that the suffering the vision describes was humanly wrought. The first verb is a niphal, like the verb which opened v. 3, which puts us on the track of the fact that in the chiasm vv. 7–9 as a whole correspond to vv. 2–3 and take up its themes. In the qal the finite verb *nāgaś* ('put in subjection') regularly means 'exact' and has money or work as its object; †Lowth thus renders 'It [the punishment]' was exacted'. This would make for a good transition to the following clause, where the pronoun *hû*ʾ can then be seen as marking the change of subject. But the other three occurrences of the niphal have a personal subject (3.5; 1 Sam 13.6; 14.24), and the qal participle ('overseers/taskmasters') often has a personal pronominal suffix. E. Lipiński suggests the translation 'seize', which can apply to property and people (*ThWAT* on *nāgaś*, III).

The noun clause that follows, introduced by *w*, is a circumstantial clause like v. 5a (see GK 141e, *TTH* 160; cf Vg *quia ipse voluit*). Its participle comes from a verb that already appeared in another participial form; it closed off v. 4, in another circumstantial clause preceding the one in v. 5a. But there the participle was pual and was thus undoubtedly passive. Here it is niphal, which could be of passive meaning (cf 58.10), but the move from pual to niphal suggests there might be a difference in meaning. The niphal is reflexive in Exod 10.3; the other occurrence in Ps 119.107 is ambiguous. Here 'submitted to affliction' makes good sense in the context (cf GK 51c; cf Vg; Sym αὐτὸς [ὑπ]ήκουσεν).

The Tg took the first verb as *nāgaš* ('draw near' and thus 'pray') rather than *nāgaś*: so also Vg *oblatus est quia ipse voluit*, which †van der Kooij (see p. 303) sees as reflecting Christian conviction; cf Sym προσηνέχθη; Syr *qrb*; on Th *audiens* (†Jerome), see *Hegermann. The LXX paraphrases the first two clauses καὶ αὐτὸς διὰ τὸ κεκακῶσθαι. *Elliger ('Textkritisches', pp. 116–17) infers that these two clauses in v. 7 need to be reversed.

The Tg then takes the second verb as *ʿānāh* I ('answer') rather than *ʿānāh* III, translating 'he was answered' (cf Heb 5.7), and understands the third clause to denote how this answer came before he had hardly opened his mouth in prayer. †Lowth combines this assumption with a non-passive understanding of the niphal, translating 'he was made answerable'. But that would be a unique meaning. 'Answered for himself' should perhaps be the meaning with *ʿānāh* I (cf GK 51c), but this would hardly fit with the subsequent colon; we might even say that the latter disambiguates this verb. In the context *ʿānāh* III is surely the verb that would come to an audience's mind.

The servant's acceptance of affliction is spelled out further in the second colon. He 'would not open his mouth' (LXX lacks the 'his', though not when the clause is repeated in v. 7b). He accepted his suffering with a strange silence. The verb is yiqtol, perhaps continuing the participial construction (cf GK 116x), or perhaps linking the continuous submission with the ever-repeated restraint over speech (cf *TTH* 31), or perhaps modal (G. I. Davies).

נגשׂ ו: †Torrey moves to the end of v. 6 as נִגָּשׂוֹ ('exacted of him').

53.7aβb. . . .like a lamb that is led to slaughter, like a ewe before her shearers. She is silent, and he would not open his mouth. The LXX begins the final clause οὕτως and thus reads these lines as the protasis and apodosis of a comparative clause ('As a lamb is led. . .so he would not. . .'; cf GK 161a), but this would require the conjunction *kaʾăšer* rather than the preposition *k* for 'as' (GK 155g). Further, the word order suggests that the verb is part of a relative clause, and the yiqtol fits with this. The LXX's understanding also gives a misleading impression of the comparison, which relates to the servant/sheep's silence, not his/its being led. In contrast, †McKenzie renders 'he was led like a lamb. . .', which has the advantage of providing the line with its own main verb, but is otherwise open to the same objections. The opening of the line must be a double simile. But it is difficult to take it as leading into 'he would not open his mouth', because the *w* on this verb is then odd. Further, in these chapters cola depending on a subsequent main clause are much less common than enjambment, lines dependent on a preceding main clause (e.g. participial clauses such as those in 46.3, 10–11, 12). More likely the MT is thus right to treat the first four cola of v. 7 together.

This leaves some questions about the last word in v. 7a, 'she is silent'. †Köhler deletes it to produce a regular 3–3 line. But we have noted that the metre of this poem as a whole is diverse rather than regular. The effect of the line as understood in the MT is a rhythmic surplus that implies an emphasis on the unexpected extra word matching the unexpected silence. The effect then continues in the further surplus of v. 7b (†Volz deletes), a closing isolated short colon that parallels the one that closes v. 6.

The Syr renders that last word of v. 7a by a masculine which suggests linking it with what follows (cf †Torrey); though *Hegermann sees the influence of the LXX which uses masculine (or neuter) words through v. 7, as does the Vg. *Dahood ('Phoenician Elements', p. 68) takes the word as an archaic third person form; in the context it seems more likely to be another feminine and thus to refer to the sheep. H. H. Rowley assumes that it then constitutes a one-word colon marked by a 'rhythmical incompleteness' like that in v. 6bβ,[25] but it surely links directly with what follows to form a straightforward 3-beat colon (like Job 4.16aα, to which Rowley refers). This might be the implication of the Vg's move from *sicut* to *quasi* for the second *k* in v. 7a. This could suggest that it sees the first *k* as introducing a clause but the second as introducing a phrase—because it links 'she is silent' with what follows. Elliger ('Textkritisches', p. 118) moves the word (emended) back into the previous line.

The Tg takes the line as a description of the fate of apparently powerful people before the Anointed, and thus prefaces the translation with 'the mighty ones of the peoples he will deliver up…' (*Hegermann compares 34.2).

כַּשֶּׂה: for asyndetic relative clauses following a noun prefixed by כ, see GK 155g, which proposes to repoint כְּשֶׂה; but for the article in comparisons, see on v. 6a.
טבח: for 'place of slaughter', one would expect מטבח (Isa 14.21; †Whitehouse). Rather cf LXX's σφαγὴν. 1QIs[a, b] have לטבוח. Sym renders θυσίαν (cf Th), which draws our attention to the fact that the Heb. is טבח not זבח (secular slaughter not religious slaughter or sacrifice).
וכרחל: 1QIs[a] omits the ו.
גזזיה: LXX, Vg, Syr have s.
נֶאֱלָמָה: the pausal form of the qatal, with the tone on the new penultimate syllable. The participle נֶאֱלָמָה keeps the stress on the final syllable.
יפתח: 1QIs[a] has פתח, recognizing that past reference is required (see on 43.9).

53.8a. He was taken by legal restraint, and who would complain at his generation? Every word in this line raises questions.

More literally the first colon reads 'from/by/without restraint and judgment he was taken'. The Syr begins from the most common meaning of *min* and renders 'from prison and from judgment he was led away', perhaps implying 'to death'. †North understands the verb thus and compares Prov 24.11, but there 'to death' is explicit. Indeed in Jer 39.14 being 'taken' from the court of the guard is a preliminary to something more like release. †Duhm assumes that the prophet refers to the servant's being taken to be with God, but the passages he compares (e.g. Gen 5.24) also make explicit that this is the point of this very common verb. 'Take' denotes being taken from life in Ezek 33.4, 6, and such a meaning may be assumed by Wis 4.11, but again the context makes the meaning clear; there it is the sword that 'takes'.

We have questioned the 'narrative' approach to the vision as a whole, and in particular the servant's 'story' does not move on through vv. 7–9. These verses offer several descriptions of the same experience, and v. 8a restates v. 7. The word *ʿōṣer* is then not a

[25] *Israel's Mission to the World* (London, 1939), p. 22; he also emends to the masculine, with Syr.

concrete word for prison but an abstract word (cf Ps 107.39; Prov 30.16); cf Vg *de angustia* ('from restraint'), also LXX's ἐν τῇ ταπεινώσει, Tg *myswryn* ('from chastisements', the people's suffering for their sins in exile, from which the servant delivers them). Some occurrences of the verb *ʿāṣar* might make possible a positive reference to the protective constraint that the law offers to the innocent person (cf the single use of the noun *ʿeṣer*, Judg 18.6, and the verb *ʿāṣar* in 1 Sam 9.17), but the other uses of *ʿōṣer* have negative implications; 'by constraint' rather than 'from constraint' therefore seems more likely. A stronger meaning such as 'oppression' would fit the usage in Ps 107.39,[26] but this is harder to fit with the collocation with 'judgment' that follows.

In chapters 40–49 *mišpāṭ* (here translated 'legal') usually referred to Yhwh's decision-making, but in chapters 50–55 it rather denotes a human activity (51.4 is the exception); the Tg has *pwrʿnw* ('retribution'). The servant has gone through the experience of being subjected to (quasi-)legal attack, has seemed to be overcome by it, but will triumph. The LXX has ἡ κρίσις αὐτοῦ ἤρθη. D. F. Payne ('Old Testament Exegesis' [see on 53.3a], p. 57) suggests that the phrase might have been a legal expression meaning 'after arrest and sentence', but we have no instances of *ʿōṣer* having this connotation.

Abrabanel (see *Neubauer) thinks of the servant as being moved from the exercise of royal rule and authority.[27] Such a notion of the degradation of a king would fit the passage, but the instances of the first root to mean 'rule' (Judg 18.17, *ʿēṣer*; 1 Sam 9.17; 2 Chr 14.10 [11], *ʿāṣar*) are problematic and there is thus little to point to this down-to-earth understanding of *mišpāṭ*. The same objection applies to †Gerleman's 'from protection and order' (p. 41).

The second colon then reads more literally 'and as for his generation, who would talk [about/to it]?'. After the copula (missing in the LXX and Vg), the colon thus opens with *ʾet*, which is most familiar as the object marker but is unusual in poetry. It does occasionally constitute an emphatic introduction to the subject of a sentence—so BDB here, though other studies do not include this passage among their lists of possible examples.[28] †Ewald rather takes *ʾet* as the preposition meaning 'with', stretched to mean 'among his generation'; but that is a stretch. In either case, there is a difficulty over what would then be the object of the verb. There are no other instances of the verb *śîaḥ* governing a *kî* clause (so RSV). More likely *ʾet* is as usual the object marker, included here precisely to make clear that the following word is the object even though it precedes its verb.

[26] Cf E. Kutsch, 'Die Würzel עצר im hebraïschen', in *VT* 2 (1952), pp. 57–69 (see p. 58).

[27] Cf more recently, e.g., P. R. Ackroyd, 'The Meaning of Hebrew דור Considered', in *JSS* 13 (1968), pp. 1–10 (see pp. 6–7).

[28] See GK 117iklm; J. Blau, 'Zum angeblichen Gebrauch von את vor dem Nominativ', in *VT* 4 (1954), pp. 7–19; P. P. Saydon, 'Meanings and Uses of the Particle את', in *VT* 14 (1964), pp. 192–210; J. Macdonald, 'The Particle את in Classical Hebrew', in *VT* 14 (1964), pp. 264–75.

The verb *śîaḥ* (polel) is a denominative, referring to the outward expression of one's inner thoughts, either in the form of appreciation or of complaint (cf LXX διηγήσεται, Vg *enarrabit*, Tg *ś*ʿʾ itp 'recount'; Aq ἐξομίλησει is more puzzling, but presumably links with the meaning of ὁμιλέω itself, 'converse' [G. I. Davies]). For the 'potential' yiqtol especially in a question, see GK 107t. The verb is usually intransitive, but it governs an impersonal direct object in Ps 145.5 and a personal one in Prov 6.22. The latter has been translated 'teach'[29] or 'reprove' (cf *Clines, pp. 18–19). Here it fits the context if the verb indicates that there is no-one complaining at people's treatment of the servant. The word *dôr* can then have its regular meaning 'generation', in the sense of a group of people living at the same time. It can also refer to a more limited circle of people, but one would then expect it to be qualified by an expression indicating who these people were, such as the company of the just or of those who seek Yhwh (e.g. Pss 14.5; 24.6; 73.15). The LXX and Aq has τὴν γενεὰν αὐτοῦ, Vg *generationem eius*. This leads Tertullian to refer it to Jesus's virginal conception (*An Answer to the Jews* 13), but Augustine behind that to his eternal generation from the Father (e.g. *The Creed: A Sermon to Catechumens* 8). The word can specifically denote a coming generation (hence 'progeny': e.g. Num 9.10), but not in quite the sense that would be required here.

The word can also denote a generation in the sense of a period of time, and †Luther renders 'length of life' (with the implication 'eternal life'), but this involves considerable stretching of the meaning. The Tg's paraphrase 'the wonders that will be done for us in his days' suggests a meaning such as 'destiny' (†Hitzig). G. R. Driver compared Akkadian *dūru* and translated 'lasting state/rank' (*JTS* 36, p. 403); †Eaton also appeals to Akkadian *dūru* in suggesting that the word here has the meaning 'company' but with the connotation 'rank'. This involves extending the meaning of the Akkadian word (see *CAD*) as well as hypothesizing its existence in Hebrew. In Isa 38.12 it has the meaning 'dwelling', related to that of the verb *dûr* ('dwell'). Out of the context the phrase might then refer to people's not caring about his home (†Duhm); when someone is found guilty by a court, their home becomes forfeit and may be demolished. But this requires us to suppose that the poet introduces this new idea in a very allusive way and does not then take it up again. In Ps 49.20 [19] *dôr* may refer specifically to the grave as a dwelling. If that were the idea, at least it is taken up in v. 9, but uncertainty regarding whether *dôr* can have this meaning at all discourages one from this understanding.

מעצר: †Marti suggests [ממשׁפט] עצור ('excluded [from justice]'); Whitley (*VT* 11, pp. 459–60) suggests מעצה ('without counsel').

[29] H.-P. Müller, 'Die hebräische Wurzel שׂיח', in *VT* 19 (1969), pp. 361–71 (see p. 366).

וממשפט: LXX's ἡ κρίσις αὐτοῦ might suggest משפטו. 1QIs[b] also lacks the ו.
לקח: 1QIs[a] לוקח, 1QIs[b] לקחו.
ואת דורו: †Marti emends את דרכו ('his way'; cf 40.27, also parallel to משפט), †Kissane to אחריתו ('his latter end'), †McKenzie to דברו את ('his case'), Whitley (*VT* 11, pp. 460) to את דויו ('his languishing').
ישוחח: †Marti emends to שוחח (dittog.).

53.8b. For he was cut off from the land of the living. Because of my people's rebellion, the blow came to him. 'Cut off' (*gāzar*) can refer to death (e.g. Ps 88.5 [6]), but it can also suggest being 'finished' while still alive (cf Ezek 37.11; Lam 3.54). King Uzziah is 'cut off' from the temple after being 'touched' by God and afflicted with a skin disease (2 Chr 26.20–21), and the goat in Lev 16.22 is driven 'to a land cut off'.[30] †Korpel and de Moor understand 'for it was cut off…'.

The phrase *ʾereṣ ḥayyîm* is also a poetic one, which could suggest 'the land of life', 'the living land', or 'the land of the living'; in some passages where the phrase occurs, any of the meanings would be possible. The first two might be ways of speaking of the land of Israel, the meaning assumed by the Tg's interpretative rendering, 'for he will take away the rule of the peoples from the land of Israel'. †Rashi refers the phrase to the Jewish people's exile from its land. Passages such as Isa 38.11 and Ezek 32.22–32 require the meaning 'the land of the living' as opposed to the dead, but generally this is not so. As 'the living' can simply refer to 'human beings' (e.g. Job 28.21), or to creatures in general, so 'the land of the living' can simply mean 'where human beings live' (e.g. Job 28.13; cf †Gerleman, pp. 41–42). Being cut off from the land of the living might then denote being killed, but might simply mean being cut off from human society (cf v. 3b; *Driver). In isolation, indeed, the niphal could suggest 'he cut himself off', but these other occurrences of the niphal with passive significance rule that out.

Who, then, speaks of 'my people'? In vv. 13–15 and 10–12, 'my/I' refers to Yhwh, and †Kaiser (p. 87) therefore argues that Yhwh speaks in vv. 7–9. †Ibn Ezra sees v. 8b as the statement of each of the world's separate peoples (cf †Torrey, who sees it as each foreign king referring to his own people). We have suggested that more likely the prophet speaks on behalf of others in vv. 1–9, and here slips into the first person (†Bonnard). The blow (*negaʿ*, lit. 'touch') comes to him 'because of' his people's rebellion, not 'for' it in the sense of paying a price (again, see on v. 5a).

חיים: LXX's αἴρεται ἀπο τῆς γῆς ἡ ζώη αὐτοῦ ('his life is taken from the earth') might imply חייו and dittog., or the suffix might be inferred from the parallelism.
מפשע עמי: in 1QIs[a], 1QIs[b], and 4QIs[d] it is difficult to tell whether the

[30] B. A. Levine, 'René Girard on Job', in *René Girard and Biblical Studies* (*Semeia* 33, ed. A. J. McKenna; 1985), pp. 125–33 (see p. 130).

reading is עמי or עמו. In 1QIs[a] the whole colon is a later addition. LXX has ἀπὸ τῶν ἀνομιῶν τοῦ λαοῦ μου ('because of the transgressions of my people'); cf Tg, but Vg, Syr have s.; Syr also adds a copula. †Budde suggested מפשעינו ('because of our rebellions'), †Volz מפשעים ('because of rebellions'), †Kissane עם פֹּשְׁעִים ('with rebels'), Sellin (*ZAW* 55, p. 209) מפשעם ('because of their rebellion'), Whitley (*VT* 11, p. 460) מִפֹּשְׁעִים ('because of rebels'), †North מפשע עַמֵּי ('because of the rebellion of peoples [to whom the blow belonged]'), *Fohrer (p. 16) מפשענו ('because of our rebellion'), *Elliger ('Nochmals', p. 138) מפשעימו ('because of their rebellions'), H. H. Rowley [ינגע] מפשע עם ('because of the people's rebellion [he was smitten]')[31] †Luzzatto suggested עמי might stand for עמים, *Clines (p. 19) for עם יהוה ('the people of Yhwh') (see the references in the next notes concerning abbreviations), M. Dahood that it is an Ugaritic-style third person -i ending (see on 46.11a).

נגע למו: the suffix is usually a pl. form, which would require the understanding 'for whom the blow [came to him]' or 'to whom the blow [belonged]': cf Sym πληγὴ αὐτοῖς; Aq, Th ἥψατο αὐτῶν. These imply the pointing נָגַע, as does Vg *percussit* and as may Tg 'the transgressions that my people committed he will transfer to them [the people]'. But the expression is particularly allusive. It is simpler to assume that this form can occasionally be s. (GK 103f, note 3; JM 103f) (cf Syr *qrbw lh*, implying נָגְעוּ). Most Vg MSS have *eum* rather than *eos*, but the latter may be the earlier reading. M. Dahood repoints לָמוֹ ('for us'; cf on 44.7b). Following 1QIs[a] נוגע (understood as pu) and LXX ἤχθη εἰς θάνατον (implying למות) produces 'he was stricken to death'. LXX's verb form may be assimilating to v. 7–8a. Its εἰς θάνατον may be assimilating to v. 12 and/or providing a contrast to חיים and/or taking למו as an abbreviation for למות, possibly rightly,[32] possibly wrongly.[33]

53.9a. He was given his tomb with the wicked, his burial mound with a rich person. *Dahood (*Bib* 63, pp. 567–68) takes 'my people' in v. 8b as the subject of the verb ('it gave'), but this is several words away and stands as part of a construct phrase. More likely the verb is impersonal ('one gave'); there is no direct referent for this 'one'. The obvious inference might seem to be that the members of the servant's community would be making the arrangements described, the same people who have taken him and failed to lament his fate in v. 8; it would indeed be 'my people'. But v. 9b may point in a different direction.

The servant's tomb is allocated, though in itself this does not mean that he is yet dead. But who are the 'wicked' among whom he will be buried? The speakers in v. 9a are Judeans, and we know nothing of divisions within the deportee community that would set righteous poor Judeans over against wicked rich members of the community. 'Wicked' is implicitly or potentially a description of the deportee

[31] *The Biblical Doctrine of Election* (London/Naperville, IL, 1950), p. 116.

[32] So G. R. Driver, 'Abbreviations in the Massoretic Text', in *Textus* 1 (1960), pp. 112–31 (see p. 123).

[33] So G. R. Driver, 'Once Again Abbreviations', in *Textus* 4 (1964), pp. 76–94 (see p. 94).

community as a whole in 48.22 and 55.7, probably as resistant to Yhwh's purpose as the prophet expounds it. But it could be a natural description of the Babylonians (cf 13.11). 'Rich', too, could have been a description of Jews who had prospered in Babylon (†Korpel and de Moor) but it would also be an uncontroversial description of Babylon and its king. 'Wicked, rich' therefore makes best sense as a description of Babylon. There is no suggestion on the part of these speakers that this burial implies a positive, fruitful identification with the wicked, though reading their words in the light of the promise in v. 15 may hint at this, and vv. 11aγ–12 may add more encouragement to such a reading. It simply means that the servant was destined to be buried in Babylon rather than (for instance) having the opportunity to leave in accordance with the commission in, for example, 52.11–12.

'Wicked' and 'rich' involve the same letters but in reverse order (*rešaʿ*/*ʿāšîr*); the actual form of the first word in the plural (*rᵉšāʿîm*) makes the two even closer. The assonance doubtless contributed to this choice of words, suggesting as it itself does an association between wicked and rich (cf *Ahlström, p. 98). The Tg assumes that the second adjective refers specifically to the 'rich in possessions that they gained by robbery'. This makes the parallelism work, perhaps by reading back from the subsequent reference to the servant not doing violence or deceit (v. 9b). Whereas the Hebrew has plural then singular, the versions mostly improve the parallelism by using two singular or two plural words.

If the two epithets are semi-independent parallel characterizations, there is no reason to be puzzled by the collocation of the two words. Indeed, even within the OT the collocation of the rich with the wicked may be seen in several contexts. Jeremiah 5.26–28 speaks of the 'wicked' among 'my people' whose houses are full of 'deceit' and who 'have become rich' through not caring about the 'judgment' of the needy. In Mic 6.10–13 the wicked person is singular and the rich plural, the opposite to here; the passage goes on to refer to Yhwh's wounding and striking, the verbs that came in v. 4 here. Job 27.13–19 begins by pairing the singular 'wicked person' with plural 'oppressors' and v. 19 refers back to this person as 'rich'. In between, v. 15 speaks of being 'buried (*qābar*) by death' (i.e. not being buried at all). Psalm 49.6–7 [5–6] characterizes the wicked as people who trust in their wealth. In an OT context the association of wicked and rich is thus not odd.

The Syr omits the copula and then apparently takes the wicked/rich as subject of the verbs, ignoring the *ʾet*. This at least indicates that at this point the translation was not affected by Christian belief: compare Išoʿ bar Nūn's attempts to explain the text (see Bundy, '"Questions and Answers"'). In contrast, the Tg understands *ʾet* (usually taken as the preposition 'with') as the object marker and translates 'he will hand over the wicked to Gehenna...'. The LXX similarly renders καὶ δώσω τοὺς πονηροὺς ἀντὶ τῆς ταφῆς αὐτοῦ... (cf Aq, Th, Sym, Vg); its first person verb perhaps follows on from the suffix of 'my people' in v. 8 (*HUB*). Christian exegetes needed to reinterpret the text (see Delekat, *Bib* 38 p. 186). The combination of plural and singular in parallelism (wicked, rich) is a common one already instanced in v. 14 (*Dahood, 'Phoenician Elements').

The LXX (in the context of a paraphrase), Vg, and Syr understand *b*^{e}*mōtāyw* ('his burial mound') to mean 'at his death'—strictly 'at his death[s]', presumably intensive plural, as in Ezek 28.8. The plural makes for another singular–plural parallelism in the line. But †Ibn Ezra takes the word to mean 'his [burial] mound', which strictly requires the repointing *bāmōtāyw*. It would again be intensive: compare the use of the plural of *miškān* ('dwelling'). The word may denote a burial mound in Ezek 43.7. 1QIs^{a} has singular *bwmtw* ('his burial mound').[34]

ויתן: 1QIs^{a} begins and indents a new line and reads ויתנו, the more common impersonal pl. The LXX and Vg have a future vb (as often in the section); so also Tg. †Marti repoints וַיִּתַּן.

ואת: 1QIs^{a} has a different reading which was corrected; both the original and the correction are unclear.

עשיר: †Ewald suggests עֹשֵׁק ('oppressor'), †Oort עָשׁוּק (cf Jer 22.3), †Kissane עֹשֵׂי־רָע ('evildoers'), Praetorius (*ZAW* 36, p. 20) שְׂעִירִים ('demons'), Whitley (*VT* 11, pp. 460) עריצים ('tyrants'), *Dahood (*Bib* 63, pp. 567–68) עֹשֵׂי רִיב ('makers of strife'; he redivides the words). J. Reider sees the word as cognate with an Arabic word for 'stumbling/corrupt/lying',[35] A. Guillaume with an Arabic word meaning 'rabble';[36] these alternative possibilities from Arabic sharpen Emerton's critique ([see footnote], p. 127).

במתיו: †Whitehouse suggests בית מותו ('his death home'), of which the MT might be an abbreviation (van Hoonacker, 'L'Ébed', p. 526), †Kissane מנתו ('his portion'). *Barrick suggests that the stress on the body in Matt 27.57–60 indicates that Matthew followed the same reading as 1QIs^{a}, 'his back', a possible meaning for במה (see *HAL*, *DCH*). *Dahood (*Bib* 63, pp. 567–68) redivides after במתי, parsing the suffix as a Phoenician-style third-person and attaching the ו as copula to the next word.

[34] W. F. Albright, 'The High Place in Ancient Palestine', in *Volume du Congrès: Strasbourg 1956* (*VT* Sup 4, 1957), pp. 242–58 (see pp. 244–48); with the refinement of J. A. Emerton, 'The Biblical High Place in the Light of Recent Study', in *PEQ* 129 (1997), pp. 116–32 (see pp. 124–28); see also P. Vaughan, *The Meaning of 'Bāmâ' in the Old Testament* (Cambridge/New York, 1974). S. Iwry, '*Maṣṣēbāh* and *bāmāh* in 1Q Isaiah^{a} 6_{13}', in *JBL* 76 (1957), pp. 225–32, notes that 1QIs^{a} also reads במה (for בם) in 6.13, where LXX has ἀπὸ τῆς θήκης αὐτῆς ('from his burial vault'). But †Barthélemy suggests that the word for burial mound or monument is strictly בָּמֶת rather than בָּמָה, and this may add to the uncertainty about this understanding at 6.13 (see also J. Sawyer, 'The Qumran Reading of Isaiah 6, 13', in *ASTI* 3 [1964], pp. 111–13).

[35] 'Etymological Studies in Biblical Hebrew', in *VT* 2 (1952), pp. 112–30 (see p. 118).

[36] 'A Contribution to Hebrew Lexicography', in *BSOAS* 16 (1954), pp. 1–12 (see p. 10).

53.9b. ...because he did no violence and no deceit with his mouth. The description of the servant as having done no violence or deceit makes for a further link with Mic 6.10–13. That passage condemns the city's people who have become 'rich' through being 'wicked': they are people who are full of 'violence' who have 'tongues of deceit in their mouths'. The word *ḥāmās* commonly means 'violence' but can refer to wrong more generally.

BDB (p. 758a) notes that *ʿal* is occasionally used as a conjunction, and suggests that here it means 'although' (cf GK 160c; JM 171e). But this is a strange meaning for the word, and the LXX and Vg give it its expected meaning 'because'. Job 16.17 is the only other alleged instance of the conjunction meaning 'although', and Bastiaens ([see on v. 4aα], p. 423) sees that as a reminiscence of this line (Job 10.7 and 34.6 are equivalent instances of the preposition *ʿal*). Perhaps the 'because' is ironic (*Clines, p. 20), or perhaps it implies that people will want to give the servant an honourable burial, because they have realized that their first attitude to him was wrong, but that this will still necessarily be a burial among the wicked/rich, in Babylon.

The LXX provides a verb in the second colon ('no deceit was found in his mouth'; cf Vg *fuerit*, EVV) but more likely the verb in the first colon also applies to the second (the verb is used with 'deceit' as its object in Dan 11.23) and the adverbial expression in the second applies to the first, in the characteristic fashion of Hebrew poetry. 'Violence' and 'deceit' will then be a hendiadys and the line will not refer to two acts (doing no violence and speaking no deceit) but to one, the doing of violence by deceptive speech, which is a characteristic fault of the rich wicked. For the powerful effectiveness of what can be done 'with the mouth', cf Prov 11.9 ('destroy'), 11 ('overthrow'). The placing of the negative before the noun rather than before the verb suggests 'he did non-violence and non-deceit...'. The repetition of the negative also adds to the emphasis on the noun rather than the verb (GK 152e), compounding the effect of locating the first noun before the verb ('no violence he did...').

The reference to his mouth forms an *inclusio* round vv. 7–9. The Tg paraphrases this second line 'so that those who commit sin might not endure [perhaps the positive counterpart to the deliverance to Gehenna of which v. 9a spoke] and might not speak of possessions/deceits [manuscripts vary] with their mouth'.

53.10aαβ. But Yhwh—he determined the crushing of the one he weakened. If the person should lay down a reparation-offering... The verb *ḥāpēṣ* and the noun *ḥēpeṣ* which comes in the next line (the LXX repeats the verb there) most often refer to a response of pleasure at something. In this context Yhwh's delight could then correspond to the motif of the turning towards a person which denotes the first stage of Yhwh's deliverance (†Westermann). But in the broader context of these chapters, the words refer not to a reactive delight but to a proactive determining (e.g. 44.28). The line thus expresses in a sharper way the point that has recurred through vv. 1–9: Yhwh was behind the servant's suffering.

The Tg applies the line to Israel and renders 'But before Yhwh it was a delight to refine and cleanse the remnant [the Reuchlin MS has 'the wicked'] of his people, in order to purify their soul from transgression'. 'Cleanse' is *dk*ʾ. As well as seeing people rather than servant as the object of the verbs, the Tg has taken *dakk*ʾ*ô* in an Aramaic sense, as if it were an alternative to *zakk*ʾ*ô*; cf LXX καθαρίσαι. Understood in the Aramaic way, the expression could alternatively mean 'his vindication', which gives excellent sense (cf 50.8). But an audience in the prophet's day could hardly be expected to infer an Aramaic usage, especially given the verb's use to mean crush in v. 5a. Perhaps all three are seeking to sidestep the 'demonic' aspect of Yhwh (see †Lust, pp. 11–13). We take the construction as more literally 'he determined his crushing [whom] he wounded'. If the word order were 'he determined he wounded his crushing' we could take the second qatal verb as coordinate with the first rather than dependent on the infinitive, suggesting 'But Yhwh willingly wounded him by crushing him' (cf GK 120gh), but the word order here makes this unlikely.

The MT links the first three cola in v. 10 and isolates the final colon. In contrast, 1QIsa indents the line which begins with the second colon, and EVV treat the first colon as a self-contained sentence and the following three cola as another. This is an unlikely structure for Hebrew poetry. *Levey (p. 65) more plausibly follows the Tg in taking the two clauses in v. 10a together, and *b. Berakot* 5a, which assumes that the second clause is an indirect question dependent on the first, '[to see] if the person would lay down'; the particle is thus interrogative ʾ*im*, not conditional ʾ*im*. Exodus 22.7, 10 [8, 11] provide parallels, though in both the particle is ʾ*im-lō*ʾ. We have concluded that both clauses connect with the line which follows, giving the verse as a whole an ABBA structure; within one unusual double line the first and last cola pair and the middle cola pair. This does actually provide some form of support for all the ways of subdividing the verse, and implies that the inside cola take the edge off the scandal implied by the first colon. We will see that v. 11aα also links with these four lines, taking up two expressions from them.

The second colon itself has been construed in a number of ways. The LXX's ἐὰν δῶτε περὶ ἁμαρτίας takes *tāśîm* ('lay down') as a second person verb and links *napšô* ('his self'; LXX has ἡ ψυχὴ ὑμῶν) with the next line. The isolated second person verb would parallel that in v. 14 in the opening subsection of the passage; as there, momentarily Yhwh speaks directly to the servant. Taking *napšô* with the next line spoils a neat 4–4 line there, though it makes for a 6-stress line in v. 10a; but the fact that this poem is very irregular in its metre makes such considerations of questionable force. More difficult is the oddness of *napšô* as subject of 'he will see'. Vg *si posuerit pro peccato animam suam* ('if he lays down his life for sin') divides the lines like the MT and produces a coherent meaning but it implies a third person masculine verb form. Thus *Wolff (p. 28) emends to *yāśîm*. While t-preformative masculine third person forms exist in Ugaritic, postulating them in Hebrew is problematic.[37]

'If you appoint his life as a reparation-offering' seems to require that the speakers address Yhwh (cf NIV), which is jerky in the context. It could have prepared for Yhwh's response in vv. 11–12 (†Laato, p. 136), but the third person references to Yhwh in the preceding clause and the succeeding line overwhelm that possibility. Further, the word order is the reverse of the usual order for this idiom: it suggests 'if you appoint a reparation-offering as his life'. 'If the person should lay down a reparation-offering' makes *napšô* the subject of the action in a way which recalls Leviticus 2–5, where *nepeš* is often the subject of sentences about a person committing an offence and thus coming to make an offering. In Leviticus *nepeš* is indefinite, but here the suffixed form makes the word definite by linking back to the same suffix in the previous colon. This consideration then answers *Whybray's objections (p. 64) to taking *napšô* as the verb's subject. 'If' is also a common introduction to prescriptions regarding the precise nature of the offerings which 'a person' brings: for example, 'if an individual person sins' in accidentally infringing one of Yhwh's commands 'and is liable [*ʾāšēm*]', this person is to bring a goat as an offering (Lev 4.27–28; cf 5.7). This makes it unlikely that *ʾim* here means 'though' not 'if' (cf 1.18; 10.22; †Muilenburg). Leviticus 5.1–4 does itself also juxtapose talk of 'carrying wrongdoing' (compare vv. 11b, 12b) and of 'being liable' (*ʾāšēm*) (*Zimmerli, p. 240). This adds to the indications that the prophet is working with a framework of thinking like that in Leviticus.

This emerges further in the prophet's reference to a reparation-offering (*ʾāšām*), which offers compensation when someone has infringed God's rights or harmed God's name or otherwise wronged God. The analogy with this ritual suggests that Yhwh gives the servant the opportunity to turn his acceptance of undeserved affliction into an offering to Yhwh which makes up for the wrongs that the people have done in relation to Yhwh. Only here does the OT talk of 'laying down' (*śîm*) a reparation-offering; one normally 'brings' it. Abraham does 'lay down' Isaac on the altar (Gen 22.9; †Barthélemy); Job asks God to 'lay down' a pledge with him (17.3).[38] The yiqtol verb is also surprising, though it introduces a sequence of yiqtol verbs running through vv. 10–12aα. This one may be implicitly the further object of Yhwh's 'determination', which was that the servant should make this offering. That might fit with the implication that the two cola in v. 10aαβ belong together.

[37] *IBHS* 31.1.1a, note 2; contrast, e.g., H. J. van Dijk, 'Does Third Masculine Singular **taqtul* Exist in Hebrew?', in *VT* 19 (1969), pp. 440–47 (see pp. 442–43); M. Dahood, 'Third Masculine Singular with Preformative *t-* in Northwest Semitic', in *Orientalia* 48 (1979), pp. 97–106.

[38] See Bentzen, *Messias*, p. 59 (ET p. 61); he is following *Nyberg (see p. 58).

חפץ: †Bonnard repoints as imper. חֲפַץ.
דכאו: Elliger (*Verhältnis*. p. 7) repoints דַּכָּאוֹ ('his crushed one'). G. R. Driver (see †North) repoints דִּכְּאוֹ ('the one he had crushed'), though חפץ is normally followed by ב before a personal obj. †Luzzatto points to Num 18.29 and 2 Sam 14.29 for similar forms allowing the MT to denote 'his crushed one'; for the adjective, cf Prov 26.22. The cl. could then mean 'Yhwh accepted his crushed one, whom he had weakened'. †Oort emends to רפא ('to heal'), *Müller to זכאו ('to cleanse').
החלי אם־תשים: †Ehrlich reworks as הֶחֱלִיאוֹ לָשׂוּם ('made him suffer in order to lay down'). †Begrich (p. 57 = 64) reworks as הֶחֱלִים אֶת־שָׂם ('he healed the one who had made [himself a reparation-offering]'). †Levy reworks as אֱמֶת שָׂם אָשָׁם ('indeed he lay down a reparation-offering') and *Battenfield notes that in the first word 1QIs[a] has medial מ rather than final ם, which supports this word division; cf also Syr *ʾttsym* for אם תשים. M. Dahood sees אם as the ptpl of אים ('the awesome one [considered his life a reparation-offering]').[39] *Sonne reworks as החל יאמו ישיב לאשם [=לאישים] ('healed him; he will return [his soul] to men'). G. R. Driver (*JTS* 36, pp. 403–4) reworked as וְהֶחֱלִיאָמוֹ תוּשַׂם ('and he made him suffer; [his life] was laid down [as a reparation-offering]') but later (see *Driver) accepted †Begrich's proposal.
החלי: on the form, see GK 74k, 75ii. *Nyberg (p. 58) derives from חלה II as an 'inwardly transitive' hi (cf GK 53d), suggesting 'he accepted appeasement'. This requires an otherwise unknown form (חלה is elsewhere piel) with an unusual meaning, and an audience could hardly be expected to understand it. 1QIs[a] has ויחללהו ('and desecrated him'), assimilating to v. 5a (†Kutscher, pp. 178–79 [ET pp. 236–37]); 4QIs[d] agrees with MT. LXX's τῆς πληγῆς ('from the blow'), Vg *in infirmitate* ('by illness'), Aq τὸ ἀρρώστημα ('the illness'), Sym ἐν τῷ τραυματισμῷ ('by the injury') might imply מֵחֳלִי (*Müller), בָּחֳלִי (†Lowth), or הָחֳלִי (but the article is odd, *pace* †North). Sym's use of τραυματισμός rather than νόσος (contrast v. 3a) suggests that it links the word with חלל I; cf *Dahood ('Phoenician Elements'), who reworks וְהַחֲלִי (hi inf. cons. with Phoenician-style third-person suffix; the copula is shared with the preceding word). Syr takes the word as an inf. parallel to the preceding one, '[desired his being crushed] and made sick'.
אם: †Eaton takes as 'surely', like Ugaritic *hm*.
תשים: †Lowth repoints as passive, '[though his life] is made'.

53.10aγb. He will see offspring. He will have a long life. Yhwh's determination will succeed by means of him. The servant has looked like someone condemned to childlessness, death, and failure. But (first) he will see offspring. 'Seeing one's grandchildren' is a sign of reaching a good age (Gen 50.23; Ps 128.6; Job 42.16). 'Seeing his children' hardly has the same implication. Indeed, it is not a natural way to refer to the servant himself having children. The Tg refers the line as a whole to Israel, though it refers these blessings to the messianic age: 'they will see the kingdom of their Anointed, they will

[39] See the paper cited in connection with v. 10aαβ, p. 100.

multiply sons and daughters...'. In the context, these offspring are the ones Second Isaiah has often been concerned about (e.g. 45.25).

The middle clause, literally 'he will lengthen days', is then ambiguous. 1QIs[a] *wyʾrk* and 4QIs[d] *whʾryk*, by the presence of a copula (cf Syr), imply the subject is the servant, as does the Tg.[40] 1QIs[b] has the same text as the MT. The LXX's σπέρμα μακρόβιον assumes that the subject is the offspring (cf Vg). The clause recalls the promise of long life (lit. 'length of days') in Ps 91.16, on which *Ginsberg (*JBL* 77, p. 155) believes v. 10 depends (cf also Pss 21.5 [4]; 23.6), and the 'length of days' of Yhwh's abandonment in Lam 5.20. The latter supports LXX's understanding, which also makes better sense in the context, particularly following on the preceding clause if it refers to the flourishing of the servant's people. Indeed, the passage's concern throughout is with the servant in connection with his ministry, and thus the implications of this ministry for other people. Comment on his own longevity would hardly be expected.

While the first colon links back to v. 10aβ, the second colon with its reference to the prospering of Yhwh's determination pairs with the opening colon, v. 10aα. It also confirms our understanding of 'he will see offspring' and supports the idea that the offspring are the subject of 'have'. Through his ministry the people will grow and flourish, and thus Yhwh's plan will be fulfilled. The Tg paraphrases 'those who perform the Teaching of Yhwh will succeed by his desire'. For '[Yhwh's determination] will succeed', the LXX has ἀφελεῖν [Yhwh determined] to take away...', leading into v. 11; this suggests it read the verb as (if it were) *yšlḥ* rather than *yṣlḥ*.

In the introduction to 52.13–53.12 we noted that v. 10 takes some its terms from Jer 22.28–30 and portrays the servant's destiny as contrasting with that of Jehoiachin, the former king long exiled in Babylon. He was not to have 'offspring' (the phrase 'see offspring' does not appear) who would 'succeed' on the throne of Judah. He himself was not to 'succeed' in 'his days'—for all the way in which he lengthened his days in Babylon (37 years, to our knowledge, according to 2 Kgs 25.27–30). Nothing of the people's *ḥēpeṣ* attached to him, but Yhwh's *ḥēpeṣ* attaches to this servant; the contrast is emphasized by the double occurrence of the divine name, as many as come in the whole of the rest of the poem.

In previous verses, any description of the servant's actual death has been allusive, and likewise the description of his restoration is not simply a description of a resuscitation. It is a description of Yhwh's purpose being fulfilled.

53.11aα. Because of his personal suffering he will see with satisfaction. C. Westermann comments that passages which refer to deep misery and sorrow are among the few where *nepeš* can properly be translated 'soul', as the suffering affects the entire humanity of the

[40] See B. Chilton's comments, 'Two in One: Readings of the Book of Isaiah in Targum Jonathan', in †Broyles and Evans, pp. 547–62 (see pp. 555–56).

person, the entire existence (*THAT*, Vol. 2, cols 79–81 [ET pp. 748–49]); †Torrey renders 'his mortal travail'. But *ʿāmāl* refers at least as much to outward and humanly-inflicted trouble as to inner pain. It first denotes Joseph's troubles, then Israel's in Egypt and in the 'judges' period; and cf the two other occurrences in Isaiah, 10.1 and 59.4. Here the word thus more likely sums up the description we have read so far. This is confirmed by the recurrence of *napšô* from v. 10: it was the outward person at least as much as the inner person who made an offering, as it was the outward person at least as much as the inner person who went through suffering.

As in English, the verb 'see' is quite commonly used thus absolutely, with the object inferred from the context (e.g. 42.18; 44.18): the object is the 'offspring' also mentioned in v. 10. Like the noun form *napšô*, the actual verb form 'he will see' (*yirʾeh*) recurs from v. 10, which adds to the hint that its implicit object is the 'offspring' mentioned there. In turn this suggests that *mēʿămal* probably implies more than merely 'after' or 'out of' his suffering (Tg: once more it sees this as the people's travail). More likely the Vg's 'because he travailed' is right to see a causal link with what precedes: the line restates v. 10 as a whole. The LXX implies the same assumption in actually linking this opening phrase with v. 10.

†Bonnard goes on to suggest that the second verb, *yiśbāʿ*, also governs an implicit object in v. 10 and means 'he will be filled [with days]' (cf, e.g., Job 42.17; 1 Chr 23.1; 2 Chr 24.15). But this requires much more inference and requires the less likely of the interpretations of that middle clause in v. 10b. The MT's accents rather link the two asyndetic verbs. Reading the first in the light of the second, *Thomas derives *yirʾeh* from a byform of *rāwāh* ('be filled'); the two verbs come in parallelism in Lam 3.15 (also Jer 31.14). †Houbigant had earlier emended to *yirweh*, while M. Dahood (*Proverbs* [see on 53.3a], p. 23) rather derives from a verb *yārāʾ* ('be sated'). It might indeed be the case that the prophet rejoiced in the paronomasia, though it is unlikely that readers could be expected to infer that this simply *was* an occurrence of *rāwāh* rather than *rāʾāh*. More likely the first of the two asyndetic verbs has its usual meaning and the second is implicitly subordinated to it, 'he will see [it and] be satisfied', implicitly 'he will see [it] with satisfaction'. When two verbs are thus co-ordinated with or without *w*, normally the first indicates the manner of the action and the second the nature of the action, but here the order is reversed (GK 120gh).

So the MT. But 1QIs[ab], 4QIs[d] supply *ʾwr* ('light') as the object of the verb, and the LXX also apparently read it (Ar. has *twʾbʾ*, 'compensation'). The word might have been omitted by haplography, but it does not appear in the Vg (which suggests that 1QIs[b] does not represent the only 'Masoretic-type' tradition of its day) nor as far as we know in Aq, Th, Sym, nor in Syr or Tg (see below), and explanation by haplography is always vulnerable to the reverse suggestion of inclusion by dittography. It might alternatively result from assimilation to a familiar usage, or specifically to 9.1 [2]; v. 12

seems to reflect 9.2 [3]. 'See light' is a figure with a number of possible meanings: it can suggest life as opposed to the darkness of Sheol (Ps 49.20 [19]; Job 33.28) or of the womb (Job 3.16), or refer to the impossibility of looking at the bright light of the sky (Job 37.21), or denote the enjoyment of God's blessings (Ps 36.10 [9]), especially after the darkness of disaster (Isa 9.1 [2]) (see further †Brownlee, pp. 226–33). The contrast 'suffering/light' here would suggest the last of these connotations, and this would fit with indications that Isaiah 9 has been taken up earlier in these chapters in references to darkness and light (see, e.g., on 42.16). If 'light' in this sense is what the servant sees, this then retrospectively implies a different understanding of the opening of the verse. He will see light not because of his travail, but after his travail, as in 9.1 [2].[41]

It also necessarily implies a different understanding of what follows, in the sense that 'he will see' no longer stands in such a close relationship with the verb which follows, which now indubitably stands independent of it with the meaning 'he will be sated' (1QIs[a] provides it with a copula; cf LXX, Vg, Syr). The LXX, Syr, Aq, Th, and Sym go on to link 'he will be sated' with the succeeding phrase; so probably does the Vg, though it preserves the MT's ambiguity (†Weber's edition links it with what follows).

But what does 'he will be sat[isfi]ed with his knowledge' mean? Does the phrase suggest his knowledge of what he has achieved or his acknowledgment of God? If so, the point is very allusively expressed. A reference back to the knowledge/experience of weakness to which v. 3 referred would be marginally less allusive, so that 'his knowledge' parallels 'his personal suffering'; the verb *śāba*ʿ then suggests being sated or full in a negative sense (cf significantly Lam 3.15, 30; also, e.g., Pss 88.4 [3]; 123.3, 4; Job 7.4; 9.18). The line would be easier if we could accept the proposal that this is an occurrence of a second root *yāda*ʿ which would imply 'by his humiliation',[42] but see on v. 3a. The Arabic evidence could perhaps generate a meaning such as '[he will be satisfied] with/by his stillness/rest' (*Williamson, *VT* 28 [1978], pp. 118–22), but this is hardly an improvement on 'with his knowledge'.

The difficulty of linking 'by his knowledge' with what precedes suggests that on balance it is best to assume that 'light' is not original and that the MT is right to link the two verbs closely together and to associate 'by his knowledge' with what follows. Verses 10–11aα then comprise five four-word cola in which the first and the fourth link in their reference to 'Yhwh' and to 'determining', the second and fifth link through the word *napšô* and the third and the fifth link through the word 'he will see'. The fourth and fifth cola are thus marked as bringing some closure by the way they take up and summarize all

[41] On the possible motivation for the addition of the word for 'light', see Tov, *Textual Criticism* (see on 44.9b), p. 266, with his reference to I. L. Seeligmann.

[42] See D. W. Thomas, 'More Notes on the Root ידע in Hebrew', in *JTS* 38 (1937), pp. 404–5.

three preceding cola. This also adds to the impact of the final asyndetic verb which brings the subsection to an end with a thumping statement of hope for the servant—'he will be satisfied'!

The Tg renders 'they will see the retribution of their adversaries and be satisfied with the spoil of their kings'.

מֵעָמָל: Syr precedes by *w*. Gelston (*VT* 21, pp. 526–27) reads מֵעָמָל יָצִיל ('he will deliver himself from suffering'), the verb having been omitted by haplog. after יָצְלָה.

יִרְאָה: *Schwarz (*ZAW* 84) adds יֵשׁ. †Kissane emends יִרְאֵהוּ ('he will see it').

יִשְׂבָּע: LXX's πλάσαι ('form') may be an inner Greek corruption (*Neubauer and Driver); Koenig (*Oracles*, p. 112) derives it from reading יִשְׂבָּע as if it were יַעֲשֵׂב understood as equivalent to יַעֲצֵב. *Schwarz (*ZAW* 84) adds טוֹב.

53.11aβb. By his knowledge my servant will show many that he is indeed just, because he bears their wrongdoing. We link *bᵉdaʿtô* with what follows, with the MT, Tg, and 1QIsᵃ (which prefixes *w* to the word). Out of this context *bᵉdaʿtô* could be an objective genitive, 'by knowledge of him'. That might then denote people's knowledge/ acknowledgment of the servant or the servant's knowledge/acknowledgment of Yhwh, though the expression is once again allusive. But the link with the opening subsection (52.13) suggests that it is rather the more common subjective genitive, 'by his knowledge'. As that first subsection opened by declaring that Yhwh's servant would act with insight, so the last subsection opens by declaring what Yhwh's servant will achieve through his knowledge.

The link with 52.13 and 53.3, and the way in which *daʿat* is among the words from this passage that reappear in Dan 12.3–4 undermines the suggestion that *bᵉdaʿtô* needs to be emended to *bᵉrāʿātô* ('by his distress') (†Ehrlich). The reference to obedience in passages such as Rom 5.19 might be linked with several of the possible understandings of *daʿat* (*Allen, 'Isaiah liii. 11', p. 26), but not with *rāʿāh*.

With this line a court scene begins. It is difficult to construe the words that follow 'by his knowledge' and open this judgment scene, *yaṣdîq ṣaddîq ʿabdî lārabbîm*. The speaker, who uses the expression 'my servant', must be Yhwh. The Vg *multos* assumes that the 'many' are the object of the verb 'justify/vindicate', but this requires *l* to be the sign of the object rather than a preposition (so GK 117n, *IBHS* 11.2.10g). The Tg similarly has 'to subject many to the Teaching', enabling them to live according to the Torah (cf †Ibn Ezra); *Hegermann sees this as a piece of anti-Christian interpretation designed to contrast with the Christian use in Mark 10.45.

There is another difficulty apart from the rarity of this use of *l*. The phrase *haṣdîq ṣaddîq* comes in 1 Kgs 8.32 with the meaning 'justify the just'; cf *hiṣdîqû ʾet-haṣdîq* in Deut 25.1. †Rashi assumes the phrase has exactly this regular meaning here: the servant will judge justly all who bring cases to him. Of course words from this root have generally had other resonances in Isaiah 40–55, and †Olley (p. 62) warns against too forensic an understanding of the Hebrew verb. But this underlines the difficulty of the traditional Christian understanding of this colon as referring to the justifying of the unjust. It is not that the OT cannot imagine God forgiving the unjust; it is that this is not language that the OT uses for such an action. Daniel 12.3 confirms this hesitation about the Vg. First, Dan 12.3 rewords the expression to remove the *l* so that 'many' is clearly the direct object, which is the expected construction if the verb means 'acquit' or 'vindicate' or 'save'. And second, Dan 12.3 takes the 'many' to be Israelites. The Tg's translation of the last colon of Isa 53.11, 'for their transgressions he will pray', implies this understanding there, and *Steck (pp. 39–41) argues that this is right. Yephet ben 'Ali (see *Neubauer) assumes that the word indicates that he leads people to repentance.

*Steck further notes that in lament psalms the 'many' are Israelites and suggests that here they are the 'we' of vv. 1–10, who confessed that the servant had been 'carrying'/'bearing' the consequences of their 'wrongdoing'/'rebellion' (vv. 4, 11b, 12b): the nouns are ones elsewhere used to describe Israel's acts, not the nations'. But the book called Isaiah has earlier spoken of the wrongdoing and failure of other nations, specifically Babylon (e.g. 13.9, 11); there is no reason why Second Isaiah should not do so. 'Rebellion' indeed applies more specifically to Israel in v. 12, but this does not affect v. 11b. Further, while *rabbîm* is common in the Psalms, it is common everywhere, and '*the* many' never occurs in the Psalms. Here the way in which vv. 11aβb–12 forms an *inclusio* with 52.13–15 and picks up motifs ('my servant', 'knowledge'/'act with insight') makes it more plausible to give 'many' the same reference as it had earlier. The article on 'many' perhaps makes that explicit—the word refers to 'the many' we were thinking of earlier. *Clines (p. 22) suggests that the word denotes 'the great ones', equivalent to the kings of v. 15, while *Wolff (p. 29) describes 'many' as a political concept.

So who gets justified/vindicated here in v. 11? One natural way to construe the clause is as meaning that 'my servant will justify the just one to many'. Out of this context it would be natural then to take 'the just one' to refer to Yhwh (cf 45.21), but this statement would take the poem in a new direction which is immediately abandoned. The need for the reworking in Dan 12.3 rather supports the LXX in assuming that the person who is justified is Yhwh's servant and that he is justified 'to the many'. In substance this assertion constitutes another link with the opening section 52.13–15: it is another way of saying that he will be exalted and that the many will shut their mouths when they see him. The person who needs vindicating is the servant.

'The just one will vindicate my servant to many' is another obvious way to construe the sentence out of the context, and it would make this point well. The LXX thus renders 'the Lord desires to vindicate a just one who is serving well' (cf Tg 'he [Yhwh] will vindicate the just';

also Sym). But this would require Yhwh to be self-referring in the third person in an artificial way. The fact that 'my servant' needs to be the verb's subject and that this servant is the person who needs to be vindicated suggests that the verb is an internal hiphil, denoting 'show himself just'. There is thus a further sense in which the line balances 52.13–15, for 'my servant' is the subject of the same kind of verb there, 'show insight'.

The LXX and Vg further assume that *ṣaddîq* ʿ*abdî* constitutes a compound expression, 'the just one, my servant'. It would be a possible but an unusual compound. It might be taken as an adjective preceding its noun, for which see GK 132b; *IBHS* 14.3.3c. †North suggests that it might be construct, suggesting 'my supremely just servant' (cf similar phrases in Exod 15.16; 1 Sam 16.7; cf GK 132c).

*Reicke (pp. 190–91) more plausibly unlinks the two words. With *yaṣdîq ṣaddîq* he compares the expression 'reign as king' (e.g. Jer 37.1), where a verb is followed by its cognate noun; here the cognate nominal adjective serves to clarify that this is indeed the way to take the verb (cf GK 117r). It is part of the predicate not part of the subject. *Reicke goes on to infer that 'for the many' means that these people can come to share in the servant's vindication. This reads too much into the preposition *l*, though something like this point is indeed made in the subsequent colon. But the point here is that it is before the 'many' that he is vindicated as they recognize his 'knowledgeable' ministry.

He does not justify them, but he does 'bear their wrongdoings'. Such language is used in various ways in the OT, but Second Isaiah's actual words correspond most closely to Lam 5.7. In years not far from Second Isaiah's, people complain that they are carrying the wrongdoing of their parents or ancestors. They are bearing the burden or the consequences of the wrongdoing that led to the fall of Jerusalem. †Olley (p. 49) assumes that Second Isaiah, while using the same words as Lam 5.7, uses them with more the connotations of Leviticus 5. But the connotations of Lam 5.7 itself are appropriate: the servant lives with the consequences of the wrongdoing of the many. The way he does that will be fruitful for them, as for the community itself.

One clue to this understanding of the last colon is the word order. †König suggests that the *w* which introduces the last colon is explicative; Mowinckel (*He That Cometh*, p. 199) goes beyond that in seeing the colon as a circumstantial clause. Usually in such a clause the subject comes first, but it may begin with another word if that requires the emphasis (*TTH* 159), and that is so here. The emphasis lies on '*their* wrongdoing'. This is indicated by its being followed by the pleonastic pronoun *hû*ʾ which serves to draw attention to the contrast with the suffix which it follows, as in v. 4a. *Dahood's instinct that the yiqtol verb must refer to the past (*Bib* 63, p. 569) is correct; in the circumstantial clause the verb takes its tense from the main clause. Th has ὑπήνεγκεν (*Hegermann sees this as an anti-Christian interpretation, but notes that Th has a future verb in v.

12b); Sym ὑπενέγκει could be present or future; but it may be a corruption of that reading (G. I. Davies).

בדעתו: LXX and Syr lack the suffix. †Begrich (p. 58 = 64) emends to בעבדתו ('with his service'), Mowinckel (*He That Cometh*, p. 199) to ברעותו ('with his desire'). On the basis of a Sabean parallel, Müller (*ZAW* 81, p. 379) sees here a noun דעה meaning 'good'. M. Dahood suggested that ידע was here a dialectal alternative to יזע 'sweat'.[43]
צדיק: †Kittel omits; *Driver moves to the end of the previous colon, which makes for an easier construction, and repoints as צֶדֶק. This makes two 3–3 lines of v. 11. We have noted that in this section metrical arguments count even less than usual. In the MT the second line focuses especially on the legal image. The repetition of the root is characteristic of the chapters.
עבדי: LXX's εὖ δουλεύοντα, Sym λατρεύοντα suggest עֹבֵד, Tg לשעבדה suggests עַבֵּד, Syr *ʿbdʾ* suggests עֲבֵד (*Hegermann). †Duhm takes עבדי as a slip for עבדו or as reflecting an original עבד יהוה; *Clines (p. 22) notes that עבדו is the 1QIsa reading, but 1QIsa may be dependent on an archetype where ו and י were hard to distinguish, and י is the more difficult reading (†Barthélemy). *Dahood ('Phoenician Elements') takes it as a Phoenician-style third-person suffix. *Coppens (*ETL* 39, p. 116) repoints to עֹבְדֵי ('those who were slaves [to the many/great]').

53.12aα. Therefore I will give him a share in the many. He will share out the powerful as spoil. Goldbaum (see on 52.6) again sees the opening *lākēn* as an asseveration, but the usual meaning is what would surely come to mind here.

The image it introduces might seem to change sharply when the vision comes to describe Yhwh's action in response to v. 11aβb. Partly this reflects the line's recollection of 9.2 [3]. North (*Suffering Servant*, p. 127) infers from the parallelism there that 'spoil' need not be a military image (cf Prov 31.11), but this is to miss the point of the imagery even in the present context: the chapter is returning to the kingly imagery of 52.13–15. *Sifre on Deuteronomy* 48 refers the passages to Moses, while chapter 355 (on Deut 33.21) adds that Moses will come at the head of every group of scholars (Bible, Mishnah, and Talmud) to receive this reward.

For *rab* ('many'), the KJV has 'great',[44] but regular usage works against this, as does the link between the five-fold occurrence of the word in the opening and closing subsections (see *Olley). 'Powerful' (*ʿāṣûm*) and 'many' are a standard pair of terms; in 21 of the 31 occurrences of 'powerful', it follows 'many', bringing out an implication of the first word. Again, the KJV takes the words to denote not the peoples whom the servant receives as spoil but those

[43] 'Northwest Semitic Philology and Job', in *The Bible in Current Catholic Thought* (ed. J. L. McKenzie; New York, 1962), pp. 55–74 (see p. 72); see further J. A. Emerton, 'A Consideration of Some Alleged Meanings of ידע in Hebrew', in *JSS* 15 (1970), pp. 145–80 (see pp. 157–59).

[44] On this meaning of רב later, see J. Carmignac, 'hrbym: les "Nombreux" ou les "Notables"?', in *RevQ* 7 (1969–71), pp. 575–86.

with whom the servant shares the spoil, but this would be an unparalleled usage of *b*. Rather the prepositional phrase parallels Job 39.17, and *ʾet* before 'the powerful' is the mark of the direct object. Thus the LXX has κληρονομήσει πολλοὺς ('he will inherit many/ cause many to inherit'), Vg *dispertiam ei plurimos* ('I will distribute many to him'); we have followed the even more literal rendering in Th and Sym, μεριῶ αὐτῷ ἐν πολλοῖς. The fact that the second noun is formally indeterminate is no objection to taking *ʾet* thus; the noun is determinate in meaning but the article is not expected in poetry (cf 41.7). In theory *ʾet* might be the preposition 'with' even on the above understanding of *b* (so *Olley) but this generates an implausible understanding of the line as a whole in which the many/mighty are both the objects and the beneficiaries of Yhwh's act.

אחלק: LXX κληρονομήσει ('he will inherit') could render יחלק (cf Driver, *JTS* 41, p. 165) but is more likely paraphrasing.
יחלק: *Driver repoints יֵחָלֵק ('he will receive a share').

53.12aβ. ...in return for the fact that he exposed himself to death when he let himself be counted with rebels. The verb *ʿārāh* can come to mean 'pour out/empty', and *nepeš* ('self/life') can be associated with blood, for the blood is the life (Deut 12.23; Lev 17.14) and the pouring out of lifeblood implies death (cf H. Seebass, *ThWAT* on *nepeš*, IV.4). The Syr thus renders *šdʾ* ('poured out [his soul to death]'), the LXX less literally παρεδόθη εἰς θάνατον. It has the same verb in v. 12b and in v. 6b), Vg *tradidit in morte*, Tg *msr lmwtʾ*. Word-for-word the MT then goes on 'and he let himself be counted with rebels', and this seems an anticlimax. *Whybray (p. 105) therefore points out that 'pour out' could be simply an extension of the meaning 'expose' (cf †Ibn Ezra here); compare the usage in Ps 141.8 where the NRSV renders 'leave defenceless'. *MHP* (p. 103) suggests 'he bared his neck to die', while †Torrey sees the phrase as a way of expressing a superlative, 'he gave himself to the uttermost', as in, for example, Judg 16.16; Jon 4.9 (cf Thomas, 'A Consideration' [see on 53.4b], p. 220).

But with suffering and the possibility of death in the context here, it is unlikely that the phrase could have been heard in a figurative sense with its reduced implications (cf *Payne, p. 137). Now the second colon again postpones the verb to the end, like v. 11b, and we have therefore rather taken the colon as another circumstantial clause, which as such would not be expected to take the argument or the narrative on. 'Rebels' presumably continues to refer to the people of God. The point is thus that the servant's willingness to be identified with them in their rebelliousness is the reason for his exaltation before the world.

The Tg applies this colon to the Messiah, in contrast to its applying the suffering in 52.13–53.12 to the community. It again takes ʾ*et* as object marker rather than preposition, and renders 'he subjected the rebels to the Teaching'.

תחת אשׁר: see BDB, pp. 1065–66; JM 170g.
נמנה: 1QIs[a] נמנא is an Aramaism with the same meaning; Th ἀπέσχετο implies נמנע ('he held back')—perhaps an anti-Christian reading (*Hegermann; contrast *Fascher, p. 14). 4QIs[d] agrees with the MT. The verb is tolerative niphal.

53.12b. . . .when he carried the faults of many, and would appeal for the rebels. This final line constitutes another circumstantial clause like those in vv. 5a and 7aα (*TTH* 160), and thus continues from v. 12aβ rather than contrasting with it. There are no other OT references to 'carrying the faults of others' (the verb is the more familiar *nāśāʾ*, the noun singular *ḥēṭʾ*), but presumably the expression restates that in v. 11b. There, the 'many' were the object of yiqtol verbs, as in 52.15, because the tense follows on that in v. 11aβ; the statements refer to something which is going to happen to them as they come to recognize and become the beneficiaries of the servant's achievement. Here the qatal verb in the poem's closing line which follows on the qatal verbs in v. 12aβ makes for a link with the poem's opening, where in v. 14 'many were appalled'. Their moment of appallment was a moment when the servant was carrying their failure. In addition, the verb *nāśāʾ* itself also recurs from the poem's opening line. The servant will be lifted up despite or because of what he lifted up.

The vision closes with a final reference to the 'rebels', the 'we' of the poem. The nature of the servant's ministry to them is given a new definition in the poem's final word, 'appeal'. The LXX, Vg, and Syr translate as if the verb were qatal (so also *Dahood, *Bib* 63, p. 569), but more likely the change to a yiqtol is again significant. The verb is implicitly taken as future in Rom 8.34; Heb 7.25; 1 John 2.1–2 (*Hegermann, p. 94). This suggests that the tense has temporal significance, as is the case with the other verbs in this verse: the verb then refers to the ministry the servant will continue to exercise as he sees offspring, as Yhwh's purpose is fulfilled, and as the servant receives his spoil. But this seems a strange reversal, and more likely the yiqtol represents an onging activity parallel to that of the previous line. The change is then no doubt partly for variation. The verb is again the hiphil of *pāgaʿ*; the hiphil comes only four other times in the OT.

The Tg reverses the sense of the two verbs in the line, 'he will pray for the transgressions of many/for many transgressions, and the rebels will be forgiven for his sake'. Its rendering of the second verb also implies it takes the verb as impersonal. Now the LXX has a passive verb, παρεδόθη ('he was given over'), while 1QIs[a]'s spelling *ypgʿ* might imply niphal (see note). †Snaith (p. 148) gives the verb the same meaning as in v. 6 but follows the Tg in taking it impersonally;

he renders 'it was caused to light'. The impersonal expression is feasible, but the use of that and the absence of an expression for 'on him' would make the line obscure, and readers would more likely reckon that the servant continues to be the subject. The verb thus needs to have a different meaning from that in v. 6. In 59.16 it will denote hostile 'pressing' of someone, corresponding to a common use of the qal to denote encounter in battle. Here Sym thus has ἀντέστη and Syr seems to use the peal form of the verb *pgʿ* which implies 'attacked'; *Hegermann (pp. 65–66) thinks this reflects a Jewish exegesis of the passage. In this context the usage corresponds more to the use of the qal to mean 'press/entreat' (Gen 23.8, with *l* 'for' as here; Jer 7.16; 27.18; Job 21.15) and of the hiphil in Jer 36.25. The sequence *nāśāʾ–hipgîaʿ* corresponds to that in vv. 4 and 6. There the two words had a similar meaning; here they have a different similar meaning.[45]

חטא: 1QIs[ab], 4QIs[d] have pl. חטאי; cf LXX ἁμαρτίας, Tg חובין, Syr *ʿwlʾ*. Sym and probably Vg (see †van der Kooij, p. 309) have s. The MT may have been assimilated to the s. in vv. 6, 8 (†Barthélemy). But the LXX, Tg, and Syr have pl. in vv. 6 and 8.
רבים: *Dahood (*Bib* 63, p. 569) repoints רָבִים ('of the quarrelers'): see on v. 9a.
ולפשעים: cf Aq, Th, Sym, Vg, Syr, Tg. 1QIs[a] has ולפשעיהמה ('and for their rebellions'); cf 1QIs[b], 4QIs[d], also LXX διὰ τὰς ἁμαρτίας αὐτῶν. Again the agreement of 1QIs[b] with the other witnesses may mean that MT has been assimilated to the previous line and/or involves an abbreviation.[46]
יפגיע: 1QIs[a] יפגע, perhaps a defectively written hi, perhaps an assimilation to the more familiar qal, perhaps ni (see †Kutscher, pp. 112, 277 [ET pp. 150, 362–63]); cf Syr *pgʿ*, perhaps peal, and LXX's passive (Koenig, *Oracles*, p. 105). †Eitan repoints יִפָּגַע.

Bibliography to 52.13–53.12

Ahlström, G. W., 'Notes to Is 53:8f', in *BZ* 13 (1968), pp. 96–98.
Allen, L. C., 'Isaiah liii 2 Again', in *VT* 21 (1971), p. 490.
—'Isaiah liii, 11 and its Echoes', in *Vox Evangelica* 1 (1962), pp. 24–28.
Alobaidi, J., *The Messiah in Isaiah 53: The Commentaries of Saadia Gaon, Salmon ben Yeruham and Yefet ben Eli on Is 52:13–53:12*. Bern: Lang, 1998.
Baars, W., 'Ein weinig bekende oudlatijnse tekst van Jesaja 53', in *NedTT* 22 (1968), pp. 241–48.
Baltzer, K., 'Jes 52, 13: Die "Erhöhung" des "Gottesknechtes", in *Religious Propaganda and Missionary Competition in the New*

45 So G. Morris, *Prophecy, Poetry and Hosea* (*JSOT* Sup 219, 1996), p. 71.
46 So G. R. Driver, 'Once Again Abbreviations', in *Textus* 4 (1967), pp. 76–94 (see p. 80).

Testament World (D. Georgi Festschrift, ed. L. Bormann and others), pp. 45–56. *Novum Testamentum* Sup 74, 1994.
Barrick, W. B., 'The Rich Man from Arimathea (Matt 27:57–60) and 1QIsa[a]', in *JBL* 96 (1977), pp. 235–39.
Battenfield, J. R., 'Isaiah liii 10', in *VT* 32 (1982), p. 485.
Beauchamp, P., 'Lecture et relectures du Quatrième Chant du Serviteur', in †Vermeylen, pp. 325–55.
Begg, C. T., 'Zedekiah and the Servant', in *ETL* 62 (1986), pp. 393–98.
Bellinger, W. H., and W. R. Farmer (eds.), *Jesus and the Suffering Servant*. Harrisburg, PA, 1998.
Bentzen, A., 'On the Ideas of "the Old" and "the New" in Deutero-Isaiah', in *ST* 1 (1947–48), pp. 183–87. Cf *Messias–Moses redidivus–Menschensohn* (Zurich, 1948), pp. 54–56; ET *King and Messiah* (London, 1955), pp. 56–59.
Betz, O., 'Die Übersetzungen von Jes 53 (LXX, Targum) und die Theologia Crucis des Paulus', in *Jesus der Herr der Kirche*, pp. 197–216. WUNT 52. Tübingen, 1990.
Blythin, I., 'A Consideration of Difficulties in the Hebrew Text of Isaiah 53:11', in *BTranslator* 17 (1966), pp. 27–31.
Brooks, R., 'A Christological Suffering Servant?', in R. Brooks and J. J. Collins (ed.), *Hebrew Bible or Old Testament?*, pp. 207–10. Notre Dame, 1990.
Brownlee, W. H., and J. Reider, 'On *mšḥty* in the Qumran Scrolls', in *BASOR* 134 (1954), pp. 27–28.
Calvin, J., 'Sermons sur la prophètie d'Esaïe Chap. liii'. 1558. Reprinted in Corpus Reformatum 63, pp. 581–688; Brunswick, 1887. ET *Sermons on Isaiah's Prophecy of the Death and Passion of Christ*. London, 1956.
Ceresko, A. R., 'The Rhetorical Strategy of the Fourth Servant Song', in *CBQ* 56 (1994), pp. 42–55.
Clines, D. J. A., *I, He, We, and They*. *JSOT* Sup 3, 1976.
Collins, J. J., 'The Suffering Servant', in *Proceedings of the Irish Biblical Association* 4 (1980), pp. 59–67.
Coppens, J., 'La finale du quatrième chant du Serviteur', in *ETL* 39 (1963), pp. 114–21.
—'Phil., ii, 7 et Is., liii, 12', in *ETL* 41 (1965), pp. 147–50.
Craig, C. C., 'The Identification of Jesus with the Suffering Servant', in *Journal of Religion* 24 (1944), pp. 240–45.
Cranfield, C. E. B., 'God's Costly Forgiveness', in *ExpT* 101 (1989–90), pp. 178–80.
Dahood, M., 'Isaiah 53, 8–12 and Massoretic Misconstructions', in *Bib* 63 (1982), pp. 566–70.
—'Phoenician Elements in Isaiah 52:13–53:12', in *Near Eastern Studies in Honor of William Foxwell Albright* (ed. H. Goedicke), pp. 63–73. Baltimore/London, 1971.
Dalman, G., *Jesaja 53*. Leipzig, 1914.
Day, J., '*Daʿat* "Humiliation" in Isaiah liii 11 in the Light of Isaiah

liii 3 and Daniel xii 4, and the Oldest Known Interpretation of the Suffering Servant', in *VT* 30 (1980), pp. 97–103.

Driver, G. R., 'Is 52 13–53 12', in *In memoriam Paul Kahle* (ed. M. Black and G. Fohrer), pp. 90–105. BZAW 103, 1968.

Eissfeldt, O., 'Neue Forschungen zum 'Ebed Jahwe-Problem', in *TLZ* 68 (1943), columns 273–80. = Eissfeldt, *Kleine Schriften*, Vol 2, pp. 443–52. Tübingen, 1963.

Elliger, K., 'Nochmals Textkritisches zu Jes 53', in *Wort, Lied und Gottesspruch* Vol. 2*: Beiträge zu Psalmen und Propheten* (J. Ziegler Festschrift, ed. J. Schreiner), pp. 137–44. Stuttgart, 1972.

—'Textkritisches zu Deuterojesaja', in *Near Eastern Studies in Honor of William Foxwell Albright* (ed. H. Goedicke), pp. 113–19. Baltimore/London, 1971.

Farmer, G., 'Isaiah liii. 9, 11', in *ExpT* 5 (1893–94), p. 381.

Fischer, M., 'Vom leidenden Gottesknecht nach Jesaja 53', in *Abraham unser Vater* (O. Michel Festschrift, ed. O. Betz and others), pp. 116–28. Leiden, 1963.

Fjärstodt, B., 'The Use of Isaiah 53 in the New Testament', in *Indian Journal of Theology* 20 (1971), pp. 109–16.

Fohrer, G., 'Stellvertretung und Schuldopfer in Jes 52,13–53,12', in *Das Kreuz Jesu* (ed. P. Rieger), pp. 7–31. Göttingen, 1969. = Fohrer, *Studien zu alttestamentlichen Texten und Themen*, pp. 24–43. BZAW 155, 1981.

Fowl, S. E. (ed.). 'Isaiah 52–53', in *The Theological Interpretation of Scripture*, pp. 173–237. Oxford/Cambridge, MA, 1997.

Galland, C., 'Structural Readings: How to Do Them', in *Structuralism and Biblical Hermeneutics* (ed. A. M. Johnson), pp. 183–208. Pittsburgh, 1979.

Gerleman, G., 'Der Gottesknecht bei Deuterojesaja', in Gerleman, *Studien zur alttestamentlichen Theologie*, pp. 38–60. Heidelberg, 1980.

Gelston, A., 'Isaiah 52:13–53:12', in *JSS* 35 (1990), pp. 187–211.

—'Knowledge, Humiliation or Suffering', in *Of Prophets' Visions and the Wisdom of Sages* (R. N. Whybray Festschrift, ed. D. J. A. Clines and H. A. McKay), pp. 126–41. *JSOT* Sup 162, 1993.

Ginsberg, H. L., 'The Arm of YHWH in Isaiah 51–63 and the Text of Isa 53 10–11', in *JBL* 77 (1958), pp. 152–56.

—'The Oldest Interpretation of the Suffering Servant', in *VT* 3 (1953), pp. 400–4.

Gordon, R. P., 'Isaiah liii 2', in *VT* 20 (1970), pp. 491–92.

Gosse, B., 'Isaïe 52,13–53,12 et Isaïe 6', in *RB* 98 (1991), pp. 537–43.

Hanks, T. D., 'The Oppressed Servant', in Hanks, *God So Loved the Third World*, pp. 73–96. Maryknoll, NY, 1983.

Hegermann, H., *Jesaja 53 in Hexapla, Targum und Peshitta*. Gütersloh, 1954.

Henning-Hess, H., "Bemerkungen zum ASCHAM-Begriff in Jes 53,10", in *ZAW* 109 (1997), pp. 618–26.

Hess, R. S., 'Isaiah 53:5', in *Vision: The Bulletin of the Glasgow Theological Forum* 3/1 (1993), pp. 7–10.

Hoad, J., 'Some New Testament References to Isaiah 53', in *ExpT* 68 (1956–57), pp. 254–55.
Hoerschelmann, W., 'Summary and Evaluation of Bultmann's View on the Use of Isaiah 53 by Jesus and the Early Church', in *Indian Journal of Theology* 20 (1971), pp. 98–108.
Hofius, O., 'Zur Septuaginta-Übersetzung von Jes 52,13b', in *ZAW* 104 (1992), pp. 107–10.
Hruby, K., 'Die rabbinische Exegese messianischer Schriftstellen', in *Judaica* 21 (1965), pp. 100–22.
Janowski, B., 'Er trug unsere Sünden', in *ZTK* 90 (1993), pp. 1–24. = Janowski, *Gottes Gegenwart in Israel*, pp. 303–26, 337. Neukirchen, 1993.
—*Stellvertretung*. Stuttgart, 1997.
Jeremias, J., 'Zum Problem der Deutung von Jes. 53 im palestinischen Spätjudentum', in *Aux sources de la tradition chrétienne* (M. Goguel Festschrift), pp. 113–19. Neuchâtel, 1950.
Johnson, R. F., 'Christ the Servant of the Lord', in *The Old and New Testaments* (ed. J. H. Charlesworth and W. P. Weaver), pp. 107–36. Valley Forge, PA, 1993.
Kapelrud, A. S., 'The Identity of the Suffering Servant', in *Near Eastern Studies in Honor of William Foxwell Albright* (ed. H. Goedicke), pp. 307–14. Baltimore/London, 1971.
Koch, K., 'Messias und Sündenvergebung in Jesaja 53-Targum', in *JSJ* 3 (1972), pp. 117–48.
Komlosh, Y., 'The Countenance of the Servant of the Lord, Was it Marred?', in *JQR* 65 (1974–75), pp. 217–20.
Kutsch, E., *Sein Leiden und Tod–unser Heil*. Neukirchen, 1967. = Kutsch, *Kleine Schriften zum Alten Testament*, pp. 169–96. BZAW 168, 1986.
Levey, S. H., *The Messiah: An Aramaic Interpretation*. Cincinnati, 1974.
Litwak, K. D., 'The Use of Quotations from Isaiah 52:13–53:12 in the New Testament', in *JETS* 26 (1983), pp. 385–94.
Livingston, G. H., 'The Song of the Suffering Servant', in *Asbury Seminarian* 24 (1970), pp. 34–44.
Luther, M., 'Enarratio 53. capitis Esaie'. 1544. Reprinted in *Werke*, Vol. 40/3 (Weimar: Böhlaus, 1930), pp. 683–746.
Marmorstein, A., 'Zur Erklärung von Jes 53', in *ZAW* 44 (1926), pp. 260–65.
Mijoga, H. B. P., 'Some Notes on the Septuagint Translation of Isaiah 53', in *Africa Theological Journal* 19 (1990), pp. 85–90.
Millard, A. R., 'Isaiah 53:2', in *TynB* 20 (1969), p. 127.
Müller, H. P., 'Ein Vorschlag zu Jes 53 10f', in *ZAW* 81 (1969), pp. 377–80.
Nehrey, J. H., 'The Thematic Use of Isaiah 42,1–4 in Matthew 12', in *Bib* 63 (1982), pp. 457–73.
Neubauer, A., and S. R. Driver. *The Fifty-third Chapter of Isaiah According to the Jewish Interpreters*. 2 vols. Oxford, 1876–77; reprinted with an introduction by R. Loewe, New York, 1969.

North, C. R., 'Who was the Servant of the Lord in Isaiah liii?', in *ExpT* 52 (1940–41), pp. 181–84, 219–21.
Nyberg, H. S., 'Smärtornas man', in SEÅ 7 (1942), pp. 5–82.
Olley, J. W., '"The Many"', in *Bib* 68 (1987), pp. 330–56.
Orlinsky, H. M., *The So-called 'Suffering Servant' in Isaiah 53*. Cincinnati, 1964. = *Interpreting the Prophetic Tradition*, pp. 225–73. Cincinnati, 1969.
Page, S. H. T., 'The Suffering Servant between the Testaments', in *NTS* 31 (1985), pp. 481–97.
Payne, D. F., 'Recent Trends in the Study of Isaiah 53', in *Irish Biblical Studies* 1 (1979), pp. 3–18.
—'The Servant of the Lord', in *EvQ* 43 (1971), pp. 131–43.
Pidoux, G., 'Le serviteur souffrant d'Ésaïe 53', in *RTP* III, 6 (1956), pp. 36–46.
Raabe, P. R., 'The Effect of Repetition in the Suffering Servant Song', in *JBL* 103 (1984), pp. 77–81.
Rad, G. von, 'Isaiah 52.13–53:12', in *Biblical Interpretations* (see 40.1–11 Bibliography), pp. 86–92.
Rembaum, J. E., 'The Development of a Jewish Exegetical Tradition Regarding Isaiah 53', in *HTR* 75 (1982), pp. 289–311.
Reicke, B., 'The Knowledge of the Suffering Servant', in *Das ferne und nahe Wort* (L. Rost Festschrift, ed. F. Maass), pp. 186–92. BZAW 105. Berlin, 1967.
Rignell, L., 'Isa. lii 13–liii 12', in *VT* 3 (1953), pp. 87–92.
Robinson, T. H., 'Notes on the Text and Interpretation of Isaiah liii. 3. 11', in *ExpT* 71 (1959–60), p. 383.
Rosenberg, R. A., 'Jesus, Isaac, and the "Suffering Servant"', in *JBL* 84 (1965), pp. 381–88.
Rubinstein, A., 'Isaiah lii 14', in *Bib* 35 (1954), pp. 475–79.
Ruppert, L., 'Der leidende (bedrängte, getötete) Gerechte', in *Die Entstehung der jüdischen Martyrologie* (ed. J. W. van Henten and others) pp. 76–87. SPB 38, 1989.
—'"Mein Knecht, der Gerechte"', in *BZ* 40 (1996), pp. 1–17.
Saadia Gaon. [see Alobaidi]
Sacchi, P., 'Ideologia e varianti della tradizione ebraica: Deut 27,4 e Is 52, 14', in *Bibel in jüdischer und christlicher Tradition* (J. Maier Festschrift, ed. H. Merklein and others), pp. 13–32. Frankfurt, 1993.
Salmon ben Yeruham. [see Alobaidi]
Scharbert, J., 'Stellvertretendes Sühneleiden in den Ebed-Jahwe-Liedern und in altorientalischen Ritualtexten', in *BZ* 2 (1958), pp. 190–213.
Schwarz, G., '"...wie ein Reis vor ihm"?', in *ZAW* 83 (1971), pp. 255–56.
—'"...sieht er... wird er satt..."?', in *ZAW* 84 (1972), pp. 356–58.
Sekine, S., 'The Concept of Redemption in Second Isaiah', in *Transcendency and Symbols in the Old Testament*, pp. 284–398. BZAW 275, 1999. Japanese original, 1994.

Soggin, J. A., 'Tod und Auferstehung des leidenden Gottesknechtes', in *ZAW* 87 (1975), pp. 346–55.

Sonne, I., 'Isaiah 53 10–12', in *JBL* 78 (1959), pp. 335–42.

Spaller, C., 'Syntaktische und stilistische Relationen im Vierten Gottesknechtslied', in *Liebe zum Wort* (L. Bernhard Festschrift, ed. F. V. Reiterer and P. Eder), pp. 275–92. Salzburg, 1993.

Spieckermann, H., 'Konzeption und Vorgeschichte des Stellvertretungsdankens im Alten Testaments', in *Congress Volume: Cambridge 1995* (ed. J. A. Emerton), pp. 281–95. *VT* Sup 66, 1997.

Steck, O. H., 'Aspekte des Gottesknechts in Jes 52,13–53,12', in *ZAW* 97 (1985), pp. 36–58. = †Steck, pp. 22–43.

Suggs, M. J., 'Wisdom of Solomon 2_{10}–5: A Homily Based on the Fourth Servant Song', in *JBL* 76 (1957), pp. 26–33.

Syrén, R., 'Targum Isaiah 52.13–53.12 and Christian Interpretation', in *JJS* 40 (1989), pp. 201–12.

Thomas, D. W., 'A Consideration of Isaiah liii in the Light of Recent Textual and Philological Study', in *ETL* 44 (1968), pp. 79–86.

Treves, M., 'Isaiah liii', in *VT* 24 (1974), pp. 98–108.

Watts, R. E., 'The Meaning of *ʿālāw yiqp^{e}ṣû m^{e}lākîm pîhem* in Isaiah lii 15', in *VT* 40 (1990), pp. 327–35.

Welshman, H., 'The Atonement Effected by the Servant', in *Biblical Theology* 23 (1973), pp. 46–49.

Whybray, R. N., *Thanksgiving for a Liberated Prophet*. *JSOT* Sup 4, 1978.

Williamson, H. G. M., '*daʿat* in Isaiah liii 11', in *VT* 28 (1978), pp. 119–22.

Wolff, H. W., *Jesaja 53 im Urchristentum*. Bethel, 1942. Reprinted Giessen, 1984.

—'Wer ist der Gottesknecht in Jesaja 53?', in *EvT* 22 (1962), pp. 338–42. = Wolff, *Wegweisung*, pp. 165–71. Munich, 1965.

Yarbro Collins, A., 'The Suffering Servant', in R. Brooks and J. J. Collins (ed.), *Hebrew Bible or Old Testament?*, pp. 201–6. Notre Dame, 1990.

Yephet ben Eli. [see Alobaidi]

Young, E. J., 'The Interpretation of יזה in Isaiah 52:15', in *WTJ* 3 (1941), pp. 125–32.

—*Isaiah Fifty-three*. Grand Rapids, 1952.

Zimmerli, W., 'Zur Vorgeschichte von Jes. liii', in *Congress Volume: Rome 1968*, pp. 236–44. *VT* Sup 17, 1969. = Zimmerli, *Studien zur alttestamentliche Theologie und Prophetie*, pp. 213–21. TBü 51, 1974.

V.b.

54.1–17a: THE RENEWING OF THE ABANDONED WOMAN/CITY

Suddenly the addressee is feminine singular, and that will be so through the chapter. GK 122i assumes that the feminine refers to the nation. This might be a plausible reading in the light of chapters 24–27 (†Lack, pp. 196–97, notes links between the two parts of the book), but more likely we should read chapter 54 in the light of 49.14–52.12 and infer that Yhwh again speaks to Madam Zion. Yet the point is never explicit (contrast the Tg's 'Sing, Jerusalem, you who were like an infertile woman...': simile thus also replaces metaphor). There is an openness about the chapter. GK's assumption that the feminine singular addresses the nation does point us to the fact that the prophet's concern is of course not merely a city of stone but a city of people.

Within chapter 54, most MT MSS provide a setuma after the twofold 'Yhwh is saying' of vv. 8 and 10, while 1QIs[a] begins a new line only after v. 10 (and then after v. 17a; it has mid-line spaces before vv. 15 and 16). This corresponds to a distinction between an address to a woman in vv. 1–8 and to a city in vv. 11–17a and to an ambiguity about vv. 9–10. Like vv. 1–8 they close with references to Yhwh's anger, commitment, and compassion, and they begin 'for', which suggests a link with vv. 1–8. But in form and content they initiate the transition from a poem addressing a woman who stands for a city to a poem addressing a city pictured as a woman; the city is personified as a woman throughout, but the manner of the personification changes and the city itself becomes more prominent as the chapter unfolds.

Rhetorically another distinction can be made. Through chapter 54 the addressee is feminine singular, and this distinguishes chapter 54 from the chapters on either side. In vv. 1–6 the verbs themselves are thus predominantly second-person and all the references to Yhwh are in the third person. Verses 7–17a, though including three further third-person references to Yhwh, is characterized more by first-person verbs. It is doubtful whether we can say that Yhwh is not really speaking through most of vv. 1–6 (*Beuken, pp. 32–33). The prophet speaks both for Yhwh and as Yhwh throughout, but in vv. 1–6 speaks more predominantly 'for', in vv. 7–17a more 'as'. This last is emphasized by the twofold 'here I am/there it was I...' in vv. 11 and 16 (on the text, see comment). There is thus a development of intimacy through the chapter, of a sense of the actual presence of Yhwh involved with the woman/city in her desolation.

Verses 1–8 comprise a series of commands, followed by the reasons that support them:

1 Sing, infertile woman: because you have children
2–3 Extend your house: because you will need more space
4–8 Do not fear: because your husband is returning.

The structure of the first subsection with its encouragement to cry out and its reasons in the form of a noun clause recalls that of a hymn (see, e.g., Pss 95.1–3; 96.1–4). But as usual the prophet adapts the form (cf 42.10–17; 44.23). Here the crying out is not explicitly worship and the noun clause is a statement about the one who is invited to sing rather than a statement about Yhwh, and the noun clause relates to the future rather than to present actuality. Succeeding verses will make this explicit, but it is already implied by the third distinctive feature of this *kî* clause, the fact that it closes with an oracle formula, 'Yhwh is saying'.

The second subsection corresponds to no traditional form. It recalls earlier commands to leave Babylon on the prophet's part (48.20–21; 52.11–12). Like them (and like v. 1) it veils a promise in the form of a command. At the same time it means the command. The addressee is not expected literally now to do that which the imperative urges, but she is expected to make a response to the prophetic word (namely, believe it and be ready to respond to its fulfilment).

As the second subsection was longer than the first, so is the third than the second. It takes up the form of a 'fear not' oracle (cf 41.8–16), but again the form is varied. Like those in 41.10–12, the reasons in due course include noun clauses and verbal statements in the qatal and the yiqtol, but here they come in the reverse order—though the yiqtol forms arguably explicate the command rather than ground it (†Schoors, p. 81). The eventual appearance of the expected qatal verbs in vv. 7–8 is part of *Steck's argument for the original unity of vv. 1–8 (or at least vv. 1, 4–8). Further, a 'fear not' oracle is usually addressed to a male leader (commonly a warrior) and promises support in some task; this 'fear not' oracle addresses an abandoned woman and refers to no task (contrast 41.14–16). Instead of shame being imposed on enemies, it is to be removed from the addressee. Verses 4–8 address an abandoned woman rather than a childless woman. The phrase 'your God is saying' (v. 6) is not a definitive marker of the end of an oracle (a phrase of this kind comes in vv. 1, 6, 8, 10), though it does set up a degree of separation between vv. 4–6 and vv. 7–8. We might then see three forms of lament in vv. 1–8, concerning bereavement or infertility, shame, and abandonment.

When Yhwh speaks directly in vv. 7–8, the defensive form of the statement recalls passages such as 42.18–25 and 43.22–28 where Yhwh grants the half-truth in a charge but counters it. Here the granting of the half-truth ('I abandoned you') takes up the description in v. 6 ('an abandoned woman'); cf more explicitly 49.14. The verbal link with v. 6 and the recurrence of 'your restorer' in v. 8 from v. 5 might suggest fortuitous collocation but more likely implies original continuity. The counter to the charge is not this time 'Yes, and I had good reason' (as in 42.18–25) but 'Yes, but it was very short-lived and will be more than made good by what follows.'

Verses 9–10 in turn take up the 'anger', 'compassion', and 'commitment' of vv. 7–8, which again might denote skilful arrangement of fortuitously available resources but more likely signifies original continuity. This perhaps adds support to the reading 'for…' rather than 'like…' in v. 9a (see comment). Verses 9–10 are another *kî*-clause, which restates vv. 7–8, but adds reference to Noah and the covenant and thus adds to the grounds for believing vv. 7–8 and also takes the subsection to a more theological closure.

The number of *kî* clauses (v. 1b, 3, 4aα, 4aβ, 4b, 5, 6a, 6b—though that one is temporal—9, 10) is a feature of vv. 1–10, indicative of the energy of its theological argument. Its closing formulae form another aspect of its armoury in seeking to clinch its argument, and these also develop, from 'Yhwh is saying' (v. 1) to 'your God is saying' (v. 6) to 'your restorer Yhwh is saying (v. 8) to 'Yhwh who has compassion on you is saying' (v. 10) (†Lack, p. 192); see also the sequence of descriptions of Yhwh in v. 5, which fulfil the same persuasive function: your maker, your husband, Yhwh armies, the holy one of Israel, your restorer, the God of the whole earth. Contrasted to these are the descriptions of the addressee: infertile, who did not bear, who did not labour, desolate, abandoned, grieved in spirit. Her plight is underlined by the multiplication of near-synonyms: shame, humiliate, disgrace. A parallel contrast is expressed in the collocation of 'abandon' and 'gather', 'anger' and 'compassion', and underlined by the paronomasia and rhymes which set up aural links between words which are linked or contrasting in meaning (vv. 1abα, 4a, 4b, 5a, 6a, 8aαβ, 10).

Verses 11–17a begin with an address which parallels that in v. 1, but without an imperative—†Mowinckel thinks the resultant abruptness is a sign that an imperative has been lost. In the MT this gives the impression of resuming from vv. 1–10 as vv. 11–17a offer a series of promises which further support the encouragement in vv. 1–10. The particle 'There' (*hinnēh*) introducing v. 11a reinforces the impression of resumptiveness (see introduction to 52.13–55.13).

The first promise, of beautification (vv. 11–12), is a new one. The second promise, of righteousness (vv. 13–14a), reaffirms the prospect of 'well-being' from v. 10. The third, of security (vv. 14b–17a) reaffirms that there is no need to fear; the verb form is the same as v. 4, but the change in the negative from *ʾal* to *lōʾ* changes its significance from exhortation to promise. Verses 11–17a have more paronomasia in vv. 11a, 11b–13, and repetitions in v. 13 (children) and v. 15 (parts of the verb *gûr*) but none of the closing formulae of vv. 1–10 and only one *kî*-clause: lyrical promise is allowed to speak for itself.

We have noted that the servant passage in 42.1–9 was followed by a summons to the world to resound, and the declarations that Yhwh is restoring servant Jacob–Israel in 42.18–44.22 were followed by a summons to heaven and earth to resound in 44.23. A summons to resounding proclamation almost closed 44.24–48.22, though the actual final words reflected the increasing ambiguity of these chapters. Once more heaven and earth were summoned to resound after 49.1–12. Then ruined Jerusalem was commissioned to resound in 52.7–10. A fifth such commission to Madam Zion now follows the final servant passage. The fact that the servant is to see offspring (53.10) is good news for her, because the offspring are also hers (v. 3). The 'many' whose failure he carried (53.12) compare with her 'many' children (v. 1). At the close of the chapter, in v. 17a, motifs from chapter 53 reappear. As Yhwh's determination will 'succeed' at the servant's hand (53.10), so no instrument used against Zion will 'succeed'. Whereas the servant was taken from 'judgment' (53.8), no judgment will prevail against her. As he would show many that he is just (*ṣdq* hi), so she will show her accusers that they are wrong (*rš*ʿ hi, the antonym).

In substance, however, chapter 54 as a whole more clearly takes up the themes of 49.14–50.3 and 51.17–52.10. The image of Zion as a woman is again expounded in superficially contradictory ways in chapter 54. Madam Zion is a woman who was infertile (v. 1a), who was abandoned (vv. 1b, 6, 7), who was widowed (v. 4b), who was bereaved of her children(?). The passage thus takes up the distinctive grievous experiences of a woman, especially in a patriarchal society.

In vv. 11–17a the personification of the city continues but the specific figure of the woman disappears. The focus now lies on the city's beauty (vv. 11–12), well-being and justice (vv. 13–14), and security (vv. 15–17a). The reality to which the images refer overlaps with that to which vv. 1–10 refers. The emphasis in vv. 1–10 lies on numerical growth which will lead to Zion's needing and being able to appropriate the nations and occupy their empty towns; in vv. 11–17a they are to be protected from their attacks and to experience the inner moral and social renewal which the community needs.

The metre of 54.1–17a is irregular, like that of 52.13–53.12, but the parallelism is especially systematic and takes varied forms (†Grimm and Dittert). There are examples of paronomasia in vv. 4, 6, 8, and 10. Elliger derives chapter 54 along with 52.13–53.12 from Third Isaiah (*Verhältnis*, pp. 135–67). Hermisson ('Einheit', p. 311) derives vv. 11–17 from the 'Deliverance is near' stratum of the work.

54.1abα. Resound, infertile woman who did not bear. Break into sound and whoop, you who did not labour. The nine words have three ways of ending: three imperatives end in *-î*, four feminines end in *-āh*, two negatives end in *-ô*.

We have noted in the introduction to 54.1–17a that the exhortation 'resound' (*rānan*) parallels that to the heavens and the rest of the world in 42.11; 44.23; 49.13, and that to wasted Jerusalem in 52.8–9 (pi), each time at the close of a section promising Yhwh's act. 'Break into sound' also appeared in 44.23 and 49.13, the verb in 52.9. In 12.6 it was accompanied by the verb 'whoop' (lit. 'neigh': cf Vg *hinni*; †Korpel and de Moor suggest 'radiate' on the basis of Ugaritic, but this gives poorer parallelism). The verbs can denote worship, but more broadly (as here) suggest simply enthusiastic joy.

The phrases 'infertile woman who did not bear' and 'who did not labour' recall a series of individuals in Israel's story—for example, Sarah, Rachel, Rebekah, and Manoah's wife. These women had their infertility reversed, and now that is to happen for the personified city. Admittedly Madam Zion has previously been a woman who was bereft rather than infertile, but within these chapters related images have been applied to her (see 49.21) even though not this precise one, and the people have already been invited to recall the experience of matriarch Sarah (51.2).

רני: 1QIs[a] רוני; the spelling recurs in the next line.
ילדה: a second person vb in the relative cl. would be more usual (JM 158n); but see comment on 44.1.
רנה: LXX omits; so also †Duhm, to regularize the metre.
לא חלה: 1QIs[a] precedes by ו; so also in the next line.

54.1bβ. For the children of the desolate are many, more than the children of the married, Yhwh is saying. For Zion as 'desolate', see 49.8, 19. The Tg has '…than the children of inhabited Rome', assuming that desolate Jerusalem is being contrasted with some other currently populous city and presupposing the background of the fall of Jerusalem in AD 70. In the prophet's own context, the other currently populous city would be Babylon (cf †Ibn Ezra's comment, though he is also prepared to generalize the reference). The desolate and the married are thus two different contemporary women, as in 1 Sam 2.5. But more likely an ellipse is presupposed: the currently desolate will regain her marital status and will have more children than she had when she was married. Being interpreted, Yhwh is restoring the relationship with Jerusalem and will bring her population back in vast numbers (cf 49.17). The promise does not say that she will bear them; in fact, Yhwh is going to bring them. Indeed, it says nothing about where they will come from, unlike chapter 49. As in 49.21, they already exist, unbeknown to their mother. There are no yiqtol verbs in the context to suggest that we should translate this noun clause as anything other than present. Yet the provision of the supporting phrase 'Yhwh is saying' (lit. 'Yhwh [has] said') reflects the fact that this is so only in vision. For similar brief buttress phrases, cf vv. 6, 8, 10; they are otherwise rare in Isaiah 40–55 (see 45.13; 48.22).

54.2aαβ. Enlarge your tent-space. Your dwelling-curtains must be spread. The two cola mirror each other: the arrangement is chiastic. A double masculine singular construct phrase is complemented by a double feminine plural construct phrase, a second-person feminine singular imperative verb is complemented by a third-person plural which the imperative in the first colon suggests is jussive. Some late medieval MSS (see *HUB*) and the Syr have plural ‘tents’, while †Bonnard resolves the difference in the persons of the verbs by rendering ‘Enlarge your tent-space and your dwelling-curtains which must be spread’. But the impersonal third person is common, not least with unnamed servants as the implicit subject of the verb. For the sequence, cf 49.13; here the variety mirrors the abundance which the words refer to (cf *CHP*, p. 32; *TTCHV*, p. 387). In substance, the first colon concerns internal living space, the second the tent’s external ‘walls’.

Within Isaiah, the application of the tent image to the city recalls 33.20. That verse also refers to the ‘stakes’ which hold the tent ropes, though otherwise the language of the two passages is not close. While Isaiah 33 thus makes a link between ‘First Isaiah’ and ‘Second Isaiah’, it is more systematically a summary of what precedes than an anticipation of what follows; conversely, Isa 54.1–3 has broader background than Isaiah 33. Comparison with Isaiah 33 helps to highlight the nature of 54.2–3. Both chapters refer both to Zion’s security and to its size, but in themselves 33.20 focuses on the former, 54.2 on the latter (†Williamson, p. 228).

הַרְחִיבִי: 1QIs[a] ארחיבי, a spelling variant.
מִשְׁכְּנוֹתַיִךְ: the word is often pl., perhaps because a tent had many parts; pl. of local extension or of amplification (cf GK 124be). LXX lacks. †Duhm omits as a prosaic gl. The equivalents to אהל and משכנות are a common pair in Ugaritic (Watson, ‘Fixed Pairs’, p. 460).
יַטּוּ: Aq, Th, Sym, ἐκταθήτωσαν may imply passive יֻטּוּ (despite the f. subject) but may equally be a (correct) interpretation of the Heb. impersonal. 1QIs[a] יטי is a composite form, combining third pl. jussive and second s. imper. הטי, also reflecting the ambiguity of י and ו in its archetype (†Barthélemy). The latter may underlie LXX πῆξον, Vg *extende*, Syr *mtwḥy*, Tg יתיבי, but this reading still likely assimilates the second colon to the first. *Dahood reworks as יַטִּ (a Phoenician-style yiphil imper.) followed by the copula.

54.2aγb. Do not hold back. Lengthen your ropes, strengthen your stakes. There is some ambiguity in v. 2 over whether it concerns the extending of an existent tent or the pitching of a tent for the first time, and this likely reflects the fact that actually it refers to the re-pitching and enlarging of a tent which has been demolished. Someone whose tent has been pulled down might be tempted not to risk pitching it again. Will the same thing happen once more? The central clause of the verse thus addresses the fundamental issue that faces such a person.

The MT links this central clause with the previous two cola, as does 1QIs[a] by the prefixing of a *w*. This is justified enough given the AABAA structure of v. 2 (*TTCHV*, p. 387). Further, it stretches the length of v. 2a (3–4 or more likely 3–3–2) in keeping with the stretching it enjoins (†Lack, p. 193). In contrast to the first, the second line is then a brisk 2–2 chiastic bicolon whose k-k-k-q sounds also mirror the hammering of stakes to which it refers (†Lack, p. 193). But the shortness of this resultant second bicolon makes it more plausible to link the single central colon with what follows rather than with what precedes; these are indeed two six-word lines, one 3–3, one 2–2–2.

The Tg again looks behind the metaphor and renders the verse as a whole 'enlarge the place of your camp and cause the cities of your land to be inhabited; do not hold back; increase the people in your camps and strengthen your rulers'. Talk of a tent suggests to the Tg a military camp, and the interpretation may link with movements such as the Bar Kochba revolt (Chilton, *Isaiah Targum*). The interpretation gains support from v. 3.

54.3. For you will break out right and left. Your offspring will dispossess nations. They will inhabit desolate towns. The 3–3–3 tricolon advertises the end of a subsection, though the MT's verse sub-division rightly implies that the parallel second and third cola belong together; both spell out the implications of the first.

'Breaking out' (*pāraṣ*) and 'dispossessing' (*yāraš*) are violent images. This reference to nations at first thus suggests a tension with the promises in Genesis and with some other parts of Isaiah 40–55. 'Nations' appear in Genesis only as the implicit or explicit objects of God's blessing (Gen 10; 18.18; 22.18; 26.4). It is in Exodus–Judges that 'nations' becomes a negative term. In Isaiah the usage has been mixed: the nations are to recognize Yhwh's revelation in Israel and Yhwh's sole deity (2.2–4; 11.10; 42.1, 6; 43.9; 49.6; 52.10, 15; cf 55.5; 60.3; 61.9, 11; 62.2; 64.2 [1]; 66.18–21), they are involved in Yhwh's service in judgment and restoration (5.26; 11.12; 13.4; 49.22; cf 60.5, 11, 16; 61.6; 66.12, 20), they are victims of more powerful nations' aggression and wear the veil of mourning (10.7; 14.6, 12, 26; 25.7; 41.2; 45.1), they are Zion's attackers judged and scattered by Yhwh and count as nothing before Yhwh (29.7, 8; 30.28; 33.3; 34.1–2; 40.15, 17; cf 60.11).

But talk of 'dispossessing nations' with its links with the story of Israel's original occupation of the land suggests a focus here on Judah's regaining control of its own land rather than looking to control the whole world. That may be background to the statement in the third colon, and may help to take the edge off the negativeness of the reference to nations.

The LXX renders the plural verb 'inhabit' by second person singular κατοικιεῖς, assimilating to the first colon and assuming that 'you' rather than 'your offspring' is the subject. The Vg renders the plural verb by third singular *inhabitabit*, assuming that 'your offspring' is the subject and producing a meaning somewhat like Ezek 36.33—though there Yhwh is the verb's subject and the promise refers to the Judeans' own cities which lie in ruins. The desolate towns are then presumably also the towns which receive the good news in 40.9, towns which had shared in the devastation of the 590s and 580s.

Such talk of the inhabiting of desolate towns again draws our attention to 6.11, where all three words came;[1] Madam Zion herself has already been described as 'desolate' in v. 1. In addition 6.12 also commented on the vast 'abandonment' of the land this involved: the word is exactly the same as the participle 'abandoned' which will describe Madam Zion here in v. 6. Then 6.13 went on to speak of the holy 'offspring' in a way which in some respect hinted at hope for the future, an explicit hope here. Verse 3 then promises a reversal of the threat of 6.11–13 and a fulfilment of its hint of hope.

But *IBHS* 7.2.1c calls *zera*ʿ a 'conventional collective', one 'almost always represented in the singular'. Thus it was singular in the previous colon. It is therefore unlikely to be the subject of the verse's closing verb. There are then two possibilities. The verb might be an impersonal third person plural, like that in v. 2a, suggesting 'desolated cities will be inhabited' (presumably by those offspring). But the presence of a third person plural masculine word in the preceding colon makes it more likely that this is the subject: it is the nations who will inhabit desolate cities (lit. 'cause them to be inhabited'). 'Desolation' can suggest ruin ar depopulation or both (cf 49.19); both are applicable here. The idea then is that other peoples will move on from the cities of which they are dispossessed to cities which are at the moment ruined and uninhabited.

Reference to people as the woman's offspring heightens the question whence they came. The prophet never says that Madam Zion will bear more children; they might seem to be children she adopts, people who come to Jerusalem from afar (from the Judean community in Babylon or elsewhere, or from the nations). Yet neither does the prophet yet refer to them as coming to her, as v. 7 will. Further, *zera*ʿ (lit. 'seed') usually denotes the offspring of a man (cf 43.5; 44.3; 45.19, 25; 48.19; 53.10), on the assumption that it is the man's seed that essentially forms the offspring.

גוים: NEB repoints גֵּוִים ('backs, wide regions'; †Brockington).
יירש: 1QIs[a] יירשו (cf †Torrey).

54.4a. Do not be afraid, for you will not be shamed. Do not be humiliated, for you will not be disgraced. Once again the four feminine verbs mean that the four main words in the line all end *-î*.

We are familiar with the exhortation not to be afraid, though it has usually been in the second person singular masculine, addressed to Jacob–Israel (41.10, 13; 43.1, 5; 44.2); exceptions which prove the rule are 41.14, where a feminine word is used to describe Jacob–

[1] See R. Rendtorff, 'Jesaja 6 im Rahmen des Komposition des Jesajabuchs', in †Vermeylen, pp. 73–82 (see p. 79); ET in Rendtorff, *Canon and Theology* (Minneapolis, 1993), p. 177.

Israel; 40.9, where the addressee is a collective embassy; 51.7, where the verb is masculine plural. Thus for the first time this feminine singular address to Zion corresponds to the earlier address to Jacob–Israel. It has new resonances when addressed to a woman who has been the victim of her husband's anger and has been abandoned by him, even if he proposes to have her back (see Hos 3). Further, Jacob–Israel has earlier been told that it will not experience shame or humiliation (see esp. 45.17; also 49.23, in the context of promises to Zion; 50.7, the servant's testimony), though this was not a reason for it not to fear. On the other hand, its invulnerability to shame was linked to its opponents' destiny of shame (e.g. 45.16–17). This latter was also a reason for Jacob–Israel not to fear (41.11) as well as for praise and confidence (42.17).

The line closes with a new word, 'disgrace' (*ḥāpar*, here hi). It is a less common one than the other two and usually follows one or both of them for variation, as here. The LXX renders the second and fourth yiqtol verbs by aorists and removes the negatives, 'because you were shamed/disgraced'.

ואל: 1QIs[b] אל.
תכלמי: †Ehrlich emends to תֵּעָלְמִי.
תחפירי: 1QIs[a] תחפורי, implying qal (cf Morgenstern, 'Isaiah 49–55', p. 22); MT is inwardly transitive hi (cf GK 53d), as in 33.9. †Ehrlich emends to תֵּחָרְפִי or תֶּחֶרְפִּי

54.4b. For you will forget the shame of your youth and no longer remember the disgrace of your widowhood. The 'for' is as much emphatic as logical. The NIV omits it and †Schoors (p. 81) calls it an adversative (cf GK 163ab) as v. 4b continues to explicate 'fear not': the motivation for the imperative will come in vv. 5–6. Shame will cease to be a memory of the past as well as a fear for the future. 'Disgrace' (*ḥerpāh*) is yet a fourth term to add to the three of v. 4a (cf 47.3; 51.7). Its letters are the same as the third; it came in Lam 3.30, 61; 5.1. 'Your youth' and 'your widowhood' rhyme.

עלומיך: LXX's *αἰώνιον* ('eternal [shame]') understands the word as if it linked with עולם. On the basis of Ugaritic *ǵlm*, *Schoors (pp. 503–5) hypothesizes yet another root עלם meaning 'bondage'.
אלמנותיך: on the pl. suffix, see GK 91l; JM 94j. ארמלותך in 4Q176 *Tanḥûmîm* is the Aramaic equivalent.

54.5a. For the one who marries you is your maker. Yhwh Almighty is his name. 'Your husband' follows on from what precedes; 'your maker' is the new element in the statement. The sentence says something about the woman's husband (namely, that he is her maker), not about her maker (namely, that he is her husband) (against *Beuken, pp. 43–44). The new statement here is that the potential husband whose existence was implied by v. 4 is the woman's maker, who can therefore be relied on; the further description of the maker in the second clause then follows naturally as a continuation of the predicate.

The verb *bāʿal* is related to the noun *baʿal* which is a common noun meaning 'lord' in the sense of husband and 'Lord' applied to Yhwh, though it is more often applied to other gods and is used as quasi-proper noun applied as a name for a key Canaanite god. It would be appropriate enough for the prophet to declare that Yhwh will now finally take the place of Baal in Madam Zion's life (cf Hosea). The LXX's κύριος and the Tg's *mryk* ('[your] lord') imply the noun, but it is noticeable that in the MT the prophet does not use the noun, perhaps rather avoiding it because of that second set of connotations (Aq, Vg also have a verbal form). Using the participle sets up the two words 'the one who marries you' and 'the one who makes you' as exactly equivalent and rhyming. But the noun and the participle probably have different implications in substance. The participle implies that Yhwh is now marrying this woman (so she is widowed or divorced). In contrast, the LXX's κύριος ὁ ποιῶν σε implies that her confidence lies in the fact that Yhwh her maker is already and still her husband; compare its reversing in v. 6. The Vg has 'The one who made you will master you'.

בעליך: is pl., perhaps assimilated to the form of the succeeding עשיך whose י is part of its root (GK 124k). 1QIs[a] בעלכי is an Aramaism (cf גואלכי which follows). In the light of Ugaritic *bʿl* ('make'), C. H. Gordon understands the verb as an equivalent of פעל.[2] But this does not take into account Ugaritic's lack of a verb *pʿl*; further, the word's meaning is thus parallel to to 'your maker' so that the suggestion seems to produce tautology (†Schoors, p. 83; and see *CP*, pp. 100–1). For כי בעליך, 4Q176 *Tanḥûmîm* has כבעליך.

54.5b. Your restorer is the holy one of Israel. He calls himself God of all the earth. Verse 5a applied to Madam Zion familiar descriptions of Jacob–Israel: Yhwh is also her maker, her sovereign. Verse 5b does the same with 'the holy one of Israel' being her 'restorer'. That image has distinctive resonances when applied to a childless widow (cf the story of Ruth). It receives extra force from the reminder that this restorer has the worldwide authority of the God of all the earth. The description comes only here, but it belongs with the series of descriptions of Yhwh's lordship over the whole world (e.g. 51.16). It is thus unlikely that the phrase denotes merely 'God of the whole land' (†Marti, who takes v. 5 as a gloss). The LXX omits 'God' and thus translates with a dative, 'to the whole earth'. The LXX and Vg render the niphal verb by a passive ('he will be called'), but the previous occurrences of the niphal in 48.1–2 were reflexive, and in parallelism with the end of v. 5a this makes good sense here (contrast the pual in 48.8, 12).

[2] *Ugaritic Textbook* (Analecta Orientalia 38; Rome, 1969), p. 375.

קְדוֹשׁ: the LXX MSS have αὐτός, probably a misreading of ἅγιος (which Ziegler reads).

54.6a. For Yhwh is calling you as a woman who has been abandoned and grieved in spirit. Once more the opening *kî* has been understood as asseverative, 'a stylistic device to express an absolute certainty';[3] but a causative sense need not be excluded. As the addressee is pictured throughout as a bereft woman, she is more likely identified 'as an abandoned woman' than compared with one ('like an abandoned woman') (†Whybray; cf GK 118x). The LXX here reuses the negatives it omitted in v. 4, 'Not like an abandoned woman. . .nor like a young woman. . .' (for the addition of the negative, †Ziegler [p. 96] compares 8.14). So Yhwh is like a man exercising compassion towards a woman in need. The woman of course is a wife, but here the prophet uses the ordinary word *ʾiššāh* which also means 'woman' in the general sense, not the patriarchal word *bᵉʿûlāh* which came in v. 1 (cf the corresponding active participle in v. 5). In the 2–2–2 line, the pual participles come next to each other and sound very like each other (*ʿăzûbāh*, *ʿăṣûbat*): the pain of abandonment is mirrored in the aural link between the two.

The reference to calling once more applies to Zion the language used of Jacob–Israel (41.9; 42.6), though once more reworks it. †Ewald assumes that this calling is the long ago one which set up the original relationship with Yhwh (cf Ezek 16), but reference to that would be irrelevant. Rather the calling is the one happening right now; the verb is another instantaneous qatal.

The Tg renders 'for the presence of Yhwh has called you' (only here does the Tg render *qārāʾ* literally).

וַעֲצוּבַת רוּחַ: On the construct (explicative genitive), see *DG* 35c.
קְרָאָךְ: on the form, see GK 58g; JM 61i.

54.6b. . . .a young woman when she has been spurned, your God is saying. With the LXX and Tg, we assume that the preposition *k* applies to the opening noun in this line which depends on v. 6a. The LXX and Tg translate the opening phrase literally, 'a woman from/of youth', which EVV take to mean 'the wife of *his* or *someone's* youth'. The image then recalls the allegory in Ezekiel 23 where Yhwh marries two women, or the allegory in Hosea 1–3 where (to beg some questions) Yhwh marries, divorces, and then remarries the same woman, or (more plausibly in terms of the way the image is worked here) an analogy with a woman who experiences a man falling in love with her when they were both young, then falling out of love with her and leaving her, and then has another man ask her to marry him. But one would expect some indication of the 'youth' being that of a

[3] A. Schoors, 'The Particle כִּי', in *Remembering All the Way*. . . (OTS 21, 1981), pp. 240–76 (see p. 260).

husband, as in Joel 1.8; Mal 2.14, 15; Prov 5.18. We have rather taken the construct as adjectival. The expression is then a little nearer to that in Hos 2.17 [15] which refers to Israel—or perhaps more likely the land of Israel—in her youth. But it is not part of an allegory.

Yet again the description of her as 'spurned' applies a term earlier applied to Jacob–Israel (cf 41.9; but also Lam 5.22, of Zion). The KJV renders the verb as second person, but the LXX and Vg render it by another passive participle, more plausibly assuming that it is third person feminine. The yiqtol verb is unexpected, and †Qimchi rather construes the line as a question, 'The wife of a man's youth—can she be spurned?'. But when *kî* introduces a question, it is normally accompanied by a further particle or some other expression which points to its interrogative significance (see BDB, p. 472). †Alexander therefore suggests ' "for she shall be spurned", said your God': that is, these are the words Yhwh uttered when spurning her. More likely the yiqtol continues the force of the participle. T. C. Vriezen understands the *kî* as concessive.[4]

Morgenstern ('Isaiah 49–55', p. 23) sees 'your God is saying [i.e. bidding]' as parallel to 'Yhwh is calling you'. But phrases such as 'your God is saying' are surely too familiar as buttressing for the prophecy (cf vv. 1, 8, 10) for this to be the phrase's significance here.

אמר: 1QIs[a] adds יהוה. †Duhm moves יהוה from v. 6a to regularize the metre.

54.7. For a little moment I abandoned you, but with great compassion I will gather you together. The two cola form a close parallelism which underlines the contrast: literally, 'in a moment little I abandoned you but in compassion great I will gather you'. The contrast is also mirrored in the word forms: 'little moment' is singular, 'great compassion' plural, while the first verb is qal qatal, the second piel yiqtol. At the same time the metre suddenly becomes very regular (3–3, 2–2–2, 3–3), mirroring the normalization of relationship which Yhwh promises (†Lack, p. 193). Yet the out-of-the-ordinariness of the lines' content is simultaneously marked by the transition to first-person speech on Yhwh's part.

Yhwh attempts to take the edge off the admission of having abandoned Zion in three ways. First, Yhwh declares that the abandonment was only momentary.

Second, this momentariness is contrasted with the greatness of the compassion Yhwh will now show. Comparison and contrast is emphasized by the reuse of the preposition in the parallel phrases at the beginning of the two cola, by the pairing of a singular and a plural noun, and by the utilizing of adjectives which are antonyms (literally 'in a small moment. . .but in big compassions'). The Tg has

[4] 'Einige Notizen zur Übersetzung des Bindeswort *kî*', in *Von Ugarit nach Qumran* (O. Eissfeldt Festschrift, ed. J. Hempel and others; BZAW 77, 1958), pp. 266–73 (see p. 271).

'in a little anger' (cf Syr *brwgzʾ zʿwrʾ*), which makes the parallelism more complete, and G. R. Driver makes a similar suggestion on the basis of an Arabic root.[5] This seems to involve reading a new meaning into the root *rgʿ* (cf on 51.15) or reading it as if were *gʿr* or reading *bĕrōgez* (cf Syr; also in v. 8; cf †Ehrlich).

Third, Yhwh promises that abandonment will be succeeded by 'gathering together' (resultative piel). Once again a verb applied to Jacob–Israel (40.11; 43.5; also the ni in 49.18) is reapplied to Zion, a little oddly. The LXX rationalizes to ἐλεήσω ('I will have mercy'), while †Ehrlich suggests 'take hold of' on the basis of the meaning of this verb in Arabic, and †Duhm emends to *ʾăḥabbᵉqēk* ('I will embrace you').

54.8aαβ. In a burst of anger I hid my face from you for a moment. Yhwh restates the point in v. 7a, once again beginning with a compound phrase introduced by the preposition *b* and this time linking two words of similar sound (*šeṣep qeṣep*). The verb *šāṣap* (or *šāsap*) means 'cut/slash' (see BDB, *DTT*) and LXX ἐν θυμῷ μικρῷ, Sym ἐν ὀξύσμῳ/ἀτόμῳ ὀργῆς, Vg *in momento indignationis* assume that the noun denotes a slash or brief moment. This fits the beginning of v. 7. The Tg indeed renders 'for a brief hour', oddly removing all reference to anger after adding it to v. 7. But the point about time is made again at the end of this line, where *regaʿ* recurs from the beginning of v. 7. This supports the idea that the poet is here (additionally?) utilizing the aural and visual link with the word for 'anger' which follows and in order to make the rhetoric work has devised a new spelling for the word 'burst' (usually *šeṭep*), or may have used an otherwise uninstanced form. The word is that used of a flash flood which bursts suddenly across countryside and then abates. Yhwh's anger is overwhelming, but short-lived. Yet once more, the language links with words used to Jacob–Israel (43.2).

The Tg has 'I took up the face of my Presence from you', while the LXX, Vg, and Syr have 'turn' rather than 'hide', as at 53.3 (Rowlands, *VT* 9, p. 188).

בשצף: †Thomas suggests בְּשֵׁפֶץ, an Akkadianism for 'in strength'; *CAD* gives 'obduracy' as the meaning of *šipṣu*.

54.8aγb. But with lasting commitment I am having compassion on you, your restorer Yhwh is saying. At the climax of vv. 1–8 Yhwh introduces the notion of *ḥesed*, which suggests an act of commitment on the part of someone in a strong position who accepts an obligation to someone in a weaker position. The LXX renders by ἔλεος and the Vg by *misericordia*, as they often do. Both thus

[5] 'Studies in the Vocabulary of the Old Testament. viii', in *JTS* 36 (1935), pp. 293–301 (see p. 299).

anticipate the root which then appears in the verb. Yhwh's *ḥesed* indeed expresses itself in mercy and forgiveness when people do not keep their side of the relationship. It is not a word which works only on the basis of the fulfilment of mutual obligation. Nevertheless these renderings miss the distinctive connotation of *ḥesed*. New Testament Greek ἀγάπη comes nearer to the idea.

'I hid my face' and 'for a moment' contrast with 'lasting commitment' and 'I am having compassion', while 'I hid' has the same three vowels as 'I am having compassion' and 'burst of anger' also links with 'commitment' as each is a noun with two short e-vowels. 'Even alliteration encourages the perception that all events took place within an ordered, symmetrical environment of divine logic' (†Willey, p. 235). 'I am having compassion' is a qatal verb, which we have taken as instantaneous qatal; the root is that of the noun 'compassion' in v. 7b. Out of context the phrase might have been related to the past ('with lasting commitment I had compassion'; cf LXX), and Yhwh might have claimed to have been having compassion even in the midst of the abandonment; 'lasting' (*ʿôlām*) can operate towards the past as well as towards the future. But given Yhwh's acknowledgment in v. 7, 'lasting' is more likely a promise than a self-defence. If *ʿôlām* can sometimes be a means of expressing the superlative, the temporal ideas in the context surely rule out this connotation here (contrast 51.11a and the comment there).

'Your restorer' picks up the description of Yhwh in v. 5.

ובחסד: 1QIs[a], 4QIs[c], 4Q176 *Tanḥûmîm* have ובחסדי, pl. construct, the form which appears in 55.3 (but see also the consonants in v. 10); Syr also has a pl. but it is *rḥmy* which is regularly pl.

54.9a. For this is the waters of Noah for me. In that I swore that the waters of Noah would not pass over the earth again... Some Masoretic MSS, also 1QIs[a], 4Q176 *Tanḥûmîm*, Vg, Tg, Aq, Th, Sym presuppose a minutely different construing of the text which changes from metaphor to simile, 'This is like the days of Noah for me...'. The prophet often utilizes *kî* clauses, especially at the close of subsections, though also at the beginning of a subsection (see esp. 45.18). On the other hand, no other subsection begins or closes with a simile (*CHP*, p. 261, says that similes are used to open sections, but none of the examples begins *k*). Although a distinctive usage might then have been assimilated to the prophet's more usual speech, the abruptness of the versions' construction makes it more appropriate to follow L and A.

The Vg then renders *zōʾt* ('this') *istud* ('that'), which implies that the demonstrative refers back to v. 8, whereas the LXX's τοῦτό more plausibly refers it forward; the MT's setuma has the same implication. But the apodosis in v. 9b will be concerned to reaffirm vv. 7–8, so the point is not affected. The line takes up an event in the OT story that the prophet has not so far appealed to and takes that as support for the belief that Yhwh will not abandon the city again.

The second colon begins with the particle *ʾăšer*. The Vg assumes that it has its usual function as a relative and takes Noah as antecedent; the Tg takes 'the days of Noah' as antecedent. The MT's verse division also implies some such understanding. But poetry does not normally use this relative, so the LXX's καθότι is more likely right to imply that *ʾăšer* looks forward. BDB (p. 83b) similarly takes it as equivalent to *kaʾăšer* (to which †Oort emends), but it might also be compared with causal *ʾăšer* (see JM 170e; *IBHS* 38.4a). BDB (p. 82b) sees it as anticipating its logical antecedent (we might render 'I swore that those waters of Noah…'), but this makes the transition to v. 9b more difficult.

We might render the niphal form of the verb *nišbaʿ* more literally 'bound myself' (the Tg typically has 'swore by my Word'). The way of expressing the oath (*min* plus the infinitive, literally 'from Noah's waters again overflowing the earth') appears only here and in the next line; on such pregnant usages, see GK 119y. As an alternative to the usual *ʾim* clause (implying 'if Noah's waters again overflow the earth [may I be punished]'), this may itself also qualify the anthropomorphic metaphor.

כי מי נח: LXX's ἀπὸ τοῦ ὕδατος seems to conflate this phrase and מי נח מעבר in the next line and is hardly evidence of a different text; it may reflect the influence of Gen 9.11 (cf *HUB*). The 'confusion' (†Ottley) continues into v. 9b.
מי נח עוד: see previous note. 4Q176 *Tanḥûmîm* omits עוד but adds עד at the end of v. 9bα, where 1QIs[a] has an extra עוד.

54.9b. …so I am swearing that I will not be angry with you. I will not blast you. The 'so' takes up from the 'in that' of v. 9a. 'I am swearing' is actually the same verb form as that in v. 9a, but it constitutes a classic example of an instantaneous qatal where the act denoted by the verb is achieved in and by the act of uttering it. The verb which follows (lit. 'from being angry') matches the equivalent in the previous line (lit. 'from overflowing'), though the verb itself takes up that in v. 8a. Then the sentence leaps on to a prepositional expression (lit. 'over you') also equivalent to what preceded ('over the earth'). And the poet completes another 2–2–2 line (if we ignore the MT's *maqqeph*) with a parallel verbal expression (lit. 'from blasting at you'). On the root, see on 50.2; the noun accompanied a word for 'wrath' in 51.20.

54.10a. For the mountains may move away, the hills may totter... JM 171b takes the *kî* to mean 'though',[6] while *Beuken (p. 50) takes it as emphatic, but the familiar causal meaning makes sense. Verse 10 brings a climax, but this can be expressed in causal terms.

Mountains and hills are a frequent pair (in Isaiah the latter appears only in parallelism with the former), combining masculine and feminine and suggesting something impressive and imposing or threatening (e.g. 2.2, 14; 41.15). But they are also a natural image for stability and security. The LXX has 'your hills', continuing from v. 9 and changing the point of the reference; 1QIs[a] lacks the article on 'the hills'. The second verb (*mûṭ*) is a familiar one to suggest instability (cf Pss 46.3 [2]; 125.1); the distinctiveness of the present line is the first verb (*mûš*). It is not an especially natural one, and it was perhaps chosen for the similarity of sound with the second. The pair recur in v. 10b in even closer forms.

תמוטנה: on the form, see JM 80b. 1QIs[a] התמוטינה: the hit was perhaps more familiar (†Kutscher, p. 275 [ET p. 359]). 4Q176 *Tanḥûmîm* has התמוטטנה.

54.10b. But my commitment will not move away from you. My covenant of well-being will not totter, the one who has compassion on you, Yhwh, is saying. In a number of ways the 3–3–3 line (if we supply a *maqqeph* in the middle colon) brings vv. 9–10 and thus vv. 1–10 to a thudding close. The effectiveness of its denial comes through the use of the tricolon with its unexpected extra colon, through the actual content of that extra colon with its buttressing through the reminder of who speaks, through the repetition of the verbs with their similarity of sound and their complementary gender (cf *TTCHV*, pp. 209, 215), and especially through their being set in the company of a sudden collection of theologically freighted nouns, *ḥesed*, *b[e]rît*, and *šālôm* (also the verb *rāḥam* in the closing colon). The Tg again makes explicit that Jerusalem is the addressee (again in v. 17). The LXX has 'your covenant of well-being'. Gerleman ([see on 41.3], p. 9) suggests that *šālôm* again denotes 'recompense'. The argument implicitly parallels that of 49.15: 'even if—*per impossibile*—I could break the Noah covenant, this new covenant would still stand'.

The closing isolated colon which makes v. 10b a tricolon also pairs with the one which opens vv. 9–10; they thus wrap four lines of more regular length, perhaps 2–2–2, 2–2–2, 3–2, 3–3. Its description of Yhwh at the end of vv. 9–10 as one who has compassion takes up the verb from the end of vv. 6–8, as v. 8b took up the description of Yhwh as restorer from v. 5.

[6] So also, e.g., T. C. Vriezen, 'Einige Notizen' [see on 54.6b]; Kaddari, 'Concessive Connectors' [see on 47.9b], p. 109.

מאתך: on the form, see GK 103b; JM 103j. Vg omits, influenced by the parallelism (*HUB*). M. Dahood reworks it as a verb form from מאה and suggests that the colon means 'my commitment which I repeat to you a hundred times will not move away'.[7]

54.11abα. Weak one, tossing, not comforted—here I am resting your stones in antimony. The MT marks by a setuma (the Reuchlin MS by a petucha) and 1QIs[a] by a new line. The MT then has the subsection beginning with a tricolon comprising v. 11, to be followed by another comprising v. 12, but the last colon of v. 11 and the first of v. 12 form a pair of their own and it seems more likely that the two verses form three bicola. The beginning of the second colon here, v. 11bα, is very heavy. The poet could have said *hēn ʾănî* and v. 11b could have been treated as a six-beat line (perhaps 2–2–2 rather than 3–3). The actual opening *hinnēh ʾānōkî* instead sets a strong assertion of the being and presence of Yhwh over against the description in v. 11a. The three descriptions in v. 11a all end *-āh*; a series of words ending *-ayik* then begins in v. 11b and will run through v. 13.

The opening phrases seem once again to take up the city's self-description from its prayers, and again the description 'weak one' (*ʿăniyyāh*) takes up a term used of Jacob–Israel (e.g. 49.13). Over against the *hinnēh saʿărāt yhwh* of Jer 23.19 and 30.23, Yhwh addresses the one who is *sōʿărah* ('tossing') by saying *hinnēh ʾānōkî*. Once again the description 'not comforted' indicates that nothing has moved on since 40.1. Once again Yhwh responds to the facts about the city's situation simply with words of promise, which are more explicit over the fact that the one addressed indeed is a city.

'Rest' (*rābaṣ*) is an odd word to use of stones, though a natural one for someone who is weak and tossing. Perhaps the expression involves a metonymy or an ellipse. Perhaps it is chosen because the consonantal sounds of the word for 'sapphires' will reverse it (*mrbṣ*/*sprm*) (†Lack, p. 196). The combining of the image of city and woman continues in the reference to antimony (*pûk*), a mineral powder applied to the eye-lids like mascara (see 2 Kgs 9.30) and also used in the construction of the temple (1 Chr 29.2). The stones are both building stones which need to have the opportunity to rest secure again, and precious stones which are set in antimony to show them off.

סערה: 1QIs[a] סחורה, reflecting weakening of and confusion between gutturals (†Kutscher, p. 42 [ET p. 57]). Vg's paraphrase *tempestate convulsa* tried to make sense of the active participle by a paraphrase (cf EVV). †Klostermann reads as pu pf ('[who] are tossed'), †Duhm takes as pu ptpl without the preformative, †Marti emends to pu ptpl מסערה.
נחמה: MT accents as a qatal vb (see GK 152a, note 1); cf LXX

[7] 'John M. Allegro... *Discoveries in the Judaean Desert*', in *Bib* 50 (1969), pp. 270–72 (see pp. 271–72).

παρεκλήθης. Contrast Th παρηγορημένη, Vg *absque ulla consolatione*. †Duhm again parses as pu ptpl.

פוך: LXX's ἄνθρακα might imply נפך ('ruby') (see BDB), but Vg *per ordinem* suggests it was also puzzled by the word in the context. Perhaps the LXX thought that parallelism required a word for a precious stone, but this is to miss the difference between this and the following cola. There the jewels are not the setting for stones; they *are* the stones. See 1 Chr 29.2. †Hessler emends to סוך ('[Yhwh's] tent'), as in Ps 76.3 [2].

אבניך: †Torrey emends אדניך, which he renders 'your foundations', though it means 'your pedestals'.

54.11bβ–12aα. . . .founding you in sapphires and making chalcedony your pinnacles. We have assumed that the finite verbs continue the participial construction of v. 11bα, though they could be read as an independent sentence ('I will found you. . .and make you. . .').

The city's foundations are made of *sappîr*, which invites equation with sapphire (cf LXX, Vg); the word is a Sanskrit loanword in Hebrew, Greek, Latin, and English. BDB notes the alternative possibility that the word refers to lapis lazuli, a deep azure blue gemstone formed by the combining of several minerals and found in limestone. An Akkadian pseudo–prophecy promises that a coming king will build the city's gates of lapis lazuli.[8]

At the other extreme, the city's highest pinnacles (lit. its 'suns') are made of sparkling chalcedony. †Ibn Ezra thinks the 'suns' are windows or apertures through which the sun came; they will be closed with semi-transparent precious stone. As the consonantal sound of the word for 'resting' is reversed in that for 'sapphires', so the consonantal sound of *kadkôd* ('chalcedony') is reverse-echoed in that of *ʾĕkdāḥ* ('sparkling'; †Lack, p. 196). BDB reckons that *kadkôd*, the parallel noun to *sappîrîm*, means 'ruby'; ruby is the other main form of corundum alongside sapphire, covering the reddish varieties. But the word (which appears in PBH as *kadkᵉdôn* and *karkᵉdôn* and in Aramaic as *kadkᵉdānāʾ*) looks like a Hebrew equivalent to χαλκηδών, 'chalcedony' (Sym; see *DTT*), though this word occurs for the first time only in Rev 21.19. Chalcedony takes various forms such as agate (so *DCH* here), onyx, cornelian, and chrysoprase. The LXX and Vg have 'jasper', another variety of quartz.

The LXX renders the colon 'I will make your pinnacles jasper' in the light of the construction of the ones which follow, as if the preposition *l* also applied in this preceding colon. But the construction 'I will make rubies your pinnacles' corresponds to regular usage (cf BDB, p. 964b). In contrast, †Eitan assimilates the second construction to the first by seeing the *l* as an emphatic particle. If v. 12aβb is actually a separate line, as we have suggested, this reduces the need to assimilate the construction of vv. 12aα and 12aβb.

[8] H. Hunger and S. A. Kaufman, 'A New Akkadian Prophecy Text', in *JAOS* 95 (1975), pp. 371–75 (see p. 372); cf M. Weinfeld, *Social Justice in Ancient Israel and in the Ancient Near East* (expanded ET Jerusalem/Minneapolis, 1995), p. 58.

4QIsaiah Pesher[d] (4Q164) applies vv. 11–12 to the community understood as living in the last days; in particular, its priests and leaders are its jewels. Revelation 21.10–21 similarly takes it as a stimulus to its description of the Jerusalem coming down out of heaven from God, perhaps partly stimulated by the text's Qumran reworking (cf *Flusser). †Grimm and Dittert also compare writings from the context of the fall of Jerusalem in the first century BC and the first century AD such as Psalms of Solomon 1–2; 4 Ezra 9–10; 2 Baruch 9–12.

ויסדתיך: 1QIs[a] ויסודותיך ('and your foundations') makes the word a noun parallel to אבניך; cf LXX's καὶ τὰ θεμέλιά. Tg, Aq, Th, Sym have a verb; Syr has a verb and a noun ('and laying your foundations').
כדכד: euphonic daghesh preceding the ד; and see GK 21d.

54.12aβb. ...your gates into sparkling stones and your entire border into delightful stones. As the participle in v. 11bα introduces the clauses which follow in vv. 11bβ–12aα, so the second of these clauses leads into two further phrases which are both dependent on it. The description of the city's gates and borders thus complements the description of its depths and heights.

'Sparkling' (*ʾeqdāḥ*) comes only here. The LXX renders 'crystal', Vg *sculptos* which suggests engraved or carved stone, BDB 'carbuncle', a red precious stone such as garnet (another silicate) cut into a boss shape, *DCH* 'beryl'. Etymologically, 'carbuncle' implies something fiery red, and this corresponds to the presumed link with the verb *qādaḥ* ('kindle'). It suggests some precious stone which glistened in the sun as it decorated the city's gates.

The word *gĕbûl* ('border') nowhere else denotes a wall (EVV); †Hessler suggests 'glacis', but it more naturally suggests the city limits (cf Tg *tḥwmk*, Vg *terminos*, Syr *tḥwmyky*; 1QIs[a] also has plural, *gbwlyk*). The LXX's τὸν περίβολόν suggests a reference to the area within the city's boundary rather than the boundary itself (†Kissane). The LXX and Syr omit 'all'. It is unlikely that *ḥēpeṣ* ('delightful') would suddenly mean merely economically or aesthetically 'precious'. Like 'rest' it carries overtones from outside building; cf occurrences in 44.28; 46.10; 48.14; 53.10 (and the verb in 42.21; 53.10; 55.11). It leads into v. 13a.

54.13–14a. All your children will be Yhwh's disciples, and the well-being of your children will be great. In rightness you will establish yourself. The LXX and Vg take v. 13 as a continuation of what preceded. This works for v. 13a ('and all your children [into] Yhwh's disciples...'; cf †Rosenbaum, pp. 169–70; †Thomas), but we have argued that vv. 11–12 are a series of bicola with a new line beginning in v. 13a, and the LXX and Vg show the difficulty of continuing the enjambment into v. 13b. The MT implies that v. 13 comprises two noun clauses; we have inferred their time reference from the context.

The transition from 'stones' to 'children' is softened by the similarity of the words (*ʾăbānîm/bānîm*) (†Simon). In 1QIs[a] the transition is softened further in v. 13b by a later hand which turned the second 'your children' (*bānāyik* in the MT, in pause) into 'your builders' (*bwnyky*). The Babylonian Talmud, *b. Berakot* 64a, encouraged the reading *bōnayik* in v. 13a, too, in order to make links with other passages about building and houses (*CP*, p. 46), while †Houbigant proposed this reading for v. 13a alone. The idea is then the plausible one that Yhwh instructs the city's builders, as Yhwh had once given instructions regarding the tent and the temple. K. Baltzer ('Stadt-Tyche', p. 117 [ET p. 56]) suggests that the passage is hinting at the construction of an actual new wall for Jerusalem. But here in vv. 11–12, Yhwh has been the builder. Further, the significance of the phrase 'Yhwh's disciples' is such that it seems unlikely that the prophet would use it with this relatively trivial significance. 'All your children' comes at the beginning of the line, not following the predicate as one would expect (see on v. 5a), and thus has some emphasis. This also suggests that the unexpected reading is the right one. Further, it means that the repetition of '[all] your children' forms an *inclusio* round the line. The prophet likes to repeat words; contrast the LXX's υἱούς...τέκνα. The situation thus resembles that at 49.13, where we reckoned that the right reading is 'your children'.

The predicate in v. 13a is also noteworthy. Even if we read 'your builders' in v. 13, the significance of the word *limmûdîm* in Isaiah suggests that the predicate hardly means merely that they will be 'taught (their craft) by Yahweh' (†North); the Tg's 'taught in Yhwh's Teaching' pushes the meaning in a more appropriate direction. The servant testimony in 49.1–6 made clear that it was only on an interim basis that the prophet was given a special position as Yhwh's servant. The servant vocation belongs to the whole people. In 50.4–11 it was implicit that the same was true of the prophet's position as Yhwh's disciple; now that is more explicit. In the double use of the word in 50.4–5 the prophet had utilized the plural *limmûdîm*, following the earlier occurrence in 8.16, and the plural recurs here (Syr has 'my disciples', as in 8.16). The people will at last give Yhwh the responsiveness that 48.18 missed, and find the well-being that they would otherwise not know (48.22).

†Hessler argues that the entire description in vv. 11–12 is of a metaphorical dwelling. This is no extravagant portrait of a material city, nor is it an otherworldly Jerusalem, but a heavenly city on earth, a new community, a counter to Ezekiel's new temple. *Beuken adds that founding (v. 11b) and establishing (v. 14a) is creation language (e.g. 45.18; 48.13), and suggests that the 'rightness' of v. 14a which parallels well-being is the rightness which Yhwh brings, which in such a context 'assumes cosmic dimensions': it is 'part of the new world order, which God is going to introduce by his creative and salvific word' (cf 45.8) (p. 62).

BDB assumes that the hitpolel of *kûn* (see note) is here passive in meaning. This fits the link with 2.2. But the hitpael and its variants are more commonly reflexive, and this makes good sense here, and in all the other occurrences of this hitpolel. In contrast, 2.2 uses the niphal; this difference draws attention to a difference in the way the theme as a whole is treated here.

ורב: LXX's καὶ ἐν πολλῇ εἰρήνῃ implies that רב is an adj. (cf Tg וסגי יהי; KJV). †Ibn Ezra sees it as a w^eqatal verb. 4QIs[d] has ורוב, Vg *et multitudinem*, which might imply a construct n.
תכונני: on the form, see GK 54c. BDB and GK 54c refer to it as a hitpoel; but see †North; JM 59a, 80h.

54.14b. You can be far from oppression and from terror, for it will not come near you and you will not be afraid. There is no need to emend the opening imperative to yiqtol (†Graetz); the imperative can express a promise (GK 110c; *IBHS* 34:4c; *TTH* 57). Literally the line reads 'Be far from oppression, for you will not be afraid, and from terror, for it will not come near you', which makes poor sense. LXX thus renders ἀπέχου ἀπὸ ἀδίκου καὶ οὐ φοβηθήσῃ, καὶ τρόμος οὐκ ἐγγιεῖ σοι ('be far from injustice and you will not fear, and trembling will not come near you'); cf Vg and Syr *ʾtrḥqy*. The potential of parallelism is utilized to interweave causes and effects in a way which makes the audience hold ideas in its head until the very end if it is to make sense of the whole. *TTCHV* (p. 249) calls this an instance of 'metathetic parallelism'. The point could have been put more prosaically as a 'fear not' oracle, but the prophet has shown an inclination to compose many variations on this theme.

The MT's verse division connects the rightness of v. 14a with this absence of oppression, which makes fine sense in itself. In the prophet's usage, the implication will then be that Yhwh's concern for *ṣ^edāqāh* issues in protection from oppressors. The LXX makes the link forward with what follows in another way, relating it to the community's own life.

'Terror' (*m^eḥittāh*) can denote the feeling of fear or the cause of fear (Tg *tbrʾ* 'breaking/shattering' might also be ambiguous). At first sight the parallel between 'from oppression' and 'from terror' and the link between 'from terror' and 'it will not come near you' would suggest the latter meaning (cf Tg 'from breaking'), but a consideration of the meaning of the line when we have resolved the parallelism, as we have suggested this above, points in the opposite direction. It is 'it will not come near you' which pairs with 'oppression' and which has oppression as its antecedent; 'terror' pairs with 'you will not be afraid'.

תיראי: †Kissane emends תראי ('you will [not] see [it]').

54.15. There, no-one need dread anything from me. Who contends with you? They will fall to you. Most of the line is systematically ambiguous. To begin with, *hēn* could mean 'there...' and make us expect a positive statement, or 'if...' and open up the possibility of a negative one. Then *ʾepes* can mean 'end' (cf Tg) or 'nothing' or 'only'. The form *gôr* could be a noun or an infinitive preceding the yiqtol *yāgûr*. Further, as †Rashi in his way notes, there are probably four verbs spelled *gûr*, meaning 'sojourn' (in PBH 'convert'), 'stir up' (a by-form of *gārāh*, which in the hitp can mean 'stir oneself', then 'wage war'), 'dread/be terrified', and 'gather'. BDB and *DCH* give 'stir up strife/quarrel/attack' as a meaning of *gûr*/*gārāh*, but when the qal verb has such a meaning it normally has an object such as a word for 'war' or 'strife'; on the other hand, the qal might be capable of meaning 'contend', by analogy with the hitpael of *gārāh*. And *DCH* omits *gûr* meaning 'gather', while BDB is also doubtful about it.

Thus LXX renders the opening with ἰδοὺ προσήλυτοι προσελεύσονταί ('lo, converts will come': the double expression renders the Hebrew infinitival construction), but it then has difficulty in making sense of *ʾepes* (Syr also omits it). It goes on σοι δι᾽ ἐμοῦ καὶ ἐπὶ σὲ καταφεύξονται ('...to you because of me and will find refuge with you'; LXX^{B} has a longer text). Cf Tg; Vg has a similar translation which incorporates the negative. The translation exemplifies the LXX's stress on conversion to Judaism (†Vande Kappelle, pp. 116–23; †Olley, pp. 148–50). *Ecclesiastes Rabbah* in its comment on 1.7 observes that people need to convert now. It will not be possible in the world to come. 'The proselyte will become a convert [here]. [But from now onwards] they are are not by me [i.e. they cannot reach me]. Whoever is converted to you [in this world] shall be attached to you [in the world to come].'

†Torrey assumes *gûr* ('sojourn') only in the second colon, but it reads oddly in the context. Assuming that *gôr* is an infinitive strengthening the main verb, the Tg renders 'There, truly they will gather to you at the end', also providing 'the exiles of your people' as the subject, and then assumes that the recurring *gûr* in v. 15b signifies a hostile 'gathering' by foreign kings. But it too seems to be reading ideas into the text. Given the verb's absolute form, 'contend' or 'gather' leave too much to explain, whereas, following on v. 14b, 'dread' makes good sense (†Rashi). The line may then be reworking Jer 20.3–10 (cf *Davis, p. 221).

In isolation one might thus understand the colon to mean 'If someone is really terrified, nothing [to terrify] is from me', though the matter is allusively expressed—but for the infinitive absolute construction in an if-clause, see *DG* 121, remark 1. But a further clue is in prospect in v. 16, which according to K also begins *hēn* (LXX repeats ἰδοὺ, Vg *ecce*). This makes vv. 15 and 16 a pair of statements which begin in the same way, like 40.15a, 15b; 50.9a and 9b and 55.4 and 5 (there are other examples which use some other particle: e.g. 40.10a, 10b and 49.12a, 12b using *hinnēh*). This fits with the fact that in any case *hēn* meaning 'if' is strictly an Aramaism; a

Hebrew-speaking audience would be inclined to hear it as meaning 'there' (cf Tg, †Rashi; 1QIs^a has *hinnēh*).[9] We can then take the colon as one clause, 'There, a person really need dread nothing from me'. For the transitive use of *gûr*, compare Deut 32.27; for 'from [with] me', cf 1 Kgs 1.27; Ps 22.26 [25]. Further, in 40.15 a double *hēn* introduces the response to *mî*-questions in 40.12–14, while the double *hēn* in 50.9 stands either side of a *mî*-clause, as here. Another *mî–hēn* sequence follows in 50.10–11. This makes it likely that the *mî*-clause here is a question and not an indefinite statement ('Whoever...'; †Rashi); we have noted in connection with 50.8, 10 that the latter is rare if it exists.

While the meaning 'dread' thus works well in the first colon, it does not work in the second, and we may infer that the prophet utilizes the existence of several verbs *gûr* (as we would put it). Elsewhere *gûr ʾet* always means 'sojourn with' (e.g. Exod 12.48; Lev 19.33, 34; Num 15.14, 16; Ezek 47.23), but 'whoever sojourns with you will fall to you' makes poor sense. We follow *Davis (p. 219) in reckoning that the meaning 'contend' works well here, though not in the assumption shared with the LXX and Vg that the verb has to have the same meaning throughout the verse and that 'contend' as the only appropriate meaning in v. 15b must be read back into v. 15a.

The LXX and Vg take the common expression *nāpal ʿal* to mean 'fall to' in the sense of 'join', but this is a watered down version of the implicit meaning of the expression, which suggests something more like 'surrender to'. It can mean 'fall on/attack', which would work here if it could be taken as a continuation of the rhetorical question ('Who contends with you [or] will fall upon you?'), but this seems too allusively put. It nowhere else means 'fall because of' (RSV). On the other hand, 'fall to' fits the prophecy's often-repeated expectation that the nations will fall down in submission and/or shame to Jacob-Israel (e.g. 45.24–25).

אפס מאותי: †Torrey repoints אָפֵס מאותי ('comes to an end at my hand'). מאותי is a common alternative to the more usual מאתי (v. 17) and need not be assimilated to the form in v. 17, with 1QIs^a and 4QIs^c (cf †Thomas); 1QIs^a's אכס is a slip. M. Dahood understands מאותי as plural of the word for 'hundreds' with a Phoenician-style third-person suffix.[10]
גר: 1QIs^a יגר (see on 43.9).
יפול: 1QIs^a יפולו, cf LXX, Tg. 4QIs^c and Vg agree with the MT.

54.16. There, it was I who created the smith, one who blows into the fire of coals and produces a tool for his work, and it was I who created the destroyer to ravage. Like 53.10 this constitutes a double bicolon in

[9] See D. M. Stec, 'The Use of *hen* in Conditional Sentences', in *VT* 37 (1987), pp. 478–86, emphasizing the demonstrative nature of *hēn* (cf BDB); C. J. Labuschagne, *Syntax and Meaning* [see on 40.15a], esp. p. 6) emphasizing the conjunctive significance of both *hēn* and *hinnēh*.

[10] 'Hebrew Lexicography', in *Orientalia* 45 (1976), pp. 327–65 (see p. 346).

which the first and last cola and the middle cola form pairs, though in this case (as the MT's verse subdivision recognizes) syntactically the middle pair links with the first colon.

Puzzled by the way the sonorous beginning 'There, it was I who created' (*hēn ʾānōkî bārāʾtî*) leads into 'the craftworker' (*ḥārāš*), the LXX renders 'There, I create you, not like a smith...'. The puzzle is made more pressing by the second colon, which further recalls the picture of the smith with his coals in 44.12, 16, 19 (see further †Ziegler, pp. 96–97). Thus †Holter (p. 37) sees the line as implying that while the worker creates an image, Yhwh creates the worker. 'Fire of coals' distinguishes this fire from the everyday wood fire. Even the third colon leaves us unclear whether we might be talking about image-making here, for *k*^e^*lî* ('tool') is a wide-ranging term which at 52.11 denoted religious artefacts, while *l*^e^*maʿăśēhû* ('for his/its work') is an allusive expression (†Ehrlich omits the suffix as dittog.). We take it that this colon refers to the result of the action described in the previous one: having prepared the fire, the smith is able to create a tool for his work. 'Fit for its purpose' reads too much into the expression, but it might be right that the tool rather than the smith is the antecedent for the pronoun ('a tool for its work') if we assume that the expression anticipates v. 17 and thus speaks of the tool as if it were a person. †North suggests that 'tool' could be a collective (see GK 123b). *Damascus Document* 6.8 quotes v. 16aγ as a description relating to the work of biblical interpretation—without the 'and', which is also missing from 1QIs^a^.

The fourth colon begins to solve the puzzle. The smith stood for the destroyer; we might render the *w*^e^*ʾānōkî* with 'Yes, it was I...'. Talk of Yhwh's creating him then parallels 45.7. Like the statement about the smith, the second statement thus refers to destroyers in general; it will apply to whatever destroyer imperils the city. It further instances the way in which *bārāʾ* suggests absolute sovereignty more than positive 'creativity'. Nevertheless the idea that God created the destroyer was perhaps too much for the copyist of the main Syriac MS, which reads 'called' rather than 'created' (*qryt* for *bryt*).

'Ravage' is the verb *ḥābal* (resultative piel according to *Piʿel*, p. 207). The verb came in 13.5; there and here J. B. Geyer suggests that it also has the connotations of twist, and hints at the Babylonian story of Marduk twisting Tiamat's tail.[11] This might be so even if Geyer is wrong that there is only one root *ḥābal* whose basic meaning is 'bind/twist', with 'destroy' as a derived meaning; *DCH* lists four verbs *ḥābal*. But there is no hint of that backgound here, especially where Israel rather than its enemy is the verb's implicit object.

[11] 'Twisting Tiamat's Tail', in *VT* 37 (1987), pp. 164–79 (see p. 172).

הן: Q has הנה, as does 1QIs[a] (matching its הנה in v. 15); 4QIs[c] agrees with K. †Watts translates הן both times 'if', but the emphatic expressions which follow each occurrence more plausibly follow the deictic 'there'.
באשׁ פחם: M. Dahood repoints as פֶּחָם ('on the fire with bellows').[12]
ומוציא: R. C. van Leeuwen suggests that this is a technical term for casting metal.[13] In 1QIs[a] the ו is a later addition.
למעשׂהו ואנכי: †Kissane links the first word with what follows and removes the copula ('for his work I myself [created the destroyer to destroy]'). 1QIs[a] למעשוהי אנוכי? But the first word is unclear (cf *HUB*).

54.17a. No tool that is formed against you will succeed. You will confute every tongue that arises with you for judgment. A line of great length closes off vv. 14b–17a and thus the chapter as a whole—if we add a *maqqeph* at the end of the first colon, it becomes a 4–4 line. The move between second and third person verbs (v. 14b) and the prepositional expressions 'with you'/'against you' (v. 15) recur, though each in reverse order. As the destroyer was parallel to the smith and ravaging was parallel to the tool's 'work', so the tool formed by the destroyer is parallel to that formed by the smith. †Ehrlich understands the first colon as 'no tool that is formed will succeed against you', but we have followed the Hebrew word order. For the verb, cf 48.15; 53.10.

The second colon begins in a way parallel to the first ('Every tool…every tongue…') and does not appear in 1QIs[a], though it leaves a space suggesting awareness of an omission; 4QIs[c] agrees with the MT. The community will again experience verbal attack as well as physical assault, of the kind that Lamentations quotes. But on future occasions, the attacks will not be justified (see vv. 13–14a), and they will be shown not to be so.

כלי: *Schwarz emends to בלי ('destruction').
יוצר: a ho form, a finite verb in an asyndetic relative cl. But there is otherwise no hi/ho of יצר and *IBHS* 22.6b hypothesizes that this is a qal passive pointed as ho. The Th variant κεραμέως implies יוֹצֵר. †Ehrlich emends to יוצא ('is produced').
תרשׁיעי: LXX amplifies by οἱ δὲ ἔνοχοί σου ἔσονται ἐν αὐτῇ/λύπῃ, part of its expansive reworking of vv. 16–17a as a whole.

Bibliography to 54.1–17a

Abma, R., 'Terms of Endearment', in *YHWH–Kyrios–Antitheism* (R. Zuurmond Festschrift, ed. K. A. Deurloo and B. J. Diebner), pp. 97–104. Amsterdam, 1996.

Beuken, W. A. M., 'Isaiah liv: The Multiple Identity of the Person Addressed', in *Language and Meaning*, OTS 19, 1974. pp. 29–70.

[12] 'Hebrew–Ugaritic Lexicography viii', in *Bib* 51 (1970), pp. 391–404 (see p. 396).
[13] 'A Technical Metallurgical Usage of יצא', in *ZAW* 98 (1986), pp. 112–13.

Brueggemann, W., '"Sing, O Barren One"', in *Hopeful Imagination*, pp. 109–30. Philadelphia, 1986/London, 1992.
Dahood, M., 'Yiphil Imperative *yaṭṭī* in Isaiah 54,2', in *Orientalia* 46 (1977), pp. 383–84.
Davis, E. F., 'A Strategy of Delayed Comprehension: Isaiah liv 15', in *VT* 40 (1990), pp. 217–20.
Derrett, J. D. M., 'Mt 23, 8–10 a Midrash on Is 54,13 and Jer 31,33–34', in *Bib* 62 (1981), pp. 372–86.
Glassner, G., 'Keine Friede für Jerusalem?', in *Liebe zum Wort* (P. L. Bernhard Festschrift, ed. F. V. Reiterer and P. Eder), pp. 155–71. Salzburg, 1993.
Korpel, M. C. A., 'The Female Servant of the Lord in Isaiah 54', in *On Reading Prophetic Texts* (F. van Dijk-Hemmes Memorial, ed. B. Becking and others), pp. 153–67. Leiden, 1996.
Martin-Achard, R., 'Ésaïe liv et la nouvelle Jérusalem', in *Congress Volume: Vienna 1980* (ed. J. A. Emerton), pp. 238–62. *VT* Sup 32. = Martin-Achard, *Permanence de l'Ancien Testament*, pp. 260–84. Geneva, 1984.
Morgenstern, J., 'Two Prophecies from 520–516 B.C.', in *HUCA* 22 (1949), pp. 365–431.
Schoors, A., 'Two Notes on Isaiah xl–lv', in *VT* 21 (1971), pp. 501–5.
Schwarz, G., '"Keine Waffe"', in *BZ* 15 (1971), pp. 254–55.
Stassen, S. L., 'Marriage (and Related) Metaphors in Isaiah 54:1–17', in *Journal for Semitics* 6 (1994), pp. 57–73.
Steck, O. H., 'Beobachtungen zur Anlage von Jes 54,1–8', in *ZAW* 101 (1989), pp. 282–85. = †Steck, pp. 92–95.

V.c.

54.17b–55.13: THE BROADENING OF THE COVENANT COMMITMENT

We follow 1QIs[a] in beginning the new section with 54.17b. Four considerations may have led to the conventional linking of 54.17b to 54.1–17a. 'Rightness' (54.17b) pairs with 'judgment' (54.17a), and recalls 'rightness' in 54.14a; 'Yhwh's oracle' (54.17b) can be a closure; 'Hey' (55.1) usually opens a section; and 'This is...' can introduce a concluding summary and appraisal at the end of a section. Further, v. 17b shares with v. 17a some links with 52.13–53.12: as the servant receives his 'allocation' (53.12), Yhwh's servants here receive their 'possession', and that is their 'rightness' or vindication as he administers justice to people like them (53.11).

On the other hand, while the 'rightness' of v. 17b pairs with the 'judgment' of v. 17a, it has different significance from the 'rightness' of v. 14a, and the plural 'servants' makes for a disjunction as much as a link with what has preceded; indeed, because Zion has not been called Yhwh's servant, the isolated comment on Yhwh's servants raises more questions than it answers. 'This is...' can as easily function as an introduction (e.g. 59.21; Jer 31.33; 44.28) as it does as a conclusion; v. 17b is not an example of the summary–appraisal form.[1] And a number of considerations suggest that 54.17b is indeed actually or also the beginning of chapter 55 (cf †Watts). First, we have noted that 54.17a constituted a particularly long 4–4 line which suggested it might mark an end. Then 'This' in v. 17b would normally point forward not backward, as in 44.21 (cf GK 136ab). It introduces a masculine plural noun (referred to in the third person), which might refer back to those in 54.13 but contrasts with the dominant feminine singular of 54.1–17a (referred to in the second person) and compares with the masculine plurals of chapter 55 (†Marti sees it as a gloss). And it closes with '(Yhwh's oracle)' which elsewhere in Second Isaiah always functions parenthetically rather than marking closure (see 41.14b). We conclude that 54.17b opens a new section; but the question which way 54.17b belongs is then mirrored in the question which way chapter 55 as a whole belongs, for †Watts links it with what follows.

The MT provides a setuma at v. 1 and at v. 6 and then a petucha or setuma at 56.1. 1QIs[a] begins a new line at v. 17b, at v. 6 (so also 1QIs[b]), and again at 56.1 (also 1QIs[b]). It leaves spaces in the line at vv. 1, 8(?), 9(?), 10(?), 10b, and 12. The main ancient divisions at vv. 1 and 6 point us to the way the plurals of v. 17b are taken up in in vv.

[1] As B. S. Childs notes, *Isaiah and the Assyrian Crisis* (London, 1967), pp. 128–36.

1–5 and 6–13. In the light of this it is possible to see chapter 55 itself as having a double structure:

1	Summons	6–7
2–3a	Reasons: the need to listen to Yhwh	8–9
3b	Promise: I will/my word will...	10–11
4–5a	Result: you will...	12–13a
5b	Aim: the acknowledgment of Yhwh	13b

Another starting point for an understanding of the chapter's structure is the parallel between the two sets of imperatives and questions in vv. 1–3a and imperatives, jussives, and statements in vv. 6–7 which constitute a double 'warning speech',[2] incorporating implicit and explicit reasons to back their exhortations. Then further implicit and explicit reasons in the form of promises follow in vv. 3b–5 and vv. 8–9. While further reasons follow in vv. 10–13, these do not specifically relate to vv. 1–9. On the basis of their sharing the imagery of new life, *Korpel ('Metaphors') suggests they belong with vv. 1–9 in such a way that the chapter comprises three related double sections, vv. 1–5, 6–9, and 10–13 (but see *Höffken's critique). Thus we might outline the chapter:

	Introduction 17b	
1–3a	Summons	6–7
3b–5	Reasons	8–9
	Promises 10–13	

The imagery and parallelism of poetry appear throughout but the chapter seems generally unmetrical.

Behind vv. 1–5 is the call of a market trader (†von Waldow, p. 22). This call had already been taken up by sages who put it onto the lips of Wisdom as a call to listen to her and thus to them. That could be expressed as an invitation to a meal and an invitation to the way which leads to life; the two come together in Prov 9.1–6 (†Begrich, pp. 52–54 = 59–61). The immediate content of the life-giving message is then a promise which is very different from Wisdom's (vv. 3b–5), though the content of vv. 6–13 will have more contact with her ways of speaking. But the fact that the promise relates to ongoing life rather than a moment of deliverance makes for more of a parallel with her words. While the language and imagery of vv. 1–3a and 3b–5 are internally unified, there are no such links between these two subsections, and they might be of separate origin (so, e.g., †Volz). On the other hand, vv. 1–3a then have a beginning but look truncated, while vv. 3b–5 begin abruptly (if we discount the copula as redactional) but close firmly.

Verses 6–13 begin with a very different summons, one which has behind it not the call of a market trader but the call of a preacher,

[2] K. A. Tångberg, *Die prophetische Mahnrede* (FRLANT 143, 1987), pp. 118–21.

explicitly expressed in Ps 105.4. That call has in turn been taken up not by sages but by prophets (cf 44.21–22; Amos 5.4–7, 14–15) (†Begrich, pp. 50–51 = 58; he associates the original call specifically with priests).[3] *Clifford understands this quite literally: the prophet is urging the people to seek Yhwh at the shrine in Zion, and was already doing so in vv. 1–5, urging them to make the journey of which vv. 12–13 will speak

†Gressmann (p. 273) saw vv. 6–9 as Second Isaiah's only 'warning address' (a form common in earlier prophets). The transition from Yhwh's speech to the prophet's speech about Yhwh at the end of vv. 1–5 is then mirrored in a transition from the prophet's speech in vv. 6–7 to Yhwh's speech in vv. 8–11; the prophet speaks again in vv. 12–13. As usual, such transitions constitute no pointer to a transition to a new oracle; indeed, the *kî* and the taking up of 'way' and 'plans' explicitly link vv. 6–7 and 8–9. Verses 8–9 also mark a transition to argumentative ways of speech. In general these were more prominent in chapters 40–48; they have been almost absent from chapters 49–55. The return to argument (†Schoors, p. 293, calls it a disputation) and its content is one sign that vv. 6–13 close off chapters 40–55 and form an *inclusio* with 40.1–11. There is another inversion here: as 40.1–11 opened the argumentative half of the material with pictures of deliverance, 55.6–13 closes off the encouraging half of the material with argument. Thus the chapter as a whole urges the people to accept the vision which has been laid out before them through chapters 40–54 (†Lack, p. 115).

Verses 10–11 and 12–13 comprise two further passages linked to what precedes them by a *kî* and by their content. Verses 8–9 concerned plans and ways; these were expressed in Yhwh's word, which vv. 10–11 declares will be effective; the fruit of that will be the events described in vv. 12–13. Further, vv. 10–11 parallel vv. 8–9 in its 'for...so...' structure. Both are thus the language of argument (†Melugin, p. 87). But vv. 10–13 are distinguished from what precedes by their focusing on two distinctive concrete figures, a simile (vv. 10–11) and a metaphor (vv. 12–13). As undertakings about the future they parallel vv. 3b–5, the 'lasting sign' which will not be cut (v. 13) paralleling the sealing (literally 'cutting') of a 'lasting covenant' (v. 5). In other ways they contribute to an ABBA structure about chapter 55 as a whole, which moves from figure to theology within vv. 1–5, then from theology to figure within vv. 6–13. A similar movement characterizes the content, a movement from the forms of reason to the content of revelation within vv. 1–5 and from the forms of revelation to the content which concerns reason within vv. 6–13. To put it another way, vv. 1–3a might have naturally led into vv. 8–13 and vv. 6–7 to vv. 3b–5. The small-scale inversion

[3] See also J. Begrich, 'Die priesterliche Tora', in *Werden und Wesen des Alten Testaments* (ed. J. Hempel), pp. 63–88. BZAW 66, 1936. = Begrich, *Gesammelte Studien zum Alten Testament* (*TBü* 21, 1964), pp. 232–60.

within the chapter thus corresponds to the large-scale inversion in its relationship with 40.1–11.

It would be natural for the Second Temple community to ask 'Where is Yhwh's word? It should come about' (Jer 17.15) (†Hessler). Verses 6–13 suggest several responses to this question. As an outside bracket to these, vv. 6–7 and 12–13 imply two. They look for a religious and intellectual response which conforms instinctive human ways of thinking with God's way of thinking (vv. 6–7), and they look for an agreement to live by God's promise (which chapters 40–55 close by reaffirming) (vv. 12–13). Inside this bracket they point out the theological fact which underlies the imperative in vv. 6–7 (vv. 8–9) but also promise that Yhwh's word *will* be fulfilled; that is its nature (vv. 10–11). †Grimm and Dittert render the fourfold *kî* in vv. 7b, 8, 10, and 12 by 'Yes', and take the passage as Yhwh's fourfold 'Yes' to the people in their uncertainty: Yes, Yhwh forgives (vv. 6–7); Yes, heaven has a plan for the people's deliverance (vv. 8–9); Yes, God's creative word will be effective (vv. 10–11); Yes, Jacob's children will return home (vv. 12–13).

*Brueggemann ('Isaiah 55') suggests that the chapter as a whole comprises a reassertion of the message of Deuteronomy and Samuel–Kings, a message perhaps recently reaffirmed by the authors of the Deuteronomistic History, though it also involves some reworking of it. It reaffirms God's covenantal promise to David, though applying it to the whole people. It calls people to seek and turn on the basis that they will find and discover God's mercy and pardon, taking up the promises and prayers of Deut 4.29–31 and 1 Kings 8. And it reaffirms the power of Yhwh's word to bring about the fulfilment of Yhwh's purpose. (Brueggemann also links vv. 12–13 with the Deuteronomic motif of blessing and curse, but here any connection is more indirect.) Chapter 55 also has some of the marks of a conclusion to chapters 40–55 as a whole, especially in the way it harks back to 40.1–11. For instance, Yhwh's lasting commitment (v. 3) contrasts with the passing nature of human commitment (40.6), while the closing comment on the effectiveness of Yhwh's word (vv. 10–11) forms an *inclusio* with 40.3–5. Croatto ('Exegesis', pp. 222–23) describes the chapters as bracketed by an inversion, for the opening reference to Jerusalem's comforting ought to come at the end, and the closing reference to departure from Babylon ought to come at the beginning. The two parts of the book have sought to persuade the deportees of Yhwh's saving power and will, and to console Zion with the promise of imminent liberation, but the bracket around them binds these two events together.

Elliger (*Verhältnis*, pp. 135–67) sees chapter 55 as a whole as coming from Third Isaiah, *Rofé (pp. 254–56) agrees on the grounds that it makes Yhwh's promises conditional on the people's behaviour in a way that Second Isaiah did not, and Sweeney ('Reconceptualization') also suggests that chapter 55 functions more to look forward to chapters 56–66 than to close off chapters 40–55. It may be more likely that vv. 6–13 were assembled from earlier raw materials of separate origin than is the case with vv. 1–5. Hermisson ('Einheit', p. 311) sees vv. 6–7 as belonging to the 'Deliverance is near' strand in chapters 40–55.

54.17b. This is the possession of Yhwh's servants, their rightness from me (Yhwh's oracle.) E. Lipiński understands *naḥălāh* here in the light of the connotation 'destiny' which it develops at Qumran (*ThWAT* on *nāḥal*, VI.2), but the affirmation that the people have a *naḥălāh* also suggests that another plaint from Lamentations (see 5.2) is reversed. Their *naḥălāh* is their 'rightness'—not the rightness of their life (as in v. 14a) but their vindication and their place in Yhwh's purpose (so, e.g., 51.6, 8). Chapter 55 is about to explicate what that place is.

'Yhwh's servants' comes for the first time in the plural. It will be taken up in 63.17; 65.8–9, 13–15; 66.14, where it will initially refer to the community as a whole, but then to the group within the community who *really* serve Yhwh. Here presumably the first meaning obtains, but the point is not explicit—that is the nature of 52.13–55.13. The significance of the plural is perhaps to underline once more that the role of servant does not belong to one individual as opposed to the community, even if this has been so on an interim basis. The plural 'servants' is taken up and developed in the plurals that run through chapter 55. Indeed the unexplicitness of the chapter makes it possible for †Torrey to reckon that 'everyone' in v. 1a is an invitation to the world as a whole.

55.1aα. Hey, everyone who is thirsty, come for water. There is some ambiguity in 54.17b over whether the prophet speaks for Yhwh (as the first colon implies) or whether Yhwh speaks in person (so the second colon). The ambiguity continues through 55.1–13. Only with v. 3 will it become clear that this invitation comes from Yhwh; compare the movement between vv. 6–7 and 8–9, and the reverse movement between vv. 10–11 and 12–13.

The call for attention, *hôy*, in the OT commonly introduces a warning and is especially associated with mourning, but it seems hazardous to infer that the usage here is an innovative reworking of such usage.[4] More likely a passage such as the present one reflects the word's more usual significance in everyday life. Proverbs 9.1–6 (see also Proverbs 8) shows how the cry of a market vender can be imitated without abandoning 3–3 metre, and F. M. Cross's reworking of the present cry shows how it could have been given a metrical form comparable to that of a Ugaritic call to a banquet, which has similar repetitions.[5] *J. A. Sanders compares a king's invitation to a

[4] So W. Janzen, *Mourning Cry and Woe Oracle* (BZAW 125, 1972), esp. p. 20. Contrast R. J. Clifford: see on 45.9, also his review of Janzen in *Bib* 55 (1974), pp. 98–100.

[5] 'Prose and Poetry in the Mythic and Epic Texts from Ugarit', in *HTR* 67 (1974), pp. 1–15 (see p. 3).

banquet on the occasion of his accession or enthronement or at the new year; such a motif would provide an especially telling introduction to vv. 3b–5.

The unmetrical form of the poetry of this cry as we have it (though †Vincent analyses it as 2–2, 3–3, 4–4) heightens the comparison with a market vendor's cry. We have taken the three occurrences of the imperative 'come' as the first clue for dividing v. 1 into three lines, with one of these summons in each. Each line then builds on, explicates, and intensifies the previous one. We have then assumed (against MT) that one of the two vocatives ('everyone who is thirsty', 'whoever has no money') links with each of the first two occurrences of this verb. †Thomas moves the *athnach* only one word, and deletes 'so come, buy'. F. Zimmermann sees that as an alternative to 'come, buy and eat', and infers that the MT combines two readings.[6] We have rather assumed that one of the two instances of the further imperative 'buy' links with each of the second and third occurrences of this verb. In order to make the parallels in the lines clear, we may lay them out as follows, changing the order of the last to show how the elements balance—actually the phrase 'without money, without price' comes in the midst of the final element in the line ('so come, buy—without money, without price—wine and milk').

Hey,	everyone who is thirsty	come	for water
	whoever has no money	come	buy and eat
	without money, without price	so come	buy wine and milk

Each of the vocative phrases ('everyone who is thirsty', 'whoever has no money') is singular, while all the verbs are plural, suggesting both the corporateness and generality of the invitation but also its individuality. The versions have more consistent plurals. The reworking of the order of the third line emphasizes the free-ness of Yhwh's offer.

'Water' became a standard figure for 'Torah', and the Tg takes 'thirsty' to denote 'wishing to learn', and continues this understanding through the following lines. †Rashi, †Ibn Ezra, and †Qimchi similarly take v. 1 as an invitation to come to learn Torah, and link the invitation with the vision in 2.2–4. *Midrash Tanḥuma* (SB) refers to this passage in connection with Exod 13.17 and 34.28 as suggesting an invitation to Pharaoh and to Moses to feed on Torah. †Theodoret takes vv. 1–2 as an invitation to baptism; †Jerome links the passage to a custom of giving wine and milk to the newly baptized. In contrast to such interpretations, *Morgenstern (*HUCA* 22, pp. 372–77) assumes that the passage refers to a literal famine which he associates with that referred to in Haggai.

Perhaps Second Isaiah would be likely to hold together the physical and the religious. On the one hand, Yhwh was the giver of

[6] 'The Perpetuation of Variants in the Masoretic Text', in *JQR* 34 (1943–44), pp. 459–74 (see p. 471).

the basics of human life, but Lamentations again shows how an event such as the fall of Jerusalem took away these basics. The people will need them for their journey home. On the other, in these chapters the promise of water has been a metaphor, and it makes sense to think of the prophet promising the meeting of all needs, outward and inward.

The LXX lacks the 'Hey' and Elliger (*Verhältnis*, p. 136) sees it as a dittograph of the word 'Yhwh' at the end of 54.17. But the LXX also omitted the *hôy* at 45.9, 10. †Willey (p. 237) suggests 'go' rather than 'come' for the verb *hālak*, in keeping with the use of this verb in 52.12. But the imperative used in such a connection is *yāṣā*ʾ (48.20; 49.9; 52.11) not *hālak*, while the latter's imperative means 'come' on the lips of Wisdom when offering bread and wine (Prov 9.5). Whereas English 'go' and 'come' both take their meaning from the location of the speaker, the Hebrew equivalents take their meaning from places: 'go' puts the focus on the place one leaves, 'come' on the place one approaches (†Ibn Ezra, with Friedländer's comment; he compares 'turn away to me' in Judg 4.18).

55.1aβbα. Whoever has no silver, come, buy, and eat. As *šeber* means 'grain', the denominative verb *šābar* etymologically suggests 'buy grain'. The verb thus hints at the buying of (the wherewithal to make) bread. The LXX has 'drink' rather than 'eat', which draws our attention to the way in which each line of the MT gives the audience something new to think about. Driver (*JTS* 36, p. 404) links *kesep* with Akkadian *kusāpu* ('bite', 'bread cake': *CAD*), which makes for good parallelism but arguably also for redundancy; *CP* (p. 153) calls the result 'a poor and stupid comic jingle'. The fact that the word has another meaning in the next line would make this an example of the prophet's utilization of homonymy, but this hardly justifies the unnecessary hypothesis (Payne, *JSS* 12, pp. 208, 223).

Cyprian (*Treatises* 3.100) comments that human ministers ought therefore to offer the grace of God without charge.

55.1bβγ. So come, buy wine and milk, without silver and without price. Yhwh or the prophet offers not only water for the thirsty, and water and bread for the penniless, but rich provision which goes beyond the basics. 1QIs[a] omits 'and eat, so come, buy', a classic instance of homoioteleuton. The LXX and Syr omit 'so come, buy', perhaps by haplography, or perhaps disliking the repetition; the prophet likes repetition, and one can see the function of the repetition within this particular line. 'Without silver…' is literally 'for not silver and for not price' (cf GK 152a, note 1). The verb *šābar* (see above) is now used as it is elsewhere in a broader sense to denote 'buy provisions' (e.g. Deut 2.6, 28; and see *DTT*).

חָלָב: LXX's στέαρ implies חֵלֶב, perhaps influenced by דשׁן in v. 2b.

55.2a. Why do you weigh out silver on what is not bread and your labour on what is not for satisfaction? The point changes again, from shortage because of deprivation to spending that is unwise. The links and differences are emphasized by the parallel in expression: 'on what is not bread' is literally 'for not-bread' as 'without silver and without price' was literally 'for not-silver and for not-price'. The LXX omits the reference to bread, having changed the reference to eating in v. 1.

Like *pᵉʿullāh* (40.10), the word for 'labour' comes to mean 'recompense for labour'. So where is the community spending its resources? †Volz suggests that the prophet refers to acquiring this-worldly goods, †Schoors to indulgence in Babylonian religion. The latter seems more plausible and would certainly count as the opposite of the word from Yhwh for which bread is a figure in Amos 8.11. *Brueggemann (*Social Reading*, p. 138) sees reference to 'the entire imperial world of Babylon' as a socio-economic and political reality. It may be that we should not press the question of the nature of this alternative. The point is that the people are not looking to Yhwh. Or it may be that we have to wait for clarification later in the chapter itself (see vv. 6–13).

לְשׂבעה: 1QIsª שבעה, assimilating to the parallel colon (†Rubinstein, p. 316).

55.2b. Listen attentively to me and eat what is good. Delight your appetite with rich food. While exhortations to 'listen' are familiar, this use of the infinitive absolute construction specifically corresponds to 6.9. But the invitation is now issued without irony. What is the relationship of this exhortation about listening to the exhortations in vv. 1–2a? By implication, the Tg has assumed that eating and drinking were figures for listening (here and in v. 3a the Tg has 'Attend to my Word'). This imperative then puts literally what has previously been put in figures. But more likely listening is what is needed if the people are to eat and drink, in the literal and metaphorical sense that v. 1 has presupposed. The imperative 'eat' is then a permissive one: 'Listen, and you can then eat'.

The third clause takes the imagery even further: literally 'your appetite is to delight itself…'. Perhaps the 'rich food' (*dešen*) is the wine and milk (not mere bread and water) of v. 1; whereas Deut 31.20 warned about the consequences of getting fat (the verb *dāšēn*) on the milk and honey of the promised land, on the edge of the people's return to the land Yhwh throws caution to the winds. But wine and milk would often be seen as everyday provision, and *dešen* more likely suggests succulence. The LXX replaces 'rich food' by ἀγαθοῖς ('good things'); as well as repeating the root from v. 2bα, it reuses it again in v. 3a. But 'good' (*ṭôb*) is itself a significant word for Second Isaiah (see 52.7).

ואכלו: 1QIs[a] ואכולו; 4QIs[c] agrees with the MT.
תתענג: on the form, see GK 54k.

55.3a. Incline your ear and come to me. Listen so that you may stay alive. The closing line of vv. 1–3a summarizes the invitation. The imperatives thus repeat the exhortation of vv. 1–2; the second and third are the very forms which appeared in v. 1 (three times) and v. 2b. Although the connection between Yhwh's speaking and the people's staying alive recalls Deut 8.3, the verbal links running through vv. 1–3a here support the view that 'listening' is one thing and 'eating and drinking' are another: this restatement seems to imply that people need to listen to Yhwh's word, in response to that word to come (to receive water, food, wine, and milk), and thus to find renewed life. In the context of reference to food in v. 2b, it seemed appropriate to understand *nepeš* to denote 'appetite', but phrases such as *ûtᵉḥî napšᵉkem* (lit. 'that your life/person may live') regularly mean 'you may stay alive' (see Gen 12.13; Jer 38.17, 20; Ps 119.175). It is quite possible for a word such as *nepeš* to emphasize different aspects of its range of meanings in successive verses (cf 53.10–12).

אלי: LXX renders with ταῖς ὁδοῖς μου, using the same idiom as in 56.11 (†Ziegler, p. 77).
שמעו: 1QIs[a] adds ו.
ותחי: LXX adds ἐν ἀγαθοῖς ('with good things'); cf v. 2b and the comment.

55.3b. I will then seal for you a lasting covenant, the faithful commitments to David. Listening in the way their predecessors did not listen will open up the way to a particular form of new future. Verse 3b begins to reveal what is signified by the water and bread, the wine and milk, the good and the rich food. Reference to a covenant takes us immediately back to 54.10 again, where also Yhwh associated covenant with commitment. While P prefers the more prosaic expression 'establish' (or 'give') a covenant, 'cutting' a covenant (the literal translation) is otherwise a standard metonymy throughout the OT; it presumably goes back to the use of ceremonies such as that in Gen 15.7–21.

In Second Isaiah's day, it looked as if the covenant between Yhwh and Israel was finished. It was inherently fragile, because conditional on the response of a people who always seemed unlikely to provide that response. Talk of a 'lasting covenant' (*bᵉrît ʿôlām*) confronts that by declaring not only that the days of a covenant relationship are not over, but also that the new covenant that Yhwh is now making will overcome the fragility of the old one. It will be like the covenant with Noah, or Abraham, or David, which (unlike the Mosaic covenant) did not break down when it did not meet with appropriate response. It is thus a covenant that Yhwh makes 'for you' not 'with you'.

Elsewhere, plural 'commitments' regularly lead into a subjective genitive, usually referring to Yhwh. Here the LXX renders τὰ ὅσια Δαυιδ, which †Olley (pp. 144–45) assumes is similarly a subjective genitive, though he is less certain whether it refers to David's holy acts or David's holy decrees. Syr *ṭybwth ddwyd* is probably also subjective genitive, and 1 Macc 2.57 presupposes this understanding (*Bordreuil) (so recently esp. *Caquot; *Beuken). But the LXX is ambiguous, as are Th, Sym ἐλέη Δαυιδ, Vg *misericordias*, Tg *ṭbwt dwyd*, and when Acts 13.34 (see *Dupont) quotes the LXX version of the phrase, the context suggests that it understands it objectively (see recently esp. *Williamson). This is more likely here in the context of reference to Yhwh's sealing a covenant and of the repetition of the qualifier 'faithful' from Ps 89.29 [28] (cf also the finite verb in 2 Sam 7.16). Reaffirmation of Yhwh's commitment accompanies reaffirmation of Yhwh's sealing a covenant. †Vincent suggests that rather the word is personal: the phrase denotes the committed people of David (cf Ps 132.9, 16). But this would be an unparalleled usage.

In what sense is Yhwh sealing with them the Davidic covenant? In the context of chapters 1–12 of this book this might suggest that God is reaffirming the commitment that a descendant of David will always rule in Jerusalem (cf †Ibn Ezra; †Vincent). 'David' means a coming Davidic ruler in Jer 30.9 and Ezek 34.23–24, though this would still be an oblique way of making the point. Further, Second Isaiah's preceding prophecies have moved in a different direction, and vv. 4–5 will take that further. It may be that the other OT promises of a lasting covenant (e.g. 61.8; Jer 32.40) are all democratizing God's commitment to David. This is explicitly so here, in keeping with the use of the Davidic motif earlier in Second Isaiah. With typical rhetorical drama, here alone at their very end do chapters 40–55 mention David (he is then not mentioned at all in chapters 56–66). While †Gerleman's thesis that the servant *is* David is implausible, his emphasis on the democratizing of David in these chapters is right. K. Heim suggests that the prophet would have had to make things clearer if vv. 3b–5 transferred the promise to David to the whole people.[7] The prophet can be brief because the promises in vv. 3b–5 say nothing new; they summarize and make absolutely explicit promises which have recurred through the chapters.

Isaiah 55 thus takes over the language of everlasting covenant, commitment, and faithfulness from Psalm 89, but omits its key motif of the promise that one of David's sons would sit on David's throne in favour of relating the Psalm's promises to the people as a whole. This does not mean the chapter's relationship with the psalm is merely 'formal and superficial' (*Eissfeldt, p. 52 [ET p. 206]; indeed, †Fohrer queries whether there is a relationship at all). It is a serious way of making a polemical point (Willey, *SBLSP* 34, p. 275). 'In thus "democratising" the tradition Deutero-Isaiah actually robbed it of its

[7] 'The (God-) Forsaken King of Psalm 89', in *King and Messiah in Israel and the Ancient Near East* (ed. J. Day; *JSOT* Sup 270, 1998), pp. 296–322 (see pp. 306–14).

specific content;' thus 'how arbitrary...Deutero-Isaiah could be in handling a time-hallowed tradition'. The same is true in the reworking of the notion of covenant, which is the subject of wide-ranging redefinition during the time of Jeremiah, Ezekiel, and Second Isaiah (cf, e.g., Jer 31.31–34; Ezek 37.26).[8] As Isaiah 40–55 affirms exodus but not Sinai, so it affirms Zion but not David.[9] Yet paradoxically it reaffirms the commitment which lay behind the covenant with David, for that was always made for the sake of the people with whom the covenant commitment is now renewed.

ואכרתה: 1QIs^a ואכרות; 4QIs^c ואכרותה; 1QIs^b has only the ה[ ]. For the cohortative following an imperative, see *DG* 87a.
חסדי: on the form, see GK 93m.
דוד: the spelling characteristic of Samuel–Kings and pre-exilic prophecy. Ezra, Nehemiah, and Chronicles spell the name דויד (†Rooker, p. 306). But דוד is also the spelling in the book called Isaiah as a whole.[10]

55.4. There, I made him a witness to nations, a leader and commander of peoples. There is a background for the application of the term 'leader' (*nāgîd*) to David (e.g. 2 Sam 5.2), and the term 'commander' is a natural extension of that, while the Davidic ruler was destined to have authority over nations and peoples (e.g. Ps 2). For 'witness', the Tg has another word for leader (*rb*), which is appropriate as a typical instance of looking below the figure for its literal reference. Yet there is a point in the MT's word 'witness'. The word is once associated with David, significantly in Psalm 89 (see v. 38 [37]), though the term's meaning there is unclear. But in Isaiah 40–55 it has already been a significant term to describe Jacob–Israel's role (43.9–12; 44.8–9), and here it is back-projected onto David in connection with the forward-projection from David's role to the people as a whole in vv. 3b and 5.

If we had other grounds for reckoning that vv. 3b–5 spoke of an individual David, then we could render v. 4 'I have made him' or 'I am making him' and refer it to Yhwh's present activity. But the fact that v. 5 will go on to use yiqtol verbs which contrast with the qatals of v. 4 confirms the impression that the prophet refers to a past individual David and a present/future corporate David. †Vincent suggests that vv. 3b–5 consistently reassert the kingship theology of the period of the monarchy. The language suggests that, on the contrary, they interweave that and Second Isaiah's own theology.

*Beuken (pp. 55–56) argues that the line rather means 'I made him, the leader and commander of peoples, into a witness to nations'. It was as international ruler that he came to bear witness.

[8] Von Rad, *Theologie* [see on 40.8], pp. 254, 276, 283; ET pp. 240, 264, 271.
[9] Cf K. D. Sakenfeld, *Faithfulness in Action* (Philadelphia, 1985), pp. 64–70.
[10] See D. N. Freedman, 'The Spelling of the Name "David" in the Hebrew Bible', in *HAR* 7 (1984), pp. 89–104.

הן: 1QIs[a] has הנה here and in v. 5a.
עד: Th συμβιβάζοντα ('teacher'), an interpretative rendering (†van der Kooij, p. 152). †Ehrlich emends to נגיד, *Morgenstern (*HUCA* 22, p. 369) to שׂר.
לאומים: the full spelling contrasts with that of לאמים in the second colon, which is always the spelling elsewhere. This suggests that the Masoretes distinguished the two words. We have taken the first as the pl. of אמה (cf Ps 117.1) with the prep. *l*. Cf †Torrey, though he takes them the other way round; this is supported by the MT's conjunctive accent in the first colon and disjunctive in the second, though the MT then oddly points מְצַוֵּה as construct (cf *HUB*). Syr *lʿmmʾ* perhaps also implies an awareness of there being two different words (rather than implying לעמים: see †Oort); cf Tg and Vg. 1QIs[a] has the full spelling both times; LXX has ἔθνεσι and ἔθνεσιν. Ar omits the second occurrence.
נתתיו: 1QIs[a], 4QIs[c] נתתיהו. 1QIs[b] agrees with the MT. Syr has *yhbtk* ('I made you'). The locating of the verb at the end of the first colon facilitates its applying to both cola (†Rosenbaum, p. 184).

55.5a. There, you will call a nation you do not acknowledge. A nation that does not acknowledge you will run to you. Who is the 'you' (singular)? A move to addressing the David of whom v. 4 spoke would be rhetorically possible, but David has never been on stage in this book and this would be a very sudden transition. Further, the addressee would have to be not the historical David of v. 4 but a coming David, so that the continuity obtained is also destroyed. All this makes it simpler to assume a different form of continuity through vv. 3–5 in which the community is addressed throughout, the move from plural to singular encouraged by that singular in v. 4; for the move between plural and singular without a change in the addressee or referent, compare, for example, 42.18–25; 43.8–13; 43.14–28; 44.1–8. Indeed, in the MT the verb which closes the line is plural (1QIs[a] has singular *yrwṣ*). This encourages us to take the singulars of the rest of the line as virtually plural/collective; cf 42.6; 49.7, 8, passages which are significantly linked in substance to vv. 3b–5. The LXX and Syr have plurals; the Vg has singular in the first colon and plural in the second.

The LXX omits 'There' (so also Syr) and has 'nations who did not know you will call on you, and peoples who are not acquainted with you will take refuge with you' (compare v. 15 for this softer attitude to Gentiles; †Vande Kappelle, pp. 116–23). The MT's point is that the people will summon to acknowledge them a people that at present they themselves do not recognize. They will come to recognize Persia as Yhwh's agent (see, e.g., 45.9–13), and Persia will hasten to submit to them (see, e.g., 45.14–25).

וגוי: 1QIs[b] adds אשר.

55.5b. . . .for the sake of Yhwh your God, of the holy one Israel, for he is glorifying you. In accordance with a common pattern, a metrical innovation marks the end of a subsection, though here the innovation takes the paradoxical form of a 'regular' 3–3 line to close a subsection which has been characterized by lines with no particular metre. The 'for the sake of' construction also points to this being the close of a subsection (cf 41.20), and the reversion to descriptions of God which are typical of the prophet ('your God, the holy one of Israel') fits this pattern. This consideration also supports the view that *l*e*ma*ʿ*an* suggests 'for the sake of' and not merely 'because of': see on 42.21a; 49.7b. 'Of the holy one. . .' is more literally 'for [the sake of] the holy one. . .' (cf JM 133d); 1QIs[b] omits the *l* ('for'); 1QIs[a] adds it above the line.

פֵּאֲרָךְ: on the m. suffix form in pause, see JM 61i; GK 58g.

55.6. Seek help from Yhwh while he is letting himself be found. Call him while he is near. The MT, 1QIs[a], and 1QIs[b] open a new paragraph. For two verses, the prophet speaks in straight 3–3 lines, perhaps reflecting the familiar speech forms of worship to which such an invitation belongs; compare the barbed version in Amos 5.4, 6, 14. The nature of such an invitation to worship is such that it does not need to name its addressees, who are there before the priest who utters the invitation; and cf the 'our God' of v. 7b.

Like *bāqaš* (pi) in 45.19 and 51.1, *dāraš* means not merely 'seek God' in the sense of seeking an experience of God, but seeking God's intervention in one's life—or seeking God's revelation for one's life. 'Call on' has similar implications. The point is made as a general one, but of course implies that Second Isaiah's community can call on Yhwh in the particular circumstances of the 540s in Babylon and Jerusalem. The LXX has 'Seek God, and when you find him call on him; so that he may draw near to you, the wicked must abandon. . .' (cf Syr). This draws attention to the different dynamic of the MT. The 'tolerative niphal' (GK 51c) of *māṣāʾ* ('find') suggests that people can seek *because* God is near not *so that* God may be near. Whenever it is impossible to maintain the tension between divine and human initiative, Second Isaiah resolves it in favour of the former, but interpreters and preachers are more inclined to resolve it in favour of the latter. The Tg's 'while you live/stand' perhaps represents a gentler form of the same phenomenon. So does Augustine's 'Seek the Lord; and as soon as you have found him, call on him; and when he has drawn near to you, the wicked must forsake their ways and the unrighteous their thoughts' (*The Trinity* XV, 2). Indeed, Psalm 103 itself threatens to deconstruct its emphasis on Yhwh's compassion by its eventual declaration that the people for whom Yhwh's commitment lasts forever are those 'who keep his covenant and apply their minds to his charges, to do them' (v. 18). *Numbers Rabbah* 11.7 (on Num 6.26) offers another take on the question in contrasting this verse with Ezek 20.31 and inferring that there is a period of grace between the writing of a decree and its sealing; during this period, prayer and penitence can cancel the decree.

בהמצאו: 4QIs[c] lacks the ו.
קראהו: 1QIs[a] קראוהי.

55.7a. The wicked must abandon their way, the evil person their plans. When the prophet turns to talk about the wicked or the 'evil person' (*ʾîš ʾāwen*; see 41.29), this is not a mere reversion to standard prophetic polemic against societal or individual wrongdoing. Wickedness and evil lies in insisting on one's own 'way' or 'plans'—over against Yhwh's 'way' or 'plans'. The word 'plan' (*maḥăšebet*; LXX renders βουλὰς; contrast Vg *cogitationes*) has a key place in vv. 7–9 (cf the verb *ḥāšab* in 40.15, 17; 53.3–4). Ezekiel documented an earlier clash between Yhwh and the Babylonian community concerning the contrast between Yhwh's way and its way[s] and issued a challenge to it to turn (e.g. 18.23–30; 33.17–20) (†McKenzie). Here, the LXX has plural 'ways', the Syr singular 'plan'; in the MT singular and plural typically complement each other in the parallelism.

55.7b. They must turn to Yhwh so that he may have compassion on them, turn to our God for he will abundantly pardon. The Syr has 'turn to me' for 'turn to Yhwh' (and then a first-person verb, perhaps reflecting the introduction and misunderstanding of an abbreviation). The LXX omits '[turn] to our God'; the Tg has '[the wicked person] must turn to the service of Yhwh…and to reverence for Yhwh…', which is true, though it imperils the prophet's distinctive concern that the community should come to think about its destiny in a new way.

The declaration constitutes another take on the relationship between divine and human action, for in 44.22 the appeal to turn was based on the fact that God had already forgiven. 'Pardon' (*sālaḥ*) is another new verb in this book. It is used only with God as subject, suggesting the forgiveness which a superior has the power to offer an inferior.

55.8–9. For your plans are not my plans and my ways are not your ways (Yhwh's oracle). For the heavens are high above the earth—so are my ways high above your ways and my plans above your plans. *EWS* (p. 163) views the first *kî* as asseverative, JM 174e as adversative. The length of the lines in vv. 8–9 and the length of the words 'your plans' and 'my plans' mirrors the point they make, which again takes up that in 45.9–13. The LXX has 'for my plans are not like your plans nor are my ways like your ways', which draws attention to the sharper way in which the MT is formulated. Having rendered 'plans' by βουλαί in vv. 7–8, the LXX renders it by διανοήματα and then by διανοίας in v. 9: one might say that the difference in the plans is reflected in the difference in the words used for them within v. 9.

In the MT the nouns in v. 9b exactly mirror those in v. 8a. In between the repetition comes the reminder in v. 8b that this is 'Yhwh's oracle': the nature of Yhwh's plans/ways as worked out in Cyrus still makes them unbelievable. The distinctive image which follows in v. 9a further underlines the prophet's claim. Verses 6–9 hold together around the difference between Yhwh's ways and the community's ways.

מחשׁבותי מחשׁבותיכם: 1QIs[b] reverses these.
כי גבהו: JM 174e is suspicious about the lack of כאשׁר ('as') in the protasis of a comparison (contrast vv. 10–11), but some other passages also omit it (see *DG* 130). The LXX has ἀλλ' ὡς ἀπέχει, Syr *mṭl dʾyk drmyn*, Tg ארי כמא דרמין. But the LXX also provides a word for 'as' in passages such as Jer 3.20 and Hos 2.20, and modern interpreters often follow. Here 1QIs[a] has כיא כגובה ('for as the height of'), which †Kutscher (p. 246 [ET pp. 320–21]) notes might be original or might also be a correction of the MT; cf one version of Sym, ὥσπερ γάρ ὑψηλός. †Kutscher (see also p. 267 [ET p. 348]) suggests that כי in fact means 'as', comparing 62.5, but this seems an unnecessary complication. Aq ἐμετεωρίσθη, along with another version of Sym, Th ὑψώθη, correspond more to the MT.

55.10. For as the rain and the snow come down from the heavens and do not return there but rather water the earth and make it bring forth and burst out, and give seed to the sower and bread to the eater... The rhythm continues to be irregular and the lines manifest some prose usage such as the object marker and the article, but the vivid imagery and the loose parallelism also mark the oracle as continuing to be poetic. The sequence of verbs with weak *w* may be co-ordinating or may be consecutive (*TTH* 132).

These chapters almost began with a gloomy figure from nature (40.6–7). They almost end with the inversion of that figure. The simile involving rain is a common middle-eastern one, though the addition of snow is novel (*Lipiński) and *Morgenstern (*HUCA* 24, p. 2) sees it as a gloss. For 'but rather', the LXX renders *kî ʾim* with ἕως ἄν ('until'), implying that after causing fruitfulness the rain and snow do return to the heavens. Literally true though this may be, it seems more likely that the Vg is right in the rendering *sed* ('but'); cf Sym ἀλλ'. The double particle introduces a contradiction of the preceding clause, not a limitation of it (BDB, p. 475a, JM 173b; contrast GK 163c).

לאכל: †Kutscher (p. 267 [ET p. 348]) suggests that 1QIs[a] לאכול ('for eating') follows Gen 28.20. But LXX has εἰς βρῶσιν, Syr *lmʾkwltʾ* ('for food'). P. Wernberg-Møller suggests that in such passages the participle can function as an infinitive so that the meaning in this line is 'for sowing...for eating'.[10] M. Dahood ([see on 40.2aβ], p. 50) links the word with a different root meaning 'grain'.

55.11a. ...so will my word be which issues from my mouth. It will not return to me fruitless. Verse 11 confirms the meaning of the *kî ʾim* in v. 10, for it hardly suggests that Yhwh's word does return fruitless after doing its work (LXX omits 'to me fruitless'). 'So will my word be effective' is probably an overtranslation of the first clause, but the 'be' is a declaring that the word will have the effectiveness suggested by the simile in v. 10 (†Koole). The reference to Yhwh's word makes a further link with 40.5–8. The wording corresponds even more closely to 45.23, though the relative particle *ʾăšer* distinguishes this line. Elsewhere we might have argued that in poetry it is hardly a pure relative and that it might be the introduction of an independent/substantive relative clause (see on 41.8a). But here the other markers of prosaic speech in vv. 10–11 suggest that it is quite natural to take the word as a pure relative.

Yhwh's word is not merely a way of referring to something. It makes things happen. The declaration expresses in other terms the key claim in chapters 41–48 about the relationship between Yhwh's sovereignty, Yhwh's words, and the events of history. *Dahms sees the formulation here as influential on John's portrayal of Jesus as one who comes from God and goes to God.

יצא: Syr *npq* suggests יָצָא.

55.11b. ...but will rather do what I determined and achieve what I sent it for. For the second clause LXX has καὶ εὐοδώσω τὰς ὁδούς σου καὶ τά ἐντάλματά μου ('I will make your ways and my commands successful'), reflecting 48.15 (†Ottley) and 16–18 (*HUB*). Vg's *prosperabitur in his ad quae*...takes *hiṣlîaḥ* as intransitive, but the LXX is surely right rather to take it transitively. The qal was intransitive at 53.10 and 54.17, but the hiphil was transitive at 48.15, and the transitive 'do' in the first colon predisposes one to another transitive (†Koole).

שלחתיו: 1QIs[b] reads שלחתי.

55.12a. For you will go out with joy and be brought in with well-being. The *kî* introduces not the grounds for what precedes but an explanation of its implications; 1QIs[a] has a space in the line before vv. 12–13. The effectiveness of Yhwh's words will be shown not merely in a departure but in an arrival. The equivalents of the two verbs used here are a common pair in Ugaritic (Watson, 'Fixed Pairs', p. 462). The Tg appropriately renders 'go out in joy from

[10] 'Observations on the Hebrew Participle', in *ZAW* 71 (1959), pp. 54–67 (see pp. 63–64).

among the peoples and be led in well-being to your land'. While there have been previous allusions to a departure from Babylon, this is the first specific reference to reaching home (but cf 40.10–11). Once more, there is no reason to infer that events have moved on. In these closing words of chapters 40–55 the prophet rather unfolds one more image that might ready the people for events when they come. The well-being which hung in the balance (48.22) but for which the servant accepted chastisement (53.5) becomes reality (cf also 54.10, 13).

ובשלום תובלון: The LXX reads ἐν χαρᾷ [under the influence of parallelism and the general context] διδαχθήσεσθε [a corruption of διαχθήσεσθε: so †Ziegler, pp. 164–65]. †Kutscher (p. 164 [ET p. 229]) sees 1QIs^{a}'s תלכו ('you shall go') as assimilated to the preceding תצאו. *Morgenstern (*HUCA* 24, p. 3) sees it as pointing to an original תלכון.

55.12b. The mountains and the hills will break into sound before you, and all the trees in the countryside will clap hands. 'Break into sound' forms an *inclusio* with 54.1; cf also 44.23 and 49.13. Flourishing nature is not merely a picture of Yhwh's provision for the people (41.17–20). It joins in the joy of the people itself.

ימחאו: 1QIs^{a} ימחוא; 1QIs^{b} ימחיו.

55.13a. Instead of the thorn will come up cypress. Instead of the brier will come up myrtle. Regular rhythm returns in the last two lines of chapters 40–55, which are 4–4, 3–3. Thorn and brier are the regular growth of the wilderness. They are in place there, but not in place in a land that is supposed to be inhabited and cultivated. There, they are marks that Yhwh's punishment has fallen (see, e.g., 7.23–25). Here, that devastation is reversed. Cypress and myrtle are the kind of trees that turn wilderness into woodland (cf 41.19).

תחת (second time): Q, 1QIs$^{a, b}$ ותחת; cf LXX, Vg, Syr, Tg.
הדס: 1QIs^{a} אדס

55.13b. It will be a memorial for Yhwh, a lasting sign which will not be cut down. The LXX has καὶ ἔσται κύριος εἰς ὄνομα...('And the Lord will be for a name...'; so †Rahlfs–Ziegler's edition has κυρίῳ, but this looks like assimilation to the MT) and Vg *et erit Dominus nominatus in signum aeternum*—more likely a free translation than suggesting a different text (†van der Kooij, p. 315). In the MT the transformation of the landscape will be a memorial and sign for God of the fulfilment of an oath on which God will not go back.

והיה ליהוה לשם לאות: 1QIs^{a} והיו ליהוה לאות ולשם.
לאות: LXX and Syr add 'and'.

Bibliography to 54.17b–55.13

Baier, W., 'Die letzten Worte eines Propheten an die Vertriebenen', in *Bibel und Kirche* 24 (1969), pp. 135–37.
Beuken, W. A. M., 'Is 55, 3–5', in *Bijdragen* 35 (1974), pp. 49–64.
Bordreuil, P., 'Les "grâces de David" et 1 Maccabées ii 57', in *VT* 31 (1981), pp. 73–75.
Boyce, R. N., 'Isaiah 55:6–13', in *Interpretation* 44 (1990), pp. 56–60.
Brueggemann, W., 'Isaiah 55 and Deuteronomic Theology', in *ZAW* 80 (1968), pp. 191–203.
—'A Poem of Summons', in *Schöpfung und Befreiung* (C. Westermann Festschrift, ed. R. Albertz and others), pp. 126–36. Stuttgart, 1989. = Brueggemann, *A Social Reading of the Old Testament*, pp. 134–46. Minneapolis, 1994.
Cameron, D., 'The Sure Mercies of David', in *ExpT* 29 (1917–18), p. 562.
Caquot, A., 'Les "grâces de David"', in *Semitica* 15 (1965), pp. 45–59.
Chiesa, B., 'Ritorno dall'esilio e conversione a Dio', in *Bibbia e oriente* 14 (1972), pp. 167–80.
Clifford, R. J., 'Isaiah 55', in *The Word of the Lord Shall Go Forth* (D. N. Freedman Festschrift, ed. C. L. Meyers and M. O'Connor), pp. 27–35. Winona Lake, IN, 1983.
Coppens, J., 'Le messianisme royale iv', in *NRT* 90 (1968), pp. 622–50.
Dahms, J. V., 'Isaiah 55:11 and the Gospel of John', in *EvQ* 53 (1981), pp. 78–88.
Dupont, J., 'Tὰ ὅσια Δαυὶδ τὰ πιστά', in *RB* 68 (1961), pp. 91–114. = Dupont, *Études sur les Actes des Apôtres*, pp. 337–59. LD 45, 1967.
Eissfeldt, O., 'Die Gnadenverheissungen an David in Jes 55, 1–5', in *Kleine Schriften* 4, pp. 44–52. Tübingen, 1968. ET 'The Promises of Grace to David in Isaiah 55:1–5', in *Israel's Prophetic Heritage* (J. Muilenburg Festschrift, ed. B. W. Anderson and W. Harrelson), pp. 196–207. New York/London, 1962.
Glynne, W., '"The Sure Mercies of David"', in *ExpT* 29 (1917–18), pp. 425–27.
Höffken, P., 'Zur Symmetrie in Jesaja lv', in *VT* 47 (1997), pp. 249–52.
Kaiser, W. C., 'The Unfailing Kindnesses Promised to David'. *JSOT* 45 (1989), pp. 91–98.
Korpel, M. C. A., 'Metaphors in Isaiah lv', in *VT* 46 (1996), pp. 43–55.
—'Second Isaiah's Coping with the Religious Crisis: Reading Isaiah 40 and 55', in *The Crisis of Israelite Religion* (ed. B. Becking and M. C. A. Korpel), pp. 90–113. OTS 42, 1999.
Lipiński, E., 'On the Comparison in Isaiah lv 10', in *VT* 23 (1973), pp. 246–47.

Morgenstern, J., 'Two Prophecies from 520–516 B.C.', in *HUCA* 22 (1949), pp. 365–431.
—'Two Prophecies of the Fourth Century B.C. and the Evolution of Yom Kippur', in *HUCA* 24 (1952–53), pp. 1–74.
Rofé, A., 'How is the Word Fulfilled?', in *Canon, Theology, and Old Testament Interpretation* (B. S. Childs Festschrift, ed. G. M. Tucker and others), pp. 246–61. Philadelphia, 1988.
Sanders, J. A., 'Is 55:1–9', in *Interpretation* 32 (1978), pp. 291–95.
Spykerboer, H. C., 'Isaiah 55:1–5', in †Vermeylen, pp. 357–59.
Williamson, H. G. M., '"The Sure Mercies of David"', in *JSS* 23 (1978), pp. 31–49.